MW00861932

Revelation

REFORMED EXPOSITORY COMMENTARY

A Series

Series Editors

Richard D. Phillips
Philip Graham Ryken

Testament Editors

Iain M. Duguid, Old Testament
Daniel M. Doriani, New Testament

Revelation

RICHARD D. PHILLIPS

P&R
PUBLISHING
P.O. BOX 817 • PHILLIPSBURG • NEW JERSEY 08865-0817

ISBN: 978-1-62995-239-0 (cloth)
ISBN: 978-1-62995-240-6 (ePub)
ISBN: 978-1-62995-241-3 (Mobi)

Printed in the United States of America

Library of Congress Cataloging-in-Publication Data

Names: Phillips, Richard D. (Richard Davis), 1960- author.
Title: Revelation / Richard D. Phillips.
Description: Phillipsburg : P&R Publishing, 2017. | Series: Reformed
  expository commentaries | Includes bibliographical references and index.
Identifiers: LCCN 2016059014| ISBN 9781629952390 (cloth) | ISBN
  9781629952406 (epub) | ISBN 9781629952413 (mobi)
Subjects: LCSH: Bible. Revelation--Commentaries.
Classification: LCC BS2825.53 .P45 2017 | DDC 228/.07--dc23
LC record available at https://lccn.loc.gov/2016059014

To Rosemary Jensen and the valiant missionary staff
of the Rafiki Foundation
and
To the Lion-Lamb of Judah,
who loved us and has freed us from our sins by his blood
(Rev. 1:5)

CONTENTS

Contents

Part 6: Final Judgment and Victory in Christ's Return

Part 7: The Great Consummation and Eternal Glory

SERIES INTRODUCTION

In every generation there is a fresh need for the faithful exposition of God's Word in the church. At the same time, the church must constantly do the work of theology: reflecting on the teaching of Scripture, confessing its doctrines of the Christian faith, and applying them to contemporary culture. We believe that these two tasks—the expositional and the theological—are interdependent. Our doctrine must derive from the biblical text, and our understanding of any particular passage of Scripture must arise from the doctrine taught in Scripture as a whole.

We further believe that these interdependent tasks of biblical exposition and theological reflection are best undertaken in the church, and most specifically in the pulpits of the church. This is all the more true since the study of Scripture properly results in doxology and praxis—that is, in praise to God and practical application in the lives of believers. In pursuit of these ends, we are pleased to present the Reformed Expository Commentary as a fresh exposition of Scripture for our generation in the church. We hope and pray that pastors, teachers, Bible study leaders, and many others will find this series to be a faithful, inspiring, and useful resource for the study of God's infallible, inerrant Word.

The Reformed Expository Commentary has four fundamental commitments. First, these commentaries aim to be *biblical*, presenting a comprehensive exposition characterized by careful attention to the details of the text. They are not exegetical commentaries—commenting word by word or even verse by verse—but integrated expositions of whole passages of Scripture. Each commentary will thus present a sequential, systematic treatment of an entire book of the Bible, passage by passage. Second, these commentaries are unashamedly *doctrinal*. We are committed to the Westminster Confession of Faith and Catechisms as containing the system of doctrine taught in the Scriptures of the Old and New Testaments. Each volume will teach, promote, and defend the doctrines of the Reformed faith as they are found in the Bible. Third, these commentaries are *redemptive-historical* in their orientation. We believe in the unity of the Bible and its central message of salvation in Christ. We are thus committed to a Christ-centered view of the Old Testament, in which its characters, events, regulations, and institutions are properly understood as pointing us to Christ and his gospel, as well as giving us examples to follow in living by faith. Fourth, these commentaries are *practical*, applying the text of Scripture to contemporary challenges of life—both public and private—with appropriate illustrations.

The contributors to the Reformed Expository Commentary are all pastor-scholars. As pastor, each author will first present his expositions in the pulpit ministry of his church. This means that these commentaries are rooted in the teaching of Scripture to real people in the church. While aiming to be scholarly, these expositions are not academic. Our intent is to be faithful, clear, and helpful to Christians who possess various levels of biblical and theological training—as should be true in any effective pulpit ministry. Inevitably this means that some issues of academic interest will not be covered. Nevertheless, we aim to achieve a responsible level of scholarship, seeking to promote and model this for pastors and other teachers in the church. Significant exegetical and theological difficulties, along with such historical and cultural background as is relevant to the text, will be treated with care.

We strive for a high standard of enduring excellence. This begins with the selection of the authors, all of whom have proved to be outstanding communicators of God's Word. But this pursuit of excellence is also reflected in a disciplined editorial process. Each volume is edited by both a series editor and a testament editor. The testament editors, Iain Duguid for the Old Testament and Daniel Doriani for the New Testament, are accomplished pastors and respected scholars who have taught at the seminary level. Their job is to ensure that each volume is sufficiently conversant with up-to-date scholarship and is faithful and accurate in its exposition of the text. As series editors, we oversee each volume to ensure its overall quality—including excellence of writing, soundness of teaching, and usefulness in application. Working together as an editorial team, along with the publisher, we are devoted to ensuring that these are the best commentaries that our gifted authors can provide, so that the church will be served with trustworthy and exemplary expositions of God's Word.

It is our goal and prayer that the Reformed Expository Commentary will serve the church by renewing confidence in the clarity and power of Scripture and by upholding the great doctrinal heritage of the Reformed faith. We hope that pastors who read these commentaries will be encouraged in their own expository preaching ministry, which we believe to be the best and most biblical pattern for teaching God's Word in the church. We hope that lay teachers will find these commentaries among the most useful resources they rely on for understanding and presenting the text of the Bible. And we hope that the devotional quality of these studies of Scripture will instruct and inspire each Christian who reads them in joyful, obedient discipleship to Jesus Christ.

May the Lord bless all who read the Reformed Expository Commentary. We commit these volumes to the Lord Jesus Christ, praying that the Holy Spirit will use them for the instruction and edification of the church, with thanksgiving to God the Father for his unceasing faithfulness in building his church through the ministry of his Word.

Richard D. Phillips
Philip Graham Ryken
Series Editors

Question:
What is the "doctrinal heritage"
of the Reformed faith?

PREFACE

Revelation needs to be preached! This conviction has motivated the writing of this commentary and its studies on John's Apocalypse. The church has been truly impoverished by its widespread ignorance of Revelation, born of confusion and fear regarding its message. But this book, perhaps above all other New Testament writings, promises hope and comfort to struggling Christians. Revelation is a book for our times! Particularly as the twenty-first century witnesses a spreading, virtually worldwide opposition to biblical Christianity, with violent oppression in the East and judicial suppression in the West, Revelation is the book especially designed by the Sovereign Christ to convey strength for perseverance unto spiritual victory.

The visions of Revelation were not intended as complex puzzles for a scholarly cadre of specialists. Instead, every Christian should know and often think about the vision of the dragon, the woman, and her child in chapter 12. Every preacher should have the vision of the angel presenting John with the scroll of God's Word emblazoned on his conscience. Believers entering into weekly worship should lift their spirits up to the vision of God's throne room in chapter 4—truly one of the great chapters of the Bible—conscious of entering into that very scene. And Christians suffering temptation or distress should turn anew to the vision of the glorified and exalted Jesus—Prophet, Priest, and King—who comes in chapter 1 as the Sovereign Lord with an urgent message for his church today, no less than in John's time.

Most Christians today neglect Revelation because they expect it to be confusing and contradictory. I hope and believe that these studies will prove exactly the opposite for readers. Many pastors shrink from preaching Revelation because they fear that it will be too obscure. I pray that they will see in this commentary the great relevance and practical value of Revelation to our times. While I am usually skeptical about purported advances in Bible scholarship, the reality is that the past several generations have seen vast progress in the study of Revelation. Today, numerous accessible resources are available to exposit John's Apocalypse in doctrinally clear and practically compelling ways. On the trajectory that began with William Hendriksen's *More than Conquerors* in 1940 and that passes through G. K. Beale's 1999 magisterial commentary, lucid and exegetically persuasive arguments have demystified Revelation. Remembering that so great an exegete as John Calvin declined to preach Revelation and that Martin Luther once argued for its removal from the canon, Christians today can be grateful for a growth in understanding that makes Revelation as accessible to them as it was to its original hearers. I offer this volume as a point of access into this scholarship, seeking to present clear expositions that not only make Revelation come alive for readers but, more importantly, make readers come alive through Christ's living Word.

I wrote this commentary as one persuaded, along the lines of Hendriksen and Beale, of the redemptive-historical and amillennial interpretation of Revelation. I was delighted to find, however, that I yet derived great value from the writings of both premillennial and postmillennial scholars. This is in large part because of the nature of apocalyptic visionary writings: even when there is disagreement about the interpretation, the primary message tends to come through clearly enough. I hope that readers who hold differing millennial views from mine will likewise find in this volume that the truth of Revelation's message is set forth in a compelling and edifying way.

It has been impossible for me to preach and write on Revelation without often thinking of my dearly beloved pastoral mentor, James Montgomery Boice. Dr. Boice was preaching through Revelation when he died—his promotion into the very scenes about which he had been preaching! We frequently traveled together during this time and often, over a lunch or dinner, reveled in the visions of this book. Readers may note that Boice's still-unpublished manuscript is occasionally cited, and I am happy to give exposure to his valuable expositions. While his references end in chapter 7, Boice's homiletical spirit will, I hope, be felt throughout, especially in Revelation's final chapter, which he so deeply loved. I often teased Jim that given his redemptive-historical approach to the text, his premillennial convictions were not likely to have survived when he arrived in Revelation 20; alas, in God's providence my opinion will have to remain a mere speculation.

I wish to express my grateful thanks to the congregation of Second Presbyterian Church, Greenville, South Carolina, to whom this material was originally preached. Their prayers, love, and support not only are invaluable to my ministry but are even more precious to my heart. My wife, Sharon, and our five children are instrumental in all the service that I offer to Christ, and this volume presents another occasion to give thanks to God for them. I am also grateful to Iain Duguid and Daniel Doriani, with whom I felt a true spirit of brotherly labor through their extensive editorial comments, together with the wonderful editorial staff at P&R Publishing. Special thanks to Mrs. Shirley Duncan for her invaluable aid in the copy edits of this volume.

This volume is dedicated to Rosemary Jensen, whose lifelong labors for the teaching of the Bible, in America and Africa especially, have done much to hasten the day of Christ's coming (2 Peter 3:12). Together with Rosemary, I wish to honor the valiant missionaries of the Rafiki Foundation, who have spread abroad the love and truth of Christ to so many needy souls on the African continent. My many years of association and friendship with them have provided some of the highest privileges of my Christian experience. Finally, I adoringly echo the apostle John's own dedication of the book of Revelation: "To him who loves us and has freed us from our sins by his blood . . . , to him be glory and dominion forever and ever. Amen" (Rev. 1:5–6).

Richard D. Phillips
Greenville, South Carolina

THE LAMB UPON HIS THRONE

PART 1

Christ amid the Lampstands

1

THE REVELATION
OF JESUS CHRIST

Jesus
↓
Angel
↓
John
↓
wrote Revel for the church

Revelation 1:1–3

*The revelation of Jesus Christ, which God gave him to show
to his servants the things that must soon take place. He made
it known by sending his angel to his servant John, who bore
witness to the word of God and to the testimony of Jesus Christ,
even to all that he saw. Blessed is the one who reads aloud the
words of this prophecy, and blessed are those who hear, and who
keep what is written in it, for the time is near. (Rev. 1:1–3)*

On November 27, 1989, the day when Communism fell in Czecho-slovakia, a Methodist church in the capital city of Prague erected a sign. For decades, the church had been forbidden any publicity, but with the winds of freedom blowing, the Christians posted three words, which summarized not only the New Testament in general but the book of Revelation in particular: "The Lamb Wins." Their point was not that Christ had unexpectedly gained victory, but that he had been reigning in triumph all along. Richard Bewes explains: "Christ is *always* the winner. He was winning, even when the church seemed to lie crushed under the apparatus of totalitarian rule. Now at least it could be proclaimed!"[1]

1. Richard Bewes, *The Lamb Wins! A Guided Tour through the Book of Revelation* (Tain, Ross-shire, Scotland: Christian Focus, 2000), 9.

Given its message, Revelation may best be understood by those who are lowly in the world. A group of seminary students were playing basketball when they noticed the janitor reading a book in the corner. Seeing that it was the Bible, they asked what part he was reading. "Revelation," he answered. Hearing this, the young scholars thought they would try to help the poor soul make sense of so complicated a book. "Do you understand what you are reading?" they asked. "Yes!" he said. When they smugly inquired about his interpretation, the lesser-educated but better-informed man answered: "Jesus is gonna win!"[2]

Not everyone in church history has shared this positive view about Revelation. Martin Luther was so dismayed by the book that in the preface to his German translation, he argued for its removal from the Bible.[3] Karl Barth, the famed twentieth-century theologian, exclaimed, "If I only knew what to do with Revelation!"[4] Barth's confusion over this book is shared by many Christians today, especially in light of the bewildering interpretations made popular in Christian literature. Ambrose Bierce spoke for many when he defined Revelation as a "famous book in which St. John the divine concealed all that he knew."[5]

Yet the opening words of the book should lead us in the opposite direction. Revelation 1:1 begins: "The revelation of Jesus Christ." This means that this book's purpose is to reveal something. God gave it "to show to his servants the things that must soon take place," and "made it known" to his servant John. It does not sound like Revelation is intended to conceal or confuse, since it reveals, shows, and makes things known.

We begin by finding that Revelation is a message from the triune God through John to seven churches in Asia. Before the salutation that begins in Revelation 1:4, John penned a prologue that provides four vital pieces of information to help us understand the book. According to the opening verses, Revelation is an apocalyptic prophecy, a historical letter, a gospel testimony, and a means of blessing for God's needy people.

---

2. Vern S. Poythress, *The Returning King: A Guide to the Book of Revelation* (Phillipsburg, NJ: P&R Publishing, 2000), 14.

3. Martin Luther, "Preface to the Revelation of St. John," in *Word and Sacrament*, ed. E. Theodore Bachmann, vol. 35 of *Luther's Works* (Philadelphia: Fortress, 1960), 398–99.

4. Quoted in Bewes, *The Lamb Wins*, 9.

5. Quoted in J. Ramsey Michaels, *Revelation*, IVP New Testament Commentary 20 (Downers Grove, IL: InterVarsity Press, 1997), 13.

In light of this blessing, John Stott comments: "This last book of the Bible has been valued by the people of God in every generation and has brought its challenge and its comfort to thousands. We would therefore be foolish to neglect it."[6]

AN APOCALYPTIC PROPHECY

The word translated as "revelation" is *apocalypse* (Greek, *apokalupsis*), which is why this book is sometimes known as the *Apocalypse of John*. The word means "the unveiling of something hidden." It might be used of a sculpture that had been covered with a cloth, which is now pulled away. Or it might be used of a grand building whose facade had been covered by scaffolding, but now with the scaffolding removed the glory of the architecture is seen. The apostle Paul used this word to describe Jesus' second coming (2 Thess. 1:7). The book of Revelation will also say much about Christ's return, yet its panorama is broader than merely the final days of history. Revelation is, more accurately, an "unveiling of the plan of God for the history of the world, especially of the Church."[7]

The word *apocalyptic* describes a kind of ancient literature, the name of which derives from this first verse of Revelation. Early forms of this genre began developing before Israel's exile in Babylon, continuing through the intertestamental period and into the first century. The Bible books of Daniel and Ezekiel are examples, and Revelation draws heavily from both. Apocalyptic books usually feature an angel who presents dramatic visions to portray the clash between good and evil. These books employ vivid symbols, including symbolic numbers, to depict the spiritual reality unfolding behind the scenes of history. An apocalypse usually contains the message that "God is going to burst into history in a dramatic and unexpected way, despite all appearances that God's people are facing oppression and defeat."[8] While there are differences between Revelation and other apocalyptic books, it fits the basic description of this literary genre.

6. John R. W. Stott, *What Christ Thinks of the Church: An Exposition of Revelation 1–3* (Grand Rapids: Baker, 2003), 10.

7. William Hendriksen, *More than Conquerors: An Interpretation of the Book of Revelation* (1940; repr., Grand Rapids: Baker, 1967), 51.

8. Steve Wilmshurst, *The Final Word: The Book of Revelation Simply Explained* (Darlington, UK: Evangelical Press, 2008), 12.

High view of scripture is literal.

The Revelation of Jesus Christ

Realizing the kind of book that Revelation is will greatly influence our approach to studying it. Some Christians seek to uphold a high view of Scripture by insisting that it always be interpreted literally. When applied to Revelation, this rule breeds only confusion. It is true that John literally received the visions recorded in Revelation, but the visions consisted of symbols that must be interpreted not literally but rather symbolically. This is true of the fantastic imagery in Revelation, such as the dragon and his beasts, and of symbolic numbers such as 7, 1,000, and 666. When we are reading the Bible's historical books, such as Samuel and Acts, we will normally take the plain, literal meaning unless there is compelling reason to interpret a passage otherwise. In studying Revelation, we should reverse this approach and interpret visions symbolically unless there is a good reason to take a passage literally. This is not to say that the visions do not depict real events, whether in John's time or in the future, but that the events are presented symbolically rather than literally in Revelation.

Why would you use a method throughout scripture + then it on us head for the last book?

Not only is Revelation an apocalypse, but it should also be understood as a book of biblical prophecy. This is how John mainly describes his book: after using the term *apocalypse* in the first verse, five times he identifies the book as a *prophecy*, starting with 1:3: "the words of this prophecy." We usually think of prophecy as foretelling distant events, but the main job of a prophet was to give a message from the Lord that demanded an obedient response. James Boice comments: "Prophets speak to the present, in light of what is soon to come, and they call for repentance, faith and changes in lifestyle."[9] It is in this respect that Revelation differs from most other apocalyptic writings, since it speaks not only of far-off events but also of those that were soon to break upon the readers. John wrote about "things that must soon take place," urging that "the time is near" (Rev. 1:1, 3). This was not just a way of saying that things, though really distant, should seem near, but rather that God was revealing challenges that were immediately before his readers. For this reason, Revelation is considered an *apocalyptic prophecy*. While taking an apocalyptic form, it delivers a prophetic message that is directly relevant to its original readers, as well as to Christians of all times.

Baloney

As a prophecy, Revelation is best understood in connection with the vision of Daniel 2, which foretold a series of four earthly kingdoms—Babylon, Medo-Persia, Greece, and Rome—that would rise up in succession, only to

9. James Montgomery Boice, *Revelation*, unpublished manuscript, n.d., chap. 1, p. 4.

8

The correct principal is it applies both ways. See chart in book by Clarence Larkin.

be destroyed in the days when "the God of heaven will set up a kingdom that shall never be destroyed" (Dan. 2:44). Daniel points out that he is revealing "what will be in the latter days" (2:28). The Greek translation of that verse used *apocalypse* for the idea of God's revealing. In using the same language, John mimics Daniel 2:28, except that he writes that the reign of Christ that Daniel foretold "in the latter days" now "must soon take place" (Rev. 1:1). This is all the more poignant when we realize that Daniel prophesied that Christ's kingdom would arise during the fourth worldly kingdom, the very Roman Empire under which John lived (Dan. 2:44). The divine kingdom that Daniel prophesied from afar, John prophesied as now happening. This shows that the book of Revelation is focused not merely on the final years before Jesus returns but on the entire church age—the reign of Christ, which began during Daniel's fourth kingdom with his resurrection and ascension into heaven—which continues until Christ's return.

In developing and expanding Daniel's vision of how the kingdom of Christ overcomes the kingdoms of this world, Revelation is organized into seven parallel sections, seven being the number of completion. Each section highlights a portion of the story as the drama advances to the final climax. This drama involves a sequence that was going to happen in John's time, that recurs through the church age, and that will take concentrated form in the final days before Christ's return.

Fairy tales begin their story of a fantasy world with the phrase "Once upon a time." In this book, John gives a visionary prophecy of the true story of the world in which we live, beginning, "The revelation of Jesus Christ" (Rev. 1:1). His visionary prophecy tells us the most important truths about our world. First, he tells us that Jesus Christ, who reigns above, has his church on earth. Did you know that Jesus is in the midst of his church, a Bridegroom seeking the love of his bride, as the vision shows him standing amid the seven lampstands (Rev. 1:12-13)? Second, did you also know the truth that the world is a dangerous place with enemies opposed to Christ and his beloved? Christ's bride, the church, is beset by a dragon, which depicts Satan, who is served by horrible, ravenous beasts, a harlot Babylon, and followers who bear his mark (Rev. 12-13). Third, what will happen to Christ's bride, the church, with such deadly foes intent on her harm? Revelation's answer is that God will defend his people, judging his enemies and sending Jesus with a double-edged sword to slay those who persecute his bride.

In succession, Christ defeats his enemies, starting with the two beasts and then the harlot Babylon, and finally casting Satan and his followers into the lake of fire (Rev. 18-20). Fourth, after Christ has come to rescue his bride, Revelation's true story of our world ends with the church living happily ever after in the glory of the royal heavenly city, awakening to life forever in the embrace of her beautiful, loving, and conquering Prince (Rev. 21-22). (You see, by the way, why fairy tales are popular, since they often tell the story of salvation that our hearts long to be true!)

The prophetic unveiling of this history is the message of Revelation. Revelation does not primarily intend to present mysterious clues about the second coming. To be sure, as Revelation advances, it narrows its focus on the return of Christ, which brings final victory. But *the message of Revelation is God's government of history to redeem his purified and persecuted church through the victory of Christ his Son.* For this reason, Revelation does not speak merely to the generation in which it was written or to a future generation when Christ returns. Rather, as William Hendriksen explains, "the book reveals the principles of divine moral government which are constantly operating, so that, whatever age we happen to live in, we can see God's hand in history, and His mighty arm protecting us and giving us the victory through our Lord Jesus Christ, . . . [so that we are] edified and comforted."[10]

A HISTORICAL LETTER

A second feature for us to realize is that Revelation is a historical letter that is firmly grounded in the times in which it was given. It begins with the customary letter format in 1:4–5, giving the name of the writer and the recipients, together with a greeting, and also ends as a letter (Rev. 22:8–21). This is why it is appropriate for Revelation to appear at the end of the New Testament Epistles. Michael Wilcock writes: "It is in fact the last and grandest of those letters. As comprehensive as Romans, as lofty as Ephesians, as practical as James or Philemon, this 'Letter to the Asians' is as relevant to the modern world as any of them."[11]

10. Hendriksen, *More than Conquerors*, 42–43.
11. Michael Wilcock, *I Saw Heaven Opened: The Message of Revelation*, The Bible Speaks Today (Downers Grove, IL: InterVarsity Press, 1975), 28.

Revelation is traditionally understood as having been written by the apostle John, the beloved disciple of Jesus, during the time of his exile on the island of Patmos. Some scholars have argued that another John may have written this book, but the testimony in favor of the apostle is impressive. Most noteworthy are the statements of the early church fathers in support of the apostle's authorship. These witnesses include second-century writers such as Justin Martyr (100–165), Melito of Sardis (c. 165), who was bishop of one of the churches to which John wrote, and Irenaeus (c. 180), who also hailed from Sardis and knew Polycarp of Smyrna, who had been a personal disciple of the apostle John. It has therefore been claimed that no other New Testament book "has a stronger or earlier tradition about its authorship than Revelation."[12]

STRONG CONSENSUS

Equally important is the date of Revelation's writing. The strong consensus among evangelical scholars holds that John wrote Revelation during the last years of the emperor Domitian's reign, probably around A.D. 95. This dating agrees with the early church tradition through Irenaeus, who said that it was given "not a very long time since, but almost in our own day, toward the end of Domitian's reign."[13]

Some scholars argue instead that Revelation was written much earlier, before the fall of Jerusalem and the destruction of the temple in A.D. 70. Most who hold this view argue that Revelation does not look forward to the return of Christ but only prophesies Jerusalem's destruction. Important to this argument is the assignment of the symbolic number 666 to the mad emperor Nero, who first persecuted Christians in Rome.

NO (min. view)

There are important reasons, along with Irenaeus's testimony, for giving Revelation the later date of A.D. 95. First, the persecution described in Revelation involves the beast's demand for worship, which corresponds not to Nero's but to Domitian's reign. Second, while there was no empirewide persecution in Domitian's reign, there is evidence that severe persecution took place in the province of Asia, where the churches of Revelation were located, whereas there was no persecution in Asia during Nero's reign. Finally, the description of the churches in Revelation 2 and 3 fits the circumstances

→Modern Day Turkey

---

12. D. A. Carson et al., *An Introduction to the New Testament* (Grand Rapids: Zondervan, 1992), giving a full exploration of Revelation's authorship on pages 468–73.

13. Alexander Roberts and James Donaldson, eds., *Ante-Nicene Fathers*, 10 vols. (Peabody, MA: Hendrickson, 1999), 1:416.

of the later date; indeed, at least one of the churches, Smyrna, may not have existed during the earlier period of Nero's persecution.[14]

When we realize that Revelation was a historical letter, we see the error of those interpreters in the so-called futurist school, who view most of Revelation as speaking only about events yet to take place. Because Revelation was a real letter to real ancient people, its meaning had to be relevant and accessible to the original audience. Hendriksen writes: "The Apocalypse has as its immediate purpose the strengthening of the wavering hearts of the persecuted believers of the first century A.D. . . . True, this book has a message for today, but we shall never be able to understand 'what the Spirit is saying to the churches' of today unless we first of all study the specific needs and circumstances of the seven churches of 'Asia' as they existed in the first century."[15]

A Gospel Testimony

A third feature of Revelation is that this book is the Word of God bearing a gospel testimony to Christ: "[God] made it known by sending his angel to his servant John, who bore witness to the word of God and to the testimony of Jesus Christ, even to all that he saw" (Rev. 1:1–2). Although John the apostle was the writer of Revelation, the message came not from him but from God, through Jesus Christ.

The description of how Revelation was transmitted gives us insight into the process known as *inspiration, that is, the way in which God used human writers to give a divine message*. Many Bible books contain a message that God gave immediately to the prophetic writer, who passed it on to other believers. Here, God the Father gave a revelation to Jesus Christ, who in turn sent an angel to show it to his servant John, so that John could write down the message for the servants of Christ in the seven churches. The obvious import of this progression is that Revelation does not consist of a message that originated in the imagination or experience of John himself. Moreover, the idea of Jesus as the Mediator of divine grace is reinforced from the book's beginning.

14. For a full discussion of the dating of Revelation, see G. K. Beale, *The Book of Revelation: A Commentary on the Greek Text*, New International Greek Testament Commentary (Grand Rapids: Eerdmans, 1999), 4–27.

15. Hendriksen, *More than Conquerors*, 44.

Hermeneutics Principles
① *Use plain - ordinary meaning when possible*
② *No conflicts in Scripture (interpret to harmonize)*
③ *Scripture interprets Scripture (look to source of ill. mention)*

REVELATION 1:1–3

The implications of the divine origin of Revelation are significant. First, since God is perfect in all things, his revealed Word is inerrant and true in all that it teaches. As God's Word, Revelation in its claims is to be reverently believed, all its promises are to be joyfully trusted, and all its commands are to be urgently obeyed. Moreover, since God is the ultimate Author not only of Revelation but also of the entire Bible, there is a unity and harmony between this book and the rest of Scripture. This means that we can interpret difficult portions of Revelation by comparison with clearer teachings elsewhere. Indeed, since the images of Revelation are derived from earlier prophetic writings, the principle of Scripture interpreting Scripture is especially important when it comes to this book.

yes!

Not only is Revelation God's Word, but John specifies it as "the testimony of Jesus Christ" (Rev. 1:2). Most commentators limit this statement to mean that Revelation is Jesus' testimony to his church (see also 19:10). But it is also true that Revelation is a testimony about Jesus as the Lord and Savior who is sufficient to meet the needs of his people. In this sense, Revelation is a gospel testimony. Martin Luther complained about Revelation that "Christ is neither taught nor known in it."[16] How wrong this is! Indeed, it is Christ, the heavenly Bridegroom, who in Revelation woos the church as his bride (1:9–3:22). Revelation proceeds to present Christ as the Sovereign over the councils of God for history, the Lamb who alone is worthy to open the seals of God's scroll, thus receiving the worship of heaven (4:1–5:14). Revelation concludes with the conquering Christ, whose sword cuts down his enemies (19:11–21), who sits on the throne of God's judgment in the last day (20:11–15), and in whose blessing the church, Christ's radiant bride, now delivered from all the trials of this world, dwells in the light of God's presence forever (21:1–22:21). This is why, over and over in Revelation, the angels and worshipers above break out in praise to Jesus. We, too, should respond to Revelation, in the words of Fanny Crosby:

Reveals Christ's God's character

> Praise him! praise him! Jesus, our blessed Redeemer!
> Sing, O earth, his wonderful love proclaim!
> Hail him! hail him! highest archangels in glory;
> Strength and honor give to his holy name!"[17]

16. Luther, *Word and Sacrament*, 399.
17. Fanny J. Crosby, "Praise Him! Praise Him!" (1869).

13

This history presented in Revelation is nothing less than *gospel*: the good news of Christ's reigning over history to save his church. Seeing this belies the idea that the gospel is only for those who are yet to be saved. Revelation is not primarily an evangelistic book; its intended audience is not the unbelieving world facing divine judgment, but the beleaguered church looking to Christ for relief. To be sure, Revelation is evangelistic—the book even concludes with an invitation to receive the free gift of salvation (Rev. 22:17)—but its gospel message is primarily given to needy believers, whom Christ calls to courageous faithfulness in light of his gospel reign.

A Means of Blessing

Finally, like the Bible in general, Revelation is a means of divine blessing for those who read, hear, and keep its message. John concludes his prologue with this invitation: "Blessed is the one who reads aloud the words of this prophecy, and blessed are those who hear, and who keep what is written in it, for the time is near" (Rev. 1:3). Since the God who originated this book is still the God who reigns over all with wisdom and power, those who read and believe Revelation will be supernaturally blessed even today.

John specifies blessing, first, on "the one who reads aloud the words of this prophecy" (Rev. 1:3). The order of the churches listed in Revelation 2–3 follows the path that a messenger would take from city to city. This suggests that John intended the letter to go from one to the next so that it could be read aloud in each congregation. In a time of persecution, this action required courage and a strong devotion to Jesus, for which the reader was sure to be blessed by God. Moreover, just as many of Revelation's visions take place largely amid the worship of heaven, so was its reading an act of worship on earth. David Chilton writes: "By showing us how God's will is done in heavenly worship, St. John reveals how the Church is to perform His will on earth."[18]

God's blessing was furthermore given to "those who hear," and specifically to those "who keep what is written in it" (Rev. 1:3). To keep the book of Revelation is to treasure its message and obey the commands of Christ given in it. This connects with John's description of his readers as God's

18. David Chilton, *Days of Vengeance: An Exposition of the Book of Revelation* (Ft. Worth, TX: Dominion Press, 1987), 54.

True Believers
(i) agree with the Bible
(ii) confirm it by faithfulness with Commands

REVELATION 1:1–3

"servants" (1:1). Literally, the word *doulos* means "slave." The point is that true believers are those who accept the obligation of obeying God's commands, and who not only give outward agreement to the Bible but also confirm it in the faithfulness of their lives. These servants, and these alone, are blessed by God through the grace that comes through his Word.

The urgency of receiving Revelation is made clear by the final words of John's prologue: "for the time is near" (Rev. 1:3). One of the lamentable tendencies in the study of Revelation is to believe that it focuses only on the return of Christ to end history. Under this reasoning, many if not most sermons on Revelation conclude with the question, "Are you ready for Jesus' coming?" It is true that Revelation foretells a great event that Christians must face. But that great event is not the second coming, at least not first of all. Rather, the event that in Revelation's view is soon to arrive is the persecution of the Christian church by the bloodthirsty world. To be sure, Christ's coming is near—either through the help he gives us now or in his final coming to end all history—but John's appeal to the urgency of his writing pertains to his church's obedience to the commands and promises of Christ in the face of violent worldly persecution.

Every Christian can be blessed now, John promises, though facing persecution and beset with weakness and sin, by hearing and keeping the saving testimony of the Bible. We are blessed in our trials by God's Word. I earlier compared Revelation to fairy tales, such as *Cinderella* and *Sleeping Beauty*, which lift up the hearts of crying children. For this same reason, God gave the revelation of Jesus Christ to his servant John for the churches of Asia. In this respect, Revelation presents the same message as given by Paul at the end of Romans 8. It is true, Paul notes, that Christians in this life are "as sheep to be slaughtered." Yet when through faith we enter the glorious kingdom of Christ's resurrection power, "we are more than conquerors through him who loved us." Receiving in Revelation the good news that "The Lamb Wins," we are blessed above all other blessings to be persuaded that nothing "will be able to separate us from the love of God in Christ Jesus our Lord" (Rom. 8:36–39).

The Lamb wins!

2

A REVELATION
CHARACTER SKETCH

Revelation 1:4–5

*Grace to you and peace from him who is and who was and who
is to come, and from the seven spirits who are before his throne,
and from Jesus Christ the faithful witness, the firstborn of the
dead, and the ruler of the kings on earth.* (Rev. 1:4–5)

One effective and interesting approach to studying history is by means of character sketches. For instance, when studying the American Revolution, one might compare and contrast George Washington, the leader of the Colonial cause, with the British monarch, King George III, or with the British military commander, General Lord Charles Cornwallis. We might consider the respective characters of able generals such as the patriot Nathanael Greene and the traitor Benedict Arnold. On the political front, one might conduct sketches of key figures in the signing of the Declaration of Independence, such as Benjamin Franklin, John Adams, and Thomas Jefferson. Through studies of leading participants, we can often help history to come alive.

The book of Revelation, which takes the form of a historical letter, can also be better appreciated if we keep in mind the people who were involved. In the salutation found in Revelation 1:4–5, we meet the main participants. Included in this greeting are John the apostle, the seven churches of the Roman province of Asia, and the triune God of grace and peace. In the background, but very much present, was the diabolical Roman emperor Domitian, whose looming persecution supplied the setting in which the book of Revelation was given. *and the future Antichrist.*

JOHN THE APOSTLE

In our study of Revelation's prologue (Rev. 1:1–3), we considered the compelling evidence that the "John" who wrote Revelation was the apostle John. John is a major figure of the New Testament, having been one of Jesus' three closest disciples, "the disciple whom he loved" (John 19:26), as well as the author of the Gospel of John and three epistles that bear his name. Revelation 1:1 identifies him as the "servant" of Jesus Christ. John MacArthur describes him further as "the elder statesman of the church near the end of the first century, . . . universally beloved and respected for his devotion to Christ and his great love for the saints worldwide."[1]

In these late days of his life, John is revealed as a *faithful* servant of Jesus. If Revelation was written around the year A.D. 95, John would have been over eighty years old. He is considered the youngest of the original twelve disciples, perhaps just a teenager when he watched Jesus die on the cross and then raced with Peter to gaze inside the empty tomb. Few people today pursue any calling single-mindedly over the entire length of their adult lives. But from the time when Jesus came to John and his brother James and pledged to make them "fishers of men" (Mark 1:17–20) until the dying moments of his elderly years, a span of over sixty years, John had served as a witness of the gospel, an apostle of Jesus, and a pastor to the church. John's faithful service was extraordinarily valuable in the first century. Likewise, the lifelong faithfulness of any Christian today—faithful in his walk of faith and in whatever calling Christ has given him in the church—will leave a legacy that honors the Lord and blesses his church.

1. John MacArthur, *Twelve Ordinary Men* (Nashville: Thomas Nelson, 2002), 97.

Early church tradition holds that in these late years of his life, John had been leading the church in the strategically important city of Ephesus. This fits the book of Revelation, since John writes this letter to churches in the province of which Ephesus was the leading city. This indicates that John was also a *humble* servant of Christ. The church in Ephesus was founded by the apostle Paul (see Acts 19). The elders of that church had been converted by Paul and had a profound loyalty to that fiery apostle (see Acts 20:37–38). Moreover, Paul had placed his protégé, Timothy, in charge of the Ephesian church (1 Tim. 1:3). So John would have accepted this charge in order to complete someone else's work and as the successor to a lesser figure in the church. Many strong leaders today would refuse such a calling, putting a priority on their own career aspirations, but John humbled himself to serve where he was most needed. Perhaps he remembered Jesus' High Priestly Prayer, in which Jesus asked the Father that "the love with which you have loved me may be in them" (John 17:26). John exemplified Christ's spirit of love in humbly accepting the calling to shepherd the precious saints of the Ephesian church.

A third characteristic of the ministry of John in Revelation is that he was still a *growing* servant of Christ. We might think that a great leader such as John would have his life completely together by this late date. Yet Revelation will reveal him as asking questions and even making mistakes as he embraces the upward call of greater communion with the Lord. If so great and veteran an apostle as John could marvel at the visions of this book and could glory so wholeheartedly in the victory of Christ, we more humble servants surely can do no less, but should eagerly desire to grow in our knowledge of and faith in Jesus Christ.

THE SEVEN CHURCHES IN ASIA

The recipients of John's letter were "the seven churches that are in Asia" (Rev. 1:4). The Roman province of Asia first appears in the New Testament when Luke describes how Paul desired to preach the gospel there but was "forbidden by the Holy Spirit to speak the word in Asia" (Acts 16:6). Instead, according to a vision he received, Paul traveled to Macedonia and brought the gospel to the great cities of Greece. Only in his third missionary journey, beginning around A.D. 53, did Paul come to the leading Asian city of Ephesus. He stayed there for three years, building that important church,

Disagree:
Read explanations of Dispensational
Theology which are very
convincing — L. Patten
of Prophecy (mean —
far)

REVELATION 1:4–5

from which the gospel seems to have spread to the other cities of the province. Two of Paul's later letters, Colossians and Philemon, are addressed to believers living outside Ephesus in the province of Asia.

John's letter was first sent to Ephesus and then advanced in a semicircle through the province from the north to the east. After Ephesus, these churches were located in Smyrna, Pergamum, Thyatira, Sardis, Philadelphia, and Laodicea. The question is raised as to why John wrote to these churches. The answer is not that these were the only churches in Asia, since there were also churches in Colosse and Hierapolis. About twenty years later, John's disciple Ignatius of Antioch would also write letters to the churches in Tralles and Magnesia. Moreover, there is no evidence to support the often-heard idea that these seven churches represent successive periods of church history.[2]

The best answer notes that the number seven in the Bible stands for completion, starting with the seven days that completed the week of creation. So while John wrote actual letters to these seven churches, their number was selected to represent the entirety of the church during the gospel age and the kinds of challenges that would beset Christians at all times. This may explain why John concludes each individual letter by writing, "He who has an ear, let him hear what the Spirit says to the churches" (Rev. 2:7, 11, 17, etc.). James Ramsey thus comments that "'John to the seven churches of Asia,' is equivalent to 'Jesus Christ to the churches of every people and age,' and therefore to us."[3]

It is obvious from Revelation that John is writing to Christians who faced violent persecution, although it seems that at the time of his writing the Asian churches had not yet suffered greatly in this way. Secular history does not record a great persecution of Christians during the reign of Domitian, although he did demand the imperial worship that led to persecution. The fact that John notes a single martyr by name, Antipas of Pergamum (Rev. 2:13), suggests that this was not yet a common event. Yet the prospect of persecution was drawing near. By the year 113, a Roman governor in Asia Minor named Pliny the Younger had written a letter to the emperor Trajan, requesting instructions regarding the Christians under his rule. He saw the spread of the gospel as a mounting problem: "A great many persons of

2. See *Scofield Reference Bible* (New York: Oxford University Press, 1909), note on Revelation 1:20.
3. James B. Ramsey, *Revelation: An Exposition of the First III Chapters*, Geneva Commentaries (Edinburgh: Banner of Truth, 1977), 42.

every age, of every social class, men and women alike, are being brought in to trial, and this seems likely to continue. It is not only the cities, but also the towns and even the country villages which are being infected with this cult-contagion."[4] The emperor, Domitian's successor, replied that convicted Christians were to be put to death. Those who denied Christianity would have to prove this claim by worshiping an image of the emperor and cursing the name of Christ. This shows that in the brief years between John's letter to the seven churches and Pliny's letter to the emperor Trajan, violent persecution did in fact descend on the Christians of Asia Minor.[5]

The letters themselves show that with persecution drawing near, the chief problem of these churches was spiritual complacency. They had grown lax in their morals and doctrinal fidelity, and in some cases there was a lost zeal for the mission of the gospel. Jesus rebukes "sexual immorality" and the eating of "food sacrificed to idols" (Rev. 2:20), some "who hold the teaching of Balaam" and the "teaching of the Nicolaitans" (2:14–15), and Christians who "are lukewarm, and neither hot nor cold" (3:16). We see in these problems how the seven letters pertain not merely to ancient believers but to all Christians. Revelation therefore addresses complacent Christians who do not realize the trial of their faith that is drawing near. J. Ramsey Michaels comments: "To a considerable extent, it is a wake-up call to Christians who do not sense that they are in any particular danger—a tract for our times no less than John's."[6]

THE GOD OF GRACE AND PEACE

While Revelation is a letter written by John to the seven churches of Asia, the chief figure of this book is the God whose message John bears. This message is the most hopeful news that anyone could ever receive: "Grace to you and peace" (Rev. 1:4). These two words formed the standard greeting of Christ's apostles, some combination of them occurring at the beginning and end of nearly every New Testament letter.

4. Pliny the Younger, "On the Christians," http://www.earlychristianwritings.com/text/pliny2.html.
5. See G. K. Beale, *The Book of Revelation: A Commentary on the Greek Text*, New International Greek Testament Commentary (Grand Rapids: Eerdmans, 1999), 5–16.
6. J. Ramsey Michaels, *Revelation*, IVP New Testament Commentary 20 (Downers Grove, IL: InterVarsity Press, 1997), 20.

Peace is the comprehensive term for the blessings that God gives to those who receive his favor. *Grace* describes the way that God grants this peace to sinners: as a free and unmerited gift through Jesus Christ. What greater need could the recipients of Revelation have than to enjoy the peace of God in a world of violent hatred and deadly temptation? Alexander Maclaren writes: "Surely the one thing that the world wants is to have the question answered whether there really is a God in Heaven that cares anything about me, and to whom I can trust myself wholly."[7] By offering this peace only through God's grace, the Bible reveals the true problem of our condition: as sinners, we are guilty before God and inwardly corrupted by sin. We can be saved only by God's initiative in extending mercy to the unworthy and the weak. The God who gives peace by his own free grace is the only God who could truly meet the needs of the seven churches of Asia or of troubled people today.

In defining the God who gives grace and peace, John employs a carefully chosen Trinitarian formula, expressing how peace and grace flow from each member of the triune Godhead. First, John says that grace and peace come "from him who is and who was and who is to come" (Rev. 1:4). These words refer to God the Father, alluding to the words that God spoke to Moses from the burning bush. Moses asked for God's name, and "God said to Moses, 'I am who i am,'" adding, "Say this to the people of Israel, 'I am has sent me to you'" (Ex. 3:14). Similarly, John represents the God "who is." God does not depend on any other source for his being, but exists by his own power. The God "who is" eternally is sovereign over all things, not only in the present but also in the past and the future: "from him who is and who was and who is to come." David Chilton writes that "as the early Christians faced what seemed to them an uncertain future, they had to keep before them the absolute certainty of God's eternal rule. . . . Threatened, opposed, and persecuted by those in power, they were nevertheless to rejoice in the knowledge of their eternal God . . . [and] His unceasing rule over history."[8] God's lordship over the future is essential to the message of Revelation, which foretells the history of the church and

---

7. Alexander Maclaren, *Expositions of Holy Scripture*, 17 vols. (Grand Rapids: Baker, 1982), 17:119.

8. David Chilton, *Days of Vengeance: An Exposition of the Book of Revelation* (Ft. Worth, TX: Dominion Press, 1987), 59.

+ God exercises sovereign control over the course of history.

declares that "by virtue of his eternal existence," God "exercises sovereign control over the course of history."[9]

Grace and peace are extended not only from the Father, but also "from the seven spirits who are before his throne" (Rev. 1:4). Some commentators suggest that the "seven spirits" are angels who go forth to do God's will, noting that John later speaks of the seven "angels of the seven churches" (1:20).[10] But the expression certainly refers to the Holy Spirit, since the "seven spirits" are presented on a par with the Father and the Son. Moreover, "it is inconceivable that *grace and peace* can originate from anyone but God."[11] G. B. Caird understood John as using "seven spirits" to signify "the Spirit of God in the fullness of his activity and power."[12] John may also have had in mind the seven aspects of the Spirit that Isaiah 11:2 said would come upon the Messiah: he is the spirit "of the LORD," "of wisdom," of "understanding," "of counsel," of "might," "of knowledge," and of "the fear of the LORD." Finally, John likely draws this image from Zechariah 4:2–6, in which the ministry of the Holy Spirit is depicted by a lampstand with seven bowls, shining light into the darkness.

The Bible teaches that the Holy Spirit goes forth from God's throne with the ministry of applying grace and peace to believers. Being perfect and complete for this ministry, the Holy Spirit is all-sufficient to empower God's people to conquer through faith in Christ. The sevenfold Spirit provides the power by which Christ's churches serve as lampstands shining a gospel light into the darkness of unbelief.

A THREEFOLD DESCRIPTION OF CHRIST

Having mentioned the grace and peace that flow from the Father and the Holy Spirit, John gives primary emphasis to God the Son: "and from Jesus Christ the faithful witness, the firstborn of the dead, and the ruler of kings on earth" (Rev. 1:5). The prominence given to Jesus here will continue throughout Revelation. We know from Scripture that the actions of the Trinity are one: whatever one divine person does, God as a whole is doing.

9. Robert H. Mounce, *Revelation*, rev. ed., New International Commentary on the New Testament (Grand Rapids: Eerdmans, 1997), 68.
10. See David E. Aune, *Revelation 1–5*, Word Biblical Commentary 52a (Dallas: Word, 1997), 34.
11. Chilton, *Days of Vengeance*, 60.
12. G. B. Caird, *The Revelation of St. John the Divine* (San Francisco: Harper, 1966), 15.

Yet we may observe that the Father and the Spirit remain relatively in the background of Revelation, which is intensely absorbed with the glorious and victorious reign of Jesus as Lord of history and Savior of his church.

Revelation comes to its conclusion with Jesus Christ offering salvation through grace alone, apart from any merit or works, simply through faith in his gospel: "Let the one who is thirsty come; let the one who desires take the water of life without price" (Rev. 22:17). Here at the beginning of Revelation, John introduces the same Savior through three key descriptions that correspond to his offices as Prophet, Priest, and King. *WITNESS*

First, Jesus is "the faithful witness" (Rev. 1:5). This means that Jesus perfectly reveals God and his salvation to a darkened world. Having come from heaven where he enjoyed close communion with the Father, Jesus is able to make him known. He preached, "Truly, truly, I say to you, we speak of what we know, and bear witness to what we have seen" (John 3:11). Hebrews 1:2 emphasizes that while formerly God spoke by other prophets, "in these last days he has spoken to us by his Son."

Jesus revealed God's holiness in the moral perfection of his life, God's wisdom in the searching teaching of his parables, and God's power in the miracles by which he cast out demons, healed the sick, and stilled the storm. But it was in dying on the cross that Jesus bore faithful witness to the grace and peace of God that sinners need. Christ's atoning death revealed how terrible is the sin by which we have offended heaven, so that only the death of God's perfect Son could gain our forgiveness. At the same time, he gave testimony to the marvel of God's grace in that the Father and Son designed this sacrifice to free believers from their sin. The grace John proclaimed is received only through faith in the gospel Jesus declared, through which we gain peace with God and are blessed with peace from God in our souls.

Moreover, John writes of Jesus as the faithful witness to encourage his people who are about to experience persecution for their testimony to Christ. Jesus gave a faithful witness before the rulers of the world and suffered death for it. But Jesus also foretold his resurrection from the grave. By trusting his Word, Christians can know that persecution will never "separate us from the love of God in Christ Jesus our Lord" (Rom. 8:39). If Jesus was "the faithful witness," declaring God's grace and peace to a sinful, dying world, let us not fail to bear our witness to the world in his name, whatever the cost.

②

Second, Jesus is "the firstborn of the dead" (Rev. 1:5). This speaks of Jesus as the One who conquered death by his resurrection and now rules as Lord over life and salvation. Moreover, as firstborn in the resurrection, Jesus guarantees that there will be a second, a third, and so on: all who are joined to him in saving faith will be resurrected with him into glory. Furthermore, it is by his resurrection that Jesus conveys grace and peace to his people today. Christ is enthroned at the right hand of the Father, ensuring by his unending high-priestly mediation that there is always grace for sinners who believe.

Realizing that we serve a Christ who lives forever, Christians today, like the churches of Asia, should be willing to suffer for the gospel. James Boice wrote: "Not many in western lands are in danger of direct physical persecution for their testimony to Christ, but we are under constant pressure to compromise in less obvious ways. Sin is treated lightly today. . . . We are pressured to adopt the politically correct stance on moral issues and treat as normal behavior sins which the Bible says will bring the unrepentant to judgment. . . . Jesus may be tolerated, . . . but woe to us if we bring him off the reservation and proclaim him as a true and relevant figure for our times."[13] It is in the face of this kind of opposition that Christians must persist in declaring the grace and peace that only Jesus can bring. Paul reasoned: "Who is to condemn? Christ Jesus is the one who died—more than that, who was raised—who is at the right hand of God, who indeed is interceding for us" (Rom. 8:34).

③

John's third description of Christ celebrates his royal authority: "and the ruler of kings on earth" (Rev. 1:5). This follows the teaching of Psalm 89:27, which proclaims, "I will make him the firstborn, the highest of the kings of the earth."

What a blessing it is to know that the true Sovereign reigning over history is Jesus, the Lord of grace and peace. Alexander Maclaren writes: "His dominion rests upon love and sacrifice. And so His Kingdom is a kingdom of blessing and of gentleness; and He is crowned with the crowns of the universe, because He was first crowned with the crown of thorns. His first regal title was written upon His Cross, and from the Cross His Royalty ever flows."[14]

---

13. James Montgomery Boice, *Revelation*, unpublished manuscript, n.d., chap. 2, p. 11.
14. Maclaren, *Expositions of Holy Scripture*, 17:124.

Jesus reigns forever, that he may send grace and peace to those who call on his name. He is the Great Prophet, who bears true testimony of God's grace and peace; he is the Great Priest, who reigns forever above to intercede in the presence of the Father, securing grace and peace for those who pray in his name; and Jesus is the Great King, under whose royal seal God provides the grace and peace that alone can secure eternal life.

To Him Who Sits on the Throne

There can be little doubt that when John completed his designation of Christ as "ruler of kings on earth" (Rev. 1:5), his mind recalled the pretender to this same title, the emperor Domitian. For though Christ sits on the throne of heaven, there sat on the throne of Rome a ruler who was the most vile and dangerous of men. Domitian, whose character is the last we will sketch, lived a life of utter debauchery, destroying those closest to him and ruling an empire by sheer terror. James Hamilton writes: "Imagine living in a world ruled by a man who would leave his brother to die, seduce his own niece, kill people for making jokes about him, and then demand to be addressed as 'Lord and God.'"[15] The Christians to whom John wrote Revelation lived in that very world, with Domitian's and subsequent emperors' malicious attention directed at them.

Revelation was written to show such frightened believers the truth of the world as seen from the throne where Jesus reigns. There is grace and peace from the Father, from the Spirit, and from Christ the Son, whose Word is truth, who conquered death, and who reigns to save his people who bear faithful witness in his name. Domitian reigned on a throne of earthly might, but enthroned as the Sovereign of heaven and earth, the Lord of all history, Jesus was able to declare of those who trust in him: "I give them eternal life, and they will never perish, and no one will snatch them out of my hand" (John 10:28).

How different Domitian was in every way from the true Sovereign, Jesus Christ. The ancient historian Suetonius writes that Domitian "became an object of terror and hatred to all, but he was overthrown at last by a conspiracy of his friends and favorite freedmen, to which his wife was also

15. James M. Hamilton Jr., *Revelation: The Spirit Speaks to the Churches* (Wheaton, IL: Crossway, 2012), 30.

privy."[16] Domitian had everything on earth, but sought to take for himself the place of God. As a result, he was despised by all, was betrayed by his wife and friends, and died to face the eternal judgment of the true and wrathful Sovereign. Meanwhile, Jesus, though himself eternally God, laid down his life to give grace and peace to sinners who receive him in faith. By his reign of love, he gained the loyalty and praise of his people forever, and as "the faithful witness, the firstborn of the dead, and the ruler of kings on earth" (Rev. 1:5), he received from his Father the name that is above every name (Phil. 2:9). For this reason, all heaven declares: "To him who sits on the throne and to the Lamb be blessing and honor and glory and might forever and ever!" (Rev. 5:13).

16. Suetonius, "Domitian," 8.14, in *Lives of the Caesars*, trans. J. C. Rolfe, rev. ed., Loeb Classical Library 38 (Cambridge, MA: Harvard University Press: 1997), 349.

3

To Him Who Loves Us

Revelation 1:5–6

*To him who loves us and has freed us from our sins by his blood
and made us a kingdom, priests to his God and Father, to him
be glory and dominion forever and ever.* (Rev. 1:5–6)

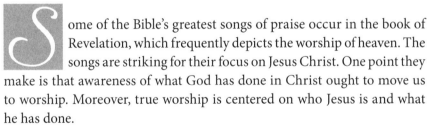

ome of the Bible's greatest songs of praise occur in the book of Revelation, which frequently depicts the worship of heaven. The songs are striking for their focus on Jesus Christ. One point they make is that awareness of what God has done in Christ ought to move us to worship. Moreover, true worship is centered on who Jesus is and what he has done.

Donald Grey Barnhouse points out that Revelation's songs of praise increase in intensity as the book advances. He compares the situation to a man who receives a package and says, "Oh, thank you." When the package is opened, he sees a wallet inside. "Oh, thank you very much," he says. Opening the wallet, he finds some large bills. "Oh, thank you very, very much," he exclaims. Finally, he finds in a side pocket a check for a very large amount and cries, "Thank you, indeed, very, very, very much."[1] Likewise, the praise

---

1. Donald Grey Barnhouse, *Revelation: An Expositional Commentary* (Grand Rapids: Zondervan, 1971), 24–25.

to Christ in Revelation 1:6 reads, "To him be glory and dominion forever and ever." In 4:11, the praise is more expansive: "Worthy are you, our Lord and God, to receive glory and honor and power." By 7:12, there is full, sevenfold praise: "Blessing and glory and wisdom and thanksgiving and honor and power and might be to our God forever and ever!"

While the doxology of Revelation 1:6 is only the beginning, it is nonetheless a great expression of praise to Jesus. When theologians think of Christ, they usually speak in terms of his person and his work. John's doxology touches on the "glory" of Christ's person, but is especially concerned with the marvel of his saving work. In praising Christ's work, John follows the same progression as when he described the Father in verse 4, as the One "who is and who was and who is to come." Similarly, Christ is glorified for his *present* love, for his *past* work of salvation, and finally for his *future* return in clouds of glory. In this chapter, we will explore the first two of these: Christ's present and past work of salvation, and the glory they gain for his name: "To him who loves us and has freed us from our sins by his blood and made us a kingdom, priests to his God and Father, to him be glory and dominion forever and ever. Amen" (Rev. 1:5–6).

Who Loves Us

When John praises Christ for his present work, he sums up the whole by speaking of Christ's love for his people: "To him who loves us" (Rev. 1:5). This is the great fact that the Bible declares to Christians: not just that Christ loved us in the past but that he loves us now. James Boice describes the love of Christ as "so great, so giving, so winsome, so victorious, so infinite, that we can only marvel at it. It is a love that reaches from the heights of divine holiness to the pit of human depravity to save and keep us from sin."[2] Perhaps this explains the popularity of one of our most enduring children's songs: "Jesus loves me, this I know, for the Bible tells me so."[3]

Christ's love is one with God's love for the world. John 3:16 asserts, "For God so loved the world, that he gave his only Son, that whoever believes in him should not perish but have eternal life." Yet the love of God may be the most misused of all Bible truths, especially since some people deny that a

---

2. James Montgomery Boice, *Revelation*, unpublished manuscript, n.d., chap. 3, p. 2.
3. Anna B. Warner, "Jesus Loves Me, This I Know" (1859).

God who loves could ever show wrath toward our sins. While "God is love" (1 John 4:8) is one of the Bible's greatest truths, J. I. Packer points out that it "is not the complete truth about God so far as the Bible is concerned."[4] By virtue of his love, God is not morally indifferent, but is holy and just. He is the God who condemns and punishes the disobedient precisely because he is a God of love: a God who loves truth, righteousness, and holiness.

I remember once meeting with a man who was about to abandon his wife and family. I urged him, among other things, to consider how angry his action would make God. After meeting with his liberal minister, he answered that he did not believe in an angry God but a God of love. I replied that God's love was precisely his problem. God loves his wife. God loves his own law. God loves the sanctity of marriage. It is precisely the God of love who is just in his condemnation of all that is faithless, evil, and unloving!

At the same time that God's love is not the only truth taught in the Bible, Packer adds, "'God is love' is the complete truth about God so far as the Christian is concerned." God sent his Son to die for the forgiveness of his people, so for believers there is nothing to stand in the way of the fullest expression of God's love. In fact, everything that God does in and through Christ is an expression of his love for his chosen people. Packer writes:

> The knowledge that this is so for him personally is the Christian's supreme comfort. . . . Knowing this, he is able to apply to himself the promise that all things work together for good to them that love God and are called according to His purpose (Rom. 8:28). Not just *some* things, note, but *all* things! Every single thing that happens to him expresses God's love to him.[5]

WHO FREED US FROM OUR SIN

In all his writings, the apostle John never mentions the love of God without immediately presenting the death of Jesus for our sins. So it is that having pointed out that Christ loves his people in the present, John praises Christ for the supreme expression of his love that took place in the past: "To him who loves us and has freed us from our sins by his blood" (Rev. 1:5). This is the first of two great saving works that John rejoices in as completed by Christ in the past. Jesus said, "Greater love has no one than this, that someone lay

4. J. I. Packer, *Knowing God* (Downers Grove, IL: InterVarsity Press, 1973), 108.
5. Ibid., 111.

down his life for his friends" (John 15:13). Jesus acted in this great love so as to remove from his people the just condemnation of their sins.

To say that Jesus "freed" us from sins, John uses the Greek verb *luo*, which normally has the meaning of "loosen" or "unfasten." It is used for the taking off of clothes or the unbuckling of armor. When used of persons, *luo* speaks of setting a prisoner free. For this reason, a noun form, *lutron*, came to mean "a ransom price that is paid." From this comes one of the main words for *redemption, apolutrosis*, which speaks of the freeing of a slave by payment of a price.

John's statement that Jesus freed us "from our sins by his blood" (Rev. 1:5) makes plain the primary meaning of Jesus' atoning death on the cross. Jesus freed us by paying the penalty for our sins, substituting himself to die in our place. This is the significance of "by his blood," which means "by his sacrificial death." Putting these ideas together brings us the doctrine of *penal substitutionary atonement*. Jesus atoned for our sins by paying the penalty of our guilt as a Substitute who made a sacrifice in our place with his own blood. Barnhouse writes: "Ours were the sins; His was the blood. Let no man wonder hereafter if salvation is sufficient."[6]

In praising Christ for freeing us from our sins, John captures the experience of Christians at the moment when they believe in Jesus and receive complete forgiveness for their sins. Charles Wesley chronicled this experience in his famous hymn "And Can It Be":

> Long my imprisoned spirit lay
> Fast bound in sin and nature's night;
> Thine eye diffused a quick'ning ray;
> I woke, the dungeon flamed with light:
> My chains fell off, my heart was free;
> I rose, went forth, and followed thee.

This stanza expresses how a believer feels when his or her sins are forgiven, and it concludes by identifying the payment that was offered to achieve that freedom from sin:

> Amazing love! How can it be
> That thou, my God, shouldst die for me?[7]

---

6. Barnhouse, *Revelation*, 24.
7. Charles Wesley, "And Can It Be That I Should Gain" (1738).

When John writes that we are "freed" by Christ's blood, he primarily means that we are set free from God's wrath on unforgiven sinners. We are likewise freed from the fear of hell and the burden of guilt and shame on our souls. Jesus said that "if the Son sets you free, you will be free indeed" (John 8:36). We are set free from fear, knowing that in Christ we have become God's beloved children, destined to live in glory forever. We are freed from the binding influence of sin's power. Although we are not free from trials, we are freed from the power of trials to steal our joy. What an incentive John provides for every sinner to turn in faith to Jesus—poor captives set free by God's gift of his Son! Only those who are so blinded by the power of sin, hardened in unbelief, and deceived in the bondage of darkness will refuse to open their hearts to Jesus. John Newton wrote:

Let us love the Lord who bought us, pitied us when enemies,
Called us by his grace, and taught us, gave us ears and gave us eyes:
He has washed us with his blood, he presents our souls to God.[8]

Who Made Us a Kingdom

When John considers Jesus' past saving work, he marvels not only at the removal of sin but also at the positive results of salvation. Having freed us by his blood, Jesus "made us a kingdom, priests to his God and Father" (Rev. 1:6).

When John spoke of Christ's blood, he evoked images of the Passover, by which the nation of Israel was delivered from death and set free in the exodus. God's angel of death came upon Egypt, visiting every home except that marked by the shed blood of a sacrificial lamb. In this way, God was pointing forward to the death of Christ that truly removes the guilt of sin. John now adds more language that looks back on the exodus when he speaks of believers as a kingdom of priests. "You shall be my treasured possession among all peoples," God told the Israelites, "and you shall be to me a kingdom of priests and a holy nation" (Ex. 19:5–6). In employing this language to speak of what Christ has done for believers, John makes clear that the New Testament church carries on the identity of Old Testament Israel. Moreover, this statement shows that Christians are saved not merely

8. John Newton, "Let Us Love and Sing and Wonder" (1774).

He gave us
Kingdom responsibilities with
fellow Believers.

into an individual relationship with God, but into kingdom responsibilities with fellow believers in the church.

First, John rejoices that Jesus has "made us a kingdom" (Rev. 1:6). Jesus is the King of kings (1:5), and Christians are the kingdom over which Jesus rules. We normally define a kingdom in terms of the territory it controls, but Jesus' kingdom is defined by obedient faith in his Word. "I am a king," he told Pontius Pilate. "For this purpose I was born and for this purpose I have come into the world—to bear witness to the truth" (John 18:37). To believe in Christ is to gain citizenship in his kingdom, transferring our allegiance from the world to him. While we live in the world, we become pilgrims on earth whose hope is in the age to come. Paul wrote that "our citizenship is in heaven, and from it we await a Savior, the Lord Jesus Christ, who will transform our lowly body to be like his glorious body, by the power that enables him even to subject all things to himself" (Phil. 3:20–21).

Not only are Christians Christ's kingdom, but all through Revelation Jesus declares that believers enter into his kingship. He states that Christians who persevere in faith will receive "authority over the nations" (Rev. 2:26) and will "sit with me on my throne" (3:21). In Revelation 5:10, the worshipers in heaven praise Christ for making his people "a kingdom and priests to our God," and John adds that "they shall reign on the earth." Kings reign by conquering, and believers conquer in Christ's name through the gospel. Kings establish their laws, and Christians enter into Jesus' reign by teaching and obeying the commands of Scripture. The key earthly institutions of Christ's kingdom are the church and the Christian family. In these realms, Christ's name is to be worshiped, his Word is to be preached and obeyed, and his gospel is to be advanced. We pray, as Jesus taught us, "Your kingdom come, your will be done, on earth as it is in heaven" (Matt. 6:10).

In addition to making his people a kingdom, Christ is praised for making them "priests to his God and Father" (Rev. 1:6). This, again, picks up the language that God used about Israel in the exodus: it was a nation that served a priestly role on earth. Whereas the Gentile peoples were "strangers to the covenants of promise, having no hope and without God in the world" (Eph. 2:12), this holy nation was to live in the light of God's presence. The priests of the Old Testament had permission to come into the tabernacle for fellowship with and service to God. Likewise, because of Christ's priestly offering to free us from our sins, Christians have liberty to draw near to God with no barriers hindering our fellowship with him.

John says that we have been made priests "to his God and Father" (Rev. 1:6), which speaks of our service to God in Christ's name. The New Testament speaks of the Christian's priestly service in three ways. First, as a kingdom of priests we render true worship to God in accordance with his Word. Hebrews 13:15 urges us: "Through him then let us continually offer up a sacrifice of praise to God, that is, the fruit of lips that acknowledge his name." This reminds us of the chief purpose for coming to church week after week. Many evangelicals today believe that the church exists either to meet the spiritual needs of Christians or to reach out to the world. Both of these are by-products of true worship: biblical worship does bless believers and evangelize the lost. But the true and primary reason to come to church is to fulfill our priestly role of offering worship to the true and living God, who is worthy of all our praise.

Second, priests bear testimony of God's glory and grace to the world. This was Peter's emphasis when he described Christians with the very language that John uses in this doxology: "But you are a chosen race, a royal priesthood, a holy nation, a people for his own possession, that you may proclaim the excellencies of him who called you out of darkness into his marvelous light" (1 Peter 2:9). Priests are those who are privileged to know God through Christ: we are then to represent God and call out to the world with his gospel so that sinners may be reconciled to God and joined to his worshiping throng.

A third passage that uses priestly language for believers is Romans 12:1: "I appeal to you therefore, brothers, by the mercies of God, to present your bodies as a living sacrifice, holy and acceptable to God, which is your spiritual worship." Christians do not offer an atoning sacrifice, since Christ has once for all freed us from our sins by his blood. Instead, we offer the priestly thank offering, using the whole of our lives to say "thank you" to God.

It is vital to emphasize that when John praises Christ for making a kingdom of priests, he is not referring to some select minority within the church. In Christ, all believers are priests unto God; one cannot be a Christian without being a priest. This teaching was known in the Reformation as *the priesthood of all believers*. This doctrine stands in stark contrast to that of the Roman Catholic Church, which sees its priests as occupying a privileged status above the people before God, serving as mediators of God's sacramental grace.

According to the Bible, however, there are only two kinds of priests in Christ's kingdom: Christ the High Priest and all his people who are a kingdom of priests in his name. Certainly, there are differences among believers. There are a variety of gifts and callings within Christ's church. There are pastor-teachers and church officers such as deacons and elders to serve and lead the church. Yet there are no priests other than the entire body of believers, who are all called into the ministries of worship, evangelism, and holy, sacrificial service. It is not merely a few who are called to worship, witness, and offer holy lives: the kingship and priesthood of all believers are essential to the life and work of the church.

On one occasion, my family was present at a swimming pool on the campus of Clemson University where Josh Davis, a three-time Olympic gold medalist, was giving a clinic on swimming technique. At the end of his instruction, Davis gave a motivational speech about how the youths could become Olympic athletes like him. He concluded with a witness that was much in keeping with John's praise to Jesus Christ. Davis pointed out that nothing achieved in a swimming pool, whether medals, sponsorships, or fame, can give true fulfillment in life. "The greatest thing that has happened to me," this Olympic champion told the crowd of youths, "was to realize that God loves me and sent Jesus Christ to die for my sins and give me eternal life." What a pleasure it was to see this energetic Christian reigning with Christ by speaking forth his gospel truth and offering priestly ministry by appealing to sinners on Christ's behalf for salvation. Every Christian, whatever our worldly calling, is likewise called into priestly service on behalf of Jesus. Paul spoke for all believers when he wrote that "we are ambassadors for Christ, God making his appeal through us. We implore you on behalf of Christ, be reconciled to God" (2 Cor. 5:20).

To Him Be Glory!

Since Revelation 1:5–6 presents the first of many praise songs to the glory of Christ in the book of Revelation, it is fitting that these verses conclude with the first doxology to his praise: "To him be glory and dominion forever and ever. Amen."

Later doxologies will add blessings to the name of Christ, such as "thanks" (Rev. 4:9), "honor" (4:11), "power," "wealth," "wisdom," "might," and "blessing" (5:12). This first doxology lifts up the glory and dominion of Christ forever.

"Glory" (Greek, *doxa*) refers to the splendor and worthiness of the exalted Christ. "Dominion" (Greek, *kratos*) refers to his right to govern as Sovereign Lord. We do not bestow these honors on Jesus, for they are his by right and by appointment of the Father. Instead, we recognize his glory and dominion and offer Jesus the praise he deserves for them. Osborne comments: "The adoration of Christ in terms of his 'glory and power' reminds the reader that only he (and not Caesar or any earthly power) is worthy of worship, for only he can effect redemption."[9]

Donald Grey Barnhouse reminds us of the liturgical context of the book of Revelation and imagines in this opening passage a worship service, with antiphonal voices singing. In 1:4, John extends to his readers grace and peace from the triune God: Father, Son, and Holy Spirit. Noting the plural and thus communal "us" and "our" of verses 5 and 6, Barnhouse envisions the congregation responding in joyful doxology, concluding: "To him be glory and dominion forever and ever. Amen." He writes:

> The grace and the peace have come upon the Church. The answer shows a yieldedness to Him. We are won by the attraction of His eternal love, though we had been captives in the chains of sin. The guilt and the chain had been dissolved together by His blood. We are freed . . . .
>
> Is it any wonder that the Church sings this great song of praise? He has redeemed us. He has made us a kingdom. We become priests to God and His Father. The redeemed Church boasts not in herself, but sings, "To him be the glory and the dominion."[10]

When we recognize that the doxology of Revelation 1:5–6 is a response to the grace and peace proclaimed in verses 4 and 5, we realize that all true worship is a response to God's revelation about himself. James Hamilton writes: "We see here the pattern of all worship: God reveals himself and his people respond with the praise due him. Glory and dominion belong to Jesus because 1) he 'loves us,' 2) he 'freed us from our sins by his blood,' and 3) he made us a kingdom and priests."[11] This shows why the idea of worship without the reading and teaching of God's Word falls so

---

9. Grant R. Osborne, *Revelation*, Baker Exegetical Commentary on the New Testament (Grand Rapids: Baker Academic, 2002), 67.

10. Barnhouse, *Revelation*, 23–24.

11. James M. Hamilton Jr., *Revelation: The Spirit Speaks to the Churches* (Wheaton, IL: Crossway, 2012), 37.

far short of the biblical ideal. All through Revelation we will witness the most exalted worship, always in response to the revelation of the glory, grace, and dominion of God in and through Jesus Christ. Jesus taught: "If you abide in my word, you are truly my disciples, and you will know the truth, and the truth will set you free" (John 8:31–32). Our greatest freedom, purchased by Christ's blood, is the worship of God as we are instructed by the revelation of his Word.

Of course, the true way to praise the glory and dominion of Christ is not merely with our lips but with our lives. Are you living as a citizen of the heavenly kingdom, or are you still selling your allegiance to the powers of this world, for the sake of its pleasures and feeble security? Do you acknowledge in your lifestyle—in your use of time, talents, and treasure—that Jesus is your Lord? Do you live like the priest you have been called to be, coming often into God's presence, helping others to know God and his gospel offer of salvation, and offering a sacrifice of praise to his glory? If we know the truth of God in Jesus Christ by believing his Word, then we should respond by living as "a kingdom, priests to his God and Father" (Rev. 1:6).

Finally, in order to live to the praise of God and of Jesus, his Son, we must begin where John began in the book of Revelation. John extends "grace and peace" from the triune God. We, too, must start with the free gift of peace with God. How can we gain this saving gift? John answers, "To him who loves us and has freed us from our sins by his blood" (Rev. 1:5).

Have you brought your sins to be cleansed by the blood of Christ? If you have not, then you are an alien to his kingdom of grace, at enmity with God and subject to his just wrath. At the end of Revelation, Jesus speaks: "Blessed are those who wash their robes, so that they may have the right to the tree of life and that they may enter the city by the gates" (Rev. 22:14). Yet even now, as the true and Great Priest, Jesus offers to free you from sin through faith in his cross, so that you might be reconciled to his God and Father and entered into his kingdom of love.

John concludes his doxology, saying with the church: "Amen." That word means "Yes, so let it be." If you will add your *amen* to the good news of Christ's shed blood for sin, you will be set free from bondage, guilt, and condemnation: free to know and worship God through Jesus Christ. With the *amen* of your faith in Jesus, you may enter his kingdom to marvel in the light of his glory and be blessed by his dominion forever.

4

COMING WITH THE CLOUDS

Revelation 1:7

Behold, he is coming with the clouds, and every eye will see him,
even those who pierced him, and all tribes of the earth will
wail on account of him. Even so. Amen. (Rev. 1:7)

round the year 553 B.C., the prophet Daniel received an angelic visit in a dream. The prophet had by now spent most of his life in exile as a reluctant servant to the kings of Babylon. Change was coming, however, because the young ruler Belshazzar was soon to be ousted by the Medo-Persian army. Daniel's vision fittingly began with "the four winds of heaven . . . stirring up the great sea" (Dan. 7:2). Just when it seemed that there would be no end to Babylonian power, God was stirring the waters of history.

As often happens, God's intervention began with initially troubling news. Daniel saw four terrible beasts rising in succession out of the waters, each representing a kingdom that would rule on earth: a winged lion for Babylon; a devouring bear for Medo-Persia; a winged leopard for Macedonia; and finally a terrifying beast with iron teeth for Rome (Dan. 7:3–8). Above these visions, Daniel then saw the "Ancient of Days," sitting on his throne, with a river of fire before him. The scene emphasized the sovereignty of God over the mighty kingdoms of earth and his judgment of their evil. Daniel saw the fourth and greatest beast "killed, and its body destroyed and given over to be burned with fire" (7:11). The vision showed heaven's victory over the evil kingdoms that dominate the earth.

Daniel's vision did not conclude, however, with God's judgment of the wicked nations. He further saw another figure, designated as "one like a son of man," coming "with the clouds of heaven" to be presented before "the Ancient of Days" (Dan. 7:13). Daniel records: "To him was given dominion and glory and a kingdom, that all peoples, nations, and languages should serve him; his dominion is an everlasting dominion, which shall not pass away" (7:14).

In our study of Revelation 1:1, we noted how John seems to have picked up language from the vision of Daniel 2, which like Daniel 7 presents earthly kingdoms overthrown by God and his kingdom. In Revelation 1:7, John makes another explicit reference to Daniel's prophecy, saying of Jesus: "Behold, he is coming with the clouds."

John's repeated appeal to Daniel in the opening section of Revelation tells us two important things. First, the apostle relates the situation of his readers, the Christians in Asia Minor in the late first century, to that of Daniel in the Babylonian captivity. Just as Daniel and his fellow exiles had been separated from God's city and forced to live under an oppressive, ungodly rule, so also were John's readers physically separated from Christ and subjected to wicked persecution. This is the usual experience of Christians, whom Peter describes as "sojourners and exiles" in this world (1 Peter 2:11). We are a pilgrim people, living as "strangers and exiles on the earth" (Heb. 11:13), journeying through this world to the world to come.

Second, by appealing to Daniel's vision of the coming Christ, John shows that Christians have this same hope of salvation. Like Daniel and John, we live in a beastly world filled with violent oppressors, tempters into evil, and ungodly opponents of God's truth. Yet these evils will not hold sway forever. According to Iain Duguid, "Our challenge is to live our lives with our eyes firmly fixed on the heavenly throne room. Instead of being terrified by the beasts we must daily live remembering the one who will deliver the final and decisive judgment."[1]

1. Iain M. Duguid, *Daniel*, Reformed Expository Commentary (Phillipsburg, NJ: P&R Publishing, 2008), 119.

Christ's Coming in Glory

The theater has a practice known as *upstaging*, when the supporting characters turn their backs on the audience, forcing their gaze on the lead actor who has entered the stage. John is doing something like this in the opening section of Revelation, drawing all our attention to the person and work of Jesus Christ. In the doxology of 1:5–6, he glorified the present and past work of Christ for our salvation: "To him who loves us and has freed us from our sins by his blood" (Rev. 1:5). Now, John completes his spotlighting of Christ by pointing to the future return: "Behold, he is coming with the clouds" (1:7). Charles Spurgeon said of this theme: "Brethren, no truth ought to be more frequently proclaimed, next to the first coming of the Lord, than His Second Coming."[2] According to the Bible, the return of Jesus is just as important as his first coming. The writer of Hebrews noted: "So Christ, having been offered once to bear the sins of many, will appear a second time, not to deal with sin but to save those who are eagerly waiting for him" (Heb. 9:28).

When John speaks of Jesus' "coming with the clouds" (Rev. 1:7), he refers to Christ in the terms of Daniel 7:13. After seeing the judgment of the wicked kingdoms, Daniel saw that "with the clouds of heaven there came one like a son of man." Like Daniel, John faced the beastly opposition of wicked earthly rulers, against which Christ will ultimately be revealed as Sovereign Conqueror in his glorious coming. Psalm 2 sets the same theme, asking, "Why do the nations rage and the peoples plot in vain?" (Ps. 2:1). This is the way it always is on the earth, whether in David's, Daniel's, John's, or our own time: "The rulers take counsel together, against the LORD and against his Anointed" (2:2). Yet however terrible earthly idolatry may seem to us, it is all laughable to God: "He who sits in the heavens laughs; the Lord holds them in derision" (2:4). God responds to violent earthly presumption by doing what he has always ordained: "As for me, I have set my King on Zion, my holy hill" (2:6). Daniel saw the glorification of Christ as the answer to the ungodly powers of history, just as Psalm 2 saw God's coronation of his Son as the answer to the plotting kings of earth. John declares to Christians that the sovereign rule of Christ at history's end is our hope as well.

---

2. Charles H. Spurgeon, *Spurgeon's Sermons on the Second Coming*, ed. David Otis Fuller (Grand Rapids: Zondervan, 1943), preface.

When Daniel, and then John, spoke of Christ's returning "with the clouds," this imagery emphasized his divine glory and authority. Psalm 104:3 tells us that God "makes the clouds his chariot; he rides on the wings of the wind." These are the same clouds that sheathed Mount Sinai when God came upon the mountain to give his law (Ex. 19:16–19) and then later filled the temple of Solomon with glory (1 Kings 8:10–11). For Jesus to come "with the clouds" is to return to earth in divine glory and power to bring his judgment on the world.

The Bible is unambiguous in declaring that Jesus Christ, who died on the cross, was raised from the grave, and ascended into heaven, will someday return to earth in divine glory and power. Paul refers to this event as "our blessed hope, the appearing of the glory of our great God and Savior Jesus Christ" (Titus 2:13). Just as Christians look to the past for salvation, trusting Jesus' death on the cross, and look to heaven for our present spiritual care, we also look to the future horizon to see the final consummation of all our hopes in Christ. We stand on the past work of Jesus' cross, are upheld by his loving intercession now in heaven, and look ahead to his glorious return when our inheritance in glory will appear.

Looking forward to Christ's return will have real implications for how believers think about their lives. For instance, a vision of Christ's coming will shape our outlook on earthly treasures. Jesus urged: "Do not lay up for yourselves treasures on earth, where moth and rust destroy and where thieves break in and steal, but lay up for yourselves treasures in heaven, where neither moth nor rust destroys and where thieves do not break in and steal" (Matt. 6:19–20). We store up treasures in heaven by serving the kingdom of Christ now: investing in ministry to others and in building up Christ's church.

A future focus on Christ's coming will produce a different lifestyle from one that is focused on earthly things. Paul saw the purpose of his life in terms of spiritual growth: "Forgetting what lies behind and straining forward to what lies ahead, I press on toward the goal for the prize of the upward call of God in Christ Jesus" (Phil. 3:13–14). Unbelievers glory in worldly pleasures, "with minds set on earthly things" (3:19). "But our citizenship is in heaven," Paul writes, "and from it we await a Savior, the Lord Jesus Christ, who will transform our lowly body to be like his glorious body, by the power that enables him even to subject all things to himself" (3:20–21). In saying that

Christians "await a Savior" from heaven, Paul means that they live lives of godly service, biblical devotion, prayer, and witness to the gospel—actions that all point us forward to the hope that we have, no longer in the world, but in the coming of Christ. Can these things be said of us? Does our manner of life suggest that we are awaiting a Savior from heaven? Or is our life fixed on earthly things?

EVERY EYE WILL SEE HIM

As John speaks of Christ's coming, he specifies that his return will be visible to all: "every eye will see him" (Rev. 1:7). This teaching rules out the idea of a merely spiritual coming of Jesus. John does not say that "every mind will perceive him," but that "every eye will see him." Spurgeon writes: "The Lord Jesus Christ will not come spiritually, for in that sense he is always here; but he will come really and substantially, for every eye shall see him, even those unspiritual eyes which gazed on him with hate."[3]

John claims that Christ's return will be visible to all people on the earth. This claim is contrary to the doctrine of Christ's secret coming, which many Christians today believe, together with the rapture of believers from the world and Christ's visible return on a second occasion. Notice that John makes no mention of two comings of Christ—one secret and one visible. In fact, the Bible consistently speaks of Christ's coming to save his people and judge his enemies as a single event. Paul writes that Christ comes both "to repay with affliction those who afflict you, and to grant relief to you who are afflicted . . . , when the Lord Jesus is revealed from heaven" (2 Thess. 1:6–8). First Thessalonians 4:16–17, the key text that teaches the rapture, or the taking up of believers from the earth, presents Christ's return as anything but a secret event. Jesus comes "with a cry of command, with the voice of an archangel, and with the sound of the trumpet of God." Not only will Christ be seen by all when he comes for his people, but he will be heard by everyone as well.

When John writes that Christ is "coming with the clouds, and every eye will see him" (Rev. 1:7), this agrees with the picture throughout Scripture of a cataclysmic, glorious event that decisively ends history as we have known it.

3. Charles H. Spurgeon, *Metropolitan Tabernacle Pulpit*, 63 vols. (Pasadena, TX: Pilgrim Publications, 1974), 33:596.

41

Jesus said that "they will see the Son of Man coming on the clouds of heaven with power and great glory" (Matt. 24:30). "For as the lightning comes from the east and shines as far as the west," Jesus added, "so will be the coming of the Son of Man" (24:27). These statements make clear that Jesus will be made visible to all the earth not by means of electronic technology, but in a decisive and sky-splitting display of divine glory.

An important implication of this teaching is that when Christ returns, there will be no further opportunity for salvation, since his coming involves the immediate resurrection and final judgment of all persons (Matt. 25:31–32; 1 Thess. 4:16). Those who rejected Jesus in this age will be forced to see how wrong they were as his sovereign glory is displayed to all. Philip Hughes writes that on that day, "there will be no escaping or hiding from the resplendent majesty of his coming; every knee will bow in submission to him and every tongue will acknowledge his lordship (Phil. 2:10f; Rom. 14:11; Isa. 45:23)."[4]

HIM WHOM THEY PIERCED

In addition to Christ's being seen by all the earth, John highlights two other features of his return. The returning Christ will be seen as the One who was crucified and rejected: "even those who pierced him." In addition, there will be great sorrow: "and all tribes of the earth will wail on account of him" (Rev. 1:7). In making these statements, John is echoing the prophecy of Zechariah 12:10: "When they look on me, on him whom they have pierced, they shall mourn for him, as one mourns for an only child, and weep bitterly over him."

There are three primary options for understanding the fulfillment of this prophecy. One approach is that of preterism, the view that understands Revelation to have been written before the fall of Jerusalem in A.D. 70 and that sees most of Revelation's prophecies as pertaining only to that event. In keeping with that approach, preterists see Revelation 1:7 not as referring to the return of Christ but as symbolically referring to God's judgment in the destruction of Jerusalem and the temple. David Chilton asserts that the language of Christ's "coming with the clouds" refers merely to "the Com-

---

4. Philip Edgcumbe Hughes, *The Book of Revelation* (Downers Grove, IL: InterVarsity Press, 1990), 21.

ing of Christ in judgment upon Israel, in order to establish the Church as the new Kingdom."[5] Likewise, "those who pierced him" refers strictly to the Jewish nation, who "wail on account of him" because of the torments of the Roman siege.

There are a number of reasons to reject the preterist reading of Revelation 1:7. We have already seen that it is unlikely that Revelation was written before A.D. 70 with the destruction of Jerusalem in mind. The persecutions described in Revelation better fit a later period, and the early church gives an extensive witness to the later dating of Revelation. We should also note that whereas the preterists see Christ's coming with the clouds as pertaining to a local judgment, Daniel and Zechariah see Christ's coming to judge the entire world. It is simply impossible to accommodate the description of Revelation 1:7 to the preterist reading, since John notes that "every eye" will see Christ and "all tribes of the earth" wail for him.

A second approach to this verse does not downplay Christ's return but adds to it the present coming of Christ through the preaching of his gospel. Under this view, the mourning over the pierced Christ takes place by those who hear the gospel, realize that Christ died for their sins, and are saved through repentance and faith. This view fits the original message of Zechariah 12:10, which undeniably looks forward to salvation through faith in Christ. Zechariah said that God will pour out "a spirit of grace and pleas for mercy, so that, when they look on me, on him whom they have pierced, they shall mourn for him." Zechariah was foreseeing the grace and mercy of God in bringing salvation to those who see Christ pierced and believe on him for their own forgiveness. This view is made all the more clear by the passage that follows: "On that day there shall be a fountain opened for the house of David and the inhabitants of Jerusalem, to cleanse them from sin and uncleanness" (Zech. 13:1).

Zechariah's message reminds us that "those who pierced him" includes more than those who were physically present at his unjust execution, since Jesus died for the sins of all his people. Likewise, "all tribes of the earth" refers to believers from all over the world who grieve over what their sins did to Christ. In his Gospel, John quoted Zechariah's prophecy as having been fulfilled by the Roman soldier who pierced Jesus and then apparently

---

5. David Chilton, *Days of Vengeance: An Exposition of the Book of Revelation* (Ft. Worth, TX: Dominion Press, 1987), 64.

repented and believed. The young John was himself a witness of Christ's piercing, and wrote that "these things took place that the Scripture might be fulfilled: . . . 'They will look on him whom they have pierced'" (John 19:36–37).

These quotations show that John saw Zechariah's prophecy as fulfilled when sinners see Christ pierced for them, believe in his gospel, and are saved. This shows that the right way to respond to the Bible's teaching of Christ's suffering for sin is to mourn over our own guilt that caused God's Son such suffering. This grieving for sin should cause us to call on God for mercy through Jesus, so that we might be forgiven and, as Zechariah went on to say, so that "a fountain [is] opened . . . , to cleanse them from sin and uncleanness" (Zech. 13:1). If we have never come to Jesus for forgiveness, we should see him now through God's Word, grieve for our sins, and call on him, the One who was pierced, to save us by his blood.

It is most likely, however, that in Revelation 1:7 John writes of Jesus' second coming as an event that catches most people unprepared and unforgiven because of their unbelief. Every eye will see his return and will look upon the One whom they pierced in mockery and rejection, "and all tribes of the earth will wail on account of him." The scene is Christ's judgment on unbelieving humanity, which experiences sorrow without repentance and mourning over the realization that there is no longer an opportunity to believe and be saved. Such mourners will no doubt lament the lives they led, and their seeing the grace of Christ for believers will make the anguish of judgment all the more keen. James Ramsey said: "Christ rejected, an offered salvation neglected, a day of grace wasted, this is the thing that will give the lost sinner his keenest anguish, and wring from him at the last a bitterer wail than devils ever uttered."[6]

John concludes Revelation 1:7 with a brief but definite response: "Even so. Amen." These words mean "Yes, so let it be." John notes how fitting it is that Christ should come to judge those who hated him, rejected his gospel, oppressed his people, and crucified him in unbelief. What John marks as certain then, however, is now still yet to come. Surely this realization urges us all to ensure that we confess our sins and come to Jesus for salvation. Donald Grey Barnhouse warns: "At His first coming, [Jesus] dealt with

6. James B. Ramsey, *Revelation: An Exposition of the First III Chapters*, Geneva Commentaries (Edinburgh: Banner of Truth, 1977), 56.

sin; at His second coming, He will deal with sinners. We must live either in verses five and six, freed by His blood, or in verse seven under His coming judgment. . . . If you will not let Him deal with you in love, He must come to you as your Judge."[7]

BEHOLD, HE COMES!

But we have a timeline revealed. The timing is ~~revealed~~ to Christians who study Daniel & Rev

For Christians, John's announcement is the most exciting news that we could ever hear. John prompts our excitement when he begins with the word "Behold" (Rev. 1:7). Since "every eye will see him," behold, we will ourselves witness Christ's returning in glory. Does this not give excitement to our lives? Does this not prove that we are personally involved in the grand story of the Bible? The prophet Isaiah foretold Christ's birth: "Behold, the virgin shall conceive and bear a son, and shall call his name Immanuel" (Isa. 7:14). None of us, however, were privileged to witness Jesus' birth. Angels came later and told the disciples about Jesus' resurrection: "Come, see the place where he lay. . . . Behold, he is going before you to Galilee; there you will see him" (Matt. 28:6–7). These are great events that we read about but did not witness for ourselves. Yet when John writes, "Behold, he is coming with the clouds," he is speaking to us as witnesses of this future event. The return of Christ in glory is not only one of the great events of redemptive history, but also the ultimate and consummate saving act of our Lord Jesus, and all people will see it. His coming is the end of the world of sin and unbelief and the beginning of an eternal age of glory in the light of God's love. Surely this event, which we all will witness, is something to be excited about!

Not only should we be excited about Christ's coming, but we should be preparing ourselves for the One who comes. Sports fans who are excited about the beginning of the football season immerse themselves in facts about their team. If we are excited about the coming of Christ, we will make it our daily passion to know him better, primarily through the prayerful study of his Word. A bride prepares for her long-awaited wedding day by making herself as beautiful as possible. We, too, anticipating the soon return of Christ, should be making ourselves daily more spiritually beautiful by laboring to remove sin and prayerfully seeking the spiritual graces—faith,

---

7. Donald Grey Barnhouse, *Revelation: An Expositional Commentary* (Grand Rapids: Zondervan, 1971), 24–25.

hope, and love (1 Cor. 13:13); righteousness, peace, and joy (Rom. 14:17)—that make our hearts lovely before the Lord. Finally, those who know that an important political election is coming will seek to persuade others of the important issues of our day. The Christian, realizing that Christ will soon come to save his people and judge those who persist in unbelief, will busy himself by bearing testimony to the grace of God in Jesus Christ, who offers salvation to all who hear and believe.

"Behold, he is coming with the clouds"! Are you ready to meet him, the holy Son of God and Sovereign Lord over all history? Are your sins washed clean in the blood of his cross? Have you been justified through faith in his gospel? The apostle Paul once addressed a man who understood the urgency of his situation. The man asked him, "What must I do to be saved?" Paul answered: "Believe in the Lord Jesus, and you will be saved" (Acts 16:30–31). He is coming soon, to gather his believing people and judge the world in its sin. Nothing is more urgent for anyone than to believe in Jesus Christ, trusting him as Savior and surrendering to him as Lord. For then, when he comes, you will see him, the One who was pierced for your sins, and you will be saved.

5

THE ALPHA AND THE OMEGA

Revelation 1:8

"I am the Alpha and the Omega," says the Lord God, "who is and who was and who is to come, the Almighty." (Rev. 1:8)

*I*n Revelation 1:8, we come to the final verse in John's introduction to this remarkable book. The prologue gives useful information about Revelation, and the most important bit is the purpose for which John is writing. There are many secondary purposes for Revelation, such as giving information about the future and exhorting the churches to which it was written. But the great purpose of Revelation is to provide Christians with a view of history from God's perspective in heaven. As James Boice elaborated, "the primary purpose of Revelation is to enable Christians from every age and in every possible circumstance to view what is happening in history from God's point of view, rather than from man's, and to be comforted and strengthened by it to live for Christ and his glory at all times."[1]

By keeping this grand purpose for Revelation in mind, we can best understand the role of 1:8 in concluding John's prologue. It might seem strange,

1. James Montgomery Boice, *Revelation*, unpublished manuscript, n.d., chap. 4, p. 1.

after all, that at the end of the apostle's introduction, God the Father himself speaks to the readers. This is more surprising when we note that the first person of the Godhead does not speak again in this long book until almost the end (Rev. 21:5–8). Why, then, does John's prologue conclude: "'I am the Alpha and the Omega,' says the Lord God, 'who is and who was and who is to come, the Almighty'" (1:8)? The answer is that since Revelation presents God's view of history, it makes sense for God to present himself as the Sovereign who is able to hold all things together and accomplish all his purposes in Christ to save his people.

THE SOVEREIGNTY OF GOD

The question of the sovereignty of God is essential to all Christians, but especially to those who are going through hard times. Boice asks: "Is God sovereign? Is he regulating affairs on earth today and at all times? Or are things somehow out of his control? Or in man's hands? Or even controlled by the devil?"[2] The evidence suggests to many that God is not in control. Perhaps no one is. History, many argue, is like a roller-coaster off the rails, careening forward by chance and momentum toward a dangerous, unsettling, but nonetheless exciting future. Wasn't it Jesus, after all, who said that history would involve wars and rumors of wars, famines, earthquakes, persecutions, and more (Matt. 24:5–12)? Someone has penned a limerick that responds to these catastrophes with a pessimistic view of history:

> God's plan made a hopeful beginning,
> But man spoiled his chances by sinning.
>> We trust that the story
>> Will end in God's glory
> But at present the other side's winning.

This poem may be funny, but its theology is dreadful. Boice points out: "If 'the other side's winning,' we are all in deep trouble. But the other side is not. What Revelation teaches is that God is sovereign over all things, including the ups and downs of human history, and that he is indeed working out everything according to the counsel of his own inscrutable yet perfect will."[3]

2. Ibid., chap. 4, p. 3.
3. Ibid.

In a world like ours, we will often feel like the prophet Isaiah, when the righteous king Uzziah died. Isaiah was reeling over Israel's loss and for the uncertainty of what would happen next. He did the right thing, however, by turning to God, entering into his temple. There, God gave the prophet the vision that his faith needed: "In the year that King Uzziah died I saw the Lord sitting upon a throne, high and lifted up; and the train of his robe filled the temple" (Isa. 6:1). Isaiah was reminded that God is the true Sovereign over his people, and that while Uzziah may have vacated his throne, God had not stepped off from his. The Lord is "high and lifted up" above the affairs of the earth, and since God's robe "filled the temple," there is no room for any other sovereign. Over all history there is only one Lord and King, and that Sovereign is God himself.

THE ETERNITY OF GOD

Revelation 1:8 supports God's sovereignty with three statements, the first of which expresses the eternity of God: "'I am the Alpha and the Omega,' says the Lord God." The point is that God reigns over all, since he is before and after all things.

"The Alpha and the Omega" is a figure of speech called a *merism*. G. K. Beale writes that "a merism states polar opposites in order to highlight everything between the opposites."[4] As the Alpha and the Omega, God is in control of everything in between. This statement echoes Isaiah 41:4, where God says: "Who has performed and done this, calling the generations from the beginning? I, the LORD, the first, and with the last; I am he."

When we speak of God's being eternal, we mean that his being exists outside time and history, which God created. A. W. Tozer writes: "Because God lives in an everlasting now, He has no past and no future. When time-words occur in the Scriptures they refer to our time, not to His. . . . Since God is uncreated, He is not Himself affected by that succession of consecutive changes we call time. God dwells in eternity but time dwells in God."[5] Peter therefore states that "with the Lord one day is as a thousand years, and a thousand years as one day" (2 Peter 3:8). Being eternal, God is the

4. G. K. Beale, *The Book of Revelation: A Commentary on the Greek Text*, New International Greek Testament Commentary (Grand Rapids: Eerdmans, 1999), 199.
5. A. W. Tozer, *The Knowledge of the Holy* (San Francisco: HarperSanFrancisco, 1992), 61–62.

One "who is and who was and who is to come" (Rev. 1:8). William Barclay comments: "He has been the God of all who have trusted in him; he is the God in whom at this present moment we can put our trust; and there can be no event and no time in the future which can separate us from him."[6]

An analogy of a river may help us to understand God as eternal. We experience time the way that a boat travels down a stream: we are on the river, are at only one place at any one time, and can see only a short distance behind and ahead. But God has an aerial view that enables him to see the entire river at once. He knows every turn, sees every narrows, and foresees every difficulty and danger. As the Alpha who started it, God knows where the river began, and as the Omega, he has ordained its destination. Likewise, everything that is, was, or will be is present to God at the same time and is subject to his rule. This is true of our individual lives, the whole of which God sees at once from beginning to end. The same is true for all history. Beale writes: "The God who transcends time guides the entire course of history because he stands as sovereign over its beginning and its end."[7] What better news could suffering Christians have than that God is "the Alpha and the Omega"?

THE SELF-EXISTENCE OF GOD

When we study the attributes of God, we find that they are all interrelated. Therefore, related to God's eternity is another attribute of God highlighted in Revelation 1:8. Repeating a phrase from verse 4, God describes himself as the Alpha and the Omega, "who is and who was and who is to come." These words reflect God's eternity, but the first of them especially declares God's self-existence. He is the God "who is." Not only does the eternal God have no beginning, but the self-existent God has no source of life other than himself.

God's self-existence is highlighted in the Greek text, which begins Revelation 1:8 with the words *ego eimi*, "I am." These words bring us to the burning bush, where God spoke to Moses. Moses asked for his name, and God answered, "I AM WHO I AM" (Ex. 3:14). In Hebrew, this is summarized by the tetragrammaton, the four Hebrew letters that make the name *Yahweh*,

6. William Barclay, *The Revelation of John*, 3rd ed., 2 vols., New Daily Study Bible (Louisville: Westminster John Knox, 2004), 1:44.

7. Beale, *Revelation*, 199.

based on the verb *to be*. "Say this to the people of Israel," God told Moses, "I am has sent me to you" (3:14).

God's self-existence is declared in the Bible's very first verse, "In the beginning, God created the heavens and the earth" (Gen. 1:1). God's being is like the fire in the burning bush that Moses saw on the mountain, which "was burning, yet it was not consumed" (Ex. 3:2). The fire did not depend on the bush but burned by its own all-sufficient life. Like the fire, God does not derive his life from any source; the fire burned in the bush, but the bush was not the source of the fire. The theological term for God's self-existence is *aseity*. This word combines the Latin *a*, meaning "from," and *se*, meaning "himself." God is "from himself." The Puritan Matthew Henry observed: "The greatest and best man in the world must say, By the grace of God *I am what I am*; but God says absolutely—and it is more than any creature, man or angel, can say—*I am that I am*."[8]

A number of implications may be drawn from the self-existence of God, starting with his self-sufficiency. Philip Ryken says: "He does not have any unmet needs or unsatisfied desires. He does not need any help. He is not codependent. He is not living on borrowed time. He does not live or move or have his being in anyone except himself."[9]

A second implication of God's self-existence involves another attribute of God: his immutability. This means that God does not and cannot change. Because God is eternal, his being is not subject to any chain of events. Because he is self-sufficient, nothing outside God is able to cause him to change. Paul wrote, "For from him and through him and to him are all things" (Rom. 11:36). Therefore, having his life entirely from himself, the God "who is and who was and who is to come" always is, was, and will be exactly who he is.

The immutability of God provides more good news to suffering Christians like the believers to whom John was writing in Revelation. It means, first, that *God's character does not change*. God is now exactly the same as he always has been and will be for all eternity. Westminster Shorter Catechism answer 4 teaches: "God is a Spirit, infinite, eternal, and *unchangeable* in his being, wisdom, power, holiness, justice, goodness, and truth" (emphasis added). This means that we can count on God to always be the same as he is revealed in the Bible. People often change and let us down. Their attitude

---

8. Matthew Henry, *Commentary on the Whole Bible*, 6 vols. (Peabody, MA: Hendrickson, n.d.), 1:284.
9. Philip Graham Ryken, *Discovering God in Stories from the Bible* (Wheaton, IL: Crossway, 1999), 94.

toward us alters without a good reason. But God is always the same in his being, attitude, and purpose. Some people counter by arguing that the Bible does show God as changing his attitude toward people. The answer is that while God responds to sin, faith, and obedience, he always responds to these in the same way. A. W. Tozer writes: "What peace it brings to the Christian's heart to realize that our heavenly Father never differs from himself. In coming to him at any time we need not wonder whether we shall find him in a receptive mood. He is always receptive to misery and need, as well as to love and faith.... Today, this moment, he feels toward his creatures, toward babies, toward the sick, the fallen, the sinful, exactly as he did when he sent his only begotten son into the world to die for mankind."[10]

Along with God's character, *God's truth does not change.* J. I. Packer writes:

> Men sometimes say things that they do not really mean, simply because they do not know their own mind; also, because their views change, they frequently find that they can no longer stand to say things that they said in the past....
>
> The words of men are unstable things. But not so the words of God. They stand forever, as abidingly valid expressions of his mind and thought. No circumstances prompt him to recall them; no changes in his own thinking require him to amend them. Isaiah writes, "All flesh is grass . . . the grass withereth . . . but the word of our God shall stand for ever" (Isa. 40:6 ff.).[11]

Moreover, *God's purposes do not change.* Our plans change, simply because we do not know the future until it arrives and we often lack the ability to do what we intended. Not so with God! Isaiah 46:9–10 proclaims: "I am God, and there is none like me, declaring the end from the beginning and from ancient times things not yet done, saying, 'My counsel shall stand, and I will accomplish all my purpose.'"

Since God's purposes never change, his purposes for Jesus Christ will never change. The Bible asserts that God's purpose is to enthrone his Son and glorify him forever (Ps. 2:6–7; Phil. 2:9–11). God has ordained his Son as the only Savior, and so the words of the apostle Peter will be true forever: "There is salvation in no one else, for there is no other name under heaven given among men by which we must be saved" (Acts 4:12). What folly it is, then, to resist Jesus Christ and withhold our faith from him, since God

---

10. Tozer, *The Knowledge of the Holy*, 82.
11. J. I. Packer, *Knowing God* (Downers Grove, IL: InterVarsity Press, 1973), 70.

"put all things under his feet and gave him as head over all things to the church" (Eph. 1:22).

Not only will God's plans for Christ never change, but his plans for his redeemed people will also never change. Paul wrote that "those whom he foreknew he also predestined to be conformed to the image of his Son, in order that he might be the firstborn among many brothers" (Rom. 8:29). Christians are ordained by God to partake of the holiness of Christ, so it makes no sense for believers to live as though they still belonged to the world. Paul stated that as children of God, believers are "heirs of God and fellow heirs with Christ" (8:17). Because God is sovereign, eternal, and unchanging, his salvation is also sovereign, eternal, and secure. Jesus said, "I give them eternal life, . . . and no one is able to snatch them out of the Father's hand" (John 10:28–29). When God forgives through faith in Christ, he does so eternally and unchangingly, promising, "I will remember their sins no more" (Heb. 8:12).

Finally, since God's purposes never change, God's plans for the wicked will not change. Revelation shows that God will judge sinners who have not been forgiven. Exodus 34:7 (NIV) teaches that God "does not leave the guilty unpunished," and the many judgments displayed in Revelation add living color to that assertion. God's unwavering wrath against sin gives a warning to anyone who refuses Jesus as Lord and Savior. A. W. Pink writes: "Those who defy him, break his laws, have no concern for his glory, but live their lives as though he existed not, must not suppose that, when at the last they shall cry to him for mercy, [having rejected Jesus], he will alter his will, revoke his word, and rescind his awful threatenings. . . . God hates sin, eternally hates it. Hence the *eternality* of the punishment of all who die in their sins."[12]

THE OMNIPOTENCE OF GOD

In proving the sovereignty of God by means of his attributes, we have considered the eternity of God, together with his self-existence, self-sufficiency, and immutability: "'I am the Alpha and the Omega,' says the Lord God, 'who is and who was and who is to come'" (Rev. 1:8). We might think that there is nothing more to say on the matter, but God points out one more essential

12. Arthur W. Pink, *The Attributes of God* (Grand Rapids: Baker, 1993), 40.

attribute that makes him sovereign over all things. Verse 8 adds an assertion of God's omnipotence, concluding with "the Almighty."

The Greek word translated as "Almighty" is *pantokrator*. This word combines *pantos*, for "all things," and *kratos*, which means both "might" and "dominion." Luke 1:51 uses *kratos* to say that God "has shown strength with his arm," and 1 Timothy 6:16 uses it to exult in God's "eternal dominion." For God to be the *pantokrator* is to exercise sovereign power and authority to rule all things, in all places, and at all times. Stephen Charnock elaborates:

> As God is Lord, he hath a right to enact; as he is almighty, he hath a power to execute; . . . in regard of his sovereignty, he hath a right to command all creatures; in regard of his almightiness, he hath power to make his commands be obeyed, or to punish men for the violation of them. . . . This dominion is a right of making what he pleases, of possessing what he made, of disposing of what he doth possess; . . . and to execute the manner wherein he resolves to dispose of his creatures.[13]

A Bible story that depicts God as Almighty is that of Joseph, the beloved son of the patriarch Jacob. Joseph's story may seem to display all that is unjust and unstable in our world. His brothers disliked him and so betrayed Joseph. Sold as a slave in Egypt, he served faithfully but was wrongly imprisoned and expended his precious youth in the darkness of a cell. Yet God was revealed as almighty over these circumstances. A fellow prisoner, Pharaoh's cupbearer, was released from jail and commended Joseph to the ruler. When God enabled Joseph to interpret Pharaoh's dreams, Jacob's son was installed as regent over the greatest nation in the world. In this almighty way, God both prepared Joseph for the role he was to play in God's plan and also used Joseph to save his people from a famine and bring them into Egypt. Joseph himself explained God's overruling sovereignty to his repentant brothers: "As for you, you meant evil against me, but God meant it for good, to bring it about that many people should be kept alive, as they are today" (Gen. 50:20).

Knowing the truth of God's almighty and sovereign rule over all things brings the greatest comfort to suffering Christians like John's audience in Revelation. How are we, in our turn, to meet the uncertainty, unfairness, and sorrows of this world of sin? In John's day, Epicurean philosophy had

13. Stephen Charnock, *The Existence and Attributes of God*, 2 vols. (Grand Rapids: Baker, 1996), 2:364.

captured large portions of society with the same kind of existentialism that tells people today to find their solace in pleasure. In this view, life is a tragedy without meaning. But for believers who know God as sovereign *pantokrator*, life possesses a great purpose beyond the trials, and our knowledge of God's eternal, unchanging, and almighty love fills us with comfort and joy. We look up from God's Word with praise to him, crying with the host of heaven: "We give thanks to you, Lord God Almighty, who is and who was, for you have taken your great power and begun to reign" (Rev. 11:17).

The God Who Speaks

The book of Revelation brings a message of great solace to Christians, good news that is centered on the sovereignty of God over all things. This was the point that John Piper sought to make when he titled a book *God Is the Gospel*.[14] The very truth of who God is provides good news for those who belong to him through faith.

We would never know that good news, however, unless God first spoke to us. This, too, is why Revelation 1:8 bears such good news, for in it God himself addresses his needy people: "'I am the Alpha and the Omega,' says the Lord God, 'who is and who was and who is to come, the Almighty.'" One reason why God speaks in this verse is to validate and verify everything that John will disclose in this apocalyptic letter to the churches. Only at the end of Revelation will God speak again, to declare his sovereign purpose and validate the message of the book: "And he who was seated on the throne said, 'Behold, I am making all things new.' Also he said, 'Write this down, for these words are trustworthy and true'" (Rev. 21:5).

When we think of God's speaking, Christians should especially think of God's revelation through his Son, Jesus Christ. Hebrews 1:1–2 says that while God formerly spoke by the prophets, "in these last days he has spoken to us by his Son." It is for this reason that when God says in Revelation 1:8, "I am," Christians hear the voice of Jesus. God says, "I am the Alpha and the Omega," an expression that Jesus will apply to himself within this very chapter: "I am the first and the last, and the living one" (1:17–18). We also hear the voice of Jesus' great "I am" sayings in John's Gospel:

14. John Piper, *God Is the Gospel: Meditations on God's Love as the Gift of Himself* (Wheaton, IL: Crossway, 2011).

I am the bread of life; whoever comes to me shall not hunger, and whoever believes in me shall never thirst. (John 6:35)

I am the light of the world. Whoever follows me will not walk in darkness, but will have the light of life. (John 8:12)

I am the door. If anyone enters by me, he will be saved. (John 10:9)

I am the good shepherd. The good shepherd lays down his life for the sheep. (John 10:11)

I am the resurrection and the life. Whoever believes in me, though he die, yet shall he live. (John 11:25)

I am the vine; you are the branches. Whoever abides in me and I in him, he it is that bears much fruit. (John 15:5)

These "I am" statements show that Jesus Christ is one with the God who says in Revelation 1:8, "I am the Alpha and the Omega, . . . who is and who was and who is to come, the Almighty." This means that Jesus was present when Moses heard God speaking from the burning bush, giving his name, "I AM THAT I AM." Exodus 3:2 declares that "the angel of the LORD appeared to him in a flame of fire" within the bush. The most likely explanation is that Moses saw the eternal Son of God in his preincarnate form, speaking with God's voice. God likewise speaks, revealing himself to us as good news through his Son, Jesus.

In fact, the only way for you to come to know the great I AM, the sovereign, eternal, unchanging, and Almighty God, is to believe in Jesus Christ. Jesus exclaimed, "I am the way, and the truth, and the life. No one comes to the Father except through me" (John 14:6). Have you met him in the way that Moses met Christ at the burning bush? God called to Moses, and he came, believed, and entered into a saving relationship with God. God now calls you through his Word. He says to you, "I am the Alpha and the Omega," the Almighty Sovereign who controls your destiny and offers you eternal life through faith in his Son. Jesus, the eternal, self-existent, and Almighty God, says to you: "Truly, truly, I say to you, whoever hears my word and believes him who sent me has eternal life. He does not come into judgment, but has passed from death to life" (John 5:24).

6

ON PATMOS, IN CHRIST

Revelation 1:9—16

Fear not, I am the first and the last, and the living one. I died,
and behold I am alive forevermore, and I have the
keys of Death and Hades. (Rev. 1:17–18)

orty miles off the coast of Asia Minor is a rocky little island, ten miles long by five miles wide, named Patmos. Because of its crescent shape it possesses a good natural harbor, and its ore mines supplied the industry of the Roman Empire. During the reign of the emperor Domitian (A.D. 81–96), Patmos was also significant as a place of exile for political prisoners.

In the year A.D. 95, Patmos housed a most significant prisoner, John, the now-aged apostle of Jesus Christ. There are differing opinions about the nature of John's imprisonment. On the easy side, exiled prisoners may have received mild treatment and been permitted relative freedom on the island, although they had lost their property and civil rights. More negatively, Sir William Ramsay paints a stark picture, arguing that John's exile was "preceded by scourging, marked by perpetual fetters, scanty clothing, insufficient food, sleep on the bare ground, a dark prison, work under the lash of the military overseer."[1] Whatever his actual circumstances, there can be little doubt that most painful to John the pastor was separation from his beloved church across the sea in Ephesus and his inability to proclaim the gospel of his Savior, Jesus.

After the introduction in Revelation 1:1–8, the vision that is introduced in verse 9 begins the main material of Revelation. This opening vision is representative of God's intention for the entire book. John is suffering oppression because of his faith in Jesus. This first vision sets before him the sovereign glory of Christ, complete with emblems of his triumphant, saving work, so that John will be encouraged to endure in worship of and service to his Lord.

JOHN, THE ENDURING CHRISTIAN

The idea that John serves in this passage as a representative Christian is confirmed in its opening verse: "I, John, your brother and partner" (Rev. 1:9). John does not set himself apart as an apostle but proclaims solidarity with his readers. What he is experiencing on Patmos is typical of what all other believers will experience. John sums up this experience in three terms: "in the tribulation and the kingdom and the patient endurance that are in Jesus."

John centers his experience on "the kingdom" of Christ. This fits his earlier emphasis, highlighting Jesus as "the ruler of kings on earth," who has made believers "a kingdom, priests to his God and Father" (Rev. 1:5–6). Christ reigns wherever his Word is believed and obeyed. Alexander Maclaren writes: "We are His kingdom in so far as our wills joyfully and lovingly submit to His authority; and then, in so far as we are His kingdom, we are kings."[2]

One of the primary ways that believers reign is by governing ourselves in accordance with God's Word. Under Christ's rule we also gain a royal freedom from the demands of the world. Peter and John showed this liberty in the early days of the church when the Jewish leaders commanded them not to witness about Christ. Peter answered that they must obey God rather than men (Acts 4:19–20; 5:29), and even when they were wrongfully beaten, the apostles gained power from Christ to rejoice for being "counted worthy to suffer dishonor for the name" (5:41).

1. William Barclay, *The Revelation of John*, 3rd ed., 2 vols., New Daily Study Bible (Louisville: Westminster John Knox, 2004), 1:48.
2. Alexander Maclaren, *Expositions of Holy Scripture*, 17 vols. (Grand Rapids: Baker, 1982), 17:153.

Our passage suggests three notes about our experience of Christ's kingdom. First, circumstances cannot inhibit this kingdom. John was a prisoner on Patmos, completely disempowered so far as the world was concerned and subject to the apparent control of his captors. In fact, however, he possessed the power of Christ to reign in triumph over sin and unbelief. However adverse our worldly circumstances may be, we, too, are free to reign with Christ through faith and obedience to his Word. We also may always enjoy the spiritual blessings of Christ's kingdom, which Paul identifies as "righteousness and peace and joy in the Holy Spirit" (Rom. 14:17).

Second, our full experience of Christ's kingdom yet remains ahead, coming to us only when Jesus returns from heaven. Even though believers now "reign on the earth" through faith (Rev. 5:10), there yet remains for us "the crown of righteousness," which the Lord "will award . . . on that Day" (2 Tim. 4:8). Only when Christ returns to consummate his kingdom fully will we experience the fullness of power, blessing, and glory befitting those who, John notes, are "partner[s] in . . . the kingdom" (Rev. 1:9).

Third, and most significant, we receive the kingdom only "in Jesus" (Rev. 1:9). Maclaren writes: "When we put the reins into His hands, when we put our consciences into His keeping, when we take our law from His gentle and yet sovereign lips, when we let Him direct our thinking; when His word is absolute truth that ends all controversy," then we experience the kingdom in and through faith in Jesus.[3]

Before John's participation in the kingdom, however, was his partnership "in the tribulation" (Rev. 1:9). John mentions the suffering of believers first because tribulation marks the path that leads us to the kingdom, just as for Jesus the cross preceded the crown. With this in mind, we may find it remarkable that many Christians read the book of Revelation as teaching that the church will be removed from the world's great tribulation. Nothing could be more contrary to the emphasis of this book, as of the entire New Testament. The great tribulation of the end times will merely intensify the tribulation that is always Christians' lot. Paul taught that "through many tribulations we must enter the kingdom of God" (Acts 14:22). John Calvin wrote: "The church of Christ has been so divinely constituted from the beginning that the Cross has been the way to victory, death the way to

---

3. Ibid.

life."[4] As Jesus himself foretold, "In the world you will have tribulation" (John 16:33). If Christians all come from the same place and are bound to the same destination, it follows that we must all take the same road. Jesus defined it: "If anyone would come after me, let him deny himself and take up his cross daily and follow me" (Luke 9:23). Just as there is a kingdom "in Jesus," together with its blessings and glory, so also there is "tribulation . . . in Jesus" (Rev. 1:9).

Christians should not be surprised by trials, "as though something strange were happening to you" (1 Peter 4:12). Paul Beasley-Murray writes: "Contrary to some modern 'prosperity' teaching, membership of Christ's kingdom does not shield us from suffering—rather, for John and his readers, membership of the kingdom was the cause of their suffering."[5] This is John's testimony concerning himself. He was "on the island called Patmos on account of the word of God and the testimony of Jesus" (Rev. 1:9). John shows that the faithful Christian will not shrink from proclaiming the truth of God's Word and the gospel message of Jesus, but will accept persecution for it. John did not conform his life or his witness to fit in with the times, and for precisely this faithful conduct he was a partner "in the tribulation."

The final item in which John is our "brother and partner" is "patient endurance" (Rev. 1:9). If tribulation is our road and the kingdom our destination, then patient endurance is our mode of travel, our manner of living. The Greek word *hupomone* suggests both passivity in the form of patience and activity in the form of endurance. It involves continual perseverance in faith and loyalty to Jesus regardless of the difficulties or cost. Paul wrote that Christ will "present you holy and blameless and above reproach before him, if indeed you continue in the faith, stable and steadfast, not shifting from the hope of the gospel that you heard" (Col. 1:22–23).

In the Greek text, there is only one definite article for "tribulation," "kingdom," and "patient endurance." This shows that they are boxed together in a set, so that we cannot have one without the others. Like John, every other Christian faces tribulation, receives a kingdom, and advances from the one to the other by patient endurance. Jesus promised that "the one who endures

---

4. Quoted in Derek Thomas, *Let's Study Revelation* (Edinburgh: Banner of Truth, 2003), 9.

5. Paul Beasley-Murray, *The Message of the Resurrection: Christ Is Risen!*, The Bible Speaks Today (Downers Grove, IL: InterVarsity Press, 2000), 195.

to the end will be saved" (Matt. 24:13). Paul adds that "if we endure, we will also reign with him" (2 Tim. 2:12).

It was said that in Napoleon's army, every French soldier carried a field marshal's baton in his knapsack. The point was that any soldier could rise from the bottom all the way to the top. We might say the same of Christians, except that every Christian has a crown in his or her possession and every one of them will certainly wear it, but only through patient endurance under the tribulation of this world. John on Patmos showed us how. Despite his imprisonment, poverty, and affliction, he continued to worship and serve Jesus, and to bear witness to his salvation. We are to do the same, as those who with John are "brother[s] and partner[s] in the tribulation and the kingdom and the patient endurance that are in Jesus" (Rev. 1:9).

THE SON OF MAN AS EXALTED DEITY

We are approaching this inaugural vision of Revelation as typical for all Christians. Just as John has described the shared Christian experience, he receives the ministry in his trials that all Christians need. John reports that he heard "a loud voice like a trumpet" and that, turning, he saw a vision of Christ as the exalted Son of Man.

John describes the situation: "I was in the Spirit on the Lord's day, and I heard behind me a loud voice like a trumpet" (Rev. 1:10). By "in the Spirit," John means that he was taken up into a trancelike, visionary state. This is not a spiritual experience common to all believers but was given to God's special messengers (see Ezek. 3:12). A New Testament example is Peter's falling "into a trance" and seeing a vision of animals that he was to slay and eat (Acts 10:10–13).

John was taken up in the Spirit "on the Lord's day." This is the Bible's only use of the expression "the Lord's day" for the Christian day of worship. The New Testament notes that the apostles moved the day of worship from the Jewish seventh-day Sabbath to the first day, presumably in order to commemorate Christ's resurrection (Acts 20:7; 1 Cor. 16:2). Since the Romans had a day in the month dedicated to Caesar, it was only fitting that Christians should have their weekly day to show that Jesus alone is Lord. The early church father Clement of Alexandria wrote: "A true Christian, according to the commands of the Gospel, observes the Lord's Day by casting out all bad thoughts, and cherishing all goodness, honoring the resurrection of the Lord, which took place on that day."[6]

We can imagine John as gazing longingly toward the north, where his church would be gathering in Ephesus. Perhaps he was praying for their worship, when he heard a voice behind him, turned, and entered a state brought upon him by the Spirit. John says that he turned to the trumpetlike voice and first saw "seven golden lampstands" (Rev. 1:12). We will consider the significance of the lampstands in the next chapter. John's attention was especially drawn to a figure standing amid the lampstands: "one like a son of man, clothed with a long robe and with a golden sash around his chest" (1:13).

Some commentators argue that the description of Jesus as "like a son of man" merely means that he appeared in human form. When we remember how closely John draws his material from the visions of Daniel, however, we find a more exalted meaning. We noted in our study of Revelation 1:7 that John drew from the vision of Daniel 7 when he spoke of Jesus' "coming with the clouds." This same vision depicted the world empires in the form of deadly beasts, but then also showed Christ's kingdom as overthrowing these powers.

The vision of Daniel 7 concluded with God as the "Ancient of Days," to whom "there came one like a son of man," riding on the clouds (Dan. 7:13). "Son of man" does not, therefore, denote the mere humanity of Jesus, but rather the fact that this One in the form of man is really God. According to Daniel, the Son of Man is the One worthy to receive "dominion and glory and a kingdom, that all peoples, nations, and languages should serve him" (7:14). According to Douglas Kelly, the Son of Man is "the sovereign Master of an indestructible kingdom that is going to crush all others."[7] Far from signifying Jesus' humble humanity, "Son of man" makes exactly the opposite point, declaring Jesus in his transcendent majesty and sovereign rule.

A number of elements in this vision not only make certain the connection with Daniel's vision, but also highlight the divine glory of Christ and the comfort that his presence brings to his struggling people. For instance, "The hairs of his head were white, like white wool, like snow. His eyes were like a flame of fire, his feet were like burnished bronze, refined in a furnace,

---

6. Quoted in Thomas, *Let's Study Revelation*, 11.

7. Douglas F. Kelly, *Revelation*, Mentor Expository Commentary (Tain, Ross-shire, Scotland: Mentor, 2012), 26.

and his voice was like the roar of many waters" (Rev. 1:14–15). The references to his hair being white like snow is interesting, since in Daniel 7:9, the Ancient of Days had hair "like pure wool" and to his throne came the Son of Man. In John's vision, the ancient and pure appearance of the Father is applied to Christ, apparently to show the union of being that Christ and the Father share in the Godhead. With eyes like flames, feet like burnished bronze, and a voice like the roaring of the waves as they crashed against the rocks of Patmos, the Christ whom John saw in his vision was nothing less than very God of very God. Here is One who holds stars in his right hand (Rev. 1:16), and therefore possesses power no less than that which created and upholds all things.

Remember John's situation as he patiently seeks to endure tribulation and then receives this vision. By the emperor's decree, John had been separated from the church and was apparently no longer in a position to influence history. But though he was on Patmos, John was in Christ, and by the Spirit he was shown the true Sovereign, the Divine Jesus, God's Son. Just as the Ancient of Days was seated in Daniel's vision as Judge of the nations, Christ is the Ruler of kings on the earth, and they will give account to him in the day of his coming.

What mattered most to John, therefore, was not the will of Domitian but the will of Christ. If Jesus desired to set John free, then just as Peter was delivered from Herod's jail by an angel (Acts 12:7), so, too, would John return to Ephesus—as he soon did, according to the early church historian Eusebius.[8] But even if John remained in exile, that would not keep God's Word from going forth from him in power. Paul wrote from his prison that he was "bound with chains as a criminal." But he added that "the word of God is not bound!" (2 Tim. 2:9). Even on Patmos, John was taken in the Spirit to receive the book of Revelation, which he would send to the churches of Asia and through the New Testament to every generation of God's people thereafter.

Does this vision not prove to us that we should never fear to live boldly for Jesus, in accordance with his Word? The world is likely to scorn us and may even persecute us, as it did John. But if the exalted Christ is with us, what will we fear? Should we not, like John, fearlessly preach the truths of

8. Eusebius, *The History of the Church* (New York: Penguin, 1989), 83.

God's Word into a dark and hostile culture? Even if we are placed in chains, the exalted Christ will send forth his Word through us. How important it is, then, that we fix our eyes on the mighty and victorious Jesus of Scripture! Remembering that John saw his vision on the Lord's Day, what is the picture of Christ that we are painting from our pulpits and worshiping in our pews? Do we preach a Jesus who relies on man's free will to achieve salvation? Do we proclaim a Jesus who exists primarily to make people comfortable or to grant their earthly whims? When the day of tribulation comes, the only way for us, like John, to patiently endure is to receive from God's Word a vision of Christ as Divine Lord, sovereign over Caesar and Christians alike, mighty to save and zealous to judge.

THE SAVIOR AS PRIEST, KING, AND PROPHET

As we consider further details from the vision of John, we should remember that he saw what Jesus is "like." This vision does not show us what Jesus *looks* like but rather what Jesus *is* like, symbolically depicting his person and work. Biblically trained Christians organize the work of Christ in his three offices of Prophet, Priest, and King. This is indeed a good way to understand this vision, starting with Jesus as the true and Great High Priest of his people.

John saw Jesus "clothed with a long robe and with a golden sash around his chest" (Rev. 1:13), reminding us of the garments made for the high priest Aaron and his sons (Ex. 28:4; Lev. 16:4). The Jewish historian Josephus described the priestly robes by using the Greek word that John employs for Christ's "long robe" (*podere*), adding that an embroidered girdle was wound around the body.[9] Further, the vision of an enrobed Christ standing among the golden lampstands recalls the priests who served in the temple and kept the lamps alight. Most importantly, priests offered sacrifices to atone for sin and assuage God's wrath. William Barclay comments: "A priest . . . was a man who himself has access to God and who opens the way for others to come to him; even in the heavenly places, Jesus, the great high priest, is still carrying on his priestly work, opening the way for all to the presence of God."[10] The same priestly Christ whom John saw is ministering for us today:

9. Cited in Barclay, *The Revelation of John*, 1:52.
10. Ibid., 1:53.

"The heart that beats beneath the golden girdle is the same that melted with pity and overflowed with love [at the cross]."[11]

Second, the vision presents Jesus as the true and reigning King. The "feet [of] burnished bronze, refined in a furnace" (Rev. 1:15), are those of a Conqueror who treads the earth in power. The eyes "like a flame of fire" (1:14) are those that pierce into every heart to judge according to truth. Christ rules with his Word, which goes forth from his mouth like a "sharp two-edged sword," while the glory of his royal face is "like the sun shining in full strength" (1:16). Here is a King fit to rule, able to conquer, all-knowing to judge, and all-glorious to demand our worship.

Third, the vision presents Jesus as the Great Prophet whose word is double-edged to save those who believe and slay those who refuse their faith. In Daniel 10, that prophet met an angelic visitor described similarly to Christ in this vision: "a man clothed in linen, with a belt of fine gold from Uphaz around his waist. His body was like beryl, his face like the appearance of lightning, his eyes like flaming torches, his arms and legs like the gleam of burnished bronze, and the sound of his words like the sound of a multitude" (Dan. 10:5–6). That messenger brought Daniel good news of a great hope for salvation, a message that pointed forward to the coming of Jesus Christ. Jesus now appeared as the substance of that good news and commissioned John to declare it to the churches of his day.

CHRIST AS THE GOSPEL

There is a word that captures the meaning of Christ as Priest, King, and Prophet: that word is *gospel*. This was what John needed in his exile: Christ in his glorious divine person and the good news of Christ in his saving work. Christ as Priest reconciles sinners to God through his blood; Christ as King conquers and judges with a two-edged sword; Christ as Prophet appears with a hopeful message of saving grace. This good news—the Bible's saving message centered on the person and work of Christ—is precisely what everyone needs today, both those who have believed and those who have not.

Albert Mohler has shown how the gospel is what everyone really needs. He gave an example of a mother who wrote to an advice columnist about her

11. Maclaren, *Expositions of Holy Scripture*, 17:147.

teenage daughter who had become an atheist. The woman said that she had raised her family under "strong Christian values" and was shocked that her child renounced her religion. As might be expected, the secular columnist advised her to accept her daughter's choice and not be upset. Wrong as this answer was, the real problem was what the Christian mother had said. How could her daughter become an atheist? Because "Christian values" are not the same as Christ himself. Mohler writes: "Hell will be filled with people who were avidly committed to Christian values. Christian values cannot save anyone and never will. . . . Salvation comes only by the gospel of Jesus Christ."[12]

Like John on Patmos, what we need is not Christian values apart from Christ himself, any more than we need a Christian social agenda, Christian lifestyle tips, or Christian worldview training unless our passion is the glorious, divine person of Christ and unless our hearts beat with a conquering joy for his all-sufficient work. Do you know Jesus as John saw him? Is your heart filled with the majesty of Christ's glorious person, so that your great longing is to know and serve him? Have you trusted in the mercy and grace of Christ, so that in him you have forgiveness of sin and acceptance into the holy presence of the Ancient of Days? And have you received the eternal life that only Jesus can give? Jesus the glorious Savior is what Christians like John need in order to patiently endure under tribulation and receive his kingdom. Jesus himself is what the world needs as well. Let his glory, his presence, and his good news be at the heart of our worship, our witness, and our own hope for salvation.

---

12. R. Albert Mohler, "Christian Values Cannot Save Anyone," September 11, 2012, http://www.albertmohler.com/2012/09/11/christian-values-cannot-save-anyone/.

7

THE CHRIST OF
THE LAMPSTANDS

Revelation 1:10–20

*As for the mystery of the seven stars that you saw in my right
hand, and the seven golden lampstands, the seven stars are the
angels of the seven churches, and the seven lampstands
are the seven churches.* (Rev. 1:20)

*I*f someone asked for the meaning of Revelation, a good place to
show the questioner is the opening vision found in chapter 1.
The apostle John was exiled on the Isle of Patmos and was
patiently enduring in faith. In John's affliction, the Lord provided for his
greatest need, which was to see Jesus in his divine glory and saving power.
Hearing a mighty voice speaking, John turned and saw Jesus as the Divine
Son of Man, dressed in his robes as the exalted High Priest. Just as Christ
appeared to strengthen John in his affliction, the book of Revelation declares
the victory of Christ to encourage Christians to endure patiently in their faith.

In addition to prompting Christian perseverance, Revelation stresses our
witness to Christ and his gospel. This message, too, is seen in this opening
vision. John saw Jesus in the midst of "seven golden lampstands" (Rev. 1:12).

This vision conveys an important message about the relationship between Christ and his church. Jesus came to give John a message to his churches, and Revelation summons believers today to carry his message to the world. Christ is reigning in our midst, ministering to his people so that our lamp will not go out but will shine the light of Christ until he returns.

SEVEN LAMPSTANDS AND SEVEN STARS

It is obvious that the lampstands in John's vision signify the churches that belong to Jesus. We see this in that the number of the churches mentioned in Revelation 1:11 corresponds to the number of lampstands in verse 12: "Write what you see in a book and send it to the seven churches, to Ephesus and to Smyrna and to Pergamum and to Thyatira and to Sardis and to Philadelphia and to Laodicea." The number seven also has the meaning of completion, so these lampstands represent not only the seven churches named to John but also the entirety of the church in all ages.

Christ's appearance with his lampstands shows that the church "is at the center of everything that God is letting happen on the world scene."[1] Whereas the world thinks its affairs in the material realm are the really important things, God asserts that the spiritual work of Christ's kingdom in and through the church is always the most significant factor. This principle was illustrated by the fall of Communism in Eastern Europe in 1989. The spark was lit when the members of a Hungarian Reformed church in Timisoara, Romania, refused to allow their faithful minister, Laszlo Tokes, to be arrested. John's vision presents the church as lampstands, and in line with this imagery the Christians surrounded their church with candles in their hands. Their defiance of evil sparked a citywide protest that spread and ultimately swept aside Communist regimes in country after country. American Rear Admiral Marmaduke Bayne stated that U.S. intelligence officers were surprised by these events "because of their blindness to the importance of God and religion."[2] Likewise, in America today, the most significant institution is not the government or the political action groups that dominate the news, but the church of Jesus Christ. If the church is silent or

---

1. Douglas F. Kelly, *Revelation*, Mentor Expository Commentary (Tain, Ross-shire, Scotland: Mentor, 2012), 25.
2. Ibid., 26.

foolishly accommodates the world, its light will burn dimly so that unbelief spreads. But if the church stands courageously as a light for God's truth, even in the face of persecution, its bright flame is the only true hope for reform.

The lampstands that John saw remind us of the golden menorah that Moses placed in the tabernacle to symbolize the light of the Lord. John's vision also corresponds closely to the vision of a golden lampstand given in Zechariah chapter 4. The prophet saw a vision of two olive trees from which pipes carried oil to a seven-bowled lamp. Zechariah was told that the olive trees represented the kingship and the priesthood, both of which pointed forward to Christ. The oil flowing from the trees signified the Holy Spirit. On that occasion, the angelic interpreter told Zechariah that the temple, which had been destroyed, would be rebuilt by the Spirit's power (Zech. 4:1–14). Zechariah's vision, given five hundred years before Christ, was now being fulfilled in the vision given to John. The true dwelling of God is not a temple building but his people as a church; just as Zechariah's vision urged the rebuilding of the temple, John's vision of Christ standing among the lampstands shows "that God will accomplish his purpose in the building of the Church."[3]

John saw the church represented not only by the seven lampstands but also by the seven stars held in Jesus' hand (Rev. 1:16). Verse 20 explains: "As for the mystery of the seven stars that you saw in my right hand, . . . the seven stars are the angels of the seven churches."

There has been considerable debate about the identity of these "angels," with two views being most likely. The first is that the angels are the pastors who serve and lead the seven churches. There are two reasons for this view. First, the Greek word for *angel* (*angelos*) means "messenger," so John could be taken as writing that "the seven stars are the *messengers* of the seven churches," that is, the pastors who deliver God's Word (see examples of *angelos* as human messengers in Matthew 11:10 and Mark 1:2). Second, this view notes that the seven letters in Revelation 2 and 3 are addressed to the "angels" of the respective churches. For instance, 2:1 says, "To the angel of the church in Ephesus." Since these letters contain rebukes for sin, it does not make sense that actual angels are being addressed but rather pastors, who do sin and fall short of their duty to Christ. Scholars who take this view

3. James M. Hamilton Jr., *Revelation: The Spirit Speaks to the Churches* (Wheaton, IL: Crossway, 2012), 46.

urge that the title *angel* helpfully reminds us that faithful pastors are God's servants and messengers (see Eph. 4:11).

Nonetheless, it is unlikely that Christ was referring to human messengers here, for the simple reason that elsewhere in Revelation the word *angel* always describes a supernatural messenger and heavenly servant of God. It is probably best, then, to see Jesus as referring to guardian angels assigned to the churches they represent. This fits the pattern of Daniel's visions, to which John has repeatedly referred, in which an angel spoke of his combat with enemy spiritual powers and referred to the angel Michael as "your prince" (Dan. 10:21). The idea of heavenly counterparts for God's earthly people seems to be reflected in the seven stars in Christ's hand. Lampstands on earth and stars in heaven both shine their light, and it seems that the angels of the churches are so closely identified with the churches themselves that the two can be spoken of as one.

LORD OF THE LAMPSTANDS

Wonderful as angels are, our focus should be on the God who sends them. In John's vision, the stars in Christ's hand revealed Jesus as the Lord of the church. Christ's present lordship is an essential point for Christians to grasp, despite his physical absence from the earth. The book of Revelation will have much to say about Christ's return, but here at the beginning it emphasizes Christ's presence with us now as a living and reigning Lord. This truth was especially important to the seven churches named in this vision. David DeSilva notes that these particular churches may have been selected because of the prominence of Caesar's imperial cult in their cities: "All but Thyatira had temples dedicated to the emperors, and all but Philadelphia and Laodicea had imperial priests and altars."[4] Domitian may be lord of the pagan Roman cult, but Jesus Christ alone is Lord of his churches even in a hostile world.

While showing Christ as Lord, this vision makes five key points about the relationship between Christ and his church: the church is under Christ's rule, receives Christ's care, is subject to Christ's judgment, relies on Christ's power, and has unity in Christ's presence.

4. Quoted in Grant R. Osborne, *Revelation*, Baker Exegetical Commentary on the New Testament (Grand Rapids: Baker Academic, 2002), 85.

First, John's vision shows *Christ's rule over his church*. The church is not under the authority of any emperor, king, president, or supreme court. This means that Christian churches must derive their teaching and practice only from God's Word, through which Christ reigns. This is a vital matter today, when evangelical churches are under pressure to conform to secular demands regarding issues such as sexuality, marriage, gender, and evolution. But if Christ is Lord, then his Word must rule in these and all other matters. In the first days of the church, Peter and John were willing to disobey civil rulers who demanded that the apostles cease preaching the gospel (Acts 4:19–20; 5:29). The rule of Christ is a vital matter for the church, and like the apostles, Christians today must accept worldly scorn rather than compromise God's Word.

One Christian who understood the necessity of Christ's ruling through his Word was a teenage English princess named Lady Jane Grey. The cousin of the godly King Edward VI, Lady Jane was thrust into prominence when the king died, leaving his Roman Catholic sister Mary next in line for the throne. Jane became a pawn of worldly lords whose opposition to Mary was primarily secular and who briefly made Jane queen of England. Before long, Mary's right to the throne prevailed, and Lady Jane became a prisoner in the Tower of London.

Mary and Jane had not gotten along, primarily because of Jane's militant refusal to accept the papal idolatries demanded by Mary. Now, with Jane her prisoner, Queen Mary sent her priest confessor, Cardinal Feckenham, to demand Jane's capitulation under threat of death. The famous interview was recorded word for word. Feckenham first sought for Lady Jane to deny salvation by faith alone. Jane refused, saying, "We are unprofitable servants, and faith only in Christ's blood saves us." Next, the cardinal sought for Jane to accept the doctrine of transubstantiation, which says that in the mass Christ's literal body and blood are presented and eaten for salvation. This Jane utterly rejected. When Feckenham insisted that Jane must yield to the pope's authority, she responded: "No, I ground my faith upon God's word, and not upon the church; for if the church be a good church, the faith of the church must be tried by God's word, and not God's word by the church. . . . And I say, that it is an evil church, and not the spouse of Christ, but the spouse of the devil, that alters the Lord's supper. . . . Shall I believe this church? God forbid!"

Disappointed, the priest took his leave, expressing sorrow, since he was sure they would never meet again. This was an unveiled threat of her impending execution. The teenage princess replied, "True it is that we shall never meet again, except God turn your heart; for I am assured, unless you repent, and turn to God, you are in an evil case; and I pray God, in the bowels of his mercy, to send you his Holy Spirit, . . . to open the eyes of your heart."[5] With little delay, Lady Jane Grey was put to death by beheading, having willingly offered her life for the sovereign rule of Christ over his church, through his Word. Her example challenges Christians today never to allow worldly powers to intimidate us into abandoning God's Word.

Second, John's vision emphasizes *Christ's care for the church*. What a comfort it must have been for John, concerned as he would have been for the beloved churches from which he was separated, to see their stars held securely and lovingly in Christ's hand—the same hand that created the heavens and was then pierced to save his people. Just as the priests in the tabernacle tended the lights of the golden lampstand—trimming the wicks, refilling the oil, and relighting any that had gone out—so Christ the true Priest "tends the [church] lampstands by commending, correcting, exhorting, and warning (see chs. 2–3) in order to secure the churches' fitness for service as lightbearers in a dark world."[6] Steve Wilmshurst writes: "Think what that vision would have meant to the persecuted churches to whom John was writing. Think of the comfort of knowing that they were held in his right hand! But then think what it means to us now. . . . He holds us in his right hand, the best and safest place we could possibly be."[7]

Third, the vision shows *Christ's judgment of his church*. This reality is emphasized by the sharp double-edged sword that comes out of his mouth and that is thus designed both to save and to judge. While Christians are set free from the judgment of condemnation for our sins, we are nonetheless subject to the chastising judgment of our Sovereign Lord, who is determined to excise sin from his people. This judgment will be prominent in the seven letters to the churches. For instance, Christ warned Sardis about its false

5. Taken from Paul F. M. Zahl, "The Examination of Lady Jane Grey, February 10, 1554," in *Five Women of the English Reformation* (Grand Rapids: Eerdmans, 2001), 110–13.

6. G. K. Beale, *The Book of Revelation: A Commentary on the Greek Text*, New International Greek Testament Commentary (Grand Rapids: Eerdmans, 1999), 208–9.

7. Steve Wilmshurst, *The Final Word: The Book of Revelation Simply Explained* (Darlington, UK: Evangelical Press, 2008), 31.

teachers: "Therefore repent. If not, I will come to you soon and war against them with the sword of my mouth" (Rev. 2:16). Christ's judgment reminds us that while Jesus is a loving, compassionate Savior, he is also an unyielding Lord who demands faithfulness from his people. How many of the woes experienced by worldly churches and unmotivated Christians today may be attributed to Christ's sovereign judgment, which calls all believers to a faith that repents and obeys God's Word.

Fourth, the connection between John's vision and the earlier vision in Zechariah 4 points out *Christ's power for his church*. Zechariah saw the two olive trees that symbolized Christ as King and as Priest, and from the trees he saw pipes conveying oil to enable the lamps to continually burn. Likewise, Christian churches will give a mighty witness to the world only as we are energized by the Holy Spirit whom Jesus sends. The spiritual power of a church relies not on finances, dynamic personalities, entertaining worship services, or clever marketing, but rather on the mighty presence of the Holy Spirit as Christ provides for his faithful church. We remember that while John was in affliction on Patmos, he was taken up "in the Spirit" (Rev. 1:10) and was thus empowered to give an undying testimony to Christ and his gospel.

I mentioned earlier the heroic fidelity of Lady Jane Grey to the rule of Jesus over his church. What happened after her death shows how faithful Christians who honor Christ's rule also experience Christ's power. When Protestant King Edward VI died, the Roman Catholic Queen Mary took the throne and immediately imposed papal teaching in the churches of England. She gained the title of Bloody Mary for her violent persecution of the faithful Protestant preachers. But these bishops and pastors had been inspired by Lady Jane Grey's martyrdom, and they, too, were willing to suffer death for Christ's truth. The valor of these servants of Christ kept the light of the gospel burning during Mary's bloody reign.

A famous example is the martyrdom of Hugh Latimer and Nicholas Ridley, two well-known preachers who were threatened with death by burning if they would not yield to unbiblical papal doctrines. This was a vital turning point: would those who had so boldly preached God's Word in the safety of their pulpits continue to do so when tied to a stake? The aged Latimer gave the answer when he and Ridley were tied and the flames were lit, with a priest taunting them with one last chance to betray their Lord. Latimer refused and called to his friend: "Be of good cheer, Master Ridley, and play the man. We shall this day light such a candle by God's grace in England as I trust shall never be put out!"[8]

What power can enable Christians to hold fast to their faith, dying with songs of joy on their lips even while being burned alive? The answer is found in the power of the Holy Spirit, which in response to prayer will enable you not only to die for Jesus, but to live for his sake and give the blazing testimony that our generation so desperately needs.

Finally, John's vision of the Lord and his lampstands shows *Christ's presence as the only basis for unity in his church*. The lampstands in the vision remind us of the seven-stemmed menorah that blazed in Moses' tabernacle. On that lampstand, the seven lamps were joined by a golden stem of great beauty. John's lampstands are joined not by a golden stem but by the Lord who stands in their midst. Michael Wilcock writes: "Perhaps we are meant to see in them the church as she appears in the world, congregations located here and there, which can be isolated and indeed destroyed (2:5). But on the heavenly level, the church is united and indestructible, for she is centered on Christ."[9] This reminds us that true church unity does not result from any institutional hierarchy, but results only from Christ as he rules and is present through prayer and his Word.

The Light and the Lamps

Perhaps the most important thing for us to note about the church as a lampstand is that the light it shines comes not from itself but from Jesus Christ. The Greek word *luxnia* describes the church not as a light for the world but rather as a stand on which a lamp is set. William Barclay writes: "It is not the churches themselves which produce the light; the giver of light is Jesus Christ; and the churches are only the vessels within which the light shines. The light which Christians possess is always a borrowed light."[10]

Moreover, we should note that while the church is the stand, the lamps are the Christians themselves on which the light of Jesus shines and reflects

8. Quoted in Sir Marcus Loane, *Masters of the English Reformation* (Edinburgh: Banner of Truth, 2005), 165.

9. Michael Wilcock, *I Saw Heaven Opened: The Message of Revelation*, The Bible Speaks Today (Downers Grove, IL: InterVarsity Press, 1975), 41–42.

10. William Barclay, *The Revelation of John*, 3rd ed., 2 vols., New Daily Study Bible (Louisville: Westminster John Knox, 2004), 1:62.

to the world. In this way we see that a church is not intended to shine its own light, in the way that so many churches today seek to market their programs, their musical style, or their friendly community. Rather, the church is where the Christian people receive Christ's light through his Word (Ps. 119:105), so that light is reflected from the lampstand of the church to the world. Jesus thus praised John the Baptist as "a burning and shining lamp" (John 5:35). This is the calling of Christians as we are together set as lamps in the stand of the church to shine forth the light of Christ.

If our light is not our own but Christ's, then our witness should also not be about ourselves but about Jesus. To be sure, it is important for us to lead lives that will commend the gospel, but our testimony is never based on what good people we are or what we ourselves have to offer non-Christians. We should be like John the Baptist, who refused to draw attention to himself but pointed to Jesus, saying, "Behold, the Lamb of God, who takes away the sin of the world!" (John 1:29).

It can be good for Christians to "give their testimony" in the sense of telling how we became Christians and what Christ has done for us. But the only witness that can save others is a biblical witness that declares the divine person and saving work of Christ. Our witness must therefore center not on our experience but on what Jesus has done to save everyone who believes.

An example of a lamp that shone the light of Christ is an English monk named "Little Bilney," so called because of his short stature. Bilney had come to believe the gospel through Martin Luther's books, and he therefore sought to advance the Protestant Reformation. He realized that he was not well educated or greatly gifted, but he had noticed a priest named Hugh Latimer who possessed great learning and ability—the same Hugh Latimer who would light a candle for Christ when he was later burned to death for the gospel.

Bilney began praying about how he might witness the gospel to Latimer, and came up with a strategy. Priests were required to hear confessions of sins. So one day, Bilney went to Latimer, tugged at his sleeve and asked him to hear his confession. After they entered the booth, Bilney confessed the gospel. He told Latimer how he was a sinner and knew his good works could not save him. He also confessed that Jesus had died for him and that the righteousness of Christ had been imputed to him through faith alone. Hearing this confession of the gospel, Latimer was converted and went on to lead many others to Christ through his faithful witness. It all began with Little Bilney, who, though short in stature and little known to history, was a bright and shining lamp who boldly reflected Christ's light.[11]

This is what our world needs today—witnesses who shine with the light of truth and burn with a passion for souls and for the glory of Christ. Surely it is in large part due to the dim light and lukewarm commitment of so many worldly Christians and churches that so few people pay attention to the gospel today. It has always been believers who shined and burned for Christ who gain the world's notice.

Have you offered yourself as a witness to reflect the light of Christ to a dark and dying world? God sent John the Baptist to Israel, and he sent Lady Jane Grey and Hugh Latimer to England. Will you be the lamp of Christ who is needed in the place where you live and work? A faithful witness to Christ is the world's greatest need because the gospel is its only salvation. "Truly, truly, I say to you," Jesus declared, "whoever hears my word and believes him who sent me has eternal life. He does not come into judgment, but has passed from death to life" (John 5:24).

---

11. Taken from James Montgomery Boice, *Acts: An Expositional Commentary* (Grand Rapids: Baker, 1997), 316.

8

FROM DEATH TO LIFE

Revelation 1:17–19

When I saw him, I fell at his feet as though dead. But he laid his
right hand on me, saying, "Fear not." (Rev. 1:17)

ne of the most hotly contested matters in the book of Revelation
is whether it describes events present in John's time or distant
future events before Christ returns. Revelation 1:19 is a key
verse in this debate: "Write therefore the things that you have seen, those
that are and those that are to take place after this." In the minds of many
twentieth-century and twenty-first-century commentators, especially those
influenced by dispensational theology, this verse outlines three sections
in the book. Chapter 1 records the vision that John saw, chapters 2 and 3
pertain to the present through the letters to the churches, and starting in
chapter 4 Revelation describes events in the distant future. The chief problem with this approach is that it fails to note how these three descriptions
pertain to material throughout the book. All of Revelation involves visions
shown to John, concerning things both present and yet to come. The best
way to understand Revelation is to see its series of visions as they pertain
to the entire church age and as they advance in focus to the events involved
with Christ's return.[1]

1. For a brief but compelling explanation of Revelation's organization, see William Hendriksen,
More than Conquerors: An Interpretation of the Book of Revelation (1940; repr., Grand Rapids: Baker,

In my opinion, overemphasis on its future orientation has diminished Revelation's influence among Christians. After all, if the book is focused on events not likely to occur during my lifetime, why should I give much attention to it, however interesting its visions may be? Contrary to this view, however, Revelation should be given, if anything, a place of precedence when it comes to the present relevance of New Testament books. Our study of the opening vision in chapter 1 has highlighted its present focus. The exalted Christ in John's vision is currently Lord over the church and over history. Appearing to John as Prophet, as King, and especially as Priest, Christ appears in the way his disciples always know and experience his saving work. Moreover, by standing amid the lampstands, Christ emphasizes his present rule over and care for the churches that proclaim his name. Finally, John's reaction to the vision, falling "at his feet as though dead" (Rev. 1:17), shows how sinners must always respond to divine holiness. Jesus' answer, "Fear not," introduces how the gospel always works in raising sinners to new and eternal life by the grace of God in Christ.

As though Dead

The opening vision of Revelation vividly presents the main actors of history. First, Christ is seen as the Sovereign Son of Man who reigns in triumph over all. Second, the church is depicted in its precious value as a golden lampstand that shines Christ's light. Third, John himself represents the people who are saved by Christ. As we now focus on him, it is startling to realize that when he saw Christ's glory, John "fell at his feet as though dead" (Rev. 1:17).

Readers who are not well versed in the Bible may find it strange that the apostle "fell apart" in Jesus' presence. In fact, John depicts how sinners always respond to a true vision of the holiness of Christ, whether in person or in the pages of Scripture. Given the way that Revelation follows the visions of Daniel, we should note that the ancient prophet had a similar experience. Daniel chapter 10 records a vision almost identical to that of Revelation 1, causing Daniel to lose all his strength and collapse to the ground (Dan. 10:9).

This experience of being undone before the majesty of God was vividly described as well by the prophet Isaiah. On the night that he was commis-

---

1967), 16–36.

sioned as a prophet, Isaiah went into the temple and "saw the Lord sitting upon a throne, high and lifted up" (Isa. 6:1). As the worshiping seraphim cried, "Holy, holy, holy is the Lord of hosts" (61:3), Isaiah responded, "Woe is me! For I am lost; . . . for my eyes have seen the King, the Lord of hosts!" (6:5).

The Bible indicates two reasons why men are slain in the presence of God's holy glory. The first is the awe of creatures in the presence of the divine. Job cried out: "I had heard of you by the hearing of the ear, but now my eye sees you; therefore I despise myself, and repent in dust and ashes" (Job 42:5–6). This overwhelming experience of seeing the Lord in glory is especially striking in the case of John, since he was the disciple most loved by Jesus and most intimate in friendship with the Lord who was now revealed to him in divine splendor (see John 13:23; 19:26; 21:7).

The John of Revelation is a mature disciple, long schooled in godliness and commended for his faithfulness under persecution. That John should fall as dead before the glorified Christ therefore amplifies the significance of the Lord's majesty. Charles Spurgeon explains: "The most spiritual and sanctified minds, when they fully perceive the majesty and holiness of God, are so greatly conscious of the great disproportion between themselves and the Lord, that they are humbled and filled with holy awe, and even with dread and alarm."[2]

A famous episode from the life of Martin Luther provides an example of this terror of the holy. After several years of training as a monk, Luther was authorized to celebrate his first mass as a Roman Catholic priest. He stepped to the altar and prepared to speak the Latin words that would supposedly turn the elements into the body and blood of Christ. At that moment, however, Luther froze solid. Years later, he explained:

> I was utterly stupefied and terror-stricken. I thought to myself, "With what tongue shall I address such majesty, seeing that all men ought to tremble in the presence of even an earthly prince? Who am I, that I should lift up mine eyes or raise my hands to the divine Majesty? The angels surround him. At his nod the earth trembles. And shall I, a miserable little pygmy, say, 'I want

2. Charles H. Spurgeon, *Metropolitan Tabernacle Pulpit*, 63 vols. (Pasadena, TX: Pilgrim Publications, 1984), 18:4.

this, I ask for that'? For I am dust and ashes and full of sin and I am speaking to the living, eternal and the true God."[3]

Psychologists in our time have looked on episodes like this and raised the question of Luther's sanity. Yet they fail to account not only for the creature's dread before the Creator's glory, but even more for the sinner's terror in the presence of the pure holiness of God. This is the second reason why John fell as dead before the Lord: because he was a sinner in the presence of perfect divine holiness.

From the biblical perspective, when we consider how grievous is a single sin in the holy presence of God, we understand how appropriate it was for Luther to tremble in God's presence. With this in mind, R. C. Sproul comments that if Luther really was insane, "our prayer is that God would send to this earth an epidemic of such insanity."[4] Since sinners who experience the death of seeing their sins before God are the only ones forgiven through faith in Christ, how much better if this shocked terror over sin were to descend on our entire race!

When we consider biblical examples of believers falling as dead before the Lord, a common element is their awareness of personal sinfulness. Isaiah was undone because, he confessed, "I am a man of unclean lips, and I dwell in the midst of a people of unclean lips" (Isa. 6:5). Job condemned himself when he saw God after chapters of complaining about the Lord. Perhaps the clearest example was that of the apostle Peter, when he first perceived the deity of Jesus. Peter had been fishing when Jesus asked to preach from his boat because of the large crowd. Afterward, Jesus told Peter where to place his nets, and when Peter obeyed, they filled with fish to the point of breaking. Through these events, Peter perceived the divine majesty of Christ. Like John on Patmos, "he fell down at Jesus' knees," and then pleaded, "Depart from me, for I am a sinful man, O Lord" (Luke 5:7–8). Perceiving the holiness of Christ, Peter was immediately overthrown by a terrifying comprehension of his own sin. Steve Wilmshurst writes: "If we had a brief glimpse of the glory and the purity of God revealed like this in Christ, we too would collapse in terror, because in that moment, like John, we would become deeply aware, horribly aware, of our own sin and his purity, his

3. Quoted in Roland H. Bainton, *Here I Stand* (New York: Penguin, 1955), 30.
4. R. C. Sproul, *The Holiness of God* (Wheaton, IL: Tyndale, 1985), 126.

majesty, his greatness. I would see what I am like; I would see what God is like—and I would react just like John."[5]

How different is this perspective on God from the easy-breezy attitude that permeates so many churches. Today, Christ is treated not with reverence but with flippant familiarity. It is true that Jesus is a friend to sinners because of his saving mercy. But Christians must realize that we come to a holy God in the person of Christ. Therefore, as the prophets Isaiah and Daniel show, together with the apostles Peter and John, true spirituality does not consist in joviality and lighthearted fun, much less in worldly enthusiasm, but is built on the awe of a holy God, a loathing for sin, and the longing for saving grace from the merciful hand of our Savior. The first matter of true godliness concerns the necessity of dealing with our sin. In this way, when John in conviction fell "as though dead" (Rev. 1:17), he reminds us that "the wages of sin is death" (Rom. 6:23). As a sinner before the Lord, John therefore fell as one who had died in terror of the holy.

FEAR NOT!

Church-growth consultants today would criticize such an emphasis on God's holiness as hindering our success in ministry. Peter's exclamation, "Depart from me, . . . O Lord," is the opposite of what church marketers are hoping to hear from visitors to the church. John's experience, however, together with the testimony of the whole Bible, shows how the dread of sinners before the holiness of God is precisely what fosters a true and saving relationship with Christ. According to the Bible, the spirit that has been crushed before God in humble repentance is the kind of spirit in which God chooses to dwell. "For thus says the One who is high and lifted up, who inhabits eternity, whose name is Holy," Isaiah wrote: "I dwell in the high and holy place, and also with him who is of a contrite and lowly spirit, to revive the spirit of the lowly, and to revive the heart of the contrite" (Isa. 57:15).

With this in mind, perhaps the most important statement about John was not what he did (falling down as though dead) but where he did it: "at [Jesus'] feet" (Rev. 1:17). Instead of turning away from God in servile terror—an ungodly fear that loathes God—he turned to the Lord in reverent

5. Steve Wilmshurst, *The Final Word: The Book of Revelation Simply Explained* (Darlington, UK: Evangelical Press, 2008), 30.

humility. In the fear of the Lord and at the feet of Jesus is always the safest, most blessed place in all the world.

The reason why we are safest when trembling before God at Jesus' feet is found in Christ's character as a tender Savior. Jesus showed this in two actions. First, John related, "he laid his right hand on me" (Rev. 1:17). This was an act of great symbolic and personal significance. All through the Gospels, when Jesus healed or raised the dead, he usually touched his suffering subject. Whether it was an unclean leper, a dead son, or a shamed sinner, Jesus not only spoke words of power but also placed his holy hand on the person in need. In this way, Jesus showed his compassion and, above all, his personal acceptance. Being perfectly holy, Jesus can touch the unclean without becoming polluted himself. Being filled with mercy, he is willing to reach out with saving grace in a personal way. If you have come to Jesus as a sinner and received the gift of saving faith, that work of his Holy Spirit was like the touch of his hand: Christ personally laid hold of you in mercy, power, and love. Imagine what it meant to John, completely undone at the vision of Christ's holy majesty, fallen as one dead before the Lord, to have Jesus reach down with a strong hand of blessing, to touch him and lay hold of him for salvation!

Second, having laid his right hand on John—the hand of strength and favor—Jesus spoke: "Fear not" (Rev. 1:17). These words may seem strange, since we have noted how right it was for John to fear. But when combined in salvation, the sinner's fear and the Savior's "Fear not" go together. Derek Thomas explains how fear and "Fear not" define the Christian's experience: "We fall down before his exalted majesty, and we feel the reassurance of his hand upon our shoulder encouraging us not to be afraid. . . . We are awed by his majesty and drawn by his grace."[6] There is no other saving Christianity than that which joins the sinner's fear of holiness with the Savior's assurance of grace.

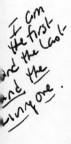

Jesus went on to explain his authority to banish our terror: "<u>Fear not</u>, I am the first and the last, and the living one" (Rev. 1:17–18). This statement connects back to the words of God the Father in verse 8: "'I am the Alpha and the Omega,' says the Lord God, 'who is and who was and who is to come, the Almighty.'" By taking up similar words, Jesus declares his oneness with the Father in deity. As "the first and the last," Jesus is sovereign over

---

6. Derek Thomas, *Let's Study Revelation* (Edinburgh: Banner of Truth, 2003), 15.

all that comes between, that is, over all time, history, and creation. As "the living one," Jesus possesses the power and life needed to cast away all fear.

Sinners will therefore find in Jesus' person all that we need for salvation. This makes the essential point that Christianity is all about Jesus Christ: past, future, and present. Sometimes people will walk away from Christianity, claiming that it no longer meets their needs. Perhaps it is a college student who is led away by sinful pleasures or vain philosophy. Perhaps it is a man or woman who is caught up in work. In every case, they have forgotten, if they ever knew, the majesty, glory, and power of Jesus Christ. There is nowhere else for us to go in order to receive life. It is true that a Christianity without the living Christ is worth little. How many Christians experience this when their religion ceases to be about Jesus and his saving grace! Jesus is the living Lord and Savior, and it is always before him that we experience the power, vitality, and joy that we ought to crave and that we truly need.

As Jesus describes himself, we see particular aspects of his all-sufficiency. There is never a time when Jesus, as the eternal God, is not present to lift us up, forgive our sins, and defeat our foes. Nothing can befall us that is contrary to his will as the Sovereign Savior. Even if the things we most fear should happen, we can know that Jesus has sovereignly willed them in order to strengthen our faith, preserve us from sin, and lead us closer in fellowship with him. Moreover, Christ in his might is able to remove our trials at the time that he knows is good for us. This was true in John's day under the Roman Empire's persecution. The trials of the seven churches could go only so far as Christ willed them, and always to serve the purposes of God. The same is true for us: as "the first and the last," our Savior not only chose us in eternity past, called us to personal saving faith, and has promised our final salvation, but will also rule all things for our eternal well-being and his own eternal glory.

Especially as "the living one," Jesus is qualified to remove the fears of one, like John, who was as dead before him. The Bible teaches that sinners are "dead in . . . trespasses" (Eph. 2:1): spiritually unable to believe the gospel or live according to God's Word. But just as Jesus possesses the purity that enables him to touch and conquer the unclean, so also does Jesus possess in himself the life that removes the curse of death. This power comes to Christians today through God's Word, where the Lord speaks with the saving power of life. To receive the life we need, we must come to him. To dwell in the power of life, we must abide in his Word. As Peter once cried, "Lord, to whom shall we go? You have the words of eternal life" (John 6:68).

Victorious over Fear

Jesus' final statement in casting out John's fear directs us not only to his person but also to his victorious saving work: "I died, and behold I am alive forevermore, and I have the keys of Death and Hades" (Rev. 1:18). Coming to the *person* of Christ in faith, we meet the One who has power to banish our fear. Then, trusting in the *work* of Christ, we see that everything we fear has been conquered, so we are freed to rejoice in the holy presence of our Savior and Lord.

First, Jesus said, "I died," in this way conquering our fear of condemnation. We have seen that when biblical figures fall in fear before Christ's majesty, it is largely as they are made aware of their sin and their dread of wrath. How can the sinner confront the holy God without the terror of condemnation? Jesus answers with reference to his atoning death on the cross: "I died."

There are two great marvels in this world, and they are found together in this passage. The first marvel—one that causes the angels to gaze downward in wonder (1 Peter 1:12)—is that sinners should be received into the loving favor of the holy God. Lawbreakers embraced by the Righteous Judge! How can this be? The answer is given in the second marvel: Jesus, "the living one," proclaims, "I died." It was to perform this second wonder—so necessary if the first wonder could ever take place—that Jesus was born of the virgin and became incarnate in true humanity. God the Son—eternal, sovereign, self-existing in life—became man in order to die for the sins of his people. "You shall call his name Jesus," the angel told Joseph about the son to be born, "for he will save his people from their sins" (Matt. 1:21). The incarnation thus found fulfillment in the atonement; the purpose of Christmas was fulfilled on Good Friday.

The power of Christ's death to cast out fear of condemnation for sin is illustrated by another curious episode from Martin Luther's life. After his famous stand on God's Word at the Council of Worms, Luther was whisked away for protection to a castle known as the Wartburg. There, while Luther was working on his translation of the Bible into German, Satan appeared to him to accuse Luther of his sins. In a letter written to his friend Philipp Melanchthon on May 24, 1521, Luther recalled his anguish as Satan unveiled a long scroll with all his sins written with care, each of them read out one by one. All the while, Satan mocked his pathetic desire to serve God, assuring him that after all he would end up in hell. Luther writhed in spiritual agony until, at last, he jumped up and cried: "It is all true, Satan, and many more sins which I have committed in my life which are known to God only; but write this at the bottom of your list." Luther then recited to the devil the glorious words of 1 John 1:7, "the blood of Jesus [God's] Son cleanses us from all sin." Then, grasping an inkwell from his table, Luther threw it at the devil, who thus fled, leaving a black spot that can still be seen there, bearing testimony to Luther's deliverance from condemnation because Jesus had died for his sins.[7]

[handwritten margin note: Do not let the accuser win. We are ✗ cleansed by Christs' blood!]

Not only did Jesus die to free us from fear of condemnation, but he rose from the dead to overcome our fear of failure and defeat: "I died, and behold I am alive forevermore" (Rev. 1:18). Many Christians, knowing that their sins are forgiven, yet live in the terror of sin's power because of their weakness in the face of temptation. Yet the Savior who rose from the dead has that same resurrection power to give to his people. In Ephesians 1:17–20, Paul prayed that his readers would know "what is the immeasurable greatness of [God's] power toward us who believe." According to Paul, weak and needy Christians receive the same might "that [God] worked in Christ when he raised him from the dead." Do you know that the power that raised Jesus from the grave enables you now to continue in faith, turn away from sin, and offer your life in worship and service to God? Christians will not ultimately fail, and we are delivered from the fear of defeat by remembering that Christ, who died, is alive forevermore in the power of life that he gives to those who call on his name in times of need.

When we think of John falling as dead before Christ's glory, believers have a special reason not only to rely on his resurrection, but also to look forward to our own resurrection. In our current sinful condition, it is not possible for even the best of Christ's disciples to see his true majesty without being undone in terror of the holy. But as John wrote in his first epistle, "we know that when he appears we shall be like him, because we shall see him as he is"

---

7. David Baron, *The Visions and Prophecies of Zechariah* (Grand Rapids: Kregel, 1972), 93–94.

(1 John 3:2). In our resurrection, the children of God will be transformed into the likeness of Christ's glory, all vestiges of sin having been removed so that we, too, are pure and radiant in holiness. Philip Hughes writes that because of our coming resurrection in Christ, "the expectation of every Christian believer is that he will see God (Jb. 19:26f.), when his own glorification has become a reality, which will be the completion of his sanctification."[8] John said that knowing this should animate our hearts with a desire to increase in holiness now: "Everyone who thus hopes in him purifies himself as he is pure" (1 John 3:3).

Third, Jesus delivers us from the final and most dreadful of our enemies, the fear of death. He concludes: "and I have the keys of Death and Hades" (Rev. 1:18). To possess keys is to control the doors and have authority over who goes in and who goes out. Jesus, by the conquest of his death and resurrection, now rules as Victor over both death and hell.

Here, then, is how Christians are freed from our greatest fears. Christ by his death has removed the legal curse that requires death, and by his resurrection has broken even the power of death. Christians therefore may live courageously before the threat of the grave. Paul Beasley-Murray writes: "He is able to lead his followers out from death into life. For those facing the prospect of martyrdom (2:13), it must have been a great comfort to know that death was not the end. Because of this they could give themselves to his service, whatever the risks, knowing that their ultimate future was secure."[9] A. W. Pitzer writes: "The Christian need not fear to die! There is one who is his friend, who has overcome death and who holds the keys of the grave and the unseen world, and who says to him: 'Fear not.'"[10]

THE GREAT "I AM"

When we consider carefully the message of Revelation chapter 1, we see that the key to understanding this book is not found by unraveling how prophecies relate to the present or the future. More important than giving

8. Philip Edgcumbe Hughes, *The Book of Revelation* (Downers Grove, IL: InterVarsity Press, 1990), 28.

9. Paul Beasley-Murray, *The Message of the Resurrection: Christ Is Risen!*, The Bible Speaks Today (Downers Grove, IL: InterVarsity Press, 2000), 199.

10. A. W. Pitzer, "Why Believers Should Not Fear," in *Southern Presbyterian Pulpit: A Collection of Sermons from the Nineteenth Century* (1896; repr., Birmingham, AL: Solid Ground, 2001), 170.

us clues to future history, Revelation directs our attention to the One who is Lord of history, the Sovereign who stands in glory among the lampstands, and the Savior whose right hand lifts up his people and declares, "Fear not."

As the key to the book of Revelation, the first chapter fixes our gaze on Jesus in his glory, the One who says, "I am" (Rev. 1:17). Our success as Christians therefore comes not by unraveling every mystery of history, but in knowing who Jesus is, entering into discipleship with him through a living faith, and relying on the all-sufficiency of his saving work to conquer every foe that besets us. He is the One who loved us and freed us from our sins by his blood (1:5). He is the glorious Son of Man, who stands in sovereign power amid his lampstands (1:13). He is coming again with the clouds, and every eye will see the One whom they pierced (1:7). Do you know Jesus? Our calling is to receive him as Lord and Savior in faith, to serve his kingdom despite all tribulation, and to trust him to meet all our needs, knowing that he will not fail in any aspect of our salvation. "Fear not," he encourages us: "I am the first and the last, and the living one. I died, and behold I am alive forevermore, and I have the keys of Death and Hades" (1:17–18). Amen. Come, Lord Jesus.

9

REKINDLING THE FIRST LOVE

Revelation 2:1–7

*But I have this against you, that you have abandoned the love
you had at first. Remember therefore from where you have
fallen; repent, and do the works you did at first.* (Rev. 2:4–5)

*I*t is common today for church leaders to spend time at a retreat evaluating their ministries and seeking a vision for their congregation. It would be interesting if Jesus were physically present for these meetings to see what he thinks about many of the emphases governing his churches. According to the book of Revelation, Christ is in fact present with his people. Jesus knows what is going on in his churches and evaluates the state of his people's hearts. Moreover, if Revelation is any indication, the Lord would not hesitate to rebuke for those things that displease him. Indeed, according to the messages in Revelation 2–3, one reason why churches may fail and even disappear is that Christ comes to them and removes their lampstands (Rev. 2:5).

Christ's messages to the churches of Revelation are relevant to us today for the same reason they were so urgent nineteen centuries ago: Christ's people need to hear Christ's voice. The tendency is for our ideas about the church to veer in a selfish or worldly direction unless we are constantly under the correction of our Sovereign Lord. This being the case, it is remarkable that the messages of Revelation 2–3 exert so little influence among Christians today. Few believers have given serious study to these chapters, and few churches would highlight these as guiding passages for their life and ministry. Yet the Christ who speaks in these chapters continues to stand in the midst of his lampstands, continues to reign as the Sovereign of his churches, and continues to hold the stars of the churches in his hand. Because the exalted Christ continues to proclaim his priorities to the church through these seven messages, Christians should study Revelation 2–3 with special care and respond with reverent obedience.

SEVEN MESSAGES TO THE CHURCHES

The so-called seven letters to the churches in Revelation are not actually letters. Instead, they form a vital portion of the book of Revelation, which forms a single letter to the churches. Note, for instance, that these messages were not divided and sent to the respective churches but rather were sent together to be read aloud in all the churches. Their form is similar to that of the Old Testament's prophetic oracles, through which God spoke with authority to his people. They are therefore better thought of as messages to these seven churches that are equally intended for the whole of the church throughout the gospel age. This was the view of the ancient church that commented on Revelation within a few generations of its writing. The Muratorian Canon, for instance, dated from A.D. 170, states that "John too, indeed, in the Apocalypse, although he writes only to seven churches, yet addresses all."[1] Each message concludes, "He who has an ear, let him hear what the Spirit says to the churches" (Rev. 2:7, etc.). The fact that they are addressed to the churches in plural, and the fact that the problems identified here are common to churches of all times, makes it clear that these letters have universal relevance to all the churches of Christ. As Ramsey Michaels writes: "Nowhere is the old saying, 'If the shoe fits, wear it,' better demonstrated than here."[2]

The seven messages follow a shared format. Christ (1) praises the churches, (2) points out areas for repentance, (3) warns the churches of his judgment,

1. Alexander Roberts and James Donaldson, eds., *Ante-Nicene Fathers*, 10 vols. (Peabody, MA: Hendrickson, 1999), 5:603.
2. J. Ramsey Michaels, *Revelation*, IVP New Testament Commentary 20 (Downers Grove, IL: InterVarsity Press, 1997), 65.

and (4) promises blessings for those who overcome in his name. Each of the letters also begins with a description of Christ that is drawn from the vision of chapter 1. These descriptions connect the seven messages to the book of Revelation as a whole, just as the continued use of these images throughout the book shows that these letters apply to the entire history it represents.

The first message, to the church in Ephesus, begins: "The words of him who holds the seven stars in his right hand, who walks among the seven golden lampstands" (Rev. 2:1). At the end of this message, Christ will threaten to come and remove the church's lampstand. He thus begins by reminding the Ephesians of his sovereignty over their place in his realm. Moreover, Jesus presents himself as standing amid the churches, whose stars he holds in his hand. Thus, when he says, "I know" (2:2), we see that he is present with his people even though he is unseen. In this way, Christ, the Chief Shepherd of his flock, sets a good example for his undershepherds. Jesus is present with his churches, and he is interested in and involved with them. Vern Poythress observes that Christ addresses "each one according to its needs, with encouragement, rebuke, exhortation, and promise."[3]

The seven messages are addressed by Christ to "the angel" of each church. This probably refers to the guardian angels assigned to the ministry of the congregations. His audience is made clear, however, when each message ends with an exhortation for the readers to hear "what the Spirit says to the churches" (Rev. 2:7, etc.). By the inspiration of the Holy Spirit, the apostle John is transmitting urgent messages from Christ to his people. The messages to the various churches will each bear their distinctive marks, yet they convey an agenda. James Hamilton summarizes: "For the glory of God, Jesus charges the churches to be zealous for the gospel, reject false teaching, and live in a manner that corresponds to the gospel."[4]

CHRIST'S PRAISE FOR FAITHFULNESS

The first of Christ's messages was directed to the church of Ephesus, the leading city of Asia. It was the gateway to the Roman Empire in the region now known as Turkey, with rivers and roads connecting it to far-flung

3. Vern S. Poythress, *The Returning King: A Guide to the Book of Revelation* (Phillipsburg, NJ: P&R Publishing, 2000), 83.
4. James M. Hamilton Jr., *Revelation: The Spirit Speaks to the Churches* (Wheaton, IL: Crossway, 2012), 53.

places. Ephesus was famous for its large harbor, a flourishing marketplace, and especially the great Temple of Artemis, one of the seven wonders of the ancient world. It was also a dissolute and greatly immoral city, in large part because of the cultic prostitution and the liberty granted to criminals at its famous temple. The ancient philosopher Heraclitus, who lived in Ephesus, was known as the "weeping philosopher" because, he explained, "no one could live in Ephesus without weeping at its immorality."[5] Just as the awesome sight of the Temple of Artemis, four times the size of the Acropolis in Athens, with 120 gilded and inlaid marble columns, each sixty feet high, dominated the views of the city, the wickedness of pagan idolatry dominated the life of this place where Christ's people dwelt.

The church in Ephesus was now a second-generation congregation, having been founded forty years earlier by Paul, who later stayed to teach for three years during his third missionary journey. It was then overseen by Paul's helper Timothy, until after Paul's death the apostle John came, probably around the year A.D. 66. Paul wrote one of his greatest epistles to this church, Ephesians, together with two of his Pastoral Epistles, 1 and 2 Timothy. From Ephesus came the Gospel of John, in addition to John's three epistles. The apostles had thus invested a great deal in this church, and it is likely that the church in Ephesus extended the gospel throughout Asia so as to plant the other churches of the region.

With such leadership and ministry, it is not surprising that Jesus finds much to praise in these believers. First, he says: "I know your works, your toil" (Rev. 2:2). This refers to their faithful efforts to spread the gospel and build up the church through ministries of love and service. They have worked hard, and they have the satisfaction of learning that Jesus has noticed. Not all Christians work hard. Not all believers put the gifts given to them by Christ to good use. The word *toil* translates a Greek word that means "hard labor" (*kopon*). None of us work as diligently as we should for Christ, but it encourages us to find that he pays attention to what we do on his behalf. We are reminded here of the words that Jesus will say to all his followers who worked hard for him while he was gone: "Well done, good and faithful servant" (Matt. 25:21).

Not only had the Ephesians performed good works in Christ's name, but they had persevered patiently under trials: "I know . . . your patient

---

5. William Barclay, *The Revelation of John*, 3rd ed., 2 vols., New Daily Study Bible (Louisville: Westminster John Knox, 2004), 1:67.

[Handwritten margin notes: Continued Believing + Stood up to the surrounding culture]

endurance . . . . I know you are enduring patiently and bearing up for my name's sake, and you have not grown weary" (Rev. 2:2–3). This commendation indicates not merely that they had continued in believing, but that they had stood up to the pressure to conform to the surrounding culture. Derek Thomas writes: "In the face of opposition, these Christians had continued in their witness to Jesus Christ. They had not yielded to the pressures to conform. They had stood firm, enduring the cross that came in the wake of their bold testimony."[6] They were like the Christians in early twentieth-century America who would not succumb to modernism and refused to water down the Bible's teaching on creation, sin, redemption, and holiness. They were like churches today that will not yield to the demands of relativistic postmodernity, but uphold the authority of Scripture, continue to preach Jesus as the only Savior of the world, and raise their children to walk in the old paths of sexual purity, sacrificial service, and obedience to God's Word.

Third, Christ commends the Ephesians for their vigilance over the truth: "I know . . . how you cannot bear with those who are evil, but have tested those who call themselves apostles and are not, and found them to be false" (Rev. 2:2). It is especially encouraging to read this, given Paul's parting words to the Ephesian elders a generation earlier, warning them of "fierce wolves" who would try to come in, "not sparing the flock" (Acts 20:29). "Therefore be alert," Paul urged them (20:31), words that the Ephesians apparently took to heart. It seems that false teachers had come among them, claiming to be apostles, but under testing they had been proved false and rejected. Jesus goes on to identify this threat in a further commendation: "Yet this you have: you hate the works of the Nicolaitans, which I also hate" (Rev. 2:6). We will gain more details about the Nicolaitans in a later chapter, but for now we can be sure that they were teaching false doctrine and encouraging compromise with worldly sensualism. William Barclay summarizes: "The Nicolaitans were not prepared to be different; they were the most dangerous of all heretics from a practical point of view, for, if their teaching had been successful, the world would have changed Christianity and not Christianity the world."[7]

Observers of culture today note that Christianity's main offense is the way that our faith will not yield to the claims of other viewpoints. Many urge

6. Derek Thomas, *Let's Study Revelation* (Edinburgh: Banner of Truth, 2003), 20.
7. Barclay, *The Revelation of John*, 1:77.

believers to relax our exclusive stance, to accommodate worldly perspectives and embrace a more pliable attitude toward matters such as gender, sexuality, and the claims of science over the Bible. In this way, it is argued, Christians will get along better and receive a less hostile hearing. There are two great errors in this advice, however. The first error is failing to realize that this unyielding attitude has always been the stance of faithful Christians. Almost a century ago J. Gresham Machen wrote a book called *Christianity and Liberalism*, in which he argued against the demands for Christians to embrace a secularist viewpoint. He answered by pointing out that the stand for exclusive biblical truth was the very thing that had caused the early Christians trouble in the Roman Empire:

> The early Christian missionaries demanded an absolutely exclusive devotion to Christ. Such exclusiveness ran directly counter to the prevailing syncretism of the Hellenistic age. . . . Salvation . . . was not merely through Christ, but it was only through Christ. In that little word "only" lay all the offense. Without that word there would have been no persecutions; the cultured men of the day would probably have been willing to give Jesus a place, and an honorable place, among the saviours of mankind. Without its exclusiveness, the Christian message would have seemed perfectly inoffensive to the men of that day. . . . All men [would] speak well of it. . . . But it [would also be] entirely futile. The offense of the Cross is done away, but so is the glory and the power.[8]

We see here the importance of how Christians define success. Those who would define it in terms of cultural approval and numerical growth need to reckon with the example of the first Christians, and with the fact that Jesus praised them for refusing to allow false teaching. Indeed, Jesus' own example was one of constantly striving for truth, without yielding to false teaching and practice. Surely Jesus' praise to the Ephesians for testing and rejecting the false teachers should disabuse us of the idea that we can remain neutral in matters of truth! Certainly we should avoid needless controversy and argument. But when truth is up for sale, there is fidelity to Christ on one side and friendship with the world on the other. "This you have," Jesus approved: "you hate the works of the Nicolaitans, which I also hate" (Rev. 2:6).

8. J. Gresham Machen, *Christianity and Liberalism* (1923; repr., Grand Rapids: Eerdmans, 1996), 123–24.

93

CHRIST'S CHALLENGE TO REKINDLE LOST LOVE

There was, however, a serious problem in Ephesus, and Jesus did not hesitate to confront it: "But I have this against you, that you have abandoned the love you had at first" (Rev. 2:4).

This rebuke is understood in two ways. Many commentators hear Jesus saying that in their zeal for correct doctrine, the Ephesians have become unloving toward people. In earlier days they warmly embraced all who named the Lord in faith, but their zealous orthodoxy has made them suspicious and harsh. The second view sees this rebuke as charging the Ephesians with growing cold in their love for Jesus and their zeal for a close relationship with him. It is likely that both are involved, especially since loss of love for God will result in less fervent affection for fellow Christians. This poses a serious challenge for doctrinally minded people: Jesus' rebuke does not say that zeal for truth must always make our love grow cold, but it certainly indicates that it is possible. This is why Paul warned: "If I have prophetic powers, and understand all mysteries and all knowledge, and if I have all faith, so as to remove mountains, but have not love, I am nothing" (1 Cor. 13:2).

We should consider this problem of abandoning our first love as it relates to churches and to individual Christians. How deadly it is to grow up in a church active in good works and sound in doctrine but devoid of love for Christ! This is the failure that results in the drifting away from the faith of young people from seemingly good churches: despite good works and faithful Bible preaching, there was no fire to enflame the soul and no grace to melt the heart.

According to James Boice, who traveled extensively to evangelical churches in America, an actual interest in God is hard to find despite vigorous activity in many churches. While there is great interest in proper organization, ministry technique, and musical performance, "God has become 'weightless' for the masses of today's alleged believers." Quoting David Wells, Boice asserts that "God rests upon us so inconsequentially as not to be noticeable."[9] In other words, Christians who were making much of building their ministries and waging a culture war with pagan secularism had taken their eyes off God himself and were in danger of forgetting his sovereign glory. "Lacking a biblical and well-understood theology," Boice observed, "evangelicals have fallen prey

9. James Montgomery Boice, *Revelation*, unpublished manuscript, n.d., chap. 6, p. 9.

to the consumerism of our times, . . . [and] modern evangelicalism has become a movement that is shaped only by popular whim and sentimentality."[10]

The remedy to otherwise good churches that have lost their fervor for Christ is given in his rebuke: "Remember therefore from where you have fallen; repent, and do the works you did at first" (Rev. 2:5). Surely this will start with preaching and worship that are centered on God and not man and that are strongly grounded on the Bible and its message of saving grace. Jesus warns: "If not, I will come to you and remove your lampstand from its place, unless you repent" (2:5). The ruins that currently occupy the former site of the Ephesian church warn us of Christ's seriousness, as should the decreasing influence and power experienced by churches in Western culture today.

This same rebuke should be directed toward Christian individuals: "I have this against you, that you have abandoned the love you had at first" (Rev. 2:4). Many Christians recognize that the enthusiasm they once had for Christ is no longer seen in their lives. In former days, perhaps when first converted, we zealously searched God's Word for truth and applied it to our lives. We thought much about Jesus, and our hearts burned with wonder for the grace of his cross. We longed to grow in godliness, and each advance was a thrilling confirmation of our salvation. But these have become commonplace themes to us now. Perhaps with the increased burden of responsibility, or a foolish tolerance of sin or worldly influences, we just do not find ourselves drawing near to the Lord as we once did. We have not turned from the faith, and we are still performing our Christian duties. But from Jesus' perspective, it is obvious that the first love has grown dim, perhaps replaced with lesser, more worldly priorities.

If we find that Jesus' rebuke fits our own situation, what should we do? He provides the answer in three points. First, he directs, we must remember: "Remember therefore from where you have fallen" (Rev. 2:5). We should think back to former times when Christ occupied a higher place in our lives. We should remember the blessing it was to have our minds filled with the light of God's Word and what a joy we had in our hearts when Christ had the first place there.

O. Henry wrote a short story about someone who began again by being reminded of what he had once been. A boy grew up in a village, and in the school there he sat beside a sweet, innocent girl who had captured his heart.

10. Ibid., chap. 6, pp. 9–10.

Later the boy found himself in the city, where he fell into bad company and became a pickpocket. One day on the street he had just lifted a purse when he spied the very girl he had once sat beside in school. Suddenly, by seeing her, he remembered the boy he had once been and realized how far he had fallen.[11] Similarly, we may notice in others the Christian we once were: maybe a recent convert or one who is filled with wonder for Christ and his grace. If so, Jesus urges us to remember our first love with longing. William Cowper writes:

> Where is the blessedness I knew, when first I saw the Lord?
> Where is the soul-refreshing view of Jesus and his word?[12]

Remembering is not enough, however. Jesus adds: "repent" (Rev. 2:5). This means that we must take action to change whatever caused us to lose our fervor for Christ. Perhaps something has come into our life that now needs to go back out. In some cases, this may require the actual removal of things such as video games, worldly magazines, hobbies that eat up our time, or worldly associations. We should ask ourselves what happened or what entered our lives so as to account for our lessened fervor for Christ. Then we should remove it or put it back into its proper place and priority.

Finally, Jesus encourages us to "do the works you did at first" (Rev. 2:5). This means that we must return again to the cross of Christ, seeking forgiveness and cleansing from sin. This was the first thing we did in our conversion to Christ, and it was in wonder for "the breadth and length and height and depth" of the cross (Eph. 3:18) that our fervor was born and thrived. Then we must return to what we used to do as his disciples. This will include things such as regular and eager attendance in church, serious time devoted to God's Word, and a focused time of prayer at the beginning and end of each day. Geoffrey Wilson points out that Christ's command "is not, 'Feel thy first feelings,' but, 'Do the first works.'" This makes the point that the way "to regain this warmth of affection is neither by working up spasmodic emotion nor by theorizing about it, but by doing its duties."[13]

11. O. Henry, "The Assessor of Success," in *One Hundred Selected Stories* (London: Wordsworth, 1997).

12. William Cowper, "O for a Closer Walk with God" (1772).

13. Geoffrey B. Wilson, *New Testament Commentaries*, 2 vols. (Edinburgh: Banner of Truth, 2005), 2:484.

Remember, repent, and return—this is Christ's call to reformation for churches that have grown dim and Christians who have abandoned their first love.

CHRIST'S PROMISE TO THOSE WHO CONQUER

The final element in the seven messages to the churches of Revelation is a promise from Christ for blessing to those who conquer through faith: "To the one who conquers I will grant to eat of the tree of life, which is in the paradise of God" (Rev. 2:7).

To conquer with Christ does not mean that all our difficulties have gone away or that believers can all expect to become thin, beautiful, wealthy, and powerful. Christians conquer by persevering to the end in faith, godliness, truth, and fervent love. This is the chief message of the entire book of Revelation, so we will gain a deeper idea of Christian overcoming as we progress in the book. Revelation 12:11 will provide us with perhaps the clearest picture of Christians' conquering in faith. The chapter depicts the warfare between Satan and the church that suffers his affliction. John writes that "they have conquered him by the blood of the Lamb and by the word of their testimony, for they loved not their lives even unto death."

To conquer in Christ is to confess our sins and seek the atoning power of his death for our forgiveness, to hold fast to the gospel truths of the Bible as the foundation of our faith, and out of love for Jesus to be willing both to live for him now and to die with him should there be a day of final testing. Do you realize what a victory this overcoming faith wins? John wrote in his first epistle that "this is the victory that has overcome the world—our faith" (1 John 5:4).

Christians conquer amid tribulation in this world, but the blessing Jesus promises is received in the world to come when he returns: "To the one who conquers I will grant to eat of the tree of life, which is in the paradise of God" (Rev. 2:7).

This promise refers back to the blessing lost by Adam and Eve through sin, as they were barred from eating from the Tree of Life (Gen. 3:22). Ever since that day, sinners have desperately sought to either find or build a paradise here on earth. Have you been trying to do that? Every earthly form of paradise fails precisely because it cannot provide the life for which we were created. Yet Jesus holds open before those who persevere with him, bearing the cross through this world, and conquering through their faith, a true paradise prepared in heaven for those who love him, where the Tree of Life blooms with leaves "for the healing of the nations" (Rev. 22:2). Jesus confronts us with our obligation to overcome through faith in him: he warns, "In the world you will have tribulation." But, together with the promised Tree of Life, Jesus offers his own presence to those who rekindle their first love for him: "Take heart; I have overcome the world" (John 16:33).

10

FAITHFUL UNTO DEATH

Revelation 2:8–11

Behold, the devil is about to throw some of you into prison, that
you may be tested, and for ten days you will have tribulation.
Be faithful unto death, and I will give you the crown of life.
(Rev. 2:10)

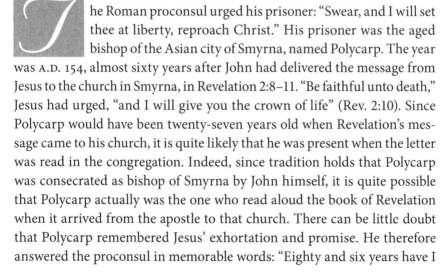he Roman proconsul urged his prisoner: "Swear, and I will set thee at liberty, reproach Christ." His prisoner was the aged bishop of the Asian city of Smyrna, named Polycarp. The year was A.D. 154, almost sixty years after John had delivered the message from Jesus to the church in Smyrna, in Revelation 2:8–11. "Be faithful unto death," Jesus had urged, "and I will give you the crown of life" (Rev. 2:10). Since Polycarp would have been twenty-seven years old when Revelation's message came to his church, it is quite likely that he was present when the letter was read in the congregation. Indeed, since tradition holds that Polycarp was consecrated as bishop of Smyrna by John himself, it is quite possible that Polycarp actually was the one who read aloud the book of Revelation when it arrived from the apostle to that church. There can be little doubt that Polycarp remembered Jesus' exhortation and promise. He therefore answered the proconsul in memorable words: "Eighty and six years have I

served [Christ], and He never did me any injury: how then can I blaspheme my King and my Saviour?"[1] With that refusal, Polycarp was executed by public burning, having been faithful to the end and being certain of the promised crown from his Lord. His obedience to the command Jesus gave to the church in Smyrna reminds us that the book of Revelation was given to address the real needs of the Christians facing adversity and trials in the apostle's day, just as it addresses the situation of afflicted believers today.

If Ephesus was the chief city of Roman Asia, then Smyrna was a shining jewel nestled on the Aegean coast. A city of over two hundred thousand residents, Smyrna possessed a fine harbor and a prominent hill known as "the Crown of Smyrna" that was surrounded by elegant estates. The city had been founded as a Greek colony around the year 1000 B.C., but was destroyed in 600 B.C. by an invasion from Lydia. Over three hundred years later, Smyrna was rebuilt in a grand style according to the plans of Alexander the Great, adorned with temples to Zeus and Cybele. As early as 195 B.C., Smyrna had thrown in its lot with the rising power in Rome, dedicating another temple to the goddess Roma. During the three hundred years between that time and the writing of Revelation, Smyrna had been one of Rome's most loyal vassals, having been lauded by Cicero as "one of our most faithful and our most ancient allies." During one war in the east, the Smyrnaeans had stripped off their own clothes to provide for a suffering Roman army, and in the year A.D. 26, Smyrna had competed for and won the honor of erecting a temple to the emperor Tiberius.[2] Given Smyrna's commitment to Rome and the cult of emperor worship, we would expect that the church here would become a particularly vulnerable target to the persecutions that the emperor Domitian was about to unleash on those who would not bow to his supposed deity.

A PERSECUTED CHURCH

Smyrna receives the shortest of Jesus' seven messages, yet one filled with praise and without any criticism from the Lord. Jesus' urgent letter to this church is dominated by his need to prepare the Smyrnaeans for

---

1. Alexander Roberts and James Donaldson, eds., *The Apostolic Fathers, Justin Martyr, Irenaeus,* in *Ante-Nicene Fathers*, vol. 1 (Peabody, MA: Hendrickson, 1999), 41.
2. Ibid., 1:82–84.

severe persecution that is drawing near: "I know your tribulation and your poverty (but you are rich) and the slander . . . . Behold, the devil is about to throw some of you into prison" (Rev. 2:9–10).

In the first letter, Jesus told the Ephesians, "I know your works" (Rev. 2:2). Jesus is equally familiar with the state of affairs in Smyrna, especially the "tribulation" that was upon the church. This word means "living under the pressure of great oppression." It is not surprising that Jesus first associated this tribulation with "poverty," since successful participation in social and economic life would probably have been impossible for those not willing to worship Caesar as Lord. G. K. Beale comments: "The imperial cult permeated virtually every aspect of city and often even village life in Asia Minor, so that individuals could aspire to economic prosperity and greater social standing only by participating to some degree in the Roman cult."[3] We can see why Jesus sends so favorable a letter to this church, since the particular word for *poverty* (Greek, *ptocheia*) indicates the crushing poverty of those who are not able to meet even their basic needs, simply because of their commitment to lead holy lives before the Lord.

How few Christians today are willing to place the affairs of Christ's kingdom ahead of their careers or financial prosperity! But the Christians of Smyrna realized that theirs was the privilege of sharing in Christ's own suffering. Paul used the same word for *poverty* when he wrote of Christ: "For you know the grace of our Lord Jesus Christ, that though he was rich, yet for your sake he became poor, so that you by his poverty might become rich" (2 Cor. 8:9). How greatly the example of both Christ and the Christians of Smyrna condemns the false teaching of today's so-called prosperity gospel, which teaches that believers who lack earthly health and riches are suffering because of their lack of faith. Douglas Kelly writes: "How dare anyone accuse [the Smyrnaeans] of lacking faith, when they are living in poverty out of self-sacrificial love to Jesus."[4]

A second form of tribulation came through the "slander" that the Christians were enduring from "those who say that they are Jews and are not" (Rev. 2:9). Another feature of Smyrna was the large and prominent Jewish community in the city. If the pattern of the apostle Paul had been followed

---

3. G. K. Beale, *The Book of Revelation: A Commentary on the Greek Text*, New International Greek Testament Commentary (Grand Rapids: Eerdmans, 1999), 240.

4. Douglas F. Kelly, *Revelation*, Mentor Expository Commentary (Tain, Ross-shire, Scotland: Mentor, 2012), 42.

when the gospel came to this city, the evangelists would first have preached the gospel to Jews, and many of the first believers may have come from the Jewish community. This would have been one reason why Jewish leaders were some of the early church's most resolute oppressors. Another reason was their resolve to retain the cherished privileges under Roman rule. Because of Jerusalem's support of Julius Caesar in the civil war, over a century earlier, Jews were granted special permission not to worship the emperor but to offer prayers to their own God on his behalf. Not wanting to share this status with converts to Christ, the Jews slandered Christians to the authorities as those who did not worship the God of the Old Testament and blasphemously denied the Christian claim that Jesus is the Messiah. Among slanders known to have been launched at Christians were the claim that Christians drowned their children and ate human flesh (these claims arising from false ideas of baptism and the Lord's Supper), that Christians were politically disloyal, and that Christians were fire-raisers, since they predicted the end of the world in flames.[5] Jesus states that Jews who slander the true Messiah and his people "are not" true Jews. This agrees with Paul's teaching in Romans 2:28–29 that true Jews are defined not by ethnicity but by faith in the message of Christ. Dennis Johnson comments that "the people of God are defined Christocentrically, not genealogically."[6]

The third and fourth forms of persecution in Smyrna go together, since imprisonment in those days was not for the sake of incarceration but merely as a brief prelude to execution: "Behold, the devil is about to throw some of you into prison . . . . Be faithful unto death" (Rev. 2:10).

The kinds of tribulation suffered by the church at Smyrna are still being suffered by Christians around the world today. For instance, under the Communist regimes of eastern Europe, Christians were often barred from attending the universities that alone offered access to well-paying jobs and important positions in society. Despite high qualifications, many faithful believers held only low-paying jobs and were subjected to frequent harassment and arrest on trumped-up charges.[7] In America today, Christians are frequently slandered as being hateful people because of our moral stance

---

5. William Barclay, *The Revelation of John*, 3rd ed., 2 vols., New Daily Study Bible (Louisville: Westminster John Knox, 2004), 1:90.

6. Dennis E. Johnson, *Triumph of the Lamb: A Commentary on Revelation* (Phillipsburg, NJ: P&R Publishing, 2001), 74.

7. Kelly, *Revelation*, 43.

against homosexuality. Simply reading the Bible's teachings on sexuality and marriage may soon be criminalized in the United States as "hate speech." In places such as central Nigeria, Sudan, and Pakistan, Christians are subjected to sudden violence and death from Muslim terrorists; and in places such as China, Iran, and Indonesia, Christians may be jailed for long periods simply for their testimony to Jesus. With the collapse of tolerance for Christians in the West, there will soon be few places where believers will not pay a price for our faith in the form of tribulation, just as Paul foretold: "All who desire to live a godly life in Christ Jesus will be persecuted" (2 Tim. 3:12).

In pointing out that the suffering of believers in Smyrna would largely come through Jewish accusation, Jesus declares not only that such people "say that they are Jews and are not," but that they are actually "a synagogue of Satan" (Rev. 2:9). We are reminded of the denunciations Jesus pronounced on the Pharisees during his earthly ministry, when those Jewish leaders accused him of falsehood despite compelling proof of his claims to be the Messiah. Jesus said: "You are of your father the devil, and your will is to do your father's desires. He was a murderer from the beginning, and has nothing to do with the truth, because there is no truth in him" (John 8:44). While the slandering Jews claimed to be the synagogue of God, they were actually serving the cause of Satan, especially as their denunciations of Christians to the Roman authorities led to the arrest and execution of Christ's people. History records that it was his Jewish enemies who denounced Polycarp to the Romans, and that Jews went so far as to violate the Sabbath in order to gather the wood used in Polycarp's execution. No wonder Christ associates them with the name of Satan, since that name refers to the devil as the false accuser of God's faithful people.[8]

Jesus goes on to say that it is "the devil" who "is about to throw some of you into prison" (Rev. 2:10), reminding believers that we face a perennial enemy of ceaseless malice and great power. G. B. Caird writes: "Throughout this book John is constantly trying to show how Satan's hand may be detected in the affairs of this world; but he is equally insistent that Satan can do nothing except by the permission of God, who uses Satan's grimmest machinations to further his own bright designs."[9]

8. Robert H. Mounce, *Revelation*, rev. ed., New International Commentary on the New Testament (Grand Rapids: Eerdmans, 1997), 118.

9. G. B. Caird, *The Revelation of St. John the Divine* (San Francisco: Harper, 1966), 36.

LORD OF THE PERSECUTED

Jesus has a message of encouragement to the persecuted church of Smyrna, which is grounded in his own glorious person. His command is "Do not fear what you are about to suffer" (Rev. 2:10). The basis for this urging is found in Christ's opening words: "To the angel of the church in Smyrna write: 'The words of the first and the last, who died and came to life'" (2:8). Jesus presents himself as the Lord of the persecuted, granting hope, provision, and victory for his saints in the tribulation of this world.

The first reason that the Christians of Smyrna should not fear the tribulation before them is that Jesus is "the first and the last" (Rev. 2:8). Some commentators suggest that this statement is meant to contrast with the reputation of Smyrna as the first city of Asia. In the city's society, men and women were busy striving to be better than everyone else so as to take the first place. Barclay notes, however: "Beside the glory of Christ, all human titles are of no importance and all human claims become ridiculous."[10] In the several uses of this expression already in Revelation, we have previously noted that "first and last" signifies God's sovereignty over all things, so Christ's meaning is also that his people should not fear in light of his sovereign control of all that they face.

A second reason why the believers should not fear is that Christ is the Lord and giver of life, by virtue of his resurrection conquest of the grave: Jesus reminds us that he "died and came to life" (Rev. 2:8). Irony is probably intended here because the city of Smyrna boasted a kind of resurrection, since after its earlier destruction the Macedonian rulers rebuilt the city in greater splendor. Jesus insists that this is little alongside his death and resurrection to free his people from sin and grant them eternal life. Having died on a cross, Jesus had already experienced the very worst that the world can do to its enemies, and Jesus had prevailed in the resurrection for the salvation of his people. Therefore, Christians should not fear to die for Jesus, since in Christ the grave is the gateway into eternal glory in heaven. Douglas Kelly summarizes Jesus' meaning as saying: "I have passed through the territory of death already. I have taken all of its terror away for believers. Now, the only thing that awaits you on the other side of death is holding my hand as we walk together into the new beauties of resurrec-

10. Barclay, *The Revelation of John*, 1:91.

tion joy."[11] Paul understood his own trials this way, writing that "this light momentary affliction is preparing for us an eternal weight of glory beyond all comparison" (2 Cor. 4:17).

Third, in light of what Jesus has said about himself, he is the Lord of the very trials being suffered by his faithful people. We see this in his declaration of the length of the trials to come: "I know," Jesus said, that "for ten days you will have tribulation" (Rev. 2:9–10). It is likely that "ten days" is a symbolic number indicating a limited and relatively brief period of suffering. The fact that Jesus was able to declare this duration in advance indicates that his sovereign control determines the bounds of the trial and limits its intensity. Michael Wilcock remarks: "There would in the goodness of God come an eleventh day, and all would be over."[12]

The duration of "ten days" may also be intended to link back to the book of Daniel, in which the young believer and his friends were tested for ten days in Babylon, while they refused to transgress the law of Israel by eating forbidden foods from King Nebuchadnezzar's table. This being the case, the Smyrnaeans would be reminded that Daniel and his friends came out of the trial "better in appearance and fatter in flesh than all the youths who ate the king's food" (Dan. 1:15). Trusting in the same Lord, the Christians in Smyrna would emerge from tribulation strengthened in faith, and they would have given public testimony to the power of their Savior and Lord.

Being reminded of Daniel, we also remember Christ's faithfulness to Shadrach, Meshach, and Abednego, when like the Smyrnaean Christians they refused to bow before the golden image of the king. For this, Daniel's friends were cast into a furnace to be burned alive. When they were thrust into the flames, however, not only were they not consumed, but onlookers saw "four men unbound, walking in the midst of the fire," with the additional figure appearing "like a son of the gods" (Dan. 3:25). We can only imagine that Polycarp, facing the flames because of his fidelity to Christ in his refusal to worship Caesar, must have thought back not only to the message of Revelation but also to Christ's faithfulness in delivering the heroes of Daniel from the flames. Polycarp was not spared physically, but

---

11. Kelly, *Revelation*, 41.

12. Michael Wilcock, *I Saw Heaven Opened: The Message of Revelation*, The Bible Speaks Today (Downers Grove, IL: InterVarsity Press, 1975), 46.

there can be no doubt that Christ was with him to grant victory through the flames. This was to fulfill Isaiah 43:2–3's promise of aid in tribulation: "When you pass through the waters, I will be with you; and through the rivers, they shall not overwhelm you; when you walk through fire you shall not be burned, and the flame shall not consume you. For I am the LORD your God, the Holy One of Israel, your Savior."

When Jesus proclaims his lordship over the trial about to be suffered in Smyrna, he not only promises a limited duration and the help of his presence in the flames, but also declares his purpose in the tribulation. There is positive significance to the trial: Jesus permits it so "that you may be tested" (Rev. 2:10). We should think of our faith being tested in trials in two ways. The first is the proving or displaying of the genuineness of our faith. Peter wrote that we should rejoice in our trials, since they "have come so that the proven genuineness of your faith—of greater worth than gold, which perishes even though refined by fire—may result in praise, glory and honor when Jesus Christ is revealed" (1 Peter 1:6–7 NIV). When Christians hold fast in faith under trial, the genuineness of our belief and the certainty of our salvation is proved. True believers will pass the test of tribulation by holding fast to Jesus, while false believers who were never truly saved are revealed by falling away under trial.

Joined to this is a second purpose of strengthening or refining our faith. Paul said that "we rejoice in our sufferings, knowing that suffering produces endurance, and endurance produces character, and character produces hope" (Rom. 5:3–4). We have seen that Peter compared the trial of faith to the refining of precious metals. The aim of refining is to purify the precious metals by removing the dross. Likewise, Christ uses trials to drive out worldliness and sin from our lives and thus purify our faith. A smith refines ore by heating it to a very high temperature, plunging it into cold water, and then scraping away the dross. He continues this process until he can look upon the gold and see a clear reflection of his own face. So it is with Christ in refining our faith: his goal is through fire and water to separate and scrape away the dross of sin and unbelief, so that he may look upon our faith and see the clear reflection of his own glorious face.

Not only does Christ use tribulation to see his reflection in our lives, but he also employs trials so that we may learn to see him more clearly. Donald Grey Barnhouse writes: "How wonderful that when we are blinded by tears, we can nevertheless see our God. In fact, our tears become crystal lenses through which He is magnified; and in the midst of suffering we realize the greatness of His power and the tenderness of His love."[13]

PERSECUTED BUT FAITHFUL

Be faithful even unto death.

Jesus places a single requirement on his persecuted church: "Be faithful," even "unto death" (Rev. 2:10). The believers were not to look at the suffering to come, so that they trembled with fear, but were to look through the suffering to the Sovereign Lord who promised to deliver them strengthened and purified after a limited duration of trial. With this perspective, remaining faithful was their single goal.

Charles Hodge worked out faithfulness in suffering in two ways. First, the afflicted believers must hold fast to what God had entrusted to them, that is, their faith in Christ and the gospel. "The thing therefore committed to the Church . . . is . . . the truth of God as revealed in his holy word."[14] They must also be faithful by maintaining their allegiance to Jesus. This was Polycarp's commitment: "How then can I blaspheme my king who saved me?" The Christians of Smyrna must not yield to the satanic demand that they worship Caesar, just as Christians today must be faithful not to bow to the gods of our age.

There are three incentives for this faithfulness in our passage, the first of which deals with a true assessment of the believers' situation even in the midst of the trial. As the world saw them, the Christians were utterly impoverished, but Jesus declares instead: "You are rich" (Rev. 2:9). The point was that they possessed spiritual riches that abundantly compensated for their material poverty. Anyone today who travels among persecuted believers will see this firsthand. In my own travels in East Africa, it is impossible to spend time with the materially poor and often-oppressed Christians without experiencing envy for the simplicity, vibrant joy, and sheer spiritual wealth of their lives.

The present wealth of the faith of the Smyrnaeans compared very poorly, however, to what awaited them through their tribulation. Jesus promised: "Be

---

13. Donald Grey Barnhouse, *Expositions of Bible Doctrines, Taking the Epistle to the Romans as a Point of Departure*, 10 vols. (Grand Rapids: Eerdmans, 1959), 4:89.

14. Charles Hodge, *Princeton Sermons* (1879; repr., Edinburgh: Banner of Truth, 1958), 321.

faithful unto death, and I will give you the crown of life" (Rev. 2:10). Smyrna had its elegant city center, its "crown," with elegant estates surrounding a lofty height overlooking the sea. But the suffering Christians anticipated a more glorious crown upon the completion of their trial, especially awaiting those who suffered death for their faith in Jesus. This promise connects to the athletic games held in Smyrna, which rivaled those of Mount Olympus in Greece. Jesus was thus promising an ornament of glory, life, and power to crown those who triumphed through faithfulness unto death and thus achieved their entrance into eternal bliss. Romans were also given laurel crowns to wear at special banquets; Christians who are faithful to Christ through the tribulations of this world will wear the crown of eternal life in the eternal banquet of heaven.[15]

Jesus gave a third incentive to faithfulness under tribulation that pertains to believers of all times: "He who has an ear, let him hear what the Spirit says to the churches. The one who conquers will not be hurt by the second death" (Rev. 2:11). The expression "second death" also appears later in Revelation, which identifies it with the eternal condemnation in hell that awaits unbelievers in the final judgment (21:8). Simon Kistemaker explains: "The saints may suffer physical death at the hand of persecutors, but they will never be separated from God. By contrast, unbelievers will be cast into the lake of fire (20:14) and suffer eternal death."[16]

The Bible speaks not only of two deaths, temporal and eternal, but also of two resurrections—of the spirit and of the body. All persons will be resurrected in the body on the last day to stand before the judgment throne of Christ (Matt. 25:31–32). But those who believe in Jesus in this present life, suffering tribulation for his name but made rich through saving faith, have received a spiritual resurrection in the new birth. Though often poor in the things of the world, afflicted believers are rich in the kingdom of God, and having been made alive to God through faith, they have no fear of the second death that is hell, having already with Jesus "passed from death to life" (John 5:24).

It was knowing his deliverance from the second death that emboldened Polycarp of Smyrna to give so bold a testimony in the face of the death of

---

15. See a detailed explanation in Grant R. Osborne, *Revelation*, Baker Exegetical Commentary on the New Testament (Grand Rapids: Baker Academic, 2002), 135.

16. Simon J. Kistemaker, *Revelation*, New Testament Commentary (Grand Rapids: Baker, 2001), 125.

his body. When the bishop refused to betray Jesus in worshiping Caesar, the proconsul threatened him with the terror of flames. Polycarp replied: "You threaten me with the fire that burns for a time, and is quickly quenched, for you do not know the fire which awaits the wicked in the judgment to come and in everlasting punishment."[17]

If you are like the proconsul in your unbelief, scorn, and perhaps even persecution of the people of Christ, Jesus has a word for you. He told his followers in Smyrna, "Do not fear what you are about to suffer" (Rev. 2:10). Likewise, Jesus tells unbelievers that their true fear is not what they will lose in this world through faith in Christ but rather God's judgment that awaits us all in death. Jesus once said: "Do not fear those who kill the body but cannot kill the soul. Rather fear him who can destroy both soul and body in hell" (Matt. 10:28). For both the Christian and the unbeliever, the Bible's antidote to fear is one and the same, along with an invitation to eternal life: "Believe in the Lord Jesus, and you will be saved" (Acts 16:31). He promises all who believe: "Be faithful unto death, and I will give you the crown of life. . . . The one who conquers will not be hurt by the second death" (Rev. 2:10–11).

17. Barclay, *The Revelation of John*, 1:85.

11

WHERE SATAN DWELLS

Revelation 2:12–17

*But I have a few things against you: you have some there
who hold the teaching of Balaam, who taught Balak to put a
stumbling block before the sons of Israel, so that they might eat
food sacrificed to idols and practice sexual immorality. (Rev. 2:14)*

he seven messages from Jesus to the churches of Revelation
seem to be organized in a chiastic pattern. *Chi* is the Greek
letter for *X*, and *chiasm* is a literary device that follows this
pattern, with the first and last items linked, the second and second-to-last
items linked, and so forth. This pattern can be seen in Revelation chapters 2
and 3 in that the first and last letters, to Ephesus and Laodicea, address
churches that have lost their first love and grown lukewarm (Rev. 2:4; 3:16).
Likewise, the second and sixth letters seem to be linked, since both Smyrna
and Philadelphia are churches for which Jesus had no criticism.

A chiastic pattern is useful not only in linking pairs but also in focusing emphasis on the items in the center. This raises a question about the
relationship of the messages to the third, fourth, and fifth churches. The
answer seems to lie in a progression that Jesus highlights as endangering not
only these churches but all his churches in all times. The third message, to

Pergamum, warns against false teaching that turns Christ's people toward worldliness. The fourth message, to Thyatira, rebukes not just false teaching but also its fruit in sinful debauchery. The fifth message, to Sardis, shows the ultimate result when false teaching leads to sinful indulgence. Jesus writes to Sardis: "You have the reputation of being alive, but you are dead" (Rev. 3:1). This seems to be the overall warning given by the exalted Christ to his church: if false teaching is permitted, the worldliness it fosters will lead to gross sinfulness, the result of which will be death. This warning not only pertained to the churches at the end of the first century, but speaks with the greatest of urgency to compromised churches at the beginning of the twenty-first century.

THE THREAT OF PERSECUTION

Christ's letter to Smyrna warned about approaching persecution (Rev. 2:10), but in the letter to Pergamum, Jesus writes to Christians who have already witnessed martyrdom for the faith. Jesus praises them: "You did not deny my faith even in the days of Antipas my faithful witness, who was killed among you" (2:13). The word for *witness* is *martus*, a form of the word that gives us *martyr*, a believer who gives his or her life in faithfulness to Christ.

It is not surprising that martyrdom had already come to Pergamum, since Jesus says that it is "where Satan's throne is" and "where Satan dwells" (Rev. 2:13). A number of reasons are suggested for why Jesus says this about Pergamum. Like Ephesus and Smyrna, Pergamum was a large and important city with a strong concentration of idolatry and false religion. Above the city streets was a high terrace filled with temples and government buildings. Four different cults had headquarters in Pergamum, including the gods Zeus, Athene, Dionysos, and especially Asklepios. The latter god was famed for healing, so that Pergamum attracted people from all over the world seeking restoration at the shrine of "Asklepios the Savior." Some have thought that this shrine is behind Jesus' reference to "Satan's throne," since Asklepios's symbol was a coiled serpent, as seen today in symbols dedicated to the medical profession.

Pergamum was also the headquarters of the Roman government in Asia. Michael Wilcock writes: "If Ephesus was the New York of Asia, Pergamum was its Washington, for there the Roman imperial power had its seat of government."[1] For this reason, Pergamum was also the city most devoted to the Roman imperial cult and the place where Christians were most likely to be persecuted for refusing to worship Caesar as God. As travelers approached Pergamum from the south, "the shape of the city-hill would appear as a giant throne towering above the plain."[2] The throne in Pergamum belonged to Caesar, who was Satan's chief instrument in persecuting Christians. In contrast to Smyrna, where the persecution arose from Jewish betrayals, in Pergamum the Christians faced the hostility of pagans who demanded conformity to their idolatrous cultural norms. It is probably for resisting pagan practices and for refusing to worship Caesar that Antipas lost his life in service to Christ.

We know from a letter from the Roman governor Pliny the Younger to the Emperor Trajan, dated around A.D. 111, that accused Christians could avoid death only by cursing the name of Jesus Christ. It is noteworthy, then, how Jesus praises the church in Pergamum: "Yet you hold fast my name" (Rev. 2:13). The Christians would not renounce Jesus or despise his name, even on pain of death. Moreover, Jesus says, "you did not deny my faith" (2:13). This means that the Christians would not accept another lord in Jesus' place, and that they would not renounce central biblical doctrines such as the deity of Christ, the atoning sacrifice on his cross, and salvation through faith alone. Though this faithful stance might threaten the Christians' lives, Jesus reminds them that he wields the true sword of judgment and that he will overturn any verdict given by the Roman proconsul. Thus Jesus begins his message: "And to the angel of the church in Pergamum write: 'The words of him who has the sharp two-edged sword'" (2:12).

Joseph Ton, a Baptist pastor persecuted by the Communist regime in Romania, wrote a book titled *A Theology of Martyrdom*. In it, he made a point about Jesus' praise for Antipas as "my faithful witness." Ton urges that just as the Lord makes Christians stewards of things such as money, time, and talents, he also makes us stewards of our witness in the face of death. A Christian who suffers for Jesus is given a precious resource with which he or she may reach multitudes for the gospel.[3] For making

---

1. Michael Wilcock, *I Saw Heaven Opened: The Message of Revelation*, The Bible Speaks Today (Downers Grove, IL: InterVarsity Press, 1975), 47.

2. Robert H. Mounce, *Revelation*, rev. ed., New International Commentary on the New Testament (Grand Rapids: Eerdmans, 1997), 96.

3. Taken from Douglas F. Kelly, *Revelation*, Mentor Expository Commentary (Tain, Ross-shire, Scotland: Mentor, 2012), 50.

the most of their persecution, the saints in Pergamum earned Christ's fervent praise.

THE THREAT OF HERESY

Persecution is not the only serious threat facing Christians and churches, however. A second threat is false teaching from within, and in this respect Jesus expresses serious concern for Pergamum: "But I have a few things against you: you have some there who hold the teaching of Balaam, who taught Balak to put a stumbling block before the sons of Israel, so that they might eat food sacrificed to idols and practice sexual immorality. So also you have some who hold the teaching of the Nicolaitans" (Rev. 2:14–15).

The strange figure Balaam is a famous biblical example of an enemy who first tried to persecute believers but found greater success by seducing them. When the Israelites were advancing through the wilderness near Moab, Balak the king of Moab sought to destroy them by having Balaam declare a curse. This attack failed because when Balaam began cursing Israel, the Holy Spirit would come upon him and change his curses into blessings (Num. 23:1–12). Like Satan in Pergamum, Balaam realized that persecution was only making God's people stronger, so he changed tactics. Jesus' message says that Balaam "put a stumbling block before the sons of Israel" (Rev. 2:14), so that they ate prohibited foods and entered into sexual sin. Balaam did this by sending the daughters of Moab into the Israelite camp to lure the men into sexual sin and idolatry. Numbers 25 records that God judged Israel for these sins, slaying twenty-four thousand people by a plague.

In referring to the example of Balaam and also the false teachers known as the Nicolaitans, it is likely that Jesus was speaking of the same persons. *Nicolaitans* and *Balaam* have the same meaning, the first a Greek word and the second a Hebrew word meaning "conqueror of the people." Jesus equates the two, saying, "So also you have some who hold the teaching of the Nicolaitans" (Rev. 2:15).

In considering Jesus' description of false teachers under the name of Balaam, we should note that Balaam wreaked his havoc by means of false teaching: he "taught Balak to put a stumbling block before the sons of Israel." In Pergamum, similar false teaching encouraged Christians to "eat food sacrificed to idols and practice sexual immorality" (Rev. 2:14). It seems, therefore, that the Nicolaitans encouraged cultural accommodation and secular living. In a place where it seemed impossible that Christians could survive by refusing to accept the imperial cult, they urged believers to say the words and participate in the ritual feasts. Perhaps they further added that since Jesus had died to forgive sins, Christians should not worry about sinful patterns such as sexual immorality that would enable us to get along in a pagan world. Robert Mounce suggests that their message may have taught "that it was possible without disloyalty to maintain a peaceful co-existence with Rome."[4] William Barclay comments that the Nicolaitans "sought to persuade Christians that there was nothing wrong with a prudent conformity to the world's standards."[5]

Pergamum reminds us, in this way, of two great strategies employed by Satan against the Christian church. The first is persecution, which the believers of Pergamum had withstood. The second was false teaching leading to unholy and worldly living, and to this Pergamum was in danger of succumbing. Jesus thus warns his people: "Therefore repent" (Rev. 2:16).

Today, Nicolaitans would be foremost among those urging the ordination of homosexuals as ministers, since this compromise is demanded by the secular culture. Evangelicals smugly condemn liberals for this patently unbiblical practice. Yet by refusing to practice biblical gender order in the church, and by refusing to teach on unpopular topics such as sin, divine wrath, and eternal judgment, they are propagating the very false approach to the Bible that has produced such radical results in other churches more advanced along the same trajectory of worldly accommodation and spiritual decline.

Jesus' warning to Pergamum teaches us that Christians and churches must be vigilant against false teaching. This was Paul's counsel when he charged the elders of Ephesus to watch out for "fierce wolves [who] will come in among you, not sparing the flock . . . . Therefore be alert" (Acts 20:29–31). The Nicolaitan spirit tells us not to be rigorous in teaching or practicing God's Word. If worship innovations are popular with unbelievers, Nicolaitans adopt them even in violation of Holy Scripture.

4. Mounce, *Revelation*, 98.
5. William Barclay, *The Revelation of John*, 3rd ed., 2 vols., New Daily Study Bible (Louisville: Westminster John Knox, 2004), 1:102.

Nicolaitanism prevails today by a general dread of controversy and doctrinal division in evangelical circles, so that leaders who contend against doctrinal error are accused of spiritual deviancy and denounced as "heresy hunters." Robert Haldane responds to this attitude: "Those who hold this opinion seem to overlook what every page of the New Testament lays before us. In all the history of the Lord Jesus Christ we never find him out of controversy."[6] Like the Christians in Pergamum, most of us today would like to get along with everyone and to enjoy the positive esteem of all. But Jesus says that this is one of the worst things that could be said about any Christian: "Woe to you, when all people speak well of you, for so their fathers did to the false prophets" (Luke 6:26). Steve Wilmshurst thus comments:

> The New Testament, in fact the whole Bible, commands us to . . . watch out for anyone and anything who will lead us astray. This is not because we are to be obsessively pedantic about our theology, . . . but because our God is the God of *truth*, because there is only one way in which we are to be saved and one written Word by which we are to live, and because false teaching destroys God's people.[7]

We remember, too, that the letter to Ephesus warns us against a cold and unloving orthodoxy (Rev. 2:1–7). Yet here in Pergamum we see the danger on the opposite side, of caring little for doctrinal truth and doing nothing to oppose false teaching when we learn of it. At Pergamum, repentance "would mean exercising church discipline, refusing to tolerate Nicolaitan teaching. The church and its leaders must confront the Nicolaitans," seeking their repentance.[8] Jesus says that unless churches are willing to oppose false doctrine and false practice, not accepting or even tolerating heresy, the Roman sword of persecution would not be needed, since Christ's own sword of discipline would fall on his church: "Therefore repent. If not, I will come to you soon and war against them with the sword of my mouth" (Rev. 2:16).

6. Quoted in D. Martyn Lloyd-Jones, *Knowing the Times: Addresses Delivered on Various Occasions 1942-1977* (Edinburgh: Banner of Truth, 1989), ix.

7. Steve Wilmshurst, *The Final Word: The Book of Revelation Simply Explained* (Darlington, UK: Evangelical Press, 2008), 42–43.

8. Dennis E. Johnson, *Triumph of the Lamb: A Commentary on Revelation* (Phillipsburg, NJ: P&R Publishing, 2001), 7.

THE PROMISE OF NEW LIFE

One form of Nicolaitan teaching that is common today among evangelical Christians claims that we should not think in terms of overcoming or conquering through our faith in Jesus. We need to accept the fact that we are really no different from others, we are told, that we will never really overcome the power of sin, and that we should therefore abandon the language of conquering together with Jesus in this world. But this argument is refuted by none other than Jesus Christ himself. He concludes his letter to Pergamum, as he concludes all seven letters, with the words, "To the one who conquers" (Rev. 2:17). To be sure, Jesus does not mean that Christians will in this life overcome all difficulties so as to become virtual gods ourselves. Rather, Jesus refers to his true people who refuse to renounce him but hold fast against all persecution, who zealously uphold true doctrine while refusing heretical teaching, and who embrace the Bible's call to holiness, refusing to capitulate to the immoral and self-serving standards of a world under God's judgment. As John put it more succinctly: "This is the victory that has overcome the world—our faith" (1 John 5:4).

To all who conquer through faith, Jesus promises three rich blessings. The point of these promises is that believers have no reason to accommodate the world or to seek the world's favor, given all that we have in Christ. Jesus concludes: "He who has an ear, let him hear what the Spirit says to the churches. To the one who conquers I will give some of the hidden manna, and I will give him a white stone, with a new name written on the stone that no one knows except the one who receives it" (Rev. 2:17).

Manna refers to the supernatural food that fell from heaven during the exodus, enabling God's people to live and making them strong to follow after God's leading. Scholars point out a Jewish legend to which Jesus may refer, which states that when Jerusalem was destroyed, the prophet Jeremiah took some of the stored manna from the exodus and hid it until the Messiah should come. Whether Jesus had this in mind or not, it is true that he offers spiritual provision out of his great, saving works to strengthen his faithful people in need. William Barclay comments that "'to eat of the hidden manna' means to enjoy the blessings of the messianic age."[9] Douglas Kelly points out the mysterious nature of manna, with its hidden origin in

9. Barclay, *The Revelation of John*, 1:105.

heaven. Of Christ's faithful people, he explains: "God provides for them, and they do not know where it came from, nor how it got there. It has a heavenly explanation. God is going to take care of you as long as he needs to. His supernatural, overruling providence will take care of you physically and spiritually."[10]

Second, Jesus promises the true believer: "I will give him a white stone" (Rev. 2:17). There were many significant uses in the ancient world of a white, ceremonial stone, called a *tessera*, which may have a connection to Jesus' meaning. In the athletic games, the most outstanding champions were given a white stone, which conveyed honor to them in the future. In this connection, Barclay writes, "This would mean that Christians are the victorious athletes of Christ who may share in the glory of their Lord."[11]

Additionally, a white stone was a token of admission, in contrast to the proverbial "black ball," which signified refusal. It was especially noteworthy to the Christians of Pergamum, whose faithfulness to Christ meant exclusion from the pagan feasts and festivals, that a white stone was given to grant admission to banquets. The stone that Jesus gives grants access to a far more sumptuous table: the great feast of the Lamb of God in the age to come (see Rev. 19:8–9).

Most importantly, in courts of law, jurors would vote for acquittal by setting forth a white stone, in contrast with a black stone for conviction. Where Satan dwelt in power, faithful Christians were accused and condemned, and some (like Antipas) were put to the sword for their conviction of fidelity to Jesus Christ. Jesus, in turn, would present a white stone to his justified people. Derek Thomas writes: "Jesus promises to give them the white stone of acquittal—an assurance of eternal life."[12]

Third, Jesus promises "a new name written on the stone that no one knows except the one who receives it" (Rev. 2:17). The new name is likely that of Christ as Lord (Phil. 2:9–11), engraved on each white stone, a name known only by those who receive salvation through faith. Revelation 14:1 speaks of the redeemed each having Christ's "name and his Father's name written on their foreheads." Knowing Christ's new name indicates the believers' intimate relationship with the Lord of glory. Moreover, just as the name of

10. Kelly, *Revelation*, 52.
11. Barclay, *The Revelation of John*, 1:107.
12. Derek Thomas, *Let's Study Revelation* (Edinburgh: Banner of Truth, 2003), 26.

the Lord made his temple holy, so also are those who receive the "new name written on the stone" signified for their holy duty, calling, and destiny in Christ. G. K. Beale adds: "Therefore, the 'new name' is a mark of genuine membership in the community of the redeemed, without which entry into the eternal 'city of God' is impossible."[13]

The importance of the blessings that Jesus promised is made vivid in the example of William Somerset Maugham, one of the greatest writers of the early twentieth century. His novel *Of Human Bondage* is a recognized classic, and his play *The Constant Wife* has received thousands of stagings. He enjoyed incredible popularity, receiving an average of three hundred fan letters a week, and had fabulous wealth. But his wildest dreams of success failed to satisfy him. His nephew, Robin Maugham, visited him shortly before his death in his villa on the Mediterranean Sea, filled with valuable furniture and works of art and served by eleven servants, including a cook who was the envy of all the other millionaires on the Riviera.

Robin was a Christian and had sent his uncle a Bible. When he arrived, he found Maugham reading Jesus' words, "What will it profit a man if he gains the whole world and forfeits his own soul?" (Matt. 16:26). Maugham said, "I must tell you, my dear Robin, that the text used to hang opposite my bed when I was a child. . . . Of course, it's all a lot of bunk. But the thought is quite interesting all the same." Yet that evening after dinner, Maugham flung himself down onto the sofa: "Oh, Robin, I'm so tired." Burying his face in his hands, he went on: "I've been a failure the whole way through my life." Robin tried to encourage him: "You're the most famous writer alive. Surely that means something?" "I wish I'd never written a single word," he answered. "It's brought me nothing but misery. . . . And now it's too late to change. It's too late . . ." At that point his face contorted with fear, and staring into space with horror, he shrieked, "Go away! I'm not ready. . . . I'm not dead yet. . . . I'm not dead yet, I tell you . . . ." Then he began to gasp hysterically. Shortly after Robin's visit, his uncle died.[14]

The point of Maugham's life and death is the very one found in the Scripture he read: "What will it profit a man if he gains the whole world and forfeits his own soul?" What a tragedy for you to live out Maugham's

13. G. K. Beale, *The Book of Revelation: A Commentary on the Greek Text*, New International Greek Testament Commentary (Grand Rapids: Eerdmans, 1999), 254–55.

14. Quoted in R. Kent Hughes, *John: That You May Believe* (Wheaton, IL: Crossway, 1999), 201–2.

choice—a choice in favor of false worldly doctrine, fleeting worldly sins, and the convicted world's destiny in judgment—when Jesus offers the hidden manna, a white stone, and his new name to all who follow him in true and saving faith.

A Church Where Satan Dwells

Since Jesus denounces Pergamum as "Satan's throne," some Christians might conclude that there is no place for the church in such a city. Jesus seems to have thought otherwise, however. So what kind of church and what kind of Christians are needed in the place "where Satan dwells"?

One answer for the kind of Christians we need to be in order to overcome through faith is found in the analogy between Jesus and the manna that long beforehand fell down from heaven. Jesus himself directed us to his own provision for eternal life: "I am the bread of life; whoever comes to me shall not hunger, and whoever believes in me shall never thirst" (John 6:35).

Let me conclude by noting four ways in which Jesus is like the manna that fell from heaven, and like the bread that gives life to our souls. First, just as manna was necessary for the life of Israel in the desert, so also Jesus is *necessary for our salvation*. Are you trying to live without Jesus? You may satisfy your ego with success, your material needs with money, or your desires with pleasure. But you will never satisfy the inescapable needs of your soul without Jesus Christ.

Second, Jesus, like bread, is *suited for everyone*. James Boice writes: "Jesus is . . . the Savior of the world, and that includes the peasant as well as the king on his throne. . . . He has what you need. What is more, he knows you and he knows how to meet that need."[15]

Third, just as bread must be chewed and swallowed, Christians must *feed on Jesus and his Word by faith*. The hearts of children are fed by the kind and loving words of their parents. An army feeds on the brave words of its leaders. A nation feeds on the inspiring speeches of its best politicians. But there is nothing compared to the Word of God to feed the soul of every man, woman, and child. If Christians or churches are weak today, easily falling prey to false teaching and foolishly seeking to accommodate worldly styles and demands, the explanation may be that we have been feeding on

15. James Montgomery Boice, *The Gospel of John*, 5 vols. (Grand Rapids: Baker, 1999), 2:478.

the world instead of on the Word. To be strong in faith and to have a strong witness to the world, we must be constantly feeding on the life-giving bread of Christ and his Word.

Finally, we are told that when Jesus fed the five thousand, he "broke the loaves and gave them to the disciples" (Matt. 14:19). Likewise, Jesus is the Bread of Life because *he was broken on the cross for our sins.* "This is my body," Jesus later explained, "which is [broken] for you" (1 Cor. 11:24). Jesus gave himself to pay the penalty of our sins, restore us to the Father in love, and grant a new kind of life to those who believe. To them, Jesus gives heavenly manna of divine provision, a white stone of justification through faith alone, and a personal relationship with himself as Lord. How can we know and experience these truths for ourselves? Psalm 34:8 gives us the best advice: "Taste and see that the LORD is good!"

12

ACCORDING TO YOUR WORKS

Revelation 2:18—29

I know your works, your love and faith and service and
patient endurance, and that your latter works exceed the first.
(Rev. 2:19)

One of the great messages of Revelation is that Christ's people are made strong and persevere by their knowledge of him. This is why Jesus appeared to John in the opening vision of chapter 1, shining forth in divine glory and garbed in the offices of Prophet, Priest, and King. Conversely, this fits the warning given by Jesus when he reproved false believers, saying: "I never knew you; depart from me, you workers of lawlessness" (Matt. 7:22–23). As Jesus saw it, a false and dead faith results from not truly knowing him, whereas a true and obedient faith flows from knowing Jesus in a personal relationship of saving faith.

This principle explains why each of the seven letters in Revelation 2–3 begins with a piece of the portrait of Christ given in chapter 1. The churches will respond to Christ's message in light of their awareness of who and what Jesus is. This shows the importance of the presentation of Christ in his fourth message, to the church in Thyatira. Here, Jesus displays himself in a way that many professing Christians will be challenged to accept but that should inspire us to holy, faithful lives. He describes himself as "the Son of God, who has eyes like a flame of fire, and whose feet are like burnished bronze" (Rev. 2:18). He is the Lord who knows our works, who hates all sin, who judges the unrepentant in his church, and who bestows glory on those who conquer in his name.

THE LORD WHO KNOWS OUR WORKS

All through the messages to his churches, Jesus says that he knows the good works of his people. This emphasis reminds us that while Christians are not saved by our works, we are able to do works that are good and pleasing to the Lord. This is part of the great difference between the unbeliever and the believer. Unbelievers are unable to do truly good works, since all is condemned by the presence of unforgiven sin. Believers are born again by the Holy Spirit and equipped by God's Word "for every good work" (2 Tim. 3:17). This being the case, Christians should be devoted to good works. "Let your light shine," Jesus said, "so that they may see your good works and give glory to your Father who is in heaven" (Matt. 5:16). Jesus reminds the church in Thyatira, "I know your works" (Rev. 2:19). Likewise, Jesus knows and will remember our good deeds when he returns from heaven. "Well done, good and faithful servant," he will tell his obedient people. "Enter into the joy of your master" (Matt. 25:21).

Having mentioned the Thyatirans' "works," Jesus specifies their "love and faith and service and patient endurance" (Rev. 2:19). Here is the kind of church that we should want to be part of. Like Ephesus, the church in Thyatira had works but added the love that the Ephesians had lost. Whereas Pergamum tolerated false teachers, Thyatira preserved the faith. Like Smyrna, these Christians were patient in enduring tribulation. Moreover, the Thyatirans show how Christian virtues work together. Where there is love, there will be service; and where faith flourishes, there God's people will patiently endure.

What particularly stands out in Thyatira is that the church was continuing to grow spiritually and in good works: Jesus says, "Your latter works exceed the first" (Rev. 2:19). These believers set a good example for us today. Part of what makes Christianity so exciting is that we are called to continually grow in terms of our knowledge of God's grace (2 Peter 3:18), our personal holiness (Eph. 4:24), our love for others, and our good works. John Stott writes: "The church of Thyatira understood that the Christian life is a life of growth, of progress, of development."[1] Knowing this, each of us should pray that our "latter works" will "exceed the first."

We know from reading this passage that Jesus is going to criticize the Thyatirans. But note that he did not therefore brush aside their achievement and their virtues. James Hamilton writes: "Sometimes when we go to address problems, even ones that are not so serious, we fail to see and acknowledge the good things that may be happening. Jesus is encouraging this church. They have problems, but those problems don't keep him from seeing and commending the fruits of the Spirit in their lives."[2] Following Jesus' gracious example, when we are dealing with churches or people who need to be corrected, we would be wise to notice their strengths and praise their virtues, in this way opening a door for the harder message that they may thus be more willing to receive. Given our own weakness and tendency toward failure, how wonderful it is to learn that Jesus knows, cares about, and appreciates all the good things taking place in our lives as his people.

THE LORD WHO DESPISES SIN

Despite the initially good impression of Thyatira, there was a very serious problem. For all its love, faith, service, and steadfastness, we heard no commendation for its holiness. This is a matter about which Jesus cares very deeply, and his rebuke and warning over tolerated sins makes this the longest of his seven messages to the churches.

Unlike the previous cities mentioned in these letters, Thyatira was not a great city. It was a market city, situated on the main route between Pergamum and Sardis. As such, Thyatira was dominated by the trade guilds that oversaw its various industries: wool, linen, dyes, clothing manufacturers, leather works, potters, bakers, and bronze works.[3] Each guild paid homage to pagan gods, especially Apollo and Artemis. This homage included attendance at the gods' sacred festivals, eating meals in their temples, and participating

---

1. John R. W. Stott, *What Christ Thinks of the Church: An Exposition of Revelation 1–3* (Grand Rapids: Baker, 2003), 67.

2. James M. Hamilton Jr., *Revelation: The Spirit Speaks to the Churches* (Wheaton, IL: Crossway, 2012), 96.

3. Sir William Ramsay, cited by Leon Morris, *The Revelation of St. John: An Introduction and Commentary*, Tyndale New Testament Commentaries 20 (Grand Rapids: Eerdmans, 1969), 69.

in the sexual immorality involved in many of the pagan rituals. Simon Kistemaker writes: "Christians who refused to honor pagan gods, eat meat sacrificed to an idol, and engage in sexual immorality jeopardized their material necessities. They were regarded as outcasts of society."[4]

It is in this context that we may understand Jesus' complaint: "I have this against you, that you tolerate that woman Jezebel, who calls herself a prophetess and is teaching and seducing my servants to practice sexual immorality and to eat food sacrificed to idols" (Rev. 2:20). Unlike Pergamum, which was tolerating a whole group of false teachers (the Nicolaitians), in Thyatira there was a persuasive woman in the church who claimed to possess prophetic gifts, and whose teaching seduced Christ's servants into becoming the slaves of sin. The designation *Jezebel* should not be taken as her name but rather describes her in terms of the famous Old Testament villainess.

In the ninth century B.C., Jezebel was an unbelieving princess from Sidon whom Israel's King Ahab married for political reasons. Jezebel brought her false gods with her, and soon her legions of pagan priests had spread the worship of Baal and Asherah throughout the land. The Israelites were seduced with the idea that these Sidonian gods, male and female, would bring economic prosperity in the form of fertile lands and wombs. Jezebel's idolatry, which involved ritual prostitution at the pagan shrines, swept through God's people.

Jesus' use of the name *Jezebel* indicates what Thyatira's false prophetess was teaching. This second Jezebel encouraged Christians to participate in the ceremonies and feasts of the trade guilds, even to participate in the sexual sin and eat the food sacrificed to idols. Just as the original Jezebel urged the Israelites to worship Baal and Ashteroth alongside the Lord, this new Jezebel urged Christians to believe that their faith in Jesus need not exclude them from the guild idolatry that was essential to prosperous living in that city. Douglas Kelly writes: "She must have said, 'Let's mingle with these people during the week; let's go to their religious services, and participate in their feasts. Then they will realize that we too know how to have fun, and are not judgmental of them.'"[5] Jezebel's doctrine stated that one might please both God and the world and that Christians do not have to be different from others just because of their faith in Jesus.

---

4. Simon J. Kistemaker, *Revelation*, New Testament Commentary (Grand Rapids: Baker, 2001), 136.
5. Douglas F. Kelly, *Revelation*, Mentor Expository Commentary (Tain, Ross-shire, Scotland: Mentor, 2012), 57.

This woman's presence in an otherwise outstanding church reminds us of the variety of attacks that Satan may launch. Revelation mentions the beast from the sea, who stands for government persecution, and the beast from the earth, who brings false teaching in the church. When these fail to hinder Christ's people, Satan has a third approach, Babylon the harlot, who seduces people through the pleasures of sin (see Rev. 13–17). John Stott writes: "If the devil cannot destroy the church by persecution or heresy, he will try to corrupt it with evil."[6] This was the role played by the Jezebel in the church of Thyatira.

Jesus' response to this Jezebel's seductive ministry reminds us of two things concerning sexual purity. First, the Bible associates sexual sin with idolatry. The Old Testament often compared idolatry to sexual infidelity. Hosea condemned Israel, saying that "the land commits great whoredom by forsaking the Lord" (Hos. 1:2). Jeremiah complained that by worshiping at Baal altars and Asherah poles, Jews "polluted the land, committing adultery with stone and tree" (Jer. 3:9). Sex is God's gift to be blessed within marriage and for the procreation of holy children. Those who engage in sexual sin divorce God's gift from God's holy purpose and thus make a god of their desires. This is why Paul wrote: "Flee from sexual immorality. . . . Do you not know that your body is a temple of the Holy Spirit within you, whom you have from God? You are not your own, for you were bought with a price. So glorify God in your body" (1 Cor. 6:18–20).

Second, Jesus' emphasis highlights the importance of sexual purity to the Christian life. In general, the idea that believers in Christ may continue to live like the world is false. James wrote: "Do you not know that friendship with the world is enmity with God? Therefore whoever wishes to be a friend of the world makes himself an enemy of God" (James 4:4). This principle is especially true when it comes to the Christian calling to sexual purity, through abstinence outside marriage and fidelity within marriage. The Bible teaches that "this is the will of God, your sanctification: that you abstain from sexual immorality" (1 Thess. 4:3). Jesus therefore rebuked the church in Thyatira: "I have this against you, that you tolerate that woman Jezebel, who . . . [is] seducing my servants to practice sexual immorality" (Rev. 2:20).

It is evident that Christ's rebuke of sexual sin needs to be heard by professing Christians today. A 2011 survey by a Christian magazine reported that

6. Stott, *What Christ Thinks of the Church*, 69.

80 percent of unmarried Christians had sinned sexually and that two-thirds of unmarried Christians between the ages of eighteen and twenty-nine had been involved in a sexual relationship within the previous year. Professing Christians were also involved in the sin of abortion. Studies show that 37 percent of women obtaining abortions identify themselves as Protestant Christians, along with another 28 percent who are Roman Catholic. The rationale for this sin was expressed in the article's title, "(Almost) Everyone's Doing It."[7]

Christians who have joined in with the sexual sin of our culture have evidently forgotten that Jesus is a holy Lord who hates all sin, and especially sexual sin. The Bible commands the Christian to "know how to control his own body in holiness and honor, not in the passion of lust like the Gentiles who do not know God" (1 Thess. 4:4–5). Sex itself, within the holy context of marriage, is neither shameful nor sinful, having been given by God to bond a husband and wife emotionally and spiritually. Therefore, Christians should grow in maturity so as to enter into a godly marriage with a fellow believer. Paul wrote: "It is better to marry than to burn with passion" (1 Cor. 7:9). Hebrews 13:4 says: "Let marriage be held in honor among all, and let the marriage bed be undefiled, for God will judge the sexually immoral and adulterous." Christians should therefore promote the sanctity of marriage by refusing to engage in sexual sin outside marriage and promoting joyful Christian marriages in which sexuality is blessed by God. To this end, Christians should prepare our sons and daughters to be godly husbands and wives, prayerfully urging them not to worship at the altars of pleasure and ego at which our generation commits idolatry against the Lord.

Jesus shows believers what price we must be willing to pay out of faithfulness to him in his comments about food sacrificed to idols. Guild membership required participation at pagan feasts, in which false gods were worshiped by receiving food at their table. William Barclay writes that refusing to join these feasts "[cut] off Christians from all social fellowship with non-Christians." Moreover, "Christians' abstention from guild membership was equivalent to commercial suicide."[8] In such a situation, Christians were to be willing to suffer for Christ, while trusting the Lord to provide for them in light of their refusal to seek prosperity by means of idolatry.

---

7. Tyler Charles, "(Almost) Everyone's Doing It," *Relevant* 53 (September–October 2011).

8. William Barclay, *The Revelation of John*, 3rd ed., 2 vols., New Daily Study Bible (Louisville: Westminster John Knox, 2004), 1:118.

The cost of being faithful to Christ was made poignant when the early church leader Tertullian rebuked a believer for participating in idolatry because of his business. The man defended his sin, saying, "After all, I must live." Tertullian answered, "Must you?"[9] There is no calling higher than our faithfulness to Christ, including our very lives. James Boice writes: "The early Christians knew that neither obeying the state, getting along or sharing in the life of those around us justifies idolatry or immorality. . . . When Paul argued that it was permissible to eat meat that had been offered to idols, he did not say that it was right to do it in a pagan temple as part of a pagan worship service. When Jesus told us to give to Caesar what is Caesar's, he limited that requirement by adding, 'and to God what is God's.'"[10]

The Lord Who Judges His Church

I said earlier that Christians may not easily accept the description of Jesus that is found in the message to Thyatira. This is particularly the case with the depiction of Christ as the Lord who judges his church. What would most evangelical Christians today think if they were told not only that Jesus hates sin but that he commands church discipline and threatens to strike dead church members who do not repent? The evidence suggests that most evangelicals would be appalled by such a portrait of Christ. Yet this is exactly how Jesus presents himself to the church in Thyatira. Speaking of their "Jezebel," Jesus writes: "Behold, I will throw her onto a sickbed, and those who commit adultery with her I will throw into great tribulation, . . . and I will strike her children dead" (Rev. 2:22–23).

Before judging his people, Christ first gives a call to repentance. This shows that his purpose is not to harm but to save his followers. Christ has goodwill even for people in serious sin, like Jezebel. He says, "I gave her time to repent" (Rev. 2:21). This indicates that church leaders had previously confronted her for her false teaching and wicked behavior. Here we see the importance of loving and faithful church discipline. Jesus reminds Christians to take biblical reproofs seriously, especially when coming from faithful pastors or church elders. "But she refuses to repent of her sexual immorality," Jesus goes on, and therefore his judgment was the only recourse.

9. Quoted in James Montgomery Boice, *Revelation*, unpublished manuscript, n.d., chap. 9, p. 9.
10. Ibid.

127

The question is raised whether Jesus is judging believers with a temporal or an eternal punishment, and thus whether they will go to heaven or hell. The answer to this question can be seen only in whether such persons can be considered true believers. In some cases in the New Testament, it seems that genuine believers who sin grievously are judged. An example is that of Ananias and Sapphira, who were slain for lying to the Holy Spirit in falsely boasting about financial gifts to the church (Acts 5:1–10). Presumably, they went to heaven after death, as true but foolish believers in Christ. It is hard to imagine how this could be said about a woman like the Jezebel of Thyatira, though it is possible. The main point is that Jesus judges his saved people in pursuit of the holiness of his church, even inflicting death on some for their sins. He says that he "will strike her children dead" (Rev. 2:23), which presumably refers to her followers in sin. The principle for Christ's judgment is given in verse 23: "I will give to each of you according to your works." Those who persist in flagrant sin, refusing to respond to biblical calls to repentance, may suffer strong chastisement from Christ both for their own preservation and for the well-being of the church.

If we find it hard to accept that Christ judges his people, the picture of Jesus given at the beginning of this letter should persuade us: "The words of the Son of God, who has eyes like a flame of fire, and whose feet are like burnished bronze" (Rev. 2:18). This is the only time the title "Son of God" is used of Christ in Revelation. Given the later quotation from Psalm 2, it is probably used to emphasize Christ's royal prerogative in judging all peoples: "Serve the LORD with fear, and rejoice with trembling. Kiss the Son, lest he be angry, and you perish in the way, for his wrath is quickly kindled" (Ps. 2:11–12). Moreover, Christ's flaming eyes can penetrate into every heart, seeing both good works and shameful sins. His feet "like burnished bronze" reveal him as being without blemish and as One who comes resolutely to punish sin.

If the believers of Thyatira had forgotten these truths about Jesus, his judgment on those committing idolatry would remind them that Jesus is not an absentee landlord but a Sovereign Ruler of his kingdom. He says of his judgment of Jezebel and her followers that "all the churches will know that I am he who searches mind and heart, and I will give to each of you according to your works" (Rev. 2:23). This calls us, first, to believe on Jesus for the forgiveness of our sins. He said, "This is the work of God, that you believe in him whom he has sent" (John 6:29). Having been saved from sin by Christ's blood, Christians must then pursue holiness and good works, knowing that Jesus will not fail to notice and bless them, and realizing that as a holy Lord, Jesus will chastise us for gross, scandalous sins that dishonor his name.

THE LORD WHO BESTOWS GLORY

This portrait of Christ provides numerous motivations to live godly lives, including our awareness that Christ hates sin and judges his church. A final reason is that Jesus is a reasonable and mild Ruler, who graciously gives glory to those who conquer in his name.

The mildness of Christ is seen in his address to those who have not participated in Jezebel's sins: "But to the rest of you in Thyatira, who do not hold this teaching, who have not learned what some call the deep things of Satan, to you I say, I do not lay on you any other burden. Only hold fast what you have until I come" (Rev. 2:24–25).

When Jesus speaks of "the deep things of Satan," he is probably noting the false prophetess Jezebel's claim that her worldly accommodation involved an advanced Christianity that only a few could comprehend. Instead, Jesus said, her teaching that Christians can safely enter into sin involves not deep Christianity but bondage to Satan. Christians are not to try to enter into esoteric knowledge or advanced states of spirituality beyond what is taught in the Bible. Instead, we are to hold fast what Christ has already revealed to us in Scripture. Christ's burdens are not actually heavy: "My yoke is easy, and my burden is light," Jesus said (Matt. 11:30). We are reminded of the commands given at the Jerusalem Council, when the apostles determined the obligation of Gentile believers. They were to "abstain from the things polluted by idols, and from sexual immorality" (Acts 15:20). Derek Thomas explains that believers "are to live by the standards of the revealed Word of God and no more. As John said elsewhere: 'His commandments are not burdensome' (1 John 5:3)."[11]

Far from being burdensome, Jesus is generous beyond all expectation. He promises two remarkable blessings to those who persevere in true, obedient faith, not mixing Christianity with idolatrous pagan practices. The first has

11. Derek Thomas, *Let's Study Revelation* (Edinburgh: Banner of Truth, 2003), 32.

to do with a share in Christ's sovereign rule: "The one who conquers and who keeps my works until the end, to him I will give authority over the nations, and he will rule them with a rod of iron, as when earthen pots are broken in pieces, even as I myself have received authority from my Father" (Rev. 2:26–27).

Here, Jesus is quoting from Psalm 2, where God tells his Son: "Ask of me, and I will make the nations your heritage, and the ends of the earth your possession. You shall break them with a rod of iron and dash them in pieces like a potter's vessel" (Ps. 2:8–9). We can understand how Christians participate in Christ's rule, but it is hard to see what it means for us to "break" others with an iron rod and "dash them in pieces" like pieces of pottery. The key to understanding this promise is to note how Jesus has modified Psalm 2 in our case, so that instead of wielding an iron rod to "break" people, authority is given us to "rule them" (Rev. 2:29). Here, the Greek word for *rule* means to "shepherd" (Greek, *poimaino*). The promise, then, is that Christ will grant his faithful people the ability to faithfully shepherd his flock, using the rod to protect them from those who would do them harm.

"Authority over the nations" is exercised through the Great Commission (Matt. 28:18–20), as Christians go throughout the world with the saving gospel that leads others to Christ. Faithful servants are empowered to shepherd, spiritually rule, and defend other believers. Jesus promises that faithful church leaders will be enabled to lead the church in godly ways, guiding Christ's sheep in paths of righteousness and wielding spiritual weapons to preserve them from every source of fear (see Ps. 23:3–4). Faithful and holy Christian parents will be able to lead their children in godly paths unto salvation. Christian men and women will have power to exercise a gracious influence in the workplace, leading others to Christ and helping them to grow in godliness.

Finally, Jesus promises to the believer who perseveres in a godly faith: "And I will give him the morning star" (Rev. 2:28). Jesus interprets the meaning of this promise in Revelation 22:16: "I am the root and the descendant of David, the bright morning star." Jesus is promising to give himself, the Light who shines brightly to cast away all darkness, as the most precious gift to his faithful people. Together with himself, however, he is promising that we ourselves will enter into that shining brightness of glory through union with Christ in faith. Even in this life, Christians are empowered by

Christ to "shine as lights in the world," as "children of God without blemish in the midst of a crooked and twisted generation, . . . holding fast to the word of life" (Phil. 2:15–16).

How bright is the light of Christ in the holy life of a faithful Christian, whether in Thyatira or in the places where we stand apart for Jesus today! But when the morning of the resurrection comes, then the light of Christ and his people will shine with a glory that we can scarcely comprehend today. Daniel 12:3 declares that "those who are wise shall shine like the brightness of the sky above; and those who turn many to righteousness, like the stars forever and ever."

13

HOW TO REVIVE
A DEAD CHURCH

Revelation 3:1—6

*I know your works. You have the reputation of being alive, but
you are dead. Wake up, and strengthen what remains and is
about to die, for I have not found your works complete
in the sight of my God.* (Rev. 3:1–2)

*T*he expression "as rich as Croesus" comes to us from an ancient
king of Sardis. This famed city in Asia Minor was once the
capital of the kingdom of Lydia and was made wealthy by
the gold that flowed in its river. Croesus went to war against the Persian
emperor Cyrus the Great, after consulting the oracle at Delphi to be sure
of his success. The oracle declared, "If you cross the River Halys, you will
destroy a great empire." Croesus assumed that Cyrus's empire would be
destroyed, but when his army was crushed, he realized that destruction
had been intended for his own empire. From that time forward, Sardis was
the story of a city famed for wealth and power that lost both. Among its
features was a necropolis known as "the city of a thousand hills," so named
because of the burial grounds that marked its skyline. Jesus picks up on this

history in rebuking the church of Sardis in Revelation 3:1: "You have the reputation of being alive, but you are dead." Just as Sardis's famous cemetery had a thousand hills, Jesus reminds us that "a church can have a thousand (or more) members and still be as dead as the inhabitants of a cemetery."[1]

A Dead Church

Seeing how Jesus uses the local history and terrain of the churches in Revelation as material for his letters reminds us that these messages were intended for actual churches in the time of the apostle John. Some scholars treat Revelation as speaking only to the distant future before Christ's return, but the seven messages of chapters 2 and 3 remind us that his first audience was the one noted in the opening greeting: "John to the seven churches that are in Asia" (Rev. 1:4).

In challenging the church at Sardis, Jesus uses the well-known history of that city. "And to the angel of the church in Sardis," he wrote: "I know your works. You have the reputation of being alive" (Rev. 3:1). Sardis was known for being overconfident and boastful. Yet behind the reputation there was no substance. This church was all name and no reality, all reputation and no life. Perhaps it was the financial stature, or the worldly influence of its members, or a great deal of activity and programs, that gave the church in Sardis its reputation for life. The reality, however, was very different: "You have the reputation of being alive, but you are dead" (Rev. 3:1).

In considering this fifth of the seven letters of Revelation, we find no threat of persecution, as at Smyrna, and no false teaching, as at Pergamum. Evidently, Satan did not consider Sardis worthy of spiritual assault. William Hendriksen writes: "Sardis was a very 'peaceful' church. It enjoyed peace, but it was the peace of the cemetery!"[2] Sardis was what we refer to today as a "nominal" church. It was Christian in name, but name only. The members professed faith in Jesus, but in reality their hearts were turned from him.

Jesus goes on to say, "Yet you have still a few names in Sardis, people who have not soiled their garments" (Rev. 3:4). This indicates that most of them had defiled themselves with sin. Simon Kistemaker writes: "Almost

---

1. James Montgomery Boice, *Revelation*, unpublished manuscript, n.d., chap. 10, p. 2.
2. William Hendriksen, *More than Conquerors: An Interpretation of the Book of Revelation* (1940; repr., Grand Rapids: Baker, 1967), 73.

133

the entire church had capitulated to the surrounding world of pagan religion and Judaism, and instead of being an influence on the culture, it had become influenced by that culture."[3]

Moreover, Jesus complains, "I have not found your works complete in the sight of my God" (Rev. 3:2). The word for *complete* (Greek, *pleroo*) is elsewhere used by John to mean "full" (see John 3:29; 16:24). While their works may have been spiritually impressive to men, in God's sight they were empty of substance. This may involve a reference to a gigantic temple to Artemis begun in Sardis but never finished. In the Old Testament, God rejected blemished lambs offered for sacrifice (Lev. 1:3; Deut. 15:21). Likewise, Christ saw that the religion in Sardis was empty of real devotion or thanks to God.

This portrait of the church in Sardis reminds us of the apostle Paul's warning in 2 Timothy 3:1–8. Paul warned Timothy that "times of difficulty" would come, characterized by selfishness, arrogance, disobedience, ingratitude, unholiness, and treachery. The church would be attacked by charlatans, false teachers, and slander. Reading Paul's description, we might think he was describing the world around him, except that what Paul says in 2 Timothy 3:5 can be said only of people within the church: they have "the appearance of godliness, but denying its power." It seems that despite its works and reputation, this was the situation in Sardis. George Eldon Ladd described this church as "outwardly prosperous, busy with the externals of religious activity, but devoid of spiritual life and power."[4]

How Churches Die

This dreadful portrait raises a question about how once-lively churches die. How did such a church with a reputation for life fall into a state of death?

At least three explanations for how the church in Sardis died may be drawn from well-known events in its history. I mentioned earlier that Sardis's King Croesus fought a losing battle against Cyrus the Great of Persia. After the battle, Croesus returned to his city and its hilltop fortress, fifteen hundred feet above the plain, which was thought to be impregnable. Cyrus besieged the city and offered a reward to anyone who could devise a way of entry. A Persian soldier named Hyeroeades was watching when a Sardian soldier

---

3. Simon J. Kistemaker, *Revelation*, New Testament Commentary (Grand Rapids: Baker, 2001), 150.
4. George Eldon Ladd, *A Commentary on the Revelation of John* (Grand Rapids: Eerdmans, 1972), 56.

knocked his helmet over the city wall and then climbed down the precipice to retrieve it. Hyeroeades spied out the way and that night led a party of Persian troops up the cliff and over the unguarded walls. Two hundred years later, the same thing happened. Sardis was besieged by one of Alexander the Great's generals, who sent a small force up the cliff. Once again, the Sardians were unwatchful, thinking themselves secure, and their fortress was overthrown.[5]

Just as Sardis was overthrown because it did not watch for enemies, churches may be overcome because they are not watching against spiritual attacks. Churches must be on guard against false teaching. Paul warned the Ephesian elders to expect doctrinal attack, urging them, "Therefore be alert" (Acts 20:31). Christians must be awake against the temptation to sin. Jesus exhorted, "Watch and pray that you may not enter into temptation" (Matt. 26:41). Churches must guard against assimilation into the spiritually dead state of the world. "Watch yourselves," Jesus warned, "lest your hearts be weighed down with dissipation and drunkenness and cares of this life" (Luke 21:34). If we are not vigilant, we may find that an enemy has scaled our walls, opened our gates, and brought us destruction. Not only are churches overthrown when pastors and elders do not watch, but families are conquered when fathers and mothers are not diligently on guard against sinful influences. Moreover, individuals are overthrown by careless neglect, having failed to watch for the devices of the enemy and be on guard against temptations to sin.

Second, like Sardis, churches can die when they rely on their impressive name, spiritual legacy, or rich heritage, but do not tend to their actual spiritual vitality. Dennis Johnson writes that "Sardis was a city with a golden past and misplaced security."[6] Churches today may try to coast on a reputation earned in past times. But no reputation can save us from our sins. Our baptism alone cannot save us. Our church membership cannot save us. Only a living faith in Jesus Christ can save any sinner. Therefore, even if we have a strong Christian reputation, we must tend to the reality and strength of our faith. James 4:8 outlines our daily calling: "Draw near to God, and he will draw near to you."

Third, churches fall away by pursuing vain and empty things in place of the true spiritual riches of salvation. Under King Croesus, Sardis exulted in

5. William Barclay, *The Revelation of John*, 3rd ed., 2 vols., New Daily Study Bible (Louisville: Westminster John Knox, 2004), 1:126.

6. Dennis E. Johnson, *Triumph of the Lamb: A Commentary on Revelation* (Phillipsburg, NJ: P&R Publishing, 2001), 82.

wealth and ease but failed to cultivate virtues such as courage and strength. Likewise, churches today may focus on their finances, their music programs, their ministry events, their lavish facilities, and many otherwise good things. Yet with all these, any church is empty without the glory of Christ present through the indwelling Holy Spirit. The substance of a church must be the gospel of Jesus and the salvation life that flows through true faith in the living Lord. Faith in Christ, worship through Christ, and genuine service to Christ must always be the primary focus of a true church. Focusing on anything else will lead to a church's losing its vitality and perhaps even its life.

CHRIST'S CALL TO REVIVAL

Not only does Sardis show us how churches die, but Jesus' message sets an agenda for how to revive a dead or dying church. Revelation 3:2–3 provides five imperatives for church revival, coupled with a warning if the church is not revived: "Wake up, and strengthen what remains and is about to die, for I have not found your works complete in the sight of my God. Remember, then, what you received and heard. Keep it, and repent. If you will not wake up, I will come like a thief, and you will not know at what hour I will come against you."

Christ's first command is for the slumbering believers at Sardis to awaken: "Wake up" (Rev. 3:2). This call shows that there was a remnant of true, if slumbering, believers in the church, since Christ would not command those who were dead to awaken from sleep. Boice comments that this command "suggests that revival begins with a few individuals who wake up to the condition of those around them and begin to be concerned for them."[7] Sardis twice fell to the sword because watchmen were asleep; its revival would correspondingly begin with Christians who woke up and began to stimulate new life.

Second, awakened Christians are to "strengthen what remains and is about to die" (Rev. 3:2). A Christian or a church that is weak needs to be strengthened by God's grace. The primary means of grace is God's Word. Peter wrote that we are born again only by "the living and abiding word of God" (1 Peter 1:23). I mentioned earlier that the description of Sardis is similar to Paul's warning in 2 Timothy. Paul advised Timothy not to seek some worldly solution but to "continue in what you have learned and have

7. Boice, *Revelation*, chap. 10, p. 8.

firmly believed, . . . the sacred writings, which are able to make you wise for salvation through faith in Christ Jesus" (2 Tim. 3:14–15). Paul added that God's outbreathed Word is "profitable for teaching, for reproof, for correction, and for training in righteousness" (3:16). This was God's command to Ezekiel when that faithful prophet was summoned to minister in the Valley of Dry Bones. Facing a grisly scene of decomposed bodies—symbolic of the situation in Sardis and many other places—God told the prophet: "Prophesy over these bones, and say to them, O dry bones, hear the word of the LORD" (Ezek. 37:4). As Ezekiel preached God's Word, "the breath came into them, and they lived and stood on their feet, an exceedingly great army" (37:10).

Here we see not only a mandate for preaching and teaching in the church, but also the way that any Christian with God's Word can be used of God. In 2006, the freestyle motorcycle champion Brian Deegan nearly lost his life in a horrible crash. Previously, his girlfriend had become pregnant and gone home to live with her Christian parents. This family reached out to Deegan in his long rehabilitation, and he began attending their evangelical church. Hearing the gospel there, he came to faith in Jesus Christ. When his physical recovery was complete, Deegan returned to the Moto-X club that he had founded, named the Metal Mulisha, which under his leadership had gained a reputation for drugs, alcohol, sexual abuse, and violence. Returning as a Christian, Deegan began inviting his fellow bikers to study the Bible. "He kept telling us how much the Bible changed his life," one recalled. "I felt like I had to listen." One after another of Deegan's biker friends came to a saving relationship with Christ, and now the Metal Mulisha is known not for riotous mayhem but for evangelism and Christian discipleship.[8]

In addition to God's Word, Christians may strengthen the church through the vital ministry of prayer. In September 1857, Jeremiah Lanphier responded to America's economic collapse by starting a prayer meeting in his Dutch Reformed Church in New York City. He printed a bulletin inviting businessmen to come and pray at noon. The first meeting began with Lanphier praying alone for the first half hour, and then being joined by six other men for the second half hour. A week later he had twenty for prayer, and three weeks later there were forty. By the next spring, there were scores of similar prayer groups throughout New York and others that had spread to other

8. Taken from Chris Palmer, "Reinventing the Wheel," *ESPN the Magazine* 11, 15 (July 28, 2008): 52–58.

cities. By Easter Sunday, New York City had to shut down every day at noon because of the tens of thousands gathering for prayer, with multitudes converted to Christ. Starting with the prayers of a few awakened believers, the 1858 Laymen's Prayer Revival spread throughout the country and resulted in hundreds of thousands of conversions to faith in Christ.

Third, besides heeding Christ's command to awaken and to strengthen what remains, Sardis was to "remember, then, what you received and heard" (Rev. 3:3). The people were, of course, to remember the gospel truths that had brought them salvation. They were also to remember Jesus himself, the grace of his salvation, and the power for new life he gives through the ministry of the Holy Spirit. This is probably the significance of the opening words of this letter: "The words of him who has the seven spirits of God and the seven stars" (3:1). Jesus holds in his hand the manifold gifts and graces of the Holy Spirit—this is the meaning of "the seven spirits of God"—just as he holds "the seven stars" of the churches in his hand. The point is that Jesus is able to grant reviving power through the Holy Spirit. Discouraged Christians are to remember this so as to go forth ministering with the Word and calling on God in prayer. The same Jesus who called his friend Lazarus out from the grave possesses power to raise spiritually dead churches back to life (John 11:43–44). If we remember our own conversions as Christ's Spirit blessed the gospel, we will be encouraged as we seek to serve others for salvation and labor to strengthen the church with the grace of God in Christ.

Finally, Jesus commands that his Word be obeyed and that sin be repented of: "Keep it, and repent" (Rev. 3:3). Boice writes: "It is not sufficient only to hear the Word of God. We must obey what we hear."[9] We show our faith in the Bible by our obedience to the Bible's teaching and to the command of Jesus Christ. Moreover, a nominal church must repent of whatever it had placed before God and turn from actual sins that had entered in. Obedience and repentance are not optional but are reinforced by a dire warning from Christ: "If you will not wake up, I will come like a thief, and you will not know at what hour I will come against you" (3:3). Christ will visit disobedient Christians and give them painful discipline. Churches that will not obey or repent may suddenly find that their lampstands have been removed and the light has fully gone out.

This warning was vividly displayed when I ministered in downtown Philadelphia, which is filled with cathedrals and preaching palaces built in

9. Boice, *Revelation*, chap. 10, p. 10.

former times that now bear testimony to death by their emptiness on Sundays. In fact, the service station where I bought gas occupies the location of one once-bustling church. The wall next door bears a mural of the lovely church that used to be there, but now is just "a shadow in the city."[10] Jesus warns that churches that will not obey his Word and repent may experience the same fate, as indeed ultimately happened in Sardis.

Walk with Christ in White

Christ's revival program shows the value of every single Christian, especially when awakened to serve the cause of Christ in the church. It is with this calling in mind that godly Christians often decide to remain in a weak or dying church, so long as that church has not entirely rejected the authority of God's Word, hoping to be used by God to stimulate new spiritual life.

Another way in which we can see the preciousness of every faithful Christian is in the fervor shown by Christ in the concluding verses of this letter. Even though the church as a whole was dead, there was a remnant of a living and holy faith: "Yet you have still a few names in Sardis, people who have not soiled their garments, and they will walk with me in white, for they are worthy" (Rev. 3:4). Here we see that true believers are those who had not fallen to secular influences and who had abstained from the gross sins into which nominal Christians fall. When Christ says that "they are worthy," he is not declaring them to be perfect, sinless Christians any more than he is suggesting that they have earned salvation by their own good works. These were, however, Christians who lived a faithful biblical lifestyle and who cleansed their daily sins by confessing them and trusting in Christ (see 1 John 1:9). Thus Paul urged the Ephesians to "walk in a manner worthy of the calling to which you have been called" (Eph. 4:1). This worthiness is "the response of gratitude and devotion to God for the new life in Christ,"[11] and is the product rather than the cause of God's saving grace in their lives.

What a blessing it is to read of Christ's calling believers "worthy"—not perfect Christians, but sincere ones who earnestly live out their faith and are accepted by the Lord. Many of us struggle with the sense that we never

10. Philip Graham Ryken, *Jeremiah and Lamentations: From Sorrow to Hope*, Preaching the Word (Wheaton, IL: Crossway, 2001), 126.

11. Philip Edgcumbe Hughes, *The Book of Revelation* (Downers Grove, IL: InterVarsity Press, 1990), 56.

measure up so as to be pleasing to the Lord. Yet all through the letters of Revelation, we have found Jesus searching out things to praise because of his love for his people. Even in the dead church of Sardis, the faithful remnant is praised as "worthy." If you have held fast in faith to God's Word and if you are leading a sincere biblical lifestyle, then be encouraged that the Lord pronounces you "worthy," all because of the mighty work of the Holy Spirit that God has bestowed on you for the eternal glory of his saving grace (Eph. 1:6).

Not only may sincere and faithful Christians rejoice to be called "worthy" by the Lord, they may especially exult in his promised reward to those who conquer by trusting and obeying his Word. Jesus concludes with three great promises, urging: "He who has an ear, let him hear what the Spirit says to the churches" (Rev. 3:6).

First, Jesus declares, "They will walk with me in white" (Rev. 3:4). He emphasizes this emblem of purity again in verse 5: "The one who conquers will be clothed thus in white garments." The white garments connect with several ideas, including the white baptismal robes sometimes worn to signify union with Christ in faith, together with the heavenly clothing described later in Revelation for those victorious souls who worship around the throne of God in heaven (7:9–14).[12] Most important is the imputed righteousness of Christ with which believers stand justified before the holy God. This pure garment is manifested in the practical holiness of a faithful, godly life, turning increasingly from sin by Christ's power. The Christian's robe is made white by the cleansing application of Christ's atoning blood. Thus the last beatitude of Christ is given in Revelation 22:14: "Blessed are those who wash their robes, so that they may have the right to the tree of life and that they may enter the city by the gates."

Not only may faithful Christians wear a white robe in the presence of God, but Jesus proclaims, "They will walk with me in white" (Rev. 3:4), signifying the highest blessing of communion with Christ, begun in this life and perfected in the unending glory of the age to come.

Second, Jesus promises, "I will never blot his name out of the book of life" (Rev. 3:5). It is important to note that this verse does not say that some elect persons may lose their salvation and have their names blotted from God's

---

12. Grant R. Osborne, *Revelation*, Baker Exegetical Commentary on the New Testament (Grand Rapids: Baker Academic, 2002), 179.

book, as many writers have claimed. Jesus' point is to amplify the security of true believers. To be sure, our names may be on the rolls of an earthly church without being in the Book of Life above. But Jesus assures those who have truly believed in Christ and persevered in obedience to God's Word that their membership in the rolls of heaven is eternally sure. Here believers have the strongest assurance of salvation: "I will never blot his name out of the book of life" (3:5). Jesus said of his true sheep in John's Gospel: "I give them eternal life, and they will never perish, and no one will snatch them out of my hand" (John 10:28). Revelation 13:8 states that believers' names were "written before the foundation of the world in the book of life of the Lamb who was slain." Unbelievers' names were never written in God's book so as to be blotted out; believers' names were inscribed by God's sovereign election in eternity past, and they will remain written there forever.

Finally, Jesus declares, "I will confess his name before my Father and before his angels" (Rev. 3:5). Here we truly see how precious is the name of everyone who possesses not merely a Christian reputation but actual eternal life through faith in Christ. His or her name was foreknown by God in divine predestination for salvation (Rom. 8:29). That name was borne on Jesus' heart as he died on the cross to atone for sins (Matt. 1:21). That name will be confessed by the lips of Christ when he stands before the Father on the last day, saying, "Behold, I and the children God has given me" (Heb. 2:13).

How can we know that Christ will confess our names before his Father on the day of judgment? The answer is that it is by God's grace, through a true, living, obedient, and persevering faith. Jesus said: "I tell you, everyone who acknowledges me before men, the Son of Man also will acknowledge before the angels of God, but the one who denies me before men will be denied before the angels of God" (Luke 12:8–9).

Do we realize how important it is that we not dabble in a nominal Christianity, one that for all its reputation before men may actually be empty and dead? Let us therefore believe in Christ's perfect work so as to receive white robes before God. Let us not soil those robes with the sins of the world. Let us confess Christ's name as courageous witnesses. And let us walk with him now in those white garments, rejoicing to know that when all is perfected in the glory of his soon return, we will walk with him in radiant white forever.

14

AN OPEN DOOR BEFORE YOU

Revelation 3:7–13

Behold, I have set before you an open door,
which no one is able to shut. (Rev. 3:8)

*D*uring the years in which I served as a pastor at Tenth Presbyterian Church in Philadelphia, I would often wonder about a sign affixed beside the door for staff entry behind the church. I would approach the locked door with my keys in hand to enter, to read on the sign the words of Revelation 3:8: "See, I have placed before you an open door that no one can shut" (NIV). I often commented to myself on the inappropriateness of that sign: a locked door with a sign saying that it can never be shut! The sign was referring, of course, to the work of preaching the gospel. It referred not to the door into the staff offices but rather to the door opened by Jesus, granting entry into his kingdom of salvation. As I entered the church building as a preacher, I was intended to remember this promise of the Sovereign Christ about the gospel opening he has provided during this present age of grace.

THE KEEPER OF DAVID'S KEY

Each of the seven messages to the churches in Revelation had the purpose of focusing the believers on the person and work of Jesus Christ. Christ himself was to be the great reality that shaped their thinking, whether they were anticipating persecution or standing up for false teaching and temptation into sin. In the sixth message, to the church in Philadelphia, Christ presents himself to a congregation that is reminded of their calling to spread the gospel. To "the angel of the church in Philadelphia," John was to write: "The words of the holy one, the true one, who has the key of David, who opens and no one will shut, who shuts and no one opens" (Rev. 3:7).

Jesus is presented as holy and true. As "holy," Jesus is set apart above all others, pure and spotless in righteousness. As the Holy One of God, he commands the reverent attention of his people, as when Moses stood before the burning bush of Mount Sinai. He is also "true." This can be taken to mean that Jesus is the *genuine* Lord and Savior of his people. The particular word used by John, however, normally emphasizes *truthfulness* (Greek, *alethinos*). Jesus is the holy and faithful Sovereign as he stands before his church in Philadelphia.

The most significant feature is that Christ "has the key of David" (Rev. 3:7). To possess a key is to control access and entry. In 1:18, Jesus said that he has "the keys of Death and Hades," referring to his conquest of death and his control over eternal life. Here, Jesus refers to the salvation kingdom over which he reigns as the heir of David. Jesus has the key to the household of God and the ancient covenant blessings promised to Israel.

The language of Revelation 3:7 refers back to an episode in the book of Isaiah. The Lord had rebuked a faithless steward named Sheba. In his place, God established a faithful servant, Eliakim, to administer the kingdom of David. The Lord added: "And I will place on his shoulder the key of the house of David. He shall open, and none shall shut; and he shall shut, and none shall open" (Isa. 22:22). This faithful steward would control access to the king and would dispense the resources of his kingdom. Eliakim was symbolic of Jesus Christ, who has "the key of David, who opens and no one will shut, who shuts and no one opens" (Rev. 3:7).

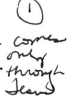

This description makes two essential statements. The first is that salvation comes only through Jesus Christ. Jesus said, "I am the door. If anyone enters by me, he will be saved" (John 10:9). "I am the way, and the truth, and the life," he insisted. "No one comes to the Father except through me" (14:6). We can therefore enter into God's kingdom of salvation only through faith in Jesus, God's Son, the Holy and True One. This teaching was especially significant in Philadelphia, where the Christians were opposed by Jews who denied Jesus Christ. Yet Jesus, as David's royal heir, possessed the only key, and he alone could open the way into the kingdom of God.

Second, since Jesus holds the key to salvation, opening and shutting the door to God's kingdom, the church relies on Christ to grant success to its ministry. John Stott comments: "If the door is the symbol of the church's opportunity, the key is the symbol of Christ's authority."[1] Realizing this, the church must faithfully preach Christ's gospel. We must pray to God in Christ's name for saving power. And what exciting news it is that Jesus holds the key to God's kingdom of salvation, since he is the Savior who has proved his love for sinners by his atoning death on the cross. Christ the heir of David, who holds the keys, calls us to minister his gospel. He grants us the great privilege of knowing that as we tell others about his saving love, we are being used by him to grant eternal life to those who believe.

A Door Opened for Salvation

If we understand what it means for Jesus to hold the keys to God's kingdom and grant success to the gospel, the message that he gave the Philadelphians is thrilling. "Behold," he told them, "I have set before you an open door, which no one is able to shut" (Rev. 3:8).

Some scholars argue that Jesus means simply that he has secured salvation for the believers in Philadelphia. Given opposition from the Jews, many of them would likely have been cast out of the synagogue for their faith in Christ. But though the synagogue door was closed, Christ opened to them the door of heaven, which none can shut. This is certainly part of Jesus' message to this church, and it is in keeping with the vision of chapter 4, which begins with "a door standing open in heaven" (Rev. 4:1).

It is likely, however, that Jesus also has in mind an open door for their ministry of the gospel to others. Paul often spoke of an open door for opportunities to bear witness to Christ. He requested prayer "that God may open to us a door for the word, to declare the mystery of Christ" (Col. 4:3; see also 1 Cor. 16:9; 2 Cor. 2:12). This interpretation is made likely when we learn that Philadelphia was a fairly young city, having been established in the

---

1. John R. W. Stott, *What Christ Thinks of the Church: An Exposition of Revelation 1–3* (Grand Rapids: Baker, 2003), 105.

second century B.C. as an outpost for Greek culture in Asia. This means that "Philadelphia was a missionary church in a missionary city. So the promise Jesus gives is that its witness to him there will be successful."[2]

History shows that Jesus' promise to Philadelphia was true in general of the entire age of the early church, as God had prepared the Mediterranean world for the rapid spread of the good news of Christ. Under the *Pax Romana*, the world from Spain to Asia was united under a well-ordered government with good roads, safe travel, and a common official language. In far-flung cities, dispersed Jewish communities had taken the Old Testament ahead of the apostles so that ideas involved in the gospel had a head start. More-over, the old gods of paganism were waning in influence, and the Roman world was prepared for a potent, challenging worldview. John Stott writes that "wherever they went, [Christian evangelists] found groping minds and hungry hearts."[3] In short, God had prepared the entire ancient world for the arrival of the gospel. Christ has opened similar doors in history at many times. The best example today may be China, where the underground-church movement has spread like wildfire and where disenchantment over Communist ideology has left a worldview vacuum that may well be filled by the gospel.

As in several of the previous letters, Jesus tells his readers, "I know your works" (Rev. 3:8). Whereas in other churches Christ had serious matters to correct, here in Philadelphia he had no criticism. He knows, however, that they are not a strong church. "I know that you have but little power," Jesus said, "and yet you have kept my word and have not denied my name" (3:8). Because of the Philadelphians' steadfast faith, and because of the saving power that Christ would unleash through their ministry, the weakness of this church would not hinder the open door that Christ had specifically granted its ministry.

It is not hard to imagine ways in which the church of Philadelphia was weak. The people may have come largely from lower economic and social classes. They probably did not have influence with the government or great material resources, and their numbers may have been fairly small. But their spiritual attainments contained a great power, as they preached and obeyed the Bible and continued their witness to Christ. In all these respects, the

2. James Montgomery Boice, *Revelation*, unpublished manuscript, n.d., chap. 11, p. 5.
3. Stott, *What Christ Thinks of the Church*, 100.

Philadelphians faced a world not much different from that facing believers today. Douglas Kelly writes that contemporary Christians

> contemplate the aggressive secularism of modern America and Western Europe, with systematic unbelief in high places, such as the universities and the media. Add to that the entrenched Modernism of the educational system, and the precipitous moral decline in once-Christian populations. It is true that over against them our strength is small. But Jesus says that we are not anxiously to worry about it. "You have little strength; use what little you have, and I am going to supernaturally multiply it by opening the right doors."[4]

Not only would the weakness of the church not hinder Christ's open door for the gospel, but neither would the opposition that the believers faced. Jesus continues: "Behold, I will make those of the synagogue of Satan who say that they are Jews and are not, but lie—behold, I will make them come and bow down before your feet and they will learn that I have loved you" (Rev. 3:9).

When Jesus refers to "the synagogue of Satan," he means that the Jewish community was mocking the faith of Christians just as the Pharisees and scribes had denied the claims of Jesus. Moreover, as the Jewish leaders had delivered Christ to the cross, the synagogue rulers sought for the Romans to persecute the church in Philadelphia. These people "say that they are Jews and are not." By this Jesus does not deny their ethnicity but rather denies their covenant status. In John 8, he made this clear to the Pharisees who were accusing him. If they were the true followers of Abraham, they would have Abraham's faith in Christ (John 8:37–40). "If God were your Father," Jesus said, "you would love me, for I came from God" (8:42).

Not only does Jesus reject the false faith of unbelieving Jews, but he promises that their opposition will not even hinder the gospel's witness to them: "Behold, I will make them come and bow down before your feet and they will learn that I have loved you" (Rev. 3:9). This is an allusion to Isaiah 45:14, where God promised Israel that the Gentiles would confess Israel's God. "They will plead with you, saying: 'Surely God is in you, and there is no other, no god besides him.'" What the Jews failed to realize was that by denying Jesus, they had themselves become Gentiles, that is, aliens to God's covenant. The Old Testament prophecy would be fulfilled

---

4. Douglas F. Kelly, *Revelation*, Mentor Expository Commentary (Tain, Ross-shire, Scotland: Mentor, 2012), 74.

as unbelieving Jews were brought to faith in Christ through the witness of the church.

Notice that it is Christ who achieves this conversion: "Behold, I will make them come and bow down," Jesus promises, and he will cause unbelievers, including unbelieving Jews, to acknowledge that God's love is upon the followers of Christ. This promise accords perfectly with Paul's description of how the church will be used to bring unbelieving Jews to faith in Christ. Paul said, "I magnify my ministry [among the Gentiles] in order somehow to make my fellow Jews jealous, and thus save some of them" (Rom. 11:13–14).

The fierce opposition may have caused the Philadelphians to back down in their witness. They may have believed that discretion called for a muted testimony, especially to the Jews. But Jesus shows that those who oppose the gospel will be those most likely to hear and be affected by its power. Having opened a gospel door for ministry, Jesus assures the church that through its bold witness to him, some of its most violent persecutors will be among those who are saved.

Christ's open door for ministry would not be hindered by the weakness of the church, by opposition against the church, or, third, by God's judgment at work in the world in which the Philadelphians lived. Jesus writes: "Because you have kept my word about patient endurance, I will keep you from the hour of trial that is coming on the whole world, to try those who dwell on the earth" (Rev. 3:10).

The hour of trial to which Jesus refers does not seem to be a local tribulation, as Jesus had foretold for Smyrna (Rev. 2:10). Jesus uses a word for *world* that means its "inhabitants" (Greek, *oikoumene*), and says that it will be "the whole world" that is tried. For this reason, most scholars believe that Jesus is referring to the worldwide tribulation foretold before the coming of Christ at the end (see 2 Thess. 2:3–12). It is not that the Philadelphia church would be removed from the tribulation to come but that it would be kept safe in and through the tribulation so as not to be overcome by God's judgment on the world. Moreover, the tribulation of the end is anticipated by God's judgment on man's rebellion throughout history (see 2 Thess. 2:7; 1 John 2:18). For this reason, the Philadelphians, like Christians now, were called to witness in a world under God's judgment. Yet Jesus had set before them an open door, and even the outworking of God's judgment would not hinder Christ from bringing men and women to salvation through faith in his Word.

One way in which Christ would empower the gospel in the midst of rebellion and judgment is by keeping his faithful people safe. Jesus notes that the Philadelphians would be preserved because "you have kept my word about patient endurance" (Rev. 3:10). Notice that it is Christ who keeps his people safe, and that this safety takes place through a living and persevering faith. Christians are kept eternally secure by God's sovereign will and power, yet this security is experienced by an active, striving faith by which Christ's people conquer in this world (see 1 Peter 1:4–5).

A historical fact makes Christ's claim here all the more remarkable. Jesus warned that the seven churches of Asia would lose their lampstands if they did not repent and believe, and history shows that these churches did ultimately cease to exist. The sole exception is the city and church of Philadelphia, which Jesus promised to keep safe even under the tribulation that would come at the end. It turns out that the city of Philadelphia was never destroyed, surviving repeated invasions until it fell to Muslim conquerors. Yet even then the Christian community endured, and in the modern Turkish city of Alasehir there remain churches descended from the original congregations, organized under their bishop whose succession is traced back to the apostolic times.[5]

How thrilling it must have been when the book of Revelation was read in Philadelphia and Christ's message for this congregation was delivered: "Behold, I have set before you an open door, which no one is able to shut" (Rev. 3:8). This door was kept open by Christ's power despite weakness, opposition, and divine judgment, to Christians who held firmly to the Bible, refused to deny Christ's name, and patiently endured in faith.

BLESSINGS IN THE CITY OF GOD

If Christ's message of an open door was thrilling to the believers, their blessing was compounded when he concluded with promises for those who endure victoriously in faith: "The one who conquers, I will make him a pillar in the temple of my God. Never shall he go out of it, and I will write on him the name of my God, and the name of the city of my God, the new Jerusalem, which comes down from my God out of heaven, and my own new name. He who has an ear, let him hear what the Spirit says to the churches" (Rev. 3:12–13).

5. Richard Bewes, *The Lamb Wins: A Guided Tour through the Book of Revelation* (Tain, Ross-shire, Scotland: Christian Focus, 2000), 33.

The history of Philadelphia had been tragically marred by its location along a dangerous fault line. Earthquakes had shattered the city, with aftershocks terrorizing the people for weeks and even years afterward, so that the city suffered from a lack of physical stability. But Jesus promises that his faithful followers will never lack for spiritual stability. Jesus promises to make every conquering Christian "a pillar in the temple of my God" (Rev. 3:12). The idea is that Christians who endure will be permanent fixtures and beautiful ornaments in the eternal temple, the church of Christ, in which God will dwell forever. In this way Jesus promises unshakable security to Christians whose faith is proved. Philip Hughes writes that "a pillar, by its very nature and function, is not removable!"[6] How wonderful it is that Christians who were acknowledged as having "little power" will through faith in Jesus be made pillars of strength in the eternal habitation of God.

Jesus further gave a threefold promise involving a new name for the faithful believers: "I will write on him the name of my God, and the name of the city of my God, the new Jerusalem, which comes down from my God out of heaven, and my own new name" (Rev. 3:12).

History records that after Philadelphia was badly damaged by the great earthquake of A.D. 17, it was rebuilt with generous financial assistance from the Roman emperor Tiberius. In gratitude, its citizens changed the city's name to Neocaesarea. Not long before John's writing, the city had been renamed once more as Flavia, the family name of the emperor Vespasian.[7] In contrast, Jesus says, Christians are under the patronage of God himself and will bear the name of God their Savior. They will also receive the name "of the city of my God, the new Jerusalem, which comes down from my God out of heaven" (Rev. 3:12). This theme will recur in Revelation. In the final chapter we see our citizenship eternally consummated: "They will see his face, and his name will be on their foreheads . . . and they will reign forever and ever" (22:4–5). Hughes writes: "This naming represents the stamp of the overcomer's authentic citizenship,"[8] showing that there is no uncertainty about a true Christian's loyalty or his right to enjoy the citizenship of God's eternal city.

6. Philip Edgcumbe Hughes, *The Book of Revelation* (Downers Grove, IL: InterVarsity Press, 1990), 62–63.
7. G. B. Caird, *The Revelation of St. John the Divine* (San Francisco: Harper, 1966), 51.
8. Hughes, *The Book of Revelation*, 62–63.

Finally, Jesus promises that the faithful believer will be marked with "my own new name" (Rev. 3:12). This new name is not unknown to believers, since Revelation 19:16 points out: "On his robe and on his thigh he has a name written, King of kings and Lord of lords." By saying that believers will receive his new name, Jesus means that through faith they are made certain of his ownership and protection, and are thus assured of the blessings of eternal life in glory. James Boice writes: "If the believers in Philadelphia are to be given this new name, it is because they have conquered in life and are now to reign with him."[9]

OPEN AND SHUT

The same Jesus who spoke to the church in Philadelphia, saying, "Behold, I have set before you an open door" (Rev. 3:8), speaks now to us through the book of Revelation. We should observe that Christ said this in the perfect tense, meaning that a past completed act has created an enduring present situation. The past act was Christ's death on the cross for the atonement of sin. The present reality is the open door for salvation to all who will confess their sin, believe the gospel, and come to Jesus in a true and living faith. People like open doors because they suggest opportunity. Here is the greatest opportunity that one could ever have: forgiveness of sins, a renewed and cleansed nature, and a destiny as a pillar in the household of God, bearing his name and enjoying his blessing forever. How can you receive this matchless salvation? The image of the open door tells you: enter salvation by believing in Christ.

But a warning goes with the opportunity of Christ and his gospel. Jesus said that no one can shut the door that he has opened. Yet Christ himself will one day shut the door, after which no one will ever come in. The Bible thus presses you with the urgency of coming to Christ in saving faith: "Behold, now is the favorable time; behold, now is the day of salvation" (2 Cor. 6:2).

Finally, Jesus gives an instruction to the believers in Philadelphia and to us today: "I am coming soon. Hold fast what you have, so that no one may seize your crown" (Rev. 3:11). It is clear that Christians do not conquer in our own strength, since Jesus knows that we have "little power" (3:8). Christians do not cast down opposition but need to be kept by Christ in

9. Boice, *Revelation*, chap. 11, p. 10.

the tribulation of this world. Yet there is something we must do. We must hold on. We must never give up.

James Boice concluded his sermon on this text with a line from the popular movie *Rocky*. The journeyman boxer Rocky Balboa was given a chance to fight the undefeated champion, Apollo Creed. People told Rocky that he could never win, but he went on training for the fight. The day of the fight came, and Rocky confided to his girlfriend, "There's no way I can beat Apollo Creed." Christians will feel this way in our witness to a hostile and rebellious world. Rocky didn't plan to win, but said, "I just want to go the distance." To everyone's astonishment, that is what Rocky did. He was not knocked out but went the full fifteen rounds in the ring against the terrifying foe.[10]

This is what we are called to do, holding fast to the Bible, honoring Christ's name, and bearing testimony to his gospel. Jesus declares, "I am coming soon" (Rev. 3:11). We say in answer, "Jesus, with your strength, I will go the distance." As we trust in him, no one will seize our crown of eternal life, but instead, as Paul said, "there is laid up for me the crown of righteousness, which the Lord, the righteous judge, will award to me on that Day, and not only to me but also to all who have loved his appearing" (2 Tim. 4:8).

Jesus,
With your strength,
I will go the distance.

10. Ibid., chap. 11, p. 12.

15

NEITHER HOT NOR COLD

Revelation 3:14–22

*Behold, I stand at the door and knock. If anyone hears my voice
and opens the door, I will come in to him and eat with him,
and he with me.* (Rev. 3:20)

*T*he seven messages to the churches of Revelation have sometimes been interpreted as outlining the history of the church
from the time of the apostles until the return of Jesus Christ.
No evidence in the text supports such a view, and as we have seen, numerous references in the letters make it clear that Christ was addressing real
churches in John's time. It is interesting, however, that those who take the
church-history view almost never associate the church of Laodicea with
their own time. Usually, they see themselves as the church of Philadelphia,
a praiseworthy church with its open door for missions and evangelism.

Yet the best fit for our time is probably the church of Laodicea. Here were
Christians whose material affluence left them little zeal for Christ and his
gospel. Likewise, the evangelical church in the West today is focused largely
on self—with worship experiences designed to make us feel good and messages geared toward self-improvement—with little apparent interest in Christ.
I experienced this a few years ago at the national convention of the Christian

Booksellers Association. I was there to do an interview on a book I had written about Jesus' approach to evangelism. The woman conducting the interview expressed surprise that my book was actually about Jesus. She told me that she had spent the entire week interviewing authors and that this was the first time that anything pertaining to Christ had come up. This situation is reminiscent of the church in Laodicea. John Stott comments: "Perhaps none of the seven letters is more appropriate to the church at the beginning of the twenty-first century than this. It describes vividly the respectable, nominal, rather sentimental, skin-deep religiosity which is so widespread among us today." [1]

CHRIST'S DISGUSTED ASSESSMENT

Laodicea was the last of the seven churches to which Jesus sent messages through the apostle John. It was one of three churches located in the Lycus valley, together with Colosse and Hierapolis, about a hundred miles east of Ephesus. These churches had been founded forty years earlier, during the apostle Paul's stay in Ephesus, probably by Epaphras, whom Paul praises in Colossians 4:13 for his work there.

Laodicea was situated along a major trade route, which is why it was a wealthy city, home to bankers, financiers, and millionaires. The city was destroyed in the great earthquake of A.D. 61, but was so wealthy that it declined government help for its rebuilding. Laodicea was home to a school of medicine that was famed for its salves, including one for eye ailments. It was further noted for the soft, raven-black wool of its sheep, in which its fashionable elites were usually dressed.

Laodicea had one main problem: it lacked a good water supply. Nearby Hierapolis had medicinal hot springs, and Colosse was blessed with a source of pure, cold water. Laodicea had to bring its water by an aqueduct from hot springs five miles away. The problem was that the water arrived tepid and brackish. Jesus picked up on this issue in writing to the Laodicean church: "I know your works: you are neither cold nor hot. Would that you were either cold or hot!" (Rev. 3:15).

The problem that Jesus notes in Laodicea was not persecution, gross sin, or false teaching. In terms of its circumstances, it seems, Laodicea was

---

1. John R. W. Stott, *What Christ Thinks of the Church: An Exposition of Revelation 1–3* (Grand Rapids: Baker, 2003), 113.

singularly blessed. For this reason, however, the people had lost their zeal for Christ. It was a spiritually apathetic church. The people gathered for worship, but they came like those today who look more frequently to their watches than to the Bible. They probably believed the right things, but those truths did not affect them deeply. When it came to Jesus, they were believers, but only lukewarmly so.

In addition to a lack of personal fervor for Christ and his Word, it is likely that the Laodicean church could show little work or witness. Jesus states, "I know your works," but then does not cite any worth mentioning. The people were probably timid in their witness, unmotivated about prayer, indifferent to the sick and imprisoned, and self-centered in their hoarding of money. They were the kind of people who believed that one should not be "fanatical" about religion, but in reality lacked the wholeheartedness that alone pleases the Lord.

Jesus' response to this lukewarm religion was to express disgust: "So, because you are lukewarm, and neither hot nor cold, I will spit you out of my mouth" (Rev. 3:16). Some commentators are distressed that Jesus would prefer coldness to a lukewarm faith. The reason, however, is not hard to fathom. It is perhaps most offensive of all for people to affirm the glories of Christ but then to live as though they meant little. Stott writes: "If he is the Son of God who became a human being, died for our sins, and was raised from death; if Christmas Day, Good Friday, and Easter Day are more than meaningless anniversaries, then nothing less than our wholehearted commitment to Christ will do."[2]

The church does not always approve the enthusiasm of a man such as John Wesley, who went into the fields preaching the gospel, but Christ does. The church may urge a man such as William Carey to shrink back from "wasting" his life among the heathens of India, but Christ was delighted and displayed his glory in the success of that gospel mission. Carey's motto—"attempt great things for God; expect great things from God"—was the very antithesis of the Laodicean malaise.

How did the Laodiceans become so lukewarm? Jesus answers that they had come to a false estimation of themselves on the basis of their outward blessings: "For you say, I am rich, I have prospered, and I need nothing, not realizing that you are wretched, pitiable, poor, blind, and naked" (Rev. 3:17).

---

2. Ibid., 114.

attempt great things for God, Expect great things from God.

The Laodiceans looked on their favorable circumstances and considered their riches as true wealth. In fact, Jesus observes that by trusting in money and living for the things of a dying world, they were wretched, pitiable, blind, and covered with shame. Anne Soukhanov has labeled this syndrome, so common in contemporary America, as "Affluenza." She defines it as "an array of psychological maladies such as isolation, boredom, passivity and lack of motivation engendered in adults, teenagers, and children by the possession of great wealth."[3] The Laodiceans, like so many churches in America today, had become sick from "Affluenza," and Jesus had become sick of them in return.

The problem was not their wealth but what their riches had done to them. Many great believers have been wealthy, such as Abraham in the Bible and such as Robert Haldane, who used his money to support a great revival in Geneva. The question is whether we hold our wealth as a stewardship from God, to be used for his glory, the good of others, and the work of the gospel. Or does wealth cause us to stop thinking about Christ's kingdom, instead musing on earthly blessings? This was the issue in Laodicea, where God's people boasted in their hearts and largely forgot about God and the kingdom of Christ.

Notice from this passage that Christians tend to estimate themselves wrongly. This is one reason why we so greatly need sound and clear teaching from the Bible, which alone will present a true portrait and convict us of our weakness and sin. The Bible tells us, "God opposes the proud but gives grace to the humble" (1 Peter 5:5). We therefore need messages such as the one to Laodicea to realize the trend of our lives and to make changes while there is still time. We need to see the truth about our corruption in sin, our toleration of false teaching, our partnership in idolatry, and our self-absorbed indifference to Christ—in order to avoid wasting our lives and even disgusting our Lord.

Second, notice that the Laodiceans drew their attitude from the secular culture around them. This happens frequently to Christians. In a sophisticated culture, Christians take on airs of superiority. In a patriotic setting, we become preoccupied with earthly kingdoms. Among pleasure-seekers, Christians live for the sake of the latest consumer goods. The rich arrogance

3. Anne Soukhanov, quoted in Dennis E. Johnson, *Triumph of the Lamb: A Commentary on Revelation* (Phillipsburg, NJ: P&R Publishing, 2001), 91n41.

of Laodicea had infected the believers' attitudes, making them spiritually poor, blind as to heavenly realities, and disgraced by a shameful absence of good works and a faithful witness. Christians should therefore be on guard against adopting the spirit of the age and of the place where we live, instead cultivating a biblical ethos and the agenda of Jesus Christ. If we do not, the danger is so great that Jesus said he would spit the Laodicean church out of his mouth. Undoubtedly, this indicates that many in that church were not even saved. Apathetic Christianity often masks a spiritually dead unbelief. In his parable of the talents, Jesus ordered that such false professors of faith be cast "into the outer darkness. In that place there will be weeping and gnashing of teeth" (Matt. 25:30).

Christ's Loving Counsel

Christ's letter to Laodicea is one of the harsher portions of Holy Scripture, and we may therefore be surprised to see the tenderness and love that Christ shows to this church. We conclude Revelation 3:17, expecting Jesus at any moment to spew out this congregation from his disgusted mouth. Instead, Jesus ministers, saying, "Those whom I love, I reprove and discipline" (3:19). Here is hope in light of our many failings and sins: Christ's love for his church. "For all their failures, this is nevertheless a church composed of his people whom he loves and whom he wants to bring to repentance."[4] It is not surprising, then, that the remedy for the Laodicean malaise comes from Jesus himself: "I counsel you to buy from me gold refined by fire, so that you may be rich, and white garments so that you may clothe yourself and the shame of your nakedness may not be seen, and salve to anoint your eyes, so that you may see" (3:18).

Before considering the particular items noted by Jesus, we should focus on the general theme of his counsel. The Christians were to stop expecting their spiritual needs to be met from the Laodicean marketplace and were instead to come to Christ and do business with him. One thing they would find is that Jesus runs a completely different economy from that of the world. This is what Jesus meant in saying that we should "buy from" him: not that his saving blessings are up for sale, but that we should come to him for the divine blessings that will save our souls. He alone can enrich our poverty, clothe

---

4. James Montgomery Boice, *Revelation*, unpublished manuscript, n.d., chap. 12, p. 7.

our nakedness, heal our blindness, and give life to the spiritually dead. No doubt Jesus had in mind the market economics expressed by Isaiah: "Come, everyone who thirsts, come to the waters; and he who has no money, come, buy and eat! Come, buy wine and milk without money and without price" (Isa. 55:1). To trade with Jesus is to come to him empty-handed, seeking saving blessings by his grace alone. Augustus Toplady put it well:

Nothing in my hand I bring, simply to thy cross I cling;
Naked, come to thee for dress; helpless, look to thee for grace;
Foul, I to the Fountain fly; wash me, Savior, or I die.[5]

First, Jesus encouraged them to "buy from me gold refined by fire" (Rev. 3:18). He was referring to the true riches of salvation and a godly life. Jesus told a parable of a rich fool who stored up wealth for his security, not realizing that his life could be forfeit at any minute. Jesus called this the folly of "one who lays up treasure for himself and is not rich toward God" (Luke 12:21). To be "rich toward God" is to have your sins forgiven, to possess justification through faith in Christ, and then to have a godly character that has been made pure and strong by enduring trials and tribulations. As Jesus pointed out, many wealthy people are pitiable in their misery and despair, while strong believers who are poor in the things of the world are rich in "righteousness and peace and joy in the Holy Spirit" (Rom. 14:17).

Second, Jesus urges his readers to gain "white garments so that you may clothe yourself and the shame of your nakedness may not be seen" (Rev. 3:18). Throughout Revelation, white garments symbolize those who are justified through faith in Christ and have confirmed their salvation by persevering to the end of life (see 3:4; 4:4; 7:9; 22:14). Here, Jesus speaks also of covering our shame. In the ancient world, the greatest humiliation was to be stripped naked, whereas the greatest honor was to be dressed in the finest clothes. The greatest glory in this world is experienced by those who know they are clothed before God in Christ's imputed righteousness and who walk in a manner worthy of their high calling to holiness.

We should remember that the standard color of Laodicea was black, from the lush wools that its sheep produced. Jesus seems to indicate, therefore, that part of being cleansed and justified through faith in him is to wear a

---

5. Augustus M. Toplady, "Rock of Ages, Cleft for Me" (1776).

different color from the world. The Christians in white were to be a public counterculture displaying the righteousness of Christ, the holy Christian calling, and the glorious hope of resurrection life in the age to come. As Christ's righteous ones, the Christians were not to fit in but were to stick out as a testimony to the gospel.

Third, Laodicea was known for its medicinal eye salves, but that did not keep the church from becoming spiritually blind. Therefore, the people should come to Jesus for "salve to anoint your eyes, so that you may see" (Rev. 3:18). With the psalmist of old, they should come to Jesus, crying, "Open my eyes, that I may behold wondrous things out of your law" (Ps. 119:18). They needed to see themselves as they really were; they needed to see anew the glory and grace of Jesus; and they needed to see the world in its true need, which can be met only through a zealous witness to the saving mercy of Christ.

All these gifts are freely given by Jesus, yet he wants something out of this transaction, demanding it as a stern and disciplining Lord: "Those whom I love, I reprove and discipline, so be zealous and repent" (Rev. 3:19). The word *zealous* means to be "boiling hot" (Greek, *zeleuo*). So Jesus wants his people to respond to his gifts by eagerly pursuing the gospel agenda of his kingdom. Paul wrote similarly in Romans 12:1: "I appeal to you therefore, brothers, by the mercies of God, to present your bodies as a living sacrifice, holy and acceptable to God, which is your spiritual worship." Since we have received everything from Jesus by free grace through his shed blood, he desires that we would give the whole of ourselves in response, as an offering of thanks and as servants of his eternal kingdom.

What will that look like for you? Will it call you to a more devoted ministry of prayer? Will it call you to step out as a witness to others? Will it energize works of service in the church or call you to the mission field? Our gifts and callings will be different, but Jesus wants each of us, in our own way, to be red-hot for his saving work.

CHRIST'S TENDER APPEAL

Jesus adds to his loving counsel a most tender appeal, which is all the more remarkable in that it is given to a church for which he has expressed disgust: "Behold, I stand at the door and knock. If anyone hears my voice and opens the door, I will come in to him and eat with him, and he with me" (Rev. 3:20).

This verse is frequently seen as an evangelistic appeal, but the context shows that this is not the case. This text does not urge unbelievers to "ask Jesus into your heart"; instead, Jesus is speaking to his church that has closed its door to him. Moreover, the idea of opening an unbelieving heart to Jesus is not the biblical idea of conversion. Biblical evangelism is the proclaiming of Christ in his person and work so that hearers believe in him as God grants them new hearts (Ezek. 36:25–26), which he opens by his Word (Acts 16:14). James Boice explains that here, Christ "is knocking at the closed hearts of those who are his but who have turned their backs on him and shut him out of their complacent, self-satisfied, worldly Christian lives. The knocking Christ is an image, not of Jesus calling unbelievers to give their hearts to him but of calling drifting, worldly believers to sincere repentance and renewal."[6]

Holman Hunt depicted Jesus at the door in his famous painting *Light of the World*, which hangs in St. Paul's Cathedral in London. Vines grow against the door, showing that it has not lately been used. Christ wears his crown of thorns and holds a lantern in his hand, the other hand raised to knock at the door. A friend complained to Hunt that the painting lacked a knob on the door, but he answered that this was the point. This is a door to be opened on the inside, which shows that Christ desires his church to show effort in their relationship with him.[7] This is a challenge to the church and to every individual in the church—"if anyone," Jesus says—to open the door to the presence, rule, and powerful blessing of Christ.

Jesus teaches that we must hear his voice and open the door. This means that Christ calls to us today through the Word, urging his people to awaken and respond with a zealous and repentant faith. Donald Grey Barnhouse comments: "The call of the Lord to Laodicea, then, is to come back to the Word of God. The poverty of this church lies in the fact that the Word of God is not given its proper place."[8] John Stott describes Christ's calling as "to surrender without conditions to his lordship. It is to seek his will in his word and promptly to obey it. It is not just attending religious services

---

6. Boice, *Revelation*, chap. 12, p. 10.

7. G. Campbell Morgan, *The Westminster Pulpit: The Preaching of G. Campbell Morgan* (Grand Rapids: Baker, 1995), 6:32–33.

8. Donald Grey Barnhouse, *Revelation: An Expositional Commentary* (Grand Rapids: Zondervan, 1971), 82.

twice a Sunday or even every day. . . . It is putting him first and seeking his pleasure in every department of life, public and private."[9]

Jesus adds a promise to his call: "If anyone hears my voice and opens the door, I will come in to him and eat with him, and he with me" (Rev. 3:20). This is an offer of enriched personal communion with Jesus. The Greeks had three meals each day, the chief of which was the *deipnon*, the evening meal where people lingered and shared the experiences and thoughts of their day. This is the meal that Jesus mentions. He offers us a living communion in daily discipleship. Some see an allusion here to the sacrament of the Lord's Supper. While this offer must not be restricted to the sacrament, it is undoubtedly true that a church that has opened itself to the living Christ through his Word is bound to enjoy rich spiritual blessings at the table of the Lord, rather than an empty ritual.

G. Campbell Morgan tells a story related to Holman Hunt's portrait of Christ at the door. A boy was viewing it and said, "Father, why don't they open the door?" His father answered, "I don't know; s'pose they don't want to!" The boy answered, "No, it isn't that. I think I know why they don't; they all live at the back of the house!"[10] The boy was describing those who come to church but have their minds on the things of the world, who are eager to be done with worship, whose bodies are present but whose hearts are not open to the Lord's coming in, since Jesus will insist on being sovereign over their priorities, affections, and choices. Christ knocks not as suppliant but as Lord, and Christians who do not open wide the door of their hearts will miss out on the rich blessing of communion that he offers.

CHRIST'S SALVATION OFFER

Christ writes to Laodicea to rebuke a lukewarm church, giving reasons for the people to repent and become hotter about him and his gospel. The first reason is that he may spit such a church out of his mouth, as evidently happened to Laodicea, which warns that many members in a lukewarm church are likely not to be saved at all. A second reason is that Jesus offers to give us true riches that the world cannot offer, together with white robes and eyes to see. Third, Jesus eagerly desires to dwell within his church and

9. Stott, *What Christ Thinks of the Church*, 121–22.
10. Morgan, *The Westminster Pulpit*, 6:33.

in Christian hearts, to reign but also to fellowship with joy and love. Finally, the most important reason to renew our zeal for Jesus is his own worthiness and glory. This is why this message began with words describing key attributes of Jesus: "And to the angel of the church in Laodicea write: 'The words of the Amen, the faithful and true witness, the beginning of God's creation'" (Rev. 3:14).

First, Jesus is the "Amen," a word that signifies solidity and truth. He is the Lord who speaks and it is so, who acts and it is established. As "the faithful and true witness," he is the One who speaks truth that we need to hear about ourselves, about the world, and about the gospel, and whose Word brings life. Moreover, Jesus is "the beginning of God's creation" (Rev. 3:14). This may also be interpreted as the "head" of God's creation. John began his Gospel by stating that Jesus is "the Word," who was in the beginning with God, and by whom "all things were made" (John 1:1–2). Jesus is able, therefore, to renew our church and restore our lives with his omnipotent, saving power.

It is in this capacity that Jesus concludes his messages to the seven churches of Asia with a final offer of salvation: "The one who conquers, I will grant him to sit with me on my throne, as I also conquered and sat down with my Father on his throne" (Rev. 3:21).

The seven messages of Revelation have included stern words that are uncomfortable for us to hear, not least the rebuke to the lukewarm church of Laodicea. But we are reminded that Jesus speaks as One who knows his church intimately and loves his people. His challenge is not for us to miss out on the best in life by yielding to him but rather to raise us up through our faith to a high communion with him. He declares that he is going to seat us beside him on his throne of glory and authority, to join his own victorious communion with God the Father forever.

For this reason, we must conquer in faith, drawing from Jesus' own victory as the One who says, "I also conquered and sat down with my Father on his throne" (Rev. 3:21). Leon Morris writes: "Christ overcame by the way of the cross and this sets the pattern for His followers. They face grim days. But let them never forget that what seemed Christ's defeat was in fact His victory over the world. They need not fear if they are called upon to suffer, for in that way they too will conquer."[11] We conquer only in his power, with

---

11. Leon Morris, *The Revelation of St. John: An Introduction and Commentary*, Tyndale New Testament Commentaries 20 (Grand Rapids: Eerdmans, 1969), 81.

the great reward of spending eternity not merely in Jesus' heaven but, he says, "with me on my throne." This is the high and glorious destiny to which Christ calls his church and his people now, saying, as John put it, "This is the victory that has overcome the world—our faith" (1 John 5:4).

Seeing the gracious offer of Christ to Laodicea, we are all the more willing to identify with this church, widely viewed as the worst of the churches in Revelation 2–3, because of the offer given to it by God's grace. Christ's message to Laodicea is the heartening message expressed by Joseph Hart in his great hymn:

> Come, ye sinners, poor and wretched, weak and wounded, sick and sore;
> Jesus ready stands to save you, full of pity joined with pow'r . . . .
> Without money, without money, without money,
> Come to Jesus Christ and buy; come to Jesus Christ and buy.[12]

Christ's calling is for us today no less than for the ancient believers of John's day. Jesus thus speaks to each of us with urgency: "He who has an ear, let him hear what the Spirit says to the churches" (Rev. 3:22).

12. Joseph Hart, "Come, Ye Sinners, Poor and Wretched" (1759).

PART 2

The Throne of God and the Seven Seals

16

A THRONE IN HEAVEN

Revelation 4:1–8

At once I was in the Spirit, and behold, a throne stood in heaven, with one seated on the throne. (Rev. 4:2)

n 593 B.C., a Jewish priest named Ezekiel was in exile outside Babylon, where he had been taken into captivity. There, beside the Chebar canal, "the hand of the LORD" came upon him (Ezek. 1:3) and he saw a remarkable vision. Emerging out of a storm came a bright light flashing with fire, together with "the likeness of four living creatures" (1:5), each with four wings and the faces of a human, a lion, an ox, and an eagle. Over their heads was a crystal sea, and, surrounded by a rainbow, "there was the likeness of a throne, in appearance like sapphire; and seated above the likeness of a throne was a likeness with a human appearance" (1:26).

Over the centuries, Ezekiel's visions so perplexed the Jewish rabbis that some sought to remove the book of Ezekiel from the canon. One rabbi, Hananiah ben Hezekiah, is said to have burned three hundred barrels of oil in his lamp by staying up late, seeking to make sense of this prophet.[1]

---

1. Iain M. Duguid, *Ezekiel*, NIV Application Commentary (Grand Rapids: Zondervan, 1999), 18.

Its true interpreter was the coming of the New Testament, and along these lines the visions in Revelation 4 and Ezekiel 1 are helpful for the interpretation of each other.

The point of Ezekiel's vision was to display the sovereignty of God in a time of woe. The Babylonian emperor ruled from his throne, but the trials facing Jerusalem ultimately came from God's more glorious throne. This was Ezekiel's great hope in his exile far from home: even in judgment, God would be faithful to his covenant promises to save.

As the book of Revelation begins its series of prophetic visions of events present and future, the apostle John receives virtually the same vision as the one presented to Ezekiel seven centuries earlier. While some details are different, the similarities between Ezekiel 1 and Revelation 4 are striking, and the message for John was the same as Ezekiel's. Though John was an exile on Patmos and though the churches of Asia faced looming persecution from the throne of Caesar in Rome, it was God who truly reigned over history. This message is important for today's Christians, who are pilgrims in a world that is not our home. As we prepare to face tribulation in our own day, we also are to know that our trials are all controlled by a faithful God and thus are certain to result in our salvation and the overthrow of evil.

THE SOVEREIGNTY OF GOD

Revelation is organized into seven sections, each presenting the history of the church age from God's perspective in heaven. These seven cycles become increasingly intense as they advance, and they increasingly narrow their focus toward the end of history. The key to identifying the sections is to note where Christ's return and the final judgment are described. Dispensationalists read Revelation as one continuous history, from chapters 1 to 22, resulting in complex and confusing explanations for the recurring depictions of Christ's return and God's final wrath. Revelation makes much better sense, however, when we recognize seven sections that present parallel depictions of history, each with its own perspective.

Revelation 4:1 begins the book's second section, a cycle that modestly begins looking forward into history. Jesus summons John, saying, "I will show you what must take place after this." Chapters 4 and 5 depict the present reality at the throne of heaven, and chapter 6 shows the breaking of the six seals of God's plan, concluding with "the wrath of the Lamb" from which the wicked vainly seek to hide (6:16–17). Chapter 7 concludes the second section with the praise of the redeemed in the glory of the age to come.

Knowing what is to come, we can understand why this vision focuses on the throne in heaven. William Hendriksen writes: "The purpose of this vision is to show us, in beautiful symbolism, that all things are governed by the Lord on the throne."[2] The visions that follow involve increasingly frightening scenes. The throne in heaven is therefore shown first to give comfort to believers in the midst of deadly trials. As Psalm 99:1 puts it: "The LORD reigns; let the peoples tremble! He sits enthroned upon the cherubim; let the earth quake!"

This vision begins with John looking and, "behold, a door standing open in heaven!" (Rev. 4:1). Like many prophets of old, such as Isaiah and Eze-kiel, and like Moses who was summoned atop Mount Sinai, John is called into God's presence by the voice of Christ: "Come up here, and I will show you what must take place" (4:1). An upward glance is often a sign of a new perspective, just as trumpets herald a new revelation, and for these John will be admitted to the heavenly tabernacle where God is enthroned in glory. This door is the third mentioned in Revelation. The first was a door of opportunity for ministry (3:8), and the second was the closed door of the church on which Christ knocked for admittance (3:20). This is a door of revelation so that John could see the things of God. Dispensationalists wrongly interpret John's summons as the rapture of the church in the end times. This completely misreads the text. Instead, John is taken up "in the Spirit" (1:10), who acted on John's senses and understanding so that John could be symbolically present in the true tabernacle above.

There, John saw "a throne" that "stood in heaven, with one seated on the throne" (Rev. 4:2). God's throne is mentioned thirty-eight times in the book of Revelation, seventeen of them in chapters 4 and 5. This is similar to the vision in which Isaiah "saw the Lord sitting upon a throne" (Isa. 6:1) during a crisis of sovereignty in Jerusalem, and aligns even more closely to Ezekiel's vision of God's throne beside the Chebar canal. G. B. Caird writes of John's vision on the Isle of Patmos: "To those who must live under the shadow of Caesar's throne, and find that that shadow is made darker by the

2. William Hendriksen, *More than Conquerors: An Interpretation of the Book of Revelation* (1940; repr., Grand Rapids: Baker, 1967), 84.

shadow of Satan's throne (2:13), the one truth that matters above all others is that there is a greater throne above."[3]

In addition to the symbolism of the throne, the vision has other indicators of God's sovereignty. Notice that Christ's voice says, "I will show you what must take place after this" (Rev. 4:1). Christ can foretell the future because he reigns sovereign over it. History does not consist of what *may* happen or even merely what *will* happen, but what *must* happen because it is ordained by the divine sovereign will. Moreover, God's sovereignty is highlighted by the placement of the throne at the center of all created reality, with angelic beings, the redeemed church, and hosts of angels around the throne of God and responding to him. When Christians think of God's sovereignty, we often think of his saving grace. But Revelation equally emphasizes God's sovereignty over the trials and persecutions facing his church, ordained by God for our good and his glory. We will see this reality emphasized throughout Revelation as the judgments and woes go forth from his throne out upon the earth (6:1–8, 16; 8:3–6; 16:17).

God's sovereign control over both judgment and salvation must have been a great comfort to exiles such as Ezekiel and the apostle John. It also gave hope to Alan Cameron, a Scottish Covenanter awaiting execution for refusing to accept the Scottish king's authority over Christ's church. The day before Cameron's execution, the royal authorities put his son, Richard, to death on the same charges. They cruelly brought the severed head and hands down to the elder Cameron's jail cell, asking if he could recognize them. "I know them, I know them," he answered. "They are my son's, my own dear son's." But instead of his faith being overthrown by this anguish, as was intended, Cameron drew strength from the sovereignty of his Lord. He said, "It is the Lord. Good is the will of the Lord, who cannot wrong me nor mine, but has made goodness and mercy to follow us all our days."[4] Believers who rejoice in God's sovereign control have peace to endure great trials. Paul wrote: "And we know that for those who love God all things work together for good" (Rom. 8:28).

The Centrality of Worship

3. G. B. Caird, *The Revelation of St. John the Divine* (San Francisco: Harper, 1966), 62.
4. Quoted in Douglas F. Kelly, *Revelation*, Mentor Expository Commentary (Tain, Ross-shire, Scotland: Mentor, 2012), 87–88.

Revelation 4 is justly considered one of the great chapters of the Bible, alongside John 3, Romans 8, and Hebrews 7. It shows not only the sovereignty of God over all history, but also the worship of God as the central activity of history. This point is depicted in verses 4–6: "Around the throne were twenty-four thrones, and seated on the thrones were twenty-four elders.... And around the throne, on each side of the throne, are four living creatures." As John's vision centers all creation on the realities of heaven, so also the heavenly occupation with the worship of God is creation's highest calling. Vern Poythress comments: "God is the all-important, all-determining spiritual center and power center for the universe." Therefore, "creatures find their consummate fulfillment, the meaning and full satisfaction of their existence, in worshiping, serving, and adoring him."[5]

Gathered around the throne in the heavenly holy of holies, John saw two remarkable gatherings. First, he mentions "twenty-four thrones, and seated on the thrones were twenty-four elders, clothed in white garments, with golden crowns on their heads" (Rev. 4:4). One theory about these elders points to 1 Chronicles 24:7–18, which organized Israel's priests into twenty-four shifts of duty, as for the temple singers (1 Chron. 25:6–31), and sees these elders as their angelic counterparts before God's heavenly throne. More likely, the twenty-four heavenly elders correspond to the twelve patriarchs of Israel combined with the twelve apostles, in this way symbolizing the redeemed church of both Testaments. This parallels the vision of Revelation 21, which reveals that "the names of the twelve tribes of the sons of Israel" are inscribed on the gates of the heavenly city and that the wall has twelve foundations on which are written the names of "the twelve apostles of the Lamb" (Rev. 21:12–14).

This vision is of great significance to believers on earth, especially those threatened with tribulation. Notice that in this heavenly depiction of history, the Christian church is given the most prominent place close to the throne of God. While the world looks upon the church and Christians as being the most insignificant people—this was especially the case of the seven churches in Asia to which John was writing—they are actually the most significant people, since they bear testimony to the gospel of Christ, and their worship is the most significant activity taking place in the world.

5. Vern S. Poythress, *The Returning King: A Guide to the Book of Revelation* (Phillipsburg, NJ: P&R Publishing, 2000), 98, 100.

Moreover, when we think of the martyrs who had already died and those of the early church threatened with death, we realize what wonderful news it must have been for them to see the redeemed church not only alive but reigning with Christ in glory.

Another reason to be confident that the twenty-four elders correspond to the church is the description that John highlights: they were "clothed in white garments, with golden crowns on their heads" (Rev. 4:4). This represents the consummation of the salvation promised and begun on earth. The white garments signify the righteousness granted to Christians through Christ as well as their calling to lives of holiness. Jesus wrote to Sardis that those "who have not soiled their garments . . . will walk with me in white, for they are worthy" (3:4). A crown is the reward for true believers, who in Christ triumph over sin: "Be faithful unto death," Jesus wrote to Smyrna, "and I will give you the crown of life" (2:10). Jesus had promised at the end of his seven letters that "the one who conquers, I will grant him to sit with me on my throne, as I also conquered and sat down with my Father on his throne" (3:21). These blessings, now dramatized in the vision of chapter 4, represent the reward not merely of certain choice believers but of all true Christians, those who not only profess faith in Jesus but live in faith to the end. Paul Gardner writes: "This is how it will be for all the redeemed. They will be in the presence of God and will reign with him and with Jesus."[6] James Ramsey declares:

> They are your representative, believer. Those thrones, and crowns, and priestly robes are yours. That position round and near to the throne of a covenant God is yours. Such is the place you occupy in the spiritual kingdom of God. Its purity, honour, power, and nearness to God are indeed, as yet, yours actually but in part; but if you are His at all in the covenant of His love, they shall be yours in actual possession, in all the glorious fullness of blessing and privilege which they imply, yours forever.[7]

In this way, John's vision reminds us of the high calling of every Christian life. Peter thus described us as "a royal priesthood, a holy nation,

6. Paul Gardner, *Revelation: The Compassion and Protection of Christ*, Focus on the Bible (Tain, Ross-shire, Scotland: Christian Focus, 2008), 71.

7. James B. Ramsey, *Revelation: An Exposition of the First III Chapters*, Geneva Commentaries (Edinburgh: Banner of Truth, 1977), 231.

a people for his own possession, that you may proclaim the excellencies of him who called you out of darkness into his marvelous light" (1 Peter 2:9). Like the faithful in Sardis, we are called to see that we do not defile our garments (Rev. 3:4), and like the saints of Philadelphia, we are urged to hold fast to what we have in Christ, in order to be assured of our heavenly crown (3:11).

Along with the joined saints of the Old and New Testaments gathered before the throne, John saw mysterious beings beside God's throne: "On each side of the throne, are four living creatures, full of eyes in front and behind" (Rev. 4:6). We would have difficulty identifying these beings if they were not present in the vision of Ezekiel 1. There, the "four living creatures" (Ezek. 1:5) have the same appearance as in Revelation 4, with only slight modifications. Moreover, in Ezekiel 10 they are identified as "cherubim," the mighty angelic attendants of God's throne. These were the glorious beings symbolized in gold atop the ark of the covenant, which was deemed the footstool of God's throne on earth. Like Ezekiel's cherubim, John's four living beings are covered in eyes and appear in four guises: "the first living creature like a lion, the second living creature like an ox, the third living creature with the face of a man, and the fourth living creature like an eagle in flight" (Rev. 4:7). These four faces represent the living creatures on earth. Along with man (the highest earthly creature) is "a lion (the highest wild animal), an ox (the highest domesticated animal), and an eagle (the highest bird)—symbolizing the fact that they embody within themselves all of the highest attributes of living creation."[8]

When you consider the four living creatures, standing for the created order of living beings, together with the redeemed church, and add the myriads of angels that Revelation 5:11 says are gathered around the believers, you have all those who will dwell in the eternal glory assembled around heaven's throne engaging in the single most important activity of all time: the worship of God. Therefore, the purpose of John's vision was to remind beleaguered believers not only of the sovereignty of God on the throne in heaven but also of the great calling of his people to give him glory in all things and at all times. James Boice summarizes: "Because God is in control

---

8. Duguid, *Ezekiel*, 58–59.

of all things we and all the creation must make it our primary activity and duty to worship him."[9]

THE CENTRALITY OF GOD IN WORSHIP

L. Frank Baum's classic book *The Wizard of Oz* tells of a girl, Dorothy, who like John on Patmos was an exile, having been blown by a tornado out of her home in Kansas. Needing help in a dangerous world, Dorothy makes a pilgrimage to the Emerald City, together with the Tin Woodman who needs a heart, the Cowardly Lion who lacks courage, and the Scarecrow missing a brain. Finally they appear before the great and powerful Wizard of Oz, attended by trumpet blasts and spouts of flame. But when the curtain is pulled back, a little man is revealed, pulling levers and pushing buttons. The mighty Wizard is a fraud who can do little to help anyone in real need.[10]

What a difference there was when John entered the inner sanctum of heaven. With the curtains drawn back and the door opened, John saw an awesome God who is almighty to accomplish all his will. John had already seen that God is enthroned as sovereign, along with the centrality of worship. Third, John's vision teaches the centrality of God in worship. Already we have observed that because of God's sovereignty, he is to be adored and served. But God is the great "because" of worship in all his attributes. John's vision displays a collage of images showing that we worship because of all that God is.

Having noted the *sovereignty* of God, we find that the next obvious thing to note about John's vision is the *glory* of God. Note how John makes no attempt to describe the "one seated on the throne" (Rev. 4:2). Paul said that God "dwells in unapproachable light, whom no one has ever seen or can see" (1 Tim. 6:16). Therefore, John describes the sounds, lights, and colors that radiate from the glory of the enthroned Lord. The closest he comes to depicting God's glory is to say that he "had the appearance of jasper and carnelian, and around the throne was a rainbow that had the appearance of an emerald" (Rev. 4:3).

---

9. James Montgomery Boice, *Revelation*, unpublished manuscript, n.d., chap. 13, p. 4.

10. This illustration is borrowed and adapted from Dennis E. Johnson, *Triumph of the Lamb: A Commentary on Revelation* (Phillipsburg, NJ: P&R Publishing, 2001), 95.

The modern-day jasper is a dull, opaque stone, but Revelation 21:11 describes it as being as "clear as crystal." Scholars thus think this was what we call a diamond. The carnelian, or sardius, stone was blood-red. These were joined with an emerald rainbow to present a staggering picture of divine beauty. "The stones intensify the light around the throne by reflecting the unapproachable brightness, and hence glory, surrounding God himself."[11] Such visible glory, which John can scarcely put into words, prompts the worship of God in heaven.

As the "because" of worship, the Lord is further revealed as the *faithful*, covenant-keeping God. This aspect of God is depicted by the emerald rainbow that encircles his throne. The rainbow was the emblem of God's covenant with Noah, which promised God's mercy to hold off judgment until the full number of the redeemed are gathered (Gen. 9:13). This vision highlights God's sovereignty as Creator, and so his faithfulness in covenant to the creation is glorified. In contrast to earthly rainbows, this bow completes a full circle, emphasizing God's eternal faithfulness. Moreover, the emerald rainbow is more than a hint that just as God provided a new, cleansed world for Noah and his family, God's covenant will usher in a new, green creation for those who trust in him. Paul Gardner writes: "Here, in picture form, is a warning not to interpret the disasters which will be talked about in the next part of the visions as if God had forgotten his promises to Noah. Even while God sits on the judgment throne, he is surrounded by his own covenant promises."[12]

God is further worshiped because of his *power*. This is probably the significance of the "sea of glass, like crystal," before God's throne (Rev. 4:6). There are numerous possible interpretations for this "sea," including the creation firmament that separated heaven from earth, which here would show God's transcendence. Or the sea could refer to the washing basins before the tabernacle, where the priests came to wash before serving, which would be a symbol of the cleansing grace of God in Christ. Most likely, however, especially in light of Revelation's later usage, the sea is a symbol for the chaos of unbelief and rebellion in the world against God. In Revelation, the first beast, which symbolizes government oppression, arises out of the sea

---

11. G. K. Beale, *The Book of Revelation: A Commentary on the Greek Text*, New International Greek Testament Commentary (Grand Rapids: Eerdmans, 1999), 321.

12. Gardner, *Revelation*, 70.

(13:1). With this in mind, we discern that the "sea of glass" represented the chaos of evil and unbelief that has been subdued by God's power. As God parted the Red Sea for Israel to pass over unscathed, God has subdued all evil and tumult so that his people can draw near to worship. In chapter 5, we find that Christ's death and resurrection have overcome the power of evil. Likewise, as Jesus once calmed the winds and the waves with his voice, he remains able today to give peace to the heart alarmed by the winds and waves of trouble in the world.

God is the great "because" of worship, not least in his *grace*, which is represented not only by the emerald rainbow but also by the seven torches of fire burning before the throne, "which are the seven spirits of God" (Rev. 4:5). Seven speaks of completion and thus the all-sufficient ministry of the Holy Spirit. Through the Spirit-inspired Word, God sends light from his throne to bring salvation to his people. In Revelation 1:4, John declared "grace . . . and peace" from God by means of "the seven spirits who are before his throne." In a similar vision, Zechariah 4:6 spoke of God's saving grace: "Not by might, nor by power, but by my Spirit, says the LORD of hosts."

Finally, God is worshiped because he is *holy*. The "flashes of lightning, and rumblings and peals of thunder" (Rev. 4:5), speak of God's glory in general but especially his holiness. The clear parallel is to the lightning and thunder that boomed from Mount Sinai when the Lord was present giving his law. The holiness of God is one of the chief reasons to worship him. The four living creatures before the throne cry: "Holy, holy, holy, is the Lord God Almighty, who was and is and is to come!" (4:8). Because of the glory of all his attributes, God is himself always at the center of worship and is alone the recipient of the adoration of his people.

CHRIST'S SUMMONS TO THE THRONE

When we remember God's holiness, see the majesty of his throne, and then spy the fearful cherubic guardians, the pressing question is how any of us could ever enter this scene of worship. We remember that images of cherubim were woven into the veil that separated Israelites from the holy of holies and kept them from the presence of God's holiness. A mighty cherub was given the flaming sword to bar fallen Adam from the Tree of Life (Gen. 3:24). How, then, will we enter the heavenly tabernacle to worship God in the presence of the four living creatures, since we have broken his laws and have stained our garments in sin?

The answer is not for us to perform works of our own to commend us to God, since the problem of our sin is too difficult and the record of our past sins condemns us. The answer for us is the same as for John. Even the apostle entered the heavenly glory only when Jesus called to him, saying, "Come" (Rev. 4:1). Jesus calls us, saying, "Come" to the cross, where his blood cleansed us from the guilt of sin once for all. Jesus invites us to the empty tomb, where his resurrection provides conquering life for those who believe. And now Jesus bids us to look into heaven and see what is ours if we come to God through faith in him alone. Christ has prepared clean garments, crowns, and thrones for all who answer his summons. Have you come to Christ? He calls you, even now, saying, "Come." The last chapter of Revelation tells us of our place in the eternal temple, and of the glory that will belong to us, if we answer Jesus' call to come and walk before God through faith in his Son:

> No longer will there be anything accursed, but the throne of God and of the Lamb will be in it, and his servants will worship him. They will see his face . . . . They will need no light of lamp or sun, for the Lord God will be their light, and they will reign forever and ever. (Rev. 22:3–4)

17

THE WEIGHT OF GLORY

Revelation 4:6–11

Worthy are you, our Lord and God, to receive glory and honor
and power, for you created all things, and by your will
they existed and were created. (Rev. 4:11)

*I*n the previous chapter I asserted that Revelation 4 should be considered one of the Bible's greatest chapters. My reasoning is that it presents what is perhaps the most informative vision of the glory of God as he reigns in heaven. Many other chapters considered among the Bible's greatest—Psalm 23, Isaiah 53, and Romans 8—focus on the vital subject of what God has done and continues to do for our salvation. But Revelation 4 presents us with God himself in the radiant glory of his enthroned being. G. B. Caird calls it a vision "of omnipotent majesty," "a mystery to be explored only by the humility of worship."[1]

Those who grow in their awareness of God inevitably wish to see him more clearly. Moses pleaded, "Please show me your glory" (Ex. 33:18). God permitted him to see only the "back" of his glory (33:23), which may be analogous to the symbolic vision given in Revelation 4. This vision of divine

1. G. B. Caird, *The Revelation of St. John the Divine* (San Francisco: Harper, 1966), 63.

176

splendor is probably the closest we will come on this side of heaven to seeing the majesty of God with our eyes.

The question is inevitably raised whether this vision, conveyed through words, shows what God and heaven "really" look like. The answer is that, like all other apocalyptic literature, Revelation presents reality in the form of symbols. Later in Revelation, Satan will be depicted as a dragon and the persecuting Antichrist as a beast. These are symbols, not photographs, yet they show what Satan and his servants are "really" like. Likewise, we would not see God and heaven more clearly even if the symbols could be replaced with the kind of unmediated vision that God told Moses is impossible for man (Ex. 33:20). Psalm 104:2 observes that God clothes himself "with light as with a garment," not to conceal but to reveal himself to us. We may be sure that John literally saw the things recorded in this vision, symbols designed to make visible the invisible God: God's jewel-refracted throne, the emerald rainbow, the four living creatures, and the enthroned elders. This symbolic vision shows the reality of how God chooses to display the glory of his countenance, in a clearer and more radiant form than perhaps anywhere else in the Bible.

GREAT THEMES IN REVELATION 4

In order to plumb some of the greatness of this chapter, let me point out some themes that should enflame our minds. The first impression we should glean from this vision is the surpassing preeminence and majesty of God. Nothing is more important or interesting than God. No subject is so mind- and soul-expanding as God. No earthly pastime should loosen the grip of our imagination from the wonder of contemplating God's glory.

One way to approach the preeminence of God is to understand the Hebrew word for *glory*. The basic meaning of the word *kabod* is "weighty." The point is that God is consequential: a heavyweight, not a lightweight. God is infinitely substantial, the very opposite of chaff that blows in the wind. Philip Ryken writes: "No one has more influence. No one has a higher position or a weightier reputation. No one is more deserving of honor, recognition and praise."[2]

2. Philip Graham Ryken, *Discovering God in Stories from the Bible* (Wheaton, IL: Crossway, 1999), 16.

As Revelation 4 presents the weighty preeminence of God, we face one of the chief ailments of Christianity today. In assessing American evangelicalism, David Wells has commented on "the weightlessness of God." Wells explains that to professing Christians, "God has become unimportant. He rests upon the world so inconsequentially as not to be noticeable."[3] Wells does not mean that something has happened to God, but rather that something has happened to our attitude toward him. In the place of God, man sees himself on the throne. Even Christians today are preoccupied not with knowing God and his will but with matching our own preferences and suiting our own needs.

If evangelicals are disinterested in God, the emerging postmodern spirituality has an especially weightless view of deity. Wells cites Sheila Larson, who answered a survey by describing her religion as "Sheilaism." This faith has no church but consists of her own personal religion. Where does Sheila find the truths of Sheilaism? She answers, "Just my own little voice." Wells comments that for postmoderns, "the self becomes the main form of reality" and the self "is what life is about."[4]

When we turn back to Revelation 4, its vision of God in his majesty smashes any pretensions to self-derived religion. The fact that the four living creatures have "eyes all around" and six wings each (Rev. 4:8) is surely related to God's supremacy. The cherubim have been everywhere and seen everything. Their sublime intelligence has concluded that God is to be the chief subject of our interest and the sole object of our worship. Seeing God enthroned in glory, we can only follow the twenty-four elders by falling on our faces (4:10), casting any crowns of ours at his feet, singing, "Worthy are you, our Lord and God, to receive glory and honor and power" (4:11).

A second impression we gain from this vision is the right longing of the human heart for glory. Christians sometimes see the Bible's call to humility as opposed to a wholesome craving for glory. In fact, man was made for glory. We were designed to be glory-seekers. This is why people exult in movie stars and sports icons. Certainly, the glorification of entertainment and sports *idols* is appropriately named: it is idolatry to grant the status of

3. David F. Wells, *God in the Wasteland: The Reality of Truth in a World of Fading Dreams* (Grand Rapids: Eerdmans, 1994), 88–90.
4. David F. Wells, *Above All Earthly Pow'rs: Christ in a Postmodern World* (Grand Rapids: Eerdmans, 2005), 150–53.

god or goddess to any creature. But the quest for glory itself is implanted in the human heart by God in order to be satisfied by none other than himself. People marvel at how thousands are religiously drawn to stadiums to cheer ecstatically for a long touchdown pass or pack into the arenas for a music concert. The reason is that we crave even a fleeting earthly experience of the glory for which we were made. Yet the only true glory is found in the person of God and in his saving works.

Christians should not only repudiate idolatry, but also open our hearts to the glory of God. This is the picture we see in Revelation 4. Blazing at the center of creation is the transcendent splendor of the glorious God. In John's vision this majesty has enthralled both the twenty-four elders and the angelic myriads surrounding them. Revelation holds before us an exalted vision of heaven's glory, and we impoverish ourselves if we do not frequently refresh our souls in meditation on the splendors of our God.

In a memorable essay, *The Weight of Glory*, C. S. Lewis noted that believers are currently on the outside of the glory we see reflected in nature. But he urges us to look on nature's lesser glory—the blazing sunrise or the burning autumn leaves—and realize that we will soon be within the true glory they signal. We should, Lewis says, "take the imagery of Scripture seriously, [and] believe that God will one day *give* us the Morning Star and cause us to *put on* the splendor of the sun." We see the echoes of a coming glory in the beauty of nature, yet we cannot now "mingle with the splendours we see." But he adds that

> all the leaves of the New Testament are rustling with the rumor that it will not always be so. Some day, God willing, we shall get in. . . . [We] will put on . . . that greater glory of which Nature is only the first sketch. . . . Nature is mortal; we shall outlive her. When all the suns and nebulae have passed away, each one of you will still be alive. . . . We are summoned to pass in through Nature, beyond her, into that splendor which she fitfully reflects.[5]

The third impression that I suggest from Revelation 4 pertains to the beauty that is so integral to this vision. Notice that the sights of this vision are surpassingly beautiful, and no doubt the angel voices, together with those of the twenty-four elders, excel the loveliness of any sound heard on

5. C. S. Lewis, *The Weight of Glory and Other Addresses* (New York: Macmillan, 1962), 16–17.

earth. All this reminds Christians to value and cultivate the classical triad of virtue: the good, the true, and the beautiful.

It is a shame that in their fervor to distance themselves from Roman Catholicism, many heirs of the Reformation set themselves against visual beauty, especially in the worship of God. But how out of place is such an attitude in light of the worship of heaven seen in this chapter. Medieval Christians built cathedrals to draw the mind upward to God; one cannot enter one of the ancient sanctuaries of Europe without feeling reverence and awe. Today, evangelicals build "worship centers" for the convenience of the "audience," drawing our eyes horizontally to the people around us rather than to God above.

The second commandment condemns the making of "a carved image, or any likeness" for the sake of bowing down to it (Ex. 20:4–5). Many Reformed Christians interpret this as a repudiation of all visual imagery in worship. They fail to note, however, that while there were to be no images of God himself, God commanded that images of great beauty should adorn the tabernacle, including the golden cherubim atop the ark of the covenant and a variety of nature images recalling the garden of Eden (Ex. 25–28). Clearly, then, God has not forbidden visual beauty in places of worship, since he has designed beauty to provoke worship. We are encouraged all through the Bible, especially in Revelation, to cultivate beauty in our worship: visually, through worship spaces designed to lift up the soul to God, and audibly, through music that adorns God's Word with beautiful sounds. The most important form of beauty for Christians to cultivate is "the beauty of holiness" (Ps. 29:2 kjv), reflecting back to God the loveliness of his own character as his grace has formed it in our hearts.

It surely is not by chance that the secularist postmodern society in which we live is resolved to mar beauty of all kinds, including the beauty of the human form. There can be little doubt that many youths today cover their bodies with tattoos and body piercings as an outward expression of a barrenness they feel in their hearts. Christians must therefore not only cultivate true and godly beauty in the things that we make and do, but also communicate the beauty and value of people who were made in God's image. Revelation 4 reminds us that we are a race designed by God to bear the image of the beauty seen in this vision: in our bodies, our character, our relationships, our deeds, and especially our worship.

WHAT WORSHIP IS

When we think of worship, Christians should realize our great need for biblical models in honoring God. One episode that reveals our need for instruction is recorded in Exodus 32. The tribes of Israel, gathered at Mount Sinai, wanted to hold a festival of honor and celebration for the Lord. They therefore brought their gold and jewels to Aaron, the high priest, and in accordance with their wishes he made a golden calf for them to worship. It is important for us to realize that this was not the worship of a false god but a false attempt to worship the true God. According to the desires and folly of their own hearts, the Israelites cast the golden calf for the worship of the Lord (Ex. 32:1–5). God responded with wrathful judgments on his people who worshiped according to their own designs.

Revelation 4 provides insights into the worship of God in heaven. Its most basic principle is that worship is praise in response to God's revelation of himself. We see this in the worship of the four living creatures, who "day and night . . . never cease" giving praise to God (Rev. 4:8). In our study of these angelic beings, we noted that with their faces of a lion, an ox, a man, and an eagle, they represent all the classes of living beings on earth. As representatives, they exhibit by their worship, as G. K. Beale puts it, "the function that all creation is meant to fulfill[:] . . . to praise God for his holiness and glorify him for his work of creation." Like the four living creatures, the whole of creation pours forth praise to God unceasingly, day and night without end. The cherubim are joined by the twenty-four elders, who "represent the purpose of redeemed humanity, which is to praise and glorify God."[6]

When we use the English word *worship*, we should notice two important things. The first is that it is a transitive, not an intransitive, verb. This means that worship must always have a direct object. Many people state that they are "just worshiping." But we always worship *someone* or *something*. In many churches today, the worship service is designed with unbelieving visitors in mind or to appeal to the tastes of the congregation. True Christian worship, however, has only one target audience: the glorious God enthroned in heaven. True worship is summarized in Revelation 5:13 as being directed to

6. G. K. Beale, *The Book of Revelation: A Commentary on the Greek Text*, New International Greek Testament Commentary (Grand Rapids: Eerdmans, 1999), 332.

"him who sits on the throne and to the Lamb," giving "blessing and honor and glory and might" to our God. While visitors and the congregation are blessed by true worship, Douglas Kelly rightly argues that the most important principle is that Christian worship "ought to be centered on God. It ought to celebrate God. It ought to turn people's hearts toward God. It ought to lift them out of their selves towards God. . . . The power and the glory, the strength and the life of a worship service is to celebrate God, to center on him."[7] This is precisely what the four living beings and the twenty-four enthroned elders are doing in Revelation 4.

Second, we should note that *worship* comes from an older English word, *worthship*. To worship God is to acclaim his worth: we praise God because he is worthy of our adoration. For this reason, we see in this vision that God is worshiped for the glory of his attributes. Revelation highlights three attributes of God, which are celebrated in the worship of the cherubim: God's holiness, power, and eternity.

The worship of the four living creatures highlights the *holiness* of God: "They never cease to say, 'Holy, holy, holy'" (Rev. 4:8). This scene echoes the angelic worship shown in Isaiah 6. We earlier compared the four living beings to the cherubim of Ezekiel 1, but they are also like the worshiping seraphim of Isaiah's vision, bearing six wings and singing what is known as the *Trisagion*, "Holy, holy, holy." In the Bible, repetition marks special emphasis, and of all of God's attributes, only holiness receives threefold repetition. Holiness is God's transcendent separation above all creation and is his preeminent attribute. Jesus addressed God as "Holy Father" (John 17:11) and taught as our first petition in prayer, "Hallowed be your name" (Matt. 6:9). Geerhardus Vos wrote: "In Jehovah's holiness his divinity as it were concentrates itself. It is exalted above the possibility of sin—in him, as the absolutely good, evil cannot enter."[8] Because of God's holiness, Moses removed his shoes before the burning bush. We should likewise worship the holy God in reverence and awe (Heb. 12:28–29).

The living creatures also praise God's *power*, calling him "Lord God Almighty" (Rev. 4:8). *Almighty* is the Greek word *pantokrator*, a title falsely employed by the Caesars. Yet it is God alone who is truly omnipotent and

---

7. Douglas F. Kelly, *Revelation*, Mentor Expository Commentary (Tain, Ross-shire, Scotland: Mentor, 2012), 103.

8. Geerhardus Vos, *Grace and Glory* (1922; repr., Edinburgh: Banner of Truth, 1994), 269.

thus able to save. Stephen Charnock writes: "How vain would be his eternal counsels, if power did not step in to execute them. His mercy would be a feeble pity, if he were destitute of power to relieve; and his justice a slighted scarecrow, without power to punish; his promises an empty sound, without power to accomplish them."[9] A. W. Pink adds: "God's power is like Himself: infinite, eternal, incomprehensible: it can neither be checked, restrained, nor frustrated by the creature."[10] We can imagine how this praise to God's power would have encouraged the churches to which John was writing, as they were about to enter a time of persecution and testing.

The third attribute for which God is praised is his *eternity*: "who was and is and is to come!" (Rev. 4:8). God's eternity emphasizes his sovereign control, since he is before and after all things. William Barclay comments: "Empires might come and empires might go; God lasts forever. Here is the triumphant affirmation that God endures unchanging amid the enmity and the rebellion of human beings."[11]

God is praised not only for what he is, but also for what he does. Revelation 5 will praise God for his redeeming work in Christ. Chapter 4 praises God for the glory of his work as Creator. We see this in the worship of the twenty-four elders, representing the redeemed church: "Worthy are you, our Lord and God, to receive glory and honor and power, for you created all things, and by your will they existed and were created" (Rev. 4:11). God made and even now upholds all that there is, and for this he is rightly to be praised.

When we look into the starry sky, we see a panoply of praise to God's glory, just as Psalm 8:1 declared, "You have set your glory above the heavens." Among the starry host are entire galaxies, shining as one because they are so distant. With the aid of telescopes, our eyes can see millions and billions of stars and galaxies. Our own galaxy, the Milky Way, contains at least two hundred billion stars and rotates majestically in space, spanning over seven hundred thousand trillion miles. The God who reveals himself to us in the Bible and sent his Son to make an atoning death for our sin is the God who made this glorious universe and sustains it now in accordance with his will. James Boice comments: "The saints in heaven praise God for

9. Stephen Charnock, *The Existence and Attributes of God*, 2 vols. (Grand Rapids: Baker, 1996), 2:15.
10. Arthur W. Pink, *The Attributes of God* (Grand Rapids: Baker, 1993), 46.
11. William Barclay, *The Revelation of John*, 3rd ed., 2 vols., New Daily Study Bible (Louisville: Westminster John Knox, 2004), 1:78.

the wonders of his creation. Shouldn't we, who are part of that creation, do so also in our worship?"[12]

When we consider how great is God's glory as Creator, we remember why our praise is given to him alone. The Christians of the first century refused to acclaim Caesar as God, suffering death for their exclusive devotion to Christ as Lord. So must Christians today refuse to bow before the idols of our age. Craig Keener writes: "God alone is God, and he alone merits first place—beyond every other love, every other anxiety, every other fear that consumes us."[13] Indeed, the logic of Revelation suggests that the best way to keep ourselves from idolatry is to gather with fellow believers to praise the holy, almighty, and eternal Creator God.

WHAT WORSHIPERS DO

① Humble ourselves

Having seen what worship is from John's vision of heaven, we should conclude with observations about what worshipers do. The four living creatures and the enthroned elders show us three things. First, their example urges us to *humble* ourselves in the presence of the holy, almighty, and eternal God.

The humility of the four living creatures is suggested by their six wings. This points back to Isaiah's vision of the seraphim, who used two wings to cover their faces, two to cover their feet, and two to fly (Isa. 6:2). Why would these angels cover their faces? The answer: to humbly show how much more glorious is the brightness of God even compared to their own blazing glory. Moreover, by covering their feet, they bore testimony to their creaturely humility. We also see humility in the elders, who "fall down before him who is seated on the throne and worship him who lives forever and ever" (Rev. 4:10). When God is lifted up, human pride is always cast down, and so it should be in worship. This is why, whether or not we are physically able to kneel in the presence of God, our hearts ought always to be prostrate before him, especially in gathered worship. The Bible says, "Humble yourselves before the Lord, and he will exalt you" (James 4:10).

② Rejoice in worshiping God

Second, God's people *rejoice* in worshiping him. This attitude is urged throughout the Psalms. Psalm 97:12 urges: "Rejoice in the LORD, O you

---

12. James Montgomery Boice, *Revelation*, unpublished manuscript, n.d., chap. 14, p. 9.
13. Craig S. Keener, *Revelation*, NIV Application Commentary (Grand Rapids: Zondervan, 1999), 182.

184

righteous, and give thanks to his holy name!" We can infer joy in Revelation 4 through the songs that the worshipers were singing. These are the first of the many hymns recorded in Revelation, all of which joyfully celebrate the glory of God's person and works, especially as he saves his beleaguered people. Congregational singing in praise to God should thus be one of our chief joys this side of heaven. Boice writes: "Music is a gift from God that allows us to express our deepest heart responses to God and his truth in meaningful and memorable ways. It is a case of our hearts joining with our minds to say, 'Yes! Yes! Yes!' to the truths we are embracing."[14]

Finally, we worship God by *confessing* him as Savior and Lord. When George Frideric Handel's *Messiah* was performed in 1743, England's King George II gave his confession by standing for the "Hallelujah Chorus," beginning a tradition that continues today. He rose with head bowed to confess that while he was sovereign of England, Jesus Christ is King of kings, the Messiah who reigns forever and ever.

The twenty-four elders gave their confession by "cast[ing] their crowns before the throne, saying, 'Worthy are you, our Lord and God'" (Rev. 4:10–11). They were acclaiming their submission to God as the only true Sovereign. They were confessing that any glory of their own as Christ's people has come from God and is for his praise only. How exciting it is for Christians to realize that by God's grace in Christ, we are in this life gaining crowns to cast at his feet, adding the testimony of our lives to the praise of the entire creation forever.

One day each of us will stand before God. If you are not a Christian, cleansed from your sin by the redeeming blood of Christ, you will hear God's dreadful pronouncement of your guilt and eternal punishment. If you are a believer in Christ, you will rejoice to hear God's admission into the holy courts of eternal praise in heaven. Will you have a crown to lay at God's feet on that day? Surely we will realize then what now so few seem to know: that our chief end and our greatest blessing is to live for the praise of God forever and be able to say, with rejoicing in our hearts, "To God alone be all the glory!"

14. Boice, *Revelation*, chap. 14, p. 2.

18

THE LION AND THE LAMB

Revelation 5:1–7

And one of the elders said to me, "Weep no more; behold, the
Lion of the tribe of Judah, the Root of David, has conquered, so
that he can open the scroll and its seven seals." (Rev. 5:5)

*T*he British philosopher Bertrand Russell is considered one of
the leading atheistic thinkers of the twentieth century. Russell
asserted that history is the chance product of a causeless series
of events. He wrote that man's "origin, his growth, his hopes and fears, his
loves and his beliefs, are but the outcome of random collocations of atoms."
Realists must accept, he insisted, "that all the inspiration, all the noonday
brightness of human genius, are destined to extinction in the vast death of
the solar system." Russell concluded: "Only within the scaffolding of these
truths, only on the firm foundation of unyielding despair, can the soul's
habitation henceforth be safely built."[1]

As we turn in our study to the fifth chapter of Revelation, we discover
the apostle John as one who briefly feels the despair of which Russell wrote.
Seeing the scroll of the divine will in the hand of God, John hears that no one

1. Bertrand Russell, *Why I Am Not a Christian* (New York: Simon & Schuster, 1957), 107.

is worthy to break the seals to open the scroll. In short, John contemplates a world without Christ, a history with no Mediator between God and man. Like Russell, John views this as a scene of deep despair. He writes: "I began to weep loudly because no one was found worthy to open the scroll or to look into it" (Rev. 5:4).

In this way, John felt how heartbreaking is the thought of a world without God and Jesus Christ. He saw what Bertrand Russell seems not to have realized, that a foundation of despair is no foundation at all. Revelation 5 shows both the necessity of Christ for hope and meaning and the good news of Christ's coming as the Lamb who conquered by being slain. James Hamilton summarizes: "By his death and resurrection Jesus has taken control of history. . . . Jesus is the one who will right the wrongs and heal the hurts and wipe away the tears."[2] John saw the good news of a Savior in Jesus Christ as the only foundation not for despair but for hope, since the gospel bears a message not of cosmic extinction but of eternal life by the saving will of God.

No One Worthy

In Revelation 4, John was admitted through a door into heaven to see the worship around God's throne. In chapter 5, John tells us what he continued to see, starting with an object in the hand of God: "Then I saw in the right hand of him who was seated on the throne a scroll written within and on the back, sealed with seven seals" (Rev. 5:1). This scroll and the opening of its seals play an important role in Revelation, providing material for the chapters to come.

There are a number of theories about this scroll, four of which are most notable. First, some believe the scroll is the last will and testament of Jesus, containing what Peter described as "an inheritance that is imperishable, undefiled, and unfading, kept in heaven for you" (1 Peter 1:4). A second view holds that the scroll in God's hand is the Book of Life that contains the names of those who have been redeemed by Christ. The problem with both of these views is that when the seals are broken, the scroll reveals not Christ's blessings on his people but the outpouring of God's judgments on the earth.

2. James M. Hamilton Jr., *Revelation: The Spirit Speaks to the Churches* (Wheaton, IL: Crossway, 2012), 151.

A third view asserts that the scroll is the Old Testament as brought to full explanation by Jesus. It is true, as Jesus insisted, that "beginning with Moses and all the Prophets, . . . all the Scriptures [teach] the things concerning himself" (Luke 24:27). Nonetheless, nothing in Revelation suggests that this scroll is the Old Testament.

The fourth and best understanding of the scroll in Revelation 5 is the entirety of God's will for history, both in judging the wicked and in redeeming his people. This scroll is written on both sides, showing that it contains the entire story of God's will. According to William Hendriksen, the scroll "symbolizes God's purpose with respect to the entire universe throughout history, and concerning all creatures in all ages and to all eternity."[3] G. B. Caird comments: "The scroll is God's redemptive plan, foreshadowed in the Old Testament, by which he means to assert his sovereignty over a sinful world and so to achieve the purpose of creation."[4]

The appearing of this scroll raised an immediate problem, however. John "saw a strong angel proclaiming with a loud voice, 'Who is worthy to open the scroll and break its seals?'" (Rev. 5:2). He realizes that there must be one with the worthiness and right to stand before God, receive the scroll, and open its seals. Unless this could happen, the content of God's book would not be revealed and the will of God for history would not be performed. Vern Poythress explains, "The destiny of John, of the church, and of the universe itself hangs in the balance over the question of whether someone can open the scroll."[5] John lamented because "no one in heaven or on earth or under the earth was able to open the scroll or to look into it" (5:3). This realization shattered him: "and I began to weep loudly because no one was found worthy to open the scroll or to look into it" (5:4).

Undoubtedly, part of the reason for John's weeping arose from his awareness of his own unworthiness and that of the entire human race. Man was created by God to exercise his authority, which is why God blessed Adam with dominion over the earth (Gen. 1:28). Adam fell from that authority, however, by violating God's commandment. When Adam sinned (3:6), he

---

3. William Hendriksen, *More than Conquerors: An Interpretation of the Book of Revelation* (1940; repr., Grand Rapids: Baker, 1967), 89.

4. G. B. Caird, *The Revelation of St. John the Divine* (San Francisco: Harper, 1966), 72.

5. Vern S. Poythress, *The Returning King: A Guide to the Book of Revelation* (Phillipsburg, NJ: P&R Publishing, 2000), 109.

plummeted himself and all his descendants into the state of guilt and corruption. As a man, John now looks upon the scroll and hears that none is worthy to open it, and he tastes the bitterness of man's sinful condition. Philip Hughes remarks how this scene shows that "there is nothing more deplorable and more calamitous in the story of mankind than our total unworthiness as sinful creatures in the presence of our Maker. Nothing is more lamentable than the fact that by our own ungodliness we have deprived ourselves of all worthiness."[6]

John must further have wept over the unopened scroll because of the blessings promised to believers that could be revealed only by the breaking of its seals. Hendriksen writes:

> You will understand the meaning of these tears if you constantly bear in mind that in this beautiful vision the opening of the scroll by breaking the seals indicates the execution of God's plan. When the scroll is opened and the seals are broken, then the universe is governed in the interest of the Church. Then, God's glorious, redemptive purpose is being realized; His plan is being carried out and the contents of the scroll come to pass in the history of the universe. But if the scroll is not opened it means that there will be no protection for God's children in the hours of bitter trial; no judgments upon a persecuting world; no ultimate triumph for believers; no new heaven and earth; no future inheritance.[7]

In a way that is analogous to John's weeping, Christians are sometimes grieved when God's will seems frustrated in our experience. We look on the church and see compromise and decline. Like the Christians to whom John was writing, we may even face persecution for our witness to the gospel. We may feel similar frustration in our families, as covenant children go astray or marriage vows are broken. How is it that we fall short of the blessings designed for God's covenant people? As John learned, the answer will often be found in our own disobedience and sin, the wages of which bring us to tears. Like John, we will find relief only through the appearing of Jesus in victory, which is the message of Revelation 5:5–7.

6. Philip Edgcumbe Hughes, *The Book of Revelation* (Downers Grove, IL: InterVarsity Press, 1990), 78.

7. Hendriksen, *More than Conquerors*, 89.

WEEP NO MORE

It is probably significant that relief comes to John not from an angel, who knows no bitterness for sin, but from a fellow redeemed believer: "One of the elders said to me, 'Weep no more.'" As one who equally relies on the saving work of Christ, the elder cries: "Behold, the Lion of the tribe of Judah, the Root of David, has conquered, so that he can open the scroll and its seven seals" (Rev. 5:5).

This is the only Bible verse that refers to Jesus as the "Lion of . . . Judah," yet the image is so inspiring that it is one of Christ's titles that is most beloved to Christians. This title sees in Jesus the fulfillment of Jacob's prophecy when he departed from his sons. "Judah is a lion's cub," Jacob said, and foresaw a royal dynasty emerging from this tribe (Gen. 49:9–10). Jesus was that promised heir from Judah, the Divine Warrior who rules history like a lion who reigns unchallenged over his domain.

Jesus is further referred to as "the Root of David" (Rev. 5:5). This title is based on the prophecy of Isaiah 11, which sees God as bringing peace to the earth: "They shall not hurt or destroy in all my holy mountain; for the earth shall be full of the knowledge of the LORD as the waters cover the sea" (Isa. 11:9). This blessed state will be secured by the One who comes as "the root of Jesse" (11:10), who was David's father. The house of David would be almost cut off because of sin, Isaiah said, yet "a shoot" would come "from the stump of Jesse, and a branch from his roots shall bear fruit" (11:1). This promise describes Jesus, who was born of the line of David when that household seemed virtually snuffed out and yet came in the power of God's Spirit to bring salvation to earth. As the Lion of Judah and the Root of David, Jesus embodies the fulfillment of the Old Testament promises and gives proof that God's saving plan is being achieved.

Hearing these words must have lifted John's heart, but the sight that followed was even more dramatic: "And between the throne and the four living creatures and among the elders I saw a Lamb standing, as though it had been slain" (Rev. 5:6). How astonishing this is: John is told of a Lion, but upon looking he sees a Lamb! One reason for this transformed appearance is where Jesus stood: "between the throne . . . and among the elders," that is, in the mediator's position between God and man. Though he is a Lion, Jesus reconciles his people to God through his ministry as the Lamb.

REVELATION 5:1–7

Jesus' appearance as both Lion and Lamb is part of his glory as the incarnate Savior for his people. We know from experience that a person is usually either lionlike, strong and dominating, or lamblike, meek in servanthood. But Christ joins these virtues in perfect balance and harmony. In a sermon titled "The Excellency of Christ," Jonathan Edwards marveled at this combination of apparent contradictions. Christ "is thus above all, yet He is lowest of all in humility. . . . In the person of Christ meet together infinite majesty and transcendent meekness."[8] As the Lion, Jesus wields God's sovereign power to rule. As the Lamb, he exercises a spirit of obedience. Jesus, alone among all mankind, could declare: "I have kept my Father's commandments and abide in his love" (John 15:10). Jesus is thus worthy as true God and perfect Man, Lion and Lamb, Lord and Servant.

It is significant that John saw the "Lamb standing, as though it had been slain." The idea is that he endured death but emerged victorious. He stands with emblems of his spiritual equipping: "with seven horns and with seven eyes" (Rev. 5:6). In the Bible, horns are symbols of power lifted up against one's enemies. "Seven horns" means complete power, that is, divine omnipotence. The seven eyes, John explains, "are the seven spirits of God sent out into all the earth" (5:6), that is, the Holy Spirit. Isaiah 11:2 says of the root of Jesse that "the Spirit of the LORD shall rest upon him, the Spirit of wisdom and understanding, the Spirit of counsel and might, the Spirit of knowledge and the fear of the LORD." Jesus is fully animated by the Holy Spirit and thus is worthy in divine power to take and open the scroll, that is, to reveal and accomplish God's saving will.

Perhaps most significant of all in this vision, Jesus the Lion, in his divine omnipotence, has conquered by the work he performed as the Lamb. The One who "conquered, so that he can open the scroll and its seven seals" (Rev. 5:5), stands as a Lamb that had been slain. Jesus is referred to as a Lamb twenty-eight times in Revelation, marking his atoning death as the central achievement that accomplished victory for his people. Vern Poythress marvels at what he calls "the central paradox and mystery of the Christian faith," that "God achieved his triumph and delivered his people not through the fireworks of military might, but through the weakness of crucifixion."[9]

8. Jonathan Edwards, *Altogether Lovely: Jonathan Edwards on the Glory and Excellency of Jesus Christ* (Morgan, PA: Soli Deo Gloria, 1997), 21–24.

9. Poythress, *The Returning King*, 109.

191

The atoning work of the slain Lamb was introduced at the scene of the first sin, in the garden of Eden. Adam and Eve had broken God's command, the penalty of which was death. God declared the gospel by providing a substitute to suffer death in their place, satisfying God's justice against their sin: "The LORD God made for Adam and for his wife garments of skins and clothed them" (Gen. 3:21). James Boice writes that the "sacrifice of the animals taught the principle of vicarious atonement, the innocent dying for the guilty, while the use of their skins to clothe Adam and Eve taught the principle of an imputed righteousness,"[10] that is, the righteousness earned by Christ but credited to those who believe in him.

Throughout the Old Testament the sacrifices of animals continued, reminding God's people that their sins could be removed only by the death of a worthy sacrifice. In the Passover, Israel was delivered from Egypt by the lamb's blood that warded against the angel of death. On the annual Day of Atonement, the high priest entered the holy of holies with the lamb's sacrificial blood to turn away God's wrath from the people. These were powerful pictures of the reality that would be achieved by Jesus when he died on the cross. Jesus explained to the Emmaus road disciples, who were dismayed by his crucifixion, that this was the central teaching of the Old Testament: "Was it not necessary that the Christ should suffer these things and enter into his glory?" (Luke 24:26). It was by stepping forth as the true sacrificial Lamb, bearing the sins of his people, that Jesus conquered and removed the barrier to God's saving will: he bore the guilt of sin under God's law and freed his people from the penalty they deserved.

Therefore, when John saw that the Lamb "went and took the scroll from the right hand of him who was seated on the throne" (Rev. 5:7), he was witnessing the exaltation of Christ to the seat of authority in heaven with the Father, after his atoning death and victorious resurrection from the grave.

Here is John's reply to Bertrand Russell and other skeptics who deny any foundation for hope in this world! William Hendriksen comments: "Christ, as Mediator, at His ascension received authority to rule the universe according to God's eternal decree. . . . As a reward for his redemptive work, Christ, on ascending into heaven, received for Himself the kingdom."[11] No wonder that John should "weep no more" (Rev. 5:5), since the enthroned

---

10. James Montgomery Boice, *Revelation*, unpublished manuscript, n.d., chap. 15, p. 8.
11. Hendriksen, *More than Conquerors*, 90–91.

Lamb will open the scroll of God's will. Moreover, John saw that despite his own failure and the failure of our entire race in sin, the Lion of Judah will rule with power to save those joined to him through faith.

Conquering through the Lamb

In observing Jesus conquering not with the Lion's teeth but with the Lamb's dying wounds, Christians gain important insights into how we are said to conquer with him through faith. In each of the seven letters to the churches in chapters 2 and 3, Jesus exhorted the readers that salvation would come only "to the one who conquers" (Rev. 2:7, 11, etc.). It is from the vantage point of chapter 5 that we can more fully understand what it means to conquer through faith in Christ.

Since Jesus conquered by dying for sin, the first step in our spiritual victory must always be to receive his saving work through faith alone. Before we do anything with or for Christ, we must be saved by his conquering work. John explained this in his first epistle. First, he reminded us that forgiveness of sins before God is the universal need of mankind: "If we say we have no sin, we deceive ourselves, and the truth is not in us" (1 John 1:8). The next verse gives the remedy: "If we confess our sins, he is faithful and just to forgive us our sins and to cleanse us from all unrighteousness" (1:9). John elaborated: "If anyone does sin, we have an advocate with the Father, Jesus Christ the righteous. He is the propitiation for our sins" (2:1–2). To *propitiate* is to turn aside wrath. Jesus must atone for our sins by his death, turning aside the wrath of God that we have deserved.

Have you confessed your sin and called on Jesus, the Lamb of God, to take away your sins? Until you have, no spiritual achievement can overcome this obstacle to your acceptance with God, and you can make no payment to remove the condemning guilt of your sin. Is your life overcome with sorrow or regret, like John's weeping when he saw the unworthiness of his and every other sinner's life? Salvation begins by coming to Jesus to be cleansed, forgiven, and renewed. John's message in the first chapter of his Gospel is therefore the first message that we must hear and believe for salvation: "Behold, the Lamb of God, who takes away the sin of the world" (John 1:29).

Having first been saved, only then are we to conquer in the example of Christ, ministering and serving not only as lions but also as lambs. The combination that we see in Jesus is possible in us only through the indwelling ministry of the Holy Spirit; it is in fact a sign of true spirituality for Christians to wield the lion's spiritual power in the gentleness and meekness of the lamb. We are to be lions in spiritual strength and faithfulness and lambs in our manner of dealing with sinners and sin. To conquer as followers of Christ is to suffer for the gospel, placing the eternal well-being of others—even enemies—ahead of our own earthly good. Peter wrote: "To this you have been called, because Christ also suffered for you, leaving you an example, so that you might follow in his steps" (1 Peter 2:21). Like Jesus, we will often make our greatest spiritual impact on the world by suffering loss out of obedience and faith. Like Jesus, we know that lions of faith must conquer in the way of the Lamb, and that the crown of eternal life is worn only by those who have first carried the cross.

Corrie ten Boom was one who learned to trust Jesus as both Lion and Lamb. When the army of Nazi Germany swept through western Europe in 1940 and its swastika-wearing tyrants took over Holland, Corrie's family faced a situation not unlike the one looming before the churches of Asia in the time of the apostle John. As caring followers of Jesus, the ten Booms risked their lives to harbor Jews from the German Gestapo, until an informer notified the Nazis and Corrie's family was arrested and sent to a concentration camp.

In the brutal Ravensbruck camp, Corrie and her sister Betsie learned to rely on Christ the Lion, whose power protected and saved them. At one point Betsie became ill and could be sustained only with drops from a small vitamin bottle. There was only a few days' worth of serum in the bottle, but Corrie found that it never ran out. She was tempted to hoard the precious medicine for her failing sister, but decided to trust Christ by sharing with everyone in need and then to pray. She later recalled that "every time I tilted the little bottle, a drop appeared at the tip of the glass stopper." The bottle lasted far beyond what was physically possible, until Betsie improved. Toward the end of the war, Corrie heard her name called out during a roll call. Certain that she was being summoned for execution, she instead received a card marked "Released." She was given back her possessions along with a railway pass to Holland. She later learned that it had been an administrative mistake and that a week afterward all the women in her cell had been put to death. In these and other ways, she witnessed the power of the Lion of Judah to overcome evil and save.[12]

12. Corrie ten Boom, *The Hiding Place* (New York: Bantam, 1971), 202–3.

It was after the war, however, that Corrie fully learned of the conquest of Jesus the Lamb. Because of her remarkable story, she became a popular speaker and often shared the gospel with her hearers. On one occasion after speaking of Christ's forgiveness, she was met at the back by one of the former SS guards at the Ravensbruck camp. He had been a brutal man, who mocked and tormented Corrie and the other women prisoners. Now he came up to her after the service, bowed, and said, "How grateful I am for your message, *Fraulein*. To think that, as you say, He has washed my sins away!" It was at this moment that Corrie fully learned to conquer in the steps of the Lamb who had been slain, the Savior who had died for those who sinned against him. She related what happened:

> His hand was thrust out to shake mine. And I, who had preached so often . . . the need to forgive, kept my hand at my side. Even as the angry, vengeful thoughts boiled through me, I saw the sin of them. Jesus Christ had died for this man; was I going to ask for more? Lord Jesus, I prayed, forgive me and help me to forgive him. . . .
>
> As I took his hand the most incredible thing happened. From my shoulder along my arm and through my hand a current seemed to pass from me to him, while into my heart sprang a love for this stranger that almost overwhelmed me.[13]

John rejoiced to see Jesus as the Lion who conquered as Lamb. Through faith in him, Christians conquer in many ways. We repent of sin, we uphold biblical truth, we witness and lead others to salvation. The power of the Lion upholds us through many trials. But we are most like Jesus when we conquer through the mercy and sacrificial love by which he took up the cross as the Lamb, forgiving those who sin against us and reaching out with grace for those who are lost. Surely it was especially for those who follow in the meek submission of the Lamb who was slain that Jesus promised: "The one who conquers, I will grant him to sit with me on my throne, as I also conquered and sat down with my Father on his throne" (Rev. 3:21).

---

13. Ibid., 215.

19

WORTHY IS THE LAMB

Revelation 5:8–14

And they sang a new song, saying, "Worthy are you to take the scroll and to open its seals, for you were slain, and by your blood you ransomed people for God from every tribe and language and people and nation." (Rev. 5:9)

Some occasions are so momentous that they warrant a new song. As an example, the Russian composer Peter Tchaikovsky was approached in 1880 to write music for a number of events occurring in Moscow. These included the dedication of the Cathedral of Christ the Savior, the twenty-fifth anniversary of Tsar Alexander II's coronation, and a commemoration of the Russian victory over Napoleon at Borodino. Tchaikovsky wrote the *1812 Overture*, famed for the resounding cannons that conclude its score. New compositions mark other special occasions, such as weddings, funerals, inaugurations, and dedications.

There has never been a more momentous event, however, than the one recorded in Revelation 5, which John said warranted a new song in heaven. This event was the ascension and enthronement of the Son of God after successfully completing his saving work. John watched as Christ approached God's throne and took the scroll of the divine will. He wrote: "And when he had taken the scroll, the four living creatures and the twenty-four elders fell down before the Lamb . . . . And they sang a new song, saying, 'Worthy are you to take the scroll and to open its seals, for you were slain, and by your blood you ransomed people for God from every tribe and language and people and nation'" (Rev. 5:8–9).

The new song that John heard in heaven is the song of redemption, celebrating the death and resurrection of Jesus. In the vision of chapter 4, John heard the song of creation sung to God's praise: "Worthy are you, our Lord and God, to receive glory and honor and power, for you created all things" (Rev. 4:11). This song is probably similar to the creation song that God spoke of in Job 38:7, when "the morning stars sang together and all the angels shouted for joy" (NIV). But with Christ's redeeming work, there is a new cause for God's praise. William Hendriksen writes: "They sing a new song . . . because never before had such a great and glorious deliverance been accomplished and never before had the Lamb received this great honor."[1] Revelation 5 adds to chapter 4, therefore, in the same way that Christ's redemption adds to the glory of God in creation. The new song is offered to Jesus "because, having redeemed his people, he has taken the scroll which will determine the flow of future history, and that means that Jesus is controlling history in the interests of those he has redeemed."[2]

WORTHY TO BE WORSHIPED

The host of heaven sang a new song not only for the greatness of the occasion but also for the worthiness of the Savior who has ascended and taken up his reign. "Worthy are you to take the scroll and to open its seals" (Rev. 5:9).

Christ's worthiness is extolled not in the sense of his glorious divine person, but in light of his successful saving mission on earth. Hebrews 5:9 similarly asserts that Christ was "made perfect" by his obedient suffering as "the source of eternal salvation to all who obey him." Christ was always perfect in his being, but now he has qualified himself to be the Savior of his people. In this sense he has become worthy to take the scroll and to be praised.

1. William Hendriksen, *More than Conquerors: An Interpretation of the Book of Revelation* (1940; repr., Grand Rapids: Baker, 1967), 91.
2. James Montgomery Boice, *Revelation*, unpublished manuscript, n.d., chap. 16, p. 4.

Revelation 5:9–10 presents the third of five songs in the vision that began in chapter 4. It contains the praise given to Christ by the twenty-four elders, who represent the redeemed church. They sing the new song: "Worthy are you to take the scroll and to open its seals, for you were slain, and by your blood you ransomed people for God from every tribe and language and people and nation." Christ is glorified for his sacrifice in death to redeem his people from their sins.

First, Christ is praised for being "slain." He did not die from an unavoidable tragedy, but died as a voluntary act of sacrificial love for his people. Ancient history lauded the philosopher Socrates, when he willingly submitted to unjust execution out of the principle of loyalty. American children extol the name of Nathan Hale, the Revolutionary War patriot who regretted that he had only one life to give to his country. Socrates died for a principle and Nathan Hale died for a cause. But the Christian has an even higher reason to love and adore God's Son, Jesus Christ, since we can say, "He died for me." He said, "I lay down my life for the sheep. . . . No one takes it from me, but I lay it down of my own accord" (John 10:15, 18). Therefore, when people ask who killed Jesus Christ, the best answer is that Jesus willed his own death, for the sake of the people he loves.

Second, Christ is worthy because of what he achieved by his death: "By your blood you ransomed people for God" (Rev. 5:9). Different English translations render *ransomed* as "purchased" (NIV) or "redeemed" (NKJV). The Greek word (*agorazo*) has the general meaning of purchasing, but often had the specific connotation of ransoming a prisoner or slave out of bondage. Here we see the essence of what Jesus Christ accomplished on the cross: at the cost of his own blood, which evidenced his death, Jesus delivered his people from the bondage and condemnation of sin. Many writers, especially in the early church, envisioned Jesus as paying a ransom to Satan. This is a mistaken idea, however, since the devil never had the true right to possess God's people. Rather, Jesus made payment to the justice of God, which demanded death as the penalty for sin (Gen. 2:17; Rom. 6:23). Jesus foretold that "the Son of Man came not to be served but to serve, and to give his life as a ransom for many" (Matt. 20:28). Paul therefore wrote, "In him we have redemption through his blood, the forgiveness of our trespasses" (Eph. 1:7).

It is significant that the adoration of the church in heaven centers on the redemptive sacrifice of Christ's cross. Similarly, when true Christians explain the substance of their faith, they always focus on his sacrificial death to purchase us from the debt of sin. In 1915, Benjamin B. Warfield made this point to incoming students at Princeton Theological Seminary, asserting that to Christ's people his most precious title is "Redeemer." The reason is, he said, that "it gives expression not merely to our sense that we have received salvation from [Jesus], but also to our appreciation of what it cost him to procure this salvation for us."[3] Warfield proved this claim not from the tomes of theology but from the volumes of the church's hymnody, listing song after song extolling Christ as Redeemer: "O for a thousand tongues to sing my great Redeemer's praise"; "All hail, Redeemer, hail, for thou hast died for me"; "I will sing of my Redeemer, and his wondrous love for me: on the cruel cross he suffered, from the curse to set me free." Warfield listed twenty-eight such hymns, and twenty-five more that used the word *ransom* to celebrate Christ's sacrifice. Warfield might have added the new song of the twenty-four elders to prove the centrality of redemption in believers' worship of Christ. James Boice writes: "Isn't that why the elders, who represent the people of God from both the Old and New Testament periods, praise Jesus as the one who 'purchased' them for God with his blood? Isn't it because they are remembering that Jesus died to redeem them personally, and the greatness of the cost?"[4]

If the death of Christ to ransom us from sin is the center of heaven's worship, it must also be at the center of the church's witness on earth. Once when I was the new pastor of a church, I decided to preach a series of sermons about redemption. After several weeks, a member came up to me after the service to complain bitterly about my emphasis on sin and salvation through Christ's blood. He protested, "If you keep preaching on sin and Christ's blood, you are going to ruin this church!" I pointed out to him that according to the Bible, the single most important reason why Christ came to earth was to die as a ransom for his people's sins. "Preaching about Christ's blood may ruin *your* church," I said, "but it will not ruin *Christ's* church." In fact, if we bear witness to the excellence of Jesus in many ways, yet neglect to proclaim the redemption of his cross, we fail to testify to the gospel, and our worship deviates from that in heaven.

3. Benjamin Breckinridge Warfield, "'Redeemer' and 'Redemption,'" in *The Person and Work of Christ* (Philadelphia: Presbyterian and Reformed, 1950), 325.

4. Boice, *Revelation*, chap. 16, p. 7.

We should notice not only the emphasis of the elders on Christ's redemption but also the kind of redemption they praised. We see this at the end of Revelation 5:9: "By your blood you ransomed people for God from every tribe and language and people and nation." The question is asked regarding *for whom* Christ paid a ransom with his blood. Universalists reply that Jesus died for everyone, so that all are forgiven even if they refuse to believe in him. This is so utterly contrary to the Bible that no serious Christian can accept it. Others assert that Jesus died for all people equally, offering his blood for their salvation, yet only those who receive this gift in faith benefit from the cross so as to be saved. This view is called *general redemption* and is associated with Arminian theology. But this also conflicts with Revelation 5:9, along with other Bible verses on Christ's redemption. The elders sing that Jesus actually "ransomed" those for whom he died, so that they no longer remain in bondage. This can describe only those who are saved. Moreover, they use a definite, not a general, term for the objects of Christ's redeeming work. He did not die for "every tribe and language and people and nation," but for "people for God from every tribe and language and people and nation" (5:9).

In other words, Christ redeemed particular people from all over the world, that is, the elect. This affirms the Reformed doctrine of limited atonement, or particular redemption. This doctrine does not state that Christ died to make redemption possible for everyone, if only they will believe, but rather that Christ died particularly for his own people, foreknown and given to him by the Father in eternity past (John 17:2; Eph. 1:4), who are actually and effectually redeemed by the blood of Christ paid as their ransom. These same persons go on to believe because the Holy Spirit applies the benefit of their redemption through the gift of saving faith (Eph. 2:8–9). Revelation 5:9 teaches an effectual redemption and a ransom that successfully purchases people for God. This argues, therefore, not that Christians are redeemed because we have believed, but rather that we have believed in Christ because by his blood he ransomed us for God.

RESTORED TO OFFER WORSHIP

This emphasis on God's sovereignty is continued in Revelation 5:10, where the elders go on praising Christ because "you have made them a kingdom and priests to our God, and they shall reign on the earth." This emphasizes what we have been saved *to* and what Christ has made us to *be*: a kingdom and priests to God.

The elders' song teaches a salvation theology of restoration. Adam was placed into the garden to be king and priest in service to God, but lost this office through his fall into sin. Israel in the exodus was established by God to be "a kingdom of priests and a holy nation" (Ex. 19:6). Israel's calling was to live out the rule of God in obedience to his Word and bear a priestly testimony of God to the nations. Instead, the Israelites turned from God's Word to follow the idols of the nations around them. But whereas Adam and Israel failed, Jesus Christ triumphed. Jesus succeeded not only through his own ministry as King of kings and true High Priest, but also in making his church "a kingdom and priests to our God" (Rev. 5:10).

How thrilling this message is when we remember that Christ's kingdom consists completely of once-condemned sinners. The church acclaims Christ's worthiness, not her own! But we celebrate that Christ cleanses and forgives prostitutes such as the woman who anointed his feet in Luke 7, murderers such as Moses and King David, and arrogant persecutors such as Paul. Paul notes the presence of others who were sexually immoral, idolaters, homosexuals, thieves, greedy, and drunkards. "But you were washed," he exclaims, "you were sanctified, you were justified in the name of the Lord Jesus Christ and by the Spirit of our God" (1 Cor. 6:9–11). Douglas Kelly points out the invitation that this presents to every sinner: "Absolutely nothing we have done in our life that is wrong, unworthy, nasty, unclean or impure disqualifies us to apply to the blood of the Lamb. You are invited to sing the song that they sing."[5]

It is noteworthy that in Revelation 5:10, "kingdom" is singular and "priests" is plural. Christ made a kingdom consisting of priests. The church is under the monarchy of Christ, so that his truth is to be taught, his commands are to be obeyed, and his saving grace is to be offered. The ancient church was not to bow to the demands of Caesar or to accommodate the tastes of pagan culture. Likewise, the Christian church today is not to affirm the edicts of Congress or of a president when they are contrary to Christ's Word. Moreover, the church serves Christ's kingdom in a priestly way. We see this in the description of Revelation 5:8: "When he had taken the scroll, the four

---

5. Douglas F. Kelly, *Revelation*, Mentor Expository Commentary (Tain, Ross-shire, Scotland: Mentor, 2012), 110.

living creatures and the twenty-four elders fell down before the Lamb, each holding a harp, and golden bowls full of incense, which are the prayers of the saints." They are worshiping him with the new song of redemption, holding the kind of small harp described in the temple worship of the Old Testament (see Pss. 33:3; 40:3; 96:1; etc.) and offering their prayers before his throne.

What a picture this presents of the church's worship! As the twenty-four elders prostrated themselves before Christ, we, too, must worship "with reverence and awe" (Heb. 12:28). The playing of harps while singing the new song shows that true worship engages not merely the mind but also the emotions and the will. As the Jewish priests daily burned incense before God, so, too, are we to pray fervently. In Revelation 6, we will see that God's judgments fall on the wicked in response to the petitions of his people (Rev. 6:10). Here in chapter 5, we should probably understand more generally the prayer lives of God's people. We are reminded that prayer is not only petition but also worship: we honor God by thanking him and by praying for his intervention; as Jesus taught us, "Your kingdom come, your will be done, on earth as it is in heaven" (Matt. 6:10).

The elders praise Christ not only for making them a kingdom and priests to God, but also because "they shall reign on the earth" (Rev. 5:10). Scholars debate when this reign takes place.[6] Premillennialists assert that the reference is future, during a literal thousand-year period when the church reigns in power on the earth before a final rebellion and the ultimate defeat of Satan. They argue that it cannot seriously be said that Christians are reigning during this present evil age of the world. Amillennialists correctly point out, however, that the church is currently described as "a kingdom and priests" and therefore currently reigns in Christ's name. Simon Kistemaker comments: "The text reads that the Lamb *made* them priests, that is, they are priests already and are in the kingdom now . . . . Through their prayers, they even now rule on the earth."[7]

It is important, then, for Christians to realize what it means to reign on earth in Christ's behalf. In response to an alarming moral decline, American Christians have sometimes sought to reign by gaining control of worldly

6. The antiquity of this argument is perhaps reflected by the conflicting manuscript evidence, which equally supports both a present and a future reading for "reign" in verse 10. See the discussion in G. K. Beale, *Revelation: A Commentary on the Greek Text*, New International Greek Testament Commentary (Grand Rapids: Eerdmans, 1999), 362–63.

7. Simon J. Kistemaker, *Revelation*, New Testament Commentary (Grand Rapids: Baker, 2001), 211.

authority structures. It is questionable whether this is even possible without a loss of spiritual integrity and legitimacy. More importantly, Christians should realize that our spiritual authority is always more potent than any worldly coercive power. We think of Polycarp of Smyrna, who inspired the early church by submitting to the fire rather than betray his Savior. We think of Martin Luther, who launched the Protestant Reformation from a pulpit, not from a princely throne. We think of Chinese house-church pastors such as Allen Yuan and Samuel Lamb, who were imprisoned in labor camps for over twenty years, but immediately resumed preaching about Jesus when they were released. "The more persecution, the more the church grows," Lamb stated. Yuan said only a few years ago, "We have a saying in Beijing. If you dare to preach, people will believe."[8]

These evangelists remind us that just as Christ said, "My kingdom is not of this world" (John 18:36), so also do Christians reign by the spiritual authority of biblical obedience and gospel proclamation. Derek Tidball comments: "The role of the church, then, is to be a faithful witness and to take an uncompromising stand for God, even to the extent of its members' laying down their lives."[9] He cites the example of the Romanian pastor Joseph Tson, who was threatened with death by his Communist interrogator. Tson answered:

> Sir, your supreme weapon is killing. My supreme weapon is dying. Sir, you know my sermons are all over the country on tapes now. If you kill me, I will be sprinkling them with my blood. Whoever listens to them after that will say, "I'd better listen. This man sealed it with his blood." They will speak ten times louder than before. So, go on and kill me. I win the supreme victory then.[10]

Before that spiritual power, Tson's jailers quailed and the Communist regime fell, largely through Christians' witness and prayers.

CREATION WELLING UP IN WORSHIP

Revelation 5 concludes with the entirety of creation responding to the adoration of the four living creatures and the twenty-four elders by welling

8. Quoted in David Aikman, *Jesus in Beijing* (Washington, DC: Regnery, 2003), 57–65.
9. Derek Tidball, *The Message of the Cross: Wisdom Unsearchable, Love Indestructible*, The Bible Speaks Today (Downers Grove, IL: InterVarsity Press, 2001), 313.
10. Ibid.

up in worship to God and the Lamb. First, we are shown the innumerable host of the angels, who offer their song to Christ: "Then I looked, and I heard around the throne and the living creatures and the elders the voice of many angels, numbering myriads of myriads and thousands of thousands" (Rev. 5:11).

In describing the angels as "myriads of myriads and thousands of thousands," the point is to show the innumerability in the very millions of God's heavenly servants. It is probably significant that they give their praise to Christ following after the twenty-four elders, for it is through the redemption of the church that the holy angels learn the glory of Christ's saving work. Peter described the gospel doctrines as "things into which angels long to look" (1 Peter 1:12). Now that they have comprehended the glory of Christ's saving work through the worship of the church, the angelic hosts offer their own praise: "Worthy is the Lamb who was slain, to receive power and wealth and wisdom and might and honor and glory and blessing!" (Rev. 5:12).

This sevenfold list of praise to Christ seems to ascribe to him all the glorious possessions properly belonging to God himself. The fact that the Greek text provides a definite article only for the first item, "the power," suggests that the whole list consists of a unified whole. Like that of the glorified church, the angels' worship responds to Christ's atoning death on the cross. Their testimony therefore shows that what once seemed like defeat for Jesus has been revealed as total victory. The cross was seen as weakness but was actually power; the cross displayed poverty but gained true riches; the cross was foolishness to the world but wisdom from God; the cross represented shame but earned the highest honor for Christ; the cross was a place of deep disgrace, yet revealed the very glory of God's grace; and the cross stood for the curse of sin but achieved eternal blessing for those on whose behalf Jesus died. "Worthy is the Lamb who was slain," the angels conclude, inviting us to enter their praise.

Finally, the worship extends to the entire creation joined together in praise of God and the Lamb: "And I heard every creature in heaven and on earth and under the earth and in the sea, and all that is in them, saying, 'To him who sits on the throne and to the Lamb be blessing and honor and glory and might forever and ever!'" (Rev. 5:13). Here we see the farthest extent of Christ's redemptive domain. As the angels comprehend the Lamb's glory in the worship of the church, so also Christ's redemption of his people undoes the curse of sin on the entire created realm. The Creator and the Redeemer together are praised by the work of their hands, the twin works of the Godhead having achieved their designed end in universal doxology.

THE SOVEREIGN IS GOOD

As we return to the world of the apostle John in writing the book of Revelation, we can see what this worship scene would have meant to the weak and threatened churches of Asia. It is Christ who reigns, not Caesar, and Christ's finished work of redemption has secured a destiny in which all things will work for the salvation of his people and the praise of God's grace. The chapter concludes with the only proper response: "And the four living creatures said, 'Amen!' and the elders fell down and worshiped" (Rev. 5:14). That was how the beleaguered Christians were to respond: by adding their own *amen* of faith in Christ's sovereign rule and by giving themselves over to joyful adoration, fulfilling their calling as a kingdom of priests.

The situation is little different for Christians today. In the year 2000, James Montgomery Boice, the famous Bible expositor and pastor of Tenth Presbyterian Church in Philadelphia, was preaching through this very section of Revelation when he realized that something was wrong with his body. A doctor's examination revealed that Boice was afflicted with a cancer that must take his life within a few short weeks. I vividly remember Dr. Boice's calling me to his office and calmly telling me this news. Shortly thereafter he addressed the congregation he had served for thirty-two years on the subject. The disease had progressed so rapidly that Boice could no longer preach and could speak only briefly. After describing his condition and thanking them for their prayers, he noted that he had been preaching the sovereignty of God for so long and that now they wanted to know whether God was sovereign over his disease. Boice responded that his illness and impending death was not accidental but was God's sovereign will for his life. Yet even that was not the point he really wanted to make. He went on: "It's possible, isn't it, to conceive of God as sovereign and yet indifferent? God's in charge, but he doesn't care. But it's not that. God is not only the one who is in charge; God is also good. Everything he does is good."[11]

11. James Montgomery Boice, "Testimony," http://www.tenth.org/articles/000507jmb.pdf.

That is the very point made in Revelation 5. It is good news that God is on the throne instead of Caesar. Yet not only is God sovereign over history, but when we see Jesus taking the scroll, we are assured that the Sovereign loves us so much as to die for our sins. We can trust him for whatever he brings into history and into our own lives.

I mentioned James Boice's farewell address to Tenth Presbyterian Church. I was seated directly behind him at the time, and when he finished speaking, we rose to sing the opening hymn of the worship service. Boice was not able to remain, so he set down his hymnal for the last time and walked to the door at the back of the chancel. As he approached the door, he passed in front of me as I was struggling with my emotions. Boice stopped, looked me in the eyes, grasped my arm, and, smiling, said, "Press on, brother. Fight the good fight."

That, too, is the message of Revelation 5. Christ is enthroned, having redeemed us by his blood. We are now a kingdom of priests to serve him on earth. Knowing that the Savior who loved us reigns over all, let us get on with the work he has given us and devote ourselves to the cause of his glory. Let us not be daunted by the winds of earthly change or the vain threats of evil powers against the gospel. Christ is sovereign, reigning over all things for our good. Let us press on in faith with the priestly work of worship, witness, and prayer for the sake of his kingdom of salvation here on earth.

20

THE FOUR HORSEMEN OF THE APOCALYPSE

Revelation 6:1–8

And I looked, and behold, a white horse! And its rider had a bow, and a crown was given to him, and he came out conquering, and to conquer. (Rev. 6:2)

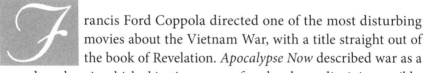rancis Ford Coppola directed one of the most disturbing movies about the Vietnam War, with a title straight out of the book of Revelation. *Apocalypse Now* described war as a crazed mayhem in which objectives are confused and morality is impossible. In one scene, an American officer arrives in the midst of a firefight. Shells are exploding everywhere, machine-gun tracers fill the air, and soldiers look wide-eyed and desperate. "Who's in charge here?" the officer asks. Nobody answers, which is Coppola's point in the film. It is a scene out of hell, with no direction, purpose, or solution.[1]

The book of Revelation presents exactly the opposite understanding of the barbarism of human history. As John's vision continues in chapter 6,

1. Adapted from James Montgomery Boice, *Revelation*, unpublished manuscript, n.d., chap. 17, pp. 1–2.

the opening of the seals on God's scroll unleashes great tribulations on the earth. Yet far from being without purpose, they are shown by John's vision as reflecting the divine will under the lordship of Jesus Christ. G. K. Beale comments: "Revelation 6:1–8 is intended to show that Christ rules over such an apparently chaotic world and that suffering does not occur indiscriminately or by chance."[2] While the four horsemen bring woe and death, they do not bring dismay to those who are trusting in Christ.

The visions of God's throne and of the glorified Lamb in chapters 4 and 5 occupy the very heart of the book of Revelation, depicting God as sovereign over history. In chapter 6, Jesus begins opening the seals of the scroll that he has been found worthy to open. Four riders go forth at his command, showing that Christ reigns not only over the hearts of those who love him but also over the dangerous forces unleashed in the world. Jesus truly is, as John has said, "the ruler of kings on earth" (Rev. 1:5), and therefore his followers can face tribulation with hope.

UNDERSTANDING THE FOUR HORSEMEN

The four horsemen of the Apocalypse have become a potent metaphor in popular culture. The 1924 Notre Dame football team under legendary coach Knute Rockne featured an all-star backfield known as the Four Horsemen of Notre Dame. The Old Testament background shows, however, a less benign significance for these images. Zechariah 1 featured horsemen who patrolled the earth for God. The prophet later wrote of four chariots, whose horses mirror the colors of those in Revelation 6, that went out into the four corners of the earth to impose God's will on his enemies (Zech. 6:1–8).

The connection with Zechariah's horsemen suggests that these in Revelation go forth to inflict punishment on a world in rebellion against God. The church, however, is in the world and is thus equally subject to these woes. The second horseman, for instance, will cause people to "slay one another" (Rev. 6:4), and the word for *slay* is used elsewhere for the slaughter of Christ and of believers (see 1 John 3:12; Rev. 5:6, 9). The judgments depicted in this vision also follow the pattern laid down in Ezekiel 14:12–23, the point of which was not only to punish idolaters but

---

2. G. K. Beale, *The Book of Revelation: A Commentary on the Greek Text*, New International Greek Testament Commentary (Grand Rapids: Eerdmans, 1999), 370.

also to purify the faith of God's people. Alan F. Johnson writes, "Each of the first four seals, then, represents conflict directed at Christians to test them and to sift out false disciples."[3] Jesus asserted that he came not "to bring peace" to the world, "but a sword" (Matt. 10:34), promising that those who lose their life for him will gain it (10:39). Therefore, while the persecution of the church may not be in the foreground of these woes, it is certainly bound up with them.

Moreover, there seems to be at least a general correspondence with the calamities foretold by Jesus in his Olivet Discourse (Matt. 24; Mark 13; Luke 21). Christ spoke of deception, war, strife, famine, and persecution, concluding that "the end is not yet. . . . These are but the beginning of the birth pains" (Matt. 24:6–8). This helps us to locate the timing of the calamities depicted in Revelation 6:1–8. Some scholars understand Jesus to be inaugurating the final days when he opens the seals of God's scroll. To the contrary, these woes occur throughout the current age of the world. Chapter 5 showed Christ as approaching God's throne to take the scroll. This corresponds to his ascension into heaven at the conclusion of his first coming and accords with the Great Commission, when Jesus declared, "All authority in heaven and on earth has been given to me" (Matt. 28:18). Revelation thus depicts Jesus as opening the seals so as to bring about God's plan for our current age. Vern Poythress writes: "Such things occurred during the tumults of the Roman Empire, are occurring now, and may be expected to occur just before the Second Coming."[4]

The most important point made by the vision of the four horsemen is the sovereignty of Christ over the tribulations on earth. Each horseman is summoned by a cherub when Jesus breaks the seal. Notice throughout the passage that the horsemen are equipped with what is "given" to them. The white horseman is given a crown, the red horseman is "permitted" to remove peace and is "given a great sword," and the pale horseman is "given authority" to slay a quarter of the earth. In each case, the evil proceeds of its own volition, so that Christ is not directly causing the calamities on earth. Yet the horsemen do only what they are assigned and permitted to do according to the plan of God and the sovereign rule of Christ.

3. Alan F. Johnson, *Revelation*, Expositor's Bible Commentary 12 (Grand Rapids: Zondervan, 1982), 473.
4. Vern S. Poythress, *The Returning King: A Guide to the Book of Revelation* (Phillipsburg, NJ: P&R Publishing, 2000), 114.

The woes unfolded in this vision are, in fact, the record of history as Christ judges the rebel world. Psalm 2:12 thus warns the ungodly: "Kiss the Son, lest he be angry, and you perish in the way." At the same time, the sovereignty of Christ provides the greatest comfort to his suffering people in the world. However hellish the affairs of earth may seem, when the Christian asks, "Who's in charge here?" the Bible points to the Lamb who was slain for our sins, who is sovereignly resolved to bring all his people to salvation in the end.

THE FIRST RIDER: CONQUERING AND TO CONQUER

Revelation 4 and 5 depict God's actions in heaven, and in chapter 6 John sees the resulting events on earth. "Now I watched when the Lamb opened one of the seven seals," John wrote, "and I heard one of the four living creatures say with a voice like thunder, 'Come!'" John then saw the first horseman: "And I looked, and behold, a white horse! And its rider had a bow, and a crown was given to him, and he came out conquering and to conquer" (Rev. 6:1–2).

Before understanding the mission of this horseman, we must first determine his identity. The three main candidates are that he is Christ going forth with his gospel in the world, the Antichrist going forth with violence, or simply the various conquerors who periodically arise in history.

Those who believe the rider is Christ point to the appearance of Jesus in Revelation 19 as a white rider who leads the armies of heaven. White is the color of righteousness, and in both John's Gospel and Revelation Jesus is frequently said to conquer (John 16:33; Rev. 5:5).[5] There are, however, reasons to doubt this view. The primary objection is that, like the celebrated Notre Dame football players, these four horsemen are all on the same team. Their purpose is tribulation, not salvation. Moreover, this rider wears the laurel crown of a conqueror rather than the "many diadems" that Jesus wears in Revelation 19:12. While the color white often speaks of righteousness, it can also represent the victorious warrior, such as the Roman conquerors who rode white horses in their triumphal parades. For these reasons, many scholars see the first rider not as Christ but as his satanic counterfeit the Antichrist,

5. For a thorough presentation of this view, see William Hendriksen, *More than Conquerors: An Interpretation of the Book of Revelation* (1940; repr., Grand Rapids: Baker, 1967), 93–96.

especially since he is also said to conquer (Rev. 11:7; 13:7). It is probably best, however, to see the first rider as neither Christ nor the Antichrist, but as the calamitous woe of military conquest. The bow was a weapon of violent warfare and was the preferred weapon of Rome's chief menace, the Parthians. Philip Hughes summarizes: "The *bow* . . . is a symbol of violence, the *crown* he is given signifies despotic rule, and the *white* colour of his horse betokens conquest, while his going forth *conquering and to conquer* expresses his lust for power and world domination."[6]

Understood this way, the first seal unleashed warlords into history— warlords who are granted authority to achieve conquest on the earth. The Roman emperors claimed a *Pax Romana* in which peace had been secured by the Roman sword. Yet the Parthians who defeated their legions in A.D. 62 showed the frailty of this claim. Throughout history Christ has sovereignly unleashed men such as Attila, Genghis Khan, Napoleon, and Hitler to over- throw human claims to peace on earth while mankind was all the while at war with God. Vern Poythress writes: "Roman peace promised prosperity, but the reality was different. Conquest, bloodshed, famine, and death have stalked the human race throughout the church age."[7]

The Red, Black, and Pale Riders

The second, third, and fourth riders depict the ravages that accompany warfare in human history. John continues with the red horse, which brings slaughter: "When he opened the second seal, I heard the second living crea- ture say, 'Come!' And out came another horse, bright red. Its rider was per- mitted to take peace from the earth, so that people should slay one another, and he was given a great sword" (Rev. 6:3–4).

The bright-red color of this second horse fits the theme of violent blood- shed. John says that its rider "was given a great sword," and with it he "was permitted to take peace from the earth." If the first rider brings military conquest, this second rider brings civil war and bloodshed within a soci- ety. Notice that Christ does not have to cause violence, but only to remove his restraint and permit it. The reason for this is the hatred within sinful

6. Philip Edgcumbe Hughes, *The Book of Revelation* (Downers Grove, IL: InterVarsity Press, 1990), 85.

7. Poythress, *The Returning King*, 115.

mankind. James explained: "What causes quarrels and what causes fights among you? Is it not this, that your passions are at war within you? You desire and do not have, so you murder. You covet and cannot obtain, so you fight and quarrel" (James 4:1–2). It is tragically ironic that a society that has turned from God is surprised by the violence of its people, since the grace of Christ is the only true restraint on sin. Our own society has unleashed the most deadly influences, from violence-glorifying entertainment to sexual "liberties" that destroy the family. Then, when these sinful forces wreak mayhem and bloodshed in our streets, schools, and homes, secular leaders express dismay. Revelation 6:3–4 informs us that the red horseman of slaughter brings judgment by permitting the expression of violent passion within unbelieving mankind.

The sword of slaughter may refer to both civil strife and persecution against Christians. The latter is particularly likely, since the fifth seal uses the same word for *slaughter* when it reveals "the souls of those who had been slain for the word of God" (Rev. 6:9). This sword of slaughter against Christ's people is quite active today, as borne out by news that regularly comes of wrongful arrests and beatings of Christians in China, savage slaughter of believers in Africa and the Middle East, and suppression of religious liberty in the West.

The third rider comes forth on a black horse, bringing famine to the earth: "Its rider had a pair of scales in his hand. And I heard what seemed to be a voice in the midst of the four living creatures, saying, 'A quart of wheat for a denarius, and three quarts of barley for a denarius'" (Rev. 6:5–6). These words depict economic collapse, so that people can barely afford the necessities of life. The province of Asia was self-sufficient in olive oil and wine, but had to import grain from Egypt and other sources. Beale reports that these prices reflect an inflation rate of 800 to 1,600 percent.[8] A quart of wheat was enough to feed one person for a day, and since it now cost an entire day's wages, many workers would be unable to feed their families. The only recourse was to eat barley, a less-nutritious grain usually reserved for livestock, so that families were existing on the margin of survival.

This third rider brings deprivation but not total starvation. Thus one cries, "Do not harm the oil and wine!" (Rev. 6:6). The preservation of olives and vineyards may indicate that only the poor are afflicted by the famine,

---

8. Beale, *Revelation*, 381.

with the more wealthy able to preserve their luxuries. The cry may also reflect a famine that struck Asia in A.D. 92, during which the emperor Domitian ordered that olive groves and vineyards be torn down to provide more land for grain. When landowners banded together to protest, the emperor revoked his order. This is at least the kind of situation that John's vision presents, with dire economic hardship producing civil strife and class conflict. Douglas Kelly reminds us of Christ's sovereignty over this woe, commenting that "a disobedient culture that rejects God's truth ultimately loses its economy."[9]

Christians often suffer during economic crises, particularly when their loyalty to Christ creates trouble with employers and government powers. In his letter to Pergamum, Jesus admonished the church not to "eat food sacrificed to idols" or "practice sexual immorality" (Rev. 2:14). This probably referred to the idolatry necessary for membership in a trade guild, so that Christians who refused to engage in these sins could not hold down well-paying jobs. Revelation will later refer to the "mark of the beast," which signified the worship of idols, without which "no one can buy or sell" (13:17). This shows that faithful Christians are sometimes forbidden to participate in economic life.

This issue is especially relevant in America today, where the federal government is requiring Christian business owners to purchase healthcare plans for their employees that provide for abortion-causing contraceptives. Failure to do this leads to crippling government fines. In a nation created to protect the religious freedoms of its people, Christians are increasingly permitted to obey Christ only in our private lives. To operate even a privately owned business, one must betray his conscience before God. Christians should be praying for legal protection against this unjust tyranny. Yet we should not be surprised, since Revelation predicts this very kind of persecution.

When the fourth seal is broken, its rider comes forth on a horse that most translations describe as "pale." More accurately, this is a sickly-green horse, the Greek term *chloros* providing the English words *chlorophyll* and *chlorine*. The color befits its purpose: "And its rider's name was Death, and Hades followed him" (Rev. 6:7). This fourth horseman is usually thought to depict disease and pestilence, which is why its victims are swift to enter the grave.

---

9. Douglas F. Kelly, *Revelation*, Mentor Expository Commentary (Tain, Ross-shire, Scotland: Mentor, 2012), 123.

It is unclear whether the final statement of Revelation 6:8 refers only to the fourth horseman or to all four. But it is clearly a summary statement of all that John has seen: "And they were given authority over a fourth of the earth, to kill with sword and with famine and with pestilence and by wild beasts of the earth." This list of deadly woes comes from Ezekiel 14:12–23, which lists these same judgments on the idolatrous people of Israel. Ezekiel spoke of wild beasts' roaming the land as a sign that human society had completely broken down under God's covenant curse; this reference probably accounts for the addition of wild beasts in Revelation 6:8. The allusion to Ezekiel also shows that Christ's judgments are in response to idol-worship and unbelief, and indicates that godly people will suffer together with the wicked.

As the fourth rider flies out from the scroll, we are reminded of the sovereignty of Christ, who has broken the seals. Terrible as they are, these woes occur for the praise of his glory. There are four living creatures who sang praise to him (Rev. 5:9), and these same four cherubim summon the four riders of doom. Their woes will continue on earth throughout the present age until Christ returns so that his purposes may be achieved. G. K. Beale writes: "Christ has made the world forces of evil his agents to execute his purposes of sanctification and judgment for the furtherance of his kingdom."[10] This is most clearly seen in the calling of the fourth rider, who is named Death and is followed by Hades. Jesus earlier declared, "I have the keys of Death and Hades" (1:18). Therefore, this rider, like the others, goes forth only at his command and is so restricted by Christ to bring only those woes that will thwart the opponents of his gospel reign.

Sovereign for Judgment and Salvation

Atheists frequently assert that the "problem of evil" is a potent challenge to the Bible. "How can there be a good God," they demand, "when evils such as these occur so frequently?" This problem exists only for the unbeliever, however. Far from being embarrassed about the existence of a holy and loving God in the presence of terrible human suffering, Revelation boldly proclaims Christ's utter sovereignty over these four horsemen. What meaning are we to take from this shocking state of affairs?

10. Beale, *Revelation*, 385.

The first message we should take from the four horsemen is the resolute anger of heaven toward the sin and rebellion of earth. James Boice writes: "The pictures painted by John in this last book of the Bible are not for our amusement or puzzles merely to exercise our minds. They are warnings of how seriously God takes sin and of how he is going to judge it fully in time."[11] Some may have concluded that Jesus is no longer concerned with sin, since he has died on the cross to make atonement. Leon Morris reminds us, however, that "Christ's death was not only salvation from sin, but condemnation of sin."[12] By pouring out his wrath on his sin-bearing Son, God showed how resolute is his hatred toward all evil. Therefore, a world that rejects Jesus and scorns his atoning death should expect nothing less than judgment from heaven. Friedrich von Schiller was thus correct when he stated, "The history of the world is the judgment of the world."[13]

It does not occur to people today that God is actively judging the world in the calamities we experience. To be sure, Christians should avoid declaring that particular events represent God's judgment on particular people. Yet John's vision shows that the secularist pursuit of a godless paradise will not be permitted by God. God cast down the Tower of Babel in Genesis 11, and he continues to smash every millennial utopia of idolatrous mankind. The Roman emperors of old and today's politicians unite in promising peace and prosperity while flouting God's commands. They forget that the purpose of the world is not the pleasure of man in sin but rather the glory of God in righteousness. Paul taught that "although [men] knew God, they did not honor him as God or give thanks to him" (Rom. 1:21). For this reason, he said, "the wrath of God is revealed from heaven against all ungodliness and unrighteousness of men" (1:18).

In our own lifetime, Western society has experienced all the woes of the four riders. Despite our initiatives for peace, we remain beset with the conquering designs of men bent on domination. The September 11, 2001, hijacking of jetliners and collapse of the World Trade Center towers may have shocked Americans, but it should not surprise the discerning reader of history. Politicians wrangle over the failure to end wars, but none will

11. Boice, *Revelation*, chap. 17, p. 12.
12. Leon Morris, *The Revelation of St. John: An Introduction and Commentary*, Tyndale New Testament Commentaries 20 (Grand Rapids: Eerdmans, 1969), 103.
13. Quoted in Geoffrey B. Wilson, *New Testament Commentaries*, 2 vols. (Edinburgh: Banner of Truth, 2005), 2:511.

address the underlying problem of sin and heaven's wrath. In the days of our founding fathers, the American government called for days of prayer and fasting when military defeats were suffered. This piety was lost in the secular humanism of the twentieth century. Demagogues called the First World War the "war to end all wars." Their hubris was exposed by the bloodiest century on record, the scourge of which continues today.

We could make similar comments about the red horse and its rider unleashing violence within society. When bullets shatter schoolrooms, we complain about guns and neglect the problem of sin in our hearts, refusing to call for repentance before God. When the sexual revolution of the '60s and '70s led to the devastation of the AIDS virus in the '80s and '90s, few would speak of repenting from sin. As economic debt soars, lawmakers refuse the truth about our mad pursuit of short-term pleasure at the expense of generations to follow. In each kind of woe represented by Revelation's horsemen, judgment is the logical result of sin and also the sovereign decree of the reigning Christ. This wrath calls the world to repent from sin and seek salvation through Jesus Christ.

A second emphasis from this vision is noteworthy especially for believers, as the horsemen of Revelation 6 reveal Christ's purpose in the calamities of history. I mentioned that some people object to God's sovereignty over evil, but the opposite is far more alarming. How terrible it would be if the message of Francis Ford Coppola's movie *Apocalypse Now* were really true, that no one is in charge and that the world's evils rage uncontrolled and unguided!

John's vision teaches Christians that these woes will continue in our world until Christ returns. Richard Bewes writes that the church should therefore "expect to live adventurously."[14] But we are also comforted that under Christ's control these woes will not destroy us. Those who trust in Jesus may suffer these trials but will be saved through them. Paul preached that "through many tribulations we must enter the kingdom of God" (Acts 14:22), and the vision of our Savior as he opens the seals proves that we will be saved, since he rules over the trials. Leon Morris concludes: "Though apocalyptic judgments be loosed against all mankind, God's people need never be dismayed. They will be preserved no matter the tribulation."[15]

---

14. Richard Bewes, *The Lamb Wins: A Guided Tour through the Book of Revelation* (Tain, Ross-shire, Scotland: Christian Focus, 2000), 54.

15. Morris, *The Revelation of St. John*, 102.

In ascribing sovereignty over history to Christ, we should remember that these woes are not caused by him, though he grants them their sphere and limitations. It is we in our sin who are the cause of these tribulations. "The point is," writes G. B. Caird, that "just where sin and its effects are most in evidence, the kingship of the Crucified is to be seen, turning human wickedness to the service of God's purpose. . . . Nothing can now happen, not even the most fearsome evidence of man's disobedience . . . , which cannot be woven into the pattern of God's gracious purpose."[16]

I noted earlier Paul's diagnosis of the problem of this world, when he said that the wrath of God is revealed against our sins (Rom. 1:18). That may be a fitting conclusion for our study of the four riders of the Apocalypse, but it was only the beginning of Paul's gospel presentation. Though man has ruined himself and brought judgment on history through his sin, God has intervened to save through his Son, Jesus Christ. Paul states the problem in Romans 3:23: "All have sinned and fall short of the glory of God." He continued, just as John will continue in Revelation, to reveal the solution from heaven, that sinners "are justified by his grace as a gift, through the redemption that is in Christ Jesus . . . , to be received by faith" (3:24–25). Therefore, as we contemplate the holy wrath of heaven against the sins of earth, we must never forget the gospel's invitation: "Everyone who calls on the name of the Lord will be saved" (Rom. 10:13). With Christ reigning over history and with his salvation offer still open, let us as his people commit our time on earth to the gospel and to the work and the glory of the only kingdom that will never fail.

16. G. B. Caird, *The Revelation of St. John the Divine* (San Francisco: Harper, 1966), 83.

21

THE FIFTH SEAL

Revelation 6:9—11

When he opened the fifth seal, I saw under the altar the souls of
those who had been slain for the word of God and for
the witness they had borne. (Rev. 6:9)

John Foxe resigned from his academic position at Oxford University in 1545 because his religious beliefs conflicted with the official position of the Church of England under King Henry VIII. When Henry's daughter Mary took the throne in 1553, Foxe's views placed him in danger, so he fled with many others to the European continent. When he learned from English refugees about the appalling persecutions of Protestants, Foxe began compiling accounts of their cruel martyrdom. He published the first edition of his *History of the Acts and Monuments of the Church* in 1554. As a result, people brought more eyewitness accounts of the execution of Christians in England, mainly by burning at the stake. When Queen Elizabeth I brought peace to the nation, Foxe returned and published a new edition of his book. Over many years he revised his records for accuracy and included martyrs from the early church and elsewhere in the world. His book became known as *Foxe's Book of Martyrs*, and became second only to the Bible in sales and in influence, playing an important role in the adherence of England to the Protestant faith.

The Bible itself records the death of faithful believers in order to strengthen those under persecution. The so-called Hall of Faith in Hebrews 11 concludes with those who "suffered mocking and flogging, and even chains and imprisonment," together with those who "were stoned, . . . sawn in two, . . . killed with the sword . . . , destitute, afflicted, [and] mistreated." Of them, says God's Word, "the world was not worthy" (Heb. 11:36–38). Martyrs like these are also remembered in the last book of the Bible. Revelation 6:9 shows "the souls of those who had been slain for the word of God and for the witness they had borne." "How long," they cry to God, "before you will judge and avenge our blood on those who dwell on the earth?" (Rev. 6:10).

The Cause of the Martyrs

When Jesus broke the first four seals on the scroll given to him in heaven, they revealed woes that occur on the earth during the church age. Opening the fifth scroll brings our attention back to heaven. Here we see the souls of the believers who died for Christ in these tribulations. This emphasis should not surprise us, since Revelation has all along been preparing its readers for persecution. In his letter to Smyrna, Jesus said, "Be faithful unto death, and I will give you the crown of life" (Rev. 2:10). Antipas of Pergamum was a faithful witness who had already died (2:13). In the Gospels, Jesus warned that "they will deliver you up to tribulation and put you to death, and you will be hated by all nations for my name's sake" (Matt. 24:9). James Boice writes: "In light of Jesus' teaching, what is surprising is not that Christians have been persecuted and killed all through the long annals of human history, . . . but that so many have not been."[1] Far from deadly persecution being unusual for Christians, it is the normal situation that Christians should expect.

With the fifth seal, John saw "under the altar the souls of those who had been slain" (Rev. 6:9). John Foxe pointed out that Jesus Christ died first, as "the inspiration and source of all martyrdom."[2] Next to die was Stephen, whose name appropriately means "crown." Stephen's murder launched "a great persecution against the church" (Acts 8:1), in which many Christians died, including John's brother the apostle James (12:1–2). Church tradition

---

1. James Montgomery Boice, *Revelation*, unpublished manuscript, n.d., chap. 18, p. 3.
2. John Foxe, *The New Foxe's Book of Martyrs*, ed. Harold J. Chadwick (Gainesville, FL: Bridge-Logos, 2001), 4.

holds that all the apostles except John suffered death for the gospel. In the middle of the first century, the Roman emperor Nero (A.D. 54–68) martyred thousands, and at the time of John's writing in Revelation, Domitian (A.D. 81–96) was preparing a new wave of violence against Christ's people. John's readers knew that the Romans dressed Christians in animal skins while lions and other wild animals were released to tear them to shreds. Some Christians were cruelly burned in torturous ways. How encouraging it must have been for those facing this kind of torment to see that the martyrs' souls were alive in heaven.

Everyone dies sometime, but these spirits are special for the *cause* of their death: they "had been slain for the word of God and for the witness they had borne" (Rev. 6:9). The martyrs died because they would not renounce the biblical revelation about Christ's divine person and saving work. The "witness" probably emphasizes the gospel testimony they received and then shared boldly with others. This is what John gave as the cause of his own exile on Patmos: "on account of the word of God and the testimony of Jesus" (1:9).

This reminds us that the basic meaning of the Greek word *martyr* is "witness." These souls died *because* of their testimony to Jesus and *as* a testimony to Jesus. In this vital sense, *martyr* describes not merely those who die for the gospel but all Christians, since we are saved by holding to the gospel and are called to witness the gospel. Bearing testimony to the gospel virtually guarantees some form of suffering in this world. George Eldon Ladd writes, "Every disciple of Jesus is in essence a martyr; and John has in view all believers who have so suffered."[3] Revelation 12:11 describes all of Christ's people as those who have "conquered . . . by the blood of the Lamb and by the word of their testimony, for they loved not their lives even unto death."

The sacrifice made by these martyrs is reflected in the symbolic location where John "saw" their souls: "I saw under the altar the souls of those who had been slain" (Rev. 6:9). When sacrifices were offered in the Old Testament temple, the blood of the victims streamed down the side of the altar and pooled at its base. Leviticus 17:11 informs us that "the life of the flesh is in the blood," so the souls beneath the altar speak of the blood they shed for Christ. This is symbolism. The martyrs did not die to make atonement for sin, but their death is so closely associated with Christ's sacrificial death

3. George Eldon Ladd, *A Commentary on the Revelation of John* (Grand Rapids: Eerdmans, 1972), 104.

that their blood is pictured as flowing down his altar. Robert Mounce writes: "Their untimely deaths on earth are from God's perspective a sacrifice on the altar of heaven" (see also 2 Tim. 4:6).[4] In this way, the altar for the burnt offerings in the temple is an emblem of their martyrdom.

We should also associate this altar with the altar of incense that signified the prayers of the saints (Rev. 5:8). Revelation 6:10 shows the martyrs praying to God, which reinforces the idea of the altar of incense. Probably it is best, then, to take the altar of verse 9 as a composite that symbolizes both altars in the temple.

A further idea is that the location of the martyrs' souls under the altar symbolizes their security in heaven under God's protection. Though rejected on earth, they are close to God's presence in heaven, kept safe by the reigning Lamb for whom they died. This would add inspiration to those facing martyrdom in John's day, just as it does for us today. Steve Wilmshurst writes:

> Down through history, thousands upon thousands of faithful servants of God have faced death because they stayed true to him. It is still happening today and it will go on happening until the end comes. They are unknowns, like the woman evangelist killed in Nigeria one day, the group beheaded in Indonesia the next, the pastor murdered in Karnataka State, . . . nameless to us but known to God.[5]

THE CRY OF THE MARTYRS

If Revelation 6:9 highlights the *cause* of the martyrs, the next verse notes the *cry* of the martyrs in heaven: "They cried out with a loud voice, 'O Sovereign Lord, holy and true, how long before you will judge and avenge our blood on those who dwell on the earth?'" (Rev. 6:10).

The martyrs cry out over the continued slaughter of the saints on earth. When Cain murdered Abel, the Lord said that the voice of his brother's blood was "crying to me from the ground" (Gen. 4:10). Now, in heaven, the souls of the martyrs cry to God not over their own deaths but over the injustice taking place on earth. This answers the supposed problem that the martyrs

4. Robert H. Mounce, *Revelation*, rev. ed., New International Commentary on the New Testament (Grand Rapids: Eerdmans, 1997), 158.

5. Steve Wilmshurst, *The Final Word: The Book of Revelation Simply Explained* (Darlington, UK: Evangelical Press, 2008), 83–84.

should cry out in vengeance, whereas Jesus prayed for God to forgive his killers (Luke 23:34), as did Stephen, the first martyr (Acts 7:60). One writer thus comments, "This is not a Christian prayer."[6] Yet the fact that glorified saints are praying this way near God's presence in heaven should alert us that this must be a biblical prayer.

The first reason that this prayer is worthy of Christians is that the martyrs were not complaining only about their own sufferings but were crying for the injustice inflicted on fellow believers. The saints in heaven want to know how long the church on earth will suffer. We, too, should pray for afflicted Christians, "O Sovereign Lord, how long?"

Second, there is nothing inherently unchristian about praying against evil and asking God to judge the wicked. Such prayers are found throughout the Psalms. David prayed, "Arise, O LORD, in your anger; lift yourself up against the fury of my enemies" (Ps. 7:6). Jesus told of a widow who kept appealing to the judge, begging, "Give me justice against my adversary" (Luke 18:3). Jesus praised her persistence, saying that our prayers to God for justice will likewise be answered: "Will not God give justice to his elect, who cry to him day and night?" Jesus asked. "I tell you, he will give justice to them speedily" (18:7–8).

Some may respond by reminding us that Paul commanded, "Beloved, never avenge yourselves, but leave it to the wrath of God, for it is written, 'Vengeance is mine, I will repay, says the Lord'" (Rom. 12:19). This is the very thing that the martyrs are doing! Christians are not to seek vengeance against people who harm us, and we should often pray for God's mercy for the salvation of the wicked. But having left vengeance to God, we do nothing wrong in asking for his justice to prevail. William Hendriksen writes: "The saint in glory does not desire personal vengeance any more than did Stephen, but he yearns for the coming of that great day when the majesty and holiness, the sovereignty and righteousness of God in Christ shall be publicly revealed."[7]

To pray for God's judgment of evil is a version of the prayer taught by Jesus: "Your kingdom come, your will be done, on earth as it is in heaven" (Matt. 6:10). Douglas Kelly urges us in our prayers to

6. Mounce, *Revelation*, 158.
7. William Hendriksen, *More than Conquerors: An Interpretation of the Book of Revelation* (1940; repr., Grand Rapids: Baker, 1967), 106.

think of what opposition to God's truth there is in the schools and in the government and in the media.... Think of the Islamic countries where to be baptized literally means beheading, if the person was previously a Muslim and the government finds out. The martyred saints above are asking: "How much longer until the truth gets out and these people can be saved?"[8]

If this is how the saints pray in heaven, their example should inspire Christians on earth not only to pray for fellow believers who suffer but also to pray against evil powers that oppose the gospel.

Third, the primary focus of this prayer is the honor of God. The martyrs pray to the Sovereign of history, knowing that his glory requires righteousness to prevail. They cry to the God who is holy and true, knowing that he cannot abide with evil and must fulfill his Word. Therefore, having prayed, "O Sovereign Lord, holy and true," they appeal to him out of concern for his honor: "How long before you will judge and avenge our blood on those who dwell on the earth?'" (Rev. 6:10). We, too, should pray for God to glorify himself in the judgment of the wicked, knowing that he certainly will. As chapter 6 goes on, John is shown that the day of judgment is God's answer to this prayer of the martyrs for vengeance (6:12–17).

THE CONDITION OF THE MARTYRS

Revelation 6:11 concludes this brief but remarkable passage by revealing the *condition* of the martyrs above: "Then they were each given a white robe and told to rest a little longer, until the number of their fellow servants and their brothers should be complete, who were to be killed as they themselves had been."

First, the martyrs are each dressed in a "white robe." Some interpreters have seen these robes as glorified bodies given to the martyrs in heaven, perhaps as a special reward for their sacrifice. The use of this imagery in Revelation argues otherwise, however. The white robe signifies righteousness. In chapter 7, John sees the great assembly of the righteous in glory, all dressed in white, because they "have washed their robes and made them white in the blood of the Lamb" (Rev. 7:14). This makes clear that the white

---

8. Douglas F. Kelly, *Revelation*, Mentor Expository Commentary (Tain, Ross-shire, Scotland: Mentor, 2012), 128.

robes of righteousness are not earned by martyrdom as a meritorious act. This point needs to be emphasized, since history has recorded numbers of Christians who sought martyrdom as a way to earn heavenly distinction. The martyrs in heaven are dressed in white not because they died for Christ but because Christ died for them, as he did for all his people. Jesus wrote to the church in Sardis to encourage all believers who persevere in faith: "The one who conquers will be clothed thus in white garments, and I will never blot his name out of the book of life" (3:5).

Together with the righteous standing of the saints above, the white robes also speak of their purity. Whenever a Christian thinks of justification through faith in Christ, he or she should also be reminded of the calling to live in the holiness of sanctification. The saints above have attained the completion of their sanctification, their white robes testifying to the glory they have attained in Christ. The writer of Hebrews thus describes the glorified saints in the heavenly Jerusalem as "the spirits of the righteous made perfect" (Heb. 12:23).

Moreover, white is "the colour of victory. The martyrs appeared to have been defeated by their enemies. Actually they were given the victory by God."[9] What a statement God makes, since the Roman emperors who persecuted the church wore white robes in their triumphal parades! The reality from heaven shows that it is the saints, though weak in the world and despised for their faith, who attain the victory through union with the crucified Christ. Wilmshurst writes: "On earth, they are helpless victims on the losing side, hated and despised by their killers. . . . But how different it looks in heaven! Their place is nearest the throne, wearing the white robes of victory."[10]

Second, the white-robed martyrs enjoy the satisfaction of rest with God in heaven: they are "told to rest a little longer" (Rev. 6:11). The word for *rest* (Greek, *anapauo*) also has the idea of being *refreshed*. They enjoy the blessedness of those who have rested from their labors and bask in the presence of the Lord. They rest in the finished work of Christ, and their joy is enriched by the treasures they stored up in heaven during a life focused not on the world below but on the world above (Matt. 6:19–20). Revelation 14:13 proclaims: "Blessed are the dead who die in the Lord from now on[,] . . . that they may rest from their labors, for their deeds follow them!"

9. Leon Morris, *The Revelation of St. John: An Introduction and Commentary*, Tyndale New Testament Commentaries 20 (Grand Rapids: Eerdmans, 1969), 109.

10. Wilmshurst, *The Final Word*, 84.

Although the martyrs are clothed in white and have entered their bliss, they have not yet arrived at the full extent of their desire. For while they rest, they are also told to wait "until the number of their fellow servants and their brothers should be complete, who were to be killed as they themselves had been" (Rev. 6:11). The martyrs long to see redemptive history come to completion and all the elect gathered in, as well as God's answer to their cry for justice.

The day has not yet come when the number of God's people is complete and the church is filled with all those called to eternal life. This reality makes clear that the ingathering of souls is the primary work of the church today. Jesus said that before the end, "the gospel must first be proclaimed to all nations" (Mark 13:10). Why has the end not come, and why has the longing of the martyrs not yet been fulfilled? The Bible answers that the world is still permitted to make its martyrs because God is still saving sinners through Jesus Christ. Peter said: "The Lord is not slow to fulfill his promise as some count slowness, but is patient toward you, not wishing that any should perish, but that all should reach repentance" (2 Peter 3:9). God tells the martyrs above to wait in their blessed rest because of his heart of mercy for sinners below.

The unbeliever should realize, however, that God's patience may end soon, after which there will be no salvation. Paul thus wrote: "Behold, now is the favorable time; behold, now is the day of salvation" (2 Cor. 6:2). The believer should more zealously embrace Jesus' Great Commission, knowing that the time may be short: "Go therefore and make disciples of all nations, baptizing them in the name of the Father and of the Son and of the Holy Spirit, teaching them to observe all that I have commanded you" (Matt. 28:19–20).

Lessons from the Martyrs

These three verses provide a great wealth of lessons for us, in large part because of the rare glimpse they offer of believers in heaven after their death and before the final resurrection. I want to conclude by highlighting four important lessons.

First, this passage teaches that *the souls of Christians who die go immediately to heaven*. This is true not only for those who suffer violent deaths for Jesus but for all those who die having trusted him for salvation. Westminster

Confession of Faith 32.1 states this teaching in powerful terms: "The souls of the righteous, being then made perfect in holiness, are received into the highest heavens, where they behold the face of God, in light and glory, waiting for the full redemption of their bodies." The final resurrection does not take place until Revelation 20, yet here are the souls of those who died for Christ with God in glory.

This is why Christians grieve with a great hope for those who have died in the Lord. In ministering to those either facing death or grieving the death of a loved one, I like to point out that in Psalm 23, "the valley of the shadow of death" appears not at the end but in the middle of the journey (v. 4). Christians do not pass *into* death but pass *through* death so as to immediately enjoy the blessing of the presence of the Lord.

Notice, as well, that these souls are depicted as being conscious and aware in heaven, as well as knowledgeable about the affairs of earth. Some Christians have taught the doctrine of soul-sleep, which says that believers are unconscious between the time of death and the resurrection day. They point to the passages in which Jesus speaks of those who have died as "asleep" (see Matt. 9:24; John 11:11), not realizing that this expression describes the appearance of the dead body and not the experience of the soul. Jesus told the believing thief on the cross that "today you will be with me in Paradise" (Luke 23:43). Paul rejoiced that to be "away from the body" is to be "at home with the Lord" (2 Cor. 5:8).

Second, the condition of the martyrs in heaven shows that *the injustice of the world is overturned by God's righteous judgment.* Christians can be bitterly frustrated to stand by watching as ungodly agendas move forward successfully and perverse ideals capture society. Although the Bible has told us that this life involves tribulation, the experience can fill us with dismay. The martyrs of the first century suffered dreadful horrors, as have countless believers who died for Christ afterward. Yet the world's persecutors achieved for these Christians exactly the opposite of what they desired. They sought to put an end to their lives, but instead they ushered the believers into glory. They condemned the Christians, but the white robes in heaven overturned their verdict. They especially sought to rid themselves of the Christians' influence. Yet look where the martyrs are now! They are close to God's throne, from which the divine decrees go forth to rule history. The world thought that martyrdom was the ultimate disempowerment of Christ's people. "But look at what actually has happened: they have only dispatched them to a place of tremendous authority that they can now exercise near their heavenly father's heart in heaven, as they are praying."[11]

Third, Revelation 6:11 shows that *the number of those saved through Christ has been predetermined by God and all of them are certain to come to faith*. God knows "the number of their fellow servants and their brothers" and has appointed a time for their gathering to be complete, just as God has ordained the manner of their lives and of their deaths. This should encourage us in our witness to the gospel, since the elect are sure to be saved and many may come to Christ through our testimony. It should also encourage us to press on in following Christ, despite all manner of difficulty and even persecution, since through our faith we can be certain of an eternity in heaven.

Fourth, these verses show *the importance of the testimony of the martyrs to God's redemptive plan for history*. Philip Hughes writes, "A martyrdom, whereby one of the Lord's faithful witnesses is silenced in death, looks like a defeat for God and a damaging setback for the church; but it leads, over and over again, to the progress of the gospel and to an increase of power and blessing for the Lord's people."[12]

I noted earlier that the word *martyr* comes from the Greek verb that means "to witness." You do not, therefore, have to die violently for Jesus in order to play a decisive role in God's redeeming plan. But you do have to be true enough to God's Word that the world notices your faith. When I was a teenager, as a nominal Christian, I received a card that asked an important question: "If you were arrested for being a Christian, would there be enough evidence to convict you?" I knew then that the answer was that I would not necessarily be convicted on the charge of Christianity. What about you? Would you be convicted?

In 1745, the Huguenot pastor Louis Rang was convicted and condemned to die. He was promised his life if only he would renounce his faith in Christ. Not only did he reject the offer, but he went forth to the scaffold singing a French version of Psalm 118:24. "Here now is the happy day, for which we have been waiting," he sang. "Sing praise to God who gives us joy, and pleasures unabating." A few weeks later, another Huguenot pastor, Jacques

11. Kelly, *Revelation*, 126.
12. Philip Edgcumbe Hughes, *The Book of Revelation* (Downers Grove, IL: InterVarsity Press, 1990), 90.

Roger, was also condemned, after many years of evading the authorities. He said, "I am he whom you have sought for thirty-nine years. It is time you should find me." As Roger was taken to execution, he sang the same verse that Louis Rang had sung before him. A later Huguenot martyr in France was Francois Rochette, who was seized in 1762. He also refused to escape death by renouncing Christ. He, too, was led through the streets singing Psalm 118:24, "Here now is the happy day, for which we have been waiting."[13]

What was the message of all these martyrs, who by faith entered into death with joy in their hearts? Their message told of life eternal in the blissful rest of heaven through faith in Jesus Christ. Each of them knew the truth of Jesus' words, which now speak to us today: "Whoever would save his life will lose it, but whoever loses his life for my sake will save it" (Luke 9:24).

---

13. Rowland E. Prothero, *The Psalms in Human Life* (New York: E. P. Dutton, 1904), 225–28.

22

The Wrath of the Lamb

Revelation 6:12—17

*When he opened the sixth seal, I looked, and behold, there was
a great earthquake, and the sun became black as sackcloth,
[and] the full moon became like blood. (Rev. 6:12)*

*T*he cycles of history that begin in Revelation 4 can be identified by their various presentations of the final judgment. The first cycle, beginning in chapter 4, presents the seven seals of history, concluding with the disruption of creation in 6:12–17 and chapter 7's corresponding vision of the assembled saints in heaven. Subsequent visions will present the blowing of the final trumpet, at which the dead are judged and the destroyers are destroyed (Rev. 11:15–19), the coming of angels to reap the earth with a great sickle (14:14–16), the pouring out of the bowls of wrath (16:17–21), the fall of Babylon the great (18:1–24), the white horseman who treads "the winepress of the fury of the wrath of God" (19:15), and the great white throne judgment in which Satan and unbelievers are cast into the lake of fire (20:11–15). These seven scenes explore different facets of the same great event, which Revelation 6:17 labels "the great day of [God's] wrath."

In terms of the first cycle of history, found in Revelation 4–7, the day of judgment appears with the opening of the sixth seal. The first four seals unleashed the horsemen of conquest, violence, famine, and death, depicting the woes that will characterize the entire church age, from Christ's ascension until his return. The fifth seal showed the souls of the martyrs in heaven who died in the midst of the woes of these four seals. The sixth seal answers the prayer of the martyrs for justice and vengeance on the dwellers of earth. God told them to wait "until the number of their fellow servants and their brothers should be complete" (Rev. 6:11), and the sixth seal shows that this waiting will be fulfilled in God's timing. Just as seven is the number of completion and salvation in Revelation, six is the number of man. Thus, when Christ "opened the sixth seal" (6:12), the day of God's wrath appeared. William Hendriksen writes: "It describes the one great catastrophe at the end of this age. The dread and terror, the awe and consternation of that day is pictured under the twofold symbolism of a crashing universe and a thoroughly frightened human race."[1]

The Disruption of Creation

As we consider the disruption of creation depicted in Revelation 6:12–14, two important questions need to be answered that must be taken together. First, are these descriptions to be taken symbolically or more or less literally, and second, what is the event they describe? There are two main answers. Those who hold the *preterist* position (the name is derived from a Latin word meaning "past") hold that this cataclysmic language is symbolic of societal upheaval and collapse rather than describing a physical dissolution. Under this view, which is coupled with an early dating of Revelation, the calamity described here is not the final judgment but the fall of Jerusalem in A.D. 70. The alternative view holds that while symbolic language is used, the sixth seal depicts literal calamities at the end of the world in the final judgment.

The arguments of the preterists in favor of a symbolic interpretation are impressive. Primarily, they show that these images of physical calamity are drawn from Old Testament passages in which these same images are used of historical events describing God's interventions and especially depicting the fall of cities and empires. An earthquake appears in Exodus 19:18

---

1. William Hendriksen, *More than Conquerors: An Interpretation of the Book of Revelation* (1940; repr., Grand Rapids: Baker, 1967), 107.

to depict God's arrival on Mount Sinai and in Nahum 1:5 to describe the conquest of Nineveh. The sun was darkened when God judged Egypt in Exodus 19:21–23, and Ezekiel 32:7 shows the moon as not giving light in a later judgment of Egypt. The falling of stars was used in Joseph's dream to depict the eclipse of his brothers (Gen. 37:9). Most of these metaphors appear in Isaiah's prediction of Babylon's fall: "Behold, the day of the LORD comes, cruel, with wrath and fierce anger. . . . For the stars of the heavens and their constellations will not give their light; the sun will be dark at its rising, and the moon will not shed its light. . . . I will make the heavens tremble, and the earth will be shaken out of its place, at the wrath of the LORD of hosts in the day of his fierce anger" (Isa. 13:9–13).

In these passages, astronomical calamities represent the fall of rulers and nations. In the case of the sixth seal, preterists apply this imagery to the fall of Jerusalem in A.D. 70, since Revelation 6:13 alludes to a fig tree, which Jesus used as an image of Israel's judgment (Matt. 21:18–19). Moreover, they point out that a literal fulfillment is not physically possible, since, for instance, stars are far too vast to literally fall to the earth. Under this view, then, the sixth seal foretells the removal of the Jewish opposition to the gospel, just as God would later remove Rome for the sin of persecuting the church. Douglas Kelly writes: "Indeed, in due time, God will shake down everything else that opposes his church to make room for the kingdom of love and grace."[2]

There are reasons, however, to take the differing view that the sixth seal foretells the literal dissolution of creation in the final judgment of God. First, while we agree that this symbolism is often used in the Old Testament for falling empires and the conquest of cities, there are other passages showing that these temporal judgments anticipate the great and final day of judgment when the earth itself will be destroyed. Isaiah 24 uses the imagery of the sixth seal in saying that "the LORD will empty the earth and make it desolate. . . . The LORD will punish the host of heaven, in heaven, and the kings of the earth, on the earth" (Isa. 24:1, 21). Most significant is the prophecy of Isaiah 34:4, which John seems to be directly quoting in Revelation 6:12–14. Here, God is addressing the entire earth: "Let the earth hear, and all that fills it . . . . For the LORD is enraged against all the nations" (Isa. 34:1–2). Isaiah

2. Douglas F. Kelly, *Revelation*, Mentor Expository Commentary (Tain, Ross-shire, Scotland: Mentor, 2012), 135.

continues with language virtually repeated by John: "All the host of heaven shall rot away, and the skies roll up like a scroll. All their host shall fall, as leaves fall from the vine, like leaves falling from the fig tree" (34:4). Isaiah is describing universal judgment in which creation itself is dissolved. This fits Revelation 6:17's description of this event as "the great day" of God's wrath. Additionally, the sixth seal answers the prayers of the fifth seal, which call for judgment on the entire world (6:10). Moreover, the language used here occurs elsewhere in Revelation to describe the final judgment of all mankind (11:13; 16:18–20; 20:11).[3]

Finally, a literal reading of the sixth seal fits Jesus' depiction in the Olivet Discourse. Jesus spoke of the sun being darkened, the moon not giving light, the stars falling, and the powers of heaven being shaken in tandem with his second coming and the end of the age (Matt. 24:29–32). There, Jesus used the metaphor of the fig tree in the same sense as Isaiah 34:4 and Revelation 6:13, as a lesson of the need to be ready for the end. This literal teaching is confirmed in Peter's second letter: "The heavens will pass away with a roar, and the heavenly bodies will be burned up and dissolved, and the earth and the works that are done on it will be exposed" (2 Peter 3:10).

Even in depicting the literal disruption of creation, there is probably symbolism in these verses. Still, a mainly literal reading is possible. A great earthquake of unprecedented violence could spew up lava and ash to darken the sky, and the falling of stars could refer to asteroids' smashing the earth. George Eldon Ladd summarizes: "The language is not merely poetical or symbolic of spiritual realities but describes a real cosmic catastrophe whose actual character we cannot conceive."[4]

Revelation 6:12–14 describes either six items, if we take the removing of the mountains and islands together, as John presents them, or seven items if we take them separately. If six items, the idea is probably that of imperfection that warrants judgment, and if seven items, the idea is that of the complete destruction visited on the earth. David Chilton writes: "Just as the salvation of God's people is spoken of in terms of creation, . . . so God's judgments

---

3. See G. K. Beale, *The Book of Revelation: A Commentary on the Greek Text*, New International Greek Testament Commentary (Grand Rapids: Eerdmans, 1999), 396–99, as well as Robert L. Thomas, *Revelation 1–7: An Exegetical Commentary* (Chicago: Moody, 1992), 450–51, for a thorough presentation of a mainly literalist interpretation. Kelly, *Revelation*, 130–36, gives the preterist view.

4. George Eldon Ladd, *A Commentary on the Revelation of John* (Grand Rapids: Eerdmans, 1972), 108.

... are spoken of in terms of de-creation, the collapse of the universe—God ripping apart and dissolving the fabric of creation."[5]

Revelation 6:12 speaks of "a great earthquake," accompanied by the sun becoming "black as sackcloth" and the full moon "like blood." Many of the cities to which John was writing had suffered devastation from earthquakes. Here, the shaking of the whole creation makes way for the new creation in the return of Christ (Hag. 2:6–7; Heb. 12:26–27). As the darkening of the sun and moon portended the fall of empires in the Old Testament, here it is the entire earth that comes under judgment. The sun's being described with reference to the black goat's hair of sackcloth adds the idea of humiliation and mourning. The blood-colored moon signified pending calamity in divine judgment.

Revelation 6:13 adds "the stars of the sky" falling to earth, "as the fig tree sheds its winter fruit when shaken by a gale." Whether this speaks of meteors or symbolically depicts the sky falling like late fruits in a gale, the image strikes terror into hearts. Jesus said that "there will be terrors and great signs from heaven" (Luke 21:11). Robert Mounce writes that the "falling of stars . . . could mean but one thing to the ancient—the end had come."[6] The same could be said about the fifth event: "The sky vanished like a scroll that is being rolled up" (Rev. 6:14). Whether the sky is broken in the center to roll back both ways or rolled up from one end to the other, the picture is the dissolution of the cosmos as viewed from the earth. Just as Jesus' first coming saw "the heavens being torn open" for his baptism (Mark 1:10), in his second coming the sky will be finally rolled up (Heb. 1:12). These images make certain that these events occur at the end of history, not merely close to the end, as dispensationalists teach, since the falling of the stars and the tearing of the sky can signal only the end of the age.

Finally, objects that have symbolized permanence for centuries, mountains and islands, are removed from their places (Rev. 6:14). This depicts what will be celebrated later in Revelation: "the former things have passed away" (21:4). Taken together, these images show the dissolving of the world corrupted by Adam's fall into sin (cf. Gen. 3:17) and condemned by its rejection of God's Son so that a new age of glory and a renewed cosmos may take its place in the return of Christ to the earth.

---

5. David Chilton, *Days of Vengeance: An Exposition of the Book of Revelation* (Ft. Worth, TX: Dominion Press, 1987), 196.

6. Robert H. Mounce, *Revelation*, rev. ed., New International Commentary on the New Testament (Grand Rapids: Eerdmans, 1997), 162.

THE DISMAY OF MANKIND

Not only does the sixth seal destroy the corrupted cosmos, but the upheavals picture the terror and dread that the condemned human race will not escape. Thus, in addition to the dissolution of creation, John sees the dismay of sinful mankind:

> Then the kings of the earth and the great ones and the generals and the rich and the powerful, and everyone, slave and free, hid themselves in the caves and among the rocks of the mountains, calling to the mountains and rocks, "Fall on us and hide us from the face of him who is seated on the throne, and from the wrath of the Lamb, for the great day of their wrath has come, and who can stand?" (Rev. 6:15–17)

Here, John sees six categories of condemned mankind (or seven, if the last couple is separated) who experience the great day of wrath. They describe all classes of society, showing that distinctions are lost in God's judgment of unbelievers. Beale writes that this list shows that "God is no respecter of persons but judges all on an equal basis regardless of their social, political, or economic standing."[7] The prominence, however, is given to judgment of the rulers and the great of the world. The martyrs prayed for God to judge and avenge "those who dwell on the earth" (Rev. 6:10), and it starts at the top.

First are the kings, who Psalm 2 said had "set themselves . . . against the LORD and against his Anointed," and are now broken "with a rod of iron" (Ps. 2:2, 9). Together with them are their deputies, "the great ones," who as princes or cabinet members shared in the earth's ungodly rule. They are joined by "the generals," who enjoyed martial glory but now face divine wrath. The "rich," who often exerted more control than kings and presidents, also face judgment, together with the influential and "powerful" (Rev. 6:15). All these kinds of people ran the world in its rebellion to God and together opposed the gospel reign of Jesus Christ. With them are the upper and lower classes of common people—"everyone, slave and free"—who face the dreadful condemnation that their rebellion against God deserves.

The dismayed human race responds to the final judgment in two ways. First is a vain attempt to flee. The people called "to the mountains and

---

7. Beale, *Revelation*, 400.

rocks, 'Fall on us and hide us'" (Rev. 6:16). In this way, they state that nothing is worse than facing the judgment that has come. Yet none will be able to escape. James Boice writes that when disaster strikes a country, "dictators will have deposited fortunes in Swiss bank accounts. Generals will have planes waiting to whisk them to a safe haven in South America. Even common people will have ways of avoiding the disaster. But not when God comes to execute his judgments."[8] In that day, all—high and low, rich and poor, free and slave—will cower before God's wrath and yet fail to escape the universal terror of the day of wrath.

Coupled with humans' attempt to flee is their terror in God's judgment. This is why they find death preferable to "the face of him who is seated on the throne" (Rev. 6:16). Like Adam and Eve fleeing from God in the garden after they had sinned (Gen. 3:8), the human race is unified in desiring above all to avoid the face of their Creator, against whom they had so viciously rebelled, and whose countenance is now revealed in wrath. Here, we are shown that "what sinners dread most is not death, but the revealed Presence of God."[9] God is revealed to condemned humanity as the enthroned Creator and as the Lamb whose offered salvation was spurned and despised. How total will their alarm be when "the great day of their wrath has come" (Rev. 6:17)!

Dismayed mankind cries in despair, "Who can stand?" (Rev. 6:17). The answer is given in chapter 7, which shows the great host of redeemed believers in heaven, who believed the gospel, confessed their need of forgiveness, embraced Jesus as Savior and Lord, and in this way were delivered from the wrath to come. John sees "a great multitude that no one could number, from every nation, from all tribes and peoples and languages, standing before the throne and before the Lamb, clothed in white robes, with palm branches in their hands, and crying out with a loud voice, 'Salvation belongs to our God who sits on the throne, and to the Lamb!'" (7:9–10).

THE GREAT DAY OF WRATH

In reflecting on the dire events depicted under the sixth seal, we should consider four applications. The first notes that *since the earth is to be destroyed*

---

8. James Montgomery Boice, *Revelation*, unpublished manuscript, n.d., chap. 19, p. 9.

9. Henry Barclay Swete, *Commentary on Revelation*, 2 vols. (1911; repr., Grand Rapids: Kregel, 1977), 2:94.

in God's judgment, we should live with an aim to the world to come and not to this present, passing world.

The New Testament is filled with this argument. Paul wrote to the Corinthians that "the present form of this world is passing away" (1 Cor. 7:31). Therefore, even though Christians are free to enjoy the things of this world, we should not live for them. This world will not last, and even its best achievements, monuments, and glories are destined to perish apart from Christ. If we believe that this world will make way for the eternal kingdom of Christ, then we should seek the treasures of his realm. We should honor Christ through obedience to his Word, serve the growth and well-being of his church, and share the gospel so that more people can inhabit eternity with us. This application urges each of us to take stock of our lives to see whether our priorities are on earth or in heaven. What would a study of your calendar, your bookshelf, your checkbook, or your Facebook page say about your heart? Is it set on earthly things or on Christ and his kingdom? Peter addressed this issue in his second letter:

> Since all these things are thus to be dissolved, what sort of people ought you to be in lives of holiness and godliness, waiting for and hastening the coming of the day of God, because of which the heavens will be set on fire and dissolved, and the heavenly bodies will melt as they burn! (2 Peter 3:11–12)

A second application was likely on John's mind as he penned Revelation to churches facing persecution. I mentioned earlier the preterist reading of Revelation, which sees the sixth seal as describing only the fall of Jerusalem in A.D. 70. Another preterist argument comes from Revelation 6:16, in which those who are judged call on the mountains and rocks, seeking refuge. Jesus spoke of this to the daughters of Jerusalem who were lamenting as he carried the cross. Jesus told them to weep for themselves and their children, since the day will come when they "say to the mountains, 'Fall on us,' and to the hills, 'Cover us'" (Luke 23:28–30). The presence of this same warning in Revelation 6:16 does not prove, as preterists claim, that the sixth seal describes only the fall of Jerusalem. It does show, however, that God's final judgment on all mankind is anticipated in judgments throughout history against those who oppose his gospel and persecute his people. God destroyed Jerusalem for its rejection of Christ and hatred for his gospel, having forewarned the Christians to escape the city (Matt. 24:15–20). God later judged and destroyed the Roman Empire after the Caesars had persecuted Christians and then corrupted the church when the gospel had been adopted.

The pattern of God's judgment on enemies of his gospel and deliverance of his people is repeated throughout history. Whether the French Revolution, Nazi Germany, or Communist Eastern Europe and China, God has judged the rulers and powers that have opposed his gospel and persecuted the church. Today, godless humanism and government hostility to Christianity can only bring divine judgment on America. Just as God answered the prayers of Revelation 6:10 with the judgment of verses 12–17, he hears and will answer the prayers of suffering believers today. Knowing that God saves his people, *Christians facing opposition and hardship should not give up or give in to the world but persevere in faith, prayer, and a loving gospel witness, knowing that redemption is near.*

Third, *believers in Christ should not fear being caught in this dreadful wrath.* Revelation 6:16 says that the final judgment reveals "the face of him who is seated on the throne." This is therefore not an overthrow of the plan of history described in the Bible but its fulfillment. The promises of God are established by this throne. Chapter 4 showed God's throne encircled by the rainbow that reminds him of his covenant of grace. Romans 8:30 proclaims that "those whom he predestined he also called, and those whom he called he also justified, and those whom he justified he also glorified." This is the will of the sovereign God enthroned in heaven for his people in Christ. Romans 5:1–2 says that "since we have been justified by faith, we have peace with God through our Lord Jesus Christ . . . , and we rejoice in hope of the glory of God." Reading this woeful passage of Revelation, we ask, "Will I survive the end of the world in judgment?" Derek Thomas writes:

> There is only one sure way to answer that question. We must believe the message of the gospel that says that faith in Jesus Christ delivers us from the wrath which is to come. The great answer of chapter 7 is that every single soul that Jesus seals in this world, will withstand the judgment of the world to come. Every single one![10]

Finally, *those who have heard the gospel but have not yet believed should realize that the present age of grace, and the opportunity for salvation, will*

10. Derek Thomas, *Let's Study Revelation* (Edinburgh: Banner of Truth, 2003), 59.

suddenly end and be followed by final judgment and divine wrath. If you have not embraced Jesus for salvation, then you will be in this picture, desperately unable to escape the wrath of the Savior whom you had personally spurned. You, above all others, should realize now that the judgment to come is the great day not only of God's justice but also of "the wrath of the Lamb" (Rev. 6:16). Mankind had rejected the Lamb who was slain for the forgiveness of sin and will now suffer God's wrath at his hands. Beale writes: "The gentle Lamb who was slain on the cross is now in an exalted position over the whole cosmos . . . to pour out his wrath. He is not only loving to his people but also a just judge of his enemies."[11] When the world's only Savior has become its wrathful Judge, there will then be no salvation for any who did not previously come to Jesus in humble, repentant faith.

In May 1980, geologists noticed warning signs that Mount St. Helens in Washington would soon blow in a colossal eruption of ash and fire. Harry Truman, named for the president, was caretaker of a lodge on Spirit Lake, five miles north of the volcanic mountain. He heard the warnings broadcast on radio and television. When the police evacuated the area, Truman refused to budge. Friends contacted him, urging him to flee, but Harry refused to heed the warnings. He even appeared on television, laughing away the danger. But at 8:31 A.M. on May 18, the mountain exploded. Millions of tons of rock flew ten miles into the sky, concussion waves crashed down the mountain faster than the speed of sound, and everything within 150 square miles was flattened. Afterward, no sign of Harry Truman was found. He was destroyed in a cataclysm that he had foolishly denied and that he could easily have escaped until the moment it came.[12]

I earlier cited Psalm 2, which notes the rebellion of the kings and rulers of earth and their destruction under the iron rod of Christ. The psalm ends with an appeal, a warning, and a promise for us: "Kiss the Son, lest he be angry, and you perish in the way, for his wrath is quickly kindled. Blessed are all who take refuge in him" (Ps. 2:12).

11. Beale, *Revelation*, 403.
12. Taken from Boice, *Revelation*, chap. 19, p. 12.

23

THE NUMBER OF THE SEALED

Revelation 7:1–12

And I heard the number of the sealed, 144,000, sealed from
every tribe of the sons of Israel. (Rev. 7:4)

*T*he book of Revelation weaves its visions in an intricate and closely knit tapestry. For instance, in chapter 6 the martyrs beneath God's throne ask when he will avenge their suffering and are told to wait "until the number of their fellow servants and their brothers should be complete" (Rev. 6:11). The opening of the next seal answers this prayer as the human race is subjected to judgment. Terrified mankind asks in dismay: "Who can stand?" (6:17). Chapter 7 answers this question, depicting "a great multitude" of God's people "standing before the throne and before the Lamb" (7:9–10). The full number of the martyrs' fellow servants is represented as "144,000, sealed from every tribe of the sons of Israel" (7:4). This imagery clearly depicts the great difference between those who trust in Jesus and those who refuse him in unbelief. The Christian suffers below but then reigns in heaven above. The unbeliever reigns in sin below but suffers heaven's wrath from above.

At the end of Revelation 6, the sixth seal has been broken, unleashing the final day of God's wrath. Before the seventh seal, which can signify only the return of Christ and the beginning of the new age, Revelation 7 provides a dramatic interlude. It shows that God's people, being righteous in Christ, are safeguarded through the tribulations of the world in order to glorify God in heaven.

SEALED AND SECURED

It is important to remember that Revelation does not present a straight-line chronology of the end times but rather gives a series of overlapping visions to present history from the perspective of heaven. Along these lines, chapter 7 cycles back to the time of the first four seals in chapter 6, which describe the calamities by which Christ judges sin and advances his kingdom. John saw "four angels standing at the four corners of the earth, holding back the four winds of the earth, that no wind might blow on earth or sea or against any tree" (Rev. 7:1). These angels are closely related to the four horsemen of chapter 6. Not only are there four of both, but in the book of Zechariah, where these images originate, God's horsemen are closely related to the four winds (Zech. 6:5). Winds present another image of judgment and disaster, as anyone who has endured a hurricane can tell you, and the four winds are a metaphor for the entirety of the earth. Here, the four angels are "holding back" the winds, that is, restraining God's judgments from utterly destroying the earth.

If we wonder why the angels are restraining the winds, a second angel appears to explain: "Then I saw another angel ascending from the rising of the sun, with the seal of the living God, and he called with a loud voice to the four angels who had been given power to harm earth and sea, saying, 'Do not harm the earth or the sea or the trees, until we have sealed the servants of our God on their foreheads'" (Rev. 7:2–3). The earth, sea, and trees depict the entirety of the earth. The point is that the final judgment, depicted under the sixth seal, is being suspended so that the whole number of God's people may be gathered. This fits God's answer to the martyrs of the fifth seal, saying that vengeance would wait "until the number of their fellow servants and their brothers should be complete" (6:11).

In the Bible, news of salvation often appears from the east, just as Ezekiel said that the Lord would enter his temple from the east (Ezek. 43:2) and as the magi who worshiped Christ came from the east (Matt. 2:1). Now from that direction comes an angel bearing "the seal of the living God" to mark "the servants of . . . God" (Rev. 7:2–3).

In the ancient world, a seal was used to *identify* an object as belonging to its master or to *authenticate* a message as coming from him. A common kind of seal was a signet ring, which bore the emblem of its owner. In the case of the angel's seal, the biblical background is Ezekiel 9. God gave the prophet a vision of his judgment of Jerusalem, but first he marked his faithful people: "Pass through the city, through Jerusalem, and put a mark on the foreheads of the men who sigh and groan over all the abominations that are committed in it" (Ezek. 9:4). Only those marked with God's seal would escape his judgment. In Revelation 14:1, we are told that the "144,000 . . . had [the Lamb's] name and his Father's name written on their foreheads." It seems likely, then, that the seal in Revelation 7 affixes the name of Christ and of the Father on their servants.

As in Ezekiel 9, the point of this sealing is that the faithful people of God will not be harmed by the calamities of the four riders or the blowing of the four winds. This does not mean that Christians will not suffer in earthly ways, since the fifth seal shows that many suffered death for God's Word. Christians in this life suffer all manner of grief—sickness, poverty, oppression, slander, and death—yet through these sufferings Christians enter salvation. James Boice writes: "What this sealing accomplishes is their perseverance in faith, God's work in them to assure that they will stand firm to the end."[1] Paul wrote: "God's firm foundation stands, bearing this seal: 'The Lord knows those who are his'" (2 Tim. 2:19). Everyone who calls on Jesus in true faith is immediately marked by God to be saved out of this world. Jesus assured us: "Truly, truly, I say to you, whoever hears my word and believes him who sent me has eternal life. He does not come into judgment, but has passed from death to life" (John 5:24).

The biblical idea of sealing not only identifies ownership and authenticates but also signifies *protection*. Jesus' grave was sealed to ensure that it would not be broken into, and God seals his people to guarantee our salvation. Paul spoke in this sense of the Holy Spirit: "When you heard the word of truth, the gospel of your salvation, and believed in him, [you] were sealed with the promised Holy Spirit, who is the guarantee of our inheritance until we acquire possession of it, to the praise of his glory" (Eph. 1:13–14). God's seal is

1. James Montgomery Boice, *Revelation*, unpublished manuscript, n.d., chap. 20, p. 3.

the indwelling Holy Spirit, whose presence accomplishes all three things that a seal does. The Holy Spirit *identifies* a true Christian by the transforming effects in his or her life. The Holy Spirit *authenticates* a Christian's testimony, enabling our lives to attest to the truth of the gospel. Finally, the Holy Spirit *protects* our faith unto salvation. His coming to regenerate believers is the beginning that guarantees the end and gives us a foretaste of the inheritance that we will fully possess in glory. William Hendriksen writes, "This sealing is the most precious thing under heaven."[2] By the seal of God's Spirit we are *identified* as belonging to him; we are *authenticated* and assured of God's saving blessing; and we are secured and *protected* against those things that would threaten our faith and separate us from God.

Since God's Spirit is the all-important seal of our salvation, how do we know that we possess the Spirit? Jesus once answered by comparing the Spirit to the wind: "You hear its sound, but you do not know where it comes from" (John 3:8). His point was that the Spirit is best known by his effects. You feel and observe tangible evidence, which tells you that the wind has blown. By the marks of the Holy Spirit we know his presence in a person's life, authenticating a profession of faith and sealing the Christian for salvation.

Perhaps the greatest book on the marks of the Holy Spirit was written by Jonathan Edwards, the eighteenth-century American preacher and theologian. Edwards was concerned about false conversions during the Great Awakening, and he conducted a biblical study of what differentiates true versus false conversions. His book was titled *The Distinguishing Marks of a Work of the Spirit of God*, and his theme verse was 1 John 4:1: "Beloved, do not believe every spirit, but test the spirits to see whether they are from God."[3]

Edwards first noted that outward evidences such as strong emotions and enthusiastic responses to God's Word can occur without the Holy Spirit. He then listed five marks that only the Spirit can produce and that thus validate a person's claim to faith in Christ. First, Edwards noted *the elevation of esteem in Jesus Christ* as the Son of God and Savior. This is the surest sign of the true operation of the Holy Spirit. "He will bear witness about me," Jesus said of the Spirit (John 15:26); "He will glorify me" (16:14). Second, a true work of the Spirit *opposes the reign of Satan and causes us to turn from*

2. William Hendriksen, *More than Conquerors: An Interpretation of the Book of Revelation* (1940; repr., Grand Rapids: Baker, 1967), 110.

3. Jonathan Edwards, *The Distinguishing Marks of a Work of the Spirit of God*, in *Jonathan Edwards on Revival* (Edinburgh: Banner of Truth, 1965).

sin (see 1 John 1:5–6). God's Spirit is a Spirit of holiness, causing believers to seek new lives that honor God. Third, a true conversion inspires *an increased interest in God's Word*, including a desire to know what the Bible teaches and to put it into practice. Fourth, the Spirit enlightens us with a *sound grasp of true doctrine* and gives a zeal to defend it against error. Fifth is *the mark of love*. Edwards writes, "If the spirit that is at work among a people operates as a spirit of love to God and man, it is a sure sign that it is the Spirit of God."[4] False spirituality is interested in self, but the Spirit gives a concern for others, an eagerness to sacrifice, and a heart that gladly forgives and happily serves.

Given the significance of God's seal, every Christian should zealously pursue the evidence of the Holy Spirit's presence. We can never earn God's seal, but by a living faith we can experience the mark of God's Spirit. And how encouraging it is to us, even under trials, to know the Spirit's indwelling. The Spirit is the "seal of the living God" (Rev. 7:2). God is not a dead idol but lives so as to protect and provide for us. The winds may blow and we may suffer, but angels are restraining judgment for our sake and God himself has pledged our salvation. For this reason, Charles Spurgeon emphasized the joyful hope that should characterize Christians in a hostile world, since even through trials we are being saved: "It is impossible that any ill should happen to the man who is beloved of the Lord. Ill to him is no ill, but only good in a mysterious form. Losses enrich him, sickness is his medicine, reproach is his honour, death is his gain."[5]

144,000 SEALED SERVANTS

Together with the vision of the angels, John heard the number of the sealed, 144,000, sealed from every tribe of the sons of Israel:

12,000 from the tribe of Judah were sealed,
12,000 from the tribe of Reuben,
12,000 from the tribe of Gad,
12,000 from the tribe of Asher,
12,000 from the tribe of Naphtali,

4. Ibid., 115.
5. Quoted in Steve Wilmshurst, *The Final Word: The Book of Revelation Simply Explained* (Darlington, UK: Evangelical Press, 2008), 96.

12,000 from the tribe of Manasseh,
12,000 from the tribe of Simeon,
12,000 from the tribe of Levi,
12,000 from the tribe of Issachar,
12,000 from the tribe of Zebulun,
12,000 from the tribe of Joseph,
12,000 from the tribe of Benjamin were sealed. (Rev. 7:4–8)

This recitation extends the vision that began with the angels, identifying the sealed servants of God.

The first question about this body concerns its identity. Some readers interpret the 144,000 literally. A prominent example is the Jehovah's Witnesses, who believe that only 144,000 people will spend eternity in heaven. They further teach that this number was achieved in 1935, so that believers after that date will not enter heaven but will make up the blessed multitude on earth, which they see described in Revelation 7:9–17. Not only is there no basis for this interpretation, but it gets the two groups exactly backward. In John's vision, the 144,000 sealed servants are undergoing trials on earth, and the vast multitude describes the Christians in heaven.

Another literal approach is taken by dispensationalists, who make up the majority of evangelical Christians in America today. Dispensationalists begin with the premise that Israel and the Christian church are separate bodies with different eternal destinies. They also interpret Revelation's visions in an exclusively futurist sense, as pertaining only to the final sequence of years before Christ's return. With these presuppositions, dispensationalists see the 144,000 as the literal number of ethnic Jews who convert to Christ after the rapture and bear witness to the gospel in the final days.[6]

There are overwhelming reasons to reject the dispensationalist approach and instead to understand 144,000 as a symbolic number. First, the dispensational view treats Revelation 7 as chronologically following chapter 6, showing what happens after the sixth seal. Yet this is impossible, since the sixth seal showed the dissolution of the heavens and the earth in the great day of God's wrath (Rev. 6:12–17). All that remains is the physical return of Christ, which the seventh seal signifies. These 144,000 are sealed not after the sixth seal but rather during the calamities of the first four seals.

6. Robert L. Thomas, *Revelation 1–7: An Exegetical Commentary* (Chicago: Moody, 1992), 463–82.

Second, dispensationalists insist that the references to Israel require a literal rendering of the 144,000, especially in light of the naming of specific tribes. This argument exposes the chief weakness of their argument: the failure to note that the Christian church is organically joined with Old Testament Israel. Whereas dispensationalists eternally separate Israel and the church, Revelation consistently refers to Christians with the imagery of Israel. The number of Christ's apostles corresponds to Israel's tribes, and Jesus promised that they would "sit on twelve thrones, judging the twelve tribes of Israel" (Matt. 19:28). Paul said that a believer in Christ is a true Jew (Rom. 2:29). He taught that Gentile Christians are grafted into the olive tree of Israel (11:17–19), and he referred to the Christian church as "the Israel of God" (Gal. 6:16). Revelation is filled with allusions to Israel, the Old Testament, and the ancient temple, all with reference to the identity and experience of John's Christian readers. It is most natural, therefore, to see Israel's tribes as referring to the church.

Questions are raised about the specific list that John cites, noting the names of twelve tribes from Israel. It is an unusual list for several reasons. For one, Judah is listed first, since Jesus was born from that tribe. The tribe of Dan is omitted, along with Ephraim. The probable reason for this is that Jeroboam's golden calves were erected in Dan and Ephraim, so that these two tribes led Israel into idolatry. Since idolaters do not enter the kingdom of God, these tribes are omitted. Moreover, this list presents the sons of Jacob's concubines before the sons of Jacob's wives: after Judah and Reuben the firstborn come Gad, Asher, Naphtali, born of concubines, and then the sons born of Jacob's wives: Simeon, Levi, Issachar, Zebulun, Joseph, and Benjamin. The most likely suggestion regarding this ordering is that the sons of Jacob's concubines signify the inclusion of the Gentiles, who are now inserted ahead of legitimate Israelite sons. At the time of John's writing, the twelve tribes no longer even existed in a literal sense, having been eradicated by God in the various exiles of Israel.[7]

These considerations make it obvious that the 144,000 sealed servants are to be taken symbolically rather than literally. The number is achieved by multiplying twelve, for Israel, by twelve, for the apostles, to signify the entirety of the redeemed church. This matches the heavenly city of chapter 21, with

7. See a thorough explanation in Dennis E. Johnson, *Triumph of the Lamb: A Commentary on Revelation* (Phillipsburg, NJ: P&R Publishing, 2001), 132–33.

twelve gates for Israel's tribes and twelve foundations for the apostles (Rev. 21:12–14), signifying the entirety of the redeemed church. This number is multiplied by a thousand probably to show the great multitude of Christ's people. The idea of Christians' being numbered like Israel's tribes may suggest that the church forms an army, carrying forth the banner of the gospel.[8] With the winds of judgment and calamity being restrained for their passage and having being sealed by God, the church triumphantly advances to heaven.

This symbolic understanding is made certain by the verses that follow: "After this I looked, and behold, a great multitude that no one could number, from every nation, from all tribes and peoples and languages, standing before the throne and before the Lamb, clothed in white robes, with palm branches in their hands" (Rev. 7:9). This language reminds us of chapter 5. There, John heard that the Lion of Judah could open the scroll, and then he looked and saw the Lamb at the throne (5:5–6). The Lion and the Lamb are the same person: John heard one thing about him and then saw another. Likewise, John hears of the 144,000, and then turns and sees the great multitude beyond counting. They are one body, the church, first depicted in battle array on earth and then as glorified in heaven.

In this way, the progression of chapter 7 is completed. First are the four angels restraining the winds of judgment and woe. The other angel comes to seal the servants of God, seen symbolically in the world as militant Israel. Finally, God's people are revealed as a vast multitude beyond human comprehension, glorified in heaven and rejoicing in the worship of their Savior God.

The Plentiful Harvest

When we think of the church in terms of Israel marching from Egypt to the promised land in the days of the exodus, we are reminded of the necessity of our perseverance in faith. Most of the Israelites who departed from Egypt under Moses never entered the promised land because of their rebellion and unbelief. Hebrews 4:2 warns that many who attend church today are like the outward members of Israel who never entered salvation, explaining that "the message they heard did not benefit them, because they were not united by faith with those who listened." This warns us that mere membership or

---

8. Grant R. Osborne, *Revelation*, Baker Exegetical Commentary on the New Testament (Grand Rapids: Baker Academic, 2002), 313.

attendance at church does not grant us salvation, but only true saving faith and the indwelling Holy Spirit. Revelation 7 assures us that true believers are sealed by God so as to persevere all the way to heaven. The question is: "Are we true believers, and do our lives bear testimony to the presence and power of God's Spirit?" The first application of Revelation 7, then, is for us to know the reality of the Spirit's presence in our lives, rather than a mere outward Christianity. Have we embraced Christ in a living faith, which alone can attest to our sealing by God for salvation?

Two more applications flow from these visions. Revelation 7:9–10 shows the church above praising God for its salvation. The great multitude is "standing before the throne and before the Lamb, clothed in white robes, with palm branches in their hands, and crying out with a loud voice, 'Salvation belongs to our God who sits on the throne, and to the Lamb!'" We will consider these verses later in greater detail. But we should notice that this scene matches that of the Feast of Tabernacles in Israel, which celebrated both the successful completion of the exodus and the ingathering of the annual harvest. We see this especially in the waving of palm branches, which was one of the chief features of this festival, praising God for the ingathered harvest. How appropriate this worship will be in heaven, when the entire harvest of Christ's people will have been gathered in.

One reason that John was shown this worship above was to inspire Christians here in this present world—during the trials signified by the first four seals—to glorify God for the salvation that is completely secured by his grace. The saints above sing to God and to the Lamb, thanking them for the salvation that is of sovereign grace alone: "Salvation belongs to our God who sits on the throne, and to the Lamb!" Our salvation is the will of the Father and the work of the Son, so they are worthy to be praised by us. There is no reason why we should wait for heaven to give this praise, since our salvation is as secure now as it will be accomplished then. Augustus Toplady wrote: "More happy, but not more secure, the glorified spirits in heav'n."[9] How we rejoice to know that we will be more happy once we are in heaven. But how we also rejoice to know that we are just as secure now amid the trials of earth as we will be forever in the splendors of heaven.

John's vision continues in Revelation 7:11–12 with the angels of heaven worshiping God because of what they have learned through our salvation:

9. Augustus M. Toplady, "A Debtor to Mercy Alone" (1771).

"Amen! Blessing and glory and wisdom and thanksgiving and honor and power and might be to our God forever and ever! Amen" (Rev. 7:12). Knowing this, we should endeavor to live now in such a way that watching angels will marvel at the power of God's grace in our lives so as to praise our Savior forever.

Finally, we are reminded of the gospel imperative that shapes the calling of every Christian. Why has judgment not yet come? Why are the angels restraining the four winds? The answer: so that the full number of God's elect people may come in. Our present history exists for the saving of the great multitude that will worship above. Like the twelve tribes in marching order, the church is sent through history on a gospel mission, to take the good news of Jesus Christ throughout the world so that countless millions will be saved.

Do we have a missional mind-set and zeal that fits this picture? Looking on the heavenly Feast of Tabernacles celebrating the final harvest, do we realize that the work in the fields is taking place right now? A zealous church should be asking, "What more can we do to reach out with the gospel to those around us and throughout the world?" What role are you playing in the great harvest of the gospel for salvation? Do you pray for specific people to be saved? Do you warmly invite neighbors to church? Are you prepared to explain the gospel message of Jesus to others, and are you willing to do so?

The gospel imperative is written across John's vision no less surely than the name of God and the Lamb are written on the foreheads of his people. The vast hosts of heaven, saints and angels alike, will spend eternity glorifying God for the salvation he has given. What a joyful privilege it is for us to be his servants on earth, sealed and protected by his Spirit, to carry the gospel to the lost. "The harvest is plentiful," Jesus told his disciples, but then sadly regretted that "the laborers are few" (Matt. 9:37).

24

WASHED IN THE BLOOD

Revelation 7:9–17

*After this I looked, and behold, a great multitude that no one
could number, from every nation, from all tribes and peoples
and languages, standing before the throne and before the Lamb,
clothed in white robes, with palm branches in their hands.*
(Rev. 7:9)

Charles Dickens's novel *A Christmas Carol* tells of Ebenezer
Scrooge, a miserly man who cared more about money than
people. Scrooge is visited by a succession of benevolent ghosts,
who take him on a mystic tour of Christmas past, Christmas present, and
Christmas future. Through these visions, Scrooge comes to a new understanding of his life and is changed from an unhappy, unpopular grouch to
a joyful and beloved benefactor.

The vision that concludes Revelation 7 has a similar intention for the
churches to which John was writing. Under the anxiety of impending persecution and other earthly trials, they are shown a vision of what they really
are in the sight of God and of the glorious future assured for them in Christ.
The logic is that if the Christians could only see themselves in terms of
their heavenly destiny, they would find strength to prevail in the contest of

faith in this world. As Christians today read and study Revelation, living in the same world as the early believers did, we are also intended to look on ourselves from the perspective of our heavenly identity and destination so that we will stand firm in faith. Douglas Kelly writes: "This passage, as well as any in the Word of God, puts our minds on heaven, where many of our loved ones already are and where all who are saved will soon be."[1]

WHO THESE ARE: OUR DESTINY

We have an expression—"Lo and behold!"—for a remarkable sight that comes before us. I remember stepping up to the rim of the Grand Canyon as a boy, or more recently my first sight of Niagara Falls, and being almost overwhelmed by the scenic majesty before my eyes. The apostle John had this kind of experience, turning to see not a landscape but a vision of the glorified church in heaven: "After this I looked, and behold, a great multitude that no one could number, from every nation, from all tribes and peoples and languages, standing before the throne and before the Lamb, clothed in white robes, with palm branches in their hands" (Rev. 7:9). We saw in our study of verses 4–8 that this great multitude is the heavenly counterpart to the 144,000 sealed servants on earth, which depicted the whole and complete church that is protected by God through trials. Like Ebenezer Scrooge's Ghost of Christmas Present, this vision informs believers of what they truly are: a multitude too great to number, standing before God's throne.

It is tempting for Christians to see themselves as an insignificant minority, unable to tip the scales of politics or world affairs. We can become despondent in the way that Elijah did when he complained to God that he was the only true believer left in Israel. The Lord informed him that there were actually seven thousand who had not bowed to the idols (1 Kings 19:14, 18). Christians are never a tiny, insignificant group but are always part of a vast host who will be elevated to positions of highest honor in heaven when history is completed.

Not only is the church a vast host, but it reflects all the diversity that is seen in the entire earth: "from every nation, from all tribes and peoples and languages" (Rev. 7:9). The church is never an ingrown ethnic or cultural

---

1. Douglas F. Kelly, *Revelation*, Mentor Expository Commentary (Tain, Ross-shire, Scotland: Mentor, 2012), 149.

enclave but is an exciting assembly of believers from every group of humanity. We are reminded of God's promise to Abraham at the beginning of the covenant of grace: "I will make of you a great nation . . . , and in you all the families of the earth shall be blessed" (Gen. 12:2–3). The multitudes of John's vision are thus "the consummate fulfillment of the Abrahamic promise."[2] Kevin DeYoung writes: "There are going to be millions of Africans in that great multitude and plenty of Brazilians and Chinese and Filipinos, and lots of Mexicans and Indians and Arabs, and there will be some white people too. . . . Heaven will be diversity without the political correctness and multiculturalism unified in one single purpose. Every heart, every head, every voice giving glory to God and to the Lamb."[3]

Here, the nations find the true peace that had eluded them on earth, now fulfilled through the person and work of Christ (Eph. 2:14). Even now, the division of the nations caused by sin at the Tower of Babel (Gen. 11) has been reversed in the church as it gathers believers from all over the earth in one creed and a shared salvation. It can often be difficult in our present world for the church to overcome barriers of race, culture, and language, but in heaven there will be true unity with the full diversity of the human race, every tongue joined in giving praise to Christ. Seeing this now should encourage churches to reach out across racial and cultural barriers, knowing that someday all Christians will be fully one.

The church is revealed not only in its vastness and diversity but especially in the victory it has received through Jesus Christ. This is the point of the white robes in which the saints are clothed, and the palm branches in their hands. Like conquerors receiving their triumphal parade, the saints above wear white robes and bear the palm branches of victory, attained through their union with Christ.

White also stands for purity and the believer's justification through faith in Christ. Jesus told the church in Sardis that the "one who conquers will be clothed thus in white garments, and I will never blot his name out of the book of life" (Rev. 3:5). The great victory over sin was won by Christ through his perfect life and sin-atoning death. Through faith we receive the victory of justification and its reward of everlasting life. Philip Hughes writes: "This is

---

2. G. K. Beale, *The Book of Revelation: A Commentary on the Greek Text*, New International Greek Testament Commentary (Grand Rapids: Eerdmans, 1999), 426–47.

3. Kevin DeYoung, "A Great Multitude and a Great Hope," *The Gospel Coalition* (blog), https://blogs.thegospelcoalition.org/kevindeyoung/2013/01/21/a-great-multitude-and-a-great-hope/.

the apparel of Christ's bride, the church triumphant, sanctified by him and cleansed from all defilement."[4] Although they may have suffered greatly in the world, some even suffering death for their faith, all Christians experience triumph in salvation. John wrote in his first letter: "This is the victory that has overcome the world—our faith" (1 John 5:4).

The white-robed multitude in heaven is occupied in the praise of God for their salvation: they are "crying out with a loud voice, 'Salvation belongs to our God who sits on the throne, and to the Lamb!'" (Rev. 7:10). The church above is centered on the sovereign grace of God and the saving work of Jesus Christ on the cross! This is what Christians should be excited about now as well, while still suffering the trials of earth. People become delirious over a football victory, a political rally, or a musical concert. But here are greater themes and a far greater victory! By ascribing salvation to God, the ones clothed in white claim that he deserves all the praise for delivering us through the tribulation of this world. Salvation relies on the grace of God and rests on the finished work of Christ, and therefore the glory belongs to them. After the Red Sea crossing, Moses sang, "The LORD is my strength and my song, and he has become my salvation" (Ex. 15:2). Knowing that we will worship this way when we have passed through to heaven, believers are urged to give God the same praise now, while still on earth.

Not only does the church give praise to God for salvation, but the angelic host gathered around responds with their own adoration: "And all the angels were standing around the throne and around the elders and the four living creatures, and they fell on their faces before the throne and worshiped God, saying, 'Amen! Blessing and glory and wisdom and thanksgiving and honor and power and might be to our God forever and ever! Amen'" (Rev. 7:11–12).

When we were studying the scene of God's throne room in Revelation 4, we noted that the twenty-four elders were probably angelic counterparts to the church, since they are seen in this passage worshiping with all the angels of heaven in response to the praise of the church. The angels begin by affirming what the church has declared: "Amen!" they cry to God's saving work. This is the great "Amen!" to acclaim the assembly of the entire vast multitude of redeemed sinners in heaven, launching the angels in praise for God's attributes as they are glorified in our salvation: "Blessing and glory

4. Philip Edgcumbe Hughes, *The Book of Revelation* (Downers Grove, IL: InterVarsity Press, 1990), 96.

and wisdom and thanksgiving and honor and power and might be to our God forever and ever!" (Rev. 7:12). God has bestowed blessing, displayed glory, exercised wisdom, earned thanksgiving and honor, and wielded power and might in saving his people from the guilt of sin and the tribulation of this world. All eternity will echo with praise like this because God has once and for all proved his grace to his people and won their hearts for worship.

This raises the question whether the angels watching our lives today see reasons to praise God. For that matter, we should ask whether other people are moved to praise God for us. They should be, since God's Spirit is at work in us to bear the fruit of salvation. Jesus said that "there is joy before the angels of God over one sinner who repents" (Luke 15:10). So be encouraged, as you follow the leading of God's Word and as, step by step, you make progress in the Christian life, that angels are praising the wisdom and power of God that is displayed in saving you from sin. Moreover, as you embrace a biblical lifestyle and more boldly spread the good news of salvation, other people will give thanks to God for the salvation he has brought through your life. Robert Mounce writes: "How unbelievably great will be the joyful adoration of the heavenly host when *all* the redeemed stand before their God!"[5] If you can see yourself in this throng—and you can through faith in Jesus Christ—doesn't the hope of glory strengthen you for the trials of your life?

How They Got There: Our Deliverance

As so often happens in Revelation, John's vision becomes more animated as one of the worshiping elders turns to ask him a question. Just as the ghosts of Dickens's *A Christmas Carol* engaged with Ebenezer Scrooge to ensure that he got the point, this angelic leader probes John's understanding. "Who are these," he asks, "clothed in white robes, and from where have they come?" John wisely gives the angel the floor: "I said to him, 'Sir, you know.'" The elder answers: "These are the ones coming out of the great tribulation. They have washed their robes and made them white in the blood of the Lamb" (Rev. 7:13–14). At first, John's vision was intended to show the suffering Christians of earth who they are as the glorified church of Christ. Now the elder wants to make clear how the church got there, highlighting the great deliverance achieved through Jesus.

---

5. Robert H. Mounce, *Revelation*, rev. ed., New International Commentary on the New Testament (Grand Rapids: Eerdmans, 1997), 172.

The elder makes two points for John and his readers to emphasize. First, the church arrives in heaven, having come "out of the great tribulation" (Rev. 7:14). Christians on earth should realize that trials and persecutions are likely to occur and that we will be saved only by persevering in faith against all opposition. Peter exhorted: "Beloved, do not be surprised at the fiery trial when it comes upon you to test you, as though something strange were happening to you. But rejoice insofar as you share Christ's sufferings, that you may also rejoice and be glad when his glory is revealed" (1 Peter 4:12–13).

The elder's statement raises a question about when this tribulation takes place. In Jesus' end-times teaching, he stated that shortly before his return "there will be great tribulation, such as has not been from the beginning of the world until now, no, and never will be. And if those days had not been cut short, no human being would be saved" (Matt. 24:21–22; see also Dan. 9:24–27). Paul likewise wrote of the man of perdition and a great apostasy within the church before the end (2 Thess. 2:3). Given this background, and since Revelation 7:14 speaks of *the* great tribulation, some scholars conclude that the elder refers to a final, relatively brief period of extraordinary trials through which these glorified saints will pass.

There are good reasons, however, to hold that the elder is referring more generally to the entirety of the church age as it is characterized by persecution, opposition, and affliction. Under this view, *the* tribulation is the general hatred displayed toward Christ and his people in this world, although it will be especially concentrated just before the end. "If you were of the world, the world would love you as its own," Jesus taught regarding the entire church age, "but because you are not of the world, but I chose you out of the world, therefore the world hates you" (John 15:19). Another reason that this general idea of tribulation is more likely is that John's vision incorporates the entirety of the church as a great multitude of believers from all ages and not merely the subset of those saved in the final time of particularly dreadful persecution.

The book of Revelation urges the churches in John's time, in the late first century, to brace for tribulation. John wrote to them as "your brother and partner in the tribulation" (Rev. 1:9). All through history, believers in Christ have suffered the grossest afflictions for the gospel, yet have prevailed because God sealed them for salvation and empowered them by his Spirit to hold fast in faith. Faithful servants of Christ were thrown to the lions in John's day, were burned at the stake in the English Reformation, were hunted through the countryside during the persecutions of Scotland, were sent to forced-labor camps in Communist China, and more recently have been bombed during their worship services in Sudan and Nigeria. Steve Wilmshurst writes: "It would be difficult to tell a Christian in China, Iraq, or North Korea today that the tribulation has not yet started!"[6] Jesus told all his disciples: "In the world you will have tribulation. But take heart; I have overcome the world" (John 16:33).

Those who wish to bear the name of Jesus in this world must reckon on tribulation of the worst kind. They can also know, as this vision shows us, that through Christ they will emerge out of the tribulation into the glorious assembly of heaven in the presence of God's throne. Heinrich Schenk wrote a hymn that asks the elder's question:

Who are these of dazzling brightness, these in God's own truth arrayed,
Clad in robes of purest whiteness, robes whose luster ne'er shall fade . . . ?

He answers:

These are they who have contended for their Savior's honor long,
Wrestling on till life was ended, foll'wing not the sinful throng;
These, who well the fight sustained, triumph through the Lamb have gained.[7]

The elder's second answer directs us to that Lamb: "They have washed their robes and made them white in the blood of the Lamb" (Rev. 7:14). The saints in heaven did not save themselves. It was not by their own prowess that they conquered through tribulation. With the clarity that belongs to those already in heaven, the elder ascribes the salvation of believers to the cleansing power of Christ's blood. Philip Bliss explains our salvation:

Bearing shame and scoffing rude,
In my place condemned he stood,
Sealed my pardon with his blood:
Hallelujah! what a Savior![8]

---

6. Steve Wilmshurst, *The Final Word: The Book of Revelation Simply Explained* (Darlington, UK: Evangelical Press, 2008), 98.

7. Heinrich T. Schenk, "Who Are These like Stars Appearing" (1719).

8. Philip P. Bliss, "Man of Sorrows! What a Name!" (1875).

In recent years, some evangelical scholars have published books urging that less attention be paid to the doctrine of Christ's atoning blood, or that we at least try to soften its gruesome implications. But the elders above know that Christ's death cannot be reduced merely to the loving sentiments of Jesus' heart. It is his blood, signifying the payment of death that he offered to God's justice, that cleanses his people from the guilt and penalty of their sins. James Hamilton writes: "How did the blood of Jesus cleanse them? When Jesus died he paid the penalty for sin, and when they trusted in Jesus, his payment of the penalty is applied to them. Their sins are washed away when they trust in Christ."[9]

We should notice three points about the cleansing of Christ's people. First, notice that not only did Christ die for sin, but his people received the cleansing benefits of his death through personal faith. They "washed their robes and made them white" by trusting in Christ's blood (Rev. 7:14). You must do the same if you will be saved. Second, realize that these are past-tense verbs, signifying completed actions. It is true that believers must persevere in faith, but it is also true that at the very moment when you believe in Christ's blood, you are washed of your sin and stand clothed in white before God. Believers still sin and need to confess their transgressions to have their consciences made clean. But true saving faith in Christ's blood "cleanses us from all sin" (1 John 1:7) once and for all. What John sees of Christ's people in heaven is true of us immediately upon our exercising faith in him. Jesus taught: "Whoever believes in the Son has eternal life" (John 3:36). Third, this vision says that the *only* way that anyone can get to heaven is by cleansing his or her sins in the blood of Jesus. John sees the entirety of the heavenly assembly of God's saved people, and they had all "washed their robes and made them white in the blood of the Lamb" (Rev. 7:14). Leon Morris comments: "The complete efficacy of Christ's atoning death is being strongly asserted. It is on the grounds of His death for men that they are able to stand before the throne properly clothed. . . . They all are saved in this way and no other."[10]

9. James M. Hamilton Jr., *Revelation: The Spirit Speaks to the Churches* (Wheaton, IL: Crossway, 2012), 194.

10. Leon Morris, *The Revelation of St. John: An Introduction and Commentary*, Tyndale New Testament Commentaries (Grand Rapids: Eerdmans, 1969), 117–18.

WHERE THEY ARE GOING: OUR DESTINATION

John's vision has given us a glorious perspective on the heavenly reality that corresponds to the suffering church on earth. Yet even these saints in heaven have a future. John has shown the heavenly destiny of believers and has learned of their deliverance through Christ's blood. He now concludes the chapter, and this entire cycle of visions that began in Revelation 4, with a spectacular description of the eternal destination to which this great multitude of Christ's people are headed.

Of the three ghosts that visited Ebenezer Scrooge in Dickens's *A Christmas Carol*, it was the Ghost of Christmas Future who most deeply affected him. Shrouded in black, this ghost enabled Scrooge to gaze upon his own funeral, to hear the disdain he had earned from people who knew him, and to contemplate the eternal condemnation he deserved. It was this frightful specter that shook his heart so that he repented and returned from his dream to lead a different life. For those who have trusted in Christ, however, the vision of our future destination is the most uplifting source of encouragement, enabling us to endure the trials and tribulations of this life with joy and hope in service to Christ. If you have not turned to Christ, the blessings awaiting his people urge you to consider the future that you will never know unless your sins are washed clean through faith in his blood.

First, John hears of the *shelter* that God provides with his own glorious presence: "Therefore they are before the throne of God, and serve him day and night in his temple; and he who sits on the throne will shelter them with his presence" (Rev. 7:15). The saints are admitted before the throne of the holy God because their sins have been washed clean and they are justified in Christ. There, "they render to Him the spontaneous, glad, and thorough devotion of the heart . . . [in] unceasing worship."[11] Worshiping in God's sanctuary, they have immediate access to the glory of his presence. They are now, as Paul put it, "filled with all the fullness of God" (Eph. 3:19).

On his part, God receives the church as his own dearly beloved children. The Sovereign Creator spreads his presence over them like a tent, so that they dwell in him forever. As a kingdom of priests, the believers fulfill the purpose for which they were made and then were redeemed in the unending

11. William Hendriksen, *More than Conquerors: An Interpretation of the Book of Revelation* (1940; repr., Grand Rapids: Baker, 1967), 114.

adoration of a God whom they more fully know as eternity stretches on forever. The apostle Paul wrote that in our present life, even the best Christians can "see in a mirror [only] dimly," but then, he adds, we will see God "face to face" (1 Cor. 13:12). Revelation 22:4–5 fills in the details: "They will see his face, and his name will be on their foreheads. . . . The Lord God will be their light, and they will reign forever and ever."

Second, John is told of the *blessing* that attends Christ's people in the shelter of God's love: "They shall hunger no more, neither thirst anymore; the sun shall not strike them, nor any scorching heat" (Rev. 7:16). Here is the bliss of the salvation rest to which Christ's people now journey in the wilderness of a sinful world. On earth, believers are subjected to every kind of deprivation and hardship, but the promise is held before us that our struggle will not be in vain. In the age to come, there is no hardship, trial, or loss, but only the gain of fullness and joy. David anticipated this bounty in the closing words of Psalm 23: "You prepare a table before me in the presence of my enemies; you anoint my head with oil; my cup overflows. Surely goodness and mercy shall follow me all the days of my life, and I shall dwell in the house of the LORD forever" (Ps. 23:5–6).

Psalm 23 connects with the third feature of our eternal destination: Christ's eternal *shepherding.* "For the Lamb in the midst of the throne will be their shepherd," John hears, "and he will guide them to springs of living water" (Rev. 7:17). All through this vision, believers have stood before God on his throne and the Lamb. In eternity, just as God makes his presence a tent for us, the Lamb shepherds us to the fullest experience of eternal life, guiding us "to springs of living water." Leon Morris writes that in heaven, "the saved will always thirst for God, and that thirst will be satisfied"[12] through the ministry of Jesus Christ. The Shepherd who leads his sheep is none other than the One who became a Lamb for us. "Come," he summons, "everyone who thirsts, come to the waters . . . , that your soul may live" (Isa. 55:1–3).

John's vision concludes, looking ahead to the final consummation recorded at the end of Revelation: "and God will wipe away every tear from their eyes" (Rev. 7:17). We think of the churches to which John was writing, which would soon suffer sore affliction so that their tears would fall. We think of people we know with tears on their cheeks. Our own eyes are often wet with the grief of this broken, fallen world. In the end, when the eternal

---

12. Morris, *The Revelation of St. John*, 119.

destination has been reached, there will be no more tears. Every loss will then have been repaid with interest, every grief answered with joy, every longing fulfilled in glory, and as we look into the eyes of God it will be his own loving hand that wipes the tears from ours. Steve Wilmshurst sums up the overall message of Revelation 7 for the suffering church of John's time and ours: "As God's people we have security today, but tomorrow is unimaginably glorious."[13]

HE WILL SAVE!

I want to conclude with an application given by the prophet Isaiah, since the last two verses of Revelation 7 quote directly from Isaiah 49:10. In an earlier vision, he rejoiced at the glorious restoration that awaits God's people in the end, saying, "They shall see the glory of the LORD, the majesty of our God" (Isa. 35:1–2). With that in mind, Isaiah urged God's people, in the same spirit with which the apostle John writes: "Strengthen the weak hands, and make firm the feeble knees. Say to those who have an anxious heart, 'Be strong; fear not! Behold, your God will come with vengeance, with the recompense of God. He will come and save you'" (35:3–4).

13. Wilmshurst, *The Final Word*, 100.

PART 3

The Seven Trumpets as Warnings of Judgment

25

SILENCE IN HEAVEN

Revelation 8:1–5

*He was given much incense to offer with the prayers of all the
saints on the golden altar before the throne, and the smoke of
the incense, with the prayers of the saints, rose before
God from the hand of the angel.* (Rev. 8:3–4)

he famous English journalist Bernard Levin was noted for his
passion for classical music, especially opera and choral music.
He reported hearing a recital of songs by Schubert that was
particularly moving. Great performances are usually met with loud applause,
but Levin said that on this occasion the audience sat in silence. Finally, still
awed by the music, they rose and quietly departed. Silence is rare in our
sound-soaked culture. At its most powerful, silence is not merely the absence
of noise but, as N. T. Wright notes, "a profound, still, deep experience in
which one can sense aspects of reality which are normally drowned out by
chatter and babble."[1]

At the end of Revelation 7, the apostle John had been treated not merely
to a great musical performance on earth but to the mixed choir of saints
and angels in heaven, giving glory to God and to the Lamb. The opening

1. N. T. Wright, *Revelation for Everyone* (Louisville: Westminster John Knox, 2011), 76–77.

of the first four seals on God's scroll had showed the riders of woe going forth into the earth. The fifth seal sounded the souls of the martyrs crying out for justice, followed by the sixth seal and the unleashing of God's judgment. Chapter 7 cut back and forth between heaven and earth, showing how God's servants are sealed below and glorified above. John's angel interpreter finally looked ahead to the ultimate bliss awaiting Christ's people, with God sheltering them with his presence and the Lamb leading them to springs of living water.

There remained one seal to be opened, however, and Christians naturally expect it to bring Jesus' appearing to end the age in judgment. At the start of chapter 8, the seventh seal is opened, yet instead of a glorious vision of Christ's return, "there was silence in heaven for about half an hour" (Rev. 8:1). At the brink of the very end, the music above is stopped and every breath is held. Dennis Johnson comments: "Silence is creation's expectant response to the Lord's impending arrival in judgment."[2] "Be silent, all flesh, before the Lord," commanded the prophet Zechariah, "for he has roused himself from his holy dwelling" (Zech. 2:13).

We should understand the silence of heaven at the opening of the seventh seal in two ways. First, it reflects awe at the glory and majesty of the Sovereign Lord who comes in splendor and might. In the Old Testament, awed silence is commanded before the coming of God to judge: "Be silent before the Lord God! For the day of the Lord is near" (Zeph. 1:7). William Hendriksen writes that the coming of God's final wrath is "so fearful and awful . . . that the inhabitants of heaven stand spell-bound, lost for a time— half an hour—in breathless, in silent amazement."[3]

In addition to expressing awe, the silent pause of the seventh seal serves the literary purpose of John in writing the book of Revelation. If we were listening to it being read for the first time, we might think that the book was concluding with the opening of the seventh seal. Yet there is more to reveal: more contours of history and more details of God's plan to save his people. Therefore, just when Christ is about to step out from the clouds of glory onto the earth, Revelation pauses with only the silence that attends his coming.

2. Dennis E. Johnson, *Triumph of the Lamb: A Commentary on Revelation* (Phillipsburg, NJ: P&R Publishing, 2001), 136.
3. William Hendriksen, *More than Conquerors: An Interpretation of the Book of Revelation* (1940; repr., Grand Rapids: Baker, 1967), 117.

SEALS, TRUMPETS, AND BOWLS

As the angels putting on the drama of Revelation pause in silence for half an hour, it is worthwhile for us to pause as well and take stock of this book. At the beginning of chapter 8, we are starting the third major section of the Apocalypse. Chapters 1–3 presented the glory of Christ as Lord of his church, and through the seven letters expressed the governing principles for the church in this age. Chapters 4–7 presented a view of history focused on the opening of the seven seals on God's scroll. After the visions of heaven in chapters 4 and 5, the seals were opened in chapter 6 to release the tribulations in history out of which the redeemed are saved. Chapter 7 showed the restraining of judgment and the sealing of the saints so that they would arrive safely in heaven. The final judgment that began in the sixth seal is paused by the opening of the seventh seal and the silence of heaven.

Chapter 8 begins the third major section of Revelation, the seven trumpets that herald God's judgment. After the symbolic histories of the fourth section (chaps. 12–14), the fifth section will feature the seven bowls of God's wrath (chaps. 15–16). It is obvious that there is a relationship between the seven seals, trumpets, and bowls. Before diving into this material, which makes up the heart of Revelation, we should seek to determine how this relationship works.

Some scholars hold the view that the seven seals, seven trumpets, and seven bowls are organized consecutively. They see a straight-line chronology in Revelation, with the seven seals followed chronologically by the seven trumpets, which are then followed in history by the seven bowls. Under this view, the opening of the seventh seal does not reveal any actual content; the scroll is opened only to show that the story moves forward to the seven trumpets.

There are good reasons to reject this view and instead to see the various cycles as covering the same period from complementary perspectives. The parallel content of these cycles is obvious, especially since the trumpets and the bowls line up almost exactly. Moreover, much of what happens when the trumpets are blown and the bowls are poured obviously precedes the final judgment revealed in the sixth seal. For instance, when the angel blows the third trumpet, a star falls from heaven to poison all the rivers (Rev. 8:10). Under a strict chronology this is impossible, since under the sixth seal (6:13) all "the stars of the sky" had already "[fallen] to the earth." Therefore, it is evident that the judgments of the trumpets and bowls take place chronologically before the sixth seal, which occurs earlier in the text of Revelation. Understood rightly, the seventh seal, the seventh trumpet, and the seventh bowl all depict aspects of the same event: the return of Christ in wrath and salvation.

Even a brief survey makes clear, then, that the cycles of seals, trumpets, and bowls are parallel representations of similar scenes of judgment. This reminds us not to read Revelation like a history book of the future. We would do better to read it as a play (actually, a musical) put on by the angels of heaven for our benefit, with its different scenes showing us important features of history from heaven's perspective. Or we might think of Revelation as a symphony, with its main melody of judgment and salvation working through each movement. There are variations on the melody within the various cycles, reflecting the different materials of the Old Testament from which John is drawing. In chapter 7, John alludes to the sealing of faithful servants depicted in Ezekiel 9. The trumpet judgments of chapter 8 will reminisce on the fall of Jericho and the plagues inflicted on Egypt in the exodus. Therefore, while the cycles cover the same ground, they do so from different angles and with an ever-increasing intensity. The theme of the seven seals is God's *restraint* of judgment for the sake of the church, the seven trumpets announce the *victory* of God's judgment over the world, and the seven bowls depict the *wrath* of God's judgment, after which the loud voice shouts from the throne, exulting, "It is done!" (Rev. 16:17).

THE SEVEN ANGELS AND THE GOLDEN CENSER

The opening of the seventh seal produces more than silence in heaven. Immediately, John is shown "the seven angels" who will appear in the next section, who "stand before God," and to whom "seven trumpets were given" (Rev. 8:2). We are not told the identity of these seven angels, although there are two notable suggestions. In chapter 1, Jesus stood amid the seven golden lampstands, with seven stars in his hand who were "the angels of the seven churches" (1:20). It may be, therefore, that the seven angels of chapter 8 are the angels of the churches to which John was writing, which together signify the whole church in the gospel age. Other scholars urge that these seven are more likely the angels of God's presence, referred to in Isaiah 63:9. Two of these archangels are named in the Bible: Michael (Jude 9) and Gabriel (Luke 1:19). Jewish apocryphal writings supply the names of the other five as Uriel, Raphael, Raguel, Sariel, and Remiel (1 Enoch 20:2–8). Since the definite article identifies these angels as "the seven," it is probably best to understand them as the seven archangels.

Before any trumpets are blown, however, another angel "came and stood at the altar with a golden censer." This bowl or fire pan contained "much incense to offer with the prayers of all the saints on the golden altar before the throne" (Rev. 8:3). As he made his offering, "the smoke of the incense, with the prayers of the saints, rose before God from the hand of the angel" (8:4). Having performed this ministry, the angel "took the censer and filled it with fire from the altar and threw it on the earth, and there were peals of thunder, rumblings, flashes of lightning, and an earthquake" (8:5).

In Luke 12:49, Jesus said, "I came to cast fire on the earth, and would that it were already kindled!" The flaming judgments of Revelation 8:5 correspond to the opening of the seventh seal, the silence of which signifies Christ's return and the fiery cleansing of the world to which Jesus looked forward. It is further obvious that his fire is cast down in response to the prayers revealed by the fifth seal. The martyrs cried, "O Sovereign Lord, holy and true, how long before you will judge and avenge our blood on those who dwell on the earth?" (Rev. 6:10). In the judgment of the seventh seal, Christ has responded to their pleas and avenged his martyred church.

The transition in 8:1–5 reveals some of the artistry of Revelation. Not only are the seven seals followed by the seven trumpets, but the end of one and the beginning of the other are interlocked, since the seven trumpets are introduced in verse 2 and the judgment of the seventh seal is shown in verses 3–5. This overlap is constructed to make a point essential to the message of Revelation as a whole. It shows that the judgments depicted by both the seals and the trumpets occur in response to the prayers of God's people. In verse 2, the angels are given trumpets to blow. In verse 3 they are interrupted by an angel who comes forward to offer the prayers of the saints, mixed with sweet-smelling incense. Only when these prayers have risen to God's throne does the angel take up the same censer that was filled with prayers and use it to cast fire on the wicked earth. This sequence gives prominence not merely to Christ's coming and God's sovereign judgment but also to the integral role played by Christians' prayers.

PRAYER AND THE PURPOSES OF GOD

The emphasis on prayer in this passage makes a number of important points. First and foremost, we see that *prayer is the means by which God accomplishes his purpose in history.* This is the point that we are to notice in Revelation 8:3–5, a point so important that the seven archangels are interrupted from blowing their trumpets. In the apocalyptic visions of the Bible, an interrupting angel appears to make a point that is not to be overlooked (see Zech. 2:3–5; Rev. 7:2–3). Here, God reveals the strength of his covenant bond with his people and his attention to their prayers by first sending the angel to offer up the prayers of the saints and only then using their container to cast fiery judgments on the world.

One reason that this needs to be emphasized is that Christians tend to rely on our own activity and to focus on what we can do against sin and evil, while we often neglect the far more important resource of prayer. In contrast, the biblical idea of holy warfare places prayer first and our own activity second. An example is provided by Judah's King Hezekiah during Sennacherib's invasion in 701 B.C. Hezekiah's army had tried to defend his kingdom, but the Assyrian host overwhelmed them, just as Christians will often be overwhelmed by worldly powers. Finally, the king and his supporters were besieged behind Jerusalem's walls. Sennacherib's herald came, mocking their defense and blaspheming Israel's God (Isa. 36). Hezekiah responded by taking the enemy's demand into the temple and spreading it before the Lord in prayer. In language reflecting the imagery of Revelation, Hezekiah prayed: "O Lord of hosts, God of Israel, enthroned above the cherubim, you are the God, you alone, of all the kingdoms of the earth; you have made heaven and earth. . . . O Lord our God, save us from his hand, that all the kingdoms of the earth may know that you alone are the Lord" (Isa. 37:16–20). In the morning, Hezekiah found that God had answered by completely destroying the enemy: "The angel of the Lord went out and struck down a hundred and eighty-five thousand in the camp of the Assyrians" (37:36).

Hezekiah's prayer is not merely a heartening story from the Old Testament but a statement of how God's people are to serve God's purposes in the world. God's sovereignty and prayer are never at odds, since God is sovereign over both the praying of his people and the answering of their prayers. Prayer is, in fact, an appeal to the sovereignty of God in accordance with the will of God.

The history of the church in recent years has provided numerous examples of how prayer is key to God's purposes. People marvel at the spiritual power of the Chinese house-church movement, through which the gospel has spread to well over a hundred million believers. How did this happen, when after the Communist takeover the missionaries were all expelled and the leading Chinese pastors were exiled to prisons for twenty years and more? Part of the answer is that those imprisoned pastors, like John on the Isle of Patmos, devoted themselves to prayer. They prayed for deliverance, precisely in the spirit of the martyrs of the fifth seal: "O Sovereign Lord, holy and true, how long before you will judge and avenge our blood . . . ?" (Rev. 6:10). They prayed with mercy for the salvation of their jailers and for the Holy Spirit to spread the gospel through their land. When they were finally released, they came with spiritual power to a land on which God's hand had been laid through prayer.[4]

Another example of how God uses prayer is the fall of the Berlin Wall in 1989. Christians in East Germany began gathering nightly for prayer at the huge Lutheran church in Leipzig where Johann Sebastian Bach once played organ. Christians from other denominations joined in, and they prayed fervently for God to do something about the terrible Communist regime ruining their country. Learning of this meeting, the authorities became alarmed. Despite their official dogma that there is no God, "they got very nervous when the Christians started talking to God about them!"[5] Finally, the army was called in, but the soldiers refused to fire on their own people, some of whom were family members and friends. The day after the troops disobeyed the order to fire on the Christians, the hated wall in Berlin was torn down by the mass revolution that followed. As Revelation 8 tells us, when Christians pray, fire is cast by God upon the earth.[6]

For this reason, the neglect of prayer is one of the great calamities and chief failings of the Western church today. Christians are more eager to

---

4. One inspiring account of the Chinese house-church movement is Ken Anderson, *Bold as a Lamb: Pastor Samuel Lamb and the Underground Church of China* (Grand Rapids: Zondervan, 1991), which recounts the suffering and ministry of Samuel Lamb.

5. Douglas F. Kelly, *Revelation*, Mentor Expository Commentary (Tain, Ross-shire, Scotland: Mentor, 2012), 165.

6. Taken from ibid., 165–66.

engage in activities that have a visible effect. We think more is accomplished by talking to one another or by taking actions that seem more beneficial. This is why it is hard to get Christians to attend prayer meetings, and why most evangelical churches today no longer have them, because you pray for half an hour, go home, and cannot be sure that anything was accomplished. But the vision of the seventh seal makes it clear not only that our prayers go up to God, but that they make the decisive difference in history according to his will.

As Christians in America face mounting threats to religious liberty and furious assaults on moral decency and truth, we must therefore recommit ourselves to the ministry of prayer. Worldly powers advance, and Christians have tried to meet them with worldly means: through the legislature, the media, and the courtroom. These are legitimate means, but means that the world is able to use more effectively than Christians can. These are the arenas in which the spirit of unbelief has power. Prayer is the arena in which Christians have a greater power than that of the world. While our own activity must fail without prayer, prayer alone in the hands of God is mighty to bring God's judgment on the enemies of his kingdom.

PRAYERS ACCEPTABLE TO GOD

A second vital point from this passage is that *the prayers of Christians are certain to be received and answered by God.* This is the point of the incense that the angel mixed with the censer of prayers to offer before God. The function of the incense was to make the prayers sweet-smelling in God's presence.

Steve Wilmshurst tells the plight of Terry Waite, an English churchman who traveled to Beirut in the 1980s, seeking to negotiate the release of Westerners taken hostage by Muslim terrorists. Waite was himself kidnapped and made a hostage for five years. During that dreadful time, family members and friends sent letters, hoping they would somehow get through to encourage him. In all those years, only a single postcard got through, sent by a woman from Bedford, England, whom Waite did not even know. Many people feel that something like this will happen to their prayers. "What chance do you honestly think your *prayers* have of getting through?" Wilmshurst asks. "Isn't it far more likely that somewhere along the way, [your prayers] will be lost or turned back, like all those letters to Terry Waite?"[7] Legions of Christians struggle with this thought, so that they pray seldom or with little fervor. The angel in John's vision shows us, however, that our prayers do get through to God, are heard by him, and make a great difference in the world and in history.

There is no doubt that something needs to be done to make our prayers acceptable to and effective with God, as were the prayers brought to God's temple by this angel. All our prayers are defective, many are selfish or foolish, and all are corrupted in some way by the sin that makes them unacceptable in God's presence. What will not only get our prayers through but make them sweet-smelling in God's presence? The answer is not found in the angel himself, since angels cannot mediate for God's people, which is why we should never pray to them. The answer is found in the mediation of Jesus Christ, through his perfect life and sin-atoning death, and by means of his present intercession on behalf of the church (Rom. 8:34; Heb. 7:25). The Bible teaches that "there is one mediator between God and men, the man Christ Jesus" (1 Tim. 2:5). Jesus told his disciples, "Whatever you ask the Father in my name, he [will] give it to you" (John 15:16).

We can see the connection of the incense to the saving ministry of Jesus by noting that the closest Old Testament parallel to this passage is found in Leviticus 16:12–13, which forms part of the temple ritual for Israel's annual Day of Atonement. In the midst of the blood sacrifices offered for sin, the high priest was to "take a censer full of coals of fire from the altar before the LORD, and two handfuls of sweet incense beaten small, and . . . bring it inside the veil and put the incense on the fire before the LORD." The Day of Atonement pointed forward to Christ's atoning blood not only to cleanse us from sin but to sanctify our prayers. Similarly, Christ's present intercession in heaven makes the prayers of his people rise before God "pure, sweet, and fragrant, like bunches of beautiful roses . . . worthy to be taken to the throne of the King."[8]

Moreover, John remarks that "the prayers of all the saints" rise fragrantly before God (Rev. 8:3). Saints are not the spiritual elite, selected and approved by some earthly pope. Rather, in the Bible, saints are sinners who have been

---

7. Steve Wilmshurst, *The Final Word: The Book of Revelation Simply Explained* (Darlington, UK: Evangelical Press, 2008), 102.

8. Kelly, *Revelation*, 164.

cleansed and sanctified by the blood of Jesus, having been set apart from sin and the world simply through faith in Christ (see 1 Cor. 1:2). If you have not come to Jesus to be saved from your sins, then you are not a saint and have no reason to believe that your prayers will be accepted by God. This is why non-Christians often ask believers they know to pray for them, since they sense their own lack of access to heaven. But the simplest Christian—each one of the saints—who prays in Jesus' name, trusting his death for sin and his never-ending reign in heaven to represent the person before God, can be certain that his or her prayers are treasured by God and will be answered according to his good and perfect will. Paul adds that in prayer, "the Spirit helps us in our weakness" (Rom. 8:26). Derek Thomas summarizes: "Our prayers rise with the Spirit's power, the Son's mediation, and the assistance of the angels of heaven."[9]

THE GREAT PRAYER OF THE CHURCH

Finally, the vision of the seventh seal shows that *the great prayer of the church is prayer for the kingdom of Christ to come.* The prayers placed in the angel's golden censer came from the martyrs who sought God's judgment to avenge them (Rev. 6:10). Jesus' teaching on prayer placed a similar priority on his kingdom. The "Lord's Prayer" includes petitions for God to meet our daily needs, to forgive our sins, and to lead us away from temptation. But Christ taught us first to pray for the holiness of God's name and his kingdom on earth: "Our Father in heaven, hallowed be your name. Your kingdom come, your will be done, on earth as it is in heaven" (Matt. 6:9–10). The prayer for Christ's kingdom to come—now through the spread of the gospel, the growth of the church, and the obedience of believers, and in the end by the sudden appearance of Christ in glory to save and to judge—is the great prayer of the church.

Christians are encouraged in the Bible to pray for our own needs and for those of friends and neighbors. But the priority of our prayer lives should be given to the spread of the gospel, the preservation and strength of the church, the ministry of God's Word, and the thwarting of godless and wicked powers in our world. Are you praying about these things? These are the prayers that according to Revelation matter the most, the prayers that God will answer

9. Derek Thomas, *Let's Study Revelation* (Edinburgh: Banner of Truth, 2003), 69.

with power from heaven at the time of his choosing, and the prayers that we should be most privileged to offer in Christ's name.

Will you commit to pray for the kingdom of Christ? Praying in his name for the cause of his gospel and for his judgment on rebellious evil, we may be heartened by the vision of the angel gathering our prayers into a golden censer, sweetened with the incense of Christ's atoning work, and offered up before God's throne, awaiting the day when our most fervent prayer will be answered. This is the prayer with which the entire book of Revelation—and the whole Bible—concludes. "Come, Lord Jesus!" we pray. He answers with words most precious to our hearts: "Surely I am coming soon" (Rev. 22:20).

26

THE FOUR TRUMPETS

Revelation 8:6—13

The first angel blew his trumpet, and there followed hail and
fire, mixed with blood, and these were thrown upon the earth.
(Rev. 8:7)

When the tribes of Israel emerged out of the exodus wilderness to claim the promised land, the trumpets of holy war sounded. God had instructed that seven priests were to blow seven trumpets for seven days. On the final day, the priests were to lead the people around the fortress city of Jericho seven times. When the seventh trumpet blew, the people were to shout and fall upon the city (Josh. 6:1–7). Led by Joshua with the ark of the covenant, Israel obeyed God's Word. When the seven trumpets blew after the seventh time around the city on the seventh day, the walls of Jericho fell down and the city was taken. Joshua had told the people, "Shout, for the LORD has given you the city" (6:16).

When Revelation 8:6 launches the third cycle of visions with the angels blowing seven trumpets, the student of the Bible looks for an intervention from God on a scale even greater than that of Jericho's fall. The trumpet visions of Revelation 8 and 9 take on a worldwide scale, showing that the worldly city, for all its might, will not bar God's covenant people from the victory of their faith. Christ will strike the fortress citadel of sin and unbelief so that it falls in terrible judgment, just as he once declared to Peter: "I will build my church, and the gates of hell shall not prevail against it" (Matt. 16:18).

THE TRUMPETS OF THE LORD

In the Bible, trumpets are blown for a variety of reasons. They are sounded as a call to the people of God to assemble for an important occasion. The feasts of Israel were hailed "with blast of trumpets," as "a holy convocation" (Lev. 23:24). Trumpets hailed Solomon's ascension to David's throne (1 Kings 1:34, 39). According to the New Testament, a trumpet blast will herald the second coming of Christ, summoning the elect to join him from all over the earth (Matt. 24:30–31). Joel associated trumpets with God's coming in judgment: "Blow a trumpet in Zion; sound an alarm on my holy mountain . . . , for the day of the LORD is coming" (Joel 2:1).

Trumpets were sounded in the Old Testament to gather Israel's hosts for battle, such as when Ehud blew trumpets to summon the tribe of Ephraim to war (Judg. 3:27). Most importantly, Israel's trumpets signified the coming of the Lord to wage warfare on the nation's behalf. This was the meaning of the trumpets that Joshua blew outside Jericho. Likewise, Gideon's three hundred blew trumpets, and God threw the host of Midian into confusion and defeat.

Against this background, when Revelation 8:6 tells us that "the seven angels who had the seven trumpets prepared to blow them," we can expect to see God intervening in history to defeat his enemies. As in the blowing of trumpets outside Jericho, God is coming with power against his foes. As at Jericho, the first six trumpets set the stage for the climactic seventh trumpet that will bring a decisive victory. Paul Gardner writes: "Certainly the holy war of Joshua 6 has its final counterpart in Revelation as God wages war against Satan and all that is evil and against those who refuse to repent."[1]

There is furthermore a clear parallel between the trumpets blasted in Revelation 8 and the horsemen of the four seals opened in chapter 6. The four horsemen unleashed warfare, violence, famine, and death, and the first four trumpets likewise unleash destructive forces on the earth. The seals

1. Paul Gardner, *Revelation: The Compassion and Protection of Christ*, Focus on the Bible (Tain, Ross-shire, Scotland: Christian Focus, 2008), 127.

and the trumpets follow the same progression: the first four seals are opened and trumpets are sounded, followed by two more, an interlude, and then the final seal and final trumpet, which depict the coming of Christ to judge. All these parallels show that the trumpets of Revelation 8 do not depict a new phase of history after the seals of chapters 6 and 7. Rather, the trumpets recapitulate from a different perspective the woes visited on earth by the seals. Whereas the judgment of the seals emphasized God's preservation of the church to arrive in heaven "out of the great tribulation" (Rev. 7:14), the perspective of the trumpets focuses on the victorious Lord's judgment of the wicked. Derek Thomas writes: "The seals view the unfolding of the redemptive purposes of God from the point of view of the Lord's own people, those who are sealed; the trumpets view this same reality from the point of view of the unsealed, those who are *not* the people of God. The opening of the seals brings great consolation to the people of God. The sounding of the trumpets brings great woes upon those who are not the people of God."[2]

INTERPRETING THE TRUMPET VISIONS

Throughout our study of Revelation, it has been important to carefully consider our approach to interpretation. It is obvious throughout the book that the visions are not to be understood literally but contain symbols that depict historical realities. This becomes vitally important in the visions of the seven trumpets. Popular Christian literature tends to look for events that present some similarity with the judgments of Revelation 8 and 9 and then declare that these prophecies have been fulfilled in our time. A classic example was the Chernobyl nuclear plant disaster that occurred in the Soviet Union in 1986. Prophecy experts soon stated that *Chernobyl* is the Ukrainian word for *wormwood* and that the prophecy contained in the third trumpet had been fulfilled. This news excited Christians, even though *Chernobyl* does not precisely mean "wormwood" and the event itself fell far short of the third trumpet's judgment.[3] Under this approach, Revelation's third trumpet could have no meaning for all the Christians living in the nineteen centuries before the Chernobyl meltdown, including the Christians to whom John has

2. Derek Thomas, *Let's Study Revelation* (Edinburgh: Banner of Truth, 2003), 73.
3. Taken from Steve Wilmshurst, *The Final Word: The Book of Revelation Simply Explained* (Darlington, UK: Evangelical Press, 2008), 114–15.

told us he was writing the book. Moreover, this kind of attempt to interpret the visions literally leads us away from the actual meaning of the text.

This is not to say, however, that Revelation does not depict literal history. First we must understand the symbols. Then we will find that what is symbolized literally happens throughout the history of which he is speaking. John draws his images from the Old Testament, and it is from there, not today's newspapers, that we will understand the visions of the seven trumpets.

What, then, do the four trumpets depict? First, they show God's judgment in the form of upheavals in nature in order to judge his enemies. In the battles that followed the conquest of Jericho, God fought against his enemies by assaults of nature. In the battle of the five kings, God rained hail on Israel's enemies, so that more enemies "died because of the hailstones than . . . with the sword" (Josh. 10:11). When the enemy army fled, the Lord caused the sun to stand still in the sky to provide extra daylight for Joshua's slaughter (10:12–13). In similar fashion, the four trumpets of Revelation 8 depict plagues on nature by which God smites his enemies. Simon Kistemaker summarizes: "The sound of the trumpets ushers in God's judgments in the form of punishments that affect the earth, the sea, the rivers and springs of water, the heavenly bodies, and the Abyss."[4]

When we think of God's defeating Israel's enemies by means of his sovereign control of nature, the greatest example is the events before the release of Israel from Egypt. In the ten plagues that preceded the exodus and in the passing of the Red Sea, God controlled natural powers to humiliate the false gods of the Nile and break the hardened will of unbelieving Pharaoh. This is important because there is a clear parallel between the plagues unleashed by the trumpets of Revelation 8 and the plagues inflicted on Egypt. This parallel reinforces the idea that Revelation's trumpets signify holy war against the ungodly nations. In particular, Revelation 8 draws from the seventh, first, and ninth plagues against Egypt, involving hail, blood, and darkness.

One of the points emphasized by the plagues on Egypt was the supernatural intervention that could be attributed only to God. Pharaoh sent his magicians to oppose Moses, but the magicians despaired, saying, "This is the finger of God" (Ex. 8:19). So also the upheavals described in Revelation 8 depict God's supernatural judgment on the unbelieving world. Just as God acted through Moses to break Pharaoh's grip of slavery on Israel,

---

4. Simon J. Kistemaker, *Revelation*, New Testament Commentary (Grand Rapids: Baker, 2001), 272.

the plagues of the first four trumpets show God as humbling unbelieving powers and punishing the world for its persecution of the church. Moreover, it is often observed that the plagues that Moses announced against Pharaoh were targeted at the false gods worshiped in Egypt. Likewise, Revelation 8 shows God as judging the idols of this world that man trusts. While the plagues against Egypt should have moved Pharaoh to repentance, instead they only hardened his heart and consigned him to final destruction. So it is in general with God's judgments in history.

We should further note the restricted character of the judgments of this chapter. With the first trumpet, a third of the earth and its trees are burned up (Rev. 8:7). The same is true for the other trumpets: a third of the sea, with its creatures and ships (8:8–9), a third of the rivers (8:10–11), and a third of the heavenly objects and their light (8:12) are judged. The point is that these are partial, not ultimate, judgments designed to announce God's wrath and warn the world against the final judgment. Michael Wilcock writes that the partial damage shows "that the Trumpets are sounding not doom, but warning. The majority of mankind is allowed to survive, being shown God's wrath against sin, and given the chance to repent."[5]

THE FOUR TRUMPETS OF REVELATION 8

With this preparation, we may consider the four trumpets of Revelation 8. The first angel blew his trumpet, "and there followed hail and fire, mixed with blood, and these were thrown upon the earth. And a third of the earth was burned up, and a third of the trees were burned up, and all green grass was burned up" (Rev. 8:7).

In Exodus 9, we read of the plague of hail and fire that God inflicted on Egypt through Moses: "There was hail and fire . . . , such as had never been in all the land of Egypt . . . . The hail struck down everything that was in the field in all the land of Egypt, both man and beast" (Ex. 9:24–25). The first trumpet includes blood as well, perhaps to show the loss of life involved. The plague strikes not just one nation but the whole earth, yet destroys only a third of the earth's surface. Grant Osborne writes: "We are supposed to picture one-third of all the great forests of the world (the

5. Michael Wilcock, *I Saw Heaven Opened: The Message of Revelation*, The Bible Speaks Today (Downers Grove, IL: InterVarsity Press, 1975), 95.

Amazon, the Congo, Yosemite, Yellowstone) burned down. It is a natural disaster beyond anything imaginable. Think of all the firefighters of the world trying to stem fires thousands of times greater than anything ever known."[6] God's judgments in history not only will be destructive of the sources of life, but will be beyond what science, organization, and human willpower can manage.

The second trumpet blows, and God's judgment falls on the earth's seas: "The second angel blew his trumpet, and something like a great mountain, burning with fire, was thrown into the sea, and a third of the sea became blood. A third of the living creatures in the sea died, and a third of the ships were destroyed" (Rev. 8:8–9). Some writers have sought to connect this plague with the eruption of Mount Vesuvius in A.D. 79 and its destruction in and near the Mediterranean Sea. But the scene depicted is far more vast, causing a third of the sea to turn to blood and destroying a third of all sea creatures and ships.

The second trumpet echoes the first of God's plagues against Egypt, when Moses plunged his staff into the Nile River and made its waters turn to blood. As a result, the fish died, the water stank, and it could no longer be used for drinking (Ex. 7:17–21). Likewise in this plague, the seas no longer provide the economic resources on which the world depends, destroying a third of the fish and trading vessels. This image would be particularly profound to subjects of the Roman Empire, the food supply of which depended on trade from the sea.

Important to this plague is the vast mountain that is set on fire and then cast into the sea. This language comes from the book of Jeremiah, where the prophet refers to Babylon in this way. God calls Babylon a "destroying mountain . . . which destroys the whole earth" (Jer. 51:25). He promises to "stretch out my hand against you . . . and make you a burnt mountain" (51:25), and then to destroy Babylon as though he had cast it into the sea (51:42). The "Babylon" of John's day was Rome, just as it had been Egypt in the time of Moses. This trumpet thus depicts the destruction of the world empires in flames as they go down to the sea and bring woe to the world.

The imagery becomes even more vivid with the third trumpet: "A great star fell from heaven, blazing like a torch, and it fell on a third of the rivers

---

6. Grant R. Osborne, *Revelation*, Baker Exegetical Commentary on the New Testament (Grand Rapids: Baker Academic, 2002), 351.

and on the springs of water. The name of the star is Wormwood. A third of the waters became wormwood, and many people died from the water, because it had been made bitter" (Rev. 8:10–11). Here, a star or flaming meteor falls not into the sea but into the inland waters so as to poison a third of the streams, killing many people. The star shows the heavenly origin of the catastrophe—it comes from God—and the star's name reveals its plague. Wormwood was a foul herb that made water undrinkable and that the Bible associates with "bitterness" (Lam. 3:15, 19).

This third plague may also allude to the fall of world imperial powers, through its connection with Isaiah 14:12–15. There, God compared the Babylonian king to a fallen star. Like Satan before him, Nebuchadnezzar would seek to exalt himself above God, saying in his heart, "Above the stars of God I will set my throne on high; . . . I will make myself like the Most High" (Isa. 14:13–14). In judgment, God declared, "You are brought down to Sheol, to the far reaches of the pit" (14:15; see also Dan. 4:28–33). The point is that God judges idolatrous imperial pretensions, whether by Babylon, Rome, Nazi Germany, Communist Russia, or secularist America. Their idolatry is embittered because it pollutes the sources of life, such as marriage, the family, communities, and civil relationships. In this way, history records God as constantly judging idolatrous man, making bitter the lives of those who seek to raise themselves above God. *Wormwood* is a biblical catchphrase for the consequences of sin in ruining all of life. God spoke this way in Jeremiah about the spiritual consequences of runaway sin: "I will feed this people with bitter food, and give them poisonous water to drink" (Jer. 9:15).

The fourth trumpet speaks of judgment in the sky that brings darkness on earth: "The fourth angel blew his trumpet, and a third of the sun was struck, and a third of the moon, and a third of the stars, so that a third of their light might be darkened, and a third of the day might be kept from shining, and likewise a third of the night" (Rev. 8:12).

This fourth plague confirms that we are not to seek a literalistic fulfillment of these trumpets, since the idea of only part of the sun and moon shining, together with a third of the day and night, does not make sense of the physical world. Some have sought to link this plague to a great solar eclipse, but this is not what the fourth trumpet describes. Geoffrey Wilson writes that it should "be obvious that John is painting a picture and not writing a treatise on astronomy!"[7] The point of the fourth trumpet is God's control over even the heavenly bodies so that he can bring the darkness of judgment on his enemies anywhere and at any time. Although God here places only a partial judgment on the sources of light, he warns mankind against a total darkness in final judgment if sinners do not repent.

Darkness describes the removal of God's blessing; it is the context of those living under sin's curse. This is why darkness descended on the cross while Jesus bore the penalty of our sins. To fall under the curse of darkness is to be condemned from sin and cut off from any blessing from God, who is light (1 John 1:5). God placed Pharaoh's Egypt under a plague of darkness for three days, while light continued to shine on the land where the Israelites lived (Ex. 10:21–23). This plague reminds us that only by coming to Christ in faith do we escape the darkness of sin and judgment. John said of Jesus: "In him was life, and the life was the light of men" (John 1:4).

We remember that Revelation is not a puzzle book but a picture book. The general impression is therefore most important. Here, the four trumpets bring plagues on the created order—the earth, the seas, the streams, and the stars and moon—to signify God's judgment on the nations that rise up in idolatry throughout history. These woes are inflicted not by "nature" but by God, and mankind is completely unable to manage them. This is precisely what a sober view of history shows, with vast portions of the human race suffering and dying at any one time because of tragedies originating from every part of creation.

These images remind me of the years that my family lived in South Florida during the most concentrated season of hurricanes in memory. For months every year, our community felt like a bull's-eye had been placed on us, targeting winds, waves, fires, and darkness that we could only desperately seek to endure. Moreover, the economic effect of those storms played an important role in the collapse of the U.S. housing market that began a national recession. The insurance companies labeled these events "acts of God," and that is precisely what they were, in keeping with the judgments of Revelation 8. The four trumpets place the bull's-eye of divine wrath on those who are alienated from God through unbelief: God is warning mankind of a greater judgment to come, with a more intense fire, destruction, and darkness that will last forever when Christ returns to judge the earth.

7. Geoffrey B. Wilson, *New Testament Commentaries*, 2 vols. (Edinburgh: Banner of Truth, 2005), 2:523.

THE TRUMPETS' SUMMONING

I have stressed that the images resulting from the four trumpets are not to be interpreted literally, yet the judgment of God on history that they depict is very real. The intention of these calamities is to show that the utopian schemes of man are doomed to failure and to warn idolatrous people of the bitterness that sin earns now and of the final judgment that will come at the end of the age.

To make this point clear, Revelation 8:13 presents an eagle flying high above the world, circling for prey, and warning that even worse judgments are yet to come: "Then I looked, and I heard an eagle crying with a loud voice as it flew directly overhead, 'Woe, woe, woe to those who dwell on the earth, at the blasts of the other trumpets that the three angels are about to blow!'" The word for *eagle* can also mean "vulture": this is a carrion-consuming bird, looking down on the earth and expecting to eat man's flesh as food. His three woes warn of the great judgments in the final three trumpets. The eagle represents how the upheavals of nature warn mankind to beware the greater spiritual consequences of sin. These spiritual judgments will begin in chapter 9.

The eagle's warning of woe concludes a chapter that makes three things vividly clear. First, *God is certain to judge sin in terrible ways.* The unbelieving world may look on the kinds of judgments symbolized in this chapter and make critical comments regarding the God of the Bible. "What kind of God is this," people scoff, "who wields fire against the earth and sea, who causes streams to be bitter, and casts the world under darkness?" The Bible's answer directs us to a holy God who burns with wrath against the sins of mankind.

When Adam fell into sin, God told him that the natural order had been cursed in judgment: "Cursed is the ground because of you," God said (Gen. 3:17). The plagues of the four trumpets show us that mankind can never escape the curse of sin apart from repentance and reconciliation with God through faith in Christ. Moreover, God did not merely curse the ground and leave Adam to it. Rather, God continues to bring judgment on sin, punishing rebellion and warning man to repent before the final judgment of the seventh trumpet. Geoffrey Wilson writes that the four trumpets "show that there are no *natural* disasters in a world which is governed by God."[8]

8. Ibid., 2:276.

Therefore, God intends that when we see natural disasters sweeping the earth with destruction virtually every day, punctuated by great calamities from time to time, we are to be reminded of God's judgment on sin so that we might repent, believe on Jesus Christ, and be saved.

Second, the constant allusions to the exodus plagues on Egypt communicate to believers that *God is determined to deliver his people from worldly oppression*. We remember that John wrote Revelation to churches on the brink of a terrible persecution launched by the great Pharaoh of their day, the Roman Emperor Domitian. The connection between the symbol of Egypt and Rome is made clear in Revelation 11:8, but the allusion is not limited to the Rome of John's day.[9] G. B. Caird writes that Revelation's "Egyptian typology is an emphatic way of saying that present disasters are but a prelude to God's great deliverance. In each of the heavenly trumpet blasts God is saying to the Pharaoh of the new Egypt, 'Let my people go!' At the same time he is saying to the Christians, 'When all this begins to happen, breathe again and hold your heads high, because your rescue is at hand' (Luke 21:28)."[10]

Christians are therefore to look on the calamities of history and be reminded not only of the judgment we escape through faith in the cross of Jesus. We are also to see them as emblems of the great deliverance by which God intends to break the will of the worldly powers that oppose the truth and grace of Christ. "Let my people go," Moses cried to Pharaoh (Ex. 7:16). Jesus said that when natural upheavals "begin to take place, straighten up and raise your heads, because your redemption is drawing near" (Luke 21:28). By the power of God, believers in Christ can be certain that just as we have been set free from the penalty and power of sin through the blood of Christ, God will set us free from the powers of history so that we will continue in faith until our salvation is achieved.

Third, in the angels' trumpet blasts we hear *our own call to arms*. The trumpets signify what God is going to do, just as the trumpets of Joshua summoned God's power to knock down the walls of Jericho. Like Joshua and the Israelites, we act in faith by advancing under God's banner. We are to go on lifting our hearts in worship, whatever restrictions the world may place

9. Revelation 11:8 describes the ungodly world as "the great city that symbolically is called Sodom and Egypt."

10. G. B. Caird, *The Revelation of St. John the Divine* (San Francisco: Harper, 1966), 115–16.

on us. We are to continue speaking the truth of God's Word, bearing witness to God's judgment on sin and God's gracious forgiveness through faith in Christ. We are to go on calling on God in prayer, knowing that through Christ God hears us and will answer even with the trumpets of heaven.

The trumpets blare to announce God's victory over the world through Jesus Christ. By his grace we are to triumph as well, not with worldly power or attainments but in the fulfillment of our calling as God's people in Christ. A later vision, between the sixth and seventh trumpets, makes our calling clear, for which the angels marvel not only at God but also at us. "They have conquered," the angels will say of Christians in our world, "by the blood of the Lamb and by the word of their testimony, for they loved not their lives even unto death" (Rev. 12:11). This is our calling—and hearing the trumpets of Revelation, we are now summoned to the battle.

27

FROM THE BOTTOMLESS PIT

Revelation 9:1–21

And the fifth angel blew his trumpet, and I saw a star fallen
from heaven to earth, and he was given the key to the
shaft of the bottomless pit. (Rev. 9:1)

*I*n the movie *National Treasure*, Benjamin Gates uses a set of glasses with specially colored lenses to decipher a message written invisibly on the back of the Declaration of Independence. Using this "ocular device," Gates's eyes widen with amazement at the images that he can now see as each lens is used. We might compare the entire book of Revelation to these multilensed glasses. The visions of Revelation enable us to look on history from the perspective of God's throne in heaven. We lower the lens of the seven seals and see God guarding his servants to pass through the great tribulation of earth to arrive safely into heaven. We then lower the lens of the seven trumpets and see God's judgments that declare the inevitable victory of Christ and call idolatrous mankind to repent of sin. When we get to the seven bowls, that lens will reveal the judging punishments from God that destroy the fortresses and pleasure palaces of this age.

As we turn to Revelation 9, the fifth and sixth trumpets reveal horrors that fill readers with dismay. The fifth trumpet summons an army of demonic locusts that could inhabit a science-fiction movie about space aliens. The sixth trumpet releases fire-breathing horses with stinging serpents for tails. These are the bizarre images that cause some Christians to avoid the book of Revelation as too disturbing and difficult. Yet the reality behind these visions is too real for us to dismiss. The lens of these visions enables us to see the spiritual dimension of our present world as it truly is and the evil powers that afflict the lives of people with misery and dread. So terrible are these visions that we may ask the dismayed question, "Why?" The reason for these woes is sin, idolatry, and the persistent rebellion of the human race against a holy God who is resolved to judge sin.

THE DEMONIC HORDE

In order to understand the message of this chapter, we must first come to grips with its bizarre images. All through our studies of Revelation, we have understood its apocalyptic visions as presenting reality through symbolic pictures. Therefore, unless we are constrained to interpret a number or an image in a literal way, we will seek its symbolic meaning. Our great resource to interpret the visions is the same resource available to John and his original readers: the Old Testament. Moreover, the visions should be expected to have relevance to the original recipients, the Christians in the churches of Asia in the Roman Empire at the end of the first century A.D.

There are dedicated Christians who teach that the Bible must always be interpreted as speaking literally. When this principle is applied to Revelation 9, however, it produces results that are not helpful. To cite one example, best-selling author Hal Lindsey, in *Apocalypse Code*, informs us that the fifth trumpet describes attack helicopters that will be deployed in our time by the Chinese army. He arrives at this conclusion by taking the details of John's vision and seeking correspondence with some feature of our current world, even though this meaning could have no significance to John's original readers and does not obviously fulfill the stated intention of the text.

So what are we to make of the locust horde summoned by the fifth trumpet? John describes what he saw:

> In appearance the locusts were like horses prepared for battle: on their heads were what looked like crowns of gold; their faces were like human faces, their

hair like women's hair, and their teeth like lions' teeth; they had breastplates like breastplates of iron, and the noise of their wings was like the noise of many chariots with horses rushing into battle. They have tails and stings like scorpions, and their power to hurt people for five months is in their tails. (Rev. 9:7–10)

It is clear that these invaders are not natural forces in our world, such as Chinese attack helicopters, because they are unleashed into history from a shaft of the bottomless Abyss where demons dwell (Rev. 9:1–2). Therefore, these locusts represent evil spiritual powers that are unleashed at God's will into our world.

The imagery in this vision derives from two Old Testament sources. The first is Exodus 10:13–15, where Moses cast a locust plague on Egypt. This fits the pattern of the previous trumpets in Revelation 8, which replicated plagues on Egypt. John's other source is Joel 2:1–11, which described the coming of the Lord's judgment in terms of an invasion of locusts. Joel described these large, devouring grasshoppers as "war horses" bringing flames and destruction, comparing them to fierce "warriors" who charge and "soldiers" who scale a wall (Joel 2:4–7).

Revelation's demonic invasion adds gruesome features to Joel's vision. John compares the locusts to war horses who wear crowns of gold and possess "human faces" (Rev. 9:7). The crowns foretell victory, and the human faces show that they are guided by a rational cunning. John adds that "their hair [is] like women's hair, and their teeth like lions' teeth" (9:8). The pleasing-looking female hair suggests seductive powers that in reality bring death. Moreover, the locusts "had breastplates like breastplates of iron, and the noise of their wings was like the noise of many chariots with horses rushing into battle" (9:9). The breastplates speak of invulnerability, and the sound of wings depicts the speed of their assault. Finally, they "have tails and stings like scorpions, and their power to hurt people for five months is in their tails" (9:10). H. B. Swete comments, "The scorpion takes its place with the snake and other creatures hostile to man, and with them symbolizes the forces of spiritual evil which are active in the world."[1] We know that John is not describing literal features because he uses the word *like* eight times. These are analogies presenting a "frightful

---

1. Henry Barclay Swete, *Commentary on Revelation*, 2 vols. (1911; repr., Grand Rapids: Kregel, 1977), 2:116.

and horrible and true picture of the operation of the powers of darkness in the souls of the wicked."[2]

The sixth trumpet summons an army that is every bit as supernatural and demonic as the locust plague. "The number of mounted troops was twice ten thousand times ten thousand" (Rev. 9:16). This number is two hundred million, which is larger than any earthly army conceivable even today. The idea is of a vast host beyond counting. John saw horses with riders: "They wore breastplates the color of fire and of sapphire and of sulfur, and the heads of the horses were like lions' heads, and fire and smoke and sulfur came out of their mouths" (9:16–17). The horses breathe fire from their lion heads and possess serpent tails: "the power of the horses is in their mouths and in their tails, for their tails are like serpents with heads" (9:19).

In keeping with the vision, the colors of the breastplates—red, yellow, and blue—signify the fire, sulfur, and smoke that accompany these riders. G. B. Caird writes: "This is an army straight from the jaws of hell. The snake-like tails of the horses indicate their Satanic nature, . . . and so do the fire, smoke, and sulphur which they exhale."[3]

LOCUSTS OF TORMENT

The vision of the fifth trumpet begins with a star "fallen from heaven to earth, and he was given the key to the shaft of the bottomless pit" (Rev. 9:1). In the imagery of Revelation, this star is an angelic being. Some scholars suggest that this is a holy angel serving God, since in chapter 20 an angel comes down from heaven to lock the Abyss with a great chain (20:1). Chapter 9 depicts a different situation, since the angel was "fallen . . . to earth." Jesus once said, "I saw Satan fall like lightning from heaven" (Luke 10:18). In the vision of Revelation 12, the great dragon Satan is "thrown down to the earth" (Rev. 12:9). It seems most likely, then, that the angel falling from heaven is a demonic archangel, who is then granted authority by God to open the great Abyss of hell. In verse 11, John tells us that the demonic host that comes forth is led by "the angel of the bottomless pit," named "Abaddon" in Hebrew and "Apollyon" in Greek (Rev. 9:11). Both of these

2. William Hendriksen, *More than Conquerors: An Interpretation of the Book of Revelation* (1940; repr., Grand Rapids: Baker, 1967), 121.

3. G. B. Caird, *The Revelation of St. John the Divine* (San Francisco: Harper, 1966), 122.

names mean "Destroyer," which shows his evil servitude to Satan, if he is not Satan himself, as well as the result of his activity. The name Apollyon derives from the same verb as the name of the Greek god Apollo. Since the Roman emperor Domitian considered himself an incarnation of Apollo, John may be tying the imperial persecution facing the churches of Asia to the tormenting plague unleashed by this trumpet.

The term "abyss" or "bottomless pit" is used throughout the Bible for the dark prison where demons are held. Jesus once found a man who was inhabited by a host of demons who called themselves "Legion." Before Jesus cast them out, the demons "begged him not to command them to depart into the abyss" (Luke 8:31). This suggests the torment of demons in the pit as they await final judgment. This idea is reinforced by the smoke that came forth from the pit, "like the smoke of a great furnace, and the sun and the air were darkened with the smoke from the shaft" (Rev. 9:2). Hendriksen comments: "It is the smoke of deception and delusion, of sin and sorrow, of moral darkness and degradation that is constantly belching up out of hell."[4]

From this Abyss comes a host of demons bringing a spiritual assault that resembles the desolation wreaked by a plague of locusts: "Then from the smoke came locusts on the earth, and they were given power like the power of scorpions of the earth" (Rev. 9:3). Locust swarms can darken the sky because of their vast numbers and devastate the land, eating all the crops and grass down to the roots, stripping bark off all the trees, and leaving a desert in their wake. As we view our world with the lens of the fifth trumpet, we see this kind of spiritual assault taking place.

Unlike literal locusts, however, these spiritual invaders do not "harm the grass of the earth or any green plant or any tree, but only those people who do not have the seal of God on their foreheads" (Rev. 9:4). This spiritual assault is God's judgment on those who rebel against him, worship idols, and make war on the church. Steve Wilmshurst explains: "Satan's hordes are at work across the earth, destroying people's lives, inciting them to commit appalling crimes against one another, making life utterly miserable for millions, holding them captive in false religions."[5]

In the terms of this vision, what demonic influences would we identify in the culture of America and the post-Christian West? Surely sexual

---

4. Hendriksen, *More than Conquerors*, 120.
5. Steve Wilmshurst, *The Final Word: The Book of Revelation Simply Explained* (Darlington, UK: Evangelical Press, 2008), 121.

promiscuity is a source of great evil, destroying marriages and families through adultery and robbing young men and women of the purity designed for them by God. Pornography should be seen as a spiritual evil that fills the hearts of men with sexual filth and violence. Racism has left its scourge across our culture, sowing needless hatred and bitterness. Drugs and alcohol abuse devastate the lives of millions. Notice that these are obviously destructive influences, yet most of them are zealously protected and even encouraged in our society! Behind the secular humanism, materialism, and self-absorbed hedonism are evil powers afflicting great portions of our population with spiritual torment and emotional affliction.

Notice three things about this spiritual plague. First, it does not directly kill but makes life such a misery that people "long to die, but death will flee from them" (Rev. 9:6). Second, these are limited judgments to warn people of the greater and final judgment for sin. The demons had "power to hurt people for five months" (9:10), which is the natural life cycle for locusts. The point is that Satan and his minions are limited by God in the judgment they can inflict.

Third, these spiritual torments afflict "only those people who do not have the seal of God on their foreheads" (Rev. 9:4). This shows that these are not physical woes that afflict all people, but spiritual torments by which God uses evil to judge those who are given over to sin. Believers are not able to stop this plague—the locusts' invulnerability is showed by the iron breastplates—but they are free from these torments as they practice godly lifestyles in the power of the Holy Spirit. Just as in the exodus, when the angel of death slew the firstborn in all of Egypt, except in the homes marked by the blood of a lamb—a marking that looked forward to faith in the cross of Christ—so also those who bear Christ's seal of the Holy Spirit today are preserved from the judgment of the demonic plague of torment.

THE DEVIL'S HORSEMEN

At the sounding of the sixth trumpet, John heard a voice "saying to the sixth angel who had the trumpet, 'Release the four angels who are bound at the great river Euphrates'" (Rev. 9:13–14). These four angels released "mounted troops" of unimaginable numbers, "to kill a third of mankind"

(9:15–16). We have seen that these horsemen are spiritual forces set loose in the world at God's command. Their judgment is not only of torment but of death, in the form of warfare and conquest. The "fire and smoke and sulfur" coming out of their mouths are the fumes of hell (9:17), and they have power to slay and wound.

The Euphrates River was the ideal boundary of Israel, as promised by God. Therefore, these horsemen represent invading enemies from the world. In the Old Testament, God sent the Assyrians and then the Babylonians across the Euphrates to bring judgment onto Israel for her idolatry. Jeremiah warned: "A great nation is stirring from the farthest parts of the earth. They lay hold on bow and javelin; they are cruel and have no mercy; the sound of them is like the roaring sea; they ride on horses, set in array as a man for battle" (Jer. 6:22–23).

Moreover, in the time of John's writing, the Euphrates was the border of the Roman Empire, beyond which were the terrifying horsemen of the Parthian Empire. Before the emperor Trajan's victory over the Parthians in A.D. 114–16, these enemies stalked the nightmares of those living within Rome's borders. It is possible that the description of these horsemen breathing fire out of their mouths and stinging with their tails would remind John's readers of the way in which Parthian horse archers fired both while advancing and while retreating.

The history of mankind shows nations repeatedly turning away from God in order to raise up their own glory. Every empire promises its own salvation on earth with peace and prosperity. History records them all as crashing before invading forces of unforeseen ferocity. Usually the origins of these conquerors are either surprising or unexplainable. Historians struggle to explain the source of the Gothic invasions that destroyed the Roman Empire under mighty leaders such as Attila the Hun. Centuries later, the hordes of Islam swept across North Africa with virtually no warning. In the early thirteenth century, the Mongol armies, led by the charismatic leader Temujin, also known as Genghis Khan, rose up with unexplained genius and vigor, conquering from China in the East to the Danube in the West. The Mongols so resembled the riders of the sixth trumpet that Christians viewed them as the literal fulfillment of Revelation, labeling them "the devil's horsemen." In the fourteenth century, the armies of England were suddenly equipped with invincible longbowmen. Historians do not know how this prowess for archery was developed in England and Wales or why it suddenly died out, but the military advantage granted to the Edwardian kings resulted in the Hundred Years' War. The twentieth century witnessed the shocking scourge of the Nazi panzer divisions, which so many people understandably compared to Revelation 9's horsemen. In the twenty-first century, a bloody passion has enflamed Islamic jihadists in a way that defies logic. These otherwise unexplainable conquerors, whose bows, swords, and bombs have killed great swaths of humanity, are hard to explain apart from the sixth trumpet's vision of warfare let loose on earth from the pits of hell.

The Peace of Christ

In studying Revelation 9, we should learn three important lessons. The first is that *because of its idolatry and sin, our world is judged by God with spiritual torments and destruction*. These plagues originate in the Abyss where demons dwell. There are times when Christian influence is strong and a wholesome culture may flower in secular society. But when a society turns away from God and rejects his Word, God will respond by judging that idolatry with spiritual forces of evil torment. Paul explained that when men turn from God to idolatry, "their foolish hearts [become] darkened" and God gives "them up in the lusts of their hearts to impurity" (Rom. 1:21–24). The very sins that they have longed for become God's judgment on them. Revelation 9 shows that God not only gives the wicked over to their sins but makes those sins a torment to them.

Revelation 9:15 reveals that the four angels at the Euphrates "had been prepared for the hour, the day, the month, and the year." This suggests definite, foreordained times when God unleashes conquest on the pride of secular powers. Given the parallels between the seals, trumpets, and bowls in Revelation, we generally interpret the trumpet visions as describing events happening throughout the gospel age. As the sixth seal focuses on the final judgment, however, this sixth trumpet vision may show that great and terribly violent warfare is reserved for the end of history at a time prepared by God.

This idea undercuts the theory of postmillennial Christians, who believe that Christian influence will increase until history ends in a crowning age of worldwide faith and godliness. The fifth and sixth trumpets suggest the opposite, that throughout history and especially at the end God will unleash plagues from the pit of hell to judge a rebellious world. Like the Roman Empire of John's day, the secular powers in every age seek security and blessing not in the God who made them but in gods of their own making. God therefore sends torments to announce the victory of his coming judgment. Hendriksen writes: "Our exalted Lord Jesus Christ . . . will again and again punish the persecutors of the Church by inflicting upon them disasters in every sphere of life."[6] The visions of Revelation 9 therefore do not promote postmillennial confidence about the world's progress but remind us instead to put our confidence only in the gospel's power to save sinners out of a world that is destined for judgment.

When we put on the lens of this chapter's visions, we see that our world is dominated by evil powers that torment with misery and utterly destroy. Paul stated that we face "spiritual forces of evil in the heavenly places" (Eph. 6:12), implacable enemies who want to ruin our lives. We see that a worldly mentality leads to misery and death, so Christians must not imbibe the world's values. Since Paul says that "the present form of this world is passing away" (1 Cor. 7:31), we ought not give our ultimate allegiance to it. John warned us in his first epistle: "Do not love the world or the things in the world. . . . For all that is in the world—the desires of the flesh and the desires of the eyes and pride in possessions—is not from the Father but is from the world. And the world is passing away along with its desires, but whoever does the will of God abides forever" (1 John 2:15–17). Because we are called to live differently from the world, Christians will be accused of being out of touch and out of style. But according to Revelation 9, our holy separation from the spirit of the age protects us from the judgments even now being inflicted on the world.

Second, *fearful as these judgments are, Christians should have no fear of them.* This passage is filled with signs of God's complete sovereignty over these plagues and torments. The chapter begins with God's granting the angel permission to open the Abyss (Rev. 9:1). Verse 10 shows that God restricts the extent of the locust plague. The sixth trumpet begins with a command that comes from "the four horns of the golden altar before God" (9:13). We have previously seen that this altar is where the prayers of the

---

6. Hendriksen, *More than Conquerors*, 123.

martyrs and saints are offered, so that these judgments are God's response to his people's pleas for deliverance. William Still stated that "God uses sin sinlessly," employing the forces of evil to render holy judgment against evildoers.[7] Fearful as these trumpet plagues may be, they are under the complete control of our covenant-keeping God, and thus they are unable to harm us. Geoffrey Wilson writes: "The children of God are strangers to the spiritual torments that plague the wicked."[8]

Moreover, Revelation 9:4 specifies that the locust plague is directed not at believers but only at "those people who do not have the seal of God on their foreheads." Many believers, however, are afflicted by their sinful lives before coming to Christ: sexual promiscuity, pornography, racism, egotism, and the like. They may therefore bear scars and enter the Christian life with habits picked up from sinful influences. But what a hope they have in Jesus Christ. Paul wrote to the Corinthians that the sexually immoral, idolaters, adulterers, homosexuals, thieves, and people like them will not enter the kingdom of God. He then said, "And such were some of you. But you were washed, you were sanctified, you were justified in the name of the Lord Jesus Christ and by the Spirit of our God" (1 Cor. 6:9–11). Those who believe in Christ are delivered from the penalty and power of sin. By living in obedience to God's Word through faith in Christ and by the power of the Holy Spirit, we are free from the bondage of sin's torment. Paul explained that "our old self was crucified with him . . . , so that we would no longer be enslaved to sin. . . . So you also must consider yourselves dead to sin and alive to God in Christ Jesus" (Rom. 6:6, 11).

Third, we find at the end of the chapter that *the purpose of these judgments is to awaken sinners to their need to repent and return to the Lord through faith in Christ*. John concludes:

> The rest of mankind, who were not killed by these plagues, did not repent of the works of their hands nor give up worshiping demons and idols of gold and silver and bronze and stone and wood, which cannot see or hear or walk, nor did they repent of their murders or their sorceries or their sexual immorality or their thefts. (Rev. 9:20–21)

7. Quoted in Douglas F. Kelly, *Revelation*, Mentor Expository Commentary (Tain, Ross-shire, Scotland: Mentor, 2012), 170.

8. Geoffrey B. Wilson, *New Testament Commentaries*, 2 vols. (Edinburgh: Banner of Truth, 2005), 2:525.

There is no reason for you to follow this self-destroying example. To worship the idols of this world—money, pleasure, power, sex—is to be in service to demons and to receive the torments reserved in judgment for this world. God intends that through the misery of the life of sin, you will realize your need to be forgiven the guilt of sin and delivered from the power of sin. God offers all of these to you as a loving gift through faith in the Savior, Jesus Christ. "For God so loved the world, that he gave his only Son, that whoever believes in him should not perish but have eternal life" (John 3:16).

I mentioned earlier how Jesus delivered a man of the Gadarenes who was possessed by a legion of demons, who begged Jesus not to cast them into the Abyss. Luke's Gospel tells us that after he had been delivered by Jesus' saving power, the man who was formerly so tormented was now a picture of one who is blessed by Christ's saving grace. The man was now "sitting at the feet of Jesus, clothed and in his right mind" (Luke 8:35). This is the salvation that Jesus offers to all who have suffered under the reign of sin. Christ will make us his disciples blessed in a personal relationship with himself. Jesus will remove our sin and clothe us with his own righteousness before God. He will restore our minds with truth and grace through power of his Word. If you have ever despaired even of living because of heartache, inward corruption, and the torments of sin, turn to Jesus Christ in faith and you, too, will be delivered.

I seldom turn to bumper stickers to make sense of complicated Bible passages. But in this case, the message of Revelation 9 is well summed up by a bumper sticker that you may have seen: "No Jesus, No Peace. Know Jesus, Know Peace." Without Jesus—without the forgiveness and cleansing from sin that he gives—there is no peace in this world of sin. But if we come to know him in saving faith, trusting his redeeming work to set sinners free from judgment and misery, we will know peace. "Peace I leave with you," Jesus said; "my peace I give to you. Not as the world gives do I give to you. Let not your hearts be troubled, neither let them be afraid" (John 14:27).

28

THE LITTLE SCROLL

Revelation 10:1–11

So I went to the angel and told him to give me the little scroll.
And he said to me, "Take and eat it; it will make your stomach
bitter, but in your mouth it will be sweet as honey." (Rev. 10:9)

*T*he *Oxford English Dictionary* defines *intermission* as "an inter-val between parts of a play, film, or concert." An intermission is designed not merely for the players to get a rest but also for the action to continue in the audience's minds and conversations. The drama of John's Apocalypse makes significant use of intermissions or interludes in the unfolding of the seven seals and the seven trumpets. In the lobby of the theater of Revelation, John received further visions to go along with the main action of the seals and trumpets, the purpose of which was to depict the situation, destiny, and calling of the church. Robert Mounce describes Revelation's interludes as "literary devices by which the church is instructed concerning its role and destiny during the final period of world history."[1]

In the intermission after the first six seals, John was shown how God sealed his church for salvation and delivered her safely out of the tribula-

---

1. Robert H. Mounce, *Revelation*, rev. ed., New International Commentary on the New Testament (Grand Rapids: Eerdmans, 1997), 207.

tion. John receives a similar vision in the intermission between the sixth and seventh trumpets. Beginning in Revelation 10, this vision depicts the church as receiving God's Word, holding fast to it, and bearing testimony on God's behalf despite persecution and even martyrdom. Chapter 10 concludes with a command for John to "prophesy about many peoples and nations and languages and kings" (Rev. 10:11). John's commission to preach, coupled with chapter 11's vision of the two persecuted witnesses, provides an explanation for the world's judgment. G. K. Beale writes: "The wicked suffer because they reject the message of the witnesses and persecute them."[2]

According to Revelation 10, Christ's true church is defined as having received and treasured God's revealed Word. Just as Israel was called to be "a light for the nations" (Isa. 49:6), the church is commissioned to bear testimony to the gospel in a hostile world. The vision of the "mighty angel" and his "little scroll" supplies us with reasons to accept this calling and remain always faithful to God's holy Word.

THE SOVEREIGN REDEEMER'S WORD

The first reason why Christians must maintain our witness to Christ and his Word is *the sovereign glory of the Redeemer* whose message it is. The vision begins with John seeing "another mighty angel coming down from heaven, wrapped in a cloud, with a rainbow over his head, and his face was like the sun, and his legs like pillars of fire" (Rev. 10:1). This is the second "mighty angel" we have encountered in Revelation, and since they both deal with the scroll of God's will, they are obviously connected (see 5:2). This angel "had a little scroll open in his hand" (10:2), and we recall the scroll earlier opened by Jesus. Since this is a "little scroll," it is not the entirety of God's will but the portion that God is revealing to John. We may thus think of the little scroll as approximating the book of Revelation.

The descriptions of this awesome angel include so many indicators of deity that many scholars believe the mighty angel is Jesus himself. The angel is "wrapped in a cloud, with a rainbow over his head, and his face was like the sun, and his legs like pillars of fire" (Rev. 10:1). All of these are emblems of deity, since God rides on the clouds, is surrounded by a rainbow, and

---

2. G. K. Beale, *The Book of Revelation: A Commentary on the Greek Text*, New International Greek Testament Commentary (Grand Rapids: Eerdmans, 1999), 536.

radiates with the sun's brightness. It is unlikely that this figure is Christ, however, since in Revelation he is described as the conquering Lamb and since the word *angel* consistently designates Christ's heavenly servants. At the very least, though, this mighty angel is intended to represent the glory of Christ whom he serves. Dennis Johnson writes: "The radiance of the angel's appearance marks him as one who bears the image of his Master, reflecting the Master's glory as he brings the Master's message."[3] The mighty angel reminds us that we, too, are to adorn our witness of Christ's gospel message with lives that are being transformed into his holy image (2 Cor. 3:18).

The details of this glorious angel further depict Christ as Israel's Redeemer in the exodus. During Israel's sojourn from bondage in Egypt to kingdom in the promised land, God's cloud descended on the tabernacle, Moses' face shone with God's radiance when he emerged from the Lord's presence, and the pillar of fire guided and protected the people. The rainbow symbolizes God's covenant mercy, signifying "not only glory and power but also deliverance for God's people."[4] In this way, the angel communicates that Christ is going to lead his people to the new and better promised land. Just as Noah emerged from the ark into a new world cleansed of sin, the angel's rainbow anticipates the new heaven and the new earth awaiting Christ's followers. James Hamilton comments: "What God did for Noah and the children of Israel by saving them through the judging of their enemies, then bringing them into a new land, he is going to do again when he saves us through the judgment of this world."[5]

The vision of this "mighty angel" emphasizes God's sovereignty. In Daniel 7:13–14, the Son of Man comes "with the clouds of heaven" to receive his eternal dominion from God. Now this angel represents Christ "wrapped in a cloud" (Rev. 10:1). Moreover, the gigantic angel "set his right foot on the sea, and his left foot on the land" (10:2). In the Bible, to have something under one's feet is to exercise dominion over it. Here, Christ's angel depicts his sovereignty over the entirety of creation, land and sea. Later in Revelation we will see Christ's enemy, Satan, raising beasts from the land and the

3. Dennis E. Johnson, *Triumph of the Lamb: A Commentary on Revelation* (Phillipsburg, NJ: P&R Publishing, 2001), 158.

4. Grant R. Osborne, *Revelation*, Baker Exegetical Commentary on the New Testament (Grand Rapids: Baker Academic, 2002), 394.

5. James M. Hamilton Jr., *Revelation: The Spirit Speaks to the Churches* (Wheaton, IL: Crossway, 2012), 223–24.

sea. Here, in advance of those beasts, we are reminded that Christ already has his foot planted on the domains from which they come.

Finally, Christ's sovereignty is depicted by the angel's great shout, "with a loud voice, like a lion roaring" (Rev. 10:3). Jesus has already been revealed as "the Lion of the tribe of Judah" (5:5). It was because Jesus conquered as Lion and Lamb that he received the heavenly scroll, a portion of which the angel now holds out to John.

We remember that the purpose of the intermission between the sixth and seventh trumpets, like that between the sixth and seventh seals, is to reveal the identity and calling of the church. The angel's exodus imagery reminds us that Christians are God's holy people on a pilgrimage through this world toward heaven. Whatever else you may be—as defined by your family, job, race, or social status—if you are a Christian, you are the object of God's eternal plan of salvation and a follower of the Sovereign Lord who redeemed you by his blood. Hamilton writes: "You are someone whom God has gone to extravagant lengths to redeem."[6] As the pillar of cloud and fire guided and protected Israel in the desert, you are being led and protected by Christ so that you will arrive safely in the new world of the age to come. The key to following Christ, which you must do for salvation, is to receive, trust, and obey God's Word, which is why the mighty angel came to John with the "little scroll" open in his hand.

The angel who depicts the glory of Christ as our sovereign Redeemer prompts us to treasure and uphold God's holy Word because of the glory of the One who gives it. The book of Revelation begins by saying that Jesus has a revelation from God to give to his people, which he made "known by sending his angel to his servant John" (Rev. 1:1). This first point of the book is now vividly depicted by the angel who brings the scroll to John. His appearance reminds us that the Word of God that we read, believe, and proclaim today comes from the One who is sovereign over the entire creation and the Savior who is delivering us to heaven.

When Christians come under fire from a hostile culture, we are tempted to compromise the Bible's message and methods in order to lessen the conflict. But if we remember that God's Word was delivered to us through the sovereign ministry of the glorified Christ, we will banish thoughts of compromise from our minds. We should remember how Jesus challenged Peter,

6. Ibid., 223.

John, and the others when the crowds rejected his teaching. Jesus pointed at the worldly despisers of his Word and said to the Twelve, "Do you want to go away as well?" (John 6:67). Peter replied, "Lord, to whom shall we go? You have the words of eternal life" (6:68). So it remains today.

When the world scorns the Bible's teaching of creation and demands an ungodly evolutionary scheme, we must hold firm to the truth revealed to us by the only One who actually witnessed the start of the world. When the twisted voices of a confused morality demand that we change our views about gender, marriage, sexuality, and the value of human life, Christians must hold firm to the teachings that come from the only perfect Man ever to live. When hostile voices express disgust as we declare God's judgment on sin and Jesus as the only Savior of the world, we must continue teaching these doctrines that are essential to the biblical way of salvation. The world may call the gospel "hate speech," but Christians must go on stating that "God so loved the world, that he gave his only Son, that whoever believes in him should not perish but have eternal life" (John 3:16). How can we dare to hold fast to God's Word before a scornful world, without capitulation or compromise? Because looking on Christ as our Sovereign Redeemer, depicted by this "mighty angel," we remember whose scroll it is and from whom God's revealed Word came to us. To reject this message is to reject Christ himself, the only Savior, and willingly to compromise the Scriptures is to betray Jesus our Lord.

The Certain Fulfillment of God's Word

Chapter 10 begins with the appearing of the mighty Christ-angel, but its message about God's Word is only heightened by the action that follows. John heard the angel shout with a lion's roar, and in answer "the seven thunders sounded" (Rev. 10:3). In the Bible, thunder signifies the majesty of God in his coming (Ps. 29:3), together with power to shatter all opposition. The addition of seven thunders to the seven seals and seven trumpets, along with the seven bowls yet to come, can only speak of more judgment on the world. We were told after the sixth trumpet was blown that idolatrous mankind still would not repent and turn from false gods and from sin (Rev. 9:20–21). Therefore, the shout of the angel is answered by seven thunders foretelling more judgments that the rebel world deserves.

As John was preparing to write down what he heard from the seven thunders, he was unexpectedly stopped: "When the seven thunders had sounded, I was about to write, but I heard a voice from heaven saying, 'Seal up what the seven thunders have said, and do not write it down'" (Rev. 10:4). John was not to record the judgment of the seven thunders. Scholars suggest a number of reasons for this command. One suggestion is that this shows that God has more plans for history than the ones he has chosen to reveal to us in the Bible. Therefore, we should not be surprised when things happen that are not accounted for by Scripture. Another suggestion is that God has canceled the judgments of the seven thunders because it has become clear that, as Robert Mounce writes, "man's adamant decision not to repent would render another series [of judgments] useless."[7]

The best explanation is the one given by the angel himself in the verses that follow: "And the angel whom I saw standing on the sea and on the land raised his right hand to heaven and swore by him who lives forever and ever . . . that in the days of the trumpet call to be sounded by the seventh angel, the mystery of God would be fulfilled, just as he announced to his servants the prophets" (Rev. 10:5–7). The angel anticipates the seventh trumpet that is about to be blown and solemnly declares that Christ will immediately return to bring the final judgment and the conclusion of the age.

The angel raises his hand to swear a solemn testimony, just as witnesses do in courtrooms today, and names the highest authority imaginable: "by him who lives forever and ever, who created heaven and what is in it, the earth and what is in it, and the sea and what is in it" (Rev. 10:6). This is the same kind of testimony that the prophets and apostles provided in the Bible. They did not give their opinions, but they swore to the Word given them by God (see Amos 3:7–8 for a clear parallel to the lion's roar and the angel's oath).

As a witness authorized to swear by God, the angel not only brings God's Word but also testifies to the certainty of its fulfillment: "that in the days of the trumpet call to be sounded by the seventh angel, the mystery of God would be fulfilled, just as he announced to his servants the prophets" (Rev. 10:7). This verse draws from the vision in Daniel 12, when that prophet wondered about the coming of the end. The angel who spoke to Daniel "raised his right hand and his left hand toward heaven and swore by him who lives

---

7. Mounce, *Revelation*, 211–12.

forever" (Dan. 12:6–7). On that occasion, the angel told Daniel that there was yet a great time of trial to be endured before the end: "it would be for a time, times, and half a time" before the end (12:7). Now, as the seventh trumpet is about to be blown, the angel—perhaps the same angel!—gives a different message. There would now be no delay, but with the blowing of the seventh trumpet "the mystery of God would be fulfilled," in accordance with Scripture (Rev. 10:7).

When the New Testament speaks of the "mystery of God," it refers not to clues for us to figure out, but rather to redemptive truths for history that can be known only as God reveals them. When the end comes, this mystery plan of judgment and salvation will be brought to complete and total fulfillment. Just as the rainbow encircles God's throne above (Rev. 4:3), his covenant will be wholly completed. The mighty angel solemnly swears the certainty of this fulfillment, just as God said in Isaiah 55:11, "so shall my word be that goes out from my mouth; it shall not return to me empty, but it shall accomplish that which I purpose, and shall succeed in the thing for which I sent it."

The angel's testimony gives us a second reason to hold fast to God's Word: *its certainty of fulfillment*. The promises of the world fall to the ground in ashes, but Jesus says, "My words will not pass away" (Matt. 24:35). The angel "swore by him who lives forever and ever, who created heaven and what is in it, the earth and what is in it, and the sea and what is in it" (Rev. 10:6). The point is that since God is eternal, he will always oversee the fulfillment of his Word. Since God is the Creator-Lord of all that is, he can ensure that his Word is accomplished. Therefore, hearing the angel's oath and testimony, Christians should resist the passing fads of worldly thinking by standing firm on the rock of God's Word.

THE COMMISSION TO PROCLAIM GOD'S WORD

In the aftermath of the First World War, William Butler Yeats wrote a poem to express the despair and chaos of Europe, especially in his dread of the Communist Revolution in Russia. Yeats used imagery from the book of Revelation to express the sense of impending calamity, naming his poem "The Second Coming." Its opening stanza memorably expresses the unsettled mind of his reeling generation:

Turning and turning in the widening gyre
The falcon cannot hear the falconer;
Things fall apart; the centre cannot hold;
Mere anarchy is loosed upon the world.[8]

Yeats's poem is an accurate description of what happens in this world, the very situation described by the judgments in Revelation. So how are Christians to stand with conviction in a world where things seem to "fall apart" and people around us reel in confusion? The answer of the angel was to open his hand and present John with the scroll of God's Word: "Then the voice that I had heard from heaven spoke to me again, saying, 'Go, take the scroll that is open in the hand of the angel who is standing on the sea and on the land'" (Rev. 10:8). Only in this same way will we face the travails of our lives and the calamities of our generation with a calm and joyful faith. The book of Proverbs declares: "The Lord gives wisdom; from his mouth come knowledge and understanding . . . . Then you will understand righteousness and justice and equity, every good path" (Prov. 2:6–9). Jesus added, "If you abide in my word, you are truly my disciples, and you will know the truth, and the truth will set you free" (John 8:31–32).

The final verses show John as being called from heaven to approach the mighty angel and receive God's Word. In the angel's hand was the little scroll that contained God's revelation to the churches through John's ministry. This vision provides four vital points about how we should receive and minister God's Word.

First, this vision depicts the Bible as a revelation from God to man. Why should Christians hold fast to God's Word, refusing to betray the Scriptures and courageously proclaiming its message? Because it is God's revelation to mankind, declaring both judgment on sin and salvation through faith in Jesus. John did not make up his message or derive it from his studies or others' opinions. Instead, he received his message from the angel's hand, showing that Scripture comes by revelation from God himself.

Second, John's example shows that we are to engage in effort in order to receive and apprehend God's message in the Bible. John is told to go and "take the scroll" (Rev. 10:8). Then he is commanded, "Take and eat it" (10:9).

8. William Butler Yeats, "The Second Coming," in *Modern American and Modern British Poetry*, ed. Louis Untermeyer, rev. ed. (New York: Harcourt, Brace and Company, 1955), 491.

This imagery is derived from Ezekiel 2:8, when that prophet was given a scroll and told, "Open your mouth and eat what I give you." Likewise, John is to identify with and ingest God's Word so that it becomes one with him. It is to be his daily bread, as he believes and relies on the message that God has given to him. Eating involves effort, and Christians must likewise apply ourselves diligently to the study of God's Word. As the Anglican Book of Common Prayer put it, we are to "read, mark, learn, and inwardly digest" God's Word as that which nourishes and enlivens our souls.

Third, we can expect God's Word to be both sweet and bitter: "Take and eat it; it will make your stomach bitter, but in your mouth it will be sweet as honey" (Rev. 10:9). There is nothing sweeter to the soul than the Bible's message of comfort and assurance to those who believe. In Psalm 19, David praises the Scriptures for "reviving the soul; . . . making wise the simple; . . . rejoicing the heart; . . . [and] enlightening the eyes." God's Word is therefore "more to be desired . . . than gold . . . ; sweeter also than honey and drippings of the honeycomb" (Ps. 19:7–10). Countless generations of believers have received these very blessings from their ingestion of God's Word.

At the same time, the Bible's message is not only of a sweet salvation but also of a bitter judgment on sin. Moreover, bitter consequences arise from believing the Bible while living in this ungodly world: the persecutions and sufferings that are clearly depicted in Revelation. Mounce writes, "Before the final triumph believers are going to pass through a formidable ordeal," which is the message of chapter 11.[9] William Hendriksen writes that the Bible believer "must experience both its sweetness and the suffering, the cross-bearing, which is always the portion of those who truthfully proclaim it."[10]

Fourth, not only do we receive God's revelation in Scripture, ingest it for our lives, and taste its bitterness and sweetness, but like John we are commissioned by Christ to proclaim it. The chapter ends with the voice from heaven commanding: "You must again prophesy about many peoples and nations and languages and kings" (Rev. 10:11). This is not the first time John has been ordained to spread God's Word, since he had long been an apostle and since Revelation began with this same commission. Therefore, the charge given to him was not unique but rings in the hearts of every believer. To be a Christian, therefore, is to receive, ingest, taste, and proclaim God's Word.

9. Mounce, *Revelation*, 218.

10. William Hendriksen, *More than Conquerors: An Interpretation of the Book of Revelation* (1940; repr., Grand Rapids: Baker, 1967), 125.

We tend to speak of two kinds of Christians—those who believe the Bible and those who do not—but the Bible knows no such distinction. The only ones who are saved by the Sovereign Redeemer, Jesus Christ, are those who humbly receive God's Word from him, obediently hold fast to Scripture in anticipation of its certain fulfillment, and faithfully fulfill Christ's commission to spread his message of judgment and salvation throughout the world.

"I Am Sending You"

We might compare John's situation to that of a baseball fan watching the World Series at Yankee Stadium in New York. John is enthralled by the action, which will determine the year's champion. Unexpectedly, in the ninth inning with the game on the line, the manager goes into the stands and approaches John. John is to come out of the stands and pitch the decisive innings! This is the angel's message for the apostle and all of Christ's people: we are to receive the Word of God's salvation, which was purchased by the blood of Christ and ordained by the eternal will of the Father, and we are to proclaim it to the world.

This commission does not mean that God has set aside his sovereignty or that Christians have replaced Christ's lordship over all affairs. Rather, the point is that God's sovereign plan calls for the decisive witness of his message to be given by sinners saved by grace to other sinners needing to be saved by grace, even though we may be persecuted by the very people whom we are seeking to save. John is commissioned to "take the scroll" and "prophesy about many peoples and nations and languages and kings" (Rev. 10:8, 11). This mission is therefore the decisive activity taking place during this entire age of world history! John is to preach judgment for sinners who will not repent and salvation for sinners who repent and believe, and we are to do the same. In this way, Christians will experience victory over the spiritual powers of darkness: "They have conquered him by the blood of the Lamb and by the word of their testimony, for they loved not their lives even unto death" (12:11).

In one of his final meetings with the disciples before his ascension into heaven, Jesus gave this same emphasis. Three things must happen, he said, for the kingdom of God to come: "Thus it is written, that the Christ should suffer and on the third day rise from the dead, and that repentance and forgiveness of sins should be proclaimed in his name to all nations, beginning from Jerusalem" (Luke 24:46–47). Notice that two of these great events have already happened—Christ's atoning death and glorious resurrection. The third event—the proclaiming of the gospel—is happening in our time. How vitally significant it is! Notice, as well, that two of these events are achieved by Jesus apart from our involvement—his death and resurrection—but that we are called to participate in the third, the preaching of repentance and forgiveness in his name. Jesus therefore added, "You are witnesses of these things" (24:48).

Our calling is to be witnesses to the gospel for the ingathering of all who will believe. We must therefore, first, receive the gospel as the glorified Christ's own Word. Second, being assured of its certain fulfillment, we must hold fast to God's Word without compromise. Third, we must fulfill the commission to proclaim God's judgment and salvation to "many peoples and nations and languages and kings" (Rev. 10:11), knowing that in this way, despite persecution, "we are more than conquerors through him who loved us" (Rom. 8:37).

29

MEASURING THE TEMPLE

Revelation 11:1—2

Then I was given a measuring rod like a staff, and I was told,
"Rise and measure the temple of God and the altar
and those who worship there." (Rev. 11:1)

*I*n John Bunyan's *Pilgrim's Progress*, Christian stops at the Interpreter's House to be shown a number of visions designed to teach important spiritual lessons. First was a picture of a man looking to heaven, holding a book, wearing a crown, and pleading with men to listen. The meaning was that Christian should listen only to faithful and holy Bible teachers. Second, he was shown a large parlor filled with dust. A man came to sweep, but the dust merely flew around the room. Then a girl came and sprinkled the room with water, after which the room was easily swept clean. This vision illustrated how the broom of the law cannot clean the heart until it has been sprinkled with the water of the gospel. Further visions illustrated a variety of spiritual lessons important to the Christian life. The reader of *Pilgrim's Progress* realizes that Bunyan is presenting allegories because of the way in which he names his characters. The man who witnesses the gospel is called Evangelist, the pilgrim is Christian, he is led astray by Pliable and Obstinate, and he receives his visions in the house of a man named Interpreter.[1]

---

1. John Bunyan, *Pilgrim's Progress* (Nashville: Thomas Nelson, 1999), 26–33.

Revelation is not an allegory like *Pilgrim's Progress*, but a book of apocalyptic visions. Still, like Bunyan's masterpiece, Revelation functions in a way that cues how we should read it. From the very beginning, Revelation employs symbols to depict redemptive-historical realities. In chapter 1, Jesus appears in the midst of golden candlesticks that represent the churches (Rev. 1:12), holding stars in his hand that symbolize angels (1:16, 20), and with a two-edged sword coming from his mouth that depicts the sharpness of his message (1:16). We are clearly to interpret these images symbolically. The same is true of John's use of numbers, including "seven" to depict the completeness of the Holy Spirit (1:4) and "144,000" to depict the vast multitude of the redeemed drawn from the twelve tribes of Israel and the twelve apostles of Christ (7:4).

As we interpret the detailed visions of Revelation chapters 11, 12, and 13, it is vital that we remember the kind of literature we are reading. Some Christians assert that we must interpret these passages literally, as giving a more or less straightforward description of historical events either past or future. This approach forgets, however, that the very nature of Revelation urges us to interpret these visions symbolically, just as the nature of *Pilgrim's Progress* compels us to interpret John Bunyan allegorically.

The passage on the measuring of the temple in Revelation 11:1–2 most clearly illustrates the significance of the differing approaches to interpreting this book. Dean Alford calls it "the *crux interpretum*," and describes this short passage as "undoubtedly one of the most difficult in the whole Apocalypse."[2] The main reason for the difficulty and importance of this passage is that it forces us to make a clear decision about how we are going to handle Revelation. It is therefore valuable here to compare the main approaches to Revelation and make clear how we are handling this book and why.

THE TEMPLE IN REVELATION

Revelation 11 begins with two verses in which John is called on to participate in the action of the book. He was "given a measuring rod like a staff," presumably by the mighty angel who had met with him in the preceding chapter. John was then told, "Rise and measure the temple of God and the altar and those who worship there, but do not measure the court outside the

2. Henry Alford, *The Greek Testament*, 4 vols. (Cambridge: Deighton, Bell, and Co., 1866), 4:655.

temple" (Rev. 11:1–2). Our first challenge is to identify what is represented by the temple, its altar, and the outer court.

The most commonly held view of this passage today may be called a literal-futurist view, associated with dispensational theology. This approach emphasizes a strictly literal reading of Scripture. Perhaps most important to dispensationalism is the belief that God's plans for Israel and for the church are fundamentally and eternally different. Anthony Hoekema explains that according to dispensationalists, "when the Bible talks about Israel it does not mean the church, and when the Bible talks about the church it does not mean Israel."[3] Under this view, the book of Revelation primarily addresses God's future plans for ethnic Israel and has no direct message about the Christian church. The dispensational commentator Donald Grey Barnhouse insists on the book of Revelation's "essential Jewishness," and urges that "it is entirely concerned with the future from the beginning of the fourth chapter."[4] In this approach, Revelation 11 speaks of future events completely unrelated to the situation and pastoral needs of the churches to which John was writing, as they faced the dire and imminent threat of Roman persecution. A more unlikely thesis for the book of Revelation is hardly imaginable.

Under dispensationalism's literal-future approach, the temple that John is told to measure is a literal building that a reconstituted Israel will erect on Mount Zion. This site is currently occupied by two Muslim mosques: the Dome of the Rock and the Al Aqsa mosque. These must be removed, probably through bloody warfare, and a new Jewish temple put in its place. Robert Thomas urges that this passage foretells "a literal temple that will exist in actuality during the future period just before Christ returns. . . . This requires a re-institution of the national life of this people, including its temple."[5] In this view, the establishment of a Jewish national state in 1948 and Israel's capture of Jerusalem in 1967 are signs of the imminent return of Christ. The application of this passage for Christians today calls for the political support of Israel and the fervent watching of the news for signs of the temple's rebuilding.

There are significant difficulties with the dispensational approach, centering on the idea of God's endorsing a rebuilt Israelite temple in Jerusalem.

---

3. Anthony A. Hoekema, *The Bible and the Future* (Grand Rapids: Eerdmans, 1979), 196.

4. Donald Grey Barnhouse, *Revelation: An Expositional Commentary* (Grand Rapids: Zondervan, 1971), 192.

5. Robert L. Thomas, *Revelation 8–22: An Exegetical Commentary* (Chicago: Moody, 1995), 82.

Unless one presupposes that references to the temple in passages such as this one must be interpreted literally, there is no New Testament teaching on the restoration of a physical temple. Jesus foretold the temple's destruction but not its rebuilding (Matt. 24:2). The reason is that the primary function of the temple was the ritual sacrifice of animals for the atonement of sin. Christ's death fulfilled this symbolism and put an end to the sacrifices, which is why God tore the veil in the temple when Jesus died (27:51). The idea of a future Israelite nation's being restored by God to its temple sacrifices contradicts Scripture, since these sacrifices would deny the sufficiency of Christ's atoning death.

God destroyed the temple in A.D. 70 precisely because he was judging the Jews' rejection of Jesus' atonement, and a rebuilt temple would merely reestablish this rejection of the blood of Christ. Even if we believe in a millennial Jewish nation, as dispensationalism teaches, the idea of God's restoring Israel to the very temple that he destroyed is simply bizarre. If such a temple were built by Jews, it would stand as a monument to the unbelieving rejection of the cross of Jesus Christ.

Because of this emphasis on God's rejection of the temple, a second approach sees our passage as foretelling Jerusalem's past destruction in A.D. 70. This is the preterist position, which for this reason believes that John wrote Revelation before the destruction of Jerusalem and the temple. Whereas dispensationalists hold a literal-future interpretation of Revelation, preterists hold a literal-past view. This is only a partially literal interpretation, however, since preterists view the temple in Revelation 11:1 as symbolizing the church and the outer court of verse 2 as symbolizing the unbelieving Jews, whereas the holy city is literally interpreted as ancient Jerusalem. Douglas Kelly thus writes that this passage foretells how God would let "unbelieving Jerusalem be trodden under for forty-two months by the Gentiles, but he has John measure the true saints, that is the real temple."[6]

There are two main problems with the preterist approach. First, it is highly unlikely that Revelation was written as early as the mid-60s, as this view requires. The witness of the early church uniformly attests to John's writing this book much later, probably in the mid-90s. Moreover, the persecution of Nero in the 60s took a different form from the persecutions described in

6. Douglas F. Kelly, *Revelation*, Mentor Expository Commentary (Tain, Ross-shire, Scotland: Mentor, 2012), 199.

Revelation and did not extend into the province of Asia. A second objection is that the preterist approach arbitrarily employs a symbolic and a literal interpretation. If this passage describes a literal event, then the temple is literal. A consistently literal-past interpretation does not fit our passage, however, since in 11:1 the temple is protected and in A.D. 70 the temple was destroyed.

This leaves a third approach to Revelation, which consistently interprets the images symbolically. Dispensationalists complain that a symbolic reading denies the literal meaning of Revelation. To the contrary, symbolism is simply Revelation's method of communicating historical reality. In this passage, John is not foretelling distant events in the future or events that must have happened before his writing, but rather the historical reality of the age in which his readers are living, both his original readers and his readers today.

The vision of Revelation 11:1–2 centers on the image of the temple, which throughout the New Testament is primarily used to describe the Christian church. James Hamilton writes: "The Bible's theology of the temple is not about a building so much as it is about God being with his people."[7] Paul told Christians that "you are God's temple and that God's Spirit dwells in you" (1 Cor. 3:16). "For we are the temple of the living God," he adds; "as God said, 'I will make my dwelling among them and walk among them, and I will be their God, and they shall be my people'" (2 Cor. 6:16). Peter said that Christians are together "being built up as a spiritual house, to be a holy priesthood, to offer spiritual sacrifices acceptable to God through Jesus Christ" (1 Peter 2:5). In this context, then, a literal understanding of *temple* is not that of a building like that which was replaced by Christ and his church, but, as G. K. Beale puts it, "the focus is now on the whole covenant community forming a spiritual temple in which God's presence dwells."[8] Some of the visions of Revelation depict God in a heavenly temple, but without exception it is Christians who gather there to worship God and the Lamb.

Understanding this vision symbolically, we realize that John is told to measure the temple to show God's commitment to preserve the church through the tribulations of this age. This vision, then, is analogous to the sealing of God's servants in Revelation 7. At the same time, John is told

---

7. James M. Hamilton Jr., *Revelation: The Spirit Speaks to the Churches* (Wheaton, IL: Crossway, 2012), 233.

8. G. K. Beale, *The Book of Revelation: A Commentary on the Greek Text*, New International Greek Testament Commentary (Grand Rapids: Eerdmans, 1999), 562.

not to "measure the court outside the temple" (Rev. 11:2), which stands for nominal Christians associated with the church but not truly belonging. This concern for false or merely outward faith, together with false teaching, was emphasized in Jesus' letters to the churches (2:5, 14–15; 3:1–2, 15–16). The "holy city" in 11:2 symbolizes the church community, which during this present age will be trampled by the nations, symbolizing the unbelieving world. G. B. Caird writes that "the trampling of the holy city is equivalent to the great martyrdom" described throughout Revelation.[9] John's command to measure the church therefore assures true believers that they will be protected and saved during the persecutions of this world, whereas merely outward professors of faith not only will be unprotected but will even join with unbelievers to persecute the true church.

THE FORTY-TWO MONTHS

When John is told that the holy city will be trampled by unbelievers, the duration given to him is "forty-two months" (Rev. 11:2). This period will repeatedly occur in Revelation—in this form, as three and a half years, or as 1,260 days, all of which equal the same length of time. In keeping with the different approaches to interpreting Revelation, there are differing views of this period. Dispensationalists interpret forty-two months as a literal period of time, in this case depicting a future attack on Jerusalem. Preterists state that forty-two months was how long Jerusalem was besieged before its destruction in A.D. 70, a claim that is disputed by critics.[10] A symbolic approach sees forty-two months and its equivalents as expressing not so much a quantity as a quality of time. This designation signifies an intense period of persecution that is limited by God's will.

The number forty-two first arises during Israel's journey through the wilderness in the exodus. Counting the two years before Israel's judgment for disobedience, God's people spent forty-two years journeying from Egypt to the promised land. Moreover, the Bible lists forty-two camps in Israel's wilderness travels (Num. 33:5–49).[11] Furthermore, when Elijah prayed for the heavens to be shut over Israel because of idolatry, there was no rain for

9. G. B. Caird, *The Revelation of St. John the Divine* (San Francisco: Harper, 1966), 132.

10. Thomas, *Revelation 8–22*, 86.

11. Leon Morris, *The Revelation of St. John: An Introduction and Commentary*, Tyndale New Testament Commentaries 20 (Grand Rapids: Eerdmans, 1969), 147.

three and a half years (Luke 4:25). This period seems to be associated with a time of rebellion during which God's faithful people are protected in the midst of trials.

The time of three and a half years plays a particularly important role in the prophecy of Daniel. Daniel 7:25 foretells the tribulation of the Jews under Antiochus Epiphanes, the Greek ruler who desecrated the temple and was defeated by the Maccabean revolt in the mid–second century B.C. This travail would last "for a time, times, and half a time," which means three and a half years. Here, again, this period symbolizes an intense period of suffering through which God's true people emerged victorious.

Perhaps the most important prophecy in Daniel takes place in chapter 9. The prophet realized that the seventy years of exile foretold by Jeremiah (Jer. 25:12) were about to end and therefore offered the prayer of repentance specified in Leviticus 26:40–42 for the return of the exiles to their land. In response to this prayer, the angel Gabriel appeared to say that the restoration would soon begin. There would be, he said, "seventy 'sevens'" before God's final redemptive purposes are achieved (Dan. 9:24 NIV). This number matched the symbolic length of Israel's seventy-year exile. For 490 years, the Israelites had neglected the seventh-year land sabbaths, so God sent them away to give the land the rest it was due (Lev. 26:34–35). By God's mercy, the period of Israel's sin, seventy times seven, would be replaced by a matching period of God's redemptive achievement, "seventy weeks," that would bring in God's final salvation (Dan. 9:24). According to Gabriel's prophecy, the Messiah would come after sixty-nine weeks and be "cut off" (9:26). This is a reference to Christ's death on the cross, after which he would establish "a strong covenant with many for one week" (9:27). This final "week" after Christ's death corresponds to the new covenant age. It, too, is divided into two halves. In the first half of this week, Christ would "put an end to sacrifice and offering," a reference to the temple's destruction in A.D. 70. This leaves a final half-week until the fulfillment of salvation.[12] This final half-week of years, or forty-two months, is the period about which Revelation is concerned, the gospel age in which we also live.

---

12. Those seeking a more in-depth treatment of these matters should consult Meredith G. Kline, "The Covenant of the Seventieth Week," in *The Law and the Prophets: Old Testament Studies in Honor of Oswald T. Allis*, ed, J. H. Skilton (Nutley, NJ: Presbyterian and Reformed, 1974), 452–69.

This is the point at which literal interpreters, especially dispensational-ists, so differ from those who interpret these numbers symbolically. First, they urge that there was a literal 69 weeks, or 483 years, from the start of this prophecy until the arrival of Jesus in Jerusalem on Palm Sunday. The problem with this view is that the numbers cannot be made to work. The angel specified the starting point of the prophecy as "the going out of the word to restore and build Jerusalem" (Dan. 9:25). This is the decree of the Medo-Persian emperor Cyrus for the Jews to return and rebuild their city. This starting point is confirmed by 2 Chronicles 36:21–22, which says that Israel's land enjoyed its sabbaths until the exile ended with the decree of "Cyrus king of Persia, that the word of the LORD by the mouth of Jeremiah might be fulfilled" (see also Ezek. 1:1). The date of Cyrus's decree is 538 B.C. However the 483 prophesied years are counted, noting the particulars of the Jewish calendar, leap years, and so on, a literal count comes nowhere near the time of Jesus' ministry. To solve this problem, dispensationalists instead use a starting time of the later decree of Artaxerxes in 457 B.C. (Ezra 7:12–26). From this date they claim to achieve a literal 483 years until Jesus' coming. The problem is that the Bible does not give historical dates for Jesus' ministry, and moreover, one can hardly be said to interpret the Bible literally when the Bible's own starting date is replaced with one that seems to work better.

Second, dispensationalists teach that the final "week" of Daniel's proph-ecy begins not after the coming of Christ, as Gabriel stated, but after a historical "parenthesis" of the church age is completed. Under this view, a seven-year tribulation begins after the secret rapture of the church, during which believing Jews are besieged at the rebuilt temple. The prophecy in Daniel 9 makes no mention of such a parenthesis, just as the New Testa-ment makes no mention of a secret rapture of Christians.[13] It is therefore imposed on the text because of the dispensational assumption regarding the separation of Israel and the church. Few Bible books more thoroughly debunk this assumption than Revelation, with its constant reference to the church by means of Old Testament symbols and its final vision in which

---

13. The main text for the rapture of believers, 1 Thessalonians 4:15–17, depicts this event as taking place not before but at the time of Christ's final return. Moreover, the last thing that could accurately be said of this rapture is that it is secret, since it is accompanied by the archangel's shout, the sounding of God's trumpet, and the visible, glorious appearing of Christ. The result of this rapture will not be a seven-year Jewish tribulation but rather the eternal state of glory, Paul concluding "and so we will always be with the Lord" (1 Thess. 4:17).

God's eternal city is designated by symbols of both the twelve tribes of Israel and the twelve apostles of Christ's church (Rev. 21:12–14).

A far better way to handle the 490 years of Daniel 9's prophecy and the forty-two months of Revelation 11:2 is symbolically, in keeping with the general principles for interpreting this book. Daniel 9:27 speaks of Christ's establishing his covenant for "one week," which corresponds to the new covenant era before his return, including the removal of the physical temple in A.D. 70, which is symbolized by the first half-week. This remaining symbolic three and a half years (forty-two months) parallels Israel's forty-two-year exodus journey and Elijah's forty-two-month exile during his drought. It represents the period in which John's readers lived and we live today and is characterized by the worldly "trampl[ing]" of the holy city, that is, the visible church. Simon Kistemaker explains that the "nations" of Revelation 11:2 are "non-Christians who trample all that is holy and make it profane." The "forty-two months" thus refer to the "persecution that Christians suffer throughout the ages."[14] This interpretation matches the vision of Revelation 12, in which the church goes out into the wilderness for three and a half years ("a time, and times, and half a time"), during which she is protected from the dragon and nourished by God (Rev. 12:14). This, too, shows the present age in which God's people face continued persecution but are kept safe by our Sovereign Lord.

SAFE IN HIS PRESENCE

This detailed analysis of the temple and the forty-two months is necessary not only to understanding our passage but also to rightly interpreting the material that is to come in the following chapters. It remains important, however, for us to apply these verses as they speak to believers today. The message is that, living in an age that is hostile to Christ and his followers, Christians must draw close to God, trusting in Christ's blood, calling on God in prayer, and gathering with fellow believers for worship. The Lord extends his measuring rod to encompass those who are close to his presence, establishing a barrier to keep them safe for a salvation that will be revealed at the end of the age.

14. Simon J. Kistemaker, *Revelation*, New Testament Commentary (Grand Rapids: Baker, 2001), 150.

A special warning is given here to merely nominal believers, those who attend church but do not belong to the spiritual body of Christ's true followers. They are like the Gentiles who were admitted to the former temple's outer courts. "Do not measure the court outside the temple," John is told (Rev. 11:2), showing that those who are Christians in name only are not protected by God. In fact, the nominal, worldly church "is given over to the nations" (11:2). The institutional church and its apparatus, apart from a living faith in Jesus and a commitment to God's Word, is annexed by the world. It is from the nominal church that much of the persecution is launched against true believers. This happens today in the false teaching pouring forth from unbelieving seminaries and worldly church pulpits.

John's vision therefore gives a challenge: are you a Christian in name only, not having received the Bible's message in an obedient faith and not embracing its message of judgment for sin and salvation through faith in Christ? Are you one who attends Christian events and uses Christian language, but has never relied on Christ for your personal salvation or surrendered your life to Jesus your Lord? If so, not only are you outside salvation, but you will not tolerate true, biblical Christianity. Revelation 11:2 gives a dreadful description of those who occupy the periphery of the church but do not worship "in spirit and truth" in the temple of Christ's true church (John 4:24).

Understanding not only how history ends but also the times in which we are currently living, we consider John's vision as urging true Christians to dwell close to God's presence. The altar that John mentions speaks both of our reliance on Christ's atoning blood for forgiveness and of the altar of prayer where we call on God for help. He further mentions "those who worship there" (Rev. 11:1), speaking of our calling to join the body of Christ's believers who worship in the holy place of the Christian congregation. There, safe in God's presence, we are measured, known, and kept safe within the holy precincts of the Christian church.

> 'Mid toil and tribulation, and tumult of her war,
> She waits the consummation of peace forevermore;
> Till with the vision glorious her longing eyes are blest,
> And the great church victorious shall be the church at rest.[15]

15. Samuel J. Stone, "The Church's One Foundation" (1866).

30

THE TWO WITNESSES

Revelation 11:3—14

*And I will grant authority to my two witnesses, and they will
prophesy for 1,260 days, clothed in sackcloth.* (Rev. 11:3)

*I*n 1685, the French king Louis XIV revoked the Edict of Nantes,
which had guaranteed religious freedom to the French Protestants known as the Huguenots. Thousands of Christians were
slaughtered in barbaric ways, and in parts of France the Reformed church
was eradicated. Louis had ordered this persecution to force the Protestants
into returning their allegiance to Roman Catholicism, bringing peace to
the kingdom. The ruthless persecution, however, embittered the Protestant
nations around him, into which thousands of Huguenots fled. Louis spent the
rest of his life mired in warfare and died, bitter and worn out, in 1715. Before
that century was over, Louis' kingdom would be bloodily savaged by the
French Revolution. During that same century, the nation of England, which
had harbored so many Huguenots, experienced a flowering of the gospel in
the ministries of John Wesley and George Whitefield. The monarchies of
those nations that rejected the gospel have disappeared. Meanwhile, blessed
by the gospel they cherished and the persecuted church they succored, the
royal houses of Britain and Holland remain to this day.

This record from church history reflects the vision of Revelation 11, which is widely regarded as one of the most difficult passages in this challenging book. This difficulty is largely removed, however, if we remember that Revelation is a visionary picture book rather than a literal narrative of future events. By means of its biblical symbols, this chapter gives a stirring depiction of the church bearing testimony during the tumultuous age of the gospel. The vision provides one of the most potent descriptions of the mightiness of the church in its witness and the violence of the world's warfare against the gospel. It concludes by depicting the witness of a resurrected Christ by the power of God, to the great consternation and despair of the opposing world.

IDENTIFYING THE TWO WITNESSES

In the opening verses of this chapter, John was told to measure the temple, with its altar and worshipers, depicting the true church of faithful believers. The outer court, depicting the false church of nominal Christians, was excluded. For forty-two months the nations will trample the church, though God's protective barrier will preserve its spiritual life. We saw in the previous chapter that forty-two months and its equivalents equal the length of Jerusalem's defilement by Antiochus Epiphanes in the second century B.C., as prophesied in Daniel 7:25. In Revelation, this number depicts not a length of time but a kind of history, namely, one of violent opposition to Christ and his church. This was the very situation that John's original readers faced in the late first century A.D. and that many Christians face in the early twenty-first century.

Revelation 11:3 begins with "And," showing that we are continuing the vision that began in verse 1: "And I will grant authority to my two witnesses, and they will prophesy for 1,260 days, clothed in sackcloth." The church is described in the figure of "two witnesses" in light of the Bible's requirement that truth be established by the testimony of two (Deut. 17:6). This emphasizes the legal validity of the church's witness to the gospel, just as God often sent two angels to announce judgment or validate truth (Gen. 19:1; Luke 24:3–9; Acts 1:10–11). We realize as well that Jesus sent out evangelists "two by two" (Luke 10:1), so the emblem of two witnesses speaks of the church in its evangelistic calling. The letters from Jesus to the churches in Revelation 2–3 made clear that the entire church is called to bear witness to Christ and his gospel (cf. Rev. 2:10, 13). When the fifth seal was opened in Revelation 6:9, John saw the martyrs from all the church "who had been slain for the word of God and for the witness they had borne." William Hendriksen therefore writes: "These witnesses symbolize the Church militant bearing testimony through its ministers and missionaries throughout the present dispensation."[1]

John is told that the church "will prophesy for 1,260 days" (Rev. 11:3). In this context, to *prophesy* means to "declare God's Word." Scholars wonder why the time is here expressed in days rather than the months of verse 2. One possible answer is that verse 2 spoke of the siege of the church, and sieges are normally measured in months. The witness of the church, however, is a day-to-day endeavor.

The two witnesses are "clothed in sackcloth" (Rev. 11:3). This rough attire expresses inward grief and repentance for sin. G. K. Beale notes that this attire "suggests mourning over the judgment that their message will result in," together with their hope that at least some of their hearers will repent.[2]

THE MIGHTY WITNESS OF THE CHURCH

It is obvious that this chapter uses symbols rather than speaking of literal future individuals, especially since Revelation 11:8 tells us to interpret the vision "symbolically." This approach is made all the more certain by the description of the witnesses as two olive trees, two lampstands, and the two Old Testament prophets Elijah and Moses. These figures describe the means of the church's witness, the effect of its witness, God's protection through its witness, and the witnessing power that the church wields through prayer. In these symbols, the vision provided the encouragement needed by the beleaguered Christians to whom John was writing and that we need today.

First, the symbolism of the two olive trees shows the means of the church's testimony. Here, Revelation draws from the visions given to the prophet Zechariah in 520 B.C. The Jews who returned to Jerusalem after the Babylonian exile had become bogged down by trials and had ceased working to rebuild the temple. God gave Zechariah visions to encourage their faith,

---

1. William Hendriksen, *More than Conquerors: An Interpretation of the Book of Revelation* (1940; repr., Grand Rapids: Baker, 1967), 129.

2. G. K. Beale, *The Book of Revelation: A Commentary on the Greek Text*, New International Greek Testament Commentary (Grand Rapids: Eerdmans, 1999), 576.

including the vision of a golden lampstand that shined with a brilliant light (Zech. 4:1–14). This was a picture of Israel in that dark time, just as Revelation used lampstands to depict the church in John's time (Rev. 1:12). Next to the golden lampstand, Zechariah was shown two olive trees (Zech. 4:3), each of which had a pipe that fed oil to the lampstand to keep its light burning (4:12). One olive tree referred to the prince Zerubbabel, representing the royal kingship. The other referred to Joshua the high priest, representing the anointed priesthood (4:14). The oil flowing from the trees stood for the Holy Spirit. God gave this message to Zerubbabel: "Not by might, nor by power, but by my Spirit, says the LORD of hosts" (4:6).

By employing the vision of the two olive trees, Revelation depicts the two means of the church's witness. Christians bear a kingly testimony to Christ by proclaiming his royal Word. The church bears a priestly testimony by offering his gospel, praying, and administering the sacraments that show forth Christ's atoning blood. The faithful church therefore witnesses by the Holy Spirit's power at work through the testimony of God's Word and the sacraments. These royal and priestly emphases fit the description of the church given throughout Revelation. John's opening doxology praised Christ as "him who loves us and has freed us from our sins by his blood and made us a kingdom, priests to his God and Father" (Rev. 1:5–6). G. B. Caird asks: "Where at the end of the first century A.D. are we to look for a Christian king and a Christian priest? Not in any two individual members of the church, but rather in the whole people of God, on which he devolved the regal and priestly functions of Christ."[3]

This description of the church's witness raises a question: Have you surrendered your life to Jesus as Lord and trusted him as the Savior who died on the cross for your sins? This is the gospel message that you must embrace in faith if you are to be saved.

Revelation 11:4 describes the purpose of the church's witness as "the two lampstands that stand before the Lord of the earth." Jesus described John the Baptist as "a burning and shining lamp" (John 5:35). A lamp does not shine its own light but reflects the light that shines on it. Christians likewise do not bear testimony to ourselves, but the church is a lampstand on which the light of Christ is to be seen. John the Baptist said of Christ: "I came baptizing with water, that he might be revealed to Israel" (1:31). As

---

3. G. B. Caird, *The Revelation of St. John the Divine* (San Francisco: Harper, 1966), 134.

lampstands stand "before the Lord of the earth" (Rev. 11:4), Christians are justified in God's presence through the blood of Christ, and then reveal the truth of his Word and the grace of his gospel to the world.

By its testimony, the church not only serves the Lord but is kept safe in the presence of danger. John is told: "And if anyone would harm them, fire pours from their mouth and consumes their foes. If anyone would harm them, this is how he is doomed to be killed" (Rev. 11:5). This is an allusion to the episode in 2 Kings 1:10–14, when the prophet Elijah called down fire from heaven to consume soldiers sent to arrest him. The point is that when the church witnesses boldly and faithfully, God's Word has power over her enemies. The Lord told Jeremiah: "Because you have spoken this word, behold, I am making my words in your mouth a fire, and this people wood, and the fire shall consume them" (Jer. 5:14). Some Christians are tempted to shrink back from boldly declaring God's Word as it comes into conflict with worldly values and practices. But we are reminded that we should not fear to declare God's Word faithfully, since God protects those who valiantly stand for his truth. Hughes writes: "The Lord's witnesses may be hated and ill-treated, and even done to death, but they cannot be harmed. Though they may appear to be overcome by enemies, yet it is they who are the overcomers."[4]

Finally, Revelation 11:6 speaks of the church's witnessing power through prayer: "They have the power to shut the sky, that no rain may fall during the days of their prophesying, and they have power over the waters to turn them into blood and to strike the earth with every kind of plague, as often as they desire." Elijah prayed in the idolatrous days of King Ahab, and the skies did not produce rain for three and a half years (1 Kings 17:1; Luke 4:25; note the parallel time reference). Moses turned the waters of the Nile into blood, along with many other devastating plagues (Ex. 7:7ff.). The witnessing church of the gospel era will not be equipped with less power than these Old Testament heroes but through prayer will wield conquering power. The apostle James urged that the "prayer of a righteous person has great power," and appealed to the example of Elijah: "Elijah was a man with a nature like ours, and he prayed fervently that it might not rain, and for three years and six months it did not rain on the earth" (James 5:16–17).

4. Philip Edgcumbe Hughes, *The Book of Revelation* (Downers Grove, IL: InterVarsity Press, 1990), 124.

Acts 12 records how Christians prayed when Peter was facing execution in Herod's prison and God sent an angel to free the apostle (Acts 12:1–17). This shows the divine power always available to faithful churches through prayer.

When Elijah prayed for the sky to be shut, he proved that he spoke for the one true God. Do you believe that the God of the Bible is the true and living God? Moses' plague "highlights the church's ability to liberate people from bondage through the proclamation of the gospel."[5] Have you been liberated from your sins through the death and resurrection of Jesus? You can be through simple faith in his gospel. If you have been set free, you have also received the calling, together with the whole church, to bear a Spirit-empowered witness of the gospel into the darkness of the world.

In 1588, a massive fleet set sail in great power from Roman Catholic Spain to conquer England and snuff out the gospel light of the Protestant Reformation. Two factors combined to destroy the Spanish Armada utterly. One was sudden violent storms that smashed many of the great ships on the rocky coast of Ireland. The other was the valiant fighting of the smaller, more nimble English ships that capitalized on the divinely appointed confusion. Behind both the storms and the English ships were the ardent prayers of countless believers in Britain, who called on the God of heaven as Elijah and Moses had done in Bible times. After Britain had been delivered, Queen Elizabeth I ordered a commemorative coin to be struck bearing the inscription *Affavit Deus*, which means "God blew." She knew that God had answered the prayers of his people, in that way bearing testimony to the Reformation's witness of the gospel.

Taken as a whole, John's vision in Revelation 11 shows the power of the witnessing church, through the Word, sacraments, and prayer by the power of God's Spirit. By these "ordinary means of grace," the church is enabled to declare the truth of God's Word, prevail over evil, and deliver sinners from judgment. James Hamilton writes: "This is what makes the church potent— not money, not political influence, not marketing gimmicks, not anything that involves worldly strategy. The church's power is in Spirit-empowered, Father-protected proclamation of Jesus Christ and him crucified."[6]

5. James M. Hamilton Jr., *Revelation: The Spirit Speaks to the Churches* (Wheaton, IL: Crossway, 2012), 239.
6. Ibid.

THE WAR AGAINST THE WITNESS

Such is God's power in the church that his witnesses cannot be defeated until Christians have given their testimony. But as Revelation 11:7 states, "when they have finished their testimony," the world will wage violent war against them. Verse 7 introduces a figure who will be prominent in the rest of Revelation, "the beast that rises from the bottomless pit," who "will make war on them and conquer them and kill them." Geoffrey Wilson writes that the beast represents "those antichristian powers in the world which seek to silence the church's witness," resulting in "the apparent triumph of the forces of evil."[7]

This image of a beast connects with the prophecy of Daniel 7. Four great empires would arise in history, each of which was represented by a deadly beast, including a lion, a bear, and a leopard. The fourth beast was terrifying and dreadful, with iron teeth and ten horns (Dan. 7:1–8). Against this background, it makes sense that the beast of Revelation is a persecuting imperial ruler, corresponding in John's time to the threat posed by the Roman emperor Domitian, since most interpreters believe that Daniel's fourth beast pointed forward to Rome. The fact that this beast "rises from the bottomless pit" indicates that it exerts a demonic power in service to the devil. Paul wrote of a "lawless one" who would appear before the return of Christ to afflict the church and deceive the nations (2 Thess. 2:8–10). John, however, uses the present tense to speak of the beast's rising: this is a menacing reality current to his readers and to Christians throughout the church age, though it seems that the beast will take a most potent form at the end of the age before Christ returns.

Once the Christians have given their witness, the beast "will make war on them and conquer them and kill them" (Rev. 11:7). Then "their dead bodies will lie in the street of the great city that symbolically is called Sodom and Egypt, where their Lord was crucified. For three and a half days some from the peoples and tribes and languages and nations will gaze at their dead bodies and refuse to let them be placed in a tomb" (11:8–9).

John places this dreadful event in a location characterized by three biblical images. The slaying of the witnesses summarizes satanic opposition to

---

7. Geoffrey B. Wilson, *New Testament Commentaries*, 2 vols. (Edinburgh: Banner of Truth, 2005), 2:534.

the gospel throughout this present age, following the pattern that will be developed more fully in later chapters of Revelation. First is the city of Sodom, which represents perverse sexual abominations and idolatrous sin. Sodom anticipates Revelation 17's description of the world as the harlot Babylon, who ensnares people for death through the cup of sensual indulgence. Second is Egypt, where God's holy people were kept in bondage and God's message was hard-heartedly despised. Egypt anticipates the first beast, who will arise in chapter 13 with tyrannical power to persecute the church. Third is the crucifixion of Jesus outside Jerusalem, representing the rejection of God's Messiah and his gospel. Here, the second beast of Revelation 13 is anticipated, the false prophet who leads the world in idolatrous, antichrist religion. Revelation 11:8 instructs that these images are to be taken "symbolically," or, more literally, "in a spiritual manner." The point is that they represent not a place in the world but the world itself in its sensual harlotry, violent persecution, and idol-worshiping false religion as it militantly opposes the gospel. For this reason, Philip Hughes aptly associates the combination of Sodom, Egypt, and Jerusalem with "the worldwide structure of unbelief and defiance against God."[8]

In this symbolic vision, the church witness lies dead in the streets for "three and a half days" (Rev. 11:9), probably representing a time limited by God. The main emphasis is on the world's attitude toward the slain church. Not just a certain kind of person but all peoples, tribes, languages, and nations unite in hatred of God's people. Contempt is shown in their refusal to grant even a decent burial to the corpses, and their hatred results in rejoicing for the slaying of the Christian witnesses: "Those who dwell on the earth will rejoice over them and make merry and exchange presents, because these two prophets had been a torment to those who dwell on the earth" (11:10). Paul Gardner explains: "The repeated witness of Christ's people to judgment and salvation, to sin and forgiveness, has deeply angered unbelievers, and so they are pleased now to have had their revenge."[9]

There is little doubt that John intended his readers to interpret the beast as a threat that they soon faced from Rome. The death of the witnesses corresponds as well to the tribulation of the Christians in France after

8. Hughes, *The Book of Revelation*, 127.
9. Paul Gardner, *Revelation: The Compassion and Protection of Christ*, Focus on the Bible (Tain, Ross-shire, Scotland: Christian Focus, 2008), 158.

Louis XIV revoked the Edict of Nantes and to similar events throughout church history. H. B. Swete says that it covers "in effect all the martyrdoms and massacres of history in which brute force has seemed to triumph over truth and righteousness."[10]

The Witness of Christ Resurrected

No doubt the beast in John's vision believed he had finally defeated the Christian witness. The Jewish leaders thought the same when they had arranged Jesus' crucifixion outside Jerusalem. Likewise, Saul of Tarsus perceived victory in the stoning of the first martyr, Stephen. But as with Jesus, so it is with his church, that crucifixion is followed by a resurrection through the power of God. John's vision thus concludes: "But after the three and a half days a breath of life from God entered them, and they stood up on their feet, and great fear fell on those who saw them" (Rev. 11:11).

John's vision, together with church history, shows that the world's victories over the church are temporary and empty because of God's resurrection power. Paul Gardner writes: "However many times churches are destroyed and God's people martyred or exiled or persecuted, and however many celebrations there are of those events among the unbelievers across the world, God will continue always to raise up for himself his church."[11]

A stirring example from recent years is the experience of the gospel in China. In 1940, William Hendriksen wrote his commentary on Revelation, using the example of the defeated church in Communist China as an example of Satan's beast's wiping out the Christian witness.[12] Just as the people of the world are said to gloat over the corpse of the church, Madame Mao famously announced that Christianity was dead during the cultural revolution of the 1960s. Great numbers of Christians were arrested, executed, or reindoctrinated to Communism. Fifty years later, the church has experienced a resurrection, the gospel sweeping China with a power that has brought as many as a hundred million people to saving faith. After a period of God's design, the church's witness in China arose in power, casting Christ's enemies into confusion and dismay.

10. Henry Barclay Swete, *Commentary on Revelation*, 2 vols. (1911; repr., Grand Rapids: Kregel, 1977), 2:137.

11. Gardner, *Revelation*, 161.

12. Hendriksen, *More than Conquerors*, 130.

John's vision further shows the church ascending to heaven: "Then they heard a loud voice from heaven saying to them, 'Come up here!' And they went up to heaven in a cloud, and their enemies watched them" (Rev. 11:12). We remember that this vision takes place between the sixth and seventh trumpets, and therefore it draws near to Christ's return and the gathering in of the saints. Yet this is far from a "secret rapture," since "their enemies watched them." The gathering of Christ's church in his return will see the vindication of his persecuted people. Throughout history this vindication takes place whenever the persecuted church is revived to stand triumphant.

Accompanying the resurrection of Christ's witnesses is a corresponding judgment on the wicked: "And at that hour there was a great earthquake, and a tenth of the city fell. Seven thousand people were killed in the earthquake, and the rest were terrified and gave glory to the God of heaven" (Rev. 11:13). The sixth seal in Revelation 6:12 unleashed a great earthquake that broke up the powers of the world. Another resulted when the angel threw the censer of fire from God's altar onto the world in Revelation 8:5. The symbolism of an earthquake shows the shaking and shattering of idolatrous power and worldly opposition to God. This effect occurs whenever the gospel is proclaimed in the power of God. Thus, when Paul witnessed in Thessalonica, his opponents complained: "These men . . . have turned the world upside down" (Acts 17:6).

In John's vision, the earthquake results in "a tenth of the city" falling and "seven thousand people" perishing. Remembering that this vision occurs just before the seventh trumpet, we know that this is near the end of history. The trumpets show how God's judgments announce Christ's victory over worldly opposition. Here, the earthquake does enough damage to make clear that God's final judgment is coming. A "tenth of the city" and "seven thousand people" seem to indicate a substantial proportion of casualties, while most people are still alive. "The rest were terrified and gave glory to the God of heaven" (Rev. 11:13). Since Christ has not yet returned, it seems that at least some will turn in repentance and faith for salvation, although many unbelievers will no doubt glorify God in their unbelieving terror as they face God's impending wrath. This dread is experienced by unbelievers whenever it is obvious that God's supernatural power has defended and then resurrected his church.

Woe or Blessing?

A knowledge of ancient church history shows how this vision accurately pictured the persecution that John's churches in Asia were about to undergo. They would be given great power to witness under tribulation, and whenever their testimony seemed to be snuffed out as leaders and martyrs were slain in the arena or by Roman swords, God would raise up even more converts to follow them in faith. Thus, the third-century leader Tertullian wrote to the Roman persecutors that "the blood of the martyrs is the seed of the church."

This testimony reminds us that what is woe for the beast is blessing for the world. The angel concludes John's vision by crying, "The second woe has passed; behold, the third woe is soon to come" (Rev. 11:14). The third woe on the world will be the final judgment when the seventh trumpet is blown and Christ returns to end the age. Until that end in final judgment, the woe on God's enemies means the continued blessing of the church's gospel witness.

God preserves his gospel witness so that sinners can yet be saved. So it was in the early church when martyrs carried the gospel banner until finally the Roman emperor Constantine yielded in faith to Christ. So it was when the destruction of the Spanish Armada enabled the gospel light to continue shining from England. So it was when the Huguenots were ejected from France but joined the witness of Reformers in England, Scotland, and Wales to carry the gospel to the world. So it has been in China in recent times and, no doubt, will be in places such as Sudan, Eritrea, and Syria where today the church suffers such violent persecution. God's preservation of the gospel offers salvation to you, if you will only repent and believe. This is the best way for you to give glory to God in light of his church's mighty witness to the gospel: not in judgment through obstinate unbelief but in salvation through faith in Jesus Christ. Then God will use you as his witness, and though you may suffer death for Jesus and his Word, God's resurrection power will raise you up to never-ending life.

31

THE SEVENTH TRUMPET

Revelation 11:15–19

Then the seventh angel blew his trumpet, and there were loud voices in heaven, saying, "The kingdom of the world has become the kingdom of our Lord and of his Christ, and he shall reign forever and ever." (Rev. 11:15)

During the Christmas season, churches of all kinds are likely to host a performance of George Frideric Handel's *Messiah*, the grand oratorio that celebrates the saving achievement of Jesus. Few realize, however, that Handel's *Messiah* was originally written and performed for the Easter season. The reason for this is seen in its triumphant "Hallelujah Chorus," which celebrates Christ's resurrection and eternal reign in glory.

Handel spoke of his experience in writing *Messiah* in words that remind us of the book of Revelation: "I did think I did see all Heaven before me and the great God Himself."[1] He had this experience not through visions but through the Word of God. Anecdotes speak of Handel's being so absorbed during the twenty-four days in which he composed *Messiah* that he often

---

1. Peter Jacobi, *The Messiah Book: The Life & Times of G. F. Handel's Greatest Hit* (New York: St. Martin's Press, 1982), 7.

forgot to eat. One servant found the composer weeping over the score for the text of Isaiah 53:3, "He was despised and rejected of men."[2] Although *Messiah* was not immediately successful, it came to inspire awed worship for the glory of Christ. Most famously, when England's King George II first heard the "Hallelujah Chorus," he sprang to his feet in order to recognize a superior Sovereign in the exalted Jesus Christ.[3] The text for the "Hallelujah Chorus" includes the great cry of Revelation 11:15, when the seventh trumpet blew and the voices of heaven proclaimed the victory of Christ: "The kingdom of the world has become the kingdom of our Lord and of his Christ, and he shall reign forever and ever."

As we conclude Revelation 11, we finally hear the seventh trumpet, for which we have been waiting since the sixth trumpet blew in chapter 9. When Joshua entered the promised land, it was the seventh trumpet that brought down the walls of Jericho (Josh. 6:20). Now the seventh trumpet of heaven blows, and the exodus journey of the church is completed with the return of Christ and the final defeat of all our foes. The cry of victory for Christ's kingdom teaches those of us who are still living in this age, before the final trumpet, that our prayer for God's kingdom to come will one day be fully answered (Matt. 6:10).

THE KINGDOM OF GOD DECLARED

In Revelation's visions of the seals, trumpets, and bowls, the seventh member of each series directs us to what happens not on earth but in heaven. This is in keeping with Revelation's purpose to show our history from the vantage point of God's throne above. When the sixth seal was opened, there was half an hour's silence in heaven (Rev. 8:1). When the seventh bowl is poured, a loud voice from God's throne will declare, "It is done!" (16:17). When the seventh trumpet is sounded, loud heavenly voices proclaim that Jesus has come into his eternal kingdom on the earth.

Paul wrote that the "last trumpet" will blow at the return of Christ, when the dead are raised for the final judgment (1 Cor. 15:52). Revelation's seventh trumpet does not describe the details of these events, which are given later in Revelation, but simply announces Christ's return to judge. Dispensationalists

2. Ibid., 33.
3. Ibid., 45.

teach that this trumpet heralds only a thousand-year reign of Christ on earth, after which another rebellion will occur, failing to note that this trumpet proclaims an eternal reign: "he shall reign forever and ever" (Rev. 11:15). Preterists see this trumpet as beginning the gospel age in which Christ spiritually reigns. Yet verse 18 defines it as "the time for the dead to be judged." The seventh trumpet therefore announces the glorious return of the King of kings, Jesus, to reign forever on earth.

Most Christians think that salvation ends with our souls going to heaven to be with Jesus. To be saved is to "go to heaven when I die." This is true, but history does not end there. The Bible teaches that Jesus will return to reign on a renewed and glorified earth. Jesus comes to "the kingdom of the world" to establish "the kingdom of our Lord and of his Christ" (Rev. 11:15). God does not retreat from the earth that he made but sin marred. Rather, God sent his Son to heal the breach of sin, paying its penalty on the cross, and after gathering his people through the gospel in the age of the church, the Son returns to resume the sovereignty of God over all creation. Isaiah foretold that "the earth shall be full of the knowledge of the LORD as the waters cover the sea" (Isa. 11:9). In that age, believers will have been resurrected in bodies like Jesus' resurrected body so that we can dwell with him forever in the renewed heavens and earth (Rev. 21:1).

When the monarchs of England come to Westminster Abbey to be enthroned, they stand before an altar on which Revelation 11:15 is written: "The kingdoms of this world have become the kingdoms of our Lord and of his Christ" (KJV). This makes the solemn point that earthly rulers must answer to God's higher authority. This is what George II acknowledged when he stood up as the same text was sung in Handel's "Hallelujah Chorus."

There is an error, however, in the King James text etched over Westminster Abbey's altar. It speaks of "the kingdoms of the world," in the plural, whereas John specifies that "the kingdom of the world," in the singular, has been conquered by Christ. Rather than saying that Christ has returned to defeat all the different kingdoms on earth, the voices speak of a single earthly kingdom that is opposed to Christ. Daniel's prophecy foretold the rising of different kingdoms in succession, each symbolized by its particular beast (Dan. 7:1–8), but in Revelation there is one beast that is a composite of them all (Rev. 13:1–2). All the secular empires are actually one earthly kingdom under the reign of Satan, including the Roman Empire, the monarchies of

Europe, Nazi Germany, the Communist regimes of Russia and China, and the pleasure-seeking humanistic societies of America and the West. When Christ returns, the "kingdom of the world" will yield to "the kingdom of our Lord and of his Christ" (11:15).

Jesus' resurrection began his saving kingdom on earth, and since that day there have been two kingdoms contesting for the hearts and minds of mankind. The resurrection kingdom of Christ is the true kingdom and the one that will endure when the worldly kingdom has been put away. Jesus therefore declared after his resurrection, "All authority in heaven and on earth has been given to me" (Matt. 28:18). Yet while the kingdom of sin and unbelief contests his rule, Christ reigns over a rebellious world even though hostility to his reign often seems to thrive. The seventh trumpet announces that Christ will then have defeated and put away all opposition to his rule, and the worldly kingdom that now seems so impressive will have perished in his coming. G. B. Caird writes: "A king may be king *de jure*, but he is not king *de facto* until the trumpet which announces his accession is answered by the acclamations of a loyal and obedient people."[4] History is racing forward, we are thus assured, to the culminating event when Christ returns, completely overthrows the wicked kingdom of the world with his own righteous kingdom, and receives the willing, joyful adoration of his resurrected people.

The coming realm is "the kingdom of our Lord and of his Christ" (Rev. 11:15). In the New Testament, *Lord* usually refers to Jesus, but in Revelation, it identifies his Lord and ours: God the Father. The coming kingdom thus involves the joint rule of "our Lord and of his Christ"; God the Father and God the Son reigning in love over their extended redeemed family; the Ancient of Days and the Son of Man (Dan. 7:9–14) exercising joint sovereignty; the One who sits on the throne and the Lamb who was slain reigning together over heaven and earth (Rev. 5:13). The Father is Lord of creation and the Son is Lord of redemption: together they rule in power and grace in divine glory. Here, the fullness of deity is ascribed to Jesus Christ, who is one with God the Father in divine rule.

Christ's kingdom comes as the final realm of history—or we might even say *after* history. Heaven exclaims: "He shall reign forever and ever" (Rev. 11:15). The readers of Revelation in the churches of Asia were persecuted

---

4. G. B. Caird, *The Revelation of St. John the Divine* (San Francisco: Harper, 1966), 141.

under the kingdom of this world, as Christians are today. They and we not only will find respite from all opposition and affliction when Christ returns, but will experience a permanent end to all evil. G. K. Beale says that the final judgment involves "a universally decisive defeat of all forces antagonistic to him,"[5] so that Christ's people will be eternally safe, eternally secure, and eternally blessed by God.

Seeing that this is the kingdom of the "Christ," we remember that this title refers to Jesus in all his anointed offices. He is not only the Great King who will reign in righteousness over his people forever. He is the Great Prophet who will eternally reveal the glory of God to believers. And he is the Great High Priest whose atoning sacrifice eternally secures our salvation. Hebrews 7:25 affirms that "he is able to save to the uttermost those who draw near to God through him, since he always lives to make intercession for them." As long as Christ lives, our salvation cannot be overthrown! No wonder that Handel placed the words "he shall reign forever and ever" (Rev. 11:15) in the "Hallelujah Chorus." The news that Christ's kingdom will replace the world's kingdom so that he can reign forever should inspire all believers to exclaim, "Hallelujah," that is, "Praise the Lord!"

THE KINGDOM OF GOD CELEBRATED

The apostle John was not the only one to hear the seventh trumpet and the declaration of Christ's kingdom. We are again shown the "twenty-four elders," who first appeared in chapter 4 as angelic representatives of the Old and New Testament church, sitting on thrones that represent the church's inclusion in Christ's reign. Whereas King George II rose for Handel's chorus, these "elders . . . fell on their faces and worshiped God" (Rev. 11:16). These angelic rulers are clothed in white to show the holiness of the church that is washed of sin in Christ's blood. Since they dwell in the very throne room of heaven, they fall at God's feet and sing: "We give thanks to you, Lord God Almighty, who is and who was, for you have taken your great power and begun to reign" (11:17). In this worship song, the kingdom of Christ announced by the seventh trumpet is celebrated.

The thanks and praise for Christ's kingdom is rendered to the Father: the "Lord God Almighty" (Rev. 11:17). The word *Almighty* is the Greek

5. G. K. Beale, *The Book of Revelation: A Commentary on the Greek Text*, New International Greek Testament Commentary (Grand Rapids: Eerdmans, 1999), 614.

pantokrator, which means "sovereign ruler" or "ruler of all." The Roman Caesars presumptuously adopted this title. But as the Creator, God is the Ruler of all history, and in his mercy he sent Jesus to reign over a kingdom of grace that would oppose the worldly kingdom of selfishness, malice, and greed. John 3:16 says that "God so loved the world, that he gave his only Son, that whoever believes in him should not perish but have eternal life." God is now praised for the final victory of the Savior he sent to be born in Bethlehem, who died on the cross, and who rose from the grave. It is because of his eternal reign that we enjoy eternal life.

Throughout the worship songs of Revelation, God is glorified in his eternity. In chapter 4, the four living creatures sang, "Holy, holy, holy, is the Lord God Almighty, who was and is and is to come!" (Rev. 4:8). In the song of Revelation 11:17, however, God is no longer acclaimed as the One who "is to come." "We give thanks to you, Lord God Almighty," they say, "who is and who was," but they do not say "who is to come." This glaring omission reflects the fact that with the return of Christ, the seventh trumpet ushers in the eternal glory. Eternity no longer "is to come" but simply "is." G. B. Caird comments that "there can be no future once futurity has been removed from the very name of God."[6] This is another reason why we can be sure that this trumpet does not bring in a temporary millennial kingdom, but heralds the end of history in the eternal state.

Where we would expect to read that God "is to come," we instead read, "For you have taken your great power and begun to reign" (Rev. 11:17). This is what used to be the future—what is still future to us now: God's taking up his almighty power and fully imposing his righteous rule. H. B. Swete calls this "that final and overwhelming display to which all prophecy points."[7] The phrase "taken your great power" is in the perfect tense, indicating a completed action with permanently enduring effects. Christ's second coming is a decisive event that results in an eternal peace and blessing.

While Revelation 11:17 thanks God for Christ's kingdom, verse 18 celebrates the outline of what happens in his coming. On one side of Christ's reign is the coming of God's final wrath on all evil and evildoers. The other side is the eternal blessing bestowed on believers, who like the twenty-four

6. Caird, *The Revelation of St. John the Divine*, 146.
7. Henry Barclay Swete, *Commentary on Revelation*, 2 vols. (1911; repr., Grand Rapids: Kregel, 1977), 2:143.

elders are clothed in white garments cleansed of sin. Daniel foretold this great event when Christ returns: "Those who sleep in the dust of the earth shall awake, some to everlasting life, and some to shame and everlasting contempt" (Dan. 12:2).

First, the elders sing, "The nations raged, but your wrath came" (Rev. 11:18). All through the visions of Revelation, we have been shown God's conflict with the unbelieving world from the perspective of history. Revelation 6:9 spoke of martyrs "who had been slain for the word of God and for the witness they had borne." This is typical of the world's entire conspiracy against the will of God, the reign of God, and especially the Word of God. Psalm 2 asked, "Why do the nations rage and the peoples plot in vain?" It makes no sense, but "the kings of the earth set themselves, and the rulers take counsel together, against the LORD and against his Anointed" (Ps. 2:1–2). In those words the entirety of human history can be charted. The same root word is used for the world's "rage" and God's "wrath" (Greek, *orgizo* and *orge*). Man was wrathful toward God and his Savior, so God responds with wrath in return. Though God had offered salvation, the Jewish leaders conspired with the Roman governor to nail Jesus to the cross and then persecuted his followers. Now, in the return of the exalted Christ, God has taken up his reign, and justice will be done on the oppressors and perverters.

In order for there to be an eternal punishment of sin, Christ's return signals "the time for the dead to be judged" (Rev. 11:18). Chapter 20 presents this scene in detail. It begins with the general resurrection of all the dead—not just believers, but all who have ever lived—in order to stand judgment in their bodies before the enthroned Christ. John writes: "I saw the dead, great and small, standing before the throne, and books were opened. . . . And the dead were judged by what was written in the books, according to what they had done" (20:12). All those found guilty of sin, without Christ's blood to forgive them, are "thrown into the lake of fire" (20:15).

Revelation 11:18 adds that Christ will conclude by "destroying the destroyers of the earth." We remember what happened when Joshua led Israel into Canaan. The first step was the utter destruction of the pagan fortress at Jericho and the cleansing of the evil Canaanites from the land. Revelation 19:11–15 shows Jesus returning to history, riding on a white horse: "In righteousness he judges and makes war. . . . He is clothed in a robe dipped in blood . . . . He will tread the winepress of the fury of the wrath of God the Almighty." The destroyers are destroyed forever by the conquering King Jesus, so that his land may enjoy blessing and peace forever.

A great king not only puts his wicked enemies to the sword but also gathers his loyal servants for praise and reward. So Jesus' coming is the time "for rewarding your servants, the prophets and saints, and those who fear your name, both small and great" (Rev. 11:18). Some commentators seek to distinguish between servants, prophets, saints, and those who fear God's name. It is more likely, however, that all these terms are intended to describe the whole of Christ's people. All faithful Christians are servants of Christ, speak forth his Word, live in a holy manner, and give reverence to God and his name. The mention of rewards does not mean that believers have merited salvation: instead, the Bible is clear that sinners can be saved only by grace alone. What we deserve is condemnation for our sins, but for Christ's sake, through faith, we are saved. The rewards therefore reflect Christ's commendation for service offered in response to his grace.

In his parable of the talents, Jesus spoke of returning to reward his people whose lives have been profitable to him: "Well done, good and faithful servant. You have been faithful over a little; I will set you over much. Enter into the joy of your master" (Matt. 25:21). John is told that these rewards will be given to all Christians, "both small and great" (Rev. 11:18). Not only is this true, but in the light of Christ's coming and reward, many Christians whose lives were considered great in the world will be seen to be rather small because they made little effort in serving Christ. Yet how many lives that now seem small will be seen in greatness and glory because of humble service to Jesus!

Since Jesus will take two opposite actions in the great judgment when he returns, there is an urgent need for us to come to him in faith now. All of us deserve to be eternally punished for our rebellion against God, and those who persist in unbelief, rejecting Christ and God's Word, are certain to receive this judgment. How greatly we should fear God's judgment! Jesus once said, "Do not fear those who kill the body but cannot kill the soul. Rather fear him who can destroy both soul and body in hell" (Matt. 10:28). The God who will speak in wrath at the end of history speaks now in his Word with an offer of salvation through his Son. The Bible promises that if we confess our sin and believe on Jesus Christ, then "the blood of Jesus

[God's] Son cleanses us from all sin" and God "is faithful and just to forgive us our sins and to cleanse us from all unrighteousness" (1 John 1:7, 9).

THE KINGDOM OF GOD CONSUMMATED

Revelation 11:19 is not only the final verse of this chapter but the conclusion to the first half of this book. By mentioning "God's temple in heaven," it bookends the vision of chapter 4, which began in the temple throne room of God. The first half of Revelation provided broad but vitally informative visions covering the grand sweep of Christian history. The visions that begin in chapter 12 focus in greater detail on the enemies of Christ and how Christ defeats them all, most significantly the false trinity of Satan and his two beasts.

The seven trumpets and the view of history they have provided concludes with God's temple opened. Christ is not yet directly shown, for more of Revelation is yet to be read, but his great Old Testament emblem is revealed: "The ark of his covenant was seen within his temple. There were flashes of lightning, rumblings, peals of thunder, an earthquake, and heavy hail" (Rev. 11:19). The seventh trumpet having declared Christ's kingdom and the song of praise having celebrated the kingdom, the kingdom is now consummated so that the way is opened for Christ's people to enter his glory.

The ark of the covenant was the most sacred object of Old Testament Israel and was lost or consumed during God's judgments on Jerusalem. Many Christians fervently hope for this ancient artifact to resurface, but the Bible gives no hint of such a thing happening. Does this vision indicate that the ark was translated out of this world into heaven sometime before Jerusalem's fall? The answer is that we cannot know. Most likely, the ark is shown here as a symbol, representing God's covenant with his people.

The ark represented God's saving presence, but the Israelites never actually saw it: even those who transported it received special instructions for how to cover the ark without looking on it. The reason lay in the holiness of God and the sinfulness of the people. Only the high priest saw the ark, once a year, when he brought the atoning blood to sprinkle on it for the forgiveness of the nation. That the ark is now open to sight indicates that the issue of sin has been done away with for believers in Jesus. When Jesus died, the temple veil that had once protected the ark was torn from top to bottom: the way into God's glorious presence is now open through Jesus Christ.

Moreover, the ark kept the tablets of God's covenant with Israel, and this ark symbolizes that God's covenant of salvation has been fulfilled. God told Moses to meet with him at the ark's "mercy seat," where the atoning blood was poured to cover Israel's sin (Ex. 25:22). We likewise meet with God through Christ's blood, shed once for all, entering into an eternity of glorious fellowship with our covenant Sovereign. Christ's saving work has not changed God's holiness: he still flashes lightning, thunder, earthquakes, and hail against all who oppose him in unbelief. For the enemies of God, the ark was a symbol of dread and woe. At Jericho, it was carried by the priests who blew their trumpets, enabling the army of God's people to advance in God's power. Henry Alford thus writes: "The ark of the covenant is seen, the symbol of God's faithfulness in bestowing grace on His people, and inflicting vengeance on His people's enemies."[8]

How wonderful it is that the trumpet visions in Revelation 8–11, like the seal visions in chapters 6–7, conclude with a reminder that believers in Christ have nothing to fear because of sin. A judgment is coming that will be unspeakably dreadful for those who oppose God and his Word. For the ungodly, history will end with the same kind of crash that brought down the walls of Jericho! But Christians, though we are so conscious of our sin, are caused to gaze on God's ark of the covenant, which can be seen only by those who are freed from sin. The message is that we should not fear the return of Christ, the great event of history yet to come and the grand conclusion of the gospel age launched by Christ's resurrection from the grave.

STANDING FOR THE KINGDOM

When Handel's *Messiah* is sung, tradition calls for the audience to follow King George's example by standing for the "Hallelujah Chorus." The Bible states that when Christ returns and sets up his throne, all humanity will stand, not by tradition but by divine compulsion for judgment. Only those who have trusted Christ and his blood for forgiveness of sin are called out of his final judgment. "Come, you who are blessed by my Father," he will say, "inherit the kingdom prepared for you from the foundation of the world" (Matt. 25:34).

8. Henry Alford, *The Greek Testament*, 4 vols. (Cambridge: Deighton, Bell, and Co., 1866), 4:666.

The seventh trumpet proclaims that Jesus, who died for sin and rose from the grave, will return in glory to establish a kingdom of righteousness that will never end. This is either the best or worst of news for you: are you sure which one it is? The Bible says that you may be declared righteous in Christ through faith, cleansed by the blood of his cross and born again by his resurrection power.

While the enemies of Christ must stand in his terrible judgment, the time for believers to stand is now. If the twenty-four elders who fell on their faces praising God are any indication, we will fall down in adoration of our Savior on that day, casting at his feet the crowns he has given us (Rev. 4:10). But now, as we await his coming, we are to stand as those who know what song will be playing when history comes to its end. We are to stand for God's truth in our teaching and living, stand for his mercy in our gospel outreach, and stand for his glory and kingdom by living holy lives and refusing to swear allegiance to the kingdom of this world in sin. If we stand in faith, by his grace, we will hear with joy the trumpet sounding on that day, and the voices from heaven crying out in wonder: "The kingdom of the world has become the kingdom of our Lord and of his Christ, and he shall reign forever and ever" (11:15).

PART 4

The Symbolic Histories

32

THE WOMAN, THE CHILD, AND THE DRAGON

Revelation 12:1–6

She gave birth to a male child, one who is to rule all the nations with a rod of iron, but her child was caught up to God and to his throne, and the woman fled into the wilderness. (Rev. 12:5–6)

O ne of the stock stories of ancient mythology is that of the evil usurper who is doomed to be slain by a royal prince yet to be born. The version of this story that would have been most familiar to John's readers concerned the birth of Apollo. When his mother Leto became pregnant, Python the dragon sought to slay her, to keep the son of Zeus from being born. Zeus, the chief god, carried Leto on winds to a secret island so as to hide the expectant mother. Finally, Apollo was born, and four days later he slew the evil dragon.

The apostle John would have known this popular story as he wrote the twelfth chapter of Revelation. Some scholars suggest that John was copying from mythology.[1] Yet John's perspective is that the history of Christ is the true story of our world. Pagan mythology partly consists of Satan's

---

1. See, for instance, Stephen S. Smalley, *The Revelation to John: A Commentary on the Greek Text of the Apocalypse* (Downers Grove, IL: InterVarsity Press, 2012), 162–63.

counterfeit of the true story of Christ in order to pervert the gospel for his own purposes.[2] Satan, John says, is the real dragon whose defeat is assured by God's promised Son, and the dragon's attempts first to stop the Messiah's birth and then to persecute the Messiah's people in fact constitute the story of the world.

Chapter 12 begins the second half of Revelation. The first half provided general overviews of history. We saw the world's opposition to the gospel, Christ's judgments on the wicked nations, and our calling to persevere in faith. The second half of Revelation homes in on the chief characters in the spiritual warfare taking place behind the scenes. The primary enemy is Satan, the dragon. He is aided by two beasts, the harlot Babylon, and the people who bear the mark of the beast. One by one, these figures are introduced in chapters 12–15, and one by one their defeat and judgment is shown in chapters 16–20.

Located as it is in the center of the book, Revelation 12 is considered by many scholars as the central and key vision. It depicts the decisive conflict between the church, the devil, and the royal child, Jesus Christ. Here is provided the background of spiritual conflict behind Jesus' words of great assurance, given on the night before his victory on the cross: "In the world you will have tribulation. But take heart; I have overcome the world" (John 16:33).

The Woman with Child

In reading Revelation, we should remember that the chapter divisions were not originally included. We should therefore hear the first half of the book concluding with the vision of the opening of God's temple to reveal the ark of the covenant, symbolizing the believers' access into God's presence, accompanied with lightning, thunder, and hail. As the book was being read aloud to its first recipients, there would likely have been a pause. So with the previous vision still lingering in the air, John continues: "And a great sign appeared in heaven: a woman clothed with the sun, with the moon under her feet, and on her head a crown of twelve stars" (Rev. 12:1). The previous vision's having concluded with heaven opened, the new vision begins with a depiction of the glorious church.

2. See G. K. Beale, *The Book of Revelation: A Commentary on the Greek Text*, New International Greek Testament Commentary (Grand Rapids: Eerdmans, 1999), 625.

John makes it clear that this is not an actual woman but rather a symbol, referring to her as a "sign" that he saw in heaven. Roman Catholics argue that this figure depicts the virgin Mary in her mediatorial glory. The details do not fit Mary's story, however, and this woman's children include all "who keep the commandments of God and hold to the testimony of Jesus" (Rev. 12:17). The woman, therefore, is the covenant community of God's faithful people, through whom God brought his Son, the long-promised Savior, into the world. She includes both Old Testament Israel and the New Testament church, "the people of God living both before and after Christ's coming."[3] Thus, this glorious woman not only gives birth to the Messiah but continues having children after his ascension. Paul spoke of spiritual Jerusalem as "our mother" (Gal. 4:26). Likewise, Scots Covenanters spoke with reverence of "Mother Kirk," the church as the bride of Christ and the mother in whose nursery God's children are raised.

The vision puts emphasis on the radiant glory of the faithful church, as God sees her according to his own will and eternal purpose. She is "clothed with the sun, with the moon under her feet, and on her head a crown of twelve stars" (Rev. 12:1). Wrapped in the sun, she is glorious, bearing the light of God; with the moon under her feet, she exercises spiritual authority; the crown of stars on her head is the laurel of victory in Christ; and as a pregnant mother, she had the task of bringing Christ into the world. The sun, moon, and stars connect her with God's covenant people. In Joseph's vision in Genesis 37:9–11, the sun was his father Jacob, the moon was his mother Rachel, and the stars were the sons who became the twelve tribes of Israel. Already in Revelation we have seen stars depicting the angels of the churches (Rev. 1:20), the new "Israel of God" (Gal. 6:16).

If we can imagine this radiant woman shining in the heavens, we are encouraged to realize that she depicts us, the Christian church, as God sees us in light of Christ's redemptive work. William Hendriksen writes: "On earth this Church may appear very insignificant and open to scorn and ridicule; but from the aspect of heaven this same Church is all-glorious: all that heaven can contribute of glory and of splendour is lavished upon her."[4] Isaiah 62:5 proclaims to the covenant people, and thus to each member in it,

---

3. Ibid., 627.

4. William Hendriksen, *More than Conquerors: An Interpretation of the Book of Revelation* (1940; repr., Grand Rapids: Baker, 1967), 136.

that "as the bridegroom rejoices over the bride, so shall your God rejoice over you." A wife is never more beautiful and precious to her husband as when she is carrying his child. And nothing so stirs up manly protectiveness as the image of his pregnant wife. God likewise speaks of his protective watch over the holy daughter Zion; Zechariah 2:8 declares that "he who touches you touches the apple of his eye."

In a world scarred by mankind's fall into sin, childbearing always involves painful travail. So it is for the covenant mother: "She was pregnant and was crying out in birth pains and the agony of giving birth" (Rev. 12:2). This statement summarizes the entire history of Israel, with all her travails, until finally the long-promised Messiah was born. Douglas Kelly writes: "Old Testament Israel was pregnant with Christ for thousands of years. Israel was being used as a womb from which the Messiah would be born."[5] Isaiah wrote: "Like a pregnant woman who writhes and cries out in her pangs when she is near to giving birth, so were we because of you, O LORD" (Isa. 26:17).

This vision of the heavenly woman reminds us of the mission of the church. She is clothed in light, and we are to shine forth with the light of God's Word. She is holy, and we are to be conformed not to the world but to the character of our Lord. Her mission is to deliver Christ, and our mission is to proclaim him as Lord and Savior. The church does not exist to provide a variety of human services to the world but to cause Christ to be born in sinners' hearts so that they may be saved. The church is the mother to God's covenant children, and we are to raise them in the nurture and admonition of the Lord. There were travails for Israel before Christ was born, and there are afflictions for the church in this present age. But we are precious to God, radiant in his redemptive purpose, and he is the strong, loving, and faithful Father who will keep the mother of all his children safe.

THE FURIOUS RED DRAGON

One of Revelation's purposes is to give explanations for what Christians experience throughout history. The first half of the book dealt with various historical realities that explain the tumults that the church will experience. They include our own sin and failure (chaps. 2–3), Christ's judgments on the

5. Douglas F. Kelly, *Revelation*, Mentor Expository Commentary (Tain, Ross-shire, Scotland: Mentor, 2012), 216.

nations to protect the church (chaps. 6–7), and further judgments designed to persuade sinners of their need to repent (chaps. 8–9). These factors—Christ's discipline, Christ's protection, and Christ's call to repentance—together with believers' prayers (Rev. 8:3–5), explain the upheavals that dominate world history.

Revelation 12 presents what may be regarded as history's primary explanation, a great spiritual conflict raging behind the scenes. Verse 3 presents a mighty and terrible monster at war with Christ: "And another sign appeared in heaven: behold, a great red dragon." Beneath all the action on the surface of history is a great spiritual enemy seeking to destroy the church. John identifies him in verse 9 as "that ancient serpent, who is called the devil and Satan."

Many people today dismiss the devil as a fantasy or myth. But you cannot take the Bible seriously without believing in this personal and powerful spirit, the fallen archangel who is the enemy of Christ and his church, nor can you make real sense of the world as it is without accounting for him. The devil first appears in the Bible as the serpent who deceived and tempted Adam and Eve into breaking God's command, plunging our race into sin (Gen. 3:1–6). In cursing him, God promised warfare between Satan's servants and the children of the woman: "I will put enmity between you and the woman, and between your offspring and her offspring" (3:15). The woman's offspring was primarily Christ, but in him it includes the entire church of the old and new covenants. The rest of history features the conflict between the devil and God's covenant people, centered on his opposition to Christ himself. "He shall bruise your head," God promised, "and you shall bruise his heel" (3:15).

John's description of Satan as a great dragon not only connects back to the serpent of the garden but also incorporates the mythological dragon imagery that symbolized chaos and evil throughout the ancient world. The Old Testament often personified evil as a dragon or sea monster. Isaiah looked back on God's defeat of Pharaoh in the exodus in these terms: "Was it not you who cut Rahab in pieces, who pierced the dragon?" (Isa. 51:9). He spoke of God's judgment on Assyria, saying that "he will slay the dragon that is in the sea" (27:1). Behind the mythical dragons of the ancient world is the real dragon, the devil. Here is the true monster who lurks in history, whom Peter described as "a roaring lion, seeking someone to devour" (1 Peter 5:8).

John sees Satan as a great red dragon, the color evidently standing for bloodshed and murder. Jesus said, "He was a murderer from the beginning" (John 8:44). The dragon is further seen "with seven heads and ten horns, and on his heads seven diadems" (Rev. 12:3). In ancient mythology, the many-headed dragon seemed impossible to defeat. Likewise, Satan has heads and fangs in many places of worldly influence, and he acts with shocking dexterity. To thwart him in one arena is to find him attacking in another. Along with the seven heads are "ten horns." In the Bible, horns symbolize strength, and the ten horns speak of the strength of evil in this world under the devil's power. Daniel's fourth and most terrible beast had ten horns (Dan. 7:7, 24), and that connection associates these horns with earthly kingdoms under Satan's control. Reinforcing this idea are "seven diadems" on his heads (Rev. 12:3). These are not like the laurel crown of victory worn by the woman but are crowns of his usurped earthly dominion. Paul thus described Satan as "the prince of the power of the air, the spirit that is now at work in the sons of disobedience" (Eph. 2:2).

Satan does not serve but only rules. His crowns are the iron crowns of tyranny. G. K. Beale writes that the diadems "represent the devil's false claims of sovereign, universal authority in opposition to the true 'King of kings and Lord of lords,' who also wears 'many diadems' (19:12, 19–21)."[6] Satan longs to hear the hymn "Crown Him with Many Crowns" sung to his glory rather than to Christ's. Paul Gardner describes Satan as "the evil angelic guide for corrupt kings, nations, and kingdoms. . . . This would include the Roman empire and its Caesars who wanted to be worshipped as God, as well as more modern examples that often come in the form of humanistic societies and governments who treat God and his Word and his people with disdain, and persecute them."[7]

John is told that the dragon's "tail swept down a third of the stars of heaven and cast them to the earth" (Rev. 12:4). Many readers jump to the conclusion that this refers to Satan's leading a host of angels into heaven in rebellion against God. It is more likely, however, that this vision symbolizes the arrogant aims of his warfare on earth against the church. This same language was used in Daniel 8:10 of Antiochus Epiphanes, the great

---

6. Beale, *Revelation*, 635.

7. Paul Gardner, *Revelation: The Compassion and Protection of Christ*, Focus on the Bible (Tain, Ross-shire, Scotland: Christian Focus, 2008), 169.

persecutor of the Jews. The point seems to be that Satan intends for his malicious actions on earth to do damage in heaven. Only a vast monster could swing his tail and knock stars from the sky. "The Dragon attacks God's order and rule. . . . He assaults heaven itself, symbolized by the effect on the heavenly bodies."[8]

The dragon especially remembers God's promise that the child of the woman would crush his head (Gen. 3:15). The vision therefore paints the gruesome picture of the mother about to give birth, and there with her is the dragon with his seven heads, lurking so as to attack the child when he is born: "And the dragon stood before the woman who was about to give birth, so that when she bore her child he might devour it" (Rev. 12:4).

This, too, is the story of the Old Testament. Immediately after receiving the curse of enmity with the woman and her child, Satan sought to cut off the line. First, he incited Cain to kill his godly brother Abel (Gen. 4:8). Later, when Israel went into Egypt, Satan led Pharaoh to order that all the male sons would be killed as soon as they left the womb (Ex. 1:8–16). Satan entered the heart of King Saul with murderous designs for David, through whom the true King would be born. In Babylon, Satan conspired through evil Haman to wipe out the Israelite community (Esth. 3:15), only to be thwarted through the resourcefulness of Queen Esther, whom God had placed near the Persian king. Finally, when the wise men came to King Herod, asking about the royal child who had been born, Herod sent soldiers to Bethlehem to slay every male child up to two years old (Matt. 2:16). All through biblical history, Satan has raged with a murderous passion focused on one object: to destroy the promised Savior before the Savior could put an end to Satan's dominion of evil.

The Child Who Will Rule

The third figure introduced in the vision is this all-important Savior: "She gave birth to a male child, one who is to rule all the nations with a rod of iron" (Rev. 12:5). In true fulfillment of the ancient myths that reflect his coming, Jesus Christ is the prophesied Son who came, as 1 John 3:8 puts it, "to destroy the works of the devil."

8. Vern S. Poythress, *The Returning King: A Guide to the Book of Revelation* (Phillipsburg, NJ: P&R Publishing, 2000), 135.

In describing Christ, John alludes to Psalm 2, which says that though the nations rage against God's Anointed One, God enthrones his Son and grants him possession of the nations. "You shall break them with a rod of iron and dash them in pieces like a potter's vessel" (Ps. 2:9), God declares. Echoing this language, the woman bears a male child who "is to rule all the nations with a rod of iron" (Rev. 12:5). The nations belong to Christ as the field of his gospel harvest. We either submit adoringly to him as Lord and Savior or fall under his rod of judgment. Moreover, his rod protects the church: as "a shepherd defends his flock against the wild beasts of prey, so will Christ at his return strike the nations which oppress and persecute his church."[9]

I mentioned earlier the biblical history of Satan's attempt to destroy the seed that would become Jesus Christ. When those efforts failed, Satan used Judas Iscariot to betray Jesus, and then manipulated the Jewish leaders and the Roman governor into the judicial atrocity of Jesus' crucifixion. Finally, the dragon had slain the Prince! Yet when Jesus cried, "It is finished," and gave up his Spirit to the Father (John 19:30), his atoning sacrifice had struck the deadly blow against Satan's tyrannical reign of sin. In John's vision, the woman's "child was caught up to God and to his throne" (Rev. 12:5). At the very cusp of Satan's apparent triumph, with Jesus lying dead in the grave, God raised his Son from Satan's clutches and exalted him in power, causing the devil's strategy to collapse in defeat.

THE WOMAN IN THE WILDERNESS

John will elaborate further details of the holy war as the chapter continues, but the opening vision connects with us now by telling what happens to the woman after her child was born and taken up safely to God's throne. John concludes: "And the woman fled into the wilderness, where she has a place prepared by God, in which she is to be nourished for 1,260 days" (Rev. 12:6).

This final verse makes three vital applications for us today. The first is that Christians must not think of this present world as home, for now is the time of our wilderness journey. This life is a time of testing in preparation for our true home when Christ returns. The world under the devil's power is hostile to faithful Christians. Jesus said, "If you were of the world, the world

9. Robert H. Mounce, *Revelation*, rev. ed., New International Commentary on the New Testament (Grand Rapids: Eerdmans, 1997), 238.

would love you as its own; but because you are not of the world, but I chose you out of the world, therefore the world hates you" (John 15:19). Christians must therefore be spiritually strong and biblically wary, for behind earthly opposition and moral perversity stand spiritual forces of evil, led by Satan himself. "For we do not wrestle against flesh and blood," Paul wrote, "but against the rulers, against the authorities, against the cosmic powers over this present darkness, against the spiritual forces of evil in the heavenly places" (Eph. 6:12). Knowing this, we should not wage war in an earthly manner, relying on things such as wealth, power, or political influence. Our spiritual warfare relies on the spiritual resources of prayer, God's Word, and holy lives (see 2 Cor. 10:3–5).

In such a conflict, our calling from God is not to overthrow the spiritual powers of darkness, for we are not the slayers of the dragon. Rather, we are simply to stand against him. We are "to withstand in the evil day, and having done all, to stand firm" (Eph. 6:13). This means that we must not accommodate worldly demands and practices, knowing that to compromise with the world in its sin is to advance the cause of our enemy, the devil. Everything in the world that is contrary to God and his Word—whether sexual immorality, secularist ideology, or consumer idolatry—is a weapon forged by Satan to afflict mankind and oppose Christ and his church. When pressed to conform to worldly ways, we should see the devil's hand at work and resolutely refuse to aid and abet the enemy of our King.

In the first battle of Manassas, the Confederate forces were being pushed off the field when Brigadier General Thomas Jackson arrived with his First Virginia Brigade. Jackson calmly ordered his regiments and stood his ground. Some of the other brigades were fleeing, when one of their leaders saw Jackson standing firm. He shouted, "There stands Jackson like a stone wall!" That is how the famous general received his name, Stonewall Jackson. Seeing him, the others regained heart. They took up solid positions beside Jackson, and the Union advance was broken on the stone wall of resolute soldiers.

Whatever your view of the American Civil War, all can admire the valor of Jackson's stance and recognize the significance of his action. We are to do likewise in the spiritual battle of our day. When you stand firm in the faith, refusing to embrace the standards and demands of a world governed by sin, you not only preserve yourself but strengthen other believers, some of whom may be wavering in fear or doubt. Let other Christians see your faith and life, saying, "There he stands like a stone wall!" While you stand resolute in simple biblical faith and obedience, you will honor God and be greatly used by him in the strife of this desert world.

Second, Revelation 12:6 emphasizes God's care for the woman who fled into the desert: "The woman fled into the wilderness, where she has a place prepared by God, in which she is to be nourished for 1,260 days." We have seen in previous studies that 1,260 days, or forty-two months, symbolizes a period of trial and tribulation. This duration depicts the church age, the limited period prescribed by God during which believers suffer affliction. But notice as well that the wilderness is designed by God as a place of safety for the woman. By stepping away from the ungodliness of the world, Christians are preserved from ravages of sin.

God's wilderness is a place not only of safety but also of his provision. God sent ravens to feed Elijah during his three-and-a-half-year exile at the brook (1 Kings 17:6), and Israel was fed in the desert by the manna that God sent from heaven (Ex. 16). God now feeds the church with his Word, making faith grow strong even in affliction (Deut. 8:3). It is, in fact, his design that the wilderness would be a place where his covenant people would draw near to him in love, learning to rely on him completely for provision and protection. God said of Israel, "I will allure her, and bring her into the wilderness, and speak tenderly to her. And there I will give her her vineyards" (Hos. 2:14–15).

Finally, we are to remember that our enemy is a defeated foe. An analogy is drawn between Christians in the church age (between Christ's conquering death and resurrection and his glorious, triumphal return) and the situation of the Allied armies between the Normandy landings on D-Day in 1944 and the final end of the war on V-Day in 1945. When Eisenhower's armies landed in France on D-Day, there was no longer any doubt that World War II would be won. The decisive blow had been struck, and the war needed only to be pursued with vigor for the enemy to collapse. The German generals were quite aware of this, and many of them sought to bring about surrender as soon as possible. Yet the war raged on for many more months, and many bloody battles had to be fought. But those battles were fought by a victorious army who knew that their cause was won.

What a difference this knowledge makes in our fight! The child of the woman has come. He has conquered sin and Satan on the cross and risen to heaven with his Father. He has promised to return and end the war in total victory. There are still battles, some of them bloody and painful, that God's people must fight. You and I must take hard stands that may prove costly. But we stand for Jesus, not only grateful for his love but certain of his victory in the end!

How inspiring it is in the trials, failures, and sorrows of this life to be shown the glorious vision of how God sees the church, clothed in glory and crowned with stars! How wondrous it is to realize that history consists of the struggle for the child to be born and his victory over the terrible dragon! And how solemn it is to realize that we have a place in this titanic struggle. John explains our contribution in Revelation 12:11: "And they have conquered him by the blood of the Lamb and by the word of their testimony." Christ, the Lamb, has conquered by his blood. What significance we find for our lives if we stand firm in faith and bear our testimony to the glory of his kingdom!

33

BY THE BLOOD OF THE LAMB

Revelation 12:7–17

*And they have conquered him by the blood of the Lamb and by
the word of their testimony, for they loved not their
lives even unto death.* (Rev. 12:11)

*T*he Cannibals! You will be eaten by the Cannibals!" These words were spoken to dissuade John G. Paton from witnessing the gospel in the New Hebrides Islands. For most Christians, the violent barbarism of the islanders was sufficient reason not to live among them as missionaries. These were islands that many supposed to belong to Satan forever and where his power was too deeply entrenched to be safely challenged. But Paton could not neglect "the awful danger of the unsaved," and prayed that he "might be the means of bringing the perishing to the Saviour." When Paton arrived on the island of Tanna in 1858, he discovered the dangers firsthand. "The depths of Satan . . . were uncovered there before our eyes in the daily life of the people," he wrote. Paton's plan was to live among the people, earn their trust, learn their language, and bear testimony to the cleansing blood of Christ.[1]

---

1. John D. Legg, "John G. Paton: Missionary of the Cross," in *Five Pioneer Missionaries* (Edinburgh: Banner of Truth, 1965), 305–11.

On the many occasions when his life was threatened by musket-wielding natives, Paton relied on prayer. A biographer writes: "He trusted only in the Lord who had placed him there and to whom had been given all power in heaven and in earth. . . . [He] prayed to Christ 'either Himself to protect me, or to take me home to His glory.' . . . Soon Paton was able to speak to them of 'sin and salvation', and this he did unceasingly."[2]

During twenty-five years on the islands of Tanna and Aniwa, Paton was used by God to convert most of the people and establish strong churches. Once when back in Scotland for fund-raising, he wrote that "my soul longed after the holy Sabbaths of Aniwa."[3] How could one person succeed against such overwhelming odds and in the midst of such satanic danger? An answer is given in Revelation 12:11, which says that Christians such as Paton "have conquered him by the blood of the Lamb and by the word of their testimony, for they loved not their lives even unto death."

THE WAR IN HEAVEN

Revelation 12 presents a grand history of the church in the form of a vision of a woman, her son, and a great red dragon. The woman stands for the church, through which God brought his Son, the Savior, into the world. The dragon is the devil, who opposed the birth of the child and persecutes the church after Christ has ascended in power. Verses 1–6 introduced the players in this holy war, showing how God overcame the devil through the birth and the saving ministry of Christ. Starting in verse 7, the vision continues by showing the devil's ongoing warfare against believers. Satan suffered a terrible defeat in the coming of Christ so that his activities are curtailed. Nonetheless, he continues to rage with the resources he has left in the spiritual warfare that marks this age between the first and second comings of Christ.

The theme of this vision, starting in Revelation 12:7, is the defeat suffered by the devil because of the death, resurrection, and ascension of Christ. John writes: "Now war arose in heaven, Michael and his angels fighting against the dragon" (Rev. 12:7). According to this verse, not only does spiritual warfare take place on the earth between Christ and his people and Satan and his servants, but there is also warfare in the spiritual realm of angels.

2. Ibid., 314.
3. Ibid., 329.

Michael is described in Daniel 10:13 as "one of the chief princes" of the angels. Daniel had prayed for God to forgive his people and restore them to Jerusalem. An angel was dispatched to tell Daniel that his prayer had been heard, but its passage was blocked by an evil angel. It was only when "Michael . . . came to help" that Daniel's angel could get through (Dan. 10:13). On that occasion, it seems that Daniel's persistence in prayer provided the spiritual resources for Michael's victory (10:2–4). The book of Daniel ends with a promise that during the trials of the church age "shall arise Michael, the great prince who has charge of your people" (12:1). Revelation 12:7–8 describes this long-foretold holy war: "Michael and his angels fighting against the dragon. And the dragon and his angels fought back."

To understand this passage, we must realize that this battle took place during the life and ministry of Jesus Christ, culminating with his ascension into heaven. Revelation 12:13 reports that after the dragon "had been thrown down to the earth, he pursued the woman who had given birth to the male child." This means that the dragon was cast down just before the church age. Jesus' victory on the cross, crowned with his ascension to heaven's throne, defeated Satan and his army, after which "there was no longer any place for them in heaven[,] . . . and Satan . . . was thrown down to the earth, and his angels were thrown down with him" (Rev. 12:8–9).

What does it mean for Satan to be "thrown down" out of heaven? Revelation 12:10 answers that "the accuser of our brothers has been thrown down, who accuses them day and night before our God." Christ has silenced Satan's attempts to accuse Christians before God. Douglas Kelly writes: "When Jesus completed his redemptive work for sinners and took his place on God's throne, Satan no longer could come before God to criticize the saints. Rather, Jesus is now there, where Satan at one time could walk in and out before God. He is there as our advocate, rather than Satan as our accuser."[4]

From this perspective, the battle between Michael and Satan might be thought of as a legal contest in the courtroom of heaven. The heavenly voices rejoice that with Satan's defeat, he "who accuses [believers] day and night before our God" has lost his court privileges (Rev. 12:10). This fits the picture in the Old Testament. Job 1:6 tells of "a day when the sons of God came to present themselves before the LORD, and Satan also came among them." As

---

4. Douglas F. Kelly, *Revelation*, Mentor Expository Commentary (Tain, Ross-shire, Scotland: Mentor, 2012), 220.

an angelic being, even the fallen Satan had authority to come with other angels into God's courtroom. God asked Satan whether he had encountered "my servant Job, . . . a blameless and upright man" (1:8). Satan responded by accusing Job, saying that he honored God only because the Lord had so richly blessed him. Satan's accusation led to the terrible sufferings of Job and Job's subsequent testimony of faith in the Lord.

Revelation 12 states that Satan is no longer able to make these accusations. In the holy war in heaven, "the great dragon was thrown down" (Rev. 12:9). John describes him as "that ancient serpent," reminding us of how the devil led our race into sin and condemnation. He "is called the devil and Satan, the deceiver of the whole world" (12:9). The word *devil* means "slanderer" or "accuser." *Satan* means "adversary" of God's people, and he works as a "deceiver" of the world in its unbelief. These names tell us how Satan wars against God and his people: he desires to deceive and especially to accuse us of sin in the courtroom of God. If you have been a Christian for long, you may know what it means for Satan to suggest evil thoughts to your mind and then afflict you with the accusation that a person with such thoughts cannot be a true Christian. But Satan has now been cast down, and while he can afflict us on earth, he can no longer accuse us in the presence of God.

The New Testament associates the casting down of Satan with the saving work of Christ. Luke 10:17 records the return of the seventy-two evangelists whom Jesus sent out. When they reported their success in preaching the gospel, Jesus cried, "I saw Satan fall like lightning from heaven" (10:18). As Jesus saw it, the news of his redeeming work removed Satan from heaven. In John 12:31, Jesus was speaking about his coming death on the cross, saying, "Now will the ruler of this world be cast out." Jesus saw his work of redeeming us from sin as the end of Satan's campaign of accusation and deceit. Now, having ascended to God's throne in heaven, Jesus by his presence forever bars Satan from appearing to accuse us. James Hamilton writes: "Christ accomplished the victory, and apparently God sent Michael to enforce it."[5] G. K. Beale writes that "what Michael does is a heavenly reflection of what Christ does on earth."[6] Christ won the victory on earth, so "Michael and

5. James M. Hamilton Jr., *Revelation: The Spirit Speaks to the Churches* (Wheaton, IL: Crossway, 2012), 251.
6. G. K. Beale, *The Book of Revelation: A Commentary on the Greek Text*, New International Greek Testament Commentary (Grand Rapids: Eerdmans, 1999), 657.

his angels" assailed Satan, defeated him, and cast him out from the courts of heaven (Rev. 12:7–8).

CHRIST'S BLOOD AND OUR TESTIMONY

Given the emphasis of this passage, it is important for Christians to understand how Christ defeated our accuser and how we overthrow him today. Revelation 12:11 tells us not only that Christ defeated Satan but that his people routed the dragon: "And they have conquered him by the blood of the Lamb and by the word of their testimony." Satan's warfare of accusation against believers has been defeated by the blood of Christ and by our gospel witness.

First, it is by Christ's blood that believers overthrow the accusations of the devil. The reason that Satan appeared in heaven to accuse us was that he was seeking our eternal condemnation under God's law. An example is provided in Zechariah 3:1, which showed "Joshua the high priest standing before the angel of the LORD, and Satan standing at his right hand to accuse him." Verse 3 states that Joshua was in fact guilty of sin: "Now Joshua was standing before the angel, clothed with filthy garments." As Israel's high priest, Joshua represented the entire nation, which had been in exile because of its sin and idolatry. Satan loved to point this out, and he urged that God could not justly bless such sinners by restoring them to Jerusalem.

This is precisely the accusation that Michael and his angels put to an end because of the conquest of "the blood of the Lamb," Jesus Christ (Rev. 12:11). Before Jesus' death, Satan had a good case against God's people. When he accused believers such as King David, he could point to actual and heinous sins that had been committed, such as David's adultery with Bathsheba and murder of her husband Uriah. When Satan prosecuted Moses, there were real sins for him to point out. So it was for all the other Old Testament believers, whom God had admitted into heaven through their faith in the gospel that pointed forward to Christ. But when Christ came and offered his own blood as the true Lamb of God, to pay the penalty for the sins of his people, there was no longer a charge against them in God's courtroom. When the law has been satisfied, there is no charge to prosecute! When the sin has been removed, there can be no accusation!

This salvation was acted out in Zechariah's vision of Satan and Joshua the high priest. Jesus appeared and commanded, "Remove the filthy garments from him." He said to Joshua, "Behold, I have taken your iniquity away from you, and I will clothe you with pure vestments" (Zech. 3:4). On this basis, Jesus said, "The LORD rebuke you, O Satan!" (3:2). Christ took Joshua's filthy garments to himself and bore the penalty of his sin on the cross. God then transferred (or imputed) Christ's righteousness to Joshua, so that he was justified before God's law. This is why Paul rejoiced in Romans 8:1, "There is therefore now no condemnation for those who are in Christ Jesus."

If you have believed in Jesus Christ, Satan has likewise lost the ability to accuse you in the court of God's justice. It is not that you have not sinned, for you have. But as 1 John 1:7 puts it, "the blood of Jesus [God's] Son cleanses us from all sin." In a previous chapter, I told the famous story of how the devil came to accuse Martin Luther. The great Reformer was performing the important work of translating the Bible into the German language, and apparently Satan wanted to discourage him. Luther reported that Satan appeared with a long list of his many sins and, pointing them out, mocked Luther's desire to serve God. Luther confessed the truth of his sins but pointed out that Christ's blood had cleansed him of them all. Luther threw his inkpot at Satan, leaving a mark on the wall that can be seen to this day.

Charles Wesley wrote of the Christian's salvation: "Amazing love! How can it be that thou, my God, shouldst die for me?" The hymn's final verse tells of our victory in Christ:

No condemnation now I dread; Jesus, and all in him, is mine!
Alive in him, my living Head, and clothed in righteousness divine,
Bold I approach th'eternal throne, and claim the crown, through Christ,
      my own.
Amazing love! How can it be that thou, my God, shouldst die for me?[7]

Second, Christians conquer by "the word of their testimony" (Rev. 12:11). Satan wants news of his defeat kept as quiet as possible! But when Christians spread the good news of forgiveness in Christ, Satan's power is diminished. Satan has a hold over our family members and friends by the accusation in their consciences that they can never be accepted by God.

7. Charles Wesley, "And Can It Be That I Should Gain" (1738).

Christians conquer this diabolical warfare by telling the truth of Christ's saving blood. After Jesus sent out his evangelists, they came back rejoicing that they had cast out demons (Luke 10:17). We, too, wield power against Satan's kingdom whenever we testify to the good news of Christ's saving work. D. A. Carson writes:

> The hosts of darkness are pushed back by Christians bearing witness— giving testimony to who God is and what he has done in Christ Jesus. How else can we push back against Satan and his forces? We will be defeated if we simply keep silent. If you never share the gospel with anybody else, you yourself are defeated. You are not pushing back the frontiers of darkness. This is how Satan is defeated—by the blood of the Lamb and by the word of your testimony.[8]

Third, Christians conquer because "they loved not their lives even unto death" (Rev. 12:11). Since Christ has saved us by his blood, we not only proclaim the gospel but hold onto it for our salvation even to the point of death. We embrace all manner of suffering for Christ's sake, including the daily battle with sin to which we are called in our sanctification. Carson points out that "suffering will take different forms for each of us. Some of us will be called to suffer intellectually. We will be mocked for taking up our cross and daily following Jesus with our minds. For others, it will be actual physical suffering that we have to endure."[9] It is not easy to suffer for Christ in this present evil age, but a true believer will endure anything rather than give up his or her faith in Jesus. James Hamilton writes that "it is better to die trusting Christ and clinging to the gospel than to go on living by denying that gospel. . . . Without the gospel, when you stand before God, all Satan's accusations will ring true, and you will be damned with Satan."[10]

This points out how important it is that each of us should confess our sin, trust in Jesus, and be cleansed at his cross. Satan wants to accuse you before God, and he has all the evidence he could possibly need. The only way for you to be delivered from the eternal wrath of God is to turn to Jesus,

---

8. D. A. Carson, "This Present Evil Age," in *These Last Days: A Christian View of History*, ed. Richard D. Phillips and Gabriel N. E. Fluhrer (Phillipsburg, NJ: P&R Publishing, 2011), 35–36.

9. Ibid., 36–37.

10. Hamilton, *Revelation*, 253.

receive in faith his death on the cross for your sins, and then live forever by trusting in his gospel.

BECAUSE THE TIME IS SHORT

The final verses of Revelation 12 explain the situation of Christians and the church after the ascension of Jesus into heaven, showing two results in our present age from Christ's victory. The first is the eternal rejoicing of heaven and its inhabitants, and the second is the temporary suffering of the church.

Christ's victory causes praise and rejoicing in heaven: "And I heard a loud voice in heaven, saying, 'Now the salvation and the power and the kingdom of our God and the authority of his Christ have come, for the accuser of our brothers has been thrown down, who accuses them day and night before our God. . . . Therefore, rejoice, O heavens and you who dwell in them!'" (Rev. 12:10–12). Christ's victory has brought the salvation promised by God, revealed the power of God to save, initiated God's blessed kingdom, and established Christ's authority as Savior and Lord. What better news could we ever hear? Satan the accuser has been cast down! "The victory has been won: salvation is secure; the kingdom of God has been launched; Christ is reigning."[11] Douglas Kelly writes of growing up in a strict North Carolina town, where dancing was forbidden. Yet when World War II ended and the soldiers came home, the rules were set aside and people danced in the streets. The greater news of Christ's victory over Satan causes our rejoicing to reach even to heaven. Kelly writes: "Therefore, we have every reason to be a joyful people, and this joy of immediate access to a reconciled, smiling Father should always be reflected in our worship."[12]

Christ's victory brings us everlasting joy in heaven, but Satan's fall to the earth causes us temporary suffering in this present age. Revelation 12:12 continues: "But woe to you, O earth and sea, for the devil has come down to you in great wrath, because he knows that his time is short!"

The final section of Revelation 12 depicts Satan's attempt to afflict the church on earth, since he can no longer accuse Christians in heaven: "And when the dragon saw that he had been thrown down to the earth, he

11. Steve Wilmshurst, *The Final Word: The Book of Revelation Simply Explained* (Darlington, UK: Evangelical Press, 2008), 156.
12. Kelly, *Revelation*, 223.

pursued the woman who had given birth to the male child" (Rev. 12:13). Satan seeks to harm believers in time because he cannot touch eternity; he seeks to thwart our earthly solicitude because he cannot thwart Christ's saving of our souls. Satan is livid about his defeat and hates nothing more than believers in Christ who obey God's Word and witness to the gospel: "Then the dragon became furious with the woman and went off to make war on the rest of her offspring, on those who keep the commandments of God and hold to the testimony of Jesus" (12:17).

I mentioned in the previous chapter that when the Allied forces landed in Normandy in June 1944, the Second World War was as good as finished. The German generals began appealing to Adolf Hitler to negotiate an end to the war. Hitler did exactly the opposite. In his mad rage against his enemies, he did all that he could to hurt them. One example is the V-2 rocket campaign that Hitler rained on the cities of England in the last months of the war. Until the rocket-launch sites were finally overrun, over a thousand V-2 rockets had landed in England, killing many people and badly damaging London. Why did Hitler do this even though the war had been lost? Revelation 12:12 answers: "Woe to you, O earth and sea, for the devil has come down to you in great wrath, because he knows that his time is short!"

The point is that Satan persecutes the church here on earth not because he thinks he can take away our salvation but because he knows that he cannot. The devil is driven by pure malice in the face of certain defeat. However disturbing it is to contemplate his malice, its futility is still encouraging to suffering Christians when friends or governments unrighteously turn against us, when false accusations hurt us, or when we are treated unfairly because of our faith! Through Christ's blood and the word of our testimony, we have the victory above, and for this reason we suffer Satan's attacks here on earth. Persecution for Christ's sake thus shows that we belong to the Savior whom the world crucified so long ago, but who has already conquered. Ours should be the attitude shown by Peter and John when they were beaten for preaching the gospel: they left, "rejoicing that they were counted worthy to suffer dishonor for the name" of Jesus (Acts 5:41). Satan's attacks against our buildings, our budgets, and our bodies show only that he can do nothing about our blessing in Christ and the fact that we now belong in the eternal glory of heaven. Satan's time to persecute us "is short," as even he knows, but our eternal rejoicing in heaven with Christ will last forever.

Finally, John was shown visions drawing from Old Testament imagery that show God's protection and provision for the woman during the dragon's persecution: "But the woman was given the two wings of the great eagle so that she might fly from the serpent into the wilderness, to the place where she is to be nourished for a time, and times, and half a time" (Rev. 12:14). The Old Testament often spoke of God's carrying his people to safety on wings of eagles (Ex. 19:4–6; Deut. 32:10–11). This symbolizes God's supernatural intervention to deliver the church from danger. As we have seen many times in our studies, "a time, times, and half a time" equals three and a half years, which symbolizes the tribulation of the church throughout this present age. God not only brings his people to safety, but causes our faith to be nourished, primarily through the heavenly manna of his Word.

Yet Satan still attempts to rage: "The serpent poured water like a river out of his mouth after the woman, to sweep her away with a flood" (Rev. 12:15). Satan's deceits are like a flood that would drown us, just as Pharaoh sought to drown Israel in the Red Sea waters, but God intervenes to save us. Revelation 1:16 spoke of a "sharp two-edged sword" that came from Jesus' mouth, speaking of his gospel message. In contrast, the flood coming from Satan's mouth highlights the false teaching by which he wants to sweep away the unsettled and unwary. John writes: "But the earth came to the help of the woman, and the earth opened its mouth and swallowed the river that the dragon had poured from his mouth" (12:16). This alludes to when God opened the earth to swallow the false witnesses Korah, Dathan, and Abiram, who opposed Moses during the exodus (Num. 16:26–33). These images encourage troubled Christians to pray, remembering how God has pledged to safeguard his church during the trials of this age. David urged us this way in Psalm 32:6–7: "Therefore let everyone who is godly offer prayer to you at a time when you may be found; surely in the rush of great waters, they shall not reach him. You are a hiding place for me; you preserve me from trouble; you surround me with shouts of deliverance."

SATAN CAST DOWN

Satan has been cast down from heaven by the victory of Christ. He can still breathe earthly affliction upon us, but he has no ability to accuse us before God or threaten our right to eternal life. This was a great truth that

John G. Paton had taught to a former cannibal named Namuri on the island of Tanna. This man had heard Paton's message of salvation through Jesus Christ and believed, experienced salvation, and became an evangelist. One day he was preaching the message of Christ's blood when a witch doctor approached and began beating him with a club. Though badly injured, Namuri escaped and fled to Paton's house. Paton nursed him back to health and urged him not to go back to his village or continue preaching. Namuri refused, reminding the missionary of how Christ's blood had conquered Satan and set him free to preach the gospel:

> Missi, when I see them thirsting for my blood, I just see myself when the missionary first came to my island. I desired to murder him, as they now desire to kill me. Had he stayed away for such danger, I would have remained heathen; but he came, and continued coming to teach us, till, by the grace of God, I was changed to what I am. Now the same God that changed me to this, can change these poor Tannese to love and serve him. I cannot stay away from them, but I will . . . do all I can . . . to bring them to Jesus.[13]

It was by the blood of the Lamb and the testimony of witnesses such as John Paton and his convert Namuri that the light of Christ conquered islands that had once been the exclusive province of Satan. What will God do where we live, if we seize by faith the victory of Christ's blood and fearlessly proclaim his gospel, without concern for suffering, loss, or even death? The answer, according to John's vision, is that Satan will be cast down from his throne, and "the salvation and the power and the kingdom of our God and the authority of his Christ" will come, causing heaven itself and those who dwell in it to rejoice with great praise to God (Rev. 12:10, 12). If we will daily embrace the cross-bearing death of Jesus, giving our testimony to his salvation, we will conquer "by the blood of the Lamb" (12:11).

---

13. Quoted in Jim Cromarty, *King of the Cannibals: The Story of John G. Paton* (Darlington, UK: Evangelical Press, 1997), 109–10.

34

THE RISING OF THE BEAST

Revelation 13:1–10

And I saw a beast rising out of the sea, with ten horns and seven heads, with ten diadems on its horns and blasphemous names on its heads. (Rev. 13:1)

*I*n studying Revelation, we constantly need to realize that we are not reading future history out of a newspaper but are learning the spiritual realities of our present age through a visionary-prophetic picture book. It is especially necessary to stress this approach today, when many Christians do not even try to understand Revelation because of the confusing teaching they have heard. Yet the visions provided to John in Revelation should be as familiar to believers as Jesus' well-known parables, such as those of the prodigal son and the good Samaritan. An example is the vision of the dragon, the woman, and the child in Revelation 12. This dramatization of spiritual warfare in the church age should provide an easy-to-understand mental picture to all Bible believers. This vision shows how Satan failed to destroy Jesus in his first coming and that now Satan vainly rages against the church in anger over his inevitable failure.

A second principle to remember is that Revelation's symbols must be interpreted not from speculations about current events but from parallels in the Old Testament. An example is seen in the final statement of chapter 12, "And he [the dragon] stood on the sand of the sea" (Rev. 12:17). The reader familiar with Old Testament imagery expects some dreadful evil to appear, since the sea is the realm of chaos and rebellion, a virtual synonym for the Abyss of hell. The vision of chapter 11 earlier spoke of "the beast that rises from the bottomless pit," who makes war on the witnessing church (11:7). Now that same warfare will be depicted from the enemy perspective, as John watches. He records, "And I saw a beast rising out of the sea" (13:1).

The Beast from the Sea

The Old Testament prophet Daniel received a vision showing four beasts who represented evil imperial powers on earth. Daniel's beasts represented the empires of Babylon, Persia, Greece, and Rome that would successively rise in history (Dan. 7:1–8). Each of these kingdoms would harm God's people, but be ultimately supplanted by Christ. Daniel was told that "the saints of the Most High shall receive the kingdom and possess the kingdom forever, forever and ever" (7:18).

As John presents a beast like Daniel's, he sees him rising slowly out of the dark water, describing each part as it breaks the surface: "And I saw a beast rising out of the sea, with ten horns and seven heads, with ten diadems on its horns and blasphemous names on its heads" (Rev. 13:1). Like Daniel's fourth beast, which represented imperial Rome, this beast has ten horns (Dan. 7:7). Like the dragon of Revelation 12, this beast has seven heads, ten horns, and royal diadems (Rev. 12:3). These parallels connect this beast with the Roman Empire and identify him as a servant who wields Satan's might.

John described this beast as having "ten horns and seven heads, with ten diadems on its horns and blasphemous names on its heads" (Rev. 13:1). More will be said about these details in Revelation 17, but for now they give the general impression of the beast as coming with powers, rulers, and thrones under his control. In Daniel's vision, the fourth beast's ten horns represented kings who would arise (Dan. 7:24). The fact that these horns each wear diadems confirms that they are royal persons. The beast has crowns on his horns, whereas the dragon of Revelation 12 had crowns on his heads. Grant

Osborne suggests that this "indicates that while the dragon is the king of the evil empire, the beast is the military arm of the king."[1]

Many commentators assert that the beast's seven heads correspond to the seven Roman emperors after Augustus Caesar: Tiberius, Caligula, Claudius, Nero, Vespasian, Titus, and Domitian. This interpretation is not certain, since there were others who briefly ruled as emperors. Simon Kistemaker therefore urges us to see the numbers ten and seven as symbolic of "completeness and fullness," indicating the comprehensive power and authority exercised by the beast.[2] The seven heads may also be intended simply to identify this beast with those of Daniel 7, since between them Daniel's four beasts had seven heads and ten horns (Dan. 7:3–7). John's own interpretation also emphasizes the general idea of royal dominion and power: "And to it the dragon gave his power and his throne and great authority" (Rev. 13:2). William Hendriksen explains: "The sea beast symbolizes the persecuting power of Satan embodied in all the nations and governments of the world throughout all history. . . . In the beast the persecuting power of Satan becomes visible."[3]

The beast had "blasphemous names on its heads" (Rev. 13:1). This points to false claims to deity made by earthly rulers. The Roman emperors gave themselves the titles of *lord*, *savior*, *son of God*, and *lord and god*. The earliest emperors were deified only after their deaths, but before long the emperors began demanding living worship. This was particularly true of Domitian, the beastly emperor of John's time, who demanded that sacrifices be offered to him in Rome and required the worship of his image throughout the empire upon pain of death.[4]

As the beast rises further, John describes it more fully: "And the beast that I saw was like a leopard; its feet were like a bear's, and its mouth was like a lion's mouth" (Rev. 13:2). This description combines the different beasts of Daniel's vision, each of which emphasized separate kingdoms. This beast, therefore, is a composite of all the beasts that Daniel saw. This suggests that John's beast is greater than any of the individual empires, even that of

1. Grant R. Osborne, *Revelation*, Baker Exegetical Commentary on the New Testament (Grand Rapids: Baker Academic, 2002), 490.

2. Simon J. Kistemaker, *Revelation*, New Testament Commentary (Grand Rapids: Baker, 2001), 377.

3. William Hendriksen, *More than Conquerors: An Interpretation of the Book of Revelation* (1940; repr., Grand Rapids: Baker, 1967), 145.

4. G. B. Caird, *The Revelation of St. John the Divine* (San Francisco: Harper, 1966), 163.

Rome. The beast from the sea represents "all the . . . empires throughout human history that have stood against God and his people."[5] The fact that this beast exercises authority for forty-two months (13:5), that is, for the entirety of the church age, shows that this beast represents more than the ancient Rome that persecuted the churches of John's time—it represents the entirety of violent earthly empires that oppose Christ's kingdom and people.

The question may be raised whether this beast from the sea should be equated with the Antichrist. The answer is yes, if the Antichrist is biblically understood. The term is used only in the epistles of John, where the apostle spoke of those who opposed the revelation of Jesus: "Children, it is the last hour, and as you have heard that antichrist is coming, so now many antichrists have come" (1 John 2:18). This verse states that the Antichrist is a figure who will appear in the end, but who is represented throughout church history by many who are like him. John added that "every spirit that does not confess Jesus is . . . the spirit of the antichrist, which you heard was coming and now is in the world already" (1 John 4:3; see also 2 John 7). This spirit is exemplified in the beast from the sea, which "was given a mouth uttering haughty and blasphemous words" (Rev. 13:5). Paul's teaching in 2 Thessalonians 2:3 indicated that there would be an ultimate Antichrist before Christ returned, whom he named as the "man of lawlessness." Yet he is represented throughout the church age by blasphemous powers in opposition to Christ.

THE BEAST AS COUNTERFEIT CHRIST

One of the most significant features of the beast in Revelation 13 is the way he parodies the death and resurrection of Jesus. In Revelation, Christ wears "many diadems" (Rev. 19:12), so the beast has his many crowns; Christ has a worthy name written on him (19:12), so the beast bears blasphemous names; Christ has people "from every tribe and language and people and nation" (5:9), so the beast assumes power "over every tribe and people and language and nation" (13:7); Christ is worshiped together with God (7:10), so the beast demands false worship together with Satan (13:4).

In keeping with these counterfeits, John says of the beast: "One of its heads seemed to have a mortal wound, but its mortal wound was healed, and the whole earth marveled as they followed the beast" (Rev. 13:3). Parallels in the

5. Osborne, *Revelation*, 492.

Greek text make clear the connection with Christ's death and resurrection. The same word is used to say that both Jesus and the beast were "slain," and the same word is used to say that Jesus "came to life" (2:8) and the beast "yet lived" (13:14). Satan's beast mimics the resurrection so that "the whole earth marveled as they followed the beast" (13:3).

Most commentators identify this slain but resurrected beast as the Roman emperor Nero, the evil ruler who savagely attacked Christians. Nero was a clear example of the self-exalting beast, and his rule was so depraved that the Roman Senate finally opposed him, after which he committed suicide, in A.D. 68. Since Nero was not publicly executed or buried, a legend developed that he had escaped. For several decades, including the time when John wrote Revelation, legends anticipated Nero's return to reclaim his empire and purge Rome. Since John identifies one of the beast's heads as receiving this wound and being healed, it is argued that Nero is the one of the Roman emperors whose myth held him to have died and risen again.[6]

There are two problems with this view. The first is that it has the apostle John believing and using a legend that is historically false, since Nero really died in A.D. 68. Second, John's beast did not commit suicide but was attacked and "mortally wounded" (Rev. 13:3 NKJV). A better approach, though one that is far from certain, sees Nero's fall as representing the death of the Roman Empire, which after Nero fell into chaos. The empire was resurrected when the Roman general Vespasian returned from besieging Jerusalem to restore order and establish himself as emperor, followed by his two sons Titus and Domitian.[7] Rome looked as though it had died, but it was revived with new life.

An even better interpretation notes that Revelation 13:14 says that the beast "was wounded by the sword and yet lived." All through Revelation, the sword is wielded by Jesus Christ (Rev. 1:16; 2:12, 16; 19:15, 21). Under this view, the beast's wound reflects the deathblow dealt to Satan by Christ's atoning death and life-giving resurrection, and by the triumphant establishment of the Christian church in the power of the Holy Spirit. Yet the persecuting emperors, beginning with Nero and continuing with Domitian, represented a revival of Satan's power in a way that would have impressed those who

---

6. For a full description of the Nero myth as it pertains to this passage, see Caird, *The Revelation of St. John the Divine*, 164–65.

7. Dennis E. Johnson, *Triumph of the Lamb: A Commentary on Revelation* (Phillipsburg, NJ: P&R Publishing, 2001), 193.

witnessed the Christians' apparent defeat. G. K. Beale writes: "Satan's wound appeared to be fatal, and, indeed, it really was. Nevertheless, the devil's continued activity through his agents makes it appear to John as though he has overcome the mortal blow dealt him at Christ's death and resurrection."[8]

While none of these explanations are conclusive, Christians can be sure that Satan and his beast will seek to confuse the world by mimicking Christ's resurrection. Jesus taught that "false christs and false prophets will arise and perform great signs and wonders, so as to lead astray, if possible, even the elect" (Matt. 24:24). Jesus added that believers must not follow anyone who claims to be the Messiah, despite apparent miracles or resurrections, since the true Christ has ascended to heaven and will return to earth only in his glorious second coming (24:25–27).

THE BEAST'S DEMAND FOR FALSE WORSHIP

John informs us that the beast has two main agendas. The first is the gathering of false worship to himself, and through himself to Satan: "And they worshiped the dragon, for he had given his authority to the beast, and they worshiped the beast, saying, 'Who is like the beast, and who can fight against it?'" (Rev. 13:4).

It is a notable fact of history that the most despicable tyrants have often been extremely popular and have elicited virtual worship from their people. Adolf Hitler set himself up as a messiah for the Aryan race and was fanatically revered by many of the German people, even as their cities were being reduced to rubble by Allied advances. The relentless conqueror Napoleon Bonaparte continues to be adored by the French, despite having bled their country dry in his ruinous wars. Steve Wilmshurst writes: "Dictators create their own personal mythology, or have others do it for them. Most of all, they demand people's unquestioning and unconditional submission—something that only God has the right to do."[9]

History records exactly what John anticipated. Equipped by Satan with power to manipulate and impress, the tyrannical rulers represented by

8. G. K. Beale, *The Book of Revelation: A Commentary on the Greek Text*, New International Greek Testament Commentary (Grand Rapids: Eerdmans, 1999), 688. See Beale's extended discussion of this matter on 687–92.

9. Steve Wilmshurst, *The Final Word: The Book of Revelation Simply Explained* (Darlington, UK: Evangelical Press, 2008), 164.

the beast virtually deify themselves. "Who is like the beast," the people ask in rapt admiration, "and who can fight against it?" (Rev. 13:4). In the Bible, these words are adoringly spoken of God alone. When God led Israel through the parted Red Sea, Moses sang, "Who is like you, O LORD, . . . majestic in holiness, awesome in glorious deeds, doing wonders?" (Ex. 15:11). The prophet Micah praised God for his saving grace: "Who is a God like you, pardoning iniquity and passing over transgression . . . because he delights in steadfast love" (Mic. 7:18). God alone is incomparable. Yet through the awesome earthly power of the beast, Satan basks in usurped divine glory.

In his first epistle, John warned believers of false signs and wonders: "Beloved, do not believe every spirit, but test the spirits to see whether they are from God" (1 John 4:1). Satan uses supernatural power to win false worship. He sought even to get Jesus to offer him worship, during the temptations in the wilderness: showing Jesus "all the kingdoms of the world and their glory," Satan said, "All these I will give you, if you will fall down and worship me" (Matt. 4:8–9).

Christians can identify the false worship of Satan and his beast when it derives from raw power and earthly glory, acting contrary to God's Word and drawing people away from faith in Jesus. Whenever we are called to give unquestioned allegiance and worship to a human ruler, we should see him as the beast behind which stands Satan in his desperate bid to usurp God's throne. This is not to say that all government is evil. Paul used his Roman citizenship and was often helped by honest Roman officials. The beast is seen when government takes the place of God in our lives. Vern Poythress notes that in democratic countries, Satan wants people to "look to the state as if it were a messiah." When the government is set forth as "the remedy for all ills—economic, social, medical, moral, and even spiritual"—then the idolatry of the state usurps the place reserved for God alone.[10] Whenever we sing the secular doxology, "Praise the state from whom all blessings flow," we will soon be serving the beast.

John argues that the beast's idolatry will not be subtle, but will include blasphemies that call for his worship: "And the beast was given a mouth uttering haughty and blasphemous words, and it was allowed to exercise

10. Vern S. Poythress, *The Returning King: A Guide to the Book of Revelation* (Phillipsburg, NJ: P&R Publishing, 2000), 139.

369

authority for forty-two months. It opened its mouth to utter blasphemies against God" (Rev. 13:5–6). The beast may be a pagan who attacks biblical teaching or an atheist who crafts cunning arguments against God's existence. Today, secularists demand that science have the last word about everything, including morality and ultimate beliefs. The Roman emperors assumed God's place more flagrantly, issuing coins with their own supposedly divine image.

The beast also blasphemes throughout the church age against God's "dwelling, that is, those who dwell in heaven" (Rev. 13:6). The wicked slander Christians, as Nero did when he blamed them for Rome's great fire in A.D. 64. The beast will have his servants mock the Christian lifestyle, amplify the sins of every prominent believer, and ridicule even the most godly and holy Christian virtues as being foolish, vain, and ignorant. Dietrich Bonhoeffer, the Lutheran pastor who stood up to Hitler in Nazi Germany and was executed in a concentration camp, wrote: "The messengers of Jesus will be hated to the end of time. They will be blamed for all the divisions which rend cities and homes. Jesus and his disciples will be condemned on all sides for undermining family life, and for leading the nation astray; they will be called crazy fanatics and disturbers of the peace."[11]

The beast goes even further than blaspheming God and Christians. His first agenda is to acquire worship for himself and for Satan, and his second agenda is to violently persecute Christians when they refuse to give the worship that belongs only to God: "Also it was allowed to make war on the saints and to conquer them" (Rev. 13:7). Notice that it is against Christians as "saints," that is, "holy ones," that the beast makes war. This reminds us that it is not for our sins and many faults that the world hates us, but for God's saving work in our lives.

The Roman emperor's demand for worship connected John and his readers directly to Daniel and his friends in the court of the Babylonian despot Nebuchadnezzar, who set up a golden image of himself and required the entire nation to bow before it. When Daniel's faithful friends refused to commit idolatry, they were thrown into a raging furnace (Dan. 3:1–23). This pattern has continued in history: Wilmshurst writes: "Whether it was Roman emperors, the Hapsburgs during the Reformation years, Louis XIV, Stalin, or Idi Amin—where there has been a faithful church which refuses

11. Dietrich Bonhoeffer, *The Cost of Discipleship* (1937; repr., New York: Macmillan, 1959), 239.

to worship the beast, the beast makes war on them."[12] We should note that John states that the bestial tyrants will generally succeed: "It was allowed to make war on the saints and to conquer them" (Rev. 13:7). So it was in the Roman Empire in the century after the apostle John: throughout the empire, persecuted Christians were driven underground while idolatry flourished everywhere. So it was in China when the Communists imprisoned virtually every Christian preacher. So it soon may be in the once-Christian West, where the advancement of moral perversions threatens to make merely reading the Bible a criminal activity.

Moreover, the beast has authority "over every tribe and people and language and nation, and all who dwell on earth will worship it" (Rev. 13:7–8). Satan's beast will entrench his influence in every corner of the world and every segment of society, ultimately gaining the worship of all who are not protected by faith in Christ. An analogy to the beast's network may be seen in the terrorist cells of al Qaeda in the early years of the twenty-first century, whose bloody web shed blood through bombings in East Africa, Arabia, Morocco, Indonesia, central Asia, Turkey, New York, Madrid, and London. "Al Qaeda is an organization that aims for nothing less than worldwide domination, where everyone will have one or two choices: to submit to it, or to be destroyed by it."[13] It is a fitting representative of the beast out of the sea, who advances Satan's idolatrous cause everywhere with demonic power and authority.

This Is the Victory!

John records his vision of the beast to warn believers of what to expect, starting with the churches of Asia that faced the bestial Roman emperor Domitian. John concludes with three applications: first, our source of hope; second, our calling in persecution; and third, the victory we win through perseverance in faith.

Where can Christians find hope for salvation against so dreadful a beast, who exercises worldwide dominion and authority? The answer is in the sovereign God who has ultimate dominion and authority over this world, over Satan and his beast, and over our lives. Notice that the beast is dependent

12. Wilmshurst, *The Final Word*, 164.
13. Ibid., 160.

on what is permitted to him: he was "allowed" to war on the saints and "was given" authority over the nations (Rev. 13:7). These things are not said of a true sovereign! God is the true Sovereign, and he employs even Satan and his beast for his own holy purposes, which include the judgment of the unbelieving world.

Most importantly, John reminds us that believers are eternally secure in God's sovereign will. He says that everyone will worship the beast, that is, "everyone whose name has not been written before the foundation of the world in the book of life of the Lamb who was slain" (Rev. 13:8). This verse teaches that all who believe on Jesus Christ as Lord and Savior were predestined by God to be saved and had their names written "before the foundation of the world in the book of life." It is by sovereign grace that anyone's name is in this book, the result of which is eternal life. Such a person belongs to Jesus Christ, "the Lamb who was slain." Christ's atoning death "made the book of life possible, for it was the slain Lamb that became the sacrifice for sin and enabled the people of God to have 'life.'"[14] By trusting in Christ for salvation and worshiping God alone through him, we can know that our souls are eternally secure, having our names in his eternal book, and thus that we will be kept from worshiping the beast.

Once, when Jesus' disciples reported that they had been able to cast out demons, Jesus urged them not to rejoice in this, but rather to "rejoice that your names are written in heaven" (Luke 10:20). What matters is our eternal destiny, not our temporal afflictions! God is sovereign over everything that happens, and his wisdom guides both our joys and our trials. What matters about you is therefore not your earthly setting—your wealth, position, acceptance in society, power, or influence—but that your name is written in the Book of Life. We can know this in only one way, by trusting Jesus as Son of God and Savior, being cleansed of our sins by the blood of the Lamb who was slain.

With God's sovereign will providing hope to suffering Christians, John next directs us to our humble calling: "If anyone is to be taken captive, to captivity he goes; if anyone is to be slain with the sword, with the sword must he be slain" (Rev. 13:10). Christ's people are told that we can expect captivity and wrongful arrest, so when this happens we should embrace it as our calling as witnesses for Christ. Even if we are slain as martyrs, this

14. Osborne, *Revelation*, 503.

is God's calling for our gospel testimony. This calling does not preclude us from taking prudent steps to avoid persecution, but it does mean that when persecution comes, Christians must embrace it with faith and a resolve to do God's will.

We are reminded of the letter God sent to the exiles in Babylon through the prophet Jeremiah. In the letter, God said that they should embrace their exile as God's plan for their ultimate salvation. He reminded them, "I know the plans I have for you, declares the LORD, plans for welfare and not for evil, to give you a future and a hope" (Jer. 29:11). Even when Christians are led to slaughter, we are to remember God's will through the death of Jesus and understand that victory is at hand. "In all these things," Paul wrote, speaking of the suffering and slaughter of believers, "we are more than conquerors through him who loved us" (Rom. 8:36–37).

John concludes this passage with one of Revelation's many stirring appeals to perseverance in faith despite all affliction: "Here is a call for the endurance and faith of the saints" (Rev. 13:10). Satan and his beast, together with their followers, think us defeated when we are put down in persecution, yet through perseverance in faith Christians have the victory through Jesus Christ. John emphasized this same principle at the end of his first epistle: "This is the victory that has overcome the world—our faith" (1 John 5:4).

I mentioned how Rome drove the Christians underground in the second and third centuries. Yet in the fourth century, the emperor himself bent the knee to Christ. I mentioned how the Communists in China arrested all the preachers. But those preachers spent twenty years in prison praying, and returned with an evangelistic power that caused the gospel to sweep the country. One of the greatest examples of triumph through persevering faithfulness was given by Daniel's friends, who refused to bow down to Nebuchadnezzar's golden idol. They were thrown into the blazing furnace, yet they were not consumed, as everyone thought would happen. Instead, Nebuchadnezzar saw them, unhurt, being accompanied by One whose appearance was "like a son of the gods" (Dan. 3:25).

Christ comes to his faithful suffering people with blessing and power. When we possess Christ by faith, despite all persecution, we gain eternal life, justification by grace, adoption as God's children, and an inheritance in glory. With these eternal blessings we also have his daily help, when we refuse to yield to the beast but persevere in faith. Jesus encourages us through Isaiah:

Fear not, for I have redeemed you;
    I have called you by name, you are mine.
When you pass through the waters, I will be with you;
    and through the rivers, they shall not overwhelm you;
when you walk through fire you shall not be burned,
    and the flame shall not consume you.
For I am the LORD your God,
    the Holy One of Israel, your Savior. (Isa. 43:1–3)

35

THE MARK OF THE BEAST

Revelation 13:11—18

*Also it causes all, both small and great, both rich and poor, both
free and slave, to be marked on the right hand or the forehead,
so that no one can buy or sell unless he has the mark, that is, the
name of the beast or the number of its name.* (Rev. 13:16–17)

*T*he movie *Valkyrie* tells the story of Major General Henning
von Tresckow and Colonel Claus von Stauffenberg, two of
the principal figures in the German conspiracy to assassinate
Adolf Hitler. Christians such as Tresckow and Stauffenberg had come to
recognize Hitler's beastly evil. Despite the oath of unconditional obedience
that they had sworn to him as Germany's supreme leader, Tresckow began
plotting Hitler's assassination early in the war. In 1941 and 1943 he put
together murder attempts that failed because of unexpected errors or sudden changes in Hitler's plans. In July 1944, his best attempt on Hitler's life
took place when Stauffenberg, a staff officer in the high command, placed
a briefcase bomb right under the dictator's feet. After Stauffenberg left the
room, another officer moved the briefcase to the other side of the table.
When the bomb went off, the stout wood of the briefing table saved Hitler's
life. Soon after, Stauffenberg and Tresckow were both dead.

These two Christians are worthy of admiration for their courage. We can sympathize with their frustration as God himself seemed to thwart their bloody efforts to remove a tyrant. Yet if they had consulted the book of Revelation more carefully, they might have discovered reasons for God's refusal to help their conspiracy. The Bible does not tell Christians who wage spiritual warfare against satanic powers of tyranny and deceit to respond with their own brand of deceit and terror. We may trust that Tresckow and Stauffenberg were justified before God by the atoning blood of Christ. But declaring obedience to Hitler and then using positions of trust to attempt to murder him will find no endorsement in the Bible. In the long run, their achievement was not in killing a monstrous tyrant but simply in being willing to face death as committed followers of Christ. That such heroic Christians struggled to respond biblically to a satanic beast like Hitler proves the apostle John's words at the end of chapter 13: our struggle with the dragon and his beasts "calls for wisdom" (Rev. 13:18).

THE SECOND BEAST AS FALSE PROPHET

The first half of Revelation 13 showed that Satan is not alone in his dragon-like warfare against Christ's church. Summoning a beast from the sea, Satan gave him power to rule on the earth. The first beast represents government tyranny working in history against Christ and his church. The second half of the chapter shows that this first beast is also not alone. He is joined by a second beast who rises "out of the earth" (Rev. 13:11). If the sea beast represented the tyrannical power of Rome that arrived in Asia out of the sea, the beast from the earth represents local forces that collaborated with Rome. If the sea beast stands for vicious tyranny, the land beast is the propagandist who encourages people to worship him. Revelation 16:13 identifies this second beast as "the false prophet." Whereas the first beast relied mainly on power, the second beast supports him with lies. J. Ramsey Michaels writes: "The relationship between the two beasts is like that between the state and a state church. The beast from the sea is a secular political power, while the beast from the earth is a religious institution fostering worship of the first beast."[1]

1. J. Ramsey Michaels, *Revelation*, IVP New Testament Commentary 20 (Downers Grove, IL: InterVarsity Press, 1997), 164.

When we speak of false religion, we should refer to this in the broadest sense of all ideology that supports unbelief and idolatry. Steve Wilmshurst sees this beast represented in "the Communism of the Soviet Union, with its spectacular parades through Red Square, . . . its party card for the privileged. . . . He is Nazism, with its Nuremberg rallies and its Hitler Youth[;] . . . the statues of Saddam which infested Iraq; the wall posters of Chairman Mao."[2] We should add to this the biased media in America that covers up the horrors of abortion, ceaselessly promotes sexual immorality, and misses no opportunity to heap scorn on Bible-believing Christianity.

In describing the second beast, John reports that it "had two horns" (Rev. 13:11). We remember that this section of Revelation began with a vision of the church in the form of two witnesses who bear testimony to Christ in this age. They are slain by the beast but rise again (11:3–11). The false prophet is their satanically inspired counterfeit, who combats the gospel with subtle philosophies and false religions that promote the cause of the beast and the dragon. The second beast "exercises all the authority of the first beast in its presence, and makes the earth and its inhabitants worship the first beast" (13:12).

John would have known this beast in the form of local provincial "elites, in city after city and province after province, who do their best not only to copy the monster at a local level but insist, in order to keep the monster's favour, that everybody in their domain should worship the monster."[3] Because of Rome's success, the leaders of Asia could not do enough to placate, imitate, and honor the imperial Caesars. In many cases, it was not the emperor who demanded worship, but the local leaders who erected idols and temples to him, vying with one another for the privilege of the most fervent imperial idolatry, to which they compelled their subjects.

Not only do the two horns form a contrast with the image of the church as two witnesses, but there is a clear parody of Christ: "It had two horns like a lamb" (Rev. 13:11). Christ rules for the good of his people, with a spirit of grace. The false prophet comes across in this way, but its actual speech is "like a dragon" (13:11). Here is the wolf in sheep's clothing about which Jesus warned us (Matt. 7:15), who teaches the doctrines of the world rather

---

2. Steve Wilmshurst, *The Final Word: The Book of Revelation Simply Explained* (Darlington, UK: Evangelical Press, 2008), 166–67.

3. N. T. Wright, *Revelation for Everyone* (Louisville: Westminster John Knox, 2011), 120. For a more extensive description of the political climate in the Asian province, see G. B. Caird, *The Revelation of St. John the Divine* (San Francisco: Harper, 1966), 171.

than the truths of God's Word. This reminds Christians not to be taken in by the outward impression of public figures, but to consider carefully what they say and do in light of the Bible. The beast represents pastors, college professors, politicians, songwriters, or media pundits who cultivate a seductive image in order to gain a hearing for a satanic message.

The second beast urges people to worship the first beast, "whose mortal wound was healed" (Rev. 13:12). This represents the world's false gospel of power and pleasure through rebellion to God. In the garden, Satan beguiled Eve into sinning; the second beast speaks with the same sin-promoting and God-blaspheming voice, urging people to make their own messiah, forge a sin-condoning salvation, and gain freedom through soul-destroying slavery to the beast.

THE SECOND BEAST AS DECEITFUL WONDER-WORKER

John forewarns that false prophets will speak deceptively to lead people into serving the first beast and its tyranny. The second beast also employs signs and wonders in this same cause: "It performs great signs, even making fire come down from heaven to earth in front of people, and by the signs that it is allowed to work in the presence of the beast it deceives those who dwell on earth, telling them to make an image for the beast that was wounded by the sword and yet lived" (Rev. 13:13–14).

Magicians and their crafts were commonplace in the Asian provinces where John's readers lived, and their chief employers were provincial pagan temples. Craig Keener cites ancient church sources who tell of moving statues, fireball explosions, and pagan magicians who could make idols appear to speak.[4] By these means, the second beast again parodies the witnessing church. Revelation 11 compared the church's witness to that of Moses and Elijah (Rev. 11:6). Here, the miracles associated with these great Old Testament figures are counterfeited by the second beast. Elijah cast fire down from heaven (1 Kings 18:37–39), and Moses performed many wonders in the presence of beastly Pharaoh (Ex. 7:9–12). G. K. Beale writes that "various pseudo-magical tricks, including ventriloquism, false lightning, and other such phenomena, . . . were effectively used in temples of John's time."[5]

---

4. Craig S. Keener, *Revelation*, NIV Application Commentary (Grand Rapids: Zondervan, 1999), 351.

5. G. K. Beale, *The Book of Revelation: A Commentary on the Greek Text*, New International Greek Testament Commentary (Grand Rapids: Eerdmans, 1999), 711.

All through Revelation, "those who dwell on earth" are people who live in sin and unbelief. The second beast deceives them into making "an image for the beast" (Rev. 13:14). Most sophisticated ancient people did not believe that idols were themselves gods, but rather thought them conduits by which the gods communicated with their servants. Through trickery, and apparently by supernatural powers that Satan was permitted to exert, these wonders promoted the prestige of idol-worship. John emphasizes the myth of the first beast's being "wounded by the sword and yet" living (13:14). We saw in the previous chapter that the "death and resurrection" of the beast likely glamorizes the renewal of Satan's and Rome's power after the victorious first coming of Christ. With pagan Rome flush with victory and earthly glory, the marvels displayed by pagan charlatans presented a compelling image of deity that captivated many worldly people into false worship.

Today, instead of cheap magic tricks, the advances of science and the achievements of government are hailed as proof of the false gospel of secular humanism. Vern Poythress writes: "Technology, then, becomes the worker of miraculous signs. . . . Worship the power of the Beast, the power of technocratic state organization, the power of the expert, because technology can work wonders like no one else."[6] In the news broadcasts, in public schools, and in movies and television, a utopian message calls us to progress beyond the narrow thinking of the Bible, with its God, its salvation, and its holy lifestyle. Of course, they never point out the reality of societal breakdown and the soul-crushing bondage of sin, since the false prophet's goal is the world's worship of a tyrannical beast and his slave-master lord, the dragon. Paul Gardner writes: "Man replaces God and Christ with himself, and in doing so succumbs to the full deception of the beast."[7]

THE SECOND BEAST AS PERSECUTOR

The beast from the earth serves the beast from the sea by false teaching and deceptive signs and wonders. Yet it could hardly be said to exercise the beast's authority if it did not also employ deadly compulsion and persecution. This is the third approach by which the second beast advances the worship

---

6. Vern S. Poythress, *The Returning King: A Guide to the Book of Revelation* (Phillipsburg, NJ: P&R Publishing, 2000), 145.

7. Paul Gardner, *Revelation: The Compassion and Protection of Christ*, Focus on the Bible (Tain, Ross-shire, Scotland: Christian Focus, 2008), 184.

of the first beast and the dragon. It persuades its followers to "cause those who would not worship the image of the beast to be slain" (Rev. 13:15). Furthermore, it causes everyone "to be marked on the right hand or the forehead, so that no one can buy or sell unless he has the mark, that is, the name of the beast or the number of its name" (13:16–17).

In writing to Pergamum, Jesus noted that a Christian named Antipas had already been slain for his faith (Rev. 2:13). Thus, murder was probably done by local authorities who wanted to display loyalty to Caesar and zeal for his cult. The situation is similar today in northern Nigeria and the Middle East, where fanatical Muslims show their zeal for Allah by bombing Christian churches and beheading converts to Christ. The point is not that all Christians are slain under the influence of the second beast, but that worshipers of false religions will often display their zeal with violence against true religion. Along with deadly force, the beast also enforces false worship by requiring everyone to receive the mark of the beast. John states that all face this requirement: small and great, rich and poor, free and slave (13:16). No class of person can evade the obligation of displaying allegiance and submission to the state tyranny of the first beast.

Popular end-times books describe the mark of the beast as something yet to appear, often a technology to implant a computer chip that will control all commerce. There are abundant reasons to believe, however, that John is referring to a phenomenon common to his own age. The Greek word for *mark* is *charagma*, a term used for the emperor's seal on official documents. In this light, the mark of the beast "alludes to the state's political and economic 'stamp of approval,' given only to those who go along with its religious demands."[8]

In the Roman world, slaves were sometimes tattooed on the forehead to mark their ownership. Similarly, the beast's mark claims those who worship him as his property. Soldiers received marks on the hand to show their allegiance to a certain general; likewise, the mark of the beast shows one's devotion as a follower.[9] John uses these examples from his own culture to make the point about what the mark of the beast involves. Deuteronomy 6:8 tells God's people to bind God's Word on their hands and before their eyes, the point of which is that we are to think and act biblically. Likewise,

---

8. Beale, *Revelation*, 715.
9. Keener, *Revelation*, 353.

the beast demands not so much a tattoo on the forehead but a mind that thinks the way he says to think. He does not care about brands on the hands so much as deeds that mimic his own evil ways.

These examples show that the mark of the beast is not something that one accidentally receives. Primarily, it is a formal acceptance of total allegiance to a person or earthly entity, rendering a devotion that only God deserves to receive. This allegiance will usually be marked with some formal recognition, such as the Nazi armband, or earn special privileges, such as those given to Communist party members in China. A notable example is recorded in the intertestamental book 3 Maccabees, which recounts how the Egyptian tyrant Ptolomy IV Philopater demanded that the Jews offer pagan sacrifices. Those who refused were put to death. Those who relented were branded with an ivy-leaf symbol for Dionysos, the Greek god of wine and sensual indulgence. Bearing this mark afforded willing Jews all the privileges of citizenship in Ptolomy's realm (3 Macc. 2:28–30).

While receiving the beast's mark is never accidental, the process may be subtle. The aristocratic officers of the German army did not vow unconditional loyalty to Adolf Hitler because they admired him. Mainly, they were motivated by patriotism and career ambitions. Later, they felt trapped by their oath into committing atrocities that they themselves knew would bring ruin to their country. In America today, businesspeople may "sell their souls" to the company out of lust for success. Some people fail to profess faith in Christ because of loyalty to family expectations. Some youths wear the tattoos of a street gang or of a rock group that they religiously follow, swearing heart and soul to the gang or the band or the subculture.

Ultimately, the mark of the beast involves a choice between the world and Christ. There is an obvious contrast between this mark and the mark that Christ's people received in chapter 7. There, suffering believers were "sealed . . . on their foreheads" as the servants of God (Rev. 7:3). Having already sought to counterfeit Christ, Satan now parodies God's sealed church with his own mark-bearing legions.

In John's day, the mark of the beast provided another way to persecute believers: "No one can buy or sell unless he has the mark, that is, the name of the beast or the number of its name" (Rev. 13:17). The Christians in the church at Pergamum could not join trade guilds without accepting idol-worship and cultic prostitution (2:14). This practically meant that

Christians there could not hold well-paying jobs. Christian businesses today may be closed down for refusing to fund abortion through their insurance. Christian military officers may forfeit promotion because they refuse to hide their faith. The point is that the beast paints Christians as being disloyal to the governing regime because of our higher allegiance to Jesus. As a result, Christians are forced to the periphery of public life, unable to be elected to office or operate small businesses. In the ancient world where the emperor's certificate was required at the marketplace, the beast might literally reduce believers to starvation. In Revelation 2:9, Jesus said that he was aware of what his people were suffering: "I know your tribulation and your poverty," Jesus stated, "but you are rich." "Be faithful unto death," he added, "and I will give you the crown of life" (2:10). How relevant are these words to so many Christians who lose out in this present world for Christ's sake, but gain an inheritance in glory with him in the world to come.

THE TWO BEASTS: A CALL FOR WISDOM

John concludes this dramatic chapter with the point of his teaching: "This calls for wisdom" (Rev. 13:18). Looking back to chapter 12, with the vision of the dragon at war with the church, and then in chapter 13 with the tyrannical beast aided by false and beguiling ideology, we see that Christians need to be very wise. We must be wise in discerning the difference between true and false prophets, by paying careful attention to God's Word. We must be wise in expecting to pay a price for our faith. All through Revelation, Jesus has promised salvation blessings only to those who persevere in faith and overcome spiritual warfare through their witness to him.

John has a final form of wisdom in mind in the final verse. This is the wisdom that enables Christians to see the enemy for what he is, so that we will not be beguiled by his deceits or intimidated by his threats. The entire Bible bears testimony to God's faithfulness in saving his people from spiritual attacks. Our wisdom thus calls us not to shrink back in our witness out of temptation or fear. John makes this point with the most well-known and most widely contested verse in this chapter: "This calls for wisdom: let the one who has understanding calculate the number of the beast, for it is the number of a man, and his number is 666" (Rev. 13:18).

Many commentators suppose that 666 is a coded reference using an ancient practice known as *gematria*. Languages such as Greek and Hebrew did not have numbers, so letters were assigned numerical values: some single digits, others tens, and still others hundreds. The idea is that John is enabling us to identify the Antichrist, or first beast, because the letters of his name in Greek add up to 666. Using this and similar systems, Christians in recent years have argued that Ronald Reagan is the Antichrist, since each of his three names had six letters. The American statesman Henry Kissinger was long considered an Antichrist candidate, not only because of his labors for a secular world peace but also because the letters of his last name add up to 666 in the Greek system. The problem is that by this approach there is virtually no limit to Antichrist candidates. One commentator fancifully made a case for Barney, the children's television figure, since the words *cute purple dinosaur* yield the calculation 666.[10]

The person most commonly associated with 666 is the Roman emperor Nero. By translating the name Caesar Nero into Hebrew, the letters add up correctly, so that some scholars see John's 666 as a code name for Nero. The point is that like him, the beast will be a popular but depraved despot who launches violent persecutions against Christians. The problem with the approach is that John's readers, being Greek converts, did not likely speak Hebrew, which this theory requires. Moreover, one must slightly misspell *Caesar* for the numbers to add up. These factors make the Nero theory unlikely.

A better approach to unpacking this number is to understand the symbolism of six. We have often encountered seven in Revelation as a number of completion and perfection (Rev. 1:11, 12, 20; 3:1). Six falls short of this number and is therefore imperfect, incomplete, and defective. This describes fallen mankind, which is why John says that this is "the number of a man" (13:18). The dragon and his two beasts set themselves forward as a fake divine trinity. God's judgment and Christ's victory will reveal them as a triple fakery and threefold failure. G. K. Beale writes that "six repeated three times indicates the completeness of sinful incompleteness found in the beast. The beast epitomizes imperfection, while appearing to achieve divine perfection."[11]

10. Ibid., 359.
11. Beale, *Revelation*, 722.

It turns out that the word *beast* in Greek (*therion*) calculates to 666. Interestingly, the name *Jesus* calculates to 888. If this was at least part of John's message, the meaning is clear: whereas Jesus superabounds in perfection (7 + 1), the beast falls short as a defective impostor (7 − 1). From this point of view, John's meaning seems to be that while Christians need to know about the two beasts, we should not take them as seriously as we might be tempted to do. Yes, they dominate this present age of the world and are able to persecute us. But in the end, the beast is doomed for failure and judgment in the lake of fire (Rev. 19:20). Whereas Christ's reign will be eternal, the beasts are mortal, and in the long run their reign will be seen to have been short-lived, permitted by God only so long as it served his purposes in judgment and redemption. Those who bear the mark of the beast partake of the failure that his name and number imply. But those who reject the beast, even under persecution, and hold fast to the perfect name of Christ will partake of his character and blessings.

One man who became wise to the beast was Boris Kornfeld, a doctor in a labor camp operated by the Soviet Union. A Christian had told him the gospel of Jesus Christ. Kornfeld was convicted of his sin, especially his hatred for the guards and for the way he had collaborated in evil, and he longed for the forgiveness that Jesus offered. When the Christian was transferred, Kornfeld turned to Jesus in faith. For some time he told no one. Yet his new allegiance required him to refuse to engage in corruption, and he began doing what he could to protect the weak and afflicted in the camp.

One night, Kornfeld was helping a patient who was recovering from a painful cancer operation. He decided that he would no longer be kept silent by fear of the Communist authorities. The words began spilling out, and he told his story about coming to faith in Christ and how God's grace had changed him. After bearing this testimony and putting the patient to sleep, Kornfeld went to his nearby room for the night. While he slept he was attacked, his skull was crushed by a hammer blow, and he died for refusing to serve the beast any longer.

Did Kornfeld's witness matter, and was his commitment to Christ worth losing his life? The answer is given by the patient who heard his last words. His name was Alexander Solzhenitsyn, and he later wrote: "Kornfeld's prophetic words were his last words on earth. And, directed to me, they lay upon me as an inheritance."[12] He realized that the mark of the beast can be renounced for the saving seal of faith in Christ. He pondered the witness and ultimately believed in Christ, was changed by God's grace, and began walking in faith. In years to come, Solzhenitsyn's writings would shake the Communist system. His famous books not only disclosed the beastly inhumanity of the Soviet system but gave light to many of the Christian hope of salvation.

John says that understanding that we are opposed by a deadly triad of Satan, together with the tyrants and false prophets who serve him, calls for wisdom among Christians. The wisdom is not how to strike back at the beast with his own weapons but how to boldly declare the gospel message of Christ. The wisdom is not how to evade the beast's tyranny but how to persevere in Christian courage and commitment. Having the beast's number, knowing his limitations and his certain defeat, we can live without fear of his assault. Even his hammer blows can do nothing but send us into the loving arms of the victorious Christ. Knowing Jesus, calculating the infinite value of his cross, and trusting his perfection in glory and salvation, we are made bold to tell others about him. John's intent is that what the angel said of the victorious believers in chapter 12 would be said of us as we triumph in faith: "They have conquered him by the blood of the Lamb and by the word of their testimony, for they loved not their lives even unto death" (Rev. 12:11).

12. See Alexander Solzhenitsyn, *The Gulag Archipelago* (New York: Harper, 1974), 310.

36

SINGING THE NEW SONG

Revelation 14:1–5

Then I looked, and behold, on Mount Zion stood the Lamb,
and with him 144,000 who had his name and his Father's name
written on their foreheads. (Rev. 14:1)

*J*ohn Bunyan's *Pilgrim's Progress* is widely considered the most-read book in the English language, after the Bible. This spiritual classic is well beloved to Christians because of its biblical accuracy in depicting the challenges of the life of faith. I suggest that another reason for *Pilgrim's Progress*'s popularity is its vision of the hope of heaven. Despite the challenges posed by the Slough of Despond, Vanity Fair, the dragon Apollyon, and Doubting Castle, every time you read the book Christian succeeds in reaching his goal by faith.

Revelation was written to convey this same message of hope to John's first-century readers. We realize this in the vision that begins chapter 14. Here, John repeats an earlier vision of the 144,000 redeemed saints, who were seen in chapter 7 amid the world's persecutions and calamities. Now the redeemed church has reached the glorified Christ. After the deadly warfare portrayed in chapters 12 and 13, chapter 14 begins: "Behold, on Mount Zion stood the Lamb" (Rev. 14:1).

Like *Pilgrim's Progress*, Revelation 14 assures struggling Christians that their perseverance in faith will lead to salvation. The reason for our confidence is not our prowess in slaying dragons or wrestling beasts, but that Jesus Christ, the Lamb who was slain, stands exalted in sovereign authority on the heavenly Zion. Simon Kistemaker writes: "The Lamb . . . stands majestically on Mount Zion as the Victor over all the anti-Christian forces in the world. Thus the saints must take heart and not despair, for they share in the victory of the Lamb."[1]

THE IDENTITY OF THE REDEEMED

In John 10:28, Jesus promised that those who follow him in faith "will never perish, and no one will snatch them out of my hand." This doctrine is graphically depicted in the vision of the 144,000 gathered with the Lamb on Mount Zion. Last seen, this assembly was beset with many dangers in the great tribulation that is the church age, including the warfare of the dragon and his two beasts. From a worldly perspective, it might seem that none of them would arrive safely in heaven. Now on Mount Zion, we find that not one of them has been lost. John sees not 129,600, which would be a 90 percent success rate, or even 143,999, with only a single precious sheep's having perished. Instead, the exact number of those who begin the journey of salvation through faith arrive safely in his presence. In the terms of Psalm 23, every one of those who begins by saying, "The LORD is my shepherd" does in fact "dwell in the house of the LORD forever."

In presenting this view, we need to prove that the 144,000 represents the entirety of Christ's people: past, present, and future. Some would argue that this glorious gathering consists only of early church martyrs—those who died for their Christian testimony—or that it literally numbers ethnic Jews converted immediately before Christ's second coming. One way to show that the 144,000 stands for all believers is to see how it represents both the Old and New Testament eras. This number joins together the twelve tribes of Israel and the twelve apostles of Christ, twelve times twelve, multiplied by a thousand to depict "a great multitude that no one could number" (Rev. 7:9). Furthermore, the descriptions given to the 144,000 in this passage are true of the entirety of the people of Christ.

1. Simon J. Kistemaker, *Revelation*, New Testament Commentary (Grand Rapids: Baker, 2001), 400.

First, John identifies them as having "his [Christ's] name and his Father's name written on their foreheads" (Rev. 14:1). Previously, we were told that everyone, "both small and great, both rich and poor, both free and slave" (13:16), received the mark of the beast on the forehead and hand. This mark represented the mark-bearers' embrace of the anti-Christian world system in their thinking and deeds. The only exceptions are those whose names were "written before the foundation of the world in the book of life of the Lamb who was slain" (13:8). According to Revelation, there are only two kinds of people: those who bear the mark of the beast in service to Satan through sin and unbelief and those who bear the seal of God, belonging to him through faith in Christ. To see the 144,000 as those marked with the seal of God is to say that they represent the entirety of believers from all ages. G. K. Beale writes: "The number 144,000 connotes the completeness of God's true people, in antithesis to the 666 on the foreheads of the beast's followers, which connotes their incompleteness in achieving the divine design for humanity."[2]

If you sat down with a Christian and a non-Christian today, there would not be a visible mark to distinguish them. Revelation is speaking in symbols of the great spiritual reality that corresponds to faith or unbelief. To say that God's name is written on someone's forehead is a figurative way of stating that the person belongs to him and is protected by his presence. What an encouragement this should provide to every believer! Having believed on Jesus, you know that God has marked you as belonging to himself for all eternity! This is a corollary to Isaiah 49:16, where God declares that he has marked himself with your name: "Behold, I have engraved you on the palms of my hands." The reason that we can speak of eternal security for those who believe in Christ is God's sovereign determination to possess and protect all those whom he has claimed for himself.

The seal is furthermore an emblem of the allegiance of those who bear it: the 144,000 consists of those whose pledge has been given to God through Christ, in contrast to those who are loyal to the world and its beastly dominion. In this way, the vision shows that you are ultimately defined by your stance regarding Jesus. To embrace him in faith requires you to renounce your allegiance to the world and sin but ensures an eternal destiny with him in glory. To deny Christ and his gospel is to remain a slave to the world and sin, enjoy-

---

2. G. K. Beale, *The Book of Revelation: A Commentary on the Greek Text*, New International Greek Testament Commentary (Grand Rapids: Eerdmans, 1999), 733.

ing in this life the poisoned pleasures that they offer but in the day of Christ's return receiving the eternal punishment reserved for his rebellious enemies.

The 144,000 are also described as those "who had been redeemed from the earth" (Rev. 14:3). The Lamb is not standing with a spiritual elite from among believers or a future gathering of ethnic Jewish believers, but with all who have been redeemed from sin by the coin of his blood. How grateful we can be that this victory with Christ is not secured by our spiritual performance as believers, by the quantity or quality of our giftedness, or by the status we enjoy in the church or the world. Instead, our position of privilege with Christ, our value to him, and our participation in his salvation depends on the blood he shed for our sins. All Christians have the glorious identity of those redeemed "with the precious blood of Christ" (1 Peter 1:19).

John further describes the 144,000 as "firstfruits for God and the Lamb" (Rev. 14:4). This might identify them as the believers already in heaven in John's time or the band of early church martyrs, since the firstfruits were the initial portion of the harvest that symbolized the whole. Yet the Bible also speaks of firstfruits as all those who belong to God in contrast with the unbelieving world. James 1:18 describes Christians as the "firstfruits of his creatures," that is, that portion of humanity that is taken by God for his own possession, and Jeremiah 2:3 describes all Israel as "the firstfruits of his harvest."[3] Since the 144,000 are the redeemed who bear God's name, it seems best to take "firstfruits" as referring to those who are precious to God, who belong to him and are offered for his glory, that is, the entirety of Christ's people, in contrast to those polluted by idolatry in the world.

How can you be numbered in this glorious body? Simply by believing in Christ. John said that he wrote his Gospel "so that you may believe that Jesus is the Christ, the Son of God, and that by believing you may have life in his name" (John 20:31).

THE LOCATION OF THE REDEEMED

Having clarified the *identity* of the 144,000, we may consider their *location*. John saw them "on Mount Zion," with "the Lamb" (Rev. 14:1). Whereas

3. For the former view, see Sam Storms, *Kingdom Come: The Amillennial Alternative* (Tain, Ross-shire, Scotland: Christian Focus, 2013), 215. For the latter view, see J. Ramsey Michaels, *Revelation*, IVP New Testament Commentary 20 (Downers Grove, IL: InterVarsity Press, 1997), 170.

Satan, the dragon, "stood on the sand of the sea" (12:17) in calling forth the beasts to aid his rebellion, Jesus stands on the rock of God's holy mountain with his saints.

Scholars debate whether this Mount Zion is on earth or in heaven. The weight of evidence points to heaven, since Christ was last seen there (Rev. 7:9–14). Revelation 14:3 mentions "the four living creatures" and the twenty-four "elders," who serve before Christ's throne above. Yet the point is that Mount Zion is located at the end of history, at the place of salvation's completion. God said in Psalm 2:6, "I have set my King on Zion, my holy hill." This statement referred not merely to the Temple Mount in Jerusalem but to "the end-time city where God dwells with and provides security" for his people.[4] Seeing the vast multitude of the church present with Christ on Mount Zion, we know that our victory is established and secured.

By seeing the divinely ordained end of our salvation, John and his readers are encouraged as they face Roman persecution. His example urges Christians to think from the end of history back to our present trials. Rather than starting where we are in our weakness, doubt, and earthly affliction, looking forward from them with anxiety over our future prospects, we should reverse the process. We should instead fix our minds on the certainty of our future, on Mount Zion where the Lamb stands in victory, working back to find hope in our present trials.

The movie *Gettysburg* relates exploits of General John Buford, who commanded the Northern cavalry during that decisive battle of the Civil War. Buford had suffered through prior defeats when the Southerners enjoyed superior terrain. He therefore growled, "We must deny the high ground to the enemy," and his fighting advance guard enabled the Union army to occupy the heights. Christians need have no anxiety when it comes to our spiritual warfare against Satan, sin, and worldly opposition. As the clouds are parted in this vision, John is enabled to look up and see Christ standing on the mount. The Lamb holds the high ground eternally, looking down on the conflict below. Seeing Jesus standing on Zion, we are assured that all of God's promises to us will be fulfilled, that those who bear his name will be kept safe, and that our lives of faith will be crowned with success. Samuel Rutherford spoke on this theme with his dying words, which Anne Cousin recorded in song:

4. Beale, *Revelation*, 732.

The Lamb with his fair army doth on Mount Zion stand,
And glory, glory dwelleth in Emmanuel's land.[5]

The Character of the Redeemed

Those who bear God's name not only enjoy his protection but partake of his attributes. John's vision thus describes the *character* of the redeemed, urging that for believers "the ultimate question is not physical prowess, or political or economic power; it is a question of true spirituality."[6] Just as it is Christ who secures the victory for his people, it is Christlikeness that not only marks them out in the world but gives them power in spiritual warfare.

The first description of Christian character has perplexed many readers: "It is these who have not defiled themselves with women, for they are virgins" (Rev. 14:4). It would be possible to take this verse in a number of erroneous ways. For instance, the 144,000 might be thought of as a spiritual elite who gained their status through celibacy as a meritorious practice. Some feminist scholars have misused this verse to complain about the Bible's supposed antipathy for women.[7] Some might also draw a negative attitude to sexuality in general, since sexual relations seem to be described as defiling.

All of these views are mistaken. Taking the last first, the Bible teaches that sexual intimacy between a husband and wife is a holy gift from God designed to bind their hearts together in marriage. Sexual purity in the Bible involves both abstinence outside marriage and faithfulness in marriage. Hebrews 13:4 commands: "Let marriage be held in honor among all, and let the marriage bed be undefiled." It is adultery, not sex itself, that defiles the marriage bed. While Paul was grateful that his singleness enabled him to be highly focused in ministry (1 Cor. 7:7), many other apostles, including Peter, were accompanied by their wives on their missionary journeys (9:5). Paul not only uses marriage as a metaphor for the union of Christ and his church (Eph. 5:32), but stresses that sexual union is essential to marital faithfulness (1 Cor. 7:5). As for women in general, the Bible presents a positive view and often highlights their contributions to the kingdom work of Christ, not least as mothers and wives. One of John's most important

5. Anne R. Cousin, "The Sands of Time Are Sinking" (1857).
6. Douglas F. Kelly, *Revelation*, Mentor Expository Commentary (Tain, Ross-shire, Scotland: Mentor, 2012), 253.
7. Michaels, *Revelation*, 170.

designations for the church is that she is "prepared as a bride adorned for her husband" (Rev. 21:2).

How, then, do we avoid taking this statement as describing the 144,000 as celibate men, who have gained their status by maintaining their virginity? The answer, familiar now to our study of Revelation, lies in taking this statement symbolically. Philip Hughes writes, "The purity in question is that of spiritual faithfulness."[8] Leon Morris adds: "It means that the people in question have kept themselves completely free from intercourse with the pagan world system. They have lived up to what is implied in their betrothal to Christ."[9]

Spiritual purity cannot be separated from moral purity, of course. The apostles lived in a Roman world that was even more sexually debauched than the decadent West today. For this reason, the apostles placed a priority on sexual purity, requiring believers to engage in determined repentance from sexual sins. Paul added the encouraging message that Christians, having been purified in Christ, can regain our virginity when it has been lost. Although Paul condemned the sexually immoral, adulterers, and practicing homosexuals, he added: "And such were some of you. But you were washed, you were sanctified, you were justified in the name of the Lord Jesus Christ and by the Spirit of our God" (1 Cor. 6:9–11).

Not only do Christians have a moral obligation to observe spiritual purity, but this matter deeply affects us in spiritual warfare. John's language may, indeed, reflect the preparation of Israel for battle, in which the spiritual purity of soldiers was represented by abstinence from sexual relations (Deut. 23:10). The symbolism of the church—including men and women, single and married—as celibate soldiers "portrays the single-minded loyalty that we all owe to our captain."[10] We should note as well that chapter 14 goes on to speak of the whore "Babylon the great, she who made all nations drink the wine of the passion of her sexual immorality" (Rev. 14:8). Therefore, verse 4's emphasis on spiritual and moral purity contrasts with the state of those who have defiled themselves through adultery with the idolatrous world system.

8. Philip Edgcumbe Hughes, *The Book of Revelation* (Downers Grove, IL: InterVarsity Press, 1990), 159.

9. Leon Morris, *The Revelation of St. John: An Introduction and Commentary*, Tyndale New Testament Commentaries 20 (Grand Rapids: Eerdmans, 1969), 177.

10. Dennis E. Johnson, *Triumph of the Lamb: A Commentary on Revelation* (Phillipsburg, NJ: P&R Publishing, 2001), 203.

In addition to being pure, Christ's 144,000 are obedient: "It is these who follow the Lamb wherever he goes" (Rev. 14:4). Where Christ calls us to go we must go; what Christ calls us to do we must do. His way becomes our way, and though it may seem narrow, it leads to eternal life. Following Christ involves belief in his teaching, submission to his commands, and the zealous promotion of his gospel cause. As Christ sacrificed himself for us, we offer ourselves as living sacrifices in service to God, as is implied by our description as "firstfruits." Seeing the Lamb exalted on Mount Zion, we are reminded that following Jesus leads us to salvation and glory.

John's vision defines Christian character, third, in terms of truthful speech: "and in their mouth no lie was found" (Rev. 14:5). H. B. Swete writes: "After purity truthfulness was perhaps the most distinctive mark of the followers of Christ, when contrasted with their heathen neighbors."[11] The ninth commandment requires believers to speak truthfully, and among those whom Revelation 21:8 sees cast into the lake of fire are "all liars." Christian salvation stems from the truth of God's Word and produces lives of truth. Whereas the world "exchanged the truth about God for a lie" (Rom. 1:25), believers reject idolatry and actively promote the gospel truth by which liars and all other sinners may be redeemed. Beale comments: "What is in mind here is not merely general truthfulness, but the saints' integrity in witnessing to Jesus when they are under pressure from the beast and the 'false prophet' to compromise their faith."[12]

John summarizes that by this Christlike character the redeemed church is "blameless" (Rev. 14:5). The point is not that godly character merits salvation but rather that it enables us to serve God as acceptable sacrifices of thanks and praise. This outline of Christian character will enable believers to make a difference for Christ's kingdom: purity, obedience, and truthfulness. Only Jesus is blameless in being without any sin (see John 8:46). But as redeemed sinners, Christians should be able to commend our testimony to Christ with lives of spiritual integrity, power, and gospel courage. Douglas Kelly points out that these attributes are not like the world's weapons of mass destruction. Instead, they "are weapons of mass resurrection. . . . Ultimately, these spiritual qualities engendered by Jesus and his army, as he is standing on

---

11. Henry Barclay Swete, *Commentary on Revelation*, 2 vols. (1911; repr., Grand Rapids: Kregel, 1977), 2:180.

12. Beale, *Revelation*, 746.

mount Zion orchestrating it all, will overcome all the violence and wicked-ness of a Satanic world system."[13]

THE ACTIVITY OF THE REDEEMED

John's vision has shown us the identity, location, and character of Christ's redeemed church. His emphasis, finally, is on the *activity* of the redeemed, as they worship God and the Lamb in joyful song: "they were singing a new song before the throne" (Rev. 14:3).

John writes that he "heard a voice from heaven like the roar of many waters and like the sound of loud thunder" (Rev. 14:2). He is referring to the worship of the redeemed, since only the 144,000 can learn this song (14:3). Many Christians have reveled in the experience of singing together with a great worshiping crowd, either in a large church or at a Christian conference. The singing in glory will excel any such experience, booming with the roar of a waterfall and the sound of thunder, since it is done by "a great multitude that no one could number, from every nation, from all tribes and peoples and languages, standing before the throne and before the Lamb, clothed in white robes," as Revelation 7:9 described the 144,000. The singing is marked only not by volume, but also by heart-uplifted passion. John compares it to "the sound of harpists playing on their harps" (14:2). William Hendriksen writes that "although it will be majestic, sublime, constant, it will at the same time be the most lovely, sweet, and tender song you have ever heard."[14]

In a sermon on this text, Jonathan Edwards noted reasons why the saints in heaven glorify God so fervently. First, it is because they finally see God in his glory, and those "who see God cannot *but* praise Him. . . . Such a glorious sight will awaken and rouse all the powers of the soul, and will irresistibly impel and draw them into acts of praise." Second, the redeemed will then "be perfect in humility. . . . A proud person is for assuming all praise to himself. . . . It is humility only that will enable us to say from the heart, 'Not unto us, not unto us, O Lord, but unto Thy name be the glory.'" Third, our "love to God and Christ will be perfect. . . . The grace of love

---

13. Kelly, *Revelation*, 256.

14. William Hendriksen, *More than Conquerors: An Interpretation of the Book of Revelation* (1940; repr., Grand Rapids: Baker, 1967), 151.

will be exalted to its greatest height and highest perfection in heaven; and love will vent itself in praise. Heaven will ring with praise because it is full of love to God."[15] Edwards's explanation for heaven's praise provides us with an agenda for worshiping God more fully now on earth: by seeing him more clearly through the study of God in his Word, by humbling ourselves before his awesome and holy majesty, and by cultivating a love for God on the basis of his redeeming love for us in Jesus Christ.

John tells us that the redeemed on Mount Zion sing "a new song before the throne and before the four living creatures and before the elders" (Rev. 14:3). This shows that our worship is directed to God and to the Lamb, whose throne is surrounded by these glorious beings. We sing a "new song" not because we have discovered something different from the salvation message taught all through Scripture, but because our experience has provided fresh instances of its power and glory. In the Old Testament, the "new song" was sung in response to a fresh instance of God's salvation (Pss. 96:1; 144:9; etc.). When our deliverance has been fully accomplished, the new song will praise the Lamb who redeemed us with his blood and made us his kingdom of priests. Katherine Hankey writes:

And when, in scenes of glory, I sing the new, new song,
'Twill be the old, old story, that I have loved so long.[16]

Because the new song celebrates Christ as Redeemer, "no one could learn that song except the 144,000 who had been redeemed from the earth" (Rev. 14:3). This statement reminds me of an occasion when my family joined with a neighborhood gathering to sing Christmas carols. The crowd celebrated the whole range of redemptive theology, yet remained spiritually unmoved. They could learn the words and the tunes, but they could not enter into the wonder and glory. Only the Christian, who has tasted the bitterness of conviction for sin, knows the joy of the song of the redeemed in Christ. Only the struggling believer, suffering the barbs of the dragon, the beast, and the false prophet in this evil world, lifts up her heart with true joy at the sight of the Lamb standing on Mount Zion.

15. Jonathan Edwards, "Praise One of the Chief Employments of Heaven," in *Altogether Lovely: Jonathan Edwards on the Glory and Excellency of Jesus Christ* (Morgan, PA: Soli Deo Gloria, 1997), 215–20.
16. Katherine Hankey, "I Love to Tell the Story" (1866).

When They Began to Sing

In applying John's vision of the Lamb enthroned on Mount Zion, in which we see the identity, the location, the character, and the activity of the redeemed in glory, I think back to another situation that took place long before John wrote Revelation. Second Chronicles 20 tells of how the godly king Jehoshaphat received news of an onslaught of armies from the east. In worldly terms it was a hopeless situation, just as was the situation that John and his churches faced with the Roman emperor, and that the church has often faced since. But Jehoshaphat lifted his face to heaven and gathered all the people to pray for salvation. In reply, God told the king to take his soldiers and advance on the enemy in faith (2 Chron. 20:17). We read that Jehoshaphat took the army forth led by priests who were singing Psalm 118: "Give thanks to the Lord, for his steadfast love endures forever" (2 Chron. 20:21). The Bible tells what happened: "And when they began to sing and praise, the Lord set an ambush against the men of Ammon, Moab, and Mount Seir, who had come against Judah, so that they were routed" (20:22).

This example does not reason that the only Christian response to spiritual opposition is to hold a hymn-sing! It does mean, however, that if we take our eyes off the daunting opposition and fix them on the glory of our mighty Savior, seeing Christ standing on Mount Zion, we may be refreshed with spiritual power and hope. With such a vision, we will not fear to proclaim God's Word in sincerity and conviction, we will not think lightly about the power of prayer, and we will not allow our worship in Christ's name to be corrupted by the world. With Christ reigning sovereign in triumph, surely when we begin to sing and praise him in the presence of every earthly foe, relying confidently on his saving provision, we will not fail to see his victory and then rejoice to sing the new song in praise to our Redeemer.

37

THE HOUR OF HIS JUDGMENT

Revelation 14:6–12

And he said with a loud voice, "Fear God and give him glory,
because the hour of his judgment has come, and worship him
who made heaven and earth, the sea and the springs of water."
(Rev. 14:7)

One of the standard plotlines in science-fiction movies involves the discovery that life as it has been known is a lie. Often, humanity has been enslaved in a hedonistic utopia that in reality enslaves them. As an example, the movie *Logan's Run* tells of a future society that lives in a pleasure dome where the people do not realize that they will be terminated at age thirty. The hero, Logan 5, saves the race by connecting with an underground community that knows the truth and destroys the controller computer. In the blockbuster *The Matrix*, the captive human race is being used as an energy source by conquering machines. The matrix is a computer-simulated reality that distracts humans from their actual slavery.

The success of these movies might be explained by the book of Revelation, which points out the substantial truth they depict. It turns out that the human race is largely controlled by unseen evil powers who use sensual pleasures to hold us in bondage. Although we have embraced the idolatries of personal autonomy and hedonistic pleasure, we realize that something does not seem quite right. Satisfaction eludes us. Empowerment feels empty. We suspect that behind the veneer of secular humanism, dark powers are at work. Using its visionary images, Revelation depicts this kind of spiritual oppression. We face the dragon, Satan, who with his servant beasts controls the unbelieving world and wars against the countercultural Christian community that has discovered the truth.

In both science fiction and Revelation, knowing the truth creates a great longing for the evil powers somehow to be defeated. This is the situation depicted by three messenger angels who appear in Revelation 14:6–12. They pronounce the overthrow of evil powers, warning of judgment for those who reject Jesus Christ and eternal wrath for those who serve the beast. William Hendriksen writes that they "have one purpose, namely, to warn mankind with respect to the coming judgment in order that men may turn to God in true faith."[1]

SPIRITUAL INDIFFERENCE JUDGED

The first angel is seen "flying directly overhead, with an eternal gospel to proclaim to those who dwell on earth" (Rev. 14:6). Advertisers rent airplanes to fly messages over crowded beaches or sporting events. John sees something like this in his vision: an angel flying in sight of the entire world, bearing a message from heaven.

John describes the angel's message as a "gospel." This seems unusual, since he says nothing directly about Jesus, his death on the cross for sins, or his offer of salvation through faith. The message, in fact, is a warning: "the hour of his judgment has come" (Rev. 14:7). This message is good news to the persecuted church about the coming defeat of ungodly powers and thus her freedom from tyrants who afflict her. Derek Thomas writes: "The downfall of all that is contrary to the purposes of God is . . . good news for the believer."[2]

Here, the gospel is presented in the form of a call to repent. We should remember the way in which Jesus introduced his ministry in the Gospels.

1. William Hendriksen, *More than Conquerors: An Interpretation of the Book of Revelation* (1940; repr., Grand Rapids: Baker, 1967), 153.
2. Derek Thomas, *Let's Study Revelation* (Edinburgh: Banner of Truth, 2003), 120.

Mark 1:14–15 says that Jesus came to Galilee "proclaiming the gospel of God," in these terms: "The time is fulfilled, and the kingdom of God is at hand; repent and believe in the gospel." The coming of Jesus is the good news, calling for repentance and faith. Jesus spoke of the coming "kingdom of God," and the first angel declares that the "hour of his judgment" has come, which amounts to the same thing. He preaches his message to all "who dwell on earth" (Rev. 14:6). In Revelation, this expression refers to unbelieving people who ignore Jesus and are comfortable with sin. This unregenerate multitude covers the globe: "every nation and tribe and language and people" (14:6). The angel shows how God calls them all to take notice and heed the message of his Son's coming. The afflicted Christian church rejoices to know that her enemies either will be converted, joining their own ranks, or will be judged by God so as to deliver his people.

The fact that the angel refers to the gospel as "eternal" raises some interesting points. There is an important sense in which the gospel is *not* eternal. The very language of "good news" points out that something new has happened to change a bad situation into a good one. Christ has come into history to save us from sin. There are, however, three senses in which the gospel may indeed be called eternal. First, the gospel message of Christ has eternal consequences. This is the point of the angel's warning: Christ's return will bring the hour of judgment, at which those who have rejected his gospel will be condemned. Second, the gospel fulfills the eternal plan of God for displaying his glory in the salvation of sinners. The gospel brings a justification that is eternally valid and secure in Christ. Third, as Revelation has often shown, the gospel message of saving grace will be the subject of eternal praises from Christ's people in glory (Rev. 5:13; 14:3).

So significant is the gospel message in light of the coming judgment that it warrants a believing response from everyone. The angel "said with a loud voice, 'Fear God and give him glory, because the hour of his judgment has come'" (Rev. 14:7). Instead of showing indifference to God's claims, people should take God seriously and grant him the honor he deserves as universal Sovereign. When the Israelite Achan was confronted for stealing contraband from the wreckage of Jericho, Joshua urged him to "give glory to the Lord God of Israel and give praise to him" (Josh. 7:19). The point was that he should confess his guilt and humble himself before God. This is basic to the message that Christians speak to the world: "There is a God!

Grant him the glory he deserves! Appeal to his mercy for the forgiveness of your sins, and then honor him with your lives!"

The situation is like that of a man who sits on the seashore painting a gorgeous landscape. He is so engrossed in his painting that he fails to notice the tide that is coming in. As a result, he is drowned. Jesus spoke this way in comparing those who died in Noah's flood to the world when he returns to judge: "Just as it was in the days of Noah, so will it be in the days of the Son of Man. They were eating and drinking and marrying and being given in marriage, until the day when Noah entered the ark, and the flood came and destroyed them all" (Luke 17:26–27). The angel thus calls the world to look up, take heed of God, and worship him instead of the creation.

The first basis of our worship of God is his glory as the Creator: "Worship him who made heaven and earth, the sea and the springs of water" (Rev. 14:7). All creatures are obligated to give worship to the Maker of all things, and Scripture notes the offense that their spiritual indifference causes: "For although they knew God, they did not honor him as God or give thanks to him" (Rom. 1:21). In light of this, the angel issues "a call to the earth's inhabitants to awake to the reality of God's rule before it is too late."[3]

THE EVIL EMPIRE FALLEN

The first angel's having warned of judgment, the second angel shouts: "Fallen, fallen is Babylon the great" (Rev. 14:8). This cry introduces a new image to Revelation, yet one that apparently was widely understood in the early church. At the end of Peter's first epistle, he included particular greetings: "She who is at Babylon," a code phrase that most scholars believe refers to the city of Rome,[4] "sends you greetings" (1 Peter 5:13). The Roman Empire of John's time was like ancient Babylon, which destroyed Jerusalem, exiled the people of Israel, and persecuted them for observing their duties to God. Both Babylon and Rome are symbols of the world system and its rulers as they oppose God and his people. Just like the Jews of Daniel's day and the early Christians of John's time, believers today live in a kind of Babylon. In science-fiction movies, Babylon would stand for the evil machines that

3. Geoffrey B. Wilson, *New Testament Commentaries*, 2 vols. (Edinburgh: Banner of Truth, 2005), 2:552.

4. This interpretation is supported by ancient documents such as 2 Baruch 11:1 and Sibylline Oracles 5:143.

control a matrix of lies and deceit. In the real world, Babylon is "the spirit of godlessness which in every age lures men away from the worship of the Creator."[5]

It is interesting for Christians to watch movies or read novels in which the plot so closely mirrors the history told by God's Word. Often we find that people who reject the Bible are passionately drawn to the biblical narrative when it is presented in another form. An example is J. R. R. Tolkien's *The Lord of the Rings*, one of the most widely read novels of all time, with millions of passionate devotees, many of them non-Christians. Toward the end of the story, Tolkien tells of two heroic figures, Eowyn, the princess of Rohan, and Faramir, a prince of Gondor, who are recuperating from their wounds while their friends have marched out to fight the decisive battle. Their dreaded enemy is Sauron, the dark lord who resembles the Bible's Satan, and his evil kingdom of Mordor, which is a kind of Babylon that mocks and threatens all free people. Day after day, Faramir and Eowyn look east over the walls of Gondor's capital city toward where the final battle is to take place. Finally a giant eagle is seen falling down from the sky, not unlike the angel that John saw flying in heaven with his good news. The eagle's message of joy is taken almost straight out of Revelation: "Sing now, ye people of the Tower of Anor, for the Realm of Sauron is ended for ever, and the Dark Tower is thrown down."[6]

Those who love Tolkien's fantasy literature should be thrilled to find that the giant eagle's cry reflects the true message of Revelation: "Fallen, fallen is Babylon the great" (Rev. 14:8). This message speaks of the future when Christ returns, assuring us of the certainty of the downfall of the evil empire that has tormented the world. Hallelujah, the dark lord Satan will be cast down!

Rome and Babylon were known not only for tyrannical oppression but also for the sinful seduction of surrounding nations. Babylon "made all nations drink the wine of the passion of her sexual immorality" (Rev. 14:8). We will learn more in chapters to come about Babylon as the great harlot of Revelation. For now, we learn that the evil world system not only oppressed people in bondage but also seduced them into soul-destroying sin. The original Babylon stood not only for power and violence, but also for luxury

---

5. Robert H. Mounce, *Revelation*, rev. ed., New International Commentary on the New Testament (Grand Rapids: Eerdmans, 1997), 274.

6. J. R. R. Tolkien, *The Return of the King* (New York: Houghton Mifflin, 1955), 942.

and sexual indulgence. If people could not beat Babylon, they would be easily led into imbibing the wine of its pleasure. Jeremiah described Babylon as "a golden cup in the Lord's hand, making all the earth drunken; the nations drank of her wine; therefore the nations went mad" (Jer. 51:7). In John's time, the same could be said of sexually indulgent Roman society. In our time, it is America and the other decadent Western nations that export sexually permissive values and provide the appetite that fuels a vast global network of prostitution and pornography. The fall of Babylon provides a sober warning of what will happen to America if it does not repent of its sin.

This second angel warns of God's judgment on those who drink from Babylon's cup. Revelation 14:8 speaks of "the wine of the passion of her sexual immorality." The word for *passion* is the Greek word for *wrath* (*thumos*), in this case referring to corruption and stupefaction. The destructive power of sexual immorality compares to the stupor brought on by drunkenness from alcohol. Those who give themselves over to sexual indulgence destroy their capacity for the purity and joy that God designed for sex in the context of marital love. This is why Proverbs warns young men to shun the seductions of the harlot, whose true purpose is to drag her victims into hell (Prov. 9:13–18).

Western society is awash in sexual sin. Virtually everything—from light bulbs to sports cars—is sold by sexual innuendo. Women find their worth calculated solely in terms of sexual appeal. Men are bombarded by images designed to send a hook through the eyes that will snare the heart for evil. What good news it is to hear of Babylon falling! The harlot who seduces so many and whose temptations afflict even God's people will be cast down when our Savior returns!

Many Christians find their struggle against the harlot Babylon to be difficult, but the angel's message pertains primarily to those who are not struggling but are lustfully indulging in sexual sin. Grant Osborne writes that the imagery of drinking the cup "refers to a participation in a lifestyle or destiny."[7] We think of young people who give themselves over to the debauchery seen on college campuses, or the legions of men whose unrestrained indulgence has made the sex trade a multibillion-dollar business. This distinction is important because Christians who have been tripped up in sexual sin but have repented, and even those who struggle sincerely

---

7. Grant R. Osborne, *Revelation*, Baker Exegetical Commentary on the New Testament (Grand Rapids: Baker Academic, 2002), 538.

but with great difficulty in this area, should not think that they are lost. Christians should take such struggles very seriously, for sexual temptation may lead to a lifestyle that ends in destruction. Meanwhile, all of a believer's sins are cleansed by Christ's blood (1 John 1:7). The angel is referring to wholehearted imbibing of sexual sin that is incompatible with the Christian faith: these indulgent sinners not only will suffer ongoing corruption but will also be condemned by God in his judgment. The third angel states that they "will drink the wine of God's wrath, poured full strength into the cup of his anger" (Rev. 14:10). The parallel is clear: sexual immorality is itself "the wine of God's wrath," and those who drink it will receive the cup of God's wrath in the final judgment. Ancient people usually diluted wine with water, but God's wrath will be "poured full strength into the cup of his anger" (14:10) for the people of Babylon to drink.

The broader point of the angels' message is the inevitability of God's judgment on all sin, the entire complex of idolatry and sinful pleasure that is promoted by this Babylonian world. The first angel warned an indifferent world to realize that judgment is coming and to fear God in repentance. The second angel adds the just condemnation of God on people who are given over to indulgence in sin, whether it is the drunkenness of wine, money, power, or sex.

Revelation 14:8 rejoices in the fall of "Babylon the great." These words recall the boast of Nebuchadnezzar, the emperor who made the original Babylon so strong. In Daniel 4:30, he crowed: "Is not this great Babylon, which I have built by my mighty power as a royal residence and for the glory of my majesty?" This is the voice of the world in its vanity and pride. James Boice compares Nebuchadnezzar's boast with Romans 11:36, where the apostle Paul ascribed all glory to God alone: "For from him and through him and to him are all things." In contrast, Nebuchadnezzar uttered "the cry of the secular humanist. It describes life as of man, by man, and for man's glory."[8] God judged Nebuchadnezzar, stripping him of his kingdom and driving him insane, to live as a wild beast for seven years (Dan. 4:31–32). Boice notes that this was not an arbitrary judgment. Through the king's insanity, God was pointing out that the man-glorifying philosophy of secular humanism is simply crazy. Boice writes: "When God caused Nebuchadnezzar to be lowered from the pinnacle of human pride and glory to the baseness of insanity, it

8. James Montgomery Boice, *Romans* (Grand Rapids: Baker, 1991), 1:196.

was God's way of saying that this is what happens to all who suppress the truth about God and take the glory of God for themselves."[9] Likewise, God is certain to judge every heart that is lifted up in idolatry and every hand that reaches out to indulge in the cup of sin.

WORLDLY IDOLATRY PUNISHED

The first angel brought a warning to the spiritually indifferent world about the coming hour of God's judgment, calling people to wake up and repent. The second angel urged the certainty of God's judgment on wicked Babylon, answering the cup of sin with God's cup of wrath. The third angel's message warns us about the severity of God's wrath in the hour of judgment:

> And another angel, a third, followed them, saying with a loud voice, "If anyone worships the beast and its image and receives a mark on his forehead or on his hand, he also will drink the wine of God's wrath, poured full strength into the cup of his anger, and he will be tormented with fire and sulfur in the presence of the holy angels and in the presence of the Lamb." (Rev. 14:9–10)

The first angel warned the spiritually negligent. The second angel threatened those who enjoy Babylon's corruption. The third angel confronts those who have given their loyalty to the world and have thus worshiped the beast, that is, the worldly power of intimidation. The Bible states that those who deny God glory must inevitably glory in the world and through it in the Evil One. Those who will not serve the true God must worship the false gods, behind which stands Satan. In John's day, the beast was manifested in the Roman emperor and his demand to be worshiped as God. Today, the beast may be political tyrants, corporate titans, entertainment idols, or anyone else to whom we give the devotion of our hearts. The angel warns that the true God responds in wrath to this idolatry. Those who worship earthly idols will "be tormented with fire and sulfur in the presence of the holy angels and in the presence of the Lamb" (Rev. 14:10).

If the first two angels foretold the certainty of judgment, the third angel warns of the reality of hell. It is always easy to go along with the world, but here we calculate the cost. Steve Wilmshurst explains that "the choices made

9. Ibid.

here on earth will have their consequences in eternity, in heaven or in hell. . . . If sin is not dealt with by Christ on the cross, its consequences must be borne by the sinner, eternally."[10]

This angel speaks of God's punishment in the form of "torment" from "fire and sulfur" (Rev. 14:10). We should remember God's punishment on Sodom and Gomorrah, when fire and sulfur fell to destroy those wicked cities (Gen. 19:24). Sulfur, or "brimstone," refers to "a type of asphalt found particularly in volcanic deposits that produced both intense heat and a terrible smell. It was an image used often in the Bible for terrible suffering under divine judgment."[11]

Some scholars urge us not to take this imagery literally.[12] Revelation speaks in symbols, after all, so "fire and sulfur" should be taken symbolically. That is surely true, but we still must ask what is being symbolized. Revelation uses the symbols of the dragon and his beasts, the reality of which is actually more deadly: Satan and his antichrist. If the fire and sulfur of hell is a symbol, the reality can only be much worse in hell's punishment of bodily and spiritual torment. Revelation 14:11 speaks of "the smoke of their torment" going up. Here, too, smoke is figurative, yet it serves as "an enduring memorial of God's punishment involving a real, ongoing, eternal, conscious torment."[13]

The angel adds that this torment takes place "in the presence of the holy angels and in the presence of the Lamb" (Rev. 14:10). This statement seems to indicate not only that the suffering of hell is physical, but that it also involves the anguish of seeing Christ, the Savior they had warred against in rebellion, exalted in triumph as Lord.

Moreover, the angel describes the torment of hell as eternal and never-ending: "And the smoke of their torment goes up forever and ever, and they have no rest, day or night, these worshipers of the beast and its image, and whoever receives the mark of its name" (Rev. 14:11). Some Christians have tried to interpret this and similar statements as describing annihilation, so

10. Steve Wilmshurst, *The Final Word: The Book of Revelation Simply Explained* (Darlington, UK: Evangelical Press, 2008), 178.

11. Osborne, *Revelation*, 541.

12. See, for instance, G. B. Caird, *The Revelation of St. John the Divine* (San Francisco: Harper, 1966), 186.

13. G. K. Beale, *The Book of Revelation: A Commentary on the Greek Text*, New International Greek Testament Commentary (Grand Rapids: Eerdmans, 1999), 763.

that the condemned do not suffer eternally but are everlastingly destroyed. The problem is that this view conflicts directly with too many Bible passages. Revelation 20:10 tells of the casting of Satan, together with the beast and the false prophet, into the lake of fire and sulfur, where "they will be tormented day and night forever and ever." Verse 15 then adds that "if anyone's name was not found written in the book of life, he was thrown into the lake of fire," which teaches that the servants of the beast suffer the same fate as their satanic masters (see also Rev. 21:8).

When people complain against the supposed immorality of the Bible's teaching of unending punishment in hell, Christians can give two answers from this passage. First, we should remind them that the warning of God's judgment calls for us to fear God, not to argue with him. The holy God will inflict his just wrath on sin whether or not we give him permission. The first angel urges us: "Fear God and give him glory, because the hour of his judgment has come" (Rev. 14:7). The second answer points out that the first angel carried an "eternal gospel" (14:6). We interpreted that statement largely as good news to God's suffering people about the defeat of their evil tormentors. But the fact that God has warned us of judgment in advance shows that he offers salvation to those who repent and believe. Even as the angel warns of the hour of judgment, John 3:16 still calls sinners to be saved: "For God so loved the world, that he gave his only Son, that whoever believes in him should not perish but have eternal life."

ENDURANCE IN FAITH AND OBEDIENCE

I have mentioned how science fiction and fantasy literature so often mirror the story line of Revelation, telling of a sinister dark power that operates in our world. Moreover, these stories nearly always mirror the Bible by telling of a savior who delivers his people through some form of atoning death and resurrection. In the movie *The Matrix*, the hero Neo offers his life for his friends and experiences a resurrection that enables him to defeat the evil agents. In Tolkien's *Lord of the Rings*, the humble hobbit Frodo Baggins offers his life to destroy the evil ring. These stories move our hearts because intentionally or not they connect with the true story of Jesus Christ, God's Son, who conquers the evil realm of sin by his self-sacrificing death and gains victory through resurrection life.

Revelation tells us that Satan counterfeits the gospel (see Rev. 13:3–4) for the sake of false worship, just as fantasy literature often does. Christians are called to tell people the true story of Jesus' death and to live out his resurrection power. This is John's application from this passage. What should we do in such a dreadful battle? John answers: "Here is a call for the endurance of the saints, those who keep the commandments of God and their faith in Jesus" (14:12).

When John urges us to continue in "faith in Jesus," he means that we must continue to look up to that gospel carried by the angel in heaven. It tells us that through faith we are forgiven by Christ's blood and reconciled to God. It bears good news that our Savior has conquered the evil power under which we have suffered. John adds that we must also "keep the commandments of God" (Rev. 14:12). The cup of sin, sexual immorality, and worldly idolatry will be offered to us by this harlot world. God's Word gives us wisdom to recognize it as poison. We remember how Jesus drank the cup filled to the brim with God's wrath on our sins so that we might be forgiven (Matt. 26:39), and out of love for him we drink the cup of life that he gives.

We can be sure that by refusing our allegiance to the world, we will suffer its wrath. But we hear the angel cry, "Fallen, fallen is Babylon the great" (Rev. 14:8), and our hearts are lifted up. In the day of Christ, faith and obedience will be crowned with eternal life in glory. The holy life of faith and obedience will present the very witness that the people we love need to see so that they may be encouraged to believe. And in the hour of God's judgment, in the presence of his holy angels, Christ will reward those who bore the mark of his name, saying, "Well done, good and faithful servant" (Matt. 25:21).

38

BLESSED IN DEATH

Revelation 14:13

And I heard a voice from heaven saying, "Write this: Blessed are
the dead who die in the Lord from now on." "Blessed indeed,"
says the Spirit, "that they may rest from their labors,
for their deeds follow them!" (Rev. 14:13)

When Jesus was on earth, he performed miracles that showed the kind of comfort and aid that only he can give. Christians can assist someone who is born blind, but Jesus can give him sight. We can sympathize with those who grieve, but Jesus can raise our loved ones back to life. Given his divine power, Jesus speaks to the churches of Revelation that are facing persecution with the greatest comfort imaginable. Others are able to bless the living, but Jesus declares: "Blessed are the dead who die in the Lord" (Rev. 14:13). In light of this comfort, his followers throughout history have been able to face death in the spirit of Romans 8:37, as "more than conquerors through him who loved us."

Christ's blessing on those facing death for him shows more clearly than ever the great difference between the Christian and the non-Christian. In life there is a profound difference between the two. The believer is at war with the devil and sin but at peace with God; the unbeliever is at peace with the devil and sin but at war with God. The divide between the two is even greater in death. Revelation 14:11 speaks of the eternal judgment of those who loved the world and rejected Christ: "The smoke of their torment goes up forever and ever, and they have no rest, day or night." In the greatest contrast, Christians are blessed in death to "rest from their labors" (Rev. 14:13).

One biblical figure who realized the distance between believers and non-believers was the mysterious enemy of Israel named Balaam. This pagan magician was sent forth to pronounce curses on Israel, but God forbade him, saying, "You shall not curse the people, for they are blessed" (Num. 22:12). Balaam thus learned of God's protection on his people during the travails of life. But it was the believers' blessings in death that he particularly envied, exclaiming: "Let me die the death of the righteous, and may my final end be like theirs!" (Num. 23:10 NIV). Revelation 14:13 states the blessing of Christ's people in death that should be envied by all.

DYING "IN THE LORD"

Revelation 14 provides a respite of good news to readers who may be reeling from the conflict described in chapters 12 and 13. There, we saw Satan as a dragon who is fanatically driven to destroy Christ's people, with the help of his terrible beasts. Chapter 14 shows the church as having been saved from this conflict, assembled on Mount Zion with the Sovereign Lamb (Rev. 14:1). Knowing Christ's triumph and seeing the fall of the harlot empire Babylon, Christians should persevere in faith and in obedience to God's Word despite their suffering. Christ expects us to be willing even to die for our faith, so a voice from heaven speaks assurance of his eternal care for our souls: "Blessed are the dead who die in the Lord" (14:13).

Given Revelation's backdrop of looming persecution, some scholars believe that the blessing of this verse is limited to martyrs.[1] After all, in Revelation 6:11, the souls of martyrs were told to "rest a little longer," just as this verse speaks of rest for those who die in Christ. Yet Christians have rightly employed Revelation 14:13 in burial rites for all who have died in the faith, whatever the circumstances of their departure. This is the correct view,

---

1. J. Ramsey Michaels, *Revelation*, IVP New Testament Commentary 20 (Downers Grove, IL: InterVarsity Press, 1997), 176.

since the voice from heaven directs God's blessing not merely on those who suffered violence for Christ but on all those "who die in the Lord."

The key to this statement is to understand what it means to "die in the Lord." This phrase refers to those who conclude their pilgrimage in life, trusting in Jesus Christ for salvation. Hebrews 11:13 says that the Old Testament patriarchs "died in faith," which is the same as to "die in the Lord." Paul frequently used the language of being "in Christ." In Philippians 3:8–9, he told how he had renounced confidence in all other things, and especially his own merit, "in order that I may gain Christ and be found in him." Being in Christ meant no longer trusting "a righteousness of my own that comes from the law, but that which comes through faith in Christ." To die in the Lord, then, is to leave this life in union with Christ through a faith that is the instrument of our justification.

This statement is the second of seven beatitudes in the book of Revelation. These promises of blessing all belong to the same people, so by considering the other six we may fully understand what it means to be blessed in the Lord. The first beatitude is directed to those who receive God's Word in faith: "Blessed is the one who reads aloud the words of this prophecy, and blessed are those who hear, and who keep what is written in it" (Rev. 1:3). The sixth blessing likewise goes to those who keep "the words . . . of this book" (22:7). To be in the Lord, then, is to believe and obey his Word. Other beatitudes speak of Christians' being born again: "Blessed and holy is the one who shares in the first resurrection" (20:6); and being forgiven of our sins through Christ's blood: "Blessed are those who wash their robes" (22:14). Revelation 16:15 blesses Christians as those who stay awake and are not swept up in the evil of this world. The blessing of Revelation 19:9 describes Christians as the friends of Christ, "who are invited to the marriage supper of the Lamb." Are these blessings directed to you? Have you believed God's Word, especially its gospel message about Jesus as God's Son and our Savior? Have you trusted in Jesus for the forgiveness of your sins? Have you been born again to a living faith? Though you are far from a perfect Christian, are you looking ahead to Christ's coming, and do you seek to live for him now? If these descriptions characterize your life, then you are "in the Lord," and he now speaks to you with words of blessing even in death.

Christ's blessing in death is directed to those who live in faith now. In fact, the only way to die in the Lord is to live in the Lord: dying in Christ is the final triumph of the believer who has lived valiantly for Jesus. Charles P. McIlvaine writes that dying in the Lord

> is the enduring to the end, of a relation formed when the Christian life began. . . . It is the Christian going through the valley and shadow of death, precisely as he went through the dangers, and trials, and sorrows, and duties, of this mortal life, saying, "The Lord is my Shepherd, I shall not want" . . . . It is faith overcoming, in the last conflict, precisely as it overcame in every previous conflict of the Christian's pilgrimage—the same faith, resting on the same promises, embracing the same Saviour just as ever before. . . . It is the child of God falling asleep in the same arms of redeeming love in which he was always embraced, and where always he was safe in the peace of God.[2]

Realizing that Christ's blessing is reserved only for those who are in him through faith exposes the tragic error of Balaam's thinking. I mentioned that Balaam wanted to die the death of the righteous. The problem is that he was not willing to live the life of the righteous. He was not willing to surrender his rebellion and submit himself in faith to the Lord. He therefore died not with the blessing of Christ on his soul but under the curse of God's wrath for sin. His fate reminds us that the way to die in the Lord is to come to Jesus now. John 3:36 states: "Whoever believes in the Son has eternal life."

THE BELIEVER'S LIFE AFTER DEATH

It is apparent from Revelation 14:13 that Christians should know the Bible's teaching about life after death, since knowing our blessing in death equips us to live boldly in life. We can summarize the Bible's teaching on this topic with three points. First, death involves the separation of the soul from the body. Second, the souls of God's people are present with him in glory. Third, immediately upon dying, the believer's soul is purified in perfect holiness so that he or she is fitted for the holy environment of God's presence in heaven.

First, immediately upon dying, *the soul is separated from the body*, until the two are rejoined in the final resurrection. This is true for the believer and the unbeliever. Often when a person has died, people will say, "He is not there anymore but has left the body." What they realize is that the soul—the con-

---

2. Charles P. McIlvaine, *Truth & Life: 22 Classic Christ-Centered Sermons* (1854; repr., Birmingham, AL: Solid Ground, 2005), 392.

411

scious self, which perceives, thinks, and experiences—has departed from the body. The body remains part of the person, though it disintegrates in death, which is why we honorably bury it, but the conscious soul is separated from it.

The Bible expresses the departure of the soul by describing the dead body as sleeping. Jesus spoke this way of a girl who had died (Matt. 9:24), and Paul wrote of the dead as having "fallen asleep" (1 Thess. 4:14). This description refers to the appearance of the body in death, but not to the soul. This is the mistake of those who teach the doctrine of "soul sleep," which says that believers enter an unconscious state in death until Christ returns. The soul is not asleep but has departed from the lifeless body.

The Bible adds, second, that *believers' souls are present with the Lord in heaven* while their bodies await the summons to the resurrection. Paul said that to be absent from the body is to be "at home with the Lord" (2 Cor. 5:8). Matthew Henry writes that the souls of those who die in the Lord "are in his presence . . . , so that they are not lost, nor are they losers, but great gainers by death, and their removal out of this world is into a better."[3] Jesus told the believing thief, "Today you will be with me in Paradise" (Luke 23:43). Paul therefore exclaimed: "For to me to live is Christ, and to die is gain" (Phil. 1:21).

Third, when believers die, *our souls are immediately perfected in holiness* so as to partake of the Lord's glory. Westminster Confession of Faith 32.1 states that "the souls of the righteous, being then made perfect in holiness, are received into the highest heavens, where they behold the face of God, in light and glory, waiting for the full redemption of their bodies." Hebrews 12:23 describes Christians in death as "the spirits of the righteous made perfect." Eric Alexander thus suggests that believers should not speak of "sudden death," but rather of "sudden glory" for those who die "in the Lord."[4]

How many Christians facing death, and especially those suffering martyrdom for their testimony, have upheld their hearts by knowing that they would soon be in the presence of the Lord! When Stephen, the first Christian martyr, was stoned to death for his testimony, he looked up and saw "the Son of Man standing at the right hand of God" (Acts 7:56). Knowing that he would shortly be with Jesus there, he died praying for God to forgive his murderers, one of whom would later become the apostle Paul (7:60–8:1).

3. Matthew Henry, *Commentary on the Whole Bible*, 6 vols. (Peabody, MA: Hendrickson, n.d.), 5:632.
4. Eric J. Alexander, *Our Great God and Saviour* (Edinburgh: Banner of Truth, 2011), 121.

Paul wrote in 1 Corinthians 13:12 that though we now perceive God only as "in a mirror dimly," in heaven we will see him "face to face." What blessing persecuted saints enjoy, along with elderly believers slowly moving toward their appointed day, along with Christians dying from disease or in sudden deadly peril, to hear the voice from heaven, saying: "Blessed are the dead who die in the Lord" (Rev. 14:13). McIlvaine writes that in death Christians are blessed "to have [Christ] specially near to them; to have most precious communion with him; to feel a freeness and a strength of faith in committing their all to him, which they have not known before; to say with a confidence, and love, and peace, sweeter than ever they realized before . . . : 'The Lord is my light and my salvation; whom shall I fear?'"[5]

RESTING FROM LABOR

John cites two particular blessings that believers enjoy in death. We should first consider, however, the statements that accompany these blessings. John heard "a voice from heaven," which told him, "Write this." Clearly, emphasis is being given to this benediction. Moreover, the Spirit adds his exclamation: "'Blessed indeed,' says the Spirit" (Rev. 14:13). So important is this teaching that God provides two heavenly witnesses, one of whom is his own Spirit. The world (and sometimes Christians, too!) presents fanciful views about death and the afterlife, but Christians should listen only to God on this most vital of subjects. "From now on," the dead in Christ are blessed, God reveals. This emphasizes that "all the saints who die while remaining true to Christ from John's time to the end of history"[6] will be blessed.

The first blessing is an end to the wearisome labor that we have known in this world of sin and toil: "'Blessed indeed,' says the Spirit, 'that they may rest from their labors'" (Rev. 14:13). We know that the Spirit always carries on the work of Christ. While in the world, Jesus called the weary, saying, "Come to me, all who labor and are heavy laden, and I will give you rest" (Matt. 11:28). Now, from heaven, the Spirit promises to fulfill that invitation in the blessing of eternal life.

The word used here for *labor* (Greek, *kopon*) means "wearisome and painful striving." This includes the arduous work that everyone experi-

5. McIlvaine, *Truth & Life*, 405.

6. Grant R. Osborne, *Revelation*, Baker Exegetical Commentary on the New Testament (Grand Rapids: Baker Academic, 2002), 544.

ences in this life, yet the context in Revelation emphasizes "the troubles which have arisen from [the Christians'] steadfastness in faith."[7] It is not easy living as a believer, contending with your own sins and those of an often-hostile world. Christians are wearied from the labors of evangelism, ministry, and prayer, and even our spiritual delights such as worship and the study of God's Word require discipline and diligence. In heaven, we will continue to worship and will work together with Christ in the fields of glory, but the toil and labor will have ended with the end of our life in this world.

Charles Spurgeon expressed some of the ways in which saints in heaven rest from earthly labor. They rest from the *toil* of labor, since heaven "will yield them refreshment and never cause them weariness." They rest from the *woe* of labor, since the sorrows of believers all end in the grave. Christians rest from the *faults* of their labor, their works no longer marred by sin. They rest from the *discouragements* and the *disappointments* of labor. In heaven there will be none to criticize our work or question our motives, and we will no longer return from labor doubting that anything has been truly accomplished. Spurgeon writes: "Here we must sow in tears: there we shall reap in joy. . . . Here we labour, there we shall enjoy the fruits of toil, where no blight or mildew can endanger the harvest. . . . Truly blessed are the dead which die in the Lord."[8]

One way to appreciate the rest that believers enjoy in death is to compare the Bible's teaching with the abominable Roman Catholic doctrine of purgatory. The pope tells his followers to expect not rest in death but purging fires of torment. McIlvaine explains what Rome teaches the dead in Christ to expect:

> Instead of resting from their labors, [they] have entered on labors and pains more severe than ever they knew before; instead of being blessed and happy with Christ, are suffering for their sins, in distant and dark separation from him; instead of finding that his blood "cleanseth from all sin," are experiencing the pains of purgatorial flames . . . ; instead of being liberated from all terrestrial things, are now dependent on the prayers, and masses,

7. Robert H. Mounce, *Revelation*, rev. ed., New International Commentary on the New Testament (Grand Rapids: Eerdmans, 1997), 278.

8. Charles Haddon Spurgeon, "A Voice from Heaven," in *Metropolitan Tabernacle Pulpit*, 63 vols. (Pasadena, TX: Pilgrim Publications, 1971), 21:116–18.

and indulgences of the Church on earth, on the will of priests, on the charity of sinners, and the payment of money to buy the priest's mediation, for the [shortening] of their years of suffering.[9]

It would be difficult to imagine a doctrine more contrary to the Bible's teaching! Here, as in so many of their teachings, the popes speak not with the voice of heaven but in brazen defiance of God's message in Scripture. This doctrine of purgatory alone should persuade us to dread the thought of being under the care of such false shepherds, who come to the deathbeds of saints with a message exactly the reverse of the comforting words of the Spirit. Yet rejecting purgatory should help Christians to see more clearly that death means resting in Christ's presence, being freed from every earthly trial and dependence, being cleansed of all sin, bathing in light and glory—as Hebrews 12:23 says, "the spirits of the righteous made perfect." "Blessed indeed," the Spirit says of "the dead who die in the Lord."

Rewarded for Works

The second blessing speaks of the reward that believers can expect in the presence of our Savior: "for their deeds follow them!" (Rev. 14:13). All our sins, trials, and torments are left behind when we die, but our good work and faithfulness to Christ in the face of persecution will follow after as a crown to our life of faith.

The Bible teaches that sinners are saved by God's grace alone, apart from any merit on our part, and that even our faith is God's free gift, "not a result of works, so that no one may boast" (Eph. 2:9). Yet the Bible also teaches that Christians will receive a reward for good deeds performed in gratitude for salvation and in obedience to God's Word. Our works earn not the reward *of* eternal life, but rather rewards *in* eternal life. Jesus urged us to "lay up for yourselves treasures in heaven" (Matt. 6:20). He promised to reward his diligent workers, saying: "Well done, good and faithful servant. You have been faithful over a little; I will set you over much. Enter into the joy of your master" (25:21). Paul urged Christians toward biblically faithful ministry: "If the work that anyone has built on the foundation survives, he will receive a reward" (1 Cor. 3:14; see also 2 Cor. 5:10).

9. McIlvaine, *Truth & Life*, 402–3.

Our verse is particularly helpful in saying that believers' "deeds follow them" (Rev. 14:13). Our works do not go before us, opening a way into heaven, but Christ and his finished work are our "forerunner" (Heb. 6:20). For this reason, Christians should never make much of their own works, spiritual attainments, or service to Christ; instead, we should make much only of Christ and what he has done for us. This is why, for all his achievements, Paul declared: "Far be it from me to boast except in the cross of our Lord Jesus Christ" (Gal. 6:14). Matthew Henry writes that the believers' works "do not go before them as their title, or price of purchase, but follow them as their evidence of having lived and died in the Lord; and the memory of them will be pleasant, and the reward glorious, far above the merit of all their services and sufferings."[10]

Many Christians think too little of their works, comparing them to the more publicized accomplishments of famous preachers, missionaries, or ministry leaders and thinking that they will be overlooked. Jesus corrects this idea in his teaching on the final judgment. Having gathered his sheep, he promises to praise their works: "For I was hungry and you gave me food, I was thirsty and you gave me drink, I was a stranger and you welcomed me, I was naked and you clothed me, I was sick and you visited me, I was in prison and you came to me" (Matt. 25:35–36). The righteous marvel, asking when they did such things for Jesus. He answers: "Truly, I say to you, as you did it to one of the least of these my brothers, you did it to me" (Matt. 25:40).

Notice that Christ mentions not great and famous Christian achievements, but the daily acts of faith and love as the works that matter most and please him the best. "Have I ever done anything worthy of Jesus' praise?" the doubtful believer wonders. When we remember that our works not only are empowered by God's grace but are assessed by the eyes of mercy, perfected by cleansing blood, and received at the throne of our loving heavenly Father, the answer is yes. Think how a loving earthly father posts his children's artwork on his office wall and adorns his bookcases with pictures of their achievements. In most cases, the art is not very good or the achievements very great, yet they are precious to the father's heart because of love for his children. This reflects the heart of God toward his children in Christ. Everything that we have ever done with a sincere desire to honor, thank, and glorify our Lord will follow after us as a blessing in heaven.

10. Henry, *Commentary on the Whole Bible*, 6:939.

Faith in Life; Blessing in Death

The last thing that the Roman Empire would say of John's beleaguered, impoverished, and soon-persecuted readers is that they were blessed. The world looks with similar eyes on believers today. But the voice of God's Spirit extols us: "Blessed indeed" (Rev. 14:13). We will rest from our labors, and our deeds in Christ will follow us.

The applications of this text are obvious. John has already urged us to endure in faith and obedience (Rev. 14:12). But here we are reminded that it matters not only that we make it to the end in the Lord. Our present lives are also invested with eternal meaning. It matters that we remain pure from the idolatries of our age. It matters that we, as Paul put it, "fight the good fight of the faith" (1 Tim. 6:12). Christians must not despise the good works before us today, though we are saved apart from works by faith alone. Life resounds in eternity. True worship on earth is recorded with angelic praises above. "Therefore, my beloved brothers," Paul urged, "be steadfast, immovable, always abounding in the work of the Lord, knowing that in the Lord your labor is not in vain" (1 Cor. 15:58).

According to the Bible, not only is today as important as eternity, but our response to Jesus Christ today determines where our eternity will be spent. Will you be accepted as righteous in the day of God's judgment or condemned for the guilt of your sins? The answer is determined by your response to Jesus. Do not be like foolish Balaam, who longed for the death of the righteous while he continued to live in rebellion and unbelief. By all means, long for the blessings of death in the Lord! For the alternative is the dreadful hell spoken of so clearly in Revelation and throughout the Bible. "The smoke of their torment goes up forever and ever, and they have no rest," Revelation has said (Rev. 14:11). But those who live in Christ and die in faith look forward to eternal blessings in heaven. And they will return the blessing to him with songs of joy in their hearts:

> For all the saints who from their labors rest,
> Who thee by faith before the world confessed,
> Thy name, O Jesus, be forever blest.
> Alleluia! Alleluia![11]

11. William Walsham How, "For All the Saints" (1864).

417

39

THE GRAPES OF WRATH

Revelation 14:14—20

So the angel swung his sickle across the earth and gathered the
grape harvest of the earth and threw it into the great
winepress of the wrath of God. (Rev. 14:19)

The expression "the grapes of wrath" has a long history in American propaganda. Its most prominent use is in "The Battle Hymn of the Republic," penned in November 1861 by Julia Ward Howe. This hymn anoints the Northern armies in the American Civil War with the sword of God's justice against their Southern neighbors:

Mine eyes have seen the glory of the coming of the Lord:
He is trampling out the vintage where the grapes of wrath are stored.

The same claim was suggested by John Steinbeck's 1939 novel *The Grapes of Wrath*, which advocated the cause of migrant workers in the California orchard fields. Steinbeck employed this title to suggest that violent labor organization and socialist economic policies represent God's righteous judgment against greedy capitalists.

The imagery of the grapes of wrath comes from Revelation 14, where it depicts Christ's judgment on a sinful world. When the angel calls for Christ to swing his sickle and gather "the grape harvest of the earth" (Rev. 14:19), he is not depicting the righteous warfare of one class of humans against another but rather the holy wrath of God against all the earth. A study of Revelation 14:14–20 shows the presumption of any people claiming to wield God's wrath against another: only the Son of Man is qualified to sit in final judgment, and the grapes of wrath represent the entire human race apart from Christ, suffering wrathful judgment for rebellion against his rule.

THE COMING OF THE SON OF MAN

The end of Revelation 14 concludes the fourth major section of the book of Revelation. In the first section (chaps. 1–3), Christ revealed his glory and addressed the seven churches of Asia. The second section introduced the seven seals (chaps. 4–7), which showed Christ as reigning throughout history for the preservation of his people. Chapters 8–11 showed the seven trumpets, with judgments announcing Christ's inevitable victory over the rebel world. The symbolic histories of the fourth section (chaps. 12–14) have shown the spiritual warfare raging behind the scenes of church history.

At the end of previous sections we have been brought to the very brink of Christ's return in glory, but now for the first time we actually see the coming of the Lord. John earlier wrote, "Behold, he is coming with the clouds, and every eye will see him" (Rev. 1:7). Now John shows us what he saw: "Then I looked, and behold, a white cloud, and seated on the cloud one like a son of man, with a golden crown on his head, and a sharp sickle in his hand" (14:14). Those who hold the preterist view of Revelation believe that this vision shows God's judgment on Jerusalem when it fell to the Roman armies in A.D. 70. But this language of the coming Son of Man belongs only to the end of the age and the final harvest of all the earth, since an emphasis on the worldwide nature of the judgment appears throughout this passage. The fall of Jerusalem was God's judgment on the unbelieving Jewish people, but as Jesus told Caiaphas during the humiliation of his trial, his deity would truly be proved when "you will see the Son of Man seated at the right hand of Power and coming on the clouds of heaven" (Matt. 26:64).

Jesus returns to earth bearing emblems of his glory and triumph. The white cloud reflects the dazzling glory of God. When Moses went into the tabernacle during the exodus, the glory cloud caused his face to shine with radiance. Jesus ascended to heaven on this cloud, and angels informed the watching disciples that he would "come in the same way" (Acts 1:11). Daniel's famous prophecy foretold Jesus' enthronement in his ascension: "With the clouds of heaven there came one like a son of man . . . to the Ancient of Days" (Dan. 7:13). Without doubt, the One who returns on the glory cloud is the same Son of Man, who now returns to finalize salvation history. The color white reflects the absolute purity of God's holiness, a holiness so bright that in Isaiah 6:2 even the holy seraphim, the burning angels that attend God's throne, cover their holy faces in awe.

Moreover, Jesus wears "a golden crown on his head" (Rev. 14:14). This is the Victor's laurel wreath (Greek, *stephanos*). Robert Mounce writes: "The golden wreath designates the Messiah as one who has conquered and thereby won the right to act in judgment."[1] The fact that Jesus comes to judge is shown by the sickle in his hand. In his parables of the kingdom, Jesus had foretold that he would return to judge, separating the righteous from the ungodly: "At harvest time I will tell the reapers, Gather the weeds first and bind them in bundles to be burned, but gather the wheat into my barn" (Matt. 13:30).

This depiction of Christ's second coming is one of many in the New Testament that link his return with the immediate judgment of the world. The premillennial view of eschatology teaches that Jesus returns to inaugurate a thousand-year earthly reign, after which there is a final rebellion that results in God's judgment. But John shows Jesus returning with the sickle already in his hand: there will be no delay, but the harvest takes place when he comes. In Matthew 25:31, Jesus likewise taught that the final judgment takes place immediately upon his return: "When the Son of Man comes in his glory, and all the angels with him, then he will sit on his glorious throne." Paul taught the same sequence: "The Lord himself will descend from heaven with a cry of command, with the voice of an archangel, and with the sound of the trumpet of God. And the dead in Christ will rise first" (1 Thess. 4:16). This is the great event for which Christians are joyfully waiting, which Paul describes as "our blessed hope" (Titus 2:13), after which comes not a confusing series of events but, Paul says, a condition in which we then "will always be with the Lord" (1 Thess. 4:17).

---

1. Robert H. Mounce, *Revelation*, rev. ed., New International Commentary on the New Testament (Grand Rapids: Eerdmans, 1997), 279.

The Harvest of the Earth

Jesus described the final judgment as a double harvest, in which believers in Christ will be separated to himself for an eternal reward while those who rejected him will be judged with an eternal punishment (Matt. 25:32–46; cf. 3:12). This twofold judgment is reflected in the vision of Revelation 14:14–20, the first half of which shows Christ's harvest of the elect for blessing and the second half shows the harvest of the ungodly for the winepress of God's wrath.

Revelation 14:15 introduces "another angel," that is, the fourth angel to appear in this chapter (see vv. 6, 8, 9). This angel comes "out of the temple," meaning that it bears a message from God the Father, "calling with a loud voice to him who sat on the cloud." The angel announces the long-awaited harvest of the saints to be gathered into the eternal glory: "Put in your sickle, and reap, for the hour to reap has come, for the harvest of the earth is fully ripe" (Rev. 14:15).

There are a number of points for us to notice in this call. First, we see Christ's receiving instructions for the final judgment from an angel sent by God the Father. The idea of an angel's commanding Jesus troubles some readers. But we remember Jesus' teaching that even he did not know the day or the hour of his appearing and the final judgment. "Concerning that day or that hour," he had said, "no one knows, not even the angels in heaven, nor the Son, but only the Father" (Mark 13:32). This is a remarkable instance of Jesus' humanity and his subordination to the Father. It reminds us that we cannot know the time of the final judgment and therefore should always be ready (13:35–37).

Second, the godly are compared to wheat. This is made clear by the word translated as "fully ripe" (Greek, *xeraino*), which means "dried out," a term used for grain that is ready to be harvested. John the Baptist contrasted the "wheat" of the godly with the "chaff" of the ungodly (Matt. 3:12). In one parable, Jesus contrasted the godly wheat with the weeds that the enemy sowed in the master's fields (13:25–30). The point is that there is a qualitative difference between those who are saved and those who are condemned long before the final harvest. This difference is evidenced by their reaction to God's Word. Jesus taught that the kingdom of God is like a farmer who "went out to sow his seed" (Luke 8:5). He said, "The seed is the word of

God" (8:11). While many hard or worldly hearts reject God's Word, believers receive it and bear fruit through faith. This qualitative difference does not result from any moral or spiritual superiority on the part of Christians, but only the grace of God at work in them. But this grace makes all the difference in the final harvest. Jesus said, "The harvest is the close of the age, and the reapers are angels," with the godly gathered into the barn and the ungodly cast into fire (Matt. 13:39–42). The way to know that you will be gathered for salvation when Christ returns is to receive God's Word in faith now and live in a way that bears godly fruit for the Lord. This faith or unbelief is the decisive mark between God's gathered wheat and the chaff that is cast off into the eternal fire.

Third, the angel notes that the harvest has come because "the harvest of the earth is fully ripe" (Rev. 14:15). This statement indicates that Christ returns when the full number of God's elect have come into the church through faith. We are thus reminded that there is a relationship between the final harvest and the ingathering of Christ's people now. Speaking of the gospel mission of the church, Jesus said, "The harvest is plentiful, but the laborers are few" (Matt. 9:37). This being the case, the great work of the church is the spread of the gospel through preaching, evangelism, and world missions (cf. Luke 24:46–47). The church is not to major in self-help tips, political critique, or feel-good stories, but in the biblical message of redemption from sin through the blood of Jesus Christ. Every Christian is called to spread the gospel, through which God is gathering the harvest of his elect.

Fourth, if our work as Christians is like preparing a harvest, we are reminded of the hard labor that this agricultural metaphor involves. We live in a machine age, when a coin is put into a slot and a soft drink comes out more or less automatically. We expect salvation to work the same way, and we often arrange our ministries around this quick-results expectation. But salvation does not ordinarily work this way. There must be careful plowing and planting, as a thoughtful biblical witness is given. Our message must be watered with prayer, often for long seasons. Early signs of growth need to be cultivated, pruned, and fertilized. This is why we should not be surprised when the growth of the church and the Christian nurture of our children require faithful labor over an extended period. The great temptation for weary Christians and churches is to give up. But faithful ministry requires patience and endurance in doing God's work in God's way, according to God's Word and by God's sovereign power, all in God's timing. Paul wrote: "Let us not grow weary of doing good, for in due season we will reap, if we do not give up" (Gal. 6:9).

Fifth, although we are workers in Christ's harvest fields, notice that Christ is actually the One who performs the harvesting. The Son of Man appears bearing his sickle, and at the summons from God, "he who sat on the cloud swung his sickle across the earth, and the earth was reaped" (Rev. 14:16). Jesus will gather his people on the last day, and he is now calling each one with the gospel. To be saved is to personally hear Christ's voice speaking to your heart through God's Word, calling, "Follow me" (Matt. 9:9). "My sheep hear my voice," Jesus said, "and they follow me. I give them eternal life, and they will never perish" (John 10:27–28). "The good shepherd lays down his life for the sheep" (10:11). Through his sin-atoning death and his saving call in the heart of every believer through the Word, Jesus is gathering his people now, just as "the saving sweep of Christ's sickle [will gather] his faithful followers"[2] on the day when he returns.

To believe in Jesus is not to be saved by the church, by the preacher, or by the person who brought you the gospel. The believer in Christ has been saved by the Lord himself and is certain to be gathered by the Lord when he returns. Douglas Kelly recalls the harvests of his boyhood in rural North Carolina and points out how uncertain they were, with the results usually not known until all was gathered in. How different is Christ's harvest! "He will gather in all the chosen, all who will ever believe in him and repent from their sins. Unlike uncertain human harvests, . . . this harvest cannot fail."[3]

The message of this chapter was intended to encourage John's readers greatly, just as it should encourage us. Psalm 2 says that the nations will rage and the rulers will conspire against God and his Savior. Kelly writes:

> Let them make all their plots to blot out the name of the Lord and of his Christ from the earth. Let them do their worst, because the Son of Man was incarnate, lived a holy life, was crucified for the sins of all his people, raised in the same body in which he was crucified, and he is now ascended up into that cloud, to the throne of God beside his Father, whence dominion over all nations has been given unto him. The beasts can never stop, nor even

2. Dennis E. Johnson, *Triumph of the Lamb: A Commentary on Revelation* (Phillipsburg, NJ: P&R Publishing, 2001), 212.
3. Douglas F. Kelly, *Revelation*, Mentor Expository Commentary (Tain, Ross-shire, Scotland: Mentor, 2012), 272.

slow down the harvest that the Son of Man is carrying on from his ascended dignity on the glory cloud.[4]

THE WINEPRESS OF GOD'S WRATH

All through Revelation, the good news of salvation includes the destruction of the enemies of Christ and his people. To this end, there is a second harvest, depicted in Revelation 14:17–20. John's vision seems to follow the sequence of Joel's prophecy: "Put in the sickle, for the harvest is ripe. Go in, tread, for the winepress is full" (Joel 3:13).

Jesus' teaching on the final judgment spoke of separating the godly from the ungodly for their different destinies (see Matt. 25:32). John's vision thus depicts two different kinds of harvest. The second harvest began with "another angel" coming "out of the temple in heaven" with "a sharp sickle" (Rev. 14:17). Yet "another angel came out from the altar, the angel who has authority over the fire" (14:18). We remember that the souls of the martyrs were gathered beneath the altar of heaven and that their prayers were offered on it (6:9–11; 8:3–4). This association indicates that the judgment of the wicked will be in part a response to the prayer of Christian martyrs for God's justice. This angel has "authority over the fire," which probably speaks to his role in judging the wicked. He therefore brings God's command to gather rebellious mankind: "He called with a loud voice to the one who had the sharp sickle, 'Put in your sickle and gather the clusters from the vine of the earth, for its grapes are ripe'" (14:18).

H. B. Swete points out the "delicate beauty" of this passage, since Christ does not himself harvest the ungodly for their judgment, but this is done by the angels.[5] This may reflect that while Jesus is immediately involved in the salvation of his people, the judgment of the rebellious, while under his authority, does not involve such personal contact. It is Christ's own hand that saves his people, but his command suffices for the judgment of rebels. This reflection should not in any way suggest that Jesus is squeamish about divine judgment, for in chapter 19 we will see him personally wielding the sword of judgment and treading the winepress of God's fury (Rev. 19:12–15). But it at least suggests the same mercy that Jesus showed throughout his

4. Ibid.
5. Henry Barclay Swete, *Commentary on Revelation*, 2 vols. (1911; repr., Grand Rapids: Kregel, 1977), 2:190.

earthly ministry and in his cry to grant his persecutors forgiveness while suffering on the cross (Luke 23:34).

Still, the angels' gathering of the nations depicts *the certainty of judgment* on all unredeemed sinners in the end: "So the angel swung his sickle across the earth and gathered the grape harvest of the earth and threw it into the great winepress of the wrath of God" (Rev. 14:19). There is no way to evade the harvest of rebellious mankind for judgment. All sin must be and will be paid in the holy court of God's almighty justice. If your sins have not been punished on the shoulders of Jesus Christ, as he died on the cross to pay the penalty that his people deserved, then your own shoulders will have to bear the infinite weight of God's condemnation. Those who have rejected God and spurned the gospel offer of Jesus will fully deserve this judgment. The harvest of wrath is the consequence of their gleeful scorning of God's honor while they lived, their withholding of worship and obedience from him, and in many cases their participation in the mocking and affliction of God's beloved people. The vision in chapter 6 shows the wicked as vainly seeking escape from this judgment harvest, finding no refuge from "the face of him who is seated on the throne, and from the wrath of the Lamb" (6:16). The angels who swing the sharp sickle will gather the entire grape harvest and cast it into the winepress of God's wrath.

The treading of the winepress further depicts *the terror of God's judgment* in the day of his wrath. In biblical times, a winepress would be built of rock or brick. Grapes were placed in an upper trough where they were trampled on by feet, so that the juice flowed down a channel into a lower trough that collected the fluid. It is hard to imagine a more vivid picture of God's terrible violence in judging his enemies. In Isaiah 63:3–4, the Lord says, "I have trodden the winepress alone, and from the peoples no one was with me; I trod them in my anger and trampled them in my wrath; their lifeblood spattered on my garments, and stained all my apparel. For the day of vengeance was in my heart, and my year of redemption had come."

John relates that the winepress was trodden "outside the city" (Rev. 14:20), which indicates the *rejection* involved in God's judgment. The ungodly are put outside the covenant precincts of God's salvation city, showing "the exclusion of the wicked from the society of the redeemed."[6] We remember

---

6. Geoffrey B. Wilson, *New Testament Commentaries*, 2 vols. (Edinburgh: Banner of Truth, 2005), 2:555.

that Jesus was crucified outside the city, in that way bearing not only the guilt but also the curse and shame of our sin. Philip Hughes writes: "It was there that he gave himself to be trodden in the great winepress of the wrath of God, bearing our sins and absorbing their punishment, so that we might be clothed with his pure and holy righteousness."[7] Now in the hour of Christ's return, judgment comes to the same place, outside God's city. There, "the rejecters of the grace that flows from the cross suffer the wrath of God that they have chosen for themselves by reason of their impenitence and ingratitude."[8]

Many people recoil in shock or loathing from such biblical descriptions of God's vengeful wrath. The imagery seems out of place with their idea of a God of love. But they fail to realize that it is precisely because of God's love for righteousness, truth, and peace that he responds so violently against all evil. Modern and postmodern humanists react against the biblical idea of God's wrath as something morally objectionable and unworthy of their embrace. But as J. I. Packer explains, the biblical idea of God's wrath

> is *righteous* anger—the *right* reaction of moral perfection in the Creator towards moral perversity in the creature. So far from the manifestation of God's wrath in punishing sin being morally doubtful, the thing that would be morally doubtful would be for Him *not* to show His wrath in this way. God is not *just*—that is, He does not act in the way that is *right*, He does not do what is proper to a *judge*—unless He inflicts upon all sin and wrongdoing the penalty it deserves.[9]

According to John's imagery, the penalty that sin deserves is truly dreadful. The reason is that it corresponds to the dreadful horror that sin is. Here we see why people find it hard to accept the Bible's pictures of God's terrible wrath: because they do not share God's revulsion for sin. Henry Ironside writes: "Sin is . . . the most loathsome thing which has blighted the whole universe, broken millions of hearts and brought dishonor to God, the One who created the world. There is nothing in His sight so hateful as sin."[10]

7. Philip Edgcumbe Hughes, *The Book of Revelation* (Downers Grove, IL: InterVarsity Press, 1990), 167.
8. Ibid.
9. J. I. Packer, *Knowing God* (Downers Grove, IL: InterVarsity Press, 1973), 166.
10. Henry A. Ironside, *Addresses on the Gospel of Luke* (Neptune, NJ: Loizeaux Brothers, 1947), 161.

For one sin, God banished Adam and Eve from Paradise. For one sin, the descendants of Canaan fell under God's curse for generations. Moses was excluded from entering the promised land for one sin, and Ananias and Sapphira were slain for a single sin. The sins that we are so accustomed to and comfortable with are appalling to the perfectly holy God whose righteous nature is personally offended by sin. Unless our sins are redeemed by the blood of Christ, through faith in his cross, then they and we must be trodden like ripe grapes in the winepress of his wrath.

Whether or not we glorify God for his judgment, or even accept the reality of this passage, we will all face God's violent wrath unless we repent and believe in Jesus Christ. Indeed, if the imagery of a winepress is not gruesome enough, John further sees a vast river of blood spreading out from the winepress. This depicts *the universal extent of God's judgment*: "blood flowed from the winepress, as high as a horse's bridle, for 1,600 stadia" (Rev. 14:20). A river of blood is seen flowing in all directions, high enough that a horse will have to swim in it, so great will be the judgment of the human race that rejected Jesus. Some commentators have argued that 1,600 stadia (about 180 miles) accounts for roughly the entire region of Palestine. It is more likely, however, that this number should be taken symbolically. The number 1,600 is arrived at through the square of four (sixteen), multiplied by one thousand, four representing the corners of the world and one thousand standing for the completeness of judgment. George Eldon Ladd writes: "The entire land is pictured as being inundated in blood to a depth of about four feet. The thought is clear: a radical judgment that crushes every vestige of evil and hostility to the reign of God."[11]

Fleeing to Life!

The applications of this passage are both urgent and obvious. Christians are reminded that we must be willing to be different now from unbelieving people, since we hope for such a different end from that which awaits them. If, in the eyes of Christ, believers are wheat compared to chaff and weeds, then there must be a spiritual substance to our lives and godly fruitfulness that corresponds to our identity in the Lord. In Psalm 73, Asaph resented

11. George Eldon Ladd, *A Commentary on the Revelation of John* (Grand Rapids: Eerdmans, 1972), 202.

the difficulty of living out an obedient faith in a world like ours. He envied the wicked for the fun they seemed to have, and even thought of going over to their side. But when he went once more into God's sanctuary, he said, "then I discerned their end. Truly you set them in slippery places; you make them fall to ruin" (Ps. 73:17–18). Never envy the ungodly, however impressive their worldliness now seems and how much they seem to enjoy a life of sin. If you belong to Jesus Christ, remember that he has separated you now in the manner of your faith and life, and he will separate you in the day of his return that you may enter into eternal life, escaping God's wrath through faith in him.

Not only must Christians gladly accept the cost of following Jesus in this world, bearing a cross as he did for us, but we must urgently warn the ungodly of the judgment that will soon appear. I mentioned earlier that since Christ is now engaged in the great harvest of salvation, we must make the witness of the gospel our chief labor. We are reminded by the closing verses of Revelation 14 that this witness must not fail to point out the terror of God's wrath. Many Christians today shy away from mentioning God's terrible judgment, thinking to make the gospel more palatable. They fail to realize that the gospel saves us from God's wrath, apart from which it is not fully clear why we should believe. We must proclaim the truth of both God's justice and Christ's redemption, trusting in his sovereign grace to call sinners through the whole counsel of God.

Finally, if you have not yet confessed your sin to God and turned to Christ for forgiveness and salvation, this is the most urgent matter of your life. John Bunyan depicted your urgent need in the opening chapter of his famous book *Pilgrim's Progress*. A sinner learned in God's book that he dwelt in the City of Destruction, on which God's wrath might fall at any moment. He found a man named Evangelist, who pointed him to the cross of Christ as the way of escape. Leaving his former life behind and with God's book open in his hand, he began running toward the cross. "Life! life!" he cried; "eternal life!"[12] Let this be your cry as well, as you flee from God's wrath on your sins, gaining at the cross both forgiveness and a place in Christ's gospel harvest. Through faith in the cross, you will find that Jesus suffered God's wrath for you, so that he might gather you into his harvest of eternal life.

12. John Bunyan, *Pilgrim's Progress* (Nashville: Thomas Nelson, 1999), 11–13.

PART 5

The Seven Bowls of God's Wrath

40

By the Sea of Crystal

Revelation 15:1–8

Then I saw another sign in heaven, great and amazing, seven
angels with seven plagues, which are the last, for with
them the wrath of God is finished. (Rev. 15:1)

T he book of Revelation, like the rest of the Bible, tells the story
of the coming of God's kingdom. In the Old Testament, this
kingdom was foretold in Daniel chapter 2, in a vision given to
Nebuchadnezzar, the emperor of Babylon and the archetypal enemy of God.
Nebuchadnezzar saw a statue, the head of which was fine gold, its breast and
arms silver, its belly and thighs bronze, its legs of iron, and its feet partly of
iron and partly of clay (Dan. 2:32–33). This statue depicted how successive
world empires would decrease in glory while increasing in power. Starting
in Daniel's time, these empires were Babylon, Medo-Persia, Greece, and
Rome. Most importantly, the vision then showed "a stone . . . cut out by no
human hand" that "struck the image on its feet of iron and clay, and broke
them in pieces" (Dan. 2:34). This stone cut without hands represents the
kingdom of Christ, which would appear during the fourth empire, Rome,
and would overthrow the kingdoms of the earth.

John's perspective throughout Revelation has been that Daniel's prophecy
of the kingdom of God was fulfilled by the ascension of Christ into heaven

after his atoning death and resurrection. In the time of the fourth empire, Rome, Christ's kingdom began, and throughout this age the gospel would prevail against the kingdoms of the world.[1] The vision of Daniel 2 concludes where the book of Revelation is leading: "The God of heaven will set up a kingdom that shall never be destroyed . . . . It shall break in pieces all these kingdoms and bring them to an end, and it shall stand forever" (Dan. 2:44).

The New Testament provides increased detail to the eschatology of the Old Testament. Thus, while Daniel's vision showed Christ's kingdom smashing the evil earthly kingdoms, the book of Revelation presents the more detailed judgments of the seals, trumpets, and bowls. These series of visions show that Christ's earthly judgments follow a sequence. First, the seven seals show Christ as judging in order to restrain the world's violence on the church, allowing his people to pass safely through this world into heaven. Second, the seven trumpet judgments serve to warn the nations of final judgment and offer them the opportunity for repentance. Third, the seven bowls pour out final judgment to destroy those wicked powers that refuse to repent. So it was for Nebuchadnezzar's Babylon, which was restrained from fully destroying Christ's people, was forewarned of God's coming judgment, and then was destroyed by the divinely ordained Medo-Persian conquerors when Babylon would not repent. The same sequence of judgment—restraint, warning, and destruction—will befall all the worldly powers that rise up against Christ, until the final judgment removes all opposition and ushers in the eternal kingdom of God.

God's Wrath Finished

Revelation 15 begins the fifth section of Revelation, presenting the judgments of the seven bowls of wrath. The first question to ask is when these judgments are taking place. Some commentators argue that these judgments pertain only to the end of history at the time of Christ's return. One reason for this view is a general inclination on the part of many to interpret Revelation in only a future sense. They also note that John now says that "the wrath of God is finished" (Rev. 15:1). Does this mean that we have moved out of the general history of the church age into the final days?

---

1. See my exposition of Revelation 1:1 for a fuller explanation of Revelation's fulfillment of Daniel's visions.

There are two reasons why the answer to this question is no. First, this section is connected with the symbolic histories of the immediately preceding chapters. The vision of the dragon and the woman in Revelation 12 described the entire church age, together with the vision of the two beasts (chap. 13). Chapter 12 began: "A great sign appeared in heaven" (Rev. 12:1). Chapter 15 begins: "Then I saw another sign in heaven, great and amazing" (15:1). Since the visions of the bowls are linked with the vision of the dragon and the woman, which describe the entire church age, it follows that the seven bowls also depict this period of history and not merely the final events at the end.

Second, we remember the relationship between the seven seals, seven trumpets, and seven bowls. There is no question that the seven seals encompassed the entire church age, with only the seventh seal corresponding to Christ's return and the final judgment. The same is true of the seven trumpets. The sense in which the seven bowls finish God's wrath corresponds to this sequence. The bowls show God as delivering final judgment on his enemies in history. Robert Mounce writes: "They are the last of the plagues in that they complete the warnings of God to an impenitent world."[2] The bowl judgments show what happens when God's initial and partial judgments are ignored. William Hendriksen explains: "When the wicked, often warned by the trumpets of judgment, continue to harden their hearts, death finally plunges them into the hands of an angry God."[3]

SALVATION THROUGH JUDGMENT

Revelation 15 opens up the visions of the bowls of wrath with a remarkable scene: "I saw what appeared to be a sea of glass mingled with fire—and also those who had conquered the beast and its image and the number of its name, standing beside the sea of glass with harps of God in their hands" (Rev. 15:2). We saw in Revelation 4:6 that the "sea of glass, like crystal," was before God's throne in heaven. The saints are now standing before that crystal sea, having arrived safely through the travails of earth. It is not certain whether this looks to the future to see the entire vast body of God's people at the

2. Robert H. Mounce, *Revelation*, rev. ed., New International Commentary on the New Testament (Grand Rapids: Eerdmans, 1997), 285.
3. William Hendriksen, *More than Conquerors: An Interpretation of the Book of Revelation* (1940; repr., Grand Rapids: Baker, 1967), 157.

end of the age or whether it envisions those who have passed from earth to heaven during the trials of this age. The sea is a biblical image for the powers of chaos and evil that rise up against God's creation and rule. It was from the sea, after all, that the dragon summoned the first beast to terrorize God's people. The raging waves have now been stilled, showing God's permanent conquest over evil and sin. The crystal sea is thus a glorious vision of God's sovereign power as Creator and his triumph as Redeemer. Since the exodus imagery of this vision is made explicit, we should also think of the glassy sea as the final version of the Red Sea passage by which God delivered Israel from the army of Pharaoh in the time of Moses. H. B. Swete writes that the saints' "exodus from the spiritual Egypt (xi. 8) has led them through the Red Sea of Martyrdom, which is now exchanged for the Crystal Sea of Heaven."[4] The sea of glass is now "mingled with fire" (Rev. 15:2). This red glow speaks "of the fire through which the Martyrs passed, and yet more of the wrath about to fall on the world which had condemned them."[5]

The saints praising God alongside the crystal sea of heaven are identified as "those who had conquered the beast and its image and the number of its name" (Rev. 15:2). The "beast" refers to the tyrannical powers in service to Satan, which in John's time were concentrated in the Roman emperor Domitian. The beast's "image" refers to his desire to be glorified as God, as Domitian demanded throughout Asia, and "the number of its name" refers to perverted worship of man-centered idolatry. Just as Moses and the Israelites sang a hymn of God's deliverance after the passage of the Red Sea, the saints in heaven "sing the song of Moses, the servant of God, and the song of the Lamb" (15:3). Moses sang beside the parted Red Sea, "The LORD is my strength and my song, and he has become my salvation" (Ex. 15:2). By the crystal sea of heaven, the glorified saints' song is also called "the song of the Lamb." Jesus referred to his own death as an "exodus" (Luke 9:31), since in sacrificing his life he was the true Passover Lamb whose blood redeemed God's people and set them free from sin to know and worship the Lord.

Many of the saints arrived in heaven having been cruelly put to death on earth by the servants of the beast. So how can they be named conquerors over him? The answer was given to John in Revelation 12: "They have conquered

---

4. Henry Barclay Swete, *Commentary on Revelation*, 2 vols. (1911; repr., Grand Rapids: Kregel, 1977), 2:195.

5. Ibid., 2:194.

him by the blood of the Lamb and by the word of their testimony, for they loved not their lives even unto death" (Rev. 12:11). The saints were victorious by holding firm in their faith to the only atonement for sin, God's gift of his Son, Jesus, to die on the cross. Since the cost of fidelity to Christ was suffering and death at the hands of the world, their willingness to experience these was their victory over the world. William Barclay writes: "It was the very fact that they died that made them victors; if they had remained alive by being false to their faith, they would have been the defeated."[6]

This vision provides yet another proof of the identification of the Christian church with Old Testament Israel, showing the fundamental error of those who regard Israel and the church as having different identities. The vision of the saints holding harps in their hands also undermines the teaching of those Christians who regard the use of musical instruments as belonging only to the Old Testament temple setting. Surely we must regard the church on earth in basic continuity with the church in heaven, and this vision links Christians today not only with the temple worship of the Old Testament but also with the rich, beautiful, and apparently instrumental worship of heaven. Most importantly, the vision links New Testament believers to the exodus salvation under Moses, which was a type of what we look forward to receiving: salvation by the atoning blood of the Lamb and by God's vengeful wrath against the persecuting world.

Some readers may question the rightness of Christians' rejoicing over the judgment of unbelievers. This passage shows, however, that it is through the judgment of the wicked world that the people of God are saved from its oppression. Just as Israel escaped the spears of Pharaoh's chariot host when the Red Sea waters drowned the enemy, so the saints in heaven stand beside the crystal sea, praising God for his power and righteousness in saving them through the plagues that the seven angels will pour on the earth.

THE FINALITY OF ETERNAL JUDGMENT

Revelation 15 joins the opening vision of the worshiping saints with a vision of the opened sanctuary of God, from which wrath comes: "After this I looked, and the sanctuary of the tent of witness in heaven was opened,

6. William Barclay, *The Revelation of John*, 3rd ed., 2 vols., New Daily Study Bible (Louisville: Westminster John Knox, 2004), 2:133.

and out of the sanctuary came the seven angels with the seven plagues" (Rev. 15:5–6). It is the sanctuary of the "tent of witness," the heavenly counterpart to the tabernacle in which God dwelt during Israel's wilderness wanderings, thus connecting the victory of God's people with the presence of God that went with them. This is the true "tent of witness in heaven," and its opening reveals the presence, power, and covenant faithfulness of God. The "testimony" of the tabernacle centered on the law of God written on the Ten Commandments kept within the ark of the covenant. It is in keeping with the testimony of God's law that the final plagues come from God's holy presence to judge nations given over to sin. The tabernacle also bore testimony to the mercy of God, since atoning sacrifices were offered there for the forgiveness of his people's sin. Now that same mercy of God for his people expresses itself in the final judgment of those who persist, like Pharaoh of old, in afflicting the church.

The appearing of this heavenly tabernacle should comfort Christians who face the threat or reality of worldly affliction. It says that no Pharaoh or Domitian can persist in the persecution of the church without in due time receiving God's terrible wrath. Today, Christians are menaced by the most savage violence in lands dominated by Islam. In the West, radically secular governments are becoming increasingly intolerant of Christian truth and morality, so that "soft" persecution is likely to become much harder. As a result, the Christian church faces a dire worldwide threat that would have been unimaginable a hundred, fifty, or even twenty years ago. But what is most important has not changed. God remains enthroned in heaven, so that nothing can transpire without his will. His holy character does not change, so that sin must always be judged, both in history and at its end. His covenant faithfulness ensures that his people will be upheld under persecution so as not to falter and that their oppressors will be cast down under plagues that come from heaven. His mercy, revealed in the Bible's covenant of grace, ensures that believers in Jesus will personally be redeemed from sin and corporately redeemed to stand beside the crystal sea of heaven rejoicing in praise.

A historical example of the inevitability of God's judgment can be seen in the differing histories of England and France. In the late medieval period there was little difference between the two kingdoms. England's Plantagenet rulers were just as cruelly violent, greedy, and ungodly as the Bourbon kings of France. Both dynasties cruelly repressed those who used the Bible to challenge Roman Catholicism. In England, the Lollards who followed the teaching of John Wycliffe by preaching the gospel were officially outlawed, and in France the Waldensians were bloodily persecuted. As Revelation predicted, neither England nor France was restrained by divine calamities that fell on them and partial judgments that warned them to repent and turn to Jesus Christ. Among these was the dreadful "black death" that killed more than a third of Europeans and was often depicted in terms of the plagues of wrath in Revelation 15.

The decisive opportunity for both kingdoms arrived in the gospel outpouring of the Protestant Reformation in the sixteenth century. The Frenchman John Calvin devoted his *Institutes of the Christian Religion* to the French king, in hopes that he might read the volume and turn France to Christ. But France so violently repressed the gospel that the academy from which Calvin sent church planters to his native land was somberly known as "Calvin's School of Death." In England, the Reformation teaching also met with bloody opposition. In reaction to Bloody Mary's burning of the Reformed preachers, however, great numbers of English people turned to the gospel during the reign of Queen Elizabeth. But the seventeenth century was very different in France. When Louis XIV revoked the Edict of Nantes in 1685, the Christians were slaughtered in thousands or driven into exile, the gospel was officially banned, and the final judgment of the French monarchy was sealed. When the winds of revolution blew in the eighteenth century, England's folly cost her the great Colonies of the United States, but the monarchy held firm and survived. France, unrepentant in rejecting the gospel, fell under the full fury of God's judgment as the Revolution's guillotines put a final end to her wicked monarchy and filled the streets of Paris with blood.

In Revelation 15:7, "one of the four living creatures gave to the seven angels golden bowls full of the wrath of God who lives forever and ever." These angels came "out of the sanctuary . . . with the seven plagues," dressed as servants who reflect the holiness and glory of God: "clothed in pure, bright linen, with golden sashes around their chests" (Rev. 15:6). Verse 7 emphasizes God's eternal being, which guarantees that his judgment of evil and his covenant faithfulness to his people will never fail. As a result, no nation or power that rebels against him and persecutes his people will be able to stand. Either they will be judged in history and destroyed or they will face the ultimate fury of Jesus Christ on the day of his return to save his church. Coming out from the presence of the ever-living God and from the tabernacle where his holy law and covenant faithfulness to his people are recorded, these angels "show that no individual or nation can defy the law of God without having to suffer the consequences."[7] The opening of the tabernacle and the appearing of the wrath-bearing angels indicate that God holds people and nations accountable to his revealed Word in the Bible. George Eldon Ladd writes: "The emphasis upon the eternity of God . . . is a reminder that, although evil may seem to dominate affairs in human history, God is the eternal one whose purposes cannot be frustrated, even by satanic and demonic evil."[8]

Revelation 15:8 concludes the chapter by stating that "the sanctuary was filled with smoke from the glory of God and from his power, and no one could enter the sanctuary until the seven plagues of the seven angels were finished." Exodus 40:35 tells us that God's glory visibly fell on the tent of meeting in a cloud of smoke and glory, so that "Moses was not able to enter" it. This recurred in the time of Solomon when God's visible glory filled the temple at its dedication (1 Kings 8:10–11). By saying that this glory cloud filled the sanctuary "until the seven plagues of the seven angels were finished," John indicates that nothing can halt God's final wrath when it comes and that no mediation remains for those whose rebellion in unbelief has brought them under the plagues of God's wrath. In the time of Moses, Pharaoh's hard-hearted rejection of God's Word brought the plagues of wrath that broke his power and set God's people free. In like manner, God sends plagues to bring unrepentant people and nations to judgment in defense of his church.

To Glorify Your Name!

The opening and the closing of Revelation 15 join in showing God's saving his people by means of his judgment on persecuting nations and unbelieving people. The heart of the chapter's message comes through the song that is sung in between: "the song of Moses, the servant of God, and the song of the Lamb" (Rev. 15:3). If the opened tabernacle in heaven provides

---

7. Ibid., 2:137.

8. George Eldon Ladd, *A Commentary on the Revelation of John* (Grand Rapids: Eerdmans, 1972), 207.

a warning to the enemies of Christ and his gospel, this song provides the chapter's application to believers.

First, this heavenly song urges believers to be preoccupied not with the changing events of earth but rather with the glory and might of the unchanging and holy God. What is true of the saints above should increasingly be true of believers here below: "They sing the song of Moses, the servant of God, and the song of the Lamb, saying, 'Great and amazing are your deeds, O Lord God the Almighty! Just and true are your ways, O King of the nations!'" (Rev. 15:3).

The entire history of God's people was summed up by the experience of Moses and Israel when their backs were to the Red Sea, with the bloodthirsty army of Pharaoh bearing down on them. Moses cried aloud, "Fear not, stand firm, and see the salvation of the Lord, which he will work for you today" (Ex. 14:13). God sent forth his power, parting the Red Sea waters for Israel to pass through, and then drowning the host of Pharaoh in the waves. God glorifies himself through great and amazing deeds that show forth his power. The same God who parted the Red Sea, caused the walls of Jericho to fall down, and converted Saul of Tarsus to become the apostle Paul is still saving his people and making a pathway for his church today.

Not only does God perform mighty deeds, but he does so in a way that is "just and true" (Rev. 15:3). It is always the wicked that he casts down in judgment and always those justified through faith in Christ that he saves. The glory and righteousness of God's mighty acts completely captivate the thoughts of those gathered into heaven, setting the example for us below. Swete writes: "In the Presence of God the martyrs forget themselves; their thoughts are absorbed by the new wonders that surround them; the glory of God and the mighty scheme of things in which their own sufferings form an infinitesimal part are opening before them; they begin to see the great issue of the world-drama, and we hear the doxology with which they greet their first unclouded vision of God and his works."[9]

Second, the song of the redeemed above reminds us that we should fear only God, and not the Pharaohs of this world. They sing: "Who will not fear, O Lord, and glorify your name? For you alone are holy" (Rev. 15:4). This was the effect on Israel of the destruction of Pharaoh's army in the Red Sea, prompting the original song of Moses: "Israel saw the great power that the

---

9. Swete, *Revelation*, 2:196.

LORD used against the Egyptians, so the people feared the LORD, and they believed in the LORD and in his servant Moses" (Ex. 14:31). Only God is to be feared, for his holiness and power, and his name alone is to be glorified.

This attitude was also seen in the earliest followers of Jesus. An example is given in Acts 12, when Herod Agrippa began persecuting the believers in deadly earnest. Herod had put the apostle James to death by the sword and had arrested Peter with the intent of taking his life as well. So how did the church respond? Did the believers seek to rise up politically or militarily against Herod? Did they seek to compromise with Herod, urging Peter to mold his doctrine to accommodate the Jewish king's demands? Did they adopt worldly styles of living, worship, and teaching, as so many evangelical churches are doing today? The answer is that they held a prayer meeting, turning their faces to God and expecting him to do great and amazing deeds. At the house of Mary, the mother of John Mark, "many were gathered together and were praying" (Acts 12:12).

An amusing scene from this chapter helps explain why Christians are so weak in prayer today. In answer to the prayers of the church, God sent an angel, who was easily able to break Peter out of Herod's jail. Peter went to the house where the Christians were praying and knocked on the door. The problem was that when the door was opened, no one would believe that it was really Peter! "You are out of your mind," they told the servant girl who announced the apostle's arrival (Acts 12:15). Like us, they forgot that God really does answer prayer. They should have been expecting the knock on the door! Perhaps the reason we are so weak in prayer is that we also doubt that God is able or willing to answer. If we learn from the Bible to fear God and not man, we will pray with greater expectancy and experience greater power from on high.

Third, the song of Moses and of the Lamb reminds us to focus our labors on serving the kingdom of God that has now come into the world through Christ and is now advancing through history. This means that in addition to prayer, we should be zealous in our commitment to the witness of the gospel and world missions. "All nations will come and worship you, for your righteous acts have been revealed," they sing (Rev. 15:4). I mentioned at the beginning of this chapter that Christ's kingdom is the rock that comes to smash the kingdoms of this world. His rule began when he ascended into heaven, beginning the church age in which we now live. Paul wrote of this:

"He must reign until he has put all his enemies under his feet" (1 Cor. 15:25). Christ is reigning and conquering now through the spread of the gospel. We should therefore be fully committed to this work, knowing that a great host from every tribe, tongue, and nation is gathering above now as the harvest of Christ's kingdom and will enter together into the glory of the age to come in worship of him.

Finally, the song of the redeemed church in heaven reminds us that the purpose of our salvation is the eternal praise of God. One of our hymns looks forward to the scene of this chapter, when the triumphant church will worship in God's presence in heaven:

> By the sea of crystal, saints in glory stand,
> Myriads in number, drawn from every land.
> Robed in white apparel, washed in Jesus' blood,
> They now reign in heaven with the Lamb of God.[10]

That hymn may look forward to the day when the whole glorified church reigns in glory with Christ. But as we sing it now, we are reminded that Christ reigns gloriously in us while we worship him on earth, amid an unbelieving world, under threat of constant opposition, and expressing through faith in his Word our confidence in the victory of Christ, which is our own hope of salvation.

10. William Kuipers, "By the Sea of Crystal" (1933).

41

THE VINDICATION OF WRATH

Revelation 16:1–7

*And I heard the angel in charge of the waters say, "Just are you,
O Holy One, who is and who was, for you brought
these judgments." (Rev. 16:5)*

nglican scholar N. T. Wright tells of an encounter with a former tutor while Wright was working on his doctoral dissertation. Both were out cycling on a day off, and the tutor asked Wright how his research on the doctrine of justification was going. "Actually," he confessed, "I'm having a hard time with wrath." "Aren't we all!" the tutor said cheerfully and rode off on his bicycle.[1]

Wright's teacher was undoubtedly correct: everyone struggles with the terrifying descriptions of God's wrath in the Bible. Even the prophet Malachi bemoaned, "Who can endure the day of his coming, and who can stand when he appears?" (Mal. 3:2). This impulse has led liberal scholars to reconstruct the biblical image of God without the notions of holiness and wrath. H. Richard Niebuhr scorned the liberal evisceration of the Bible's message, describing it in these terms: "A God without wrath brought men without sin into a kingdom without judgment through the ministrations of a Christ

1. N. T. Wright, *Revelation for Everyone* (Louisville: Westminster John Knox, 2011), 141.

without a cross."[2] However palatable such a message may be to secularist trend-setters, it is very far from the Christianity of the Bible.

WRATH UNDER FIRE

For writers unhappy with the biblical portrait of God, two approaches are taken in pronouncing judgment on the biblical doctrine of wrath. The first is to highlight the Bible's teaching of wrath and retributive justice, gleefully using this fact to malign the Bible as primitive and immoral. Atheist provocateur Christopher Hitchens thus describes the book of Revelation as "deluded fantasies" from the mind of the apostle John.[3] He says that "nothing proves the man-made character of religion as obviously as the sick mind that designed hell."[4] Richard Dawkins writes that teaching children "to believe in something like the punishment of . . . sins in an eternal hell" is a worse form of "child abuse" than their sexual molestation by Roman Catholic priests.[5]

A second approach places divine wrath under fire from some evangelical scholars, who seek to deny that the Bible teaches a God who burns with anger against sinners and sin. As an example, Joel Green and Mark Baker write: "The Scriptures as a whole provide no ground for a portrait of an angry God needing to be appeased in atoning sacrifice."[6] Steve Chalke states that the idea of divine wrath "makes a mockery of Jesus' own teaching to love your enemies and to refuse to repay evil with evil."[7] These and similar views have recently been expressed in books printed by evangelical publishers.

It is hardly necessary, when preaching from the later chapters of Revelation, to argue that the Bible does in fact speak of God's angry and violent judgment on sin. This is true not only of Revelation: hundreds of references to God's wrath are found throughout the Bible. Yet one need only read Revelation 16:1 to prove the Bible's teaching on this subject: "Then I heard a loud voice from the temple telling the seven angels, 'Go and pour out on

2. H. Richard Niebuhr, *The Kingdom of God in America* (1937; repr., New York: Harper & Row, 1959), 193.

3. Christopher Hitchens, *God Is Not Great: How Religion Poisons Everything* (New York: Twelve Books, 2007), 56.

4. Ibid., 219.

5. Richard Dawkins, *The God Delusion* (New York: Houghton Mifflin Harcourt, 2006), 328.

6. Joel B. Green and Mark D. Baker, *Recovering the Scandal of the Cross: Atonement in New Testament & Contemporary Contexts* (Downers Grove, IL: InterVarsity Press, 2000), 51.

7. Steve Chalke and Alan Mann, *The Lost Message of Jesus* (Grand Rapids: Zondervan, 2003), 182–83.

the earth the seven bowls of the wrath of God.'" The command comes from the inner sanctuary of the very heavenly temple where God dwells in his eternal being. The angels are his servants and the bowls contain his wrath that is to be poured out in vengeful judgment. So the Bible plainly teaches the terrible doctrine of divine wrath.

With the Bible's teaching of wrath, the question turns to the moral acceptability of divine anger. This question is also answered in the opening section of Revelation 16. Not only does the angel who speaks in verses 5 and 6 defend God, but he praises God profusely for his wrath: "Just are you, O Holy One, who is and who was, for you brought these judgments" (Rev. 16:5). He further explains the reason why God's wrath is to be praised: "For they have shed the blood of saints and prophets, and you have given them blood to drink. It is what they deserve!" (16:6).

If the book of Revelation is any guide, the doctrine of God's wrath and judgment on all sin needs to be proclaimed by Christians today. Believers also need to defend these truths against atheistic scorn and scholarly confusion. In this cause, the opening section of Revelation 16 highlights four aspects of God's wrath that are worthy of praise: the holiness of wrath, the vengeance of wrath, the justice of wrath, and the benefits of God's wrath.

THE HOLINESS OF WRATH

Revelation 16:1–4 describes the outpouring of the bowls of God's wrath on the earth, beginning with his command: "Then I heard a loud voice from the temple telling the seven angels, 'Go and pour out on the earth the seven bowls of the wrath of God'" (Rev. 16:1). Chapter 15 concluded with a picture of the inner sanctuary so filled with smoke that "no one could enter the sanctuary until the seven plagues of the seven angels were finished" (15:8). This being the case, none other than God himself could be speaking from within his temple. This inner sanctuary is the most holy place in the entirety of creation. According to Psalm 27:4, to gaze inside this temple is to see "the beauty of the LORD" in all his holiness. It is from this place of perfect beauty, love, and divine splendor that the bowls of wrath come to be poured on the earth. This fact tells us the most important thing for us to know about God's anger: it is a holy wrath that responds in terrible violence precisely because of God's moral perfection and the morally heinous nature of sin.

When critics ask how God can react so violently against his creatures, the first and most important answer is that God is infinitely and perfectly holy and that therefore the sins of man have elicited God's wrath. God is not angry with man as such, but at man as sinner. His holiness must abhor evil, and therefore the evil of sin alone explains God's wrath. David wrote: "For you are not a God who delights in wickedness; evil may not dwell with you. . . . You destroy those who speak lies; the LORD abhors the blood-thirsty and deceitful man" (Ps. 5:4–6). Stephen Charnock writes: "A love of holiness cannot be without a hatred of everything that is contrary to it. As God necessarily loves himself, so he must necessarily hate everything that is against himself: and as he loves himself for his own excellency and holiness, he must necessarily detest whatsoever is repugnant to his holiness because of the evil of it."[8]

An emphasis on God's holiness reminds us not to compare God's wrath to man's often-sinful and petulant anger. God's wrath is never an uncontrolled rage. John Stott explains: "God's anger is absolutely pure and uncontaminated by those elements which render human anger sinful. . . . Dr. Charles Cranfield's summary is that God's *orgē* is 'no nightmare of an indiscriminate, uncontrolled, irrational fury, but the wrath of the holy and merciful God called forth by, and directed against, men's *asebeia* (ungodliness) and *adikia* (unrighteousness).'"[9] Stott adds, "The wrath of God . . . is his steady, unrelenting, unremitting, uncompromising antagonism to evil in all its forms and manifestations."[10] Benjamin Warfield writes that without wrath for sin, God "would not be a moral being: for every moral being must burn with hot indignation against all wrong perceived as such. If we do not react against the wrong when we see it, in indignation and avenging wrath, we are either unmoral or immoral."[11] Therefore, it is not God's wrath that warrants our chastisement, but instead an absence of God's wrath that would bring his holiness into question.

As we see God's wrath poured out on the earth, the sea, and the rivers and springs, we are reminded of his obligations as Creator. A. W. Tozer explains:

8. Stephen Charnock, *The Existence and Attributes of God*, 2 vols. (Grand Rapids: Baker, 1996), 2:118.
9. John R. W. Stott, *The Cross of Christ* (Downers Grove, IL: InterVarsity Press, 1986), 106, quoting C. E. B. Cranfield, *The Epistle to the Romans* (Edinburgh: T&T Clark, 1975), 1:111.
10. Ibid., 173.
11. Benjamin Breckinridge Warfield, *Faith and Life* (1916; repr., Edinburgh: Banner of Truth, 1974), 28.

"The holiness of God, the wrath of God, and the health of the creation are inseparably united. God's wrath is His utter intolerance of whatever degrades and destroys. He hates iniquity as a mother hates the polio that takes the life of her child."[12] Here, the wrath of God is linked to his love, since he does not simply walk away in disgust from his fallen creation. The world belongs to him and was created for the display of his glory. God in his love for his own work is utterly, irreconcilably opposed to sin, is resolved to stamp it out, and through his wrathful judgment is determined to cleanse the world for its holy destiny in the glorious return of Jesus Christ (Rom. 8:19–21).

In Revelation 16:5, "the angel in charge of the waters" vindicates God's wrath. It is not entirely clear what it means for this angel to have charge of the waters: it could mean that he is the one who pours the bowls of wrath on the waters, or just as there are angels at the four corners of the earth (Rev. 7:1) there may be an angel in charge of the earth's waters. What matters is not his identity but his acclamation of God's character: "Just are you, O Holy One, who is and who was, for you brought these judgments" (16:5). The eternity of God and the holiness of God work together in ensuring that God must always respond to sin with burning wrath. Charnock writes: "He can no more cease to hate impurity than he can cease to love holiness. . . . [God] should renounce himself, deny his own essence and his own divinity, if his . . . aversion from evil could be changed."[13]

From the perspective of God's holiness, it is not divine wrath but rather the criticism of it that reveals a morally defective attitude. The reason that people react so violently against God's wrath is that they lack God's utter revulsion for evil.

THE VENGEANCE OF WRATH

The second reason for God's wrath is his vengeance against his enemies. Who are the recipients of God's vengeful wrath? They are "the people who bore the mark of the beast and worshiped its image" (Rev. 16:2). God's wrath falls on the unbelieving world as the servants and worshipers of his supreme opponent, the dragon and his beasts. Jesus said, "Whoever is not with me is against me" (Luke 11:23). Revelation shows this by depicting all

12. A. W. Tozer, *The Knowledge of the Holy* (San Francisco: HarperSanFrancisco, 1992), 166.
13. Charnock, *The Existence and Attributes of God*, 2:121.

mankind as bearing either the mark of the beast in idolatry or the mark of Christ through faith (Rev. 13:17–14:1). The world on which the bowls of God's wrath are poured is a world that rejected God in rebellious unbelief and chose instead to worship the evil powers under Satan.

Moreover, God's enemies "have shed the blood of saints and prophets" (Rev. 16:6). God's wrath is thus in part a repayment for the violence inflicted against his people. Paul urged suffering Christians never to avenge themselves, "but leave it to the wrath of God, for it is written, 'Vengeance is mine, I will repay, says the Lord'" (Rom. 12:19). This vengeance is now seen in the bowls of God's wrath. Revelation 6:10 showed the souls of the martyrs in heaven asking God, "How long before you will judge and avenge our blood on those who dwell on the earth?" Therefore, in the background of God's wrath are the prayers of his suffering people. In 16:7, John reports that he "heard the altar saying, 'Yes, Lord God the Almighty, true and just are your judgments!'" The martyrs' souls were earlier seen beneath the altar, and on it their prayers for vengeance were offered (8:3), so this cry probably reflects the suffering church's satisfaction regarding the vengeful wrath of God for her foes.

When we speak of the vengeance of God's wrath, we are noting its necessity in saving his people from the wicked. Jesus taught his disciples to pray, "Deliver us from evil" (Matt. 6:13), and it is by his wrath on the ungodly that God fully answers this prayer. Therefore, God's *vengeful* wrath is also his *redeeming* wrath. This comes through in the exodus background for the judgments poured out in this chapter. The first bowl of wrath brought "harmful and painful sores" on the ungodly (Rev. 16:2). This corresponds to the sixth plague on Pharaoh and Egypt, when God inflicted boils and sores on their skin (Ex. 9:8–12). The second bowl made the sea become "like the blood of a corpse," so that "every living thing died that was in the sea" (Rev. 16:3). The third bowl was poured "into the rivers and the springs of water," so that "they became blood" (16:4). These judgments correspond to the first plague on Egypt, when the Nile was turned to blood so that all the fish died (Ex. 7:21). The point is that just as God poured his wrath onto Egypt so as to free his people from bondage and suffering, so do all of God's judgments in history deliver the Christian church from the afflictions of the world. The cataclysmic outpouring of wrath that will end the history of this age will have the result of finally delivering the people of God and granting them the victory of eternal rest.

Christians know that God is going to judge all evil and save his people from the afflictions of the wicked. Knowing this frees believers to serve as agents of mercy and grace in the world for the sake of the gospel. Paul thus urged: "'If your enemy is hungry, feed him; if he is thirsty, give him something to drink . . . .' Do not be overcome by evil, but overcome evil with good" (Rom. 12:20–21).

THE JUSTICE OF WRATH

A third feature that vindicates God's anger is the justice of his wrath. "Just are you, O Holy One," the angel cries. God is praised for judging those who shed the blood of his saints and prophets, since "it is what they deserve!" (Rev. 16:5–6). "True and just are your judgments!" adds the voice of the martyrs (16:7).

We may notice that the judgments of the seven bowls correspond closely to the previous judgments of the seven trumpets. Particularly, the second and third bowls line up with the second and third trumpets. The second trumpet caused "a third of the sea" to become blood and "a third of the living creatures in the sea" to die (Rev. 8:8–9). The third trumpet caused "a third of the rivers" and "springs of waters" to be polluted (8:10). The fourth, fifth, and sixth trumpets also line up roughly with the corresponding bowls of wrath. The main difference is that while the trumpet judgments affected only a third of their targets, since they were judgments of warning, the bowl judgments affect the entirety of their targets, since they are judgments of wrath and destruction.

The point for us to grasp is that these bowl judgments exact a just retribution for sin. They represent God's justice acting in punishment for violations of God's law. Revelation 16:6 says that since the wicked shed the blood of God's servants, they are given blood to drink in return. They receive in God's wrath exactly "what they deserve" (Rev. 16:6). This is in keeping with the pattern of judgment taught all through the Bible. Scholars may assert, as Stephen Travis has done, that "the judgment of God is to be seen not primarily in terms of retribution, whereby people are 'paid back' according to their deeds,"[14] yet this is precisely what the Bible shows over and over again. When Achan stole gold, silver, and precious cloths from fallen Jericho, God had him punished in retribution for his sins. Others who received plain retribution from God include Jeroboam, Ahab and Jezebel, Nebuchadnezzar, and Ananias and Sapphira. Israel herself received retributive justice from God when her idolatry was punished by exile into an idol-worshiping land.

Objections, however, are still raised. Some complain that under this theory, God is the One from whom Christians must be saved. Biblically considered, this statement must be reverently affirmed. The chief and ultimate threat against sinful mankind is indeed God himself: the holy, righteous, and just God who must and will personally judge sin by pouring out the bowls of his holy wrath. This is why the writer of Hebrews urges us to embrace Jesus for salvation, since "it is a fearful thing to fall into the hands of the living God" (Heb. 10:31).

Another objection to God's just wrath is that it conflicts with Jesus' teaching in the Sermon on the Mount. Did not Jesus teach his followers to turn the other cheek? Did he not say, "Love your enemies and pray for those who persecute you, so that you may be sons of your Father who is in heaven" (Matt. 5:39, 44–45)? If God teaches nonretaliation but then pours out wrath in retributive justice, is this not an example of God's telling us to do one thing while he does another? The answer is yes, for the very reason that God is different from us and so able to dispense justice perfectly. In Paul's teaching, we are not to exact revenge precisely because we know that God will: "Vengeance is mine, I will repay, says the Lord" (Rom. 12:19). Garry Williams thus observes, "God would have us not do what he does precisely because he does it. God says, 'do as I say, not as I do,' and justly so, since he is God and we are not."[15]

In considering the first three bowls of wrath, we can see that they involve just recompense for human sin. The worshipers of the beast bore its mark thinking to partake of earthly beauty and pleasure, so God pours out sores and boils on their flesh. They shed the blood of the righteous, so God turns their waters into cesspools of blood and death. The dwellers of earth sought peace and rest in alliance with the powers of hell, so in the fourth bowl God scorches them with fire from heaven (Rev. 16:8–9). Douglas Kelly points

14. Stephen H. Travis, *Christ and the Judgment of God: Divine Retribution in the New Testament* (Basingstoke, UK: Marshall Pickering, 1986), preface.

15. Garry J. Williams, "Penal Substitution: A Response to Recent Criticisms," in *The Atonement Debate*, ed. Derek Tidball, David Hilborn, and Justin Thacker (Grand Rapids: Zondervan, 2008), 178.

out that this is a warning to us if we have not received Jesus as our Savior through faith: "All these future judgments against us will come out of the holy beautiful place in heaven. Proud sinners will be smitten to the ground in horror when it occurs, except they repent before it happens."[16]

THE BENEFITS OF WRATH

The fourth way to see God's wrath vindicated in these verses is to note that the testimony of the angel and the martyrs joins to rejoice in the beneficial results of God's wrath: "Yes, Lord God the Almighty, true and just are your judgments!" (Rev. 16:7). God's wrath is beneficial because it upholds God's law for the well-being of all creation. The world cannot be whole, good, and at peace while evil is in play. What good news it is that God's wrath is directed at all sin and evil so that the world will be cleansed in the end and that God's righteousness will finally reign over all.

N. T. Wright imagines a village in the country outside the big city, which seldom receives the attention of government officials. In the absence of law-keepers, a builder is cheated by his customer. A widow has her purse stolen, and no one has power to help her. A family is evicted from their home by a greedy landlord who violates the contract. All kinds of these injustices wreak misery and loss without anyone to come and set things right.

Finally, however, a judge arrives in town with his officers. He hears each case carefully and renders effective justice, with a special eye to the care of those who are weak and needy. Under his rule, judgment is done, the guilty are punished, and unjust losses are restored. The cheat will make his payment. The thief will return the stolen purse with recompense. The landlord will give way to the obligations of his agreements. Now, what will be the response of this community to the judge and his officials who have come? Wright answers: "The village as a whole will heave a sigh of relief. Justice has been done. The world has returned into balance. A grateful community will thank the judge from the bottom of its collective heart."[17]

If we magnify this village's experience to the global level, we see how good it is that God judges all evil with wrath and judgment. How blessed it is when

---

16. Douglas F. Kelly, *Revelation*, Mentor Expository Commentary (Tain, Ross-shire, Scotland: Mentor, 2012), 297.

17. Wright, *Revelation for Everyone*, 138.

divine judgment achieves this in history, and how completely wonderful it will be when God concludes history in a holy, vengeful, and just wrath that puts everything to rights! David anticipated this joyous achievement in Psalm 58:11: "Mankind will say, 'Surely there is a reward for the righteous; surely there is a God who judges on earth.'" And because of the goodness of God's wrath in judging evil, the redeemed people of God will add their voices to those of the angels in worshiping God with great praise: "Just are you, O Holy One, who is and who was, for you brought these judgments. For they have shed the blood of saints and prophets, and you have given them blood to drink. It is what they deserve!" (Rev. 16:5–6).

SALVATION FROM WRATH

N. T. Wright told his tutor that he was having a hard time with wrath while he was researching the doctrine of justification. Yet that very doctrine provides the solution to sinners in need of escape from God's wrath. Indeed, when sinners struggle with the terrible doctrine of divine judgment, we might point them to one verse in the book of Romans as solving their plight. In Romans 3:25, Paul says of Christ Jesus that "God put [him] forward as a propitiation by his blood, to be received by faith." Everything in Romans before that verse is bad news, given God's anger against sin. Paul started by saying that "the wrath of God is revealed from heaven against all ungodliness and unrighteousness of men" (1:18). He added, "None is righteous, no, not one" (3:10). Paul summarized that "all have sinned and fall short of the glory of God" (3:23), and that therefore all are under God's wrath. But the good news that we need declares that God sent his Son, Jesus, to be a propitiation for our sin, that is, a sacrifice to bear the wrath of God in the place of those who receive him in faith. Before this statement, everything is bad news because of God's wrath on sin. After this provision of God's grace, everything is good news because of the saving sufficiency of Jesus Christ. Revelation 16 has answered complaints against the wrath of God by showing that it is a holy, vengeful, just, and beneficial wrath. But for sinners themselves who are under the threat of God's wrath, the true solution is to believe in Jesus so as to be freed from the righteous judgment that our sins deserve.

Indeed, once we find a refuge from sin in the cross of Christ, believers no longer marvel at the problem of God's wrath. Seeing the evil of sin and the holiness of God, we realize that his wrath is the most logical and most reasonable thing in the world! Our marvel is instead directed to the wonder of the redeeming grace by which the very God we have offended sent his Son to bear the penalty of our sins. No one ever wrote a hymn to "amazing wrath," since wrath is the most obvious response of God to sin. But grace is truly amazing: of it we sing, "Amazing grace!—how sweet the sound—that saved a wretch like me!"[18]

Moreover, once we have received the grace of God through faith in Christ, the very characteristics that made God's wrath so terrible become now the source of our greatest hope. God is holy, and through faith in Christ sinners are forgiven and cleansed to be the holy ones of God. The wrath of God is vengeful, but those who believe in Jesus become the children of God who receive his watchful care (John 1:11–12). The wrath of God is just, so that every sin will receive its just retribution. But for those who are covered and forgiven through his Son, God "cancel[ed] the record of debt that stood against us with its legal demands. This he set aside, nailing it to the cross" (Col. 2:14). Therefore, having been cleansed, sanctified, adopted, and forgiven, Christians may join in wondering adoration of the righteous God. "Yes, Lord God the Almighty," we say, "true and just are your judgments!" (Rev. 16:7). Even more, we rejoice with great glory that the righteous God has brought us salvation, for God shed the blood of his only Son, that we who deserve his wrath might receive instead the glory of his grace.

---

18. John Newton, "Amazing Grace!" (1779).

42

ARMAGEDDON

Revelation 16:8—16

They were scorched by the fierce heat, and they cursed the name
of God who had power over these plagues. They did not
repent and give him glory. (Rev. 16:9)

*I*n 852 B.C., the Moabites rebelled against Judah's King
Jehoshaphat, forming a warring coalition with the Ammonites
and the Meunites. Jehoshaphat did not learn of their assault
until the enemy army had assembled at Engedi, a relatively short march from
Jerusalem (2 Chron. 20:2). He was stunned by this sudden calamity, which
threatened total destruction to his nation. With nowhere else to turn, he
called on the Lord, summoning one of the great prayer meetings of the Old
Testament: "All Judah stood before the LORD, with their little ones, their
wives, and their children" (20:13). The king prayed for deliverance: "O our
God, will you not execute judgment on them? For we are powerless against
this great horde that is coming against us. We do not know what to do, but
our eyes are on you" (20:12). God answered by urging him to remain strong
in faith: "Stand firm, hold your position, and see the salvation of the LORD"
(20:17). The next day, when the king and the people looked out on the enemy
camp, "there were dead bodies lying on the ground; none had escaped"
(20:24), and they enriched themselves on the spoil of the enemy (20:25–30).

God's deliverance of Jehoshaphat was anything but an isolated event in the Old Testament. The scenario was virtually repeated in 701 B.C., when King Hezekiah's prayer resulted in God's routing of the Assyrian army of King Sennacherib that was besieging Jerusalem, slaying 185,000 soldiers in the enemy host. The Bible records a similar episode in the book of Judges, when Jabin the king of Canaan and his general Sisera held the people of Israel in subjugation. God used Deborah to summon Barak to rise up in faith and defend God's people.

These scenarios of God's salvation do not belong only to the Old Testament. The book of Revelation, together with the whole New Testament, makes clear that this scenario of disastrous opposition and divine rescue is the manner in which God will save his church at the end of history. According to Deborah's song, Barak's victory occurred "at Taanach, by the waters of Megiddo," where "from heaven the stars fought . . . against Sisera" (Judg. 5:19–20). The book of Revelation seems to make this victory the model for Christ's end-times rescue of his people, saying that the forces bent on destroying the church "assembled . . . at the place that in Hebrew is called Armageddon" (Rev. 16:16), that is, "the mount of Megiddo."

The Fourth and Fifth Bowls

As we have studied Revelation's visions of the seven seals, trumpets, and bowls, we have noted that these generally refer to God's judgments taking place throughout the church age. The sixth in these series, however, refers to events shortly before the end of the age, and the seventh brings us to the return of Christ. In considering the fourth and fifth bowls of wrath, therefore, we should see them as characterizing the world's ungodly response throughout the age as it leads up to the climactic final events.

The fourth bowl of wrath was poured out "on the sun," to make it "scorch people with fire" (Rev. 16:8). The key to this bowl is to note it as the opposite of what the Bible promises to God's faithful people. Psalm 121:5–6 says, "The LORD is your keeper; the LORD is your shade on your right hand. The sun shall not strike you by day, nor the moon by night." Similarly, Revelation 7:16 promised that the redeemed "shall hunger no more, neither thirst anymore; the sun shall not strike them, nor any scorching heat." Here, the Lord is doing exactly the opposite in judging the sinful world. G. K. Beale thus observes that the fourth bowl "symbolizes a covenantal judgment. . . . The people are judged because they have altered God's moral laws, usually through idolatry."[1] In his Sermon on the Mount, Jesus taught that God is kind in making his sun "rise on the evil and the good" (Matt. 5:45). Yet the time comes when God removes the blessing of life from those who rebel against him, so that what is normally a source of blessing becomes a vehicle for divine judgment.

As a judgment for sin, the fourth bowl addresses the situation of Western society today. Our secularist world has deliberately rejected God and tried to bar his influence. As Revelation envisions, we have replaced God with the beast of all-pervasive government, the false prophet of secular humanism, and the seductions of the harlot Babylon. But God is not actually dethroned or excluded. Instead of hearing the Bible's words of covenant blessing—"The Lord bless you and keep you; the Lord make his face to shine upon you" (Num. 6:24–25)—sin-serving mankind receives God's covenant curse. Paul said that "the wrath of God is revealed from heaven against all ungodliness and unrighteousness of men" (Rom. 1:18). Notice the present tense of this judgment, which goes on to note how God gives idolaters over to the misery of perverse living (1:26–31). The fourth bowl depicts this same judgment by scorching the world with "fierce heat" from a divinely cursed sun. In sin, the world becomes harsh and painful.

What is the response of the sin-corrupted secularist to the misery that results from God's judgment on sin? We hear the answer all the time today, as media figures unceasingly blaspheme against God. John writes: "They cursed the name of God who had power over these plagues. They did not repent and give him glory" (Rev. 16:9). On this same basis, "religion" and Christianity are publicly maligned today. Angry atheists point to widespread poverty, ignorance, disease, lawlessness, and relationship breakdowns—all of which are rooted in sin—and then curse God for them. "Where is this kind and loving God that you Christians speak of?" the secularists revile. The answer is that man's own idolatry and sin have turned God's face away in anger.

Some Christians today are foolishly tempted to downplay the reality of God's wrath. They insist that God would never inflict judgment, deny

---

1. G. K. Beale, *The Book of Revelation: A Commentary on the Greek Text*, New International Greek Testament Commentary (Grand Rapids: Eerdmans, 1999), 821.

or minimize God's sovereignty, and announce God's tolerance of moral abominations. In contrast, the Bible is clear in declaring God's furious judgment on the wicked, symbolized in the fourth bowl by the sun's being made to scorch the earth. America today savagely murders her babies, actively promotes sexual indecency, and legislatively wars against God's created design for mankind. What other biblical explanation can there be for the ensuing collapse of our society but indignant divine judgment? This argument infuriates the secularist, who will not admit his guilt or the justice of God's wrath, exactly as portrayed in the fourth bowl of Revelation 16. Douglas Kelly writes: "People who refuse to repent are determined not to recognize any connection between a life that displeases God and the pains and sores that follow,"[2] yet this is precisely the explanation given by the Bible.

God not only places his curse of judgment on a faithless world, but also targets the leaders of spiritual opposition: "The fifth angel poured out his bowl on the throne of the beast, and its kingdom was plunged into darkness" (Rev. 16:10). This judgment is based on the fourth plague on Egypt in the exodus, when God brought darkness on the realm of Pharaoh. The intent was to disgrace the Egyptian sun god Ra, whom Pharaoh was thought to represent. In a similar way, God will shame the satanic dominion behind the governments that oppose the gospel. John's original readers might have connected this darkness to the chaos that engulfed Rome in the years after the suicide of the evil ruler Nero, which shook the empire's confidence. G. K. Beale points out that "world rulers who oppress the saints and foster idolatry" may expect to suffer "internal rebellion" and the "removal of political and religious power."[3] Such divinely ordained setbacks cast a shadow over the secular ideologies behind the beast's power. The plague of darkness in the exodus showed God's sovereignty over Egypt, and God likewise shows his sovereignty over Satan's rule by sowing confusion among his earthly servants.

Today, our public figures seem to acknowledge God by speaking of calamities as "acts of God." Yet a political leader would be reviled if he suggested that disasters such as hurricanes, tornadoes, terrorist attacks, and stock-market crashes are actually divine acts of judgment. Yet all these calamities are well

---

2. Douglas F. Kelly, *Revelation*, Mentor Expository Commentary (Tain, Ross-shire, Scotland: Mentor, 2012), 307.

3. Beale, *Revelation*, 824.

within the scope of woes described in Revelation precisely as God's judgment. Although sinful people would not "repent of their deeds," they still "gnawed their tongues in anguish and cursed" God (Rev. 16:10–11). Having their sources of security toppled—whether financial, political, or ideological—they are portrayed by John as gnawing on their tongues, seeking to maintain self-control. "There is no peace," the Bible says, "for the wicked" (Isa. 57:21). The anxiety of sin is especially intense when God's shadow brings dismay to the dominion of Satan, afflicting the spirits of those who will not forsake their sin or give God the glory he deserves.

THE SIXTH BOWL

While the first five bowls show God's judgment in striking satanic powers throughout the church age, the sixth bowl, like the sixth seal (Rev. 6:12–17) and sixth trumpet (9:13–19), moves us forward to the climactic events preceding Christ's return. The vivid picture of this penultimate vision begins with the angel's pouring "out his bowl on the great river Euphrates, and its water was dried up, to prepare the way for the kings from the east" (16:12).

The Euphrates River was the border between the lands that God gave to Israel and her enemies beyond it. Similarly, in John's time, the Euphrates was the border between Rome and the dreaded Parthian Empire. The city of Babylon was located on the Euphrates, and in Revelation Babylon symbolizes the idolatrous world system. In the Old Testament, the parting or drying up of waters was an act of God's intervention in order to advance the cause of his people. Here, he dries up the Euphrates "to prepare the way for the kings from the east."

There are differing views regarding these "kings from the east" (Rev. 16:12). Most scholars consider them to symbolize warfare among the world's powers. This would be the idea if the Parthians were in view, since they were Rome's chief enemies. It is also pointed out that Cyrus the Great fulfilled Isaiah's prophecy of the fall of Babylon (Isa. 44:26–45:3) by damming up the Euphrates, using its dry channel as a highway for his troops to attack under the city walls.[4] In both these scenarios, the removal of the river obstacle allows one pagan empire to attack another, to the benefit of God's afflicted

---

4. This event, fulfilling the prophecy of Isaiah, was recorded by Herodotus, *History*, 1.191.

people. It was Cyrus, after all, who issued the decree restoring the Jewish people to Jerusalem, ending their exile and captivity.[5]

We need to be reminded again that Revelation presents visionary symbols, not a straightforward narrative of historical events. This becomes clear when we see Satan's response to this assault from worldly powers: "And I saw, coming out of the mouth of the dragon and out of the mouth of the beast and out of the mouth of the false prophet, three unclean spirits like frogs" (Rev. 16:13). By means of his unholy counterfeit trinity—the dragon, the beast, and the false prophet, signifying Satan, the tyrannical rule of the Antichrist, and false teachers in society and within the organized church—Satan unleashes a spiritual assault. Demons, called "unclean spirits," go forth "like frogs." This points again to the exodus, when God sent a plague of frogs on Egypt (Ex. 8:2–14). The frogs penetrated every household, spreading defilement and making a mind-numbing sound. It is for both the corruption and the deception of their slick and slippery speech that the demons are compared to frogs.

Added to their success in misrepresenting truth, the spirits are "performing signs," going "abroad to the kings of the whole world, to assemble them for battle on the great day of God the Almighty" (Rev. 16:14). In this way we see both Satan's and God's purposes in these events. In response to assault from worldly powers, Satan deceives all the nations into gathering for the climactic battle against God. It was for this very purpose that God dried up the river, which symbolizes the removal of his restraint that had kept earthly forces from uniting against his church. Satan's spiritual deception thus succeeds in the grand humanistic quest to unify the nations, assembling them for the day of their destruction and judgment at Christ's return. The title "kings of the whole world" reminds us of Psalm 2: "The kings of the earth set themselves, and the rulers take counsel together, against the LORD and against his Anointed . . . . He who sits in the heavens laughs; the Lord holds them in derision" (Ps. 2:2–4). Beale explains: "The nations are deceived into thinking that they are gathering to exterminate the saints, but they are gathered together ultimately by God only in order to meet their own judgment at the hands of Jesus."[6]

5. Another view understands the kings of the east as crossing the Euphrates simply to join in battle against God and his people. See William Hendriksen, *More than Conquerors: An Interpretation of the Book of Revelation* (1940; repr., Grand Rapids: Baker, 1967), 163; Philip Edgcumbe Hughes, *The Book of Revelation* (Downers Grove, IL: InterVarsity Press, 1990), 176.

6. Beale, *Revelation*, 835.

The Battle of Armageddon

The name given to this final battle symbolizes the cataclysmic end of the world. John writes: "And they assembled them at the place that in Hebrew is called Armageddon" (Rev. 16:16).

The meaning of *Armageddon* is not seriously in doubt. The Hebrew to which John refers means "Mount Megiddo."[7] *Har* is the Hebrew word for "mount," and Megiddo was a fortress city overlooking the plain to the northwest of Jerusalem that hosted great battles in antiquity and as recently as Napoleon and the British army of World War I. Large armies could amass in the plain of Esdraelon, following the Valley of Jezreel to advance from the seacoast into the heartland of Israel and the Jordan River. Derek Thomas writes, "It was *the* battlefield of Israel."[8] Overlooking it on one side was Mount Tabor, from which Deborah and Barak launched their assault on the Canaanites. Across the valley was Mount Gilboa, where King Saul was slain by the Philistines. Behind Megiddo itself was Mount Carmel, where Elijah conquered the false priests of Baal in service to Jezebel. It was in this plain that Gideon blew his trumpet and overthrew the Midianites. It was also here that Israel's last godly king, Josiah, died in battle with Pharaoh Neco of Egypt. Thomas writes: "It is, then, altogether appropriate that Megiddo should symbolize the location of the battle of the Lord against the forces of darkness and that the final, cataclysmic battle should be pictured as taking place here."[9]

Some scholars envision a literal battle taking place in the future at Megiddo, in which the armies of the entire earth will be gathered to assault a future Jewish state. This approach does not fit the symbolic nature of Revelation's visions. Moreover, large as the plain around Megiddo was for ancient warfare, it could not hold even a single large military formation today, much less the combined armies of the world. Moreover, Revelation specifies the symbolism at work in this passage. Chapter 17 states that the reference to the Euphrates River was a symbol for "peoples and multitudes

7. Meredith G. Kline has advocated the view that *Armaggedon* refers to Har-Moed, the "mount of assembly," that is, Jerusalem. Despite Kline's skillful argument, however, no textual evidence supports this interpretation. See Meredith G. Kline, "Har Magedon: The End of the Millennium," *JETS* 39, 2 (1996): 207–22.

8. Derek Thomas, *Let's Study Revelation* (Edinburgh: Banner of Truth, 2003), 131.

9. Ibid.

and nations and languages" (Rev. 17:15). Even the name Armageddon, or Mount Megiddo, is symbolic, since Megiddo is not a mountain but was a city set on a small mound. Beale writes: "The battles in Israel associated with Megiddo . . . become a typological symbol of the last battle against the saints and Christ, which occurs throughout the earth."[10]

While Har-Megiddo is a symbol, it depicts a very real future event. The Bible gives abundant witness to a final conflict in which the forces of the world unite under a satanically inspired Antichrist to wage war on God's people. Jesus spoke of the deceiving spirits referred to in Revelation 16:14, saying that in the last days "false christs and false prophets will arise and perform great signs and wonders, so as to lead astray, if possible, even the elect" (Matt. 24:24). Paul foretold a great tribulation on the church, when many will fall away from their outward profession of faith. He spoke of "the man of lawlessness," "the son of destruction, who opposes and exalts himself . . . , proclaiming himself to be God" (2 Thess. 2:3–4). This Antichrist appears "by the activity of Satan with all power and false signs and wonders, and with all wicked deception for those who are perishing" (2:9–10). Revelation depicted this same final onslaught, when "the beast . . . will make war" on believers of the witnessing church "and kill them" so that "their dead bodies will lie in the street of the great city" (Rev. 11:7–8).

Revelation 20 says that at the end of this age, Satan will be permitted to deceive the nations one last time (Rev. 20:3). He will "gather [the nations] for battle," marching "up over the broad plain of the earth and surround[ing] the camp of the saints and the beloved city" (20:8–9). Christ appears at this moment to save his church, mounted on a white war horse: "In righteousness he judges and makes war. . . . From his mouth comes a sharp sword with which to strike down the nations" (19:11–15). Robert Mounce writes: "The great conflict between God and Satan, Christ and Antichrist, good and evil, which lies behind the perplexing course of history will in the end issue in a final struggle in which God will emerge victorious and take with him all who have placed their faith in him. This is Har-Magedon."[11] It is, 16:14 proclaims, "the great day of God the Almighty," to which the Scriptures so often looked, when Christ returns to destroy Satan and his evil powers,

10. Beale, *Revelation*, 838.
11. Robert H. Mounce, *Revelation*, rev. ed., New International Commentary on the New Testament (Grand Rapids: Eerdmans, 1997), 302.

to rescue his church, and through the final resurrection and judgment to establish his eternal reign over a rescued and renewed creation that will fully display his glory.

AWAKE AND CLOTHED

At least three important lessons clearly flow from this text. The first lesson is that Christians are to understand the biblical model for the end of history in terms of the besieged city that is rescued by the sudden appearing of Christ. The Bible does not look forward to Christians' winning over the world before Christ's return. Rather, following an age in which the gospel has gone forth to the nations, history will end with Satan's orchestrating a worldwide persecution of Christians. Our situation will be like that of Deborah and Barak, facing in weakness the armed might of a terrible world bent on domination. Deborah sang that as Barak fought "by the waters of Megiddo," the stars of heaven fought to destroy their enemy (Judg. 5:19–20). So it will be in the end, when the sky opens to reveal Christ, returning in omnipotent power with wrath against the oppressors of his church. Our situation will be like Jehoshaphat's when massed hordes appeared from the east, which he had no power to withstand. But in answer to the prayers of God's people, the Lord slew the enemy host and Jehoshaphat and the people saw the salvation of their God. Our situation will be like Hezekiah's when Sennacherib's hordes mockingly besieged Jerusalem, until the angel of the Lord appeared to slay the entire enemy host.

Because of this teaching, when persecution arises Christians are to respond not with dismay but with anticipation of the Lord's coming. Revelation emphasizes that the final tribulation, though great, will be relatively short: symbolically, it is "three and a half days" (Rev. 11:11), that is, "half a time" (12:14). Jesus said, "Now when these things begin to take place, straighten up and raise your heads, because your redemption is drawing near" (Luke 21:28).

This teaching of Christ's sudden rescue should especially comfort downcast believers today. It would be a mistake to think that Bible figures such as Deborah, Jehoshaphat, and Hezekiah succeeded by doing everything right. That is far from the case. The Israelites of Deborah's time had suffered oppression because of their idol-worship. Jehoshaphat was militarily vulnerable because of the disaster of his foolish alliance with wicked King Ahab. Hezekiah had unfaithfully waged rebellion against his Assyrian overlords. God rescued them not because they had deserved salvation by outstanding achievements, but because of his grace for the humble who call on him in faith. Like them, and like the church at the end, you may find that when all seems lost, God is about to arrange your salvation. God saves sinners! So when you are dismayed because of failures in marriage or as a parent, or when your foolish dabbling in sin has left you broken in despair, Har-Megiddo urges you to call on God. You will find that his comforting answer to the saints of old will speak to you as well:

> Fear not, for I have redeemed you;
> I have called you by name, you are mine.
> When you pass through the waters, I will be with you;
> and through the rivers, they shall not overwhelm you;
> when you walk through fire you shall not be burned . . . .
> For I am the LORD your God,
> the Holy One of Israel, your Savior. (Isa. 43:1–3)

The second lesson is so important that Jesus breaks into John's vision to speak directly to his people: "Behold, I am coming like a thief! Blessed is the one who stays awake, keeping his garments on, that he may not go about naked and be seen exposed!" (Rev. 16:15). Here we have both a word of comfort, assuring us that Jesus will come unexpectedly, appearing to his enemies the way that a thief comes in the night, and a word of vital exhortation.

This exhortation answers the question about what Christians are to do while we await the awesome events that will come at the end. Some might respond to the Bible's teaching of Christ's return and conclude that the end is safely in the distant future. Jesus directly confronts this attitude, urging instead constant vigilance. George Eldon Ladd writes: "The whole emphasis is upon the unexpectedness of the Lord's return, and in light of the uncertainty of the times, believers must never relax and sleep but must always be awake."[12] We are not to be deceived by the world's lies or caught up in the sinfulness of the world's ways. Christians are not to buy into

---

12. George Eldon Ladd, *A Commentary on the Revelation of John* (Grand Rapids: Eerdmans, 1972), 215.

the world's vision of peace, prosperity, and success. Having been granted through faith Christ's own garment of righteousness, we are not instead to put on the uniform of the world, nor abandon our fidelity to Christ so that we are shamed like those caught naked in public. Our calling as Christians, therefore, is to live as Christians, bearing the hope of Christians, applying the faith of Christians to a genuine Christian life, seeking by the power of God's grace to live for his pleasure and with an eye on Christ's coming to take us to be with God forever.

Christ's comment about our garment leads to the third application, which is addressed to the unbeliever. According to the Bible, you will stand before God for judgment. In what are you clothed before him? The Bible teaches that we are clothed either in the guilt of our sin or in the free gift of the righteousness of Jesus Christ, which we receive through faith in him. This means that you must stand apart from the attitude of the masses of people in the world, who are so hardened in sin that they refuse in the face of all evidence to repent and glorify God. They reject God despite all the evidence that creation gives to the glory of its Creator. They refuse to admit that history reveals the lordship of a holy God, who casts down evil and preserves his church. At the end of history, the deceit of secular humanism will have betrayed these unbelievers, so that they are gathered for the return of Christ, who comes to save his suffering people, whose tribulation has brought them to the brink of eternal glory. Now is still the day of salvation! If you will repent and believe on Jesus Christ, he will wash you of your sins through the atoning blood of his cross. He will receive you into the presence of God the Father, giving you his own robe of righteousness to wear "on the great day of God the Almighty" (Rev. 16:14). "Truly, truly, I say to you," Jesus taught, "whoever hears my word and believes him who sent me has eternal life. He does not come into judgment, but has passed from death to life" (John 5:24). This is a call to you today, by God's grace, to repent, believe, and give God the glory he deserves, so that you may be saved.

43

THE END HAS COME

Revelation 16:17–21

The seventh angel poured out his bowl into the air, and a loud
voice came out of the temple, from the throne, saying,
"It is done!" (Rev. 16:17)

he final verses of Revelation 16 conclude the fifth major section of Revelation. As we draw closer to the end of the book, we also focus more clearly on the end of history and especially on God's judgment of his enemies. In reading Revelation, Christians may therefore become weary of the unrelenting scenes of divine wrath, as God brings down his enemies one by one. Some readers may even think that John's gospel focus has wavered or been forgotten.

More careful attention, however, will reveal that the bad news of God's wrath on his enemies is organically tied to God's good news for believers. Looking ahead to upcoming chapters, we find that God's judgment on Babylon avenged and vindicated "the blood of prophets and of saints" (Rev. 18:24). The casting down of the harlot Babylon precedes the arrival of Christ's glorious bride for the marriage feast of the Lamb (19:6–8). A blood-drenched Jesus who slays his enemies is also the Savior, mounted on a white horse, who is called "Faithful and True" (19:11). Moving back into our passage, as the seventh bowl of wrath is poured out, the voice from heaven's throne shouts words that thrill the hearts of biblical believers: "It is done!" (16:17).

Readers familiar with John's Gospel inevitably associate the "It is done!" from our passage with Jesus' cry of victory on the cross, "It is finished," after atoning for our sins (John 19:30). After all, John was the writer of both books: if readers today connect the sayings, it is hard to imagine that John himself would not have done so. Moreover, the "loud voice" coming "out of the temple, from the throne" (Rev. 16:17), can only be Christ's. We were earlier told that while the bowls of wrath were being poured, only God could be in the sanctuary (15:8), and parallel passages have named these judgments "the wrath of the Lamb" (6:16). By connecting this cry of divine judgment with the crucified Christ's cry of salvation, we join judgment and salvation as the two sides of Christ's double-edged gospel sword (1:16).

Indeed, there is a profound redemptive-historical relationship between Christ's cry from the cross and this loud call from heaven. Having accomplished redemption by his atoning death, Jesus uttered the Greek word *tetelestai*, meaning "It is accomplished." Now, from heaven at the end of the gospel age, at the brink of his return, Jesus shouts *gegonen*, meaning "It has come to pass." This perfectly fits the redemptive relationship between the two events: the salvation that Christ accomplished on the day of his crucifixion will come fully to pass only in the crowning victory of his day of return.

What results, then, will occur at the end of this age when Christ returns? Our passage presents four endings that arrive with the coming of Jesus and the final judgment: the end of the world, the end of worldly society, the end of sin, and the end of the gospel opportunity for salvation.

THE END OF THE WORLD

First, a clear emphasis of these verses is that Christ's return spells *the end of the world* in its present form. When the seventh bowl was poured, "there were flashes of lightning, rumblings, peals of thunder, and a great earthquake such as there had never been since man was on the earth, so great was that earthquake" (Rev. 16:18). These violent phenomena intensify descriptions that we have previously seen about the end of the world. Revelation 6:12–14 spoke of "a great earthquake" and the sky vanishing "like a scroll that is being rolled up." Now, with the seventh bowl of wrath thrown into the air,

465

the physical world is assaulted by lightning, thunder, and an earthquake to end all earthquakes.

This is not merely *a* great earthquake but *the* great earthquake that Haggai foretold, saying, "In a little while, I will shake the heavens and the earth and the sea and the dry land" (Hag. 2:6). The writer of Hebrews explained that this "indicates the removal of things that are shaken—that is, things that have been made—in order that the things that cannot be shaken may remain" (Heb. 12:27). Revelation 16:20 tells how sweeping is the upheaval of this final great earthquake: "every island fled away, and no mountains were to be found." Objects that symbolize permanence— mountains and islands—are swept away in destruction. Revelation 21:4 says of this that "the former things have passed away." The earth that was corrupted together with mankind in Adam's sin (Gen. 3:17) and con- demned by its rejection of God's Son is shattered in the coming of Christ and the final judgment.

Some scholars argue that the present world is removed in order to be replaced by a completely new one. But it is best to understand that this present physical order will be shaken and purged so as to be renewed and glorified in the new age after Christ's return. Jesus himself referred to the new world as the "regeneration" (NASB) or "renewal" (NIV) (Matt. 19:28—Greek, *palingenesia*). Paul spoke of the undoing of the world as its "redemption" (Rom. 8:23), when "the creation itself will be set free from its bondage to corruption" (8:21).

The fact that the earth itself must be undone reminds us of the gravity of sin in all its forms. When Cain murdered Abel, God cursed him, say- ing, "The voice of your brother's blood is crying to me from the ground" (Gen. 4:10). So does every sin find a witness in the earth on which it was committed, above all the blood of Calvary where God's own Son was ridiculed, tortured, and slain. Therefore, if nothing else will persuade us of the horror of sin, the smashing of the world at the end of the age should prove to us how horrific in God's holy sight is the stain of every sin committed by man.

Paul urged another application from the future end of the world. Writing to the Corinthians, Paul pointed out that "the present form of this world is passing away" (1 Cor. 7:31). Christians should therefore live here with an aim for the new world to come in the kingdom of Christ. Paul explained:

The appointed time has grown very short. From now on, let those who have wives live as though they had none, and those who mourn as though they were not mourning, and those who rejoice as though they were not rejoicing, and those who buy as though they had no goods, and those who deal with the world as though they had no dealings with it. (1 Cor. 7:29–31)

His point was not for Christians to reject the affairs of this present life, but rather that we avoid being preoccupied by them. All that we do *here and now* should serve the *then and there* to which we are called in the kingdom of Christ, as well as the advancement of the gospel, which alone grants admission into the glory to come.

THE END OF WORLDLY SOCIETY

Even more pointed than the world's end is *the end of worldly society*: "The great city was split into three parts, and the cities of the nations fell, and God remembered Babylon the great, to make her drain the cup of the wine of the fury of his wrath" (Rev. 16:19).

Scholars suggest that in John's day, "the great city" would have referred to Rome, the capital of the Mediterranean world. If that is so, Rome was identified as a symbol of the world system, together with Babylon, a city that had been deserted by then for centuries. It is not merely one city or one nation that falls under this judgment but "the cities of the nations," that is, the entire corrupt world system in service to Satan and opposition to Christ. Leon Morris writes that the great city "stands for . . . man ordering his affairs apart from God," along with "the pride of human achievement, the godlessness of those who put their trust in man."[1]

The fact that the seventh bowl was poured out "into the air" (Rev. 16:17) strengthens the idea of the great city as the anti-Christian world society, since Satan is called "the prince of the power of the air" (Eph. 2:2). The devil has manipulated and empowered worldly opposition to God since he led our first parents into sin in the garden of Eden. But now his spiritual realm and the worldly culture that he has led into rebellion against God come under final judgment. Matthew Henry writes: "[Satan] had used all

---

1. Leon Morris, *The Revelation of St. John: An Introduction and Commentary*, Tyndale New Testament Commentaries 20 (Grand Rapids: Eerdmans, 1969), 201.

possible means to preserve the antichristian interest, and to prevent the fall of Babylon—all the influence that he has upon the minds of men, blinding their hearts, raising their enmity to the gospel as high as could be. But now here is a vial poured out upon his kingdom, and he is not able to support his tottering cause and interest any longer."[2]

John sees the great city, the ungodly world culture, "split into three parts" (Rev. 16:19), showing the complete destruction of the city of man. Simon Kistemaker writes: "All the human arguments and philosophical allegations that have been raised against the knowledge of God are utterly demolished."[3] The universal scope of this destruction is seen in the falling of "the cities of the nations." "It is not just Rome or some later great capital of evil that is decimated but all the world's cultural, political, economic, and sociological centers. They fall because they are part of the Babylonian world system."[4] The great city of the human-Satan alliance against God has fallen, together with all its tributaries that cover the earth, so that its pieces topple to the ground. This judgment "symbolizes the shattering of its power as it meets with the overmastering judgment of Almighty God whose supreme authority its citizens have presumed to defy."[5]

John adds the provocative statement that "God remembered Babylon the great" (Rev. 16:19). How often it has seemed that God has forgotten the affairs of this world, including the terrible injustices against his people and the high-handed sins of wicked people in positions of worldly power. This will be especially true during the great tribulation that precedes the end, when evil seems victorious and all hope seems lost. But God has not forgotten. He has heard the cry of his people under affliction (Ex. 2:24–25). And when he chooses to remember so as to act against the wicked, those who opposed Christ and his gospel and persecuted the church will receive their just due in a devastating judgment.

This judgment reminds believers today not to be intimidated by the menacing power of the world or enticed by the seductive pull of its sinful pleasures. When Christians are tempted to desire worldly approval, we should

---

2. Matthew Henry, *Commentary on the Whole Bible*, 6 vols. (Peabody, MA: Hendrickson, n.d.), 6:943.

3. Simon J. Kistemaker, *Revelation*, New Testament Commentary (Grand Rapids: Baker, 2001), 454.

4. G. K. Beale, *The Book of Revelation: A Commentary on the Greek Text*, New International Greek Testament Commentary (Grand Rapids: Eerdmans, 1999), 843.

5. Philip Edgcumbe Hughes, *The Book of Revelation* (Downers Grove, IL: InterVarsity Press, 1990), 179.

remember this end that is in store for the city of the world. In Psalm 73, Asaph admitted that he envied the wicked until he remembered their end: "Truly you set them in slippery places; you make them fall to ruin. How they are destroyed in a moment, swept away utterly by terrors!" (Ps. 73:18–19). Judgment awaits the worldly society of unbelief and immorality, as surely as God is waiting at the end of history. H. B. Swete writes: "The mills of God, if they grind slowly, are never stopped except by human repentance."[6] The destruction of mountains, often associated with idolatry in the Bible, together with the islands, probably shows the full extent of this destruction. Richard C. H. Lenski writes: "No city, even on the most remote island, no fortress of the antichristian empire on a single mountain height escaped the destructive final wrath."[7]

Paul urged Christians to realize, therefore, that "our citizenship is in heaven" (Phil. 3:20). Christian parents should thus be raising their children not for the world but for the kingdom of Christ. While believers live in the world, we must not be of the world so as to enter into its way of thinking and acting. We must not dream worldly dreams of earthly glory, financial security, and self-centered recreation. Churches must not try to put on a worldly facade or adopt styles of worship designed to win approval of the great worldly city. Since our citizenship is not in worldly society but in Christ's kingdom, Paul points out the great incentive and hope that we cherish: "From [heaven] we await a Savior, the Lord Jesus Christ, who will transform our lowly body to be like his glorious body, by the power that enables him even to subject all things to himself" (3:20–21).

THE END OF SIN

Together with the destruction of the worldly society, this passage also shows Christ's return as bringing *the end of sin*. The reason that God remembered Babylon is that God keeps a close record of all sin. The Old Testament presents countless examples of God's noting, recording, and remembering sin, as well as his obligation to punish it. From Cain to Lamech, from Eli's sons Hophni and Phinehas to Ahab and his wife Jezebel, God brought in time

6. Henry Barclay Swete, *Commentary on Revelation*, 2 vols. (1911; repr., Grand Rapids: Kregel, 1977), 2:211.

7. Richard C. H. Lenski, *The Interpretation of St. John's Revelation* (1943; repr., St. Louis: Augsburg Fortress, 2008), 485.

the terrible destruction he threatened for sin. Often God patiently provides a long opportunity for repentance and salvation through faith. Paul writes that "in his divine forbearance he had passed over former sins" (Rom. 3:25), not fully punishing them immediately. Lenski observes: "God restrains his wrath and hopes for and invites to repentance for a long time . . . . He also lets the wicked fill up the measure of his wickedness and thus eliminates any charge that he is hasty and strikes too soon at men who might after all repent. Humanly speaking, this looks like forgetting. When judgment then strikes at last, this looks like sudden remembering."[8] But the law of God has never been abrogated: "The soul who sins shall die" (Ezek. 18:20); and "the wages of sin is death" (Rom. 6:23).

In the end, sin itself will be brought to an end. Paul wrote that after ascending to heaven, Christ "must reign until he has put all his enemies under his feet" (1 Cor. 15:25). In the cataclysmic end of the world, including the final judgment and its punishments, we see the end of sin in the creation made by God. No wonder the angels sing, "Hallelujah! For the Lord our God the Almighty reigns" (Rev. 19:6).

God judged the sin of Babylon by making her "drain the cup of the wine of the fury of his wrath" (Rev. 16:19). This shows that our sins do not merely deviate from the owner's manual of life in some impersonal way, but rather give personal offense to the holy God who made us. God responds to sin with "the fury of his wrath." It also shows the perfect justice by which God makes an end of sin. The punishment of Babylon fits the crime: she made others drink to be intoxicated by her abominations, so now she must be intoxicated with the terrors of divine judgment, drinking the cup of God's wrath down to the dregs.

It is often said that God hates the sin but loves the sinner. This is true, so long as we understand what it means that God loves sinners. John 3:16 says, "God so loved the world, that he gave his only Son, that whoever believes in him should not perish but have eternal life." God loved sinners by sending Jesus as the offered Savior, through faith in his gospel. But sinners who refuse God's loving offer of salvation in Christ will find that in the end even the creation itself rises up in violence against them for bringing so great a curse on the earth.

The destruction of wicked Babylon proves that all who drink the wine of sinful pleasure and remain unforgiven will receive a punishment from God that they deserve. The cup of the fury of God's wrath can produce only

8. Ibid.

infinite condemnation and eternal woe. When God came down on Mount Sinai to give his law to Moses and Israel, lightning and thunder filled the air and earthquakes shook the ground. These phenomena threatened God's judgment on any who broke God's holy law. Now, at the end of the age, God finally shatters the realm of sin, together with all sinners who have neglected the great salvation offered through Jesus Christ.

At the same time, this end to sin should give a great solace to those suffering under a world system that is practically governed by sin and evil. The civil-rights leader Martin Luther King Jr. spoke of his encouragement from knowing that God will defeat and remove all sin one day. He encouraged others of this, writing:

> We must be reminded anew that God is at work in his universe. He is not outside the world looking on with a sort of cold indifference. . . . As we struggle to defeat the forces of evil, the God of the universe struggles with us. Evil dies on the seashore, not merely because of man's endless struggle against it, but because of God's power to defeat it.[9]

Knowing that sin will be defeated at the end of the age should decisively shape the lifestyles of those who look to Christ for salvation. This was Peter's point as he considered the violent end of history:

> Since all these things are thus to be dissolved, what sort of people ought you to be in lives of holiness and godliness, waiting for and hastening the coming of the day of God, because of which the heavens will be set on fire and dissolved, and the heavenly bodies will melt as they burn! But according to his promise we are waiting for new heavens and a new earth in which righteousness dwells.
>
> Therefore, beloved, since you are waiting for these, be diligent to be found by him without spot or blemish, and at peace. And count the patience of our Lord as salvation. (2 Peter 3:11–15)

THE END OF GOSPEL OPPORTUNITY

We have seen that the great cataclysm that accompanies the return of Christ brings the end of the world, the end of worldly society, and the end

9. Martin Luther King Jr., "The Death of Evil upon the Seashore," in *Strength to Love* (New York: Harper & Row, 1963), 64.

of sin. This being the case, it is evident that this same event heralds *the end of the gospel opportunity* by which sinners can be forgiven and cleansed through faith in Jesus Christ. The writer of Hebrews made this point: "And just as it is appointed for man to die once, and after that comes judgment, so Christ, having been offered once to bear the sins of many, will appear a second time, not to deal with sin but to save those who are eagerly waiting for him" (Heb. 9:27–28). This states that Christ's first coming, culminating with his atoning death for sin on the cross, establishes a present opportunity for salvation, through faith in him. During this age, sinners who die without believing in Jesus face the immediate prospect of divine judgment. Then, when Christ returns at the end of the age, the opportunity of salvation is no longer offered. Instead, Jesus delivers those who have been waiting for him even as he brings a destructive end to all those who have rebelled against him.

Another way to say this is that God's plan holds two answers to sin. The first was defined by Christ's cry on the cross, "It is finished" (John 19:30). Jesus' death accomplished forgiveness and salvation for all who come to him in saving faith. For those who confess their sins and turn to Christ for salvation, Paul writes, "There is therefore now no condemnation for those who are in Christ Jesus" (Rom. 8:1). John wrote: "If we confess our sins, he is faithful and just to forgive us our sins and to cleanse us from all unrighteousness" (1 John 1:9). But if we do not turn to the cross for forgiveness, God's second way of dealing with sin is defined by Christ's loud call "It is done!" in Revelation's scenes of final judgment (Rev. 16:17). Likewise, the cup of God's wrath is poured out for all sins. Either Jesus Christ drank it for you when he suffered God's wrath on the cross or you will be made to drink to your eternal ruin on the dreadful day of judgment soon to come.

John's vision showed that even as the terrible judgment falls on the last day, Christ's enemies "cursed God" for this severe plague (Rev. 16:21). This reaction to God's just punishment confirms their enmity to God. As unrepentant enemies and sinners, they are smitten to the ground with "great hailstones, about one hundred pounds each," which "fell from heaven" on them (16:21). Great hail attacks from heaven are a biblical symbol of wrathful judgment on the enemies of God (see Josh. 10:11; Isa. 28:2). Hailstones of this colossal size would easily have enough force to slay all those beneath them, utterly silencing the lips that curse their God. Craig Keener writes, "The world dies in its sin, unwilling to repent."[10]

This judgment shows the need for the renewing grace of the Holy Spirit through the ministry of God's Word. Not even the cataclysms of the end of the age can motivate Satan's minions to repent and give God the glory he deserves, even as the last seconds of gospel opportunity flee from history forever. Keener tells of a man who miraculously survived an air crash. He "always expected people who were dying to cry out to God for mercy in their final moments, but noted that he heard many respond with cursing, following the habits they had spent their life developing."[11] Their example should help persuade you that now is the time to repent before your heart is so hardened in sin and unbelief that you are no longer able to do so. This call is especially urgent if you angrily rise against God in response to minor trials and judgments that you have already experienced. Matthew Henry warns you: "To be hardened in sin and enmity against God by his righteous judgments is a certain token of utter destruction."[12]

At the same time, the annals of the Christian church are filled with stories of those who realized their peril in sin and did receive grace from God to repent, believe, and be saved. One was John L. Girardeau, a student at the College of Charleston who heard the preaching of God's Word about sin and salvation. He spent a month's conflict wrestling with his sin and the looming prospect of hell. Finally, standing at the north corner of King Street and Price's Alley in Charleston, he experienced the light of forgiveness through the blood of Jesus as it broke through, and he cast himself on Christ for salvation. He related, "The heavens and the earth seemed to be singing psalms of praise for redeeming love," and he went on to lead a life of extraordinary usefulness to his Savior and Lord.[13] The same joy and peace can be yours by confessing your sin to Jesus and calling on his name for forgiveness. God's covenant of grace promises all who seek forgiveness through Christ: "I will be merciful toward their iniquities, and I will remember their sins no more" (Heb. 8:12).

---

10. Craig S. Keener, *Revelation*, NIV Application Commentary (Grand Rapids: Zondervan, 1999), 397.

11. Ibid., 400.

12. Henry, *Commentary on the Whole Bible*, 6:943.

13. Quoted in David B. Calhoun, *Our Southern Zion: Old Columbia Seminary (1828–1927)* (Edinburgh: Banner of Truth, 2012), 222.

PART 6

Final Judgment and Victory in Christ's Return

44

Unveiling the
Great Prostitute

Revelation 17:1—6

*Come, I will show you the judgment of the great prostitute who
is seated on many waters, with whom the kings of the earth
have committed sexual immorality. (Rev. 17:1–2)*

*I*n an earlier chapter I compared the book of Revelation to
Charles Dickens's popular story *A Christmas Carol*. Dickens'
classic is a rare example in English literature of the apocalyptic
style seen in Revelation. In *A Christmas Carol*, Ebenezer Scrooge is swept
up by three successive ghosts, who present him with visions of Christmas
past, Christmas present, and Christmas future. These visions leave Scrooge
a changed man: no longer the champion of humbug, but a paragon of charity and joy.

In the book of Revelation, the apostle John is swept up from his grim
exile on the Isle of Patmos for a guided tour of the church history to come,
escorted not by ghosts but by angels. The book began with John's being "in
the Spirit" (Rev. 1:10), when the glorified Jesus appeared with a message
for his churches. In chapter 4, an angel called John, saying, "Come," and he
passed "in the Spirit" through a door into heaven, to see visions of the seven

seals, seven trumpets, and seven bowls. The expression "in the Spirit" occurs only twice more in the book, both times joined to a summons to "Come," signaling important revelations for which John is placed into a heightened state of spiritual awareness. These are the major section breaks in the book of Revelation. Having been shown the meaning of history through the visions of chapters 4–16, John will now see the end-times judgment of Christ's enemies. An angel cries, "Come," and John is carried "in the Spirit" to see "the great prostitute" of the world system being cast down (17:1–3). The final section of Revelation will also see John summoned "in the Spirit," this time to come and see the harlot world's opposite, the church, not a prostitute but "the Bride, the wife of the Lamb" (21:9).

Like the messages of the three ghosts that changed Ebenezer Scrooge, these four summonses "in the Spirit" outline the message that John was to give to the troubled church: a vision of Christ in his sovereign glory, a vision of history under his sovereign control, a vision of the world in its violent decadence, and a vision of the church in her holy beauty.

MEET THE GREAT HARLOT

Chapter 17 begins a new section of Revelation, and for it John's tour guide is one of the seven angels who poured the bowls of wrath on the earth. This indicates that this sixth cycle will culminate in the judgment of Christ's enemies: "Then one of the seven angels who had the seven bowls came and said to me, 'Come, I will show you the judgment of the great prostitute'" (Rev. 17:1). Before God brings an end to the idolatrous world system, he wants John and his readers to see it for what it is. John sees worldly culture personified as a detestable harlot, awash in iniquity and violence, who has not only turned from godly virtue but used her sinful pleasures to lead multitudes into idolatry. The opening verses of chapter 17 present five notable features in describing the great prostitute: her *location*, her *mount*, her *adornment*, her *cup* of abominations, and her *name*, which unfolds the mystery of her role in history.

First, her location is given: John relates that the angel "carried me away in the Spirit into a wilderness" (Rev. 17:3). The wilderness has several meanings in Scripture. It depicts the barren results of sin. In Matthew's Gospel, the wilderness is inhabited by demons (Matt. 12:43) and Jesus was led into the wilderness to be tempted by the devil (4:1). Isaiah described the desert as the place from which invaders would come to destroy Babylon (Isa. 21:1–10). Later, Babylon will herself be turned into a wilderness (Rev. 18:2). Earlier in Revelation, the desert was where God prepared a refuge for the church to be kept safe during the great tribulation (12:6). Since Babylon is "the great city" where sin festers (17:18), the wilderness is also a place where John can view the harlot while being out of reach of her sinful allures. Persecution or social rejection will often cause Christians to be excluded from worldly society, but this very seclusion offers a refuge from the allure of sin. Dennis Johnson thus writes: "For John and the church the wilderness combines physical suffering and spiritual safety; for Babylon, it is her destiny of desolation."[1]

Second, the brazen woman is mounted "on a scarlet beast that was full of blasphemous names, and it had seven heads and ten horns" (Rev. 17:3). There is no question that this beast is the persecuting tyrant of earlier visions, the antichrist government rulers of the earth (see 13:1). The seven heads correspond to the four beasts of Daniel 7, which stood for violent world kingdoms, and the ten horns identify Daniel's fourth beast, the Roman Empire (Dan. 7:7). This composite beast thus symbolizes all "the great persecuting power which rules by brute force and is the supreme enemy of Christ and the church."[2] The beast's scarlet color identifies him with Satan, the red dragon, and reflects his bloody persecution of the saints. The blasphemous names reflect his idolatrous demand to be worshiped, the very danger facing John's readers from the bestial Roman emperor.

The fact that the harlot rides the beast shows an alliance in which the aims of sinful debauchery and the aims of violent tyranny are bound together. Moral indecency and tyrannical government work together in gaining the submission of "the kings of the earth," like the proverbial velvet glove hiding an iron fist. Some are intimidated by worldly power to cooperate in the decadent economic system, and others are enticed by fleshly pleasure so as to tolerate the loss of their rights to a tyrannical state idolatry. This vision thus depicts how tyrannies will always foster immorality and how immorality will always promote the acceptance of tyranny. America's founding fathers

1. Dennis E. Johnson, *Triumph of the Lamb: A Commentary on Revelation* (Phillipsburg, NJ: P&R Publishing, 2001), 244.

2. Robert H. Mounce, *Revelation*, rev. ed., New International Commentary on the New Testament (Grand Rapids: Eerdmans, 1997), 309.

understood that an immoral nation will soon lose its freedom, a lesson that is likely to be bitterly learned in years to come.

This picture is amplified, third, with the harlot's adorning: "The woman was arrayed in purple and scarlet, and adorned with gold and jewels and pearls" (Rev. 17:4). William Hendriksen writes, "She is gorgeously arrayed and excessively adorned[,] . . . clothed with purple and scarlet, for she sits as queen."[3] The first thing we notice is the costliness of her garb: scarlet dye was expensive, and purple was so costly that it was the symbol of aristocracy and royalty. She adds the gaudy shimmer of jewels and pearls to complete the impression of wealth and carnal beauty. G. K. Beale writes, "She is the symbol of a culture that maintains the prosperity of economic commerce," as well as reflecting "the outward attractiveness by which whores try to seduce others."[4] In a similar way today, decadent worldly cultures advertise their wealth not only as a justification for their immorality but also to urge the supposed benefits of ungodliness.

The harlot's luscious depravity contrasts with the true beauty of the church as the bride of Christ. Revelation 12:1 described her beauty as reflecting the holiness of God: "a woman clothed with the sun, with the moon under her feet, and on her head a crown of twelve stars." Later, Christ's bride will bear a beauty that outshines the world's tawdry counterfeit: "having the glory of God, its radiance like a most rare jewel, like a jasper, clear as crystal" (Rev. 21:11). The harlot Babylon dresses seductively, so as to lure the worldly kings to their destruction. In contrast, the outward beauty of a Christian woman is modest, seeking to edify rather than allure, and her most precious beauty is inward and spiritual: "the imperishable beauty of a gentle and quiet spirit, which in God's sight is very precious" (1 Peter 3:4). Christian men will likewise be advised to avoid women whose appeal is primarily sensual, valuing instead the beauty of a noble feminine character in which Christ dwells by the Spirit.

Fourth, we are shown the harlot's cup: "holding in her hand a golden cup full of abominations and the impurities of her sexual immorality" (Rev. 17:4). The golden cup suggests riches and glory—"one expects the most

3. William Hendriksen, *More than Conquerors: An Interpretation of the Book of Revelation* (1940; repr., Grand Rapids: Baker, 1967), 167.

4. G. K. Beale, *Revelation: A Commentary on the Greek Text*, New International Greek Testament Commentary (Grand Rapids: Eerdmans, 1999), 854.

precious drink from such a precious vessel"[5]—while its contents impoverish the soul and disgrace those who drink of it. "Abominations" speaks of things especially offensive to God, such as false worship (Deut. 27:15), occult practices (18:10–11), and sexual perversions such as homosexuality (Lev. 18:22) and gross indecency (20:13), while "impurities" refers to sinful corruptions in general. The point is not merely imbibing of impiety and sin but their intoxicating influence in promoting idolatry in the place of faith in the true God. Hendriksen summarizes: "Whatever is used by the world to turn believers away from their God is in this cup: pornographic literature, sports in which one becomes completely absorbed, luxuries, worldly fame and power, the lusts of the flesh, and so on. . . . It includes things that are bad in themselves as well as things which become bad because one does not view them as a means but as an end in themselves."[6] Secular culture holds forth this very cup, in all the apparent glitter of gold, so as to seduce people by its contents, making them slaves of the consumer enterprise and willing servants of the idolatrous state. Douglas Kelly warns: "It looks fabulous! What this modern world-system can offer me is tremendous! But wait till you see what is inside the cup; it is full of abominations and filthiness of her fornications!"[7]

John has seen the desert location of the harlot, her bestial mount, her seductive adornment, and her cup of abominations. Finally, he learns her name: "And on her forehead was written a name of mystery: 'Babylon the great, mother of prostitutes and of earth's abominations'" (Rev. 17:5). Harlots in Rome were said to wear headbands bearing their names. Here, the name is "Babylon the great." Going back to the earliest recesses of history, Babylon symbolized satanic powers arrayed against God. Its famous tower was raised to heaven until God overthrew it in confusion (Gen. 11). It was Babylon that destroyed Jerusalem under Nebuchadnezzar and into Babylon that God's people were sent into captivity as punishment for idol-worship. Nebuchadnezzar coined the phrase "Babylon the great" in his boast of secular-humanistic idolatry (Dan. 4:30). John describes this as "a name of mystery" (Rev. 17:5), the point of which is the symbolic meaning of this name. James Hamilton

---

5. Hendriksen, *More than Conquerors*, 169.

6. Ibid.

7. Douglas F. Kelly, *Revelation*, Mentor Expository Commentary (Tain, Ross-shire, Scotland: Mentor, 2012), 326.

writes: "This symbol of the oppressive kingdoms of the world that disregard God and do not recognize Christ as King is here personified as a human female who sells herself and gives birth to abominations."[8]

In addition to being named "Babylon the great," she is named "mother of prostitutes and of earth's abominations" (Rev. 17:5). Not only is the harlot herself a prostitute, "with whom the kings of the earth have committed sexual immorality, and with the wine of whose sexual immorality the dwellers on earth have become drunk" (17:2), but she is "the mother superior over all those who commit spiritual prostitution by worshiping the beast."[9] It does not stretch the imagination to think of young American girls who imbibe the values of secular society and early in life take on the appearance and values exemplified by this harlot. This symbolizes the spiritual harlotry of a culture that has turned from God. Just as Christian women are to possess a virtue completely opposite the harlot's debauchery, the Christian church as a whole is to live in holy separation from the sinful corruptions that will dominate any culture given over to secular-humanistic ideology, to a consumer economy driven by sensual pleasure, and to a state idolatry in which the powers of the world are worshiped in the place of God.

WHAT TO EXPECT FROM THE WORLD

The point of John's vision of the harlot is for Christians to see the truth of the world for what it is. It works like a fairy tale in which the magic of the beautiful seductress wears off to reveal a hideous and evil witch. "Do you see the world for what it is?" Revelation asks. The problem is not the world itself but the secular-humanistic world system in rebellion to God. Apart from God's rule of grace and truth, the world falls to the deadly alliance of the prostitute's moral corruption and the tyrant's abuse of power.

The model for this decadent world system is the ancient Rome that dominated the world in John's time. This chapter alludes directly to Rome several times. Rome is Daniel's fourth beast with ten horns (Dan. 7:7; Rev. 17:3). Rome was identified by Christians under the code name *Babylon* (1 Peter 5:13). Revelation 17:9 speaks of the seven hills, which can only mean Rome,

---

8. James M. Hamilton Jr., *Revelation: The Spirit Speaks to the Churches* (Wheaton, IL: Crossway, 2012), 326.

9. Simon J. Kistemaker, *Revelation*, New Testament Commentary (Grand Rapids: Baker, 2001), 466.

symbolizing the dominant world system of political, cultural, economic, and military power in all times. She is the prostitute who "is seated on many waters" (17:1), speaking of Rome's pervasive influence on world culture and power.

Rome provides an apt symbol for worldly idolatry especially in the two great threats she posed to the church, threats that organize Satan's assaults in every age. The first of these is persecution. John's readers could not forget the shocking torment of Christians in the reign of Nero, and they now faced the deadly threat of the emperor Domitian if they continued to refuse to worship his idolatrous images. The second form of satanic attack on Christians is moral corruption. Rome was a cesspool of the worst debaucheries, especially sexual. The historian Tacitus described Rome as the place "where all the horrible and shameful things in the world congregate and find a home."[10] A famous example was seen in Messalina, wife of the emperor Claudius, who was reputed to spend her evenings selling her body in a common brothel, symbolizing how the decadence of the imperial family forced debauchery on others in society. These two strategies—persecution and corruption—continue to be used by Satan in his attempt to destroy the Christian church and witness.

The harlot's role in persecution is described in Revelation 17:6: "I saw the woman, drunk with the blood of the saints, the blood of the martyrs of Jesus. When I saw her, I marveled greatly." John is horrified that Christians should be made to suffer so terribly for refusing to participate in filth and abomination. Just as virtuous Joseph was tempted and betrayed by Potiphar's wife, so the church is afflicted for refusing to participate in moral evil. Simon Kistemaker writes: "Not satisfied with what she already controls and unable to deceive the elect (Matt. 24:24), she relentlessly torments and kills the saints so that their blood is spilled on the face of the earth."[11]

Persecution has spread all over the world today, just as it loomed over John's churches and appeared throughout the early centuries of the church. More Christian blood was spilled in the twentieth century than any previous century, and the twenty-first is seeing Christian martyrdom reach new heights. If John marveled in horror at the blood of saints spattering the harlot's rich clothing, he would grieve the slaughter of believers today, especially in nations governed by Islam.

10. Quoted in Mounce, *Revelation*, 310.
11. Kistemaker, *Revelation*, 467.

On the whole, however, persecution is not a very effective strategy for harming the church. While making Christians suffer, persecution actually strengthens the church, weeding out false converts and turning suffering saints to their Lord in prayer. Finally, the great tribulation will cause Jesus to return to save and avenge his bride. His call to Christians in the face of persecution is simple: "Be faithful unto death, and I will give you the crown of life" (Rev. 2:10).

The second strategy of the world against the church is not outward but inward; it involves not persecution but infiltration, through moral corruption and false doctrine. This strategy was successfully employed by Balaam during Israel's exodus. Forbidden by God from casting curses on Israel, Balaam set loose the lovely daughters of Moab, who tempted the Israelite men into sin and through sin into idolatry (Num. 25:1–3). Jesus mentions this strategy in his letter to the church of Pergamum: "You have some there who hold the teaching of Balaam, who taught Balak to put a stumbling block before the sons of Israel, so that they might eat food sacrificed to idols and practice sexual immorality" (Rev. 2:14). His letter to Thyatira included a similar warning, using a similar Old Testament figure: "I have this against you, that you tolerate that woman Jezebel, who calls herself a prophetess and is teaching and seducing my servants to practice sexual immorality and to eat food sacrificed to idols" (2:20).

Satan infiltrates the church not only with immoral practices but also with false doctrine. Jesus complained to Pergamum: "So also you have some who hold the teaching of the Nicolaitans" (Rev. 2:15). Paul wrote to the Galatians to warn of the serious danger of false teaching on salvation: "If anyone is preaching to you a gospel contrary to the one you received, let him be accursed" (Gal. 1:9). Today, the church is beset with theological liberalism that submits the Bible to worldly critiques, with health-and-wealth prosperity teaching that degrades the gospel to mere worldly blessings, and with a therapeutic gospel that is driven by pop psychology and that downplays the importance of sin, redemption, and the biblical call to holiness in a lifestyle of costly obedience.

Whereas persecution often makes the church strong, the successful infiltration of immorality and false doctrine always makes the church weak and ineffective. This is why Jesus especially warned against unbiblical influences in the church: "Beware of false prophets, who come to you in sheep's clothing but inwardly are ravenous wolves. You will recognize them by their fruits" (Matt. 7:15–16).

PSALM 1: THE TWO WAYS

When Christ's people see the abominations of the great harlot world culture, what is to be their response? The answer is obvious from the nature of this vision, but it is explicitly given in Revelation 18:4–5: "Come out of her, my people, lest you take part in her sins, lest you share in her plagues, for her sins are heaped high as heaven."

Probably the best advice ever given on how to avoid the pollution of sin and the enticements of a harlot world is found in the very first chapter of the book of Psalms. The Psalms are intended to guide the spirituality of believers, and Psalm 1 provides the very gateway to a wholesome lifestyle of godliness. It begins with instruction that every Christian should have memorized: "Blessed is the man who walks not in the counsel of the wicked, nor stands in the way of sinners, nor sits in the seat of scoffers; but his delight is in the law of the LORD, and on his law he meditates day and night" (Ps. 1:1–2). This says that Christians are shaped by the influence of their associations. The messages to which we open our ears and our hearts will end up determining the way of life that we will follow. On the one hand are those who live close to the world, receiving its ideas and following its fads, who then begin walking in that way and end up seated, or confirmed, in worldly corruption. On the other hand are those who live close to God's Word, listening to the counsel of God and practicing a lifestyle that is pleasing to him. These are the two ways that will yield two different lives. Jesus picked up on this approach when he taught: "For the gate is wide and the way is easy that leads to destruction, and those who enter by it are many. For the gate is narrow and the way is hard that leads to life, and those who find it are few" (Matt. 7:13–14).

In David McCullough's celebrated biography of John Adams, he writes of the shock that his virtuous wife, Abigail, received when she joined him in decadent Paris, where Adams was America's first ambassador to France. When Abigail became lonely, however, she began attending the Parisian opera with friends. At first, she was scandalized by the virtual nudity and the sensuality of the ballet dancers. But she noted in her letters the effect of frequent exposure. At first, she wrote, "I was shamed to be seen looking at them," describing the extremely revealing dress of the dancing girls. But later, she wrote, "I have found my taste reconciling itself to habits, customs and fashions which at first disgusted me."[12] The same influence is exerted today on college campuses, in movie theaters, and through music videos, slowly acclimating America's youths into sinful habits that will destroy their souls.

Psalm 1 goes on to describe the two lifestyles and then the two differing eternal destinies that arise from the two ways—that of the world and that of God's Word. The one who draws truth from the Bible "is like a tree planted by streams of water that yields its fruit in its season, and its leaf does not wither. In all that he does, he prospers" (Ps. 1:3). In contrast, "The wicked are not so, but are like chaff that the wind drives away" (1:4). Finally, eternal matters are decided by the path on which we allow ourselves to tread: "Therefore the wicked will not stand in the judgment, nor sinners in the congregation of the righteous; for the LORD knows the way of the righteous, but the way of the wicked will perish" (1:5–6).

Notice that this progression is determined at the start by the counsel you accept and the influences to which you expose yourself. The counsel of the world leads you into the embrace of the harlot and the tyranny of the beast. The Scripture directs you not only to godly obedience but most significantly to Jesus Christ, the Savior of the lost, the Redeemer of those condemned in sin, the Lord who gives life and beauty to his church. His message is founded on promises that overthrow the realm of the harlot and of the beast for those who believe. What encouragement for salvation Jesus gives for those who have known the pollution of sin and the tyranny of worldliness. He says: "If you abide in my word, you are truly my disciples, and you will know the truth, and the truth will set you free" (John 8:31–32). "If anyone thirsts, let him come to me and drink. Whoever believes in me, as the Scripture has said, 'Out of his heart will flow rivers of living water'" (7:37–38). In 1 Corinthians 6:9, Paul writes that "the unrighteous will not inherit the kingdom of God," including "the sexually immoral," "idolaters," "adulterers," and "men who practice homosexuality." Then he adds, "Such were some of you. But you were washed, you were sanctified, you were justified in the name of the Lord Jesus Christ and by the Spirit of our God" (1 Cor. 6:11).

12. David McCullough, *John Adams* (New York: Simon and Schuster, 2001), 307.

Jesus said, "I came that they may have life and have it abundantly" (John 10:10). The harlot Babylon allures with pleasure that leads to the embrace of death and despair. The Savior Jesus calls with life from God for those who believe. The only blood he bears is the blood he shed in our place, to free us from the penalty of our sin. The key to Christian living, then, is in part to see the ugly destruction of the harlot who rides the beast. An even greater key is to see Jesus, who is altogether lovely, and who imparts true beauty, life, and glory to those who take the cup of life from his hands. David knew this, and his conviction provides the best remedy to the deadly traps of worldly allure: "You make known to me the path of life; in your presence there is fullness of joy; at your right hand are pleasures forevermore" (Ps. 16:11).

45

THE MYSTERY OF THE WOMAN AND THE BEAST

Revelation 17:7–18

*They will make war on the Lamb, and the Lamb will conquer
them, for he is Lord of lords and King of kings, and those with
him are called and chosen and faithful.* (Rev. 17:14)

One of the great figures of the Scottish Reformation was Samuel
Rutherford, who spent much of his life under persecution. As
a young man, he was exiled for teaching salvation by grace,
and as an old man, he was condemned to die for insisting that the king was
subject to God's law. Observers have wondered at how Rutherford maintained his life of joyful faith amid such troubles. The answer is found in a
hymn that paraphrases Rutherford's dying words and his hope in Christ:

The sands of time are sinking, the dawn of heaven breaks,
The summer morn I've sighed for, the fair sweet morn awakes;
Dark, dark hath been the midnight, but dayspring is at hand,
And glory, glory dwelleth in Emmanuel's land.[13]

13. Anne R. Cousin, "The Sands of Time Are Sinking" (1857).

488

The vision of Revelation 17 is intended to promote a similar attitude. John had seen the great prostitute Babylon, riding the scarlet beast and drenched in the blood of the saints. "When I saw her," he said, "I marveled greatly" (Rev. 17:6). It seems that John was set back by the appalling vision. The angel followed up: "Why do you marvel? I will tell you the mystery of the woman, and of the beast with seven heads and ten horns that carries her" (17:7). This interpretation of this vision was designed to comfort John's fear and encourage him to persevere in faith.

The angel's message is organized by the three main portions of this passage. First, John needs to recognize the beast and the manner of his appearing. Second, he must understand the powers arrayed by the beast for war against Christ. Third, he is to marvel at the destruction that God has ordained to be at work between the harlot and the beast, displaying his sovereign power. The perspective we gain from studying this difficult chapter is intended to give us, like Rutherford, boldness to stand for God in this hostile world.

RECOGNIZING THE RETURNING BEAST

By this time in Revelation, we are familiar with the beast, who represents violent worldly power arrayed against God and his people. He was first mentioned in chapter 11, where he briefly had power to slay the two witnesses, symbolizing the martyr church (Rev. 11:7–8), until they were raised from the dead before God's judgment on the beast (11:11–13). In chapter 12, we learn that the beast's master, the seven-headed dragon, Satan, makes unsuccessful war against the church, which conquers him by the blood of Christ and "the word of their testimony" (12:11). In chapter 13, John again sees this beast making war on the saints, being permitted by God to conquer them for a limited period (13:5–7).

This background material fits in with the description of Revelation 17:8: "The beast that you saw was, and is not, and is about to rise from the bottomless pit and go to destruction." The pattern follows the record of Satan in history. The devil was and then was not, that is, he reigned over the nations in sin until Christ defeated him on the cross and overthrew his kingdom. This does not minimize the evil activity of Satan in our own time, but points out that his power has been restrained so that the gospel may go forth to the world (Rev. 20:3). Although his reign was and now is not, there will be a brief time at the end of history when he will once more be permitted "to deceive the nations" and "gather them for battle" against Christ (20:7–8). Therefore, Satan "was, is not, and is about to rise" again.

When it comes to the beast, this same pattern recurs in history. There was Pharaoh of Egypt, then Sennacherib of Assyria, and then Nebuchadnezzar of Babylon in the Old Testament. Between the two Testaments there was Antiochus Epiphanes, who persecuted the Jews, and Herod the Great, who tried to slay the Christ child. All these beastly tyrants had their bloody day of power, until God cast them down. They were and then were not. But always the beast rose again, as in Nero and his persecution of the Christians and now in John's time in the menace of the emperor Domitian. G. K. Beale writes: "This situation will continue until [Christ's] final [coming], at which time the beast's success over God's people will seem even greater than before."[14] Robert Mounce adds: "Down through history he repeatedly 'comes up from the abyss' to harass and, if it were possible, to destroy the people of God."[15] Recognizing this pattern, Christians who live in godly times should be aware that evil is only waiting to come back. Likewise, Christians who are suffering under persecution can know that the beast who has arisen is soon to be defeated. Just as it is certain that the beast will "rise from the bottomless pit," he will also "go to destruction" (Rev. 17:8). The Abyss is the place of darkness that is the very opposite of heaven. The beast's rise from the Abyss is always a prelude to his return to the Abyss in defeat and disgrace.

John's vision further points out that the beast's appearing will gain fervent support from the world: "And the dwellers on earth whose names have not been written in the book of life from the foundation of the world will marvel to see the beast, because it was and is not and is to come" (Rev. 17:8). Worldly people, lacking the discernment of the Holy Spirit, are awed by the power and ability of the bestial tyrant. One need only think of the fanatical masses at the Nuremberg rallies in the early days of Hitler's Nazi Germany. This is hardly surprising, since unbelievers belong to the great idol-worshiping, Babylonian city of man. Philip Hughes writes: "The feats of despotic empire

---

14. G. K. Beale, *The Book of Revelation: A Commentary on the Greek Text*, New International Greek Testament Commentary (Grand Rapids: Eerdmans, 1999), 866.

15. Robert H. Mounce, *Revelation*, rev. ed., New International Commentary on the New Testament (Grand Rapids: Eerdmans, 1997), 312.

builders who aspire to world dominion always evoked the wonder and the worship of the citizens of Babylon the great."[16]

In seeking this devotion, the beast mimics the resurrection of Jesus in his sudden appearing and ascension to power. We encountered this theme in Revelation 13, where one of the beast's "heads seemed to have a mortal wound, but its mortal wound was healed, and the whole earth marveled as they followed the beast" (Rev. 13:3). If we wonder how humanity can fall for this charade, we should remember that because they are alienated from God, sinners are eager to replace him, and on the slightest pretext they will give their allegiance to an impostor.

Where is the comfort for us in such a passage? One comfort comes from realizing that Satan and his beast are so bankrupt that they can amaze the world only by pretending to be like Jesus. In this way, the history of the beast's appearing proves the truth about Christ. Second, we are comforted, having believed in Jesus, that our names were written in his Book of Life before all eternity. Simon Kistemaker writes: "Despite the havoc the beast wreaks, and notwithstanding the adoration the world showers on the beast, God's people are safe and free from fear. Their eternal destiny is established."[17]

Understanding the Beast's War on Christ

The angel's second point to John unfolds the meaning of the seven heads and ten horns, in order to show the powers joined with the beast for the war against Christ. This passage is so difficult that we are not surprised at the way the angel introduces it: "This calls for a mind with wisdom" (Rev. 17:9). A similar statement was made when the number of the beast was given (13:18). Wisdom is needed not only to understand the material but also to keep its meaning in focus.

The angel begins by saying that "the seven heads are seven mountains on which the woman is seated" (Rev. 17:9). This seems to be a clear reference to Rome, the city of seven hills, which was in John's time the main representative of the beast and the seat of the harlot's seductions. Some scholars point to other cities with seven hills, such as Jerusalem. But "seven-hilled city"

---

16. Philip Edgcumbe Hughes, *The Book of Revelation* (Downers Grove, IL: InterVarsity Press, 1990), 184.

17. Simon J. Kistemaker, *Revelation*, New Testament Commentary (Grand Rapids: Baker, 2001), 470.

was practically a name for Rome, just as Chicago is the "Windy City" and New York is the "Big Apple" today. Moreover, mountains are often used in the Bible to depict spiritual powers arrayed against God (see Isa. 2:2; Jer. 51:25; Ezek. 35:3). This image perfectly fits John's warning to the churches in Revelation: the beast is about to rise again from the Abyss, centering his power in Rome, using emperor-worship to persecute the church.

If the seven hills are easy to understand, what follows is not: "They are also seven kings, five of whom have fallen, one is, the other has not yet come, and when he does come he must remain only a little while" (Rev. 17:10). There are three main theories for interpreting this verse, two of which are historical and one of which is symbolic.

The first historical approach sees the seven kings as successive Roman emperors. The idea is that five emperors have fallen, one currently reigns, and one will briefly reign in the future.[18] The problem with this approach is that Domitian was the twelfth Roman emperor, not the sixth. If we start with Augustus Caesar, the list includes Tiberius, Caligula, Claudius, and Nero as five fallen rulers. The sixth would then be Vespasian, which does not fit if Revelation was written during the reign of Domitian, as most scholars believe. Even this approach leaves out three emperors who ruled briefly after the fall of Nero: Galba, Otho, and Vitellius. It is therefore virtually impossible to make this theory work without arbitrary manipulation.

The second historical approach sees the seven kings as world empires in history. Here, too, it is not certain which names ought to be included. William Hendriksen lists ancient Babylon, Assyria, new Babylon, Medo-Persia, and Greece as the five fallen empires, with Rome as the sixth that was then reigning.[19] Henry Alford lists Egypt, Nineveh, Babylon, Persia, and Greece as the five fallen kingdoms.[20]

The main problem with this approach is the seventh empire, which "has not yet come, and when he does come he must remain only a little while" (Rev. 17:10). One approach is to identify this as the church-state empire that began with Constantine the Great in A.D. 312, including all the subsequent history of Europe. It seems arbitrary, however, to include all the empires of

---

18. See, for instance, David Chilton, *Days of Vengeance: An Exposition of the Book of Revelation* (Ft. Worth, TX: Dominion Press, 1987), 436.

19. William Hendriksen, *More than Conquerors: An Interpretation of the Book of Revelation* (1940; repr., Grand Rapids: Baker, 1967), 170.

20. Henry Alford, *The Greek Testament*, 4 vols. (Cambridge: Deighton, Bell, and Co., 1866), 4:710–11.

two millennia, including Attila, Charlemagne, the English dynasties, Napoleon, Adolf Hitler, the American Republic, and the Communist tyrannies, under one heading. Moreover, it is hard to see how this history describes one who "must remain only a little while."

The problems with the historical approaches lead us to consider a symbolic approach, especially since the numbers seven and ten have been used this way throughout Revelation. Seven stands for completeness and here would represent the totality of antichrist government throughout history. Picture a beast with seven heads, five of which have been cut off. The idea is that Christ's first coming inflicted a deadly blow to Satan and his beast, who continues fighting undaunted, employing the power of his deadly sixth head, with a seventh yet to come. The point is that war is getting closer to its end. John's readers were not at the end—theirs was the sixth head—but the last phase was beginning. This fits Paul's teaching that with the church, "the end of the ages has come" (1 Cor. 10:11). The conflict will be fierce, but the end is not far off. This image of the beast thus mirrors the earlier statement that Satan is filled with wrath at the church, "because he knows that his time is short" (Rev. 12:12). There will be great suffering in John's time and in the church's future, with a great need for courage and perseverance, but Christians face the conflict, knowing that its duration is limited and that the end is near.

When the end comes, the church will face an eighth head: "As for the beast that was and is not, it is an eighth but it belongs to the seven, and it goes to destruction" (Rev. 17:11). Eight is the number of resurrection, which fits the Antichrist's attempt to masquerade as Christ. Like all the previous horns, he is bent on world domination in rebellion to God. But he is different in that he is the genuine beast. "He is not a human ruler through whom the power of evil finds expression—he is that evil power itself. He belongs to the cosmic struggle between God and Satan which lies behind the scenes of human history. Yet he will appear on the stage of history as a man."[21]

Revelation 17:12 says that the seventh king has "ten horns," which "are ten kings who have not yet received royal power, but they are to receive authority as kings for one hour, together with the beast." In the 1990s, it was common for dispensationalists to identify the ten horns with the European Common Market, on the premise that a reunified Europe would be the seventh head

---

21. Mounce, *Revelation*, 316.

of the beast, having ten horns. Since there were then nine member nations, preachers assured their hearers that the entry of a tenth nation would signal the final tribulation and Christ's return. Today, when the European Union consists of twenty-eight nations, this theory seems less plausible.

Instead, the ten horns are best taken symbolically. Ten is another number for completion, this time representing the subordinate powers that assist the imperial beast. In John's day, Rome was organized in ten provinces, and it was mainly provincial leaders who persecuted the Christians. More generally, the ten horns symbolize "the mighty ones of this earth in every realm: art, education, commerce, industry, government, in so far as they serve the central authority."[22] With such allies exercising his authority, the Antichrist will dominate all society for a brief time—"for one hour"—during which period he will exalt himself in power. Being "of one mind," the horns will "hand over their power and authority to the beast. They will make war on the Lamb" (Rev. 17:13–14). With this global force at his command, the beast will seek to eradicate the Christian church and claim the lordship that belongs to Jesus. Christians often marvel at the apparent delusion of the media, educators, entertainers, and legislators in support of agendas that are obviously immoral and self-destructive. The explanation is that in their moral rebellion against God and their rejection of Christ, they enter (usually unknowingly) into the service of the beast, who animates them with the deceitful spirit of the Abyss.

The only possible result of this warfare, however greatly the church may briefly suffer, is the total victory of Christ: "The Lamb will conquer them, for he is Lord of lords and King of kings" (Rev. 17:14). In a previous vision, worldly society worshiped the beast, marveling, "Who is like the beast, and who can fight against it?" (13:4). In the appearing of Jesus, the world receives its answer!

In high school, I played on a large and powerful football team. We occasionally traveled to play smaller programs. All week, our rivals had been preparing for the game, sometimes boasting about how they would defeat us. But as soon as our team came onto the field for pregame warm-ups and the size and strength of our players was displayed, the opponents realized that they were in for a beating. How much greater will be the dismay of those who have joined the mocking ranks of the beast, strik-

22. Hendriksen, *More than Conquerors*, 171.

ing out against the church in its apparent weakness, when Jesus returns in divine power and glory! Kistemaker writes: "The name *King of kings* denotes sovereignty and authority; the name *Lord of lords* signifies majesty and power."[23] At the coming of Christ, the forces of the Antichrist receive a shattering defeat, the details of which are provided in the visions yet to come in Revelation.

Worldly powers will unite under the beast to bring great affliction to Christians for periods during history and in an intense way at the very end. But just when the Antichrist seems to be grasping victory, Christ will appear and bring him to utter and final ruin, while delivering believers into his kingdom of glory. As John was earlier told, "Here is a call for the endurance and faith of the saints" (Rev. 13:10). It is also a call for sinners to surrender to Christ in faith while time remains. Psalm 2 tells of the nations' raging vainly in their conspiracy against God, who "holds them in derision" and "will speak to them in his wrath" (Ps. 2:4–5). It concludes with this call to repentance and faith that is the emphasis of the entire Bible: "Serve the LORD with fear, and rejoice with trembling. Kiss the Son, lest he be angry, and you perish in the way" (2:11–12).

MARVELING AT THE SELF-DESTRUCTION OF EVIL

John is to recognize the beast when he rises from the Abyss as well as the Antichrist's gathering of forces for war. The final lesson calls for John to marvel at the self-destructive nature of worldly society.

Revelation 17:9 showed the harlot sitting on the seven mountains, as the mighty ones became drunk from her corrupting wine. Verse 18 now describes her as "the great city that has dominion over the kings of the earth." The harlot symbolizes the entire economic and cultural system on which the world depends. Verse 15 describes her spread of immoral culture throughout the world: "The waters that you saw, where the prostitute is seated, are peoples and multitudes and nations and languages." Steve Wilmshurst writes: "Satan is building his *anti*-church from every nation, just as the Lord is building the *true* church from every nation and language."[24] Like polluted waters

---

23. Kistemaker, *Revelation*, 476.
24. Steve Wilmshurst, *The Final Word: The Book of Revelation Simply Explained* (Darlington, UK: Evangelical Press, 2008), 214.

flowing from Babylon, the harlot's decadent culture spreads through "her arrogant confidence, through the heart-stealing seduction of her promises of prosperity and through the brute force of the beast's military might."[25]

Given his close relationship with the harlot, we would expect the tyrannical beast to care for and protect her. Instead, the opposite happens: "And the ten horns that you saw, they and the beast will hate the prostitute. They will make her desolate and naked, and devour her flesh and burn her up with fire" (Rev. 17:16). Having enjoyed her allurements, the worldly powers turn in hatred on the harlot. They strip her of her gorgeous clothing and jewelry to stand naked in disgrace. They hack and devour her flesh. They consign her to flames to be consumed. Why is this? One reason is that the pleasures of sin ultimately disappoint, turning evil men on one another in frustration. Another reason is that the beast and his worldly rulers do not love the people they have used. Grant Osborne writes: "Satan and his fallen angels have no love for human beings, who are made in the image of God and are still loved by God."[26]

This vision supplies vital lessons. First, young people are warned against the dream of becoming a movie star or popular singer, receiving the world's adoring worship. Not only is it wrong in itself to desire a place in the harlot's idolatry, but experience shows that virtually all the stars and starlets are first corrupted and then cast off by a contemptuous world. Second, we find here the principle that those who are unfaithful to God cannot be trusted by anyone. Those who embrace ungodly culture will be betrayed by it. Satan and his client powers have no love to give, and those who wield the beast's tyrannical power soon lose all respect for human dignity and life.

The ultimate reason why the beast turns on the harlot is God's will: "for God has put it into their hearts to carry out his purpose by being of one mind and handing over their royal power to the beast" (Rev. 17:17). In the Old Testament, God often confounded his enemies by bringing them into confusion and causing them to strike one another. God does not permit evil to flourish, or for the harlot and the beast to enjoy harmonious union. Isaiah wrote: "The wicked are like the tossing sea . . . . 'There is no peace,'

---

25. Dennis E. Johnson, *Triumph of the Lamb: A Commentary on Revelation* (Phillipsburg, NJ: P&R Publishing, 2001), 252.

26. Grant R. Osborne, *Revelation*, Baker Exegetical Commentary on the New Testament (Grand Rapids: Baker Academic, 2002), 625.

says my God, 'for the wicked'" (Isa. 57:20–21). God himself has placed a self-defeating principle within all ungodliness. Derek Thomas writes: "There is no resolution of the insecurity that is at the heart of rebellion. Finding no way to defeat the Lamb, the forces of evil turn upon each other.... It is only in Jesus that fullness and light are to be found."[27]

Rejoicing at the Sovereign Victory of God

The bulk of this chapter describes the anti-Christian forces at work in history. John is to recognize the appearing of the beast, even when he seemed to have been defeated; he is to understand the beast's power in warring on the church; and he is to marvel at the self-destructive tendency at work among the ungodly. Two statements, however, directly relate to believers and urge Christians to be steadfast and faithful during evil times.

First, when Revelation 17:14 tells of the Lamb's conquest, it adds that "those with him are called and chosen and faithful." Here is a good definition of a Christian. The followers of Christ are those who have answered the call of the gospel to saving faith. They are those chosen by God's sovereign grace, which ensures their eternal salvation. Their duty is simply to be faithful to their Savior and Lord. Moreover, the faithfulness of Christians in opposing evil not only proves their salvation but makes a real contribution to Jesus' victory in the end.

In 480 b.c., the vast Persian army under Xerxes launched an invasion of Greece. Realizing that the scattered city-states needed time to mobilize, the Spartan king Leonidas agreed to take three hundred volunteer warriors on a desperation mission to hold the narrow gap of Thermopylae. For two vital days, the tiny force held the gap until being surrounded and destroyed, giving the Athenian navy time to defeat the Persian fleet near the island of Salamis. Without his fleet, Xerxes could no longer support his army, and Greece was saved. The Christian church in the world is like that small but choice Spartan band. We occupy the fighting ground that God has given. We stand against sometimes seemingly desperate odds. We face suffering and death not only believing in our cause, and not only burning with love for our fellow believers, but also knowing that Christ will suddenly appear to save us and cast all evil into the lake of fire. If we realize the importance

27. Derek Thomas, *Let's Study Revelation* (Edinburgh: Banner of Truth, 2003), 142.

of our role in history, defending truth from error, godliness from evil, and gospel light from pagan darkness, then like the Spartans who trained ceaselessly for war, we will train ourselves in faith and godliness through prayer and God's Word.

Second, we should note what the angel said about God's sovereignty: "God has put it into their hearts to carry out his purpose . . . until the words of God are fulfilled" (Rev. 17:17). This means that God is not surprised by anything that happens in this evil age. The apparent advance of evil does not mean that God has lost control. He knows the end from the beginning, since he is the Alpha and the Omega (1:8). Believers can trust him, including his wisdom in working both against evil and through evil to glorify himself and eternally bless his people. Moreover, God's Word is certain to be fulfilled. The angel said that his vision "calls for a mind with wisdom" (17:9). Our wisdom comes by carefully observing, believing, and practicing everything revealed in God's Word, the teaching of which is "perfect, reviving the soul," and "sure, making wise the simple" (Ps. 19:7).

Samuel Rutherford challenged the bestial power of Britain's king, who sought to usurp Christ's authority in the church. When an official came to take him for execution, the infirm Rutherford pointed out that he was already too close to death to go. He said, "Tell them I have got a summons already before a superior Judge and judicatory, and I behove to answer my first summons, and ere your day come I will be where few kings and great folks come."[28] Rutherford had seen the crown beyond the cross, so he feared neither to live nor to die in faith in Christ. The hymn that records his dying testimony reveals his living hope:

The Lamb with his fair army doth on Mount Zion stand,
And glory, glory dwelleth in Emmanuel's land.[29]

---

28. Samuel Rutherford, *The Letters of Samuel Rutherford* (1664; repr., Edinburgh: Banner of Truth, 2006), 20.

29. Cousin, "The Sands of Time Are Sinking."

46

Christianity and Culture

Revelation 18:1–8

*Then I heard another voice from heaven saying, "Come out of
her, my people, lest you take part in her sins, lest you
share in her plagues." (Rev. 18:4)*

n 1951, H. Richard Niebuhr published his seminal study *Christ
and Culture*, pointing out that one of the most difficult and
important decisions for Christians to make is their relationship
to the world. He wrote that "the question of Christianity and civilization is
by no means a new one. . . . The problem has been an enduring one through
all the Christian centuries." Moreover, he said, "the repeated struggles of
Christians with this problem have yielded no single Christian answer."[1] His
book outlined the different answers that church leaders tend to give, tracing
each in Christian thought.

The first option that Niebuhr presented is "Christ against Culture." Here,
Christianity opposes the culture and seeks to avoid worldly influences.
Second is "the Christ of Culture," in which Christianity adapts to societal
standards and demands. Another view is "Christ above Culture," in which

---

1. H. Richard Niebuhr, *Christ and Culture* (1951; repr., San Francisco: HarperSanFrancisco, 2001), 2.

Christians partner with the world for its betterment. A fourth view is "Christ the Transformer of Culture," in which believers seek to Christianize society so that it more and more reflects the kingdom of Christ. All these views are advocated today by Christians who claim the Bible as God's Word.

WHAT ATTITUDE TOWARD THE WORLD?

In setting forth his first option, "Christ against Culture," Niebuhr notes that this view is exemplified in the writings of the apostle John. Indeed, one could hardly find a stronger statement of biblical opposition to the world than is stated in Revelation 18. "Fallen, fallen is Babylon the great!" it cries, and demands, "Come out of her, my people, lest you take part in her sins, lest you share in her plagues" (Rev. 18:2, 4). A simple reading of these verses would seem to urge Christians to adopt a very negative attitude toward the world.

The angel bearing the message of Babylon's fall is remarkable even by the book of Revelation's standards. John writes: "After this I saw another angel coming down from heaven, having great authority, and the earth was made bright with his glory" (Rev. 18:1). This seems to be an angel that we have not yet seen. He is noted for his great authority and glorious brightness. His authority enables him to carry out his important mission, and his brightness reflects the glory of God into the shadowed and depraved earth. He sings a dirge over the fallen world, not in lament but to taunt the defeated enemies of God.

This attitude of opposition to worldly culture is not the only view in the Bible. Paul urged us to appreciate good things wherever we find them: "Whatever is true, whatever is honorable, whatever is just, whatever is pure, whatever is lovely, whatever is commendable, if there is any excellence, if there is anything worthy of praise, think about these things" (Phil. 4:8). Christians should not be inhibited from enjoying the musical genius of Mozart, however ungodly the composer was. We likewise fall short of our humanity if our hearts do not stir at the romance of Andrew Lloyd Webber's *Phantom of the Opera*, our voices do not cheer a diving touchdown catch, or our fingers do not feverishly turn the pages of a brilliant mystery novel.

Indeed, the dirge "Fallen, fallen is Babylon the great!" (Rev. 18:2) takes note of what the world was before it fell. The world was made good by God and was precious to him as his own possession (Ps. 24:1). The angel's hostility is directed not to the physical earth but to sinful worldly culture. What God hates is Babylon as a symbol of the idol-worshiping, sensually perverse world system in rebellion to heaven. The world is not evil in itself but only in rebellion and sin. The most virulent atheist today, the most arrogantly seductive cultural harlot, and the most cynical abortion doctor all bear the stamp of the image of God. It was in this world that Jesus taught, "Love your enemies and pray for those who persecute you" (Matt. 5:44).

Nonetheless, because of its wickedness, the glorious angel sings triumphantly, "Fallen, fallen is Babylon the great!" (Rev. 18:2). This cry repeats the prophecy that Isaiah spoke over the original Babylon, when he looked ahead to its destruction by the Medo-Persian conqueror Cyrus. Isaiah wrote, "Fallen, fallen is Babylon; and all the carved images of her gods he has shattered to the ground" (Isa. 21:9). Just as Isaiah looked ahead to the coming of Cyrus, the angel looks ahead to the coming of Christ and sees the final overthrow of evil as an accomplished fact. When John wrote Revelation, the earthly city of Babylon had been lying under the sands for centuries. The Babylon that he writes of symbolizes "the world-wide, humanistic system that is hostile to God; that rejects his Word and refuses to accept the salvation that he offers through his Son."[2] The entire Babylonian world will fall to the sword of Christ's wrath in his return just as the city of Babylon fell to Cyrus's mounted warriors.

In calling forth Babylon's fall, the angel condemns the depravity of its condition: "She has become a dwelling place for demons, a haunt for every unclean spirit, a haunt for every unclean bird, a haunt for every unclean and detestable beast" (Rev. 18:2). This statement mirrors Isaiah's prophecy that foretold Babylon's complete desolation to the extent that "wild animals will lie down there, and their houses will be full of howling creatures . . . . Hyenas will cry in its towers, and jackals in the pleasant places" (Isa. 13:20–22). Revelation takes this same imagery to its ultimate extreme, saying that worldly Babylon will be haunted by demons, unclean spirits, and defiled beasts.

This imagery of occupation by violent and unclean animals symbolizes what happens in a society whenever God is rejected. Douglas Kelly points out that just as "nature abhors a vacuum," so does the spiritual condition of a society. "When a culture turns its back on God, the Holy Spirit, to some

2. Douglas F. Kelly, *Revelation*, Mentor Expository Commentary (Tain, Ross-shire, Scotland: Mentor, 2012), 336.

degree, is withdrawn, leaving a vacuum. Guess who rushes in to fill it? The evil one and those fallen created beings, former angels, who now are demons."[3] Behind the idols of a godless culture are spiritual powers of evil, who make that society a haunt of tortured spirits.

Imagine a society turning its back on God and outlawing the public influence of his Word. Imagine further that in the generation afterward the following trends resulted: births to unmarried girls increased 500 percent; reported child abuse increased 2,300 percent; the divorce rate rose by 350 percent; illegal drug use among youths increased by 6,000 percent; teenage suicide rose by 450 percent; and in 25 percent of viable pregnancies the babies were surgically killed at the mother's request. Would it not be fair to suggest that such a society, having publicly rejected God's rule and experiencing such a complete breakdown of moral order, had become "a dwelling place for demons" and a haunt for unclean spirits? Would it not further be fair to suggest, according to our passage, that such a society had fallen under the just judgment of God and would soon fall to his wrath unless it repented?

This situation is not imaginary, of course, for the statistics cover the United States of America in the years between 1962 and 2003, after the Supreme Court banned prayer and Bible teaching in public school, establishing an officially secularist national religion.[4] In 1962, the city of Detroit was the fifth-largest city in America and boasted the highest per capita income. Now, after a generation of ungodliness and greed, Detroit has had to file for bankruptcy and is so widely deserted that many neighborhoods have become overrun with coyotes. Other cities may not have Detroit's wild "jackal" problem, but even America's most affluent suburbs have become such a "haunt for unclean spirits" that they now are prey to mass violence, such as the 1999 Columbine High School massacre, and throughout the country children may no longer play outside unsupervised for fear of murderous child sexual predators. "The wages of sin is death," the Bible says (Rom. 6:23), including the death of any society that knowingly turns against God and falls under his judgment.

The living death depicted in Babylon is caused by the reign of moral depravity in rebellion to God. First, Babylon is condemned for exporting

3. Ibid.
4. These statistics, covering the years 1962–2003, are provided by the Traditional Values Coalition, based on statistics from the U.S. Department of Commerce, Bureau of the Census.

a culture of sexual indulgence and perversion throughout the world: "For all nations have drunk the wine of the passion of her sexual immorality" (Rev. 18:3). This statement suggests that those who lead masses of people into sin will be especially accountable to God's wrath. Moreover, "the kings of the earth have committed immorality with her" (18:3). Tyrannical governments rely on the sensual inducements of immorality to gain allegiance and strengthen their power. Furthermore, "the merchants of the earth have grown rich from the power of her luxurious living" (18:3). The point is not to condemn honest gain from business, but to oppose merchants and corporate titans who so worship money that they traffic in the poison of sin. The angel's condemnation of Babylon warns both citizens engaged in public service and those engaged in private enterprise that God is keeping tabs on their practice, and will hold them especially to account for their promotion of sexual immorality and other abuses of their fellow man.

This depiction of worldly society helps us to sort through the question of Christianity and culture. If Babylon presents "a picture of a world completely devoid of God and his Word,"[5] then we certainly must not accommodate the church to its ways. Christians must never allow such a spiritually desolate world to dictate doctrines, standards, values, and practices to the people of God. Simon Kistemaker writes, "How different is the city of God, where the Holy Spirit dwells in the hearts and lives of the saints! There the light of the gospel shines brightly and the people live in joy and happiness."[6]

SEPARATION—HOW?

After the first angel's rejoicing dirge for fallen Babylon, another voice is heard from heaven that either belongs to God or certainly represents God. This voice is directed to John and his readers, who live in the very Babylon under judgment. Their call is both simple and urgent: "Come out of her, my people" (Rev. 18:4).

Just as the previous angel quoted Isaiah's prophecy about Babylon's fall, this second voice cites Jeremiah's call for the people of Israel to depart from Babylon before its fall (Jer. 51:9, 45). In fact, this call for God's people to live separately from the world permeates the Bible. When God chose Abraham,

5. Simon J. Kistemaker, *Revelation*, New Testament Commentary (Grand Rapids: Baker, 2001), 487.
6. Ibid.

he commanded, "Go from your country and your kindred and your father's house to the land that I will show you" (Gen. 12:1). Paul similarly urged separation to the first Christians, writing: "Do not be unequally yoked with unbelievers. For what partnership has righteousness with lawlessness? Or what fellowship has light with darkness?" (2 Cor. 6:14).

This call to separation must be understood in light of the Bible's full teaching. An important example is the letter that God sent through Jeremiah to the Jewish exiles sent to Babylon. The Lord urged them to settle down in the midst of the pagans: "Build houses and live in them; plant gardens and eat their produce. Take wives and have sons and daughters." God further told the Jews to "seek the welfare of the city where I have sent you into exile, and pray to the LORD on its behalf, for in its welfare you will find your welfare" (Jer. 29:4–7). In terms of Niebuhr's *Christ and Culture*, this passage supports the "Christ above Culture" view, in which the moral and cultural resources of God's kingdom are employed for the general aid of society. The exiles were not called to transform or somehow redeem pagan Babylon, but rather called to be good and loyal citizens, serving its king so long as no conflict arose in their obligations to God. This was Daniel's policy as he loyally served Nebuchadnezzar, while refusing to obey commands that conflicted with God's Word. Jesus likewise encourages Christians to do good in the world: "You are the light of the world. . . . Let your light shine before others, so that they may see your good works and give glory to your Father who is in heaven" (Matt. 5:14–16). These passages show that the Christian call to separation does not mean absolute withdrawal from society. Derek Thomas writes: "Some form of involvement in the world is a responsibility and duty. The church is to be salt and light in the world."[7]

Christians sometimes make classic mistakes in the name of biblical separation. One is to physically separate from the world, as the monks did during the medieval era. Another mistake is that of the Amish communities, which associate holiness with abstaining from modern technology. Both the monks and the Amish fail to realize that physical separation from the world cannot preserve us from sin, since we ourselves are sinners. Yet another mistake is the kind of fundamentalism that forbids certain cultural activities, such as watching movies or eating at restaurants that serve alcohol, as though such merely external behavior constituted separation from the world.

---

7. Derek Thomas, *Let's Study Revelation* (Edinburgh: Banner of Truth, 2003), 147.

Christians seeking to "come out" from culture can fail to realize how deeply permeated they are by their culture. The very languages into which we translate God's Word involve structures and expressions that are culturally rooted. People raised in Japan, France, Africa, and America all have deeply ingrained social habits and life expectations that are shaped by their native society. Niebuhr writes that the Christian "cannot rid himself of political beliefs and economic customs by rejecting the more or less external institutions; these customs and beliefs have taken up residence in his mind."[8] Therefore, even if we were physically to leave our culture, we would still be products of the culture and would carry our cultural outlook with us.

So how do Christians obey the command, "Come out of her, my people"? The answer is given as the voice continues: "lest you take part in her sins, lest you share in her plagues" (Rev. 18:4). Christians need to avoid two dangers in relating to worldly Babylon: the danger of participating in its sin and the danger of suffering its judgment.

Christians must understand the idolatries at work in their society, and they must resist pressures to enter into the culture's sinful attitudes and practices. When it comes to America today, these idolatries include money, beauty, youth, pleasure, and power. When we consider temptations to sin, the entire Ten Commandments come into play. Our attitude toward worship, to God's holy name, to our use of time, to authority figures, to the lives of others, to possessions, to sexuality and marriage, to property, to truth, and to contentedness must all be shaped by God's Word rather than by the world. Sometimes this will require us to refuse to participate in cultural activities that aggressively promote ungodliness. A prime example today is the unwillingness of many Christians to send their children to public schools, given the aggressive secular ideology promoted there.

Separation from sin can be achieved only by both a no to the world and a yes to God's Word. Christians who imbibe the ideas, the images, and the dreams of the pagan world are likely to walk down the worldly path. This is why Psalm 1 begins: "Blessed is the man who walks not in the counsel of the wicked" (Ps. 1:1). But we must also positively apply our minds and hearts to God's Word. Psalm 1 says of the blessed man that "his delight is in the law of the Lord, and on his law he meditates day and night" (1:2). So important is this principle of thinking and acting by God's Word that it was

8. Niebuhr, *Christ and Culture*, 69.

Paul's first exhortation in the long book of Romans: "Do not be conformed to this world, but be transformed by the renewal of your mind, that by testing you may discern what is the will of God, what is good and acceptable and perfect" (Rom. 12:2).

In a culture such as ours in America today, which so closely resembles both cursed Babylon and pagan Rome, Christians who thoughtlessly use the world's products and mindlessly enjoy worldly entertainment, without carefully discriminating according to God's Word, live in grave danger of sinful defilement. William Hendriksen writes: "To depart from Babylon means not to have fellowship with her sins and not to be ensnared by her allurements and enticements."[9]

If we wonder how Christians may share in Babylon's judgment, we need only recall the experience of Abraham's nephew Lot. While a believer himself, Lot moved into Sodom, since its area of the Jordan valley seemed so lush and productive. When God sent angels to destroy Sodom, they first rescued Lot, who suffered greatly because of his assimilation into that wicked culture. Lot escaped the evil city before the fires of judgment fell, but God turned his wife into a pillar of salt when she looked back with longing, and his two daughters led Lot into such deplorable sexual sins that his offspring were mocked by God's people (Gen. 19:1–38). Likewise, many worldly Christians not only will accomplish little for the gospel, but will leave a wretched spiritual legacy. "Remember Lot's wife," Jesus warns every Christian who looks longingly on the world (Luke 17:32).

The voice from heaven aids Christians in this calling by pointing out that Babylon's "sins are heaped high as heaven, and God has remembered her iniquities" (Rev. 18:5). This statement warns us against taking a casual view of sin, especially in light of the Bible's teaching about God's mercy and grace. "God is a gracious God, and because of the sacrificial death of his Son he not only forgives the repentant sinner but also remembers his or her sins no more (Heb. 8:12; 10:17). But sins committed by unrepentant sinners he recalls one by one."[10] The sins that are so flagrantly discounted by a depraved society are each an infinite and eternal offense to the heart of the holy God.

9. William Hendriksen, *More than Conquerors: An Interpretation of the Book of Revelation* (1940; repr., Grand Rapids: Baker, 1967), 174.
10. Kistemaker, *Revelation*, 489.

Some years ago, an elder at the church where I served attended a meeting at a luxury hotel in South Florida. When he arrived, he found that a convention of pornographers was meeting there. He called me to express his revulsion at their boastful smiles and the super-luxurious limousines they parked outside. What was particularly galling was his awareness that some of the money fueling this dirty enterprise was being provided by Christians who imbibe their filthy wares. This should not be. "Come out of her, my people," God commands (Rev. 18:4).

OUR HIGHEST CALLING

Beyond the call to come out from the sinful ways of the Babylonian world, we may make three more specific applications, each of which is tied to the statements of judgment in Revelation 18:6–8.

First, since the sinful world is destined for judgment, Christians should not invest our ultimate dreams or seek our true treasures in this world. Jesus taught, "Do not lay up for yourselves treasures on earth." We should not set our hearts on earthly things because they are inherently unstable. Even in this life, Jesus warned, moths and rust destroy, and thieves break in and steal (Matt. 6:19–20). More importantly, he said, "Where your treasure is, there your heart will be also" (6:21). You can know where your heart is by asking what you think about in idle moments. What ambitions are most important to you? What endeavors are most exciting? While we are in this world, we are bound to have a good many interests here. But those who know the grace and glory of Christ should hold him as our highest treasure. Our minds should be interested in the work of his church and of the gospel. And our chief interests should be those bound up with the kingdom of heaven.

The voice from heaven gives another reason for us not to place our treasures in this world, since God has resolved its condemnation and judgment: "Pay her back as she herself has paid back others, and repay her double for her deeds; mix a double portion for her in the cup she mixed" (Rev. 18:6). Having recorded each sin, God has prepared a perfect corresponding judgment. The idea of *double* here is not that of twice the judgment but of a duplicate portion, a double in judgment for what was committed in sin. Why should Christians and the church be preoccupied with the fads, opinions, and priorities of the world, when the sin involved in them all is certain to be judged by our God? Rather than placing our treasures in the vaults of Sodom and Babylon, we should seek treasures that Jesus safeguards. He urged: "But seek first the kingdom of God and his righteousness, and all these things will be added to you" (Matt. 6:33).

Second, since this judgment reveals God's hatred of the world's sinful priorities, Christians should increasingly take on an attitude that is pleasing to God and contrary to the spirit of the world. Some believers are reluctant to be different from the world because they fear being discovered as Christians. But what does this say about our commitment to the Lord? Seeing his response to Babylon's arrogance and sins, we should cultivate instead the holy humility that characterized Jesus and pleases our God.

God's revulsion for the sinful world is vividly displayed in Revelation 18:7: "As she glorified herself and lived in luxury, so give her a like measure of torment and mourning, since in her heart she says, 'I sit as a queen, I am no widow, and mourning I shall never see.'" Here, it is especially the self-glorifying attitude of the world that offends God. Babylon boasts of her self-sufficiency and lives for her own praise. By speaking of herself as a queen, she exalts her autonomy in rebellion to God. By repudiating widowhood and mourning, she mocks God's threats of judgment. Similar attitudes are prevalent in secular society today, and Christians should turn their hearts instead toward God in humility, using the things of the world in stewardship to him.

Finally, Christians are always to remember the fate in store for the ungodly world: "For this reason her plagues will come in a single day, death and mourning and famine, and she will be burned up with fire; for mighty is the Lord God who has judged her" (Rev. 18:8). Like the world that Noah departed before the flood that rose suddenly, and like Sodom, which fell in a day to the fire and brimstone crashing down from God, the entire world awaits a judgment that will utterly destroy everything that sinners hold dear. When judgment comes, there will be no escape for those who have rejected the gospel offer of salvation through Jesus Christ.

Why should you live differently from the world in sin? First, for God's sake; second, for the world's sake. Our world desperately needs the testimony of a lived Christianity that bears witness to the God of salvation, his judgment on sin, and the forgiveness he offers through the blood of Jesus Christ. This gives the most important answer to the question of Christianity and culture, as commanded by Jesus himself: "Go therefore and make disciples of all nations, baptizing them in the name of the Father and of the Son and of the Holy Spirit, teaching them to observe all that I have commanded you" (Matt. 28:19–20).

John Bunyan's *Pilgrim's Progress* provides a model for sinners who learn of impending judgment and their need for a Savior. Christian heard the warning and fled to the cross, crying, "Life! life! eternal life!" That is what you must do, not looking back to the world but looking only to Jesus in faith and fleeing to him for forgiveness and life. But *Pilgrim's Progress* also provides a model for those who have believed and found salvation, and who for a time have an opportunity to help others to be saved. His name was Evangelist, and he gave the pilgrim a verse from Christ's gospel, "Flee from the wrath to come" (Matt. 3:7). Evangelist directed the endangered sinner to the shining lamp of God's Word, where he would learn of salvation through the narrow gate at the cross of Jesus Christ.[11] However unpopular it may be, Evangelist cited the words of Hebrews 12:25: "See that you do not refuse him who is speaking. For if they did not escape when they refused him who warned them on earth, much less will we escape if we reject him who warns from heaven."

11. John Bunyan, *Pilgrim's Progress* (Nashville: Thomas Nelson, 1999), 12–13.

47

ALAS FOR THE GREAT CITY

Revelation 18:9–24

Rejoice over her, O heaven, and you saints and apostles and prophets, for God has given judgment for you against her!
(Rev. 18:20)

n the morning of June 3, 1942, two squadrons of American torpedo bombers spotted the main force of Japanese aircraft carriers about seven hundred miles west of Midway Island. The American bombers launched an immediate attack, but fifty Japanese Zero fighters shot them all down, without a single torpedo even scratching a Japanese ship. The only surviving American pilot was Ensign George H. Gay. Floating in the water with a rubber seat cushion, Ensign Gay watched the unfolding events of the great battle of Midway, cheering on as three of four vital Japanese carriers were set aflame and sunk.[1]

Revelation 18 presents a similar perspective on the fall of the great world city, Babylon the great. John's account is modeled on Ezekiel's lament for the fall of the mercantile city of Tyre (Ezek. 26–27). Revelation 18 imitates this lament, featuring the kings, merchants, and seafarers whose alliance

---

1. Taken from Sir Basil Liddell Hart, ed., *History of the Second World War* (New York: Exeter Books, 1980), 225–28.

with wicked Babylon is ended by God's judgment. This scene of despair is contrasted at the end with the rejoicing of heaven and the people of God. Like Ensign Gay in battle with the Japanese Imperial Fleet, God's people had been victims of Babylon's great might, but now they would gaze marveling as the great evil power sank beneath the waves.

THE MOURNERS' LAMENT

When John wrote the book of Revelation, the city of Babylon had long since been destroyed. Babylon symbolized imperial Rome, the powerful and decadent city that dominated the first-century Mediterranean world. Rome itself was symbolic, standing along with Babylon as a symbol of the satanic realm of secularism in idolatrous opposition to God. Her judgment is lamented in these verses by those who had feasted from her table.

The first to lament Babylon's fall are "the kings of the earth" (Rev. 18:9). These are the client princes who relied on the empire for their prestige and power, including the rulers in the province of Asia, where John's churches were located. These rulers had embraced the corruption of Rome so as to gain power from her. They "committed sexual immorality and lived in luxury with her," and now they "weep and wail over her when they see the smoke of her burning" (18:9). The kings lamented Rome's greatness and might: "Alas! Alas! You great city, you mighty city, Babylon!" (18:10). With the great city fallen, they grieve not for her but for their lost patronage.

The second mourners are the merchants, who grieve over losing the great market for their luxurious products: "And the merchants of the earth weep and mourn for her, since no one buys their cargo anymore" (Rev. 18:11). Paul Gardner writes: "They see their whole livelihood and purpose for living disappearing before their eyes. All that they have counted valuable is gone."[2]

Historians describe the staggering amount of trade that flowed into Rome. People compare today's Western decadence with that of ancient Rome, but there is no comparison. The citizens of Rome led lives of spectacular wealth and stunning opulence. The riches of the ancient world were poured into the lap of Rome. Aristides wrote: "Merchandise is brought from every land and sea, everything that every season begets, and every country produces,

---

2. Paul Gardner, *Revelation: The Compassion and Protection of Christ*, Focus on the Bible (Tain, Ross-shire, Scotland: Christian Focus, 2008), 241.

the products of rivers and lakes, the arts of the Greeks and the barbarians, so that, if anyone were to wish to see all these things, he would either have to visit the whole inhabited world to see them—or to visit Rome . . . ; everything flows to Rome; merchandise, cargoes, the products of the land, the emptying of the mines, the product of every art that is and has been."[3] With such wealth, Romans vied for the most outlandish extravagance. The historian Suetonius wrote of the emperor Caligula: "In reckless extravagance he outdid the prodigals of all times in ingenuity, inventing a new sort of baths and unnatural varieties of foods and feasts; for he would bathe in hot or cold perfumed oils, drink pearls of great price dissolved in vinegar, and set before his guests loaves and meats of gold."[4] The emperor Nero never wore the same garment twice, never traveled with less than a thousand carriages, and had his mules' hooves shod with silver horseshoes.[5]

Against this backdrop, we are not surprised at the wealthy cargo that the merchants lament as lost: "cargo of gold, silver, jewels, pearls, fine linen, purple cloth, silk, scarlet cloth, all kinds of scented wood, all kinds of articles of ivory, all kinds of articles of costly wood, bronze, iron and marble, cinnamon, spice, incense, myrrh, frankincense, wine, oil, fine flour, wheat, cattle and sheep, horses and chariots, and slaves, that is, human souls" (Rev. 18:12–13). The general impression of wealthy extravagance is most important, but the categories merit comment. In addition to gold, silver, and jewels, there are the costliest fabrics and most rare dyes so that Romans could wear the latest and highest fashion. Rich woods and ivory supplied the most costly furniture. Spices of all kinds provided flavor and scents, and the richest foods provided variety and sensual delight to the dining table. The list concludes with human slaves. The word for *slaves* literally means "bodies" (Greek, *soma*), showing how little regard the Romans had for the dignity of human life. These "souls" were possessions to be used and misused at the whim of their wealthy owners. Dennis Johnson writes that "commerce in human flesh is the last of Babylon's imports, the culmination of a decadent culture's ruthless pursuit of pleasure, whatever the cost to others."[6]

3. Quoted in William Barclay, *The Revelation of John*, 3rd ed., 2 vols., New Daily Study Bible (Louisville: Westminster John Knox, 2004), 2:176.

4. Ibid.

5. Ibid., 2:176–77.

6. Dennis E. Johnson, *Triumph of the Lamb: A Commentary on Revelation* (Phillipsburg, NJ: P&R Publishing, 2001), 257.

If the rulers valued power, the merchants loved splendor and beauty. They cry, "The fruit for which your soul longed has gone from you, and all your delicacies and your splendors are lost to you, never to be found again!" (Rev. 18:14). Verse 16 views the great city as a sumptuously beautiful woman dressed in the most alluring clothes and the richest jewelry: "Alas, alas, for the great city that was clothed in fine linen, in purple and scarlet, adorned with gold, with jewels, and with pearls!" Philip Hughes writes that "the materialistic extravagance and carnal voluptuousness of her existence, and for which she had sold her soul, are now suddenly and irretrievably lost. Before the Judge of all the world she is empty and naked."[7]

The third group of mourners consists of the seafarers, whose ships carried the merchants' cargo: "And all shipmasters and seafaring men, sailors and all whose trade is on the sea, stood far off and cried out as they saw the smoke of her burning, 'What city was like the great city?'" (Rev. 18:17–18). The ship captains and their crews see from afar the smoke of the great burning city. "They recall its former greatness and splendour. They can hardly believe their eyes when they see the total ruin and thorough collapse of all their hopes and desires. They heap dust on their heads as a token of grief."[8]

Unlike the kings, who sought power from Rome, and the merchants, who relished the luxurious living of Rome, the shipmasters care only for the money they made from Rome: "Alas, alas, for the great city where all who had ships at sea grew rich by her wealth!" (Rev. 18:19). There will be no further chance for them to get rich quick and make such lavish profits. Contrary to Jesus' advice in the Sermon on the Mount, they had stored up treasure on earth, rather than in heaven, and the time had now come when all their riches would be lost (Matt. 6:19–20). In the judgment of the Babylonian world system, those whose hearts are fixed to the things of the world will suffer total loss.

Notice two things about these laments. First, the mourners remained at a distance, not coming to the rescue because of their fear: "They will stand far off, in fear of her torment" (Rev. 18:10). Their lament is entirely for themselves—what they are losing—and not for Babylon or her people, and they do nothing to stretch out a hand in mercy or love. This demonstrates

7. Philip Edgcumbe Hughes, *The Book of Revelation* (Downers Grove, IL: InterVarsity Press, 1990), 193.
8. William Hendriksen, *More than Conquerors: An Interpretation of the Book of Revelation* (1940; repr., Grand Rapids: Baker, 1967), 175.

that the more worldly you are, the less real fellowship you will enjoy in relationships. William Barclay notes: "It is one of the laws of life that, if people place all their happiness in material things, they miss the greatest things of all—love and friendship with others."[9] These mourners were poor even before Babylon fell, since they had abandoned the true riches of love for God and friendship with their fellow man for the sake of mere material riches.

We should remember that this vision is symbolic of the final judgment, when not merely Babylon and Rome will fall but the entire idolatrous world and its decadent system. When the final judgment comes to history, none will be outside watching the fall of destruction and fire, except those spared that judgment through their saving relationship with Jesus Christ.

Second, notice how swiftly and suddenly judgment came upon the great city: "Alas! Alas! You great city, you mighty city, Babylon! For in a single hour your judgment has come" (Rev. 18:10). The false god that they boasted would last forever instead fell at a single blow from heaven. When God's patient delay has run its course, judgment will come immediately and bring a sudden end to the powers of the world.

After the battle of Midway, the Japanese commander, Vice Admiral Nagumo, admitted that he had not believed it possible for his mighty fleet to be defeated. His confidence was reinforced in the midmorning when a second flight of American torpedo planes arrived. Nagumo's fighters smashed this assault, shooting down many of the American planes. At this very moment of casual triumph, however, two squadrons of American dive bombers arrived high overhead. While the Japanese fighters were away destroying the torpedo planes, the screaming sound of diving bombers was heard above the precious aircraft carriers *Kaga*, *Soryu*, and *Akagi*, their decks jammed with refueling planes. Massive bombs rained down on the carriers, bursting into flames, one after another, streaming fire and death on the ships. One historian writes: "Thus, in five brief, searing minutes, half of Japan's entire fleet carrier force, her naval *corps d'elite*, had been shattered."[10]

When God's sovereign hand of providence decrees judgment, the fall can be swift and the destruction utterly devastating. This is a picture of how God's wrath will fall on the rebellious world in sin with the coming of Jesus Christ. "In a single hour she has been laid waste," cried the mourners of

---

9. Barclay, *The Revelation of John*, 2:185.
10. Liddell Hart, *History of the Second World War*, 228.

Babylon (Rev. 18:19). The time to escape God's judgment is therefore before it falls. This is why Paul urged his readers in Corinth: "Behold, now is the favorable time; behold, now is the day of salvation" (2 Cor. 6:2).

REJOICE, O HEAVEN!

The lament of the kings, merchants, and seafarers is not the only perspective on the fall of mighty Babylon. Revelation 18:20 interrupts with the voice of John's angel-interpreter: "Rejoice over her, O heaven, and you saints and apostles and prophets, for God has given judgment for you against her!"

In dramatizing Babylon's fall, John leaves us in no doubt that this was God's doing. John shows this by adapting a scene from Jeremiah's ministry. In Jeremiah 51:60, the prophet wrote in a book all the judgments that would befall evil Babylon. He then gave the book to one of the leading Jews who was going to exile in Babylon so that God's judgment could be proclaimed when the people of God arrived there in chains. He then was to tie a stone to the book and cast it into the river Euphrates to symbolize that Babylon would sink and rise no more because of God's cataclysmic judgment (Jer. 51:61–64).

Now, as John looks to the end of history when the Babylonian world system will come under judgment, "a mighty angel" appears with "a stone like a great millstone." He throws the great stone "into the sea, saying, 'So will Babylon the great city be thrown down with violence, and will be found no more'" (Rev. 18:21). The great millstone crashes into the water and sinks to the bottom of the deepest sea. This symbolizes the utter ruin of the evil world, which perishes forever because of idolatry and sin. This total judgment fell on Rome in due time, as the empire was completely engulfed by the barbarian hordes that flooded out of the East. G. K. Beale points out that the historical judgments of Tyre, Babylon, and Rome "typify the fall of the final world kingdom." All these judgments reflect "that of Egypt at the Red Sea," when God drowned the chariot army of Pharaoh.[11] Nehemiah 9:11 says, "You cast their pursuers into the depths, as a stone into mighty waters." What Moses said of his Egyptian enemies will be true for the entire evil world: "The floods covered them; they went down into the depths like a stone" (Ex. 15:5).

11. G. K. Beale, *The Book of Revelation: A Commentary on the Greek Text*, New International Greek Testament Commentary (Grand Rapids: Eerdmans, 1999), 918.

The angel follows up this symbolic gesture with a eulogy recounting the judgment befalling every aspect of Babylonian life. In Revelation 18:21–23, he intones the words "no more" six times. Babylon herself "will be found no more." With her fall the sound of music, the busy noise of craftsmen, and the clanging sounds of daily industry "will be heard in you no more" (Rev. 18:22). Moreover, "the light of a lamp will shine in you no more," and the sounds of merriment and joy would no more be heard in Babylon the great (18:23).

First, "the sound of harpists and musicians, of flute players and trumpeters, will be heard in you no more" (Rev. 18:22). Music is a cherished blessing of life. The harpists and singers performed on happy occasions, and the trumpet sounded for ceremonies and games. But now God's covenant curse falls in the silencing of all music (see Isa. 24:8). The contrast with heaven is obvious and severe: whereas the glorified choirs above sing hallelujahs to the Lord, the music of earth that glorified idolatry and sin will be silenced forever.

Another delight on earth is the sound of craftsmanship and industry, as men and women apply their skills to building an economy and making a prosperous future. This sound will also be silenced: "A craftsman of any craft will be found in you no more" (Rev. 18:22). Hands that were raised up in rebellion to God will no longer be permitted to make things of value and beauty. This judgment may in part represent God's rebuke on the trade guilds of Asia from which Christians were barred because they would not render worship to Caesar and to the patron idols (see 2:9). Added to this is the curse that "the sound of the mill will be heard in you no more" (18:22). This is the noise of daily provision in busy communities and homes. There is now no reason to meet life's basic needs.

God's curse is seen even more keenly as all light is removed from fallen Babylon: "and the light of a lamp will shine in you no more" (Rev. 18:23). Whereas God promised to make "his face to shine upon" his people in the blessing of grace (Num. 6:25), there is only darkness for those under his curse. Lights bathed the streets of wealthy Tyre, luxurious Babylon, and glorious imperial Rome, just as garish lamps assault the eyes in today's New York City and Las Vegas. Without light, who could enjoy, or even notice, the lavish wealth symbolized by gold, silver, and precious jewels? William Hendriksen writes: "Utter darkness reigns supreme, a darkness that can be felt, a darkness which symbolizes the final and complete effusion of God's wrath upon this wicked, pleasure-loving, seductive world!"[12]

Finally, Babylon will hear no more of "the voice of bridegroom and bride" (Rev. 18:23). The blessings of love and merriment, the covenant bonds of human fidelity, and the voice of tender romance will be stilled in the great city (see Jer. 25:10–11), for even love, man's highest blessing, will have ended for those consigned to hell.

THE CASE FOR JUDGMENT

Given the horror of this judgment, some might wonder why the angel calls on believers to "rejoice over her" (Rev. 18:20). The reason does not lie in any vindictiveness that Christians harbor against the unbelieving world or any delight in the judgment of those who are, after all, our fellow sinners. Rather, the answer is found in the three causes for judgment given in verses 23 and 24: "for your merchants were the great ones of the earth, and all nations were deceived by your sorcery. And in her was found the blood of prophets and of saints, and of all who have been slain on earth." Given these evils that were spawned from worldly Babylon, God's people should welcome her demise with much the same spirit that Ensign Gay cheered the sinking of the Japanese aircraft carriers at the battle of Midway.

The first cause for the great judgment is the idolatry of worldly Babylon, who turned from giving glory to God to taking glory for herself. Notice how Babylon is spoken of by the kings, merchants, and seafarers as "great" and "mighty" (Rev. 18:10), and the worship that is given to her "splendors" (18:14) and "wealth" (18:17). They not only had forgotten God and ceased giving him glory but had banned the knowledge of God and persecuted his true worship. The kings exclaimed, "What city was like the great city?" (18:18), speaking in terms that the Bible elsewhere uses only for God (see Ex. 15:11; Mic. 7:18). John's depiction shows how worldly people make "the good things in life" their gods, being driven not by love or fidelity, but by their own comfort and security. These cries of praise to Babylon are heard in the claims of secular humanism today, which denies the glory that God desires and foolishly ascribes all sovereignty to man. Beale states simply,

12. Hendriksen, *More than Conquerors*, 177.

"To focus on humanity as the center of everything and to forget God is the greatest sin."[13]

Second, Babylon is judged because "all nations were deceived by [her] sorcery" (Rev. 18:23). While this verse no doubt contains a condemnation of occult magic, more generally Rome cast a spell of temptation that lured all around her into the grossest depravity. Jesus warned that it would be better to have a millstone tied around one's neck and be cast into the sea than to face God's judgment for leading even one child into sin (Matt. 18:6). The use of a millstone here suggests that it is especially for seducing others into wickedness that Rome and the Babylonian world would be so thoroughly removed by God. While Christians grieve to know that others have suffered judgment when they could have been saved, they rejoice to see God's removing from the world a source of stumbling and corruption.

Third, the people of God above and on earth rejoice that he has put an end to their sufferings at the hands of the Babylonian world: "And in her was found the blood of prophets and of saints, and of all who have been slain on earth" (Rev. 18:24). Not only will music, light, and love be no more in wicked Babylon, but by God's judgment there will be no more idolatry, seduction, and persecution for believers. Not only is the violent bloodshed that so characterized pagan society in general put to an end, but the blood of God's servants is vindicated by his corresponding judgment on their enemies. "Rejoice over her, O heaven, and you saints and apostles and prophets," says the angelic voice, "for God has given judgment for you against her!" (18:20). Christians rejoice in the justice of God's judgment, which vindicates his holy character in light of history. Moreover, this judgment will prove that while the church was despised and convicted on earth, believers are accepted and vindicated by God.

Lessons from Babylon's Fall

We may conclude with three lessons from Babylon's judgment and fall. The first is that Christians must learn how to use the things of the world rightly, enjoying God's good gifts without falling into the world's idolatry. Just as the kings, merchants, and seafarers stood far off from Babylon in

---

13. Beale, *Revelation*, 922.

fear, Christians must keep distance from the materialism that characterizes Babylon's spirit.

Christians are perfectly free, of course, to enjoy good things in the world and even to appreciate luxuries, so long as we do so in gratitude to God and with generosity toward those in need. We will find, for instance, that when we see the radiant bride of Christ in Revelation 19 and 21, she is also clothed in "fine linen" (Rev. 19:8) and is adorned with jewels (21:11–14). There is nothing drab about the glory of Christ's people, and the church's beauty actually excels that of harlot Babylon (see 12:1). If we have money, or high position, or pleasant activities, let us be grateful to God for them and be stewards of them for God's work in the world. Let our true treasure always be God and his blessings in Christ. John warns us, "Do not love the world or the things in the world. . . . For all that is in the world—the desires of the flesh and the desires of the eyes and pride in possessions—is not from the Father but is from the world" (1 John 2:15–16). Let us therefore not be proud in possessions or boastful about worldly things, but content like the apostle Paul. He wrote: "I know how to be brought low, and I know how to abound. . . . I can do all things through him who strengthens me" (Phil. 4:12–13). Jesus adds, "Where your treasure is, there your heart will be also" (Matt. 6:21).

A second lesson from this passage is that we should never doubt the certainty of God's judgment on the wicked. Long years after John recorded this vision, it seemed to many that Rome would never fall but would endure forever. Yet the day came, in A.D. 410, when the Visigoth chieftain Alaric overran and sacked the city of Rome, bringing the empire to an end. Many Christians were utterly dismayed in the insecurity of the moment, just as many Christians today tremble for the collapse of Western society. But when the Christian leader Augustine of Hippo received the news about Rome's fall, he pointed out how inevitable this judgment was: "There will be an end to every earthly kingdom. You are surprised that the world is losing its grip and full of pressing tribulations. Do not hold on to the old man, the world; do not refuse to regain your youth in Christ who says to you: 'The world is passing away, the world is short of breath. Do not fear, thy youth shall be renewed as an eagle.'"[14]

14. Quoted in Richard Bewes, *The Lamb Wins: A Guided Tour through the Book of Revelation* (Tain, Ross-shire, Scotland: Christian Focus, 2000), 121.

Finally, Christians should realize that in the midst of this very world, with its history moving forward to certain judgment, Christ is building his church that will endure eternally in glory. Jesus promised, "I will build my church, and the gates of hell shall not prevail against it" (Matt. 16:18). These judgments display God's sovereignty and power. Those same almighty attributes ensure that the work he is doing now in our midst through the gospel is certain to succeed. Knowing this, we labor in the world for eternity. We seek first his kingdom and his righteousness, as Jesus said, confident that all other things will be given to us with him (6:33).

48

SALVATION TO GOD

Revelation 19:1–5

After this I heard what seemed to be the loud voice of a great multitude in heaven, crying out, "Hallelujah! Salvation and glory and power belong to our God." (Rev. 19:1)

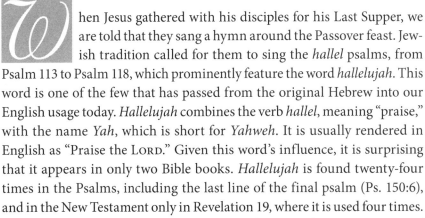hen Jesus gathered with his disciples for his Last Supper, we are told that they sang a hymn around the Passover feast. Jewish tradition called for them to sing the *hallel* psalms, from Psalm 113 to Psalm 118, which prominently feature the word *hallelujah*. This word is one of the few that has passed from the original Hebrew into our English usage today. *Hallelujah* combines the verb *hallel*, meaning "praise," with the name *Yah*, which is short for *Yahweh*. It is usually rendered in English as "Praise the LORD." Given this word's influence, it is surprising that it appears in only two Bible books. *Hallelujah* is found twenty-four times in the Psalms, including the last line of the final psalm (Ps. 150:6), and in the New Testament only in Revelation 19, where it is used four times.

There seems to be a connection, however, between these appearances of "Hallelujah." Revelation 19 contains the last songs of the book of Revelation and thus of the New Testament. Therefore, just "as the Heb[rew] Psalter closes with God's chosen people singing 'Hallelujah,' the N[ew] T[estament]

closes with God's redeemed in heaven singing 'Hallelujah.'"[1] Moreover, it is likely that Jesus sang the *hallel* with his disciples during the Last Supper, at the culmination of his earthly ministry to save his people from the guilt of sin. In Revelation 19, his redeemed people sing "Hallelujah" in response to Christ's saving his people from the power and dominion of sin, after the fiery judgment of Babylon the great in chapter 18. Revelation 19 begins with "After this," speaking of the judgments of the prior chapters, which are now followed by the adoring worship of heaven. John heard "what seemed to be the loud voice of a great multitude in heaven, crying out, 'Hallelujah!'" (Rev. 19:1). The angels' *hallelujah* "indicates the desire of the heavenly multitude to praise the Lord for the downfall of evil's tyranny."[2]

God Glorified in Salvation

In Revelation 19:1, the heavenly throng rejoices in the glory that God has won by saving his people: "Hallelujah! Salvation and glory and power belong to our God."

When we speak of salvation glorifying God, we mean that his saving achievement shines light on his wonderful attributes. A similar worship scene in Revelation 7:12 noted seven attributes of God for praise: "Blessing and glory and wisdom and thanksgiving and honor and power and might be to our God forever and ever! Amen." Here in chapter 19, the heavenly host celebrates three of God's attributes that are marvelously displayed: his salvation, glory, and power.

In rejoicing that "salvation . . . belong[s] to our God," the heavenly singers note God's sovereignty over *salvation*. Salvation belongs to God in that he alone accomplished it. We do not save ourselves either by good works or by our efforts to defeat evil, since we are ourselves sinners who need to be saved. Rather, we are like Jonah, when his sin resulted in his being cast into the sea and God's sending a great fish to swallow him and save him from drowning. Jonah recognized God's sovereign mercy and cried in praise, "Salvation belongs to the LORD!" (Jonah 2:9). We are also like Jehoshaphat and his generation when God saved them from a mass invasion of enemies. Jehoshaphat

---

1. Guy B. Funderburk, quoted in Simon J. Kistemaker, *Revelation*, New Testament Commentary (Grand Rapids: Baker, 2001), 509.
2. Derek Thomas, *Let's Study Revelation* (Edinburgh: Banner of Truth, 2003), 152.

was overwhelmed and dismayed, as we often are, so he called a great prayer meeting for the nation. He prayed, "O our God, . . . we do not know what to do, but our eyes are on you" (2 Chron. 20:12). God sent a prophet to answer, saying, "Do not be afraid and do not be dismayed at this great horde, for the battle is not yours but God's" (20:15). The next day, the believers went out to see God's victory, finding that the Lord had routed the enemy and left a great heap of spoils for his people. Like Jonah, Jehoshaphat, and the entire host of biblical witnesses, Christians should praise God as the Redeemer who has saved us by his own sovereign action, apart from any merit or contribution on our part, and we should give him all the glory from the very depths of our hearts.

Since the expression "Salvation . . . belong[s] to our God" emphasizes God's sovereignty in our salvation, it reminds us of the aim of God's will for believers. Christians sometimes wonder what God's will for them is, especially when they are going through hard times. "To what purpose is God working in my life," they ask, "and how do I make sense of these trials?" The answer is that God has sovereignly willed and is presently working out our salvation to the praise of his *glory*. He has arranged marvelous ways in which each of our lives displays his sovereign grace, so that forever in heaven the angels will marvel at how we each bear our own unique testimony that "salvation belongs to God!"

God's salvation also magnifies his *power*. Doubters ask, "We see that God wills salvation, but is he able to do it?" The destruction of the satanic world system in the coming of Christ, which our passage celebrates in praise, will put an end to such questions. The Bible shows throughout that God has power to save his people. God enabled Samson to slay a host of Philistines with the jawbone of a donkey to display his abundant power to deliver his people (Judg. 15:15). When the Israelites needed a way of escape, God parted the Red Sea (Ex. 14:26–30) and then made the mighty walls of Jericho crash down at their feet (Josh. 6:20). All through the Bible, God proves his power to save. Paul states that the greatest example is the resurrection of Jesus Christ, when God overcame the power of sin and death. He thus prayed that believers would know "the immeasurable greatness of his power toward us who believe, according to the working of his great might that he worked in Christ when he raised him from the dead" (Eph. 1:19–20). We may add to this the praise of the angels in Revelation 19, magnifying God for the display of his power in overthrowing the Babylonian harlot that is our world. Anticipating this end, we should rely on God's power now without doubting.

Paul Gardner writes: "God's power enables him to do all that he promises and to ensure that his purposes come to fulfillment."[3] That truth alone is ample reason to sing "Hallelujah" to God today!

At the center of heaven's praise is the *glory* of God that is displayed in salvation: "Hallelujah! Salvation and glory and power belong to our God" (Rev. 19:1). We can grasp the significance of God's glory by considering the two Bible words used for this attribute. The Hebrew word for *glory* is *kabod*, which originally meant that something is "weighty." To speak of the glory of God, then, is to celebrate his weightiness. We live in a time when thoughts of God exercise little influence. Secular people do not consider God to be very consequential, so that one may believe whatever one wants about God and do whatever one desires without fear of God's judgment. The events at the end of history will display both the folly of this attitude and the infinite weightiness of God! God is the true heavyweight, and those who have ignored him will suffer a great fall in the last judgment. The Greek word for *glory* is *doxa*. This comes from the verb *dokeo*, which means "to seem." It came to be used for something that we esteem or that is especially impressive. It is rightly used of God, since he is the most seemly of all beings. The events at the end of the age will prove that nothing is more significant than our relationship with God. Nothing is more important now than that we should live in God's favor through faith in Jesus, the Savior whom he has sent.

At the end of history, God's salvation will prove that only he deserves our praise. The kings of the earth glorified the powers of the world, saying, "What city was like the great city?" (Rev. 18:18). But when Babylon the great has been brought to ruin and believers in Christ have been gathered into God's loving presence, the only remaining voices will exclaim from heaven: "Salvation and glory and power belong to our God" (19:1). Anticipating this end, we should give God alone the ultimate place of worship and authority in our lives, and we should live now for the glory that he will display then.

GOD GLORIFIED IN JUDGMENT

The end of history will see God glorified not only in saving his people but also in judging the wicked. The angels thus praise God's holy justice:

3. Paul Gardner, *Revelation: The Compassion and Protection of Christ*, Focus on the Bible (Tain, Ross-shire, Scotland: Christian Focus, 2008), 250.

"for his judgments are true and just; for he has judged the great prostitute" (Rev. 19:2).

God is glorified in his wrath for sin, since "his judgments are true and just." God is not capricious or unfair in judging, but exercises perfect justice in accord with his law. Even those who reject God's Word tend to agree in the punishment of murderers, thieves, and cheats. God enforces the entirety of his law, upholding it perfectly in his judgment of sin. Especially in places where injustice widely prevails and evil goes unchecked, the cry goes up for justice to be done. At the end of history, when Christ has returned and put an end to the sinful world, this cry for justice will be satisfied to the praise of God.

Two primary causes are cited in the judgment of the Babylonian world system. First, Babylon "corrupted the earth with her immorality" (Rev. 19:2). The world tempts people by making actions seem attractive and pleasing when they are in fact immoral and ultimately destructive. This is heinously offensive to God, who made mankind to live in holiness and blessing. Genesis 3 shows how sin came into the world by means of deception, ruining the world and placing mankind under the shadow of corruption and death. Every time sin is similarly advanced by deceitful enticements, God is infuriated once more. How terrible it is to lead a person into sin, especially those who are young and impressionable. Jesus declared that it would be better to be drowned in the sea with a millstone around one's neck than to lead a child into evil (Matt. 18:6), and Revelation 18:21 shows this very judgment as befalling Babylon. Today, how great is the sin of the entertainment industry, advertisers, and government officials who promote immorality in order to gain money and power. In the end, God will vindicate his law by judging the entire Babylonian world for this kind of corruption.

Second, Babylon is judged because her hands are red with "the blood of [God's] servants" (Rev. 19:2). In many places in the world today, the most dangerous thing one can do is to speak the Word of God or worship openly in Jesus' name. Christians are killed and imprisoned for telling others the good news of salvation. Milder forms of persecution have now arrived in the West. Businesses are closed because their Christian owners refused to violate their consciences by glorifying the sin of homosexuality. Others are threatened by the government for refusing to fund the slaughter of infants in the womb. Worldly Babylon lashes out against faithful witnesses to the grace and truth of Christ, but God has promised to avenge their sorrow and blood. In the end, the world's persecution of believers, together with its crucifixion of Jesus, will be a chief cause of God's wrath. For judging those who shed his servants' blood, God's faithfulness will be praised.

The heavenly choir adds praise for the eternity of God's justice on the wicked: "Once more they cried out, 'Hallelujah! The smoke from her goes up forever and ever'" (Rev. 19:3). This language draws from Old Testament judgments. Abraham stood above the plain of Sodom and Gomorrah when God judged those wicked cities with fire and brimstone: "He looked and, behold, the smoke of the land went up like the smoke of a furnace" (Gen. 19:28). Isaiah spoke similarly about the judgment of Edom: "Night and day it shall not be quenched; its smoke shall go up forever" (Isa. 34:10).

These judgments merely symbolized the reality that is eternal judgment in hell. Paul spoke of the final judgment after Christ's return as "the punishment of eternal destruction, away from the presence of the Lord and from the glory of his might" (2 Thess. 1:9). "Eternal destruction" does not mean the annihilation or eradication of the wicked but their everlasting torment under God's just wrath. Revelation 20:10 will later speak of the wicked as being cast by God "into the lake of fire and sulfur where . . . they will be tormented day and night forever" (see also Rev. 20:15).

Some Christians find it difficult to accept such a brutal doctrine of eternal judgment. It has thus become popular to downplay the Bible's objectionable teaching on hell. Such people fail to realize, however, that they are denigrating God's Word and corrupting all the doctrines that are inseparably related to the eternal punishment of hell. To deny eternal punishment is inevitably to downplay the horrible nature of sin. Those who suggest that there may be salvation for those who died rejecting Christ undermine the Bible's urgent call to believe the gospel now. Those who wish to soften the idea of hell's sufferings minimize the sacrifice offered by Jesus on the cross for our sins.

Revelation 19:4 shows the response of the worship leaders of heaven to God's eternal judgment of the wicked: "And the twenty-four elders and the four living creatures fell down and worshiped God who was seated on the throne, saying, 'Amen. Hallelujah!'" The twenty-four elders are angelic counterparts to the twelve tribes of Israel and the twelve apostles of the church, who thus represent the entirety of the redeemed people of God in history. The "four living creatures" are the cherubim who are closest to God's throne and represent the submission of all creation (see Rev. 4:4–6). Therefore, "a song of praise from the twenty-four elders and the four living creatures is a hymn of praise to God from the whole Church and the whole of nature."[4]

If our thoughts and feelings about God's final judgment differ from this song of praise above, it calls for us to ask how worldly ideas have shaped our thoughts concerning sin, God's holiness, salvation, and judgment. When we think of people—perhaps those we love—having to suffer such eternal torment, we ought to resent not the justice of a holy God, but rather the evil of sin. The Bible will not compromise the truth of God's righteous wrath on the wicked. Instead, Christians should resolve to speak more boldly of the salvation that this same God so lovingly offers to the world through the blood of his Son. If we are not yet believers, we must urgently consider our own peril of eternal judgment for our sins. How great is the need of every sinner to be delivered from God's righteous, holy, and glorious wrath by embracing God's gracious provision of salvation through faith in Jesus, our Savior and Lord!

A SUMMONS TO PRAISE

This opening section of Revelation 19 concludes with a summons to praise God: "And from the throne came a voice saying, 'Praise our God, all you his servants, you who fear him, small and great'" (Rev. 19:5). Having believed in God's Word concerning his glory in salvation and judgment, we not only should ensure that we are saved through faith, but should then live in such a way that expresses thanksgiving and praise to him.

Three statements are made here about those who worship God. First, God is worshiped by his servants. This title does not describe a certain class of Christians, such as those who hold vocational positions in ministry, but rather describes all believers. To be a Christian is to be a servant of God.

The Greek word *doulos* is best translated as "slave." The point is not only that Christians serve God but that we serve him as those who are his possessions. This truth is illustrated by a boy who longed for a model sailboat. He spent weeks building one from a kit. When it was finally complete, he took the boat to the lake, where it sailed so beautifully that it kept going, right

4. William Barclay, *The Revelation of John*, 3rd ed., 2 vols., New Daily Study Bible (Louisville: Westminster John Knox, 2004), 2:192.

out of sight. Despite all his efforts, the boy could not find the boat. Several weeks later he was walking past a store window when to his amazement he saw his own boat, with an expensive price tag on it. He went into the store and explained to the shopkeeper, but the owner said, "I'm sorry, but I paid a great deal of money for this toy boat and I cannot give it to you for free." So the boy took up jobs and worked until he had the money to buy back his boat. Finally, he walked out of the store with the precious toy in his hand. He said, "Now you are twice mine—once because I made you and once because I bought you." So it is with God. He created us, and then when we were lost in sin he purchased us with the precious blood of Jesus. How wonderful it is to be twice his and thus to be God's willing servant forever![5]

Christians today have been taught by the world that their lives belong to themselves. But this is not true. We belong to God and are his possessions. When he chooses for our lives to take difficult paths, sometimes for long stretches of time, and when he gives us sacrifices to make on his behalf, we should remember first his right to do so as our Maker and Lord and also his grace that sustains us now and that will lead us to victory in the return of our Savior.

Second, worshipers are those who "fear him" (Rev. 19:5). True servants of God worship him with reverence and are careful to obey God's Word. The believer's fear of God is not a servile terror, but the respectful attitude of a son for a father whose rule is accepted and whose punishment is dreaded. The wise Christian knows that "the Lord disciplines the one he loves, and chastises every son whom he receives" (Heb. 12:6). Therefore, he is careful how he lives, and while he delights in the Lord's kindness and love, he worships "with reverence and awe," knowing that "our God is a consuming fire" (12:28–29).

Third, the God-fearing servants who are summoned to worship God include people of all kinds, both "small and great" (Rev. 19:5). This includes the new believer and the spiritually mature. It summons people from every race, nationality, and economic class. What matters is no longer how the world classifies and divides us, but how believers are united as one people in the saving grace of Christ. No matter who you are in the world or in the church, your calling in life is to give praise to God through your worship, service, and reverent obedience, all of which display the glory of God's grace in you. Just as our voices unite in the congregational singing of the worship

---

5. Taken from R. Kent Hughes, *John: That You May Believe* (Wheaton, IL: Crossway, 1999), 308.

service, each of our lives and our testimony of God's grace is needed to form the true *hallelujah* chorus that will praise the Lord in unending ages to come.

AMEN! HALLELUJAH!

I mentioned that *hallelujah* is one of the few Hebrew or Aramaic words that has passed directly into the church's use, crossing into our language. Another of these words is seen in Revelation 19:4: "Amen." This word expresses agreement with God, responding to his truth by saying, "Yes, it is so!" Although the words *amen* and *hallelujah* are joined together only here in the New Testament, the two words fit well together. It is the *amen* of faith that motivates Christians to the *hallelujah* of praise.

Can you give your *amen* to the praise of the angels in Revelation 19:1, crying, "Hallelujah! Salvation and glory and power belong to our God"? If you can, then you should live in gratitude to God for his sovereign, glorious, and all-powerful salvation, offering your life freely to his service. Can you further give your *amen* to the praise for his true and just judgments in verse 2? If you can praise God for his holy justice in punishing sin, then you will first seek forgiveness for your own sins by believing in Jesus and appealing to his death on the cross. You will further express your *amen* by telling other sinners how they can be saved, as you look upon the world, knowing in advance its terrible judgment under the just wrath of God for rebellion and sin.

Revelation 19:1 speaks of "the loud voice of a great multitude in heaven" giving their *hallelujah* to God. But here on earth, there are comparatively few who give their *amen*. Yet while not everyone will praise God from the heart, everyone will give glory to God at the end of history. God is sovereign and almighty, so his glorious purposes in salvation and judgment are certain to be fulfilled. Therefore, James Boice writes:

> Every person who has ever lived or will ever live must glorify God, either actively or passively, either willingly or unwillingly, either in heaven or in hell. You will glorify him as the object of his mercy and glory, which will be seen in you. Or you will glorify him in your rebellion and unbelief by being made the object of his wrath and power at the final judgment.[6]

6. James Montgomery Boice, *Romans* (Grand Rapids: Baker, 1993), 3:1108–9.

Given the truth of this claim, how vital it is that we should glorify God now by giving our *amen* to Jesus Christ, looking in faith to him as our Savior and Lord.

I mentioned that the words *amen* and *hallelujah* are joined only here in the New Testament. But they are also joined together in Psalm 106, which concludes by summing up the attitude we should have in desiring that by his mercy to us, God should have the praise of our lives: "Save us, O Lord our God, and gather us from among the nations, that we may give thanks to your holy name and glory in your praise. Blessed be the Lord, the God of Israel, from everlasting to everlasting! And let all the people say, 'Amen!' Praise the Lord!" (Ps. 106:47–48).

49

The Marriage Supper of the Lamb

Revelation 19:6–10

Let us rejoice and exult and give him the glory, for the marriage
of the Lamb has come, and his Bride has made herself ready.
(Rev. 19:7)

ccording to the ESPN sports network, the loudest crowd noise at a college football game took place at Clemson University's famed Death Valley stadium during the 2005 contest between the Clemson Tigers and the Miami Hurricanes. During the final minutes of that closely contested game, the noise reached the ear-shattering level of 126.6 decibels. It is likely, however, that even the Clemson football crowd could not compete with the heavenly chorus resounding in praise for the victory of Jesus Christ. After the Lamb's conquest of the great harlot Babylon, the apostle John "heard what seemed to be the voice of a great multitude, like the roar of many waters and like the sound of mighty peals of thunder" (Rev. 19:6).

If a great football crowd helps us to anticipate the volume of heaven's choir, the best foretaste of its beauty must be the "Hallelujah Chorus" in

George Frideric Handel's *Messiah*. Peter Jacobi wrote of it: "All the energy so far contained, all the emotions so far restrained, are released in an explosion of choral splendor."[1] This is the very kind of scene that John describes: the choir of assembled millions of holy voices in heaven, singing out in joy, crying, "Hallelujah!"

FOR THE LORD ALMIGHTY REIGNS!

In Revelation 18, we noted how difficult it is for Christians to rejoice fully in the downfall of worldly Babylon, in part because of the compassion for sinners that Jesus himself displayed. We know that God's wrath is both just and glorious, but hell remains less than a cheerful thought. Now, as the heavenly choir sings "Hallelujah," we find more positive reasons to rejoice in God's final judgment. The overthrow of the ungodly is a means to the glorious, universal, and unimpeded reign of Jesus Christ over all things. "Hallelujah!" heaven sings, "For the Lord our God the Almighty reigns" (Rev. 19:6).

The title "Lord our God the Almighty" emphasizes the sovereignty and omnipotence of God. In an important sense, there has never been a moment when God has not been reigning. Psalm 2 emphasizes that even when the earthly rulers conspire against God and his Word, God yet "sits in the heavens," holding them "in derision," establishing the sovereign reign of his Son (Ps. 2:1–7). God's plan for history merely permitted sin so that in the end his Son, Jesus Christ, would reign in grace with a people purchased by his blood. When this victory is achieved, when the opposition of Satan, sin, and death is conquered and put away, leaving nothing to hinder the blessed kingdom of Christ in all creation, no wonder that heaven rejoices.

All through history, mankind has sought to achieve a utopia of our own design. Even today, this secularist dream influences public policy and finds expression in literature and the arts. History shows, however, that with the problem of sin unresolved, the kingdoms of man's glory inevitably end up in blood-soaked tyranny and moral chaos. Even in the church, which as the assembly of the redeemed offers our best foretaste of heaven's society, the corruption of sin and our immaturity as pilgrims along the way leave

---

1. Peter Jacobi, *The Messiah Book: The Life & Times of G. F. Handel's Greatest Hit* (New York: St. Martin's Press, 1982), 78.

us longing for the purer and more perfect fellowship that will be ours when Jesus returns.

Edward Hicks was a famous nineteenth-century American folk painter and a minister in the Society of Friends, known as the Quakers. To express his longing for the reign of God, every one of Hicks's paintings is dedicated to the theme of Christ's "Peaceable Kingdom," depicting a lion lying down with a lamb and a little child leading (see Isa. 11:6). Art historians group Hicks's paintings into four periods, which more or less chart the conflict that grew in his life and ministry. Toward the end, when his churches had suffered bitter division, Hicks painted the animals fighting and the believers at odds. His last painting expresses his depressed state over the failure to achieve peace on earth, showing a lion hunched over in utter exhaustion.[2]

What the Babylonian world will never see because of its rebellious rejection of Christ and his Word, and what the church can only partially achieve before his coming, the heavenly choir celebrates with the greatest joy as Jesus comes finally and fully to reign. No wonder the entire holy assembly sings out "Hallelujah!" and cries, "Let us rejoice and exult and give him the glory" (Rev. 19:6–7).

THE MARRIAGE OF THE LAMB

When believers seek to understand the blessings that await us in glory, the Bible provides a variety of images. Psalm 23 depicts Christ's sheep grazing on the lush green grass of the high tablelands after their annual journey. What Christian has not reveled in blessed anticipation of the psalm's final verse: "Surely goodness and mercy shall follow me all the days of my life, and I shall dwell in the house of the LORD forever" (Ps. 23:6)! Revelation 19:7 adds a glorious vision of a wedding banquet after Christ has taken his bride. The choir sings: "Let us rejoice and exult and give him the glory, for the marriage of the Lamb has come, and his Bride has made herself ready."

Throughout the Bible, salvation is presented as a love relationship between God and his people. God told Israel, "I will betroth you to me in righteousness and in justice, in steadfast love and in mercy. I will betroth you to me in faithfulness" (Hos. 2:19–20). Paul sees this marriage promise fulfilled

2. Taken from Philip Graham Ryken, *My Father's World: Meditations on Christianity and Culture* (Phillipsburg, NJ: P&R Publishing, 2002), 117–20.

in the saving work of Jesus: "Christ loved the church and gave himself up for her, that he might sanctify her, . . . so that he might present the church to himself in splendor, without spot or wrinkle or any such thing" (Eph. 5:25–27). Douglas Kelly writes: "The Almighty Father planned to give his Son the finest gift a father could give a son: a beautiful bride. So why did God make the world? Why did he put me in it? It was because he wanted his son to have a marvelous bride and he has invited us to be part of that."[3]

A wonderful picture of this appears in the love story of Ruth the Moabitess and Boaz of Bethlehem. Ruth comes to him with nothing—with no name, no heritage, no wealth, and no honor. When she appeals to righteous Boaz in faith at the urging of Naomi, what does he do? He does not exploit her, but he spreads his garment over her to cover her, provide for her, and be her redeemer (Ruth 3:7–13). And having redeemed her, he joins with her in the intimate purity of marital love. This is a picture of Christ's covenant love for us.

I pointed out that Revelation 19 rejoices in the judgment of wicked Babylon because it makes way for Christ's reign. We further rejoice in the removal of the seducing harlot so that the holy bride of Christ may come forth. We may remember that Jesus' first miracle was at the wedding of Cana (John 2:1–11), a beginning that was not incidental: we find that "the entire ministry of Jesus is a preparation for a wedding."[4] Now that Christ has conquered, the wedding feast begins.

Wedding practices in biblical times were different from ours today. First, parents arranged the betrothal of their children, and once the terms of marriage were publicly accepted, the couple was legally married. This was followed by an interval of varying lengths, even years, between the betrothal and the wedding. During this time the groom would pay the dowry to the father of the bride (Gen. 34:12) or provide an arranged period of servitude (29:20). The wedding itself took the form of a processional in which the bride was taken from her father's house to the home of her husband. As the wedding drew near, the bride prepared and adorned herself to be presented to her groom. Upon her arrival, the groom received his bride from her father and the wedding feast began, a banquet that might last as long as

---

3. Douglas F. Kelly, *Revelation*, Mentor Expository Commentary (Tain, Ross-shire, Scotland: Mentor, 2012), 357.

4. Derek Thomas, *Let's Study Revelation* (Edinburgh: Banner of Truth, 2003), 155.

seven days.[5] William Hendriksen summarizes how this wedding practice pertains to Christ and his church:

> In Christ the bride was *chosen* from eternity. Throughout the entire Old Testament dispensation the wedding was *announced*. Next, the Son of God assumed our flesh and blood: the *betrothal* took place. The price—the *dowry*— was paid on Calvary. And now, after an *interval* which in the eyes of God is but a little while, the Bridegroom returns and "It has come, the wedding of the Lamb." Then we shall be with Him forevermore. It will be a holy, blessed, everlasting fellowship: the fullest realization of all the promises of the gospel.[6]

The question may rightly be asked how sinners can ever fill the role of the holy, virgin bride of Jesus Christ. Indeed, most of the biblical references to Israel as God's bride are made to point out her adultery in sin (see Jer. 3:9, etc.; Ezek. 16:38, etc.). The most poignant example was God's calling to the prophet Hosea, who would illustrate God's abused love for Israel by falling in love with and marrying a prostitute named Gomer. "Go, take to yourself a wife of whoredom and have children of whoredom," God told his prophet, "for the land commits great whoredom by forsaking the LORD" (Hos. 1:2).

This description could be applied to the entire human race, as Revelation has done by condemning the world as the harlot Babylon. So how can sinners from that very world, who have ourselves betrayed God in sin and idolatry, ever qualify to be Christ's spotless and radiant bride? The answer is given in Revelation 19:8: "It was granted her to clothe herself with fine linen, bright and pure." This sums up the Bible's gospel teaching, that God so loved the world, and Christ so loves his bride, that he came to cleanse his chosen people from sin by dying on the cross. Jesus further achieved a perfect righteousness on our behalf by means of his own spotless life. Sinners are justified by means of the imputed righteousness that Jesus gives, so that through faith alone we receive the spotless garment of the righteousness of Christ (see Rom. 4:4–6; 2 Cor. 5:21). A popular hymn puts it this way:

The church's one foundation is Jesus Christ, her Lord;
She is his new creation by water and the Word:

5. See William Hendriksen, *More than Conquerors: An Interpretation of the Book of Revelation* (1940; repr., Grand Rapids: Baker, 1967), 180.
6. Ibid., 181.

From heav'n he came and sought her to be his holy bride;
With his own blood he bought her, and for her life he died.[7]

Revelation 19:7–8 presents both sides of Christian salvation, involving our justification and our sanctification. The emphasis on sanctification, that is, our active calling to live holy and godly lives, is clear. First, we read that the "Bride has made herself ready" (Rev. 19:7). Every bride works diligently to present herself in maximum beauty on her wedding day. The bride exercises to fit into a slimmer dress. She spends a small fortune on makeup, perfume, and hairstyling and exhausts a small team of helpers in ensuring that she walks down the aisle as beautifully as she possibly can. This corresponds to the spiritual labor that all Christians are to exert as we prepare for the coming of Jesus and our wedding as he takes the church to be his bride. We prepare ourselves by putting sin to death and ridding ourselves of habits that are ugly and offensive to our holy Lord. We cultivate the inward graces of faith, hope, and love so as to bless our Savior. This is the calling that every Christian has entered into when we through faith were betrothed to Jesus Christ.

Moreover, in contrast to the gaudy and alluring dress of the harlot Babylon, the bride of Christ is clothed "'with fine linen, bright and pure'—for the fine linen is the righteous deeds of the saints" (Rev. 19:8). The dress given to Christ's bride reflects the way she lives in this world through faith in him. We tend to think of personal holiness in terms of our rejection of sin, and that is profoundly true. But "righteous deeds of the saints" probably refers especially to acts of mercy and love that we offer through the grace of Christ. In Matthew 25, Jesus anticipates the praise he will lavish on his people when he returns: "For I was hungry and you gave me food, I was thirsty and you gave me drink, I was a stranger and you welcomed me, I was naked and you clothed me, I was sick and you visited me, I was in prison and you came to me" (Matt. 25:35–36). The astonished saints marvel at this praise. When did they ever perform these kinds of ministries for Jesus Christ? He answers, "Truly, I say to you, as you did it to one of the least of these my brothers, you did it to me" (25:40). Here we see the value to Christ of every loving deed we perform, whether we are noticed in the world or not. The "righteous deeds of the saints" mirror the mercy that Jesus showed to the weak and broken and the grace by which we were forgiven and saved.

7. Samuel J. Stone, "The Church's One Foundation" (1866).

536

Some readers might conclude that Christians must therefore earn their acceptance with Christ by our own works and self-righteousness. This completely misses the point. Notice that this radiant dress is "granted her" (Rev. 19:8). Notice that the grammar is passive, not active; the gown is given to her, not earned. It is God through Christ who provides the bright and pure fine linen of a spotless righteousness before his throne. Simon Kistemaker writes: "The bride can prepare herself only when God provides the wedding gown for her, because this garment is beautiful and pure. Her own clothes are but filthy rags, but Christ cleanses and presents her to himself 'without stain or wrinkle or any other blemish' (Eph. 5:26–27)."[8]

Our covenant relationship with Jesus Christ equally involves his righteous work *for us* to justify us from sin and his sanctifying work *in us*, in which we participate to present ourselves beautifully to him. In the language of our passage, a spotless wedding garment is "granted" by God to every sinner who believes. Henceforth, we are to put it on and wear it—that is, we are to live in accordance with the righteous standing we have received through faith in Christ. Paul spoke precisely this way in outlining the Christian's duty in preparing for Christ: "You . . . were taught in him . . . to put off your old self, which belongs to your former manner of life and is corrupt through deceitful desires, and to be renewed in the spirit of your minds, and to put on the new self, created after the likeness of God in true righteousness and holiness" (Eph. 4:21–24). Having been saved by the blood of Christ from the judgment of the harlot world to which we formerly belonged, we are by grace alone granted a spotless wedding garment of righteousness, and henceforth we are to live as his holy people. Robert Mounce summarizes that "a transformed life is the proper response to the call of the heavenly bridegroom."[9]

BLESSINGS NOW AND FOREVER

Revelation 19 does not show the actual marital bliss that Christ and his bride will enjoy in eternity: that description comes in chapters 21 and 22. But the angel did point out a particular blessing that belongs to the people

---

8. Simon J. Kistemaker, *Revelation*, New Testament Commentary (Grand Rapids: Baker, 2001), 515.

9. Robert H. Mounce, *Revelation*, rev. ed., New International Commentary on the New Testament (Grand Rapids: Eerdmans, 1997), 340.

of Christ even now: "Write this: Blessed are those who are invited to the marriage supper of the Lamb" (Rev. 19:9). This is the fourth beatitude of the book of Revelation. So far, blessing has been pronounced on those who read and hear the message of this book (1:3), on "the dead who die in the Lord," who "rest from their labors" (14:13), and on those who keep their garments on, remaining ready for the return of Christ (16:15). Now, Christians are described not only as the bride of Christ but also as the wedding guests who are invited to attend the feast. We are blessed in looking forward to the wedding and the feast, both of which will continue forever.

Even though the wedding between Christ and his church is yet to come, believers are blessed now because through faith in Jesus they possess the invitation needed to reserve a seat at that feast. This makes the vital point that our present salvation through faith in Jesus renders our future salvation in the wedding feast to come absolutely secure. We know this because of the inviolable authority of God's Word. John adds: "And he said to me, 'These are the true words of God'" (Rev. 19:9). John 3:36 speaks of our salvation as a present established fact: "Whoever believes in the Son has eternal life." Paul added that believers have been "sealed with the promised Holy Spirit," who, having regenerated us, is henceforth "the guarantee of our inheritance until we acquire possession of it" (Eph. 1:13–14). Everyone who believes in Jesus now and lives as his disciple has "an inheritance that is imperishable, undefiled, and unfading, kept in heaven for you, who by God's power are being guarded through faith for a salvation ready to be revealed in the last time" (1 Peter 1:4–5).

Knowing this, Christians do not need to wait for the wedding feast before we join the heavenly choir of praise. We may worship just as fervently now, with a present assurance of salvation in Christ: "Hallelujah! For the Lord our God the Almighty reigns. Let us rejoice and exult and give him the glory" (Rev. 19:6–7). Now we await the sudden appearing of our Lord. But our invitation to his feast is certified by the Word of God and secured by the sealing ministry of the Holy Spirit. What a cause believers have to live in joyful praise of God and offer our lives in fervent preparation for his coming! This awareness of the coming feast in glory should spiritually enliven the gathering of the church during our celebration of the Lord's Supper. David Chilton writes that believers gather at Christ's table as those "saved from the whoredoms of the world to become the Bride of [God's] only begotten

Son."[10] How wonderful that we may come to Jesus even now to be renewed and strengthened by the gospel Word that binds our hearts to him.

Revelation 19:10 adds a surprising episode that highlights how glorious it is to anticipate our future union with Christ. Having heard God's blessing on those invited to the wedding feast, John "fell down" at the feet of the angel "to worship him." The angel stopped John, crying in alarm: "You must not do that! I am a fellow servant with you and your brothers who hold to the testimony of Jesus." This verse reminds us that however glorious any person or angel may appear to be, we must never grant worship to anyone but God. Moreover, this verse states that having been redeemed by Christ's blood, Christians are now "fellow servants" with the angels in proclaiming the gospel and bringing praise to God's throne.

While this is a fascinating episode in itself, it connects to the main passage by showing how glorious even the anticipation of our future marriage to Christ ought to be. To be sure, we should never venerate a preacher because of the glorious message he is given to proclaim, or the author of a book that wonderfully explains our gospel blessings, however much gratitude we may have for God's creaturely servants. But if we have never been tempted to do so—if we have never been so overwhelmed at the privileges, glories, and wonderful love that are given to us through Jesus Christ that we almost transfer our worship of God to the messenger he has sent—then we have probably never exulted as we should in the glories that await us in Jesus Christ. Such a glorious anticipation gripped the apostle who once leaned his head on Jesus' breast that he fell down to adore the messenger, having to be rebuked: "You must not do that! . . . Worship God" (Rev. 19:10).

This kind of keen anticipation will make the rigors of the present Christian life seem as nothing compared to the glories ahead. Douglas Kelly writes: "The best experiences we can have on earth: good marriages, professional accomplishments, loving friendships, family lands, and ancestral heritage—all of these at best are pale pointers beyond themselves to the supreme happiness of being part of the bride of Christ on that glorious day."[11] As we grow in Christian faith, that future should loom ever clearer

10. David Chilton, *Days of Vengeance: An Exposition of the Book of Revelation* (Ft. Worth, TX: Dominion Press, 1987), 475.

11. Kelly, *Revelation*, 360.

in our minds, so that the glory and love awaiting us become more real to our hearts than the poisoned delights of a harlot world that desires to lead us astray.

Finally, while we celebrate the coming day when "the Lord our God the Almighty" will reign (Rev. 19:6), let us never forget that Jesus reigns now through the ministry of his Word. The angel concludes: "For the testimony of Jesus is the spirit of prophecy" (19:10). This statement can be taken in two equally valid ways. It may mean that wherever the testimony of Jesus' love is given, there is the true spirit of prophecy. Alternatively, it may state that those who believe in the gospel testimony receive the spirit of prophecy to tell others about the saving grace of Christ. Both as the gospel comes to us and as we bring it to others, Christ reigns in our present world, bringing sinners to himself through faith, and securing for everyone who believes a place in the wedding feast that will resound in joy and praise forever. How exciting it is to be a Christian, even as we wait in this darkened world for the glorious light of Jesus' soon appearing: "Let us rejoice and exult and give him the glory" (19:7).

The Redeeming Love of Christ

I mentioned earlier the biblical episode in which God commanded his prophet Hosea to marry a harlot named Gomer. Soon after their wedding, Gomer turned away to chase after her lovers. This was God's picture of Israel in its sin of idolatry. Gomer's sin plunged her into such a depraved state that she was being sold as a slave in the market. There, as the various men bid on her exposed body, the voice of her husband was heard once more. One man bid thirteen shekels, but the voice of Hosea cried out a bid of fourteen. Another man countered with a bid of fifteen shekels, but Gomer's husband cried out, "Fifteen shekels of silver and a homer and a lethech of barley" (Hos. 3:2). It was clear that no one would outbid the prophet, so his wife Gomer became his once again. "Then I told her," he said: "You are to live with me many days; you must not be a prostitute or be intimate with any man, and I will behave the same way toward you" (3:2–3 NIV).

If you have not turned in faith to the love of Jesus Christ, this episode describes your condition and the redeeming love he offers for your soul. James Boice explains:

We were created for intimate fellowship with God and for freedom, but we have disgraced ourselves by unfaithfulness. First we have flirted with and then committed adultery with this sinful world and its values. The world even bid for our soul, offering sex, money, fame, power and all the other items in which it traffics. But Jesus, our faithful bridegroom and lover, entered the market place to buy us back. He bid his own blood. There is no higher bid than that. And we became his. He reclothed us, not in the wretched rags of our old unrighteousness, but in his new robes of righteousness. He has said to us, "You must dwell as mine . . . you shall not belong to another . . . so will I also be to you."[12]

What higher love can you ever discover than the redeeming love of Jesus Christ? If you respond to his call, offering your faith and love to him, then Jesus will take you to himself for eternity. He will be your beloved Savior and glorious Lord, and by his grace at work in you, you will respond in faithful covenant love and worship back to him. Every believer of the gospel will be blessed together with the Son of God, along with the entire glorious host of his blessed church, so long as you both eternally live.

12. James Montgomery Boice, *Foundations of the Christian Faith* (Downers Grove, IL: InterVarsity Press, 1986), 329–30.

50

THE RIDER ON A WHITE HORSE

Revelation 19:11—16

*Then I saw heaven opened, and behold, a white horse! The one
sitting on it is called Faithful and True, and in righteousness
he judges and makes war.* (Rev. 19:11)

hen I was a boy, many years ago now, we would walk down to
the local theater with fifty cents and watch the latest Western
movie. Most of the plots were virtually the same, and we loved
them every time. A prairie town was besieged by a bloodthirsty gang who
had run off the law. But then, followed by a cloud of dust, a rider on a white
horse appeared, and there was a new sheriff in town. In short order, the hero
would produce a pile of bodies of the wicked men he had slain. The women
and children could return to the town streets, and hope was reclaimed.

Revelation 19:11 says that John "saw heaven opened, and behold, a white
horse!" with its righteous rider. The image is largely that of the old-time
Western movie, with the new sheriff who comes to town and cleans out
the evil gang. Sadly, this image is seldom attached to Jesus Christ, in large
part because of the tendency of artistic renderings to present him as passive and weak. Charles Wesley's hymn has taught us, "Gentle Jesus, meek
and mild, look upon a little child."[1] That verse accurately describes Jesus'

---

1. Charles Wesley, "Gentle Jesus, Meek and Mild" (1742).

attitude toward repentant sinners who believe, but not wicked sinners who continue to rebel. Another hymn balances our portrait:

Who is this that comes in glory, with the trump of jubilee?
Lord of battles, God of armies, he has gained the victory.[2]

The Warrior Messiah

We remember that Revelation presents a series of visions depicting the church age and final judgment. The seven seals, trumpets, and bowls each provided a perspective on Christ's reign throughout the age of the gospel to restrain, warn, and finally punish evil. Each of these vision cycles concluded at the very brink of Christ's return. In Revelation 6:12–17, the sky was rolled up like a scroll and the wicked vainly hid from the wrath of the Lamb. When the seventh trumpet blew, angels sang, "The kingdom of the world has become the kingdom of our Lord and of his Christ" (Rev. 11:15). Later, a white cloud appeared with "one like a son of man" who harvested the earth with a sharp sickle (14:14–16). These were veiled allusions to the second coming of Christ to overthrow and judge evil once and for all. In Revelation 19:11, the veil is lifted and John writes: "Then I saw heaven opened, and behold, a white horse!" No longer do we look through windows or doors into heaven, but this time heaven itself opens so that the Lord and his armies may come out.

The Christ who comes forth from heaven is the Warrior-Messiah foretold in the Old Testament. This was the Savior who slew the hosts of Pharaoh after parting the Red Sea for Israel to pass through. Moses sang, "The Lord is a man of war; the Lord is his name" (Ex. 15:3). This is the battle captain who appeared to Joshua "with his drawn sword in his hand" (Josh. 5:13). "I am the commander of the army of the Lord," Jesus declared, and Joshua worshiped him (5:14). Like a medieval knight who defends his damsel against a lurking dragon, the heavenly Warrior Jesus arrives on a white stallion, wielding a sword to slay the enemies of his church. The white horse symbolizes victorious conquest in battle. In his first coming, Jesus dealt with sin by offering his own blood in sacrifice. He now returns in glory, "and in righteousness he judges and makes war" (Rev. 19:11).

2. Christopher Wordsworth, "See, the Conqueror Mounts in Triumph" (1862).

A MANY-CROWNED CONQUEROR

At first glance, we might think that this vision shows only Christ's victory in bringing judgment to the unbelieving world. But just as Christ wears a crown of "many diadems" (Rev. 19:12), the victory that he comes to proclaim has a number of facets.

For instance, Jesus arrives as the Savior who has already conquered by his cross. John sees him "clothed in a robe dipped in blood" (Rev. 19:13). Some scholars argue that Christ's robe is spattered with the blood of his enemies.[3] Isaiah 63:1–6 supports this view as it presents the Lord as "mighty to save" (Isa. 63:1) and clothed in crimson garments. When asked why he comes as one stained from the winepress, he answers: "I trod them in my anger and trampled them in my wrath; their lifeblood spattered on my garments, and stained all my apparel" (Isa. 63:3). Yet there are also good reasons to see this blood as representing Christ's own atoning blood for the cleansing of his people. In Revelation 19:11–13, Jesus presents himself before entering into battle with his enemies. He is joined by "the armies of heaven, arrayed in fine linen, white and pure, . . . following him on white horses" (Rev. 19:14). This army includes the assembled host of the redeemed (see 17:14), who are cleansed and arrayed in white because Jesus shed his blood for their sins. Indeed, Revelation has emphasized that the saints conquered the dragon Satan "by the blood of the Lamb" (12:11). Paul Gardner therefore writes: "The blood on his robe will always be a reminder of where the victory was actually won, on the cross."[4]

When Jesus died on Calvary, it appeared that the world had prevailed over him. But though he returns bearing the emblems of his atonement, the world possesses no weapon that can now harm him. J. W. Alexander writes: "Jesus can agonize no more; . . . no more can he be slapped in the face, hoodwinked and spit upon; no more can he be torn with Roman scourges and nailed to the cursed cross . . . . Christ still bears the tokens of a sacrificial death; and even when he comes up to victory and vengeance, he is red in his apparel."[5] While the sight of Christ's blood moves his people to praise and adoration,

3. For this view, see G. K. Beale, *The Book of Revelation: A Commentary on the Greek Text*, New International Greek Testament Commentary (Grand Rapids: Eerdmans, 1999), 958.

4. Paul Gardner, *Revelation: The Compassion and Protection of Christ* (Tain, Ross-shire, Scotland: Christian Focus, 2008), 261.

5. J. W. Alexander, *God Is Love: Communion Addresses* (Edinburgh: Banner of Truth, 1985), 343–44.

this image in his return will drive his enemies to despair. John wrote at the beginning of Revelation: "Behold, he is coming with the clouds, and every eye will see him, even those who pierced him, and all tribes of the earth will wail on account of him" (Rev. 1:7).

Jesus further conquers by means of his covenant faithfulness in obedience to God the Father. John says that the rider of the white horse "is called Faithful and True" (Rev. 19:11). Jesus appears as the new and righteous Adam who receives the nations as his inheritance (see Ps. 2:8). Paul notes in Philippians 2:8–11 that Jesus took up a human form and "humbled himself by becoming obedient to the point of death, even death on a cross." In response, "God has highly exalted him . . . , so that at the name of Jesus every knee should bow, in heaven and on earth and under the earth, and every tongue confess that Jesus Christ is Lord." God had promised in Isaiah that in consequence of Jesus' covenant-fulfilling death, "I will divide him a portion with the many, and he shall divide the spoil with the strong" (Isa. 53:12).

Furthermore, Christ appears, having conquered by his Word. John writes that "the name by which he is called is The Word of God" (Rev. 19:13). It seems that "Word of God" is used here to signify Christ's authority to exercise the will of God for his redemptive conquest. Revelation 5 showed that only the Lamb could open the scroll of God's will. It is in view of his obedience in suffering death and his righteousness in fulfilling God's covenant that Jesus is now granted the right to wield God's omnipotent decree. As God's appointed and faithful Messiah, Jesus has authority to proclaim God's final judgment against his foes. Philip Hughes writes: "As the Word of God the Son is both the revealer of the divine mind and also the agent of the divine will. Since the word of God never fails to effect what it decrees (cf. Isa. 55:11), it is through him who is the eternal Word that the will of God is brought to pass."[6]

In Righteousness to Judge

The Chinese military theorist Sun Tsu famously taught that a wise general does not enter battle seeking victory but only enters battle having already achieved it. By his standard, there was never a greater general than the Lord

6. Philip Edgcumbe Hughes, *The Book of Revelation* (Downers Grove, IL: InterVarsity Press, 1990), 204.

Jesus Christ. Jesus appears from heaven to meet his wicked foes, having already conquered by his death, by fulfilling God's covenant, and as the Word who bears God's decreed will. Appearing in this way, Jesus then achieves the victory highlighted in this passage: the conquest of his final judgment over evil. Riding the white horse of victory, Jesus "is called Faithful and True, and in righteousness he judges and makes war" (Rev. 19:11).

Numerous details are provided about Jesus' victory in judging his enemies. Some of them emphasize Jesus' person and the attributes that enable his conquest. For instance, it is in his "righteousness" that "he judges and makes war" (Rev. 19:11). John's readers were familiar with unjust tyrants who took bribes to pervert justice and who wielded the sword in tyranny and for personal gain. But Christ makes war in perfect righteousness and true justice. This is especially important when we realize that his chief battlefield is not one of literal warfare but rather a legal contest in the courts of God. Justice is on Jesus' side, in both his own righteousness and his just condemnation of sin. The ungodly will suffer conquest in the shame of knowing that Jesus is right to slay them with the sword of his righteousness.

Jesus is further seen with eyes "like a flame of fire" (Rev. 19:12). This may speak in general of Jesus' deity, but it specifically depicts his penetrating sight that discovers all sin. Hebrews 4:13 speaks this way about God's Word: "No creature is hidden from his sight, but all are naked and exposed to the eyes of him to whom we must give account." Because of this, faithful preachers are sometimes accused of prying into people's private affairs to discover and expose their secret sins in the sermon, when what actually happens is that the Word of God penetrates to expose the secret corruptions of the heart. How complete will be the exposure of all sin when Jesus returns with eyes of flaming fire to judge all whose sins are not forgiven!

Moreover, Jesus "has a name written that no one knows but himself" (Rev. 19:12). There are questions about the meaning of this statement, but the best solution seems to be that there are depths in the deity of Christ that are beyond our fathoming. There are resources in his infinite being that his enemies have scarcely considered and a wisdom that is deeper than the wells of creation. Jesus conquers in judgment because, as the Nicene Creed put it, he is "very God of very God; begotten, not made." Furthermore, in the ancient world, to know someone's true name was a basis of power over him. Jesus remains beyond the grasp of his foes, but he has their name and number, allowing him to place them wholly under his spell.

Further details in this passage emphasize not only Jesus' supreme person but also his authority in coming to judge. This authority is displayed in the crown of "many diadems" on his head (Rev. 19:12). Two words for *crown* are used in Revelation. One is *stephanos*, the laurel crown of victory. The other is *diadema*, which signifies ruling authority. The evil dragon appeared with "seven diadems" (12:3), showing his aim to usurp the authority that belongs only to Christ. The beast then appeared with "ten diadems on its horns" (13:1). In John's day, these crowns were usually ribbons tied around the sovereign's head, each bearing the name of territories that he ruled. Today, the Queen of Great Britain rules over the separate realms of England, Scotland, Wales, and Northern Ireland. The list of nations over which Jesus rules as Lord is vast, given his unassailable sovereignty over every realm in all creation.

When Jesus ascended into heaven after his resurrection, the Father "seated him . . . far above all rule and authority and power and dominion, and above every name that is named, not only in this age but also in the one to come. And he put all things under his feet and gave him as head over all things to the church" (Eph. 1:20–22). Jesus thus appears in judgment not to *become* Ruler over all, but already *possessing* ultimate lordship, wearing many diadems of rule and dominion on his sovereign head. What he is by right he now enforces by actual rule, taking the ends of the earth as his possession (Ps. 2:8).

Jesus' authority is further seen in his command of the mounted hosts of heaven: "And the armies of heaven, arrayed in fine linen, white and pure, were following him on white horses" (Rev. 19:14). Included are the legions of angels, since Paul wrote that Jesus will be "revealed from heaven with his mighty angels" (2 Thess. 1:7). According to Revelation 17:14, however, they are joined by those who "are called and chosen and faithful," that is, the glorified church. The spiritual power of this army is seen in the fine white linen of their holiness before God and their righteousness in Christ, the saints wearing the uniform of their priestly status in Christ's kingdom.[7]

The authority of Christ to judge is especially emphasized in the title written on his robe at the thigh: "King of kings and Lord of lords" (Rev. 19:16). The thigh symbolizes manly strength, and thus Christ's robe bears titles

---

7. Beale, *Revelation*, 961.

upon his thigh that proclaim his supreme rule. There are lesser kings, but he is the King of kings. There are other lords, but he is Lord of lords. Robert Mounce comments: "This name emphasizes the universal sovereignty of the warrior Christ in his eschatological triumph over all the enemies of God."[8]

Not only is Jesus qualified to judge by his person and his authority, but he also appears with overwhelming power to destroy his enemies completely and immediately. John says, "From his mouth comes a sharp sword with which to strike down the nations" (Rev. 19:15). We know from 1:16 that the "sharp two-edged sword" of his Word comes from Jesus' mouth. Wielding this weapon, Jesus does not trade blows with the powers of evil but immediately slays them. In Paul's teaching on the end-times Antichrist, he states that "the Lord Jesus will kill [him] with the breath of his mouth and bring [him] to nothing by the appearance of his coming" (2 Thess. 2:8). Jesus wipes out the enemy opposition by the mere word of his authoritative will and sovereign, righteous condemnation of sin. Martin Luther expressed this memorably in his most famous hymn, "A Mighty Fortress Is Our God":

> The prince of darkness grim, we tremble not for him;
> His rage we can endure, for lo! his doom is sure;
> One little word shall fell him.[9]

Jesus' power also "will rule them with a rod of iron" (Rev. 19:15). This weapon is the rod of the shepherd by which he protects his sheep from predatory animals. Jesus wields this rod to shatter all opposition, fulfilling the promise of Psalm 2:9: "You shall break them with a rod of iron and dash them in pieces like a potter's vessel." It was because of this punishment of the wicked that Paul commanded Christians not to retaliate against evil: "Beloved, never avenge yourselves, but leave it to the wrath of God, for it is written, 'Vengeance is mine, I will repay, says the Lord'" (Rom. 12:19). As a rod of iron, Christ's vengeance on the oppressors of his people is mighty and unyielding. Evil must in the end be crushed and destroyed if Christ's flock is to lie down in the green pastures beside the still waters of eternal glory.

Finally, John writes that Jesus comes with power to vent the fury of God's wrath on the wicked rebel powers of earth: "He will tread the winepress of the

---

8. Robert H. Mounce, *Revelation*, rev. ed., New International Commentary on the New Testament (Grand Rapids: Eerdmans, 1997), 347.
9. Martin Luther, "A Mighty Fortress Is Our God" (1529).

fury of the wrath of God the Almighty" (Rev. 19:15). Like a man trampling grapes in a winepress, the Warrior-Messiah will trample the wicked in his divine strength, with their blood pouring out in floods of just retribution for evil and sin. Of course, this is symbolism. But the reality it depicts ought to terrify sinners as they ponder having to suffer the judgment of the righteous and avenging Jesus Christ. G. K. Beale writes: "Christ's conviction of the impious will lead to his destruction of them, which will be as thoroughgoing as the crushing of grapes in a winepress."[10]

Isaiah forewarned that this day of judgment is coming, in which Christ will save his people while crushing his enemies. First, the question is asked, "Who is this who comes . . . splendid in his apparel, marching in the greatness of his strength?" The Messiah answers, "It is I, speaking in righteousness, mighty to save." But he is asked, "Why is your apparel red, and your garments like his who treads in the winepress?" Christ replies: "I have trodden the winepress alone . . . ; I trod them in my anger and trampled them in my wrath; their lifeblood spattered on my garments, and stained all my apparel" (Isa. 63:1–3).

These verses show that Jesus is not squeamish when it comes to judgment, nor is he aloof from the inflicting of God's personal wrath. The same cannot be said of all who read the Bible. Many recoil at such anti-humanistic teaching, with human lives symbolically squashed like ripe and bloody grapes. There are many replies to this objection. One is to point out that this righteous Lord has previously come as the Savior who offers to save these very sinners by shedding his own blood in a sacrifice of love on his cross. Jesus has offered a free and full forgiveness by the terrible cost to himself that he bore on the cross. But if we refuse his salvation, we deserve his condemnation. Steve Wilmshurst writes: "Either judgment is done *on* him at the cross, or else, failing that, judgment is done *by* him as people's unforgiven sin sends them to hell."[11] It is pointless for us to object out of our low view of the offense of sin when the Bible plainly declares the fury of God's wrath. We may turn our eyes from the rivers of blood that are shed on earth in human violence, warfare, and unrighteous oppression, no small part of which is the blood of the persecuted and martyred church, but unless we face the wickedness

---

10. Beale, *Revelation*, 963.
11. Steve Wilmshurst, *The Final Word: The Book of Revelation Simply Explained* (Darlington, UK: Evangelical Press, 2008), 238.

of sin and repent, we will behold in bloody terror the treading of the grapes in the violent retribution of a holy God. Robert Mounce writes: "Any view of God which eliminates judgment and his hatred of sin in the interest of an emasculated doctrine of sentimental affection finds no support in the strong and virile realism of the Apocalypse."[12]

THE CONQUERING POWER OF TRUTH

The most urgent application of this passage is that instead of arguing with the Bible's images of wrath and final judgment, we must instead "flee from the wrath to come" (Matt. 3:7) by confessing our sin and gaining forgiveness at the cross of Jesus Christ. Jesus' gracious offer is simple and clear: "Whoever hears my word and believes him who sent me has eternal life. He does not come into judgment, but has passed from death to life" (John 5:24).

Another application of great importance concerns the conquering power of truth in the hands of its Author, Jesus Christ. Jesus comes riding on a white horse, bearing the names "Faithful and True," is called "The Word of God," and slays the wicked with nothing more than the "sharp sword" that comes from his mouth (Rev. 19:11–15). Christ's Word will not fail in the contest with the deceiving powers of unbelief but will, in the end, slay them in total condemnation. Why, then, should Christians fear to speak this same truth from the Word of God in the Bible in the face of hostile cultural unbelief? We live in a generation whose voices of darkness, unbelief, and idolatry are bold in declaring falsehood and perversion. How great is the need for Christians not to shrink back but to speak out in the spirit taught by the apostle Paul: "For the weapons of our warfare are not of the flesh but have divine power to destroy strongholds. We destroy arguments and every lofty opinion raised against the knowledge of God, and take every thought captive to obey Christ" (2 Cor. 10:4–5). The foundation of all evil is deception and lies; let Christians fight valiantly with the sword of the Spirit that is the Word of God.

Christians should wield the power of truth especially against atheistic assaults on the Christian religion, all of which engage in the most blatant falsehood. One example was the best-selling book *The Da Vinci Code* with its many claims to debunk the so-called myths of Christianity. One of author

---

12. Mounce, *Revelation*, 347.

Dan Brown's characters, Leigh Teabing, brazenly declares, "The Bible is a product of man my dear, not of God. . . . The Bible as we know it today was collated by the pagan Roman emperor Constantine the Great."[13] Elsewhere, Teabing states that the deity of Jesus was never thought of until theologians invented the doctrine at the Council of Nicaea in A.D. 325.[14] These challenges raise questions that Christians welcome, since we can easily show the simple and intentional falsehood of these claims, which no credible scholar would attempt in the light of day. Christians stand on the truth, even as Jesus said, "I am . . . the truth" (John 14:6). In the end, he will slay the wicked with his sword of truth, and with that sword Christians are to oppose the darkness of unbelieving powers today.

Christians must rely on the conquering power of truth not only in the world but also in the church. How often doctrines such as sin, judgment, Christ's atoning blood, and sanctification are opposed from the pulpits of supposedly Christian churches. What should faithful believers, and especially pastors, do? The answer was given by Paul to Timothy as he faced just this situation: "Preach the word; be ready in season and out of season; reprove, rebuke, and exhort, with complete patience and teaching" (2 Tim. 4:2). Not only will faithful preaching correct false doctrine, but God's Word will give spiritual vitality to a lifeless church. God sent Ezekiel to the valley of dry bones and commanded him to preach: "Say to them, O dry bones, hear the word of the LORD" (Ezek. 37:4). As God's Word went forth from God's faithful servant, the bones began moving and came together. Finally they took on flesh and "stood on their feet, an exceedingly great army" (37:10). If the Christian church is to regain vigor in its witness today, it will happen through the faithful ministry of the conquering Word.

Not only is Christ going to judge the world by the sword of his Word, but he is going to judge you by his truth. If you are wise, you will stand under that judgment now, confessing your sin, believing his gospel offer of salvation, and embracing in faith the mercy that forgives you through the loving sacrifice of Jesus' blood. It is by the Word that believers are called (John 10:27), born again (1 Peter 1:23), sanctified (John 17:17), enlightened (Ps. 19:8), and in the end finally delivered (2 Thess. 2:8). In his gospel, Jesus comes humbly on a colt of a donkey, signifying mercy to sinners who repent

13. Dan Brown, *The Da Vinci Code* (New York: Doubleday, 2003), 231.
14. Ibid., 233–34.

and believe (Matt. 21:5). He returns riding on a white horse to slay the wicked and cleanse the world of sin. Let us call him Faithful and True now. Let us invite his gracious rule into our hearts. And let us joyfully anticipate his coming by crowning him with our faith and love, joining the praise that is sung by his church:

> Awake, my soul, and sing of him who died for thee,
> And hail him as thy matchless King through all eternity.[15]

15. Matthew Bridges, "Crown Him with Many Crowns" (1851).

51

THE LAST BATTLE

Revelation 19:17–21

And I saw the beast and the kings of the earth with their armies gathered to make war against him who was sitting on the horse.
(Rev. 19:19)

n the last of his seven *Narnia* books, C. S. Lewis concluded his fantasy series with themes drawn from the final chapters of Revelation. Lewis's *The Last Battle* describes the conquest of Narnia by the tyrannical Calormene army, whose leader the Tarkaan represents Revelation's villainous beast. This despot could never have taken over Narnia, however, without the help of another figure who represents Revelation's false prophet, whom Lewis depicts as a talking monkey named Shift. The ape had found a lion's skin and draped it over his reluctant conspirator, a donkey named Puzzle. When the donkey was seen in poor lighting, the Narnians were persuaded that this false Christ was really their divine king, the lion Aslan. "You will pretend to be Aslan," the monkey explained to the donkey, "and I'll tell you what to say."[1] Soon, Shift had secured power for the sake of the Calormene invaders, and, supposedly at Aslan's command, the evil soldiers began destroying forests and otherwise devastating Narnia.

---

1. C. S. Lewis, *The Last Battle* (New York: Collier, 1970), 10.

The false prophet had succeeded not only in passing power to the tyrant, but also in tarnishing the faith of many who had believed in Aslan.

Lewis's allegory captures the satanic strategy that Revelation foretells for the end of history. The apostle John writes that, supported by the false prophet, "the beast and the kings of the earth with their armies gathered to make war" (Rev. 19:19). Lewis highlighted the role played by the false prophet's deceptions, even as he mocked him as "the cleverest, ugliest, most wrinkled Ape you can imagine."[2] As the book moves to its climax, brave King Tirian calls the legendary Narnian heroes from all the previous books— Polly, Digory, Edmund, Lucy, Jill, Eustace, and the High King Peter—who together represent the faithful, militant church. In the end, their struggle is crowned with victory by the appearing of Aslan, who brings Narnia to an end in final judgment and the coming of a new world.

WHEN IS THE LAST BATTLE?

One question we should ask about Lewis's depiction is whether Revelation 19 intends for its last battle to represent a final end-times conflict. Scholars who hold to a postmillennial view of history tend to assign this vision to the church age, similar to the earlier visions of the seals, trumpets, and bowls. The bloody conquest of the sinful world by the sword-wielding Christ is seen to describe the church's success in conquering the world. Peter Leithart has written that "by His victory, the Warrior cleanses the earth of the influence of the beast and the false prophet, and this, combined with the fall of Babylon and the binding of the dragon, inaugurates a period of unprecedented power for the Church."[3] Under this view, Christians should view the military images of conquest and slaying as depicting the church's present warfare against unbelief and evil in society.

Careful study of the text will show, however, that this is not the best understanding of this portion of Revelation. Previous visions in Revelation did summarize the whole of church history, such as the seal, trumpet, and bowl visions in chapters 4–16. But while the visions in chapters 17–20 review the activity of Christ's enemies throughout history, they highlight their

2. Ibid., 1.
3. Peter J. Leithart, "Biblical-Theological Paper: Revelation 19:17–18," quoted in David Chilton, *Days of Vengeance: An Exposition of the Book of Revelation* (Ft. Worth, TX: Dominion Press, 1987), 490–91.

final judgment at the end of the age. It is with a summons to witness final judgment that this section begins: "Come, I will show you the judgment of the great prostitute who is seated on many waters" (Rev. 17:1). This command to "come" marks a new section in Revelation. The previous command to "come" began the vision cycles of chapters 4–16, which dramatized the tribulations of the church age. "Come up here," John was told, "and I will show you what must take place after this" (4:1). The "come" of Revelation 17:1 transitions us to the final judgment, just as the final summons to "come" will begin visions of the glorified church in eternal blessing: "Come, I will show you the Bride, the wife of the Lamb" (21:9).

One reason why we must rightly place the visions of holy warfare in our chapter is to avoid a wrongly hostile attitude toward our present world. Some readers of Revelation will see Christ smiting the nations, and vultures feasting on the flesh of unbelievers, and conclude that Christians should adopt a similarly antagonistic attitude toward non-Christians. It was under this inspiration, together with their medieval notions of honor, that Crusaders massacred the Muslim and Jewish inhabitants when they captured Jerusalem in A.D. 1099. To be sure, Revelation calls Christians to stand up to evil, and especially to persevere in faith despite persecution. But the church conquers in this present age not by militant assaults against the ungodly but by our testimony to the saving blood of Jesus (see Rev. 12:11).

Consider the conversion of Rosaria Butterfield. Describing herself as "a leftist, lesbian professor," she despised Christians and the Bible for what she saw as "their politics of hatred against queers like me." In 1997, she wrote an article in a local newspaper attacking the values of the Christian men's ministry known as the "Promise Keepers." She received a great deal of mail, including abusive letters from supposed Christians, assuring her that she would go to hell. But one letter was sent by the pastor of a conservative Presbyterian church. He courteously challenged her to defend the presuppositions of her argument, which were inconsistent with her claims as a postmodern secular humanist. Realizing that he had made a point, she responded, beginning a dialogue that changed her life. She later described how the pastor and his wife reached out to her:

> They entered my world. They met my friends. We did book exchanges. We talked openly about sexuality and politics. They did not act as if such

conversations were polluting them. . . . When we ate together, Ken prayed in a way I had never heard before. His prayers were intimate. Vulnerable. He repented of his sin in front of me. He thanked God for all things. Ken's God was holy and firm, yet full of mercy.[4]

This pastor plainly did not sidestep God's judgment on the sinful life that Rosaria had been living. But he also pointed out that this holy God has offered the gospel of Jesus for forgiveness of sin. He knew that in this age Christ has commissioned his church to be a herald of grace to the lost. The time will come when Christ returns and wields the sword of justice against all unbelief and evil. But now is the time of salvation, when Christians face the evil of the world with the love of Christ and his gospel. In response to the loving witness of these Christians who had become friends, Rosaria began reading the Bible inquiringly. Despite opposition from friends and her own battle against the truth, she writes: "One Sunday morning, I rose from the bed of my lesbian lover, and an hour later sat in a pew at the Syracuse Reformed Presbyterian Church."[5] She began worshiping the God she had previously reviled, confessed her faith in Jesus, and is today married to a Presbyterian minister, reaching out with gospel truth to those captured in the bondage of sin.

CARRION BIRDS SUMMONED

One reason for Christians to seek the salvation of the lost is our awareness that the offer of salvation will end when Christ returns. Although we are reviled as hatemongers for our witness of God's wrath against sin, Christians are motivated by the forewarning of destruction for those who deny Jesus and reject his salvation. The horrific nature of that destruction was foretold to John with an image of an angel summoning carrion birds to the future battlefield:

Then I saw an angel standing in the sun, and with a loud voice he called to all the birds that fly directly overhead, "Come, gather for the great supper of God, to eat the flesh of kings, the flesh of captains, the flesh of mighty men,

4. Rosaria Champagne Butterfield, "My Train Wreck Conversion," *Christianity Today* 57, 1 (January–February 2013): 112.
5. Ibid., 114.

the flesh of horses and their riders, and the flesh of all men, both free and slave, both small and great." (Rev. 19:17–18)

The main point of this vision is to figuratively depict the certainty of defeat for those who oppose Jesus now but must face his glorious return. The angel stands in midair, an appropriate place from which to summon the eagles and vultures to descend on those slain by the judicial sword of Christ. This image is symbolic, but what it represents is correspondingly devastating: the utter shame, destruction, and condemnation suffered at the end of history by those who opposed Christ and afflicted his people during history. The imagery of carrion birds is adapted from a similar vision in Ezekiel 39, when that prophet summoned vultures to eat the flesh of the defeated armies of Gog (Ezek. 39:17–20). Robert Thomas describes it as "a horrible picture of human carnage designed to accentuate the greatness of Christ's victory."[6] The point is that divine retribution for sin is just as certain as the arrival of vultures to devour flesh that dies in the desert. "There is an endless battlefield, strewn with millions of corpses, where the only movement to be seen is the birds tearing at the flesh of the dead."[7] As Jesus stated, "Wherever the corpse is, there the vultures will gather" (Matt. 24:28).

The details of these two verses are worth noting. First, there is a clear and ironic contrast with the earlier summons of believers to the wedding feast of the Lamb. This carnage is named "the great supper of God" (Rev. 19:17), making the point that God is glorified in judgment just as in salvation. One of these two destinies is the end toward which every single person is heading, depending on his or her response to the saving offer of Jesus Christ. The ungodly, whose sins are not forgiven because of their unbelief, "will go away into eternal punishment," Jesus said, "but the righteous into eternal life" (Matt. 25:46).

Second, this fundamental contrast pertains equally to every single person. The carrion birds are summoned to devour "the flesh of kings, the flesh of captains, the flesh of mighty men, the flesh of horses and their riders, and the flesh of all men, both free and slave, both small and great" (Rev. 19:18).

---

6. Robert L. Thomas, *Revelation 8–22: An Exegetical Commentary* (Chicago: Moody, 1995), 394.

7. Steve Wilmshurst, *The Final Word: The Book of Revelation Simply Explained* (Darlington, UK: Evangelical Press, 2008), 239.

This proves that whatever earthly distinctions we may recognize, the entire human race is united in the guilt of sin and in our need for a Savior in order to escape God's judgment. When that judgment comes, those who have refused Jesus will find that no earthly status matters at all, but only their guilt before the scorned Savior who has now returned as Judge.

It will accomplish little to complain about the gruesomeness of the Bible's warnings of judgment. These warnings are given during the age of grace, when you can still be saved by seeking forgiveness at the cross of Jesus Christ. Have you done that? If you refuse to humble yourself, confessing your sins and believing on Jesus for salvation, then you will have no choice but to face his judgment and the cursed end figuratively depicted in the terrible imagery of these verses.

THE LAST BATTLE JOINED

Revelation 19:19 presents the final battle itself, which was described earlier in Revelation as the battle of Armageddon (Rev. 16:16). Revelation 17:14 foretold that the beast and his vassal kings "will make war on the Lamb, and the Lamb will conquer them." Revelation 19:19 presents the same epic final confrontation: "And I saw the beast and the kings of the earth with their armies gathered to make war against him who was sitting on the horse and against his army." Jesus' teaching clarifies that this great battle symbolizes a worldwide persecution before his return: "There will be great tribulation, such as has not been from the beginning of the world until now, no, and never will be. And if those days had not been cut short, no human being would be saved" (Matt. 24:21–22).

This shows that C. S. Lewis's depiction in *The Last Battle* is largely on target. Lewis's false prophet, the monkey Shift, deceived the Narnians with a false-Aslan donkey, so that they obeyed the Calormene tyrant. Likewise, history will climax with a false prophet's deceiving people so effectively that even believers would be fooled if Christ did not prevent it (Matt. 24:24). Nations will exalt the tyrannical Antichrist, who will seek to destroy the true church through worldwide persecution. Is this conceivable? A hundred years ago, the Bible commentator H. B. Swete wrote: "Those who take note of the tendencies of modern civilization will not find it impossible to conceive that a time may come when throughout Christendom the spirit of Antichrist will, with the support of the State, make a final stand against a Christianity which is loyal to the Person and teaching of Christ."[8] From our perspective today, such a worldwide persecution of Christians is not only conceivable but apparent on every continent. When it happens, the rebellion of Psalm 2 will have fully unfolded: "The kings of the earth set themselves, and the rulers take counsel together, against the LORD and against his Anointed" (Ps. 2:2).

The imagery of the last battle varies in different Bible passages, but the result is the same. Psalm 2 tells us: "He who sits in the heavens laughs; the Lord holds them in derision" (Ps. 2:4). By the mere word of his decree, God establishes the reign of his Son, who "shall break them with a rod of iron and dash them in pieces like a potter's vessel" (2:9). Paul asserted that Christ will slay the Antichrist "with the breath of his mouth and bring [him] to nothing by the appearance of his coming" (2 Thess. 2:8). Revelation 17:14 states, "They will make war on the Lamb, and the Lamb will conquer them, for he is Lord of lords and King of kings." Just as the waters of the Red Sea suddenly parted for Israel to pass through and closed in again just as suddenly to drown the host of Pharaoh (Ex. 14:19–30), just as the walls of mighty Jericho fell down immediately when the trumpets of Israel blew (Josh. 6:20), and just as the angel of the Lord slew the 185,000 of Assyria's army in a single night when godly Hezekiah prayed (2 Kings 19:35), so will Christ appear and suddenly, immediately rout those who besiege his church. Robert Mounce states that John "is not describing the gradual conquest of evil in the spiritual struggles of the faithful, but a great historic event which brings to an end the Antichrist and his forces and ushers in the long-awaited era of righteousness."[9]

AFTER THE LAST BATTLE

John is shown the immediate aftermath of the last battle and the devastating effects of Christ's coming: "The beast was captured, and with it the false prophet who in its presence had done the signs by which he deceived those who had received the mark of the beast and those who worshiped its

---

8. Henry Barclay Swete, *Commentary on Revelation*, 2 vols. (1911; repr., Grand Rapids: Kregel, 1977), 2:256.

9. Robert H. Mounce, *Revelation*, rev. ed., New International Commentary on the New Testament (Grand Rapids: Eerdmans, 1997), 349.

image. These two were thrown alive into the lake of fire that burns with sulfur" (Rev. 19:20).

Revelation 17–18 witnessed the downfall of the great harlot Babylon when Christ returns. The last battle also sees the arrest of the beast and his false prophet. How great is the guilt of this tyrant and this deceiver! The beast's hands were red with the blood of the saints. The false prophet had arranged counterfeit miracles, deceiving people to accept the mark of the beast and worship the image of the beast (see also Rev. 13:13–17). Throughout history, Christ has brought down beasts and false prophets, whether they were Adolf Hitler and his propagandist Joseph Goebbels or Saddam Hussein and his bombastic information minister. In the end, the final beast and false prophet will be captured by Christ, leaving only Satan to face his judgment in the very end.

Having been disarmed, the beast and false prophet "were thrown alive into the lake of fire that burns with sulfur" (Rev. 19:20). This is the first of four references to "the lake of fire" at the end of Revelation. The idea of God's judgment arriving with fire looks back to the destruction of Sodom and Gomorrah, as God's anger found expression in burning sulfur from heaven (Gen. 19:24), as well as Daniel's teaching that in the final judgment a "stream of fire issued and came out from before [God]" (Dan. 7:10). The lake of fire manifests the wrath of God, inflicting the burning punishment of hell. John specifies that the beast and false prophet "were thrown alive" into the lake, making the point that their punishment will consist not of eradication but of eternal suffering as the just penalty of sin. When the devil receives his punishment, he, too, is cast "into the lake of fire and sulfur where the beast and the false prophet were, and they will be tormented day and night forever and ever" (Rev. 20:10).

It is hard even for believers to face the biblical images of eternal torment in hell. The Bible describes hell in terms of both negative and positive punishments. Negatively, every pleasure that sinners enjoyed in this world will have been stripped away. "The worldly person, who lived only for the temporal advantages of 'the world, the flesh, and the devil,' now find that those fleshly pleasures are eternally out of reach."[10] Positively, the Bible speaks of a dreadful existence as the just punishment on a life of sin. The most common New

---

10. Douglas F. Kelly, *Revelation*, Mentor Expository Commentary (Tain, Ross-shire, Scotland: Mentor, 2012), 371.

Testament image of punishment is the torment of fire, an expression used twelve times by Jesus to describe hell. Moreover, there is no exit from hell for those who go into it. The same word used in the Bible to depict eternal life is also used for the eternal torments in the lake of fire (see Matt. 18:8; John 3:16—Greek, *aionion*).

Whether or not we like the idea of such a hell, the fact is that God's revealed Word teaches it. Douglas Kelly writes: "If we believe in Jesus, then we by definition accept his teaching on hell, and on everything else. . . . Hell is part of the reality we must face, and to deny reality is a disaster for us, sooner or later."[11] In 1912, the captain of the *Titanic* arrogantly boasted that icebergs could not harm his great ship. Hundreds died because he denied reality. Many more who blithely dismiss the biblical teaching of hell will suffer something far greater than mere death, because they denied the awful reality of hell for those who sin and reject the gospel of Jesus Christ.

Revelation 19:21 makes clear that the beast and false prophet will not suffer alone. All their allies "were slain by the sword that came from the mouth of him who was sitting on the horse, and all the birds were gorged with their flesh." Revelation later states that all who worship the beast and serve in his army will be cast into the lake of fire, together with everyone who has not believed in Jesus Christ (Rev. 20:15). The slaying sword appears here to represent "a decree of death"[12] as the punishment for sin. Philip Hughes notes: "The word of grace they have rejected becomes the word of judgment by which they are condemned."[13] The New Testament teaches that "the wages of sin is death" (Rom. 6:23), and these images depict that death in terms of eternal condemnation, eternal suffering, and eternal shame.

These symbolic images—the lake of fire and the carrion birds who eat the flesh—combine to show the torment and shame that God will inflict on his enemies when Christ returns. The solemn scene with which Revelation 19 concludes confirms the warning of Hebrews 10:31, "It is a fearful thing to fall into the hands of the living God."

11. Ibid., 373.
12. G. K. Beale, *The Book of Revelation: A Commentary on the Greek Text*, New International Greek Testament Commentary (Grand Rapids: Eerdmans, 1999), 970.
13. Philip Edgcumbe Hughes, *The Book of Revelation* (Downers Grove, IL: InterVarsity Press, 1990), 208.

THE VICTORY THAT OVERCOMES THE WORLD

According to the Bible, you can avoid a destiny of punishment in the lake of fire in one of two ways. The first is to live a life of perfect obedience to God's law, never sinning in the least degree and doing all things over the entirety of your life for the glory of your Creator. If you have not done that—if you have sinned in the least degree (and the wisdom of Solomon reminds us that "there is no one who does not sin" [1 Kings 8:46])—then you need the second way of salvation. You need a Savior to deliver you from God's holy justice. The only Savior available is the very Son of God, who did live a perfect life to provide righteousness for his needy people, and who died a sin-atoning death so that those who believe in him may be forgiven of their sins.

Notice that Revelation 19:20 speaks of the people who bore "the mark of the beast and those who worshiped its image." According to Revelation, there are two marks that determine one's ownership and destiny, and everyone bears either one or the other. Revelation 7:2–3 says that God has marked his servants with a seal, a mark that only he can see and that signifies true and saving faith. Revelation further teaches that "those people who do not have the seal of God" (Rev. 9:4) all bear the "mark" of the beast (14:9, 11). These are those who worship the beast's false gods—pleasure, power, wealth, and beauty—and belong to the world in rebellion to Christ. The point is that unless you are gathered to Jesus for salvation, having believed on him in this life, you must in the day of his return be consigned to the judgment reserved for the servants of rebellion to Christ's kingdom. Jesus said that when he returns, he will gather his people into eternal glory, but that to those who refused him he will declare, "Depart from me, you cursed, into the eternal fire prepared for the devil and his angels" (Matt. 25:41). With this punishment looming before you, the most urgent issue in your life is to act on the counsel given by the apostle Paul: "Believe in the Lord Jesus, and you will be saved" (Acts 16:31).

The outcome of the last battle not only urges us to believe, but also teaches believers not to fear the power of evil in this world. The Bible says that Christians will face tribulation and, in the end, a dreadful conspiracy of worldwide persecution. Yet the last battle will bring a stunning end to all evil. William Hendriksen writes: "At Christ's second coming Satan's persecution of the Church and his power to deceive on earth shall cease for ever. Every influence of Satan—whether in the direction of persecution or deception—goes with him to hell, never again to appear anywhere outside hell."[14] So the appeal of the writer of Hebrews aptly suits the exhortation of Revelation: "Let us hold fast the confession of our hope without wavering, for he who promised is faithful" (Heb. 10:23).

As we await Christ's return and the last battle, Christians have a war to wage in this world. Paul said, "I have fought the good fight," speaking of a life of godliness and faith (2 Tim. 4:7). Christians also wage warfare through the kind of loving witness that the pastor and his wife extended to the militantly anti-Christian professor Rosaria Butterfield. Her response in taking a public stance for Jesus was no less a triumph in Christian warfare. She later wrote:

> When I became a Christian, I had to give up everything—my life, my friends, my writing, my teaching, my clothes, my speech, my thoughts. I was tenured to a field that I could no longer work in. . . . I was writing a book that I no longer believed in. And, I was scheduled in a few months to give the incoming address to all of Syracuse University's graduate students. What would I say to them?[15]

The question, she knew, was whether she was willing to suffer reproach for the gospel of Christ, standing up publicly against the beast and the false prophet as they reign in the unbelieving circles of academic prestige. Her address, originally scheduled to be on the topic of "Queer Theory," was instead presented as her coming-out statement of faith in Jesus Christ. It was received with hostility. It resulted in her losing her faculty assignments. It cost Rosaria most of her friends. And it was, as John said in his first epistle, "the victory that has overcome the world, even our faith" (1 John 5:4 NIV).

---

14. William Hendriksen, *More than Conquerors: An Interpretation of the Book of Revelation* (1940; repr., Grand Rapids: Baker, 1967), 183.

15. Rosaria Champagne Butterfield, *The Secret Thoughts of an Unlikely Convert* (Pittsburgh: Crown & Covenant, 2012), 26.

52

THE THOUSAND YEARS

Revelation 20:1–3

And he seized the dragon, that ancient serpent, who is the devil and Satan, and bound him for a thousand years. (Rev. 20:2)

here are many distinctions among Christians according to their views of nonessential subjects. Notable differences are between those who practice infant baptism and those who administer baptism only upon a profession of faith. Another distinction is between those who practice a congregational form of church government versus those who practice presbyterianism (elder rule) or episcopalianism (bishop rule). In describing these differences as *nonessential*, I do not mean that they are unimportant. Rather, these are positions regarding which Christians may disagree and still accept one another as fellow believers in Jesus and in the Bible.

When it comes to eschatology, the doctrine of the end times, Bible-believing Christians hold differing views about the thousand years referred to in Revelation 20:1–9. While there are innumerable variations, we can identify three main views regarding the millennium. The *premillennial* view holds that Christ returns before the millennium. There are two versions of premillennialism. The *historic premillennial* view holds that resurrected

Christians will enjoy a thousand years of earthly bliss after Jesus returns. *Dispensational premillennialism* holds that a restored Jewish state will reign with the Messiah for a literal thousand years. A second main view is *post-millennialism*, which sees Christ as returning after the thousand years of Revelation 20:1–9. In general, postmillennialists believe that the thousand years is a symbolic period toward the end of the gospel age, when the church has conquered all other religions throughout the world. The third view is called *amillennialism*. While this name means "no millennium," the view actually holds that the thousand years is a symbolic way of speaking of the entire present age, between the ascension and Christ's glorious return. In sum, *premillennialism* believes that Christ returns before the thousand years, *postmillennialism* holds that Christ returns after a millennial era of crowning victory for the church, and *amillennialism* teaches that Christ returns at the end of the church age, which is numerically symbolized as a thousand years.

It is important to note that these differing millennial views do not justify deep rifts among believers who all anticipate Christ's return. Church leaders holding opposing millennial views may cheerfully serve in the same denominations and even congregations. Still, the issues are significant, and the teaching of the controversial verses that open Revelation chapter 20 warrants careful attention. In order to give this attention and still consider the practical significance of this material, we will approach chapter 20 in four studies: the binding of Satan for a thousand years (Rev. 20:1–3), the reign of the saints with Christ (20:4–6), the great battle of Gog and Magog (20:7–10), and the great white throne judgment (20:11–15).

THE PREMILLENNIAL ARGUMENT

In order to handle the material in Revelation 20, we must come to conclusions regarding the nature and timing of the thousand years, which is mentioned six times in verses 1–9. Since premillennialism has been the most popular evangelical approach in recent years, it serves to begin with this understanding of the millennium.

Revelation 20 begins with John seeing "an angel coming down from heaven, holding in his hand the key to the bottomless pit and a great chain. And he seized the dragon, that ancient serpent, who is the devil and Satan, and bound him for a thousand years" (Rev. 20:1–2). The premillennial view of these verses holds that Satan is bound for a thousand literal years *after* the second coming of Jesus Christ. Thus, Christ's return is *premillennial*. There are three main arguments in these verses for the premillennial view (other points are made from verses 4–9): the relationship of chapter 20 to chapter 19, the nature of Satan's binding, and the question of the literal or symbolic understanding of the number one thousand.

According to the premillennial view, Revelation chapters 17–20 follow a chronological progression, so that first the great harlot Babylon is judged and destroyed (chap. 18), then the beast and false prophet are conquered when Christ returns (chap. 19), and then the thousand years begin as described in chapter 20. After this millennial period of earthly blessing, there will be a brief crisis in Satan's final rebellion, and then, as chapter 20 ends, the final judgment arrives.[1]

A second argument employed by some premillennialists holds that the number one thousand must be interpreted as a literal period of history and that this precludes us from assigning it to the church age, which has already lasted much longer than a thousand years.[2]

The third argument concerns the language used about Satan's binding in Revelation 20:1–2. An angel comes from heaven with "a great chain." He "seized the dragon . . . and bound him for a thousand years." According to Robert Thomas, this passage "requires a complete termination of [Satan's] activity in the sphere of the earth."[3] This cannot seriously be claimed about our present age, to which the Bible itself ascribes a wide range of satanic activity, opposition, and power. Therefore, the thousand years of Satan's binding must result from and take place after Christ's return from heaven.

Based on these arguments—the chronology of Revelation 19 and 20, the literal view of the number one thousand, and the absolute binding of Satan—premillennialists look for a golden age on earth that follows the return of Christ. Dennis Johnson describes it: "Believers, who will have received their new sin-free and curse-free bodies, will have returned with Christ to earth

1. See George Eldon Ladd, *A Commentary on the Revelation of John* (Grand Rapids: Eerdmans, 1972), 261.

2. See Robert L. Thomas, *Revelation 8–22: An Exegetical Commentary* (Chicago: Moody, 1995), 407–9.

3. Ibid.; see also Alan F. Johnson, *Revelation*, Expositor's Bible Commentary 12 (Grand Rapids: Zondervan, 1982), 581.

and will rule with him. Because of Christ's rule on the present earth during that time much, though not all, of the curse against human sin—injustice, violence, disease, sorrow, death—will be radically suppressed."[4]

THE AMILLENNIAL RESPONSE

The most powerful critique of premillennialism is made today by those holding the amillennial position, who teach instead that the thousand years of Revelation 20 is a symbolic description of the entire church age. This assessment begins by denying that Revelation 20 should be understood as following chronologically from chapter 19. Instead, it understands these visions as recapitulating the history of the spiritual opposition to Christ. Revelation 19 shows the judgment of the enemies of Christ who were introduced in the symbolic histories of chapters 12–14. In reverse order from their appearance, the harlot Babylon is first considered, and her judgment takes place to make way for the marriage feast of the Lamb, which occurs in the return of Christ (Rev. 19:6–10). Then the career of the beast and his false prophet is summarized, and they are destroyed by Jesus, returning on his white horse (19:11–21). At this point there is one more enemy to be defeated, the dragon Satan, and chapter 20 reveals his defeat and final judgment in the return of Jesus. These visions therefore follow one another not chronologically, but topically: the judgment of Babylon, then the beasts, and finally Satan.

The text contains ample evidence to show that these visions must describe the same period of history, rather than successive periods. For instance, Revelation 19:15 refers to "the nations" being struck down by Christ's rod and subjected to the winepress of God's wrath. If Revelation 20 chronologically follows this event, it is difficult to see how these nations can still exist when Revelation 20:3 states that they will no longer be deceived and when they are gathered for a final battle in 20:8.[5] Moreover, the battle described in 20:7–10 is clearly the same battle depicted in 19:17–21. Both battles involve the nations'

---

4. Dennis E. Johnson, *Triumph of the Lamb: A Commentary on Revelation* (Phillipsburg, NJ: P&R Publishing, 2001), 279.

5. Premillennialists respond either that "the nations" of Revelation 19:15 were only those unbelievers who actually joined in the beast's armed forces (see Ladd, *A Commentary on the Revelation of John*, 263) or that "the nations" of chapter 20 are the reprobate offspring of the believers who in 19:11–21 were saved by the return of Christ (see Thomas, *Revelation 8–22*, 404).

gathering at the end of history to war against the Lord and his saints, only to be destroyed by fire in Christ's coming. Notably, in both accounts John draws material from the same Old Testament passage, Ezekiel 39, where the prophet foretells doom for the armies of "Gog and Magog" (Ezek. 39:1–6; Rev. 20:8) and calls for the carrion birds to eat their flesh (Ezek. 39:17–18; Rev. 19:17). Since chapters 19 and 20 provide complementary visions of the same event, chapter 20 does not follow chapter 19, and its vision of the millennium does not follow but precedes the return of Jesus.[6]

Second, we consider whether the thousand years of Revelation 20 must be viewed as a literal period. We have noted all through Revelation that these visions beg to be interpreted symbolically, not literally. This is true of numbers, such as seven, ten, and a thousand, just as it is true of features in this passage such as the angel's chain and the image of Satan as a dragon. Satan is by nature an angelic spirit who could not be bound by a physical chain, however stout. If the chain and the dragon imagery of these verses is manifestly symbolic, it makes little sense that the number one thousand must be literal. The symbolic meaning of this number is not difficult to discern, since a thousand years represents a long but definite span of time. Moreover, noting that a thousand is a perfect cube of the number ten, we see that this number represents perfect completeness. Thus, the millennium is a long but definite time in which the work of the gospel is completed.

The most important premillennial argument pertains to the actual binding of Satan in Revelation 20:1–3. Here, postmillennialists are agreed with the premillennial view in stating that this binding cannot describe the situation of the entire church age. Both hold that "this binding must be understood as an action that completely curtails the actions of Satan," which plainly is not yet the case.[7] This is why postmillennialists ascribe the thousand years to a golden age of total victory at the end of the church age, rather than the entire church age itself. Amillennialists reply that this binding of Satan in fact describes the entire age of the gospel with great accuracy, showing the spiritual results of Christ's first coming with his conquering death, resurrection, and ascension into heaven. The key to understanding the spread of

---

6. For a detailed argument in favor of the recapitulation theory of these visions, see G. K. Beale, *The Book of Revelation: A Commentary on the Greek Text*, New International Greek Testament Commentary (Grand Rapids: Eerdmans, 1999), 974–84.

7. Cornelis P. Venema, *The Promise of the Future* (Edinburgh: Banner of Truth, 2000), 317.

the gospel and the growth of the church in this age is the binding of Satan as a result of Christ's saving work.

Christians today may not realize how much of a revolution resulted from the first coming of Jesus. In the old covenant, God called Abraham from Ur of the Chaldees and then brought salvation primarily to the nation of Israel. The spread of the gospel to the nations was promised but never begun before Christ. All the nations, except the Jews, were bound in darkness by Satan. In Acts 14:16, Paul said, "In past generations [God] allowed all the nations to walk in their own ways." But in the coming of Christ, John 1:9 informs us, "the true light, which enlightens everyone, was coming into the world." The gospel age has seen the mighty spread of salvation to every continent and nation—lands previously dominated by Satan in spiritual blindness and evil. The record of missionary expansion during the church "millennium" precisely fits the effects of Satan's binding. William Hendriksen explains:

> Through this gospel age the devil's influence on earth is curtailed. He is unable to prevent the extension of the Church among the nations by means of an active missionary programme. During this entire period he is prevented from causing the nations—the world in general—to destroy the Church as a mighty, missionary institution. . . . In regions where the devil had been allowed to exercise almost unlimited authority, during Old Testament times, he is now compelled to see the servants of Christ gaining territory little by little.[8]

When one asks how Satan can be described as being bound during our present age, there are two answers. The first answer notes that Revelation 20:3 specifies the particular effect of Satan's binding: "so that he might not deceive the nations any longer." This verse does not state that Satan is bound in every way, or that he is physically kept in a chained cell, but it symbolizes that he is bound in the particular way of no longer being able to prevent belief in Jesus. Cornelis Venema writes:

> This is the one great purpose and effect of Satan's binding, so far as the explicit language of Revelation 20 is concerned. Satan is bound so that he can neither prevent the spread of the gospel among the nations nor effectively deceive them. This vision confirms the teaching that the period between Christ's first

8. William Hendriksen, *More than Conquerors: An Interpretation of the Book of Revelation* (1940; repr., Grand Rapids: Baker, 1967), 188–89.

coming and his second coming is one in which the gospel of the kingdom will powerfully and effectively go forth to claim the nations for Jesus Christ.[9]

A second way to see that this binding of Satan depicts the church age is to note how this vision echoes the language used elsewhere of Satan's defeat in Christ's first coming. Consider Matthew 12:29, where Jesus spoke of Satan in this same way: "How can someone enter a strong man's house and plunder his goods, unless he first binds the strong man? Then indeed he may plunder his house." The word for *bind* is the same here as in Revelation 20:2 (Greek, *deo*), and the plundering of Satan's house undoubtedly refers to the salvation of sinners through the gospel. Other New Testament passages use similarly forceful language in describing the victory of Christ's first coming. In John 12, Jesus spoke of his approaching death on the cross: "Now is the judgment of this world; now will the ruler of this world be cast out" (John 12:31). Earlier, Jesus spoke of Satan's downfall when the seventy evangelists returned from preaching the gospel, declaring, "I saw Satan fall like lightning from heaven" (Luke 10:18). This fits the vision of Revelation 12, in which Satan "the great dragon was thrown down, . . . the deceiver of the whole world—he was thrown down to the earth" (Rev. 12:9), after which the saints conquered "by the blood of the Lamb and by the word of their testimony" (12:10–11). Hebrews 2:14 states that Jesus became man, "that through death he might destroy the one who has the power of death, that is, the devil." Paul said that by the cross, Christ "disarmed the rulers and authorities and put them to open shame, by triumphing over them" (Col. 2:15). All this language unmistakably speaks of the stripping of Satan's power by Christ's death and resurrection and the granting of authority to Jesus in his ascension so that his gospel may go forth through the church.

None of these dramatic statements denies Satan's continued activity in this current age. According to the New Testament, Satan still blinds the minds of unbelievers (2 Cor. 4:4), prowls like a roaring lion (1 Peter 5:8), "is now at work in the sons of disobedience" (Eph. 2:2), and oversees "the cosmic powers" of this present darkness and "the spiritual forces of evil" for the sake of warfare against the church (Eph. 6:12). Satan remains a dreadful and active foe. Yet when it comes to the work of missions and the witnessing power of the church among the nations, Satan is described as being "cast out" (John

9. Venema, *The Promise of the Future*, 319.

12:31), "fall[en]" (Luke 10:18), "thrown down" (Rev. 12:9), "destroy[ed]" (Heb. 2:14), "disarmed" (Col. 2:15), and "b[ound]" (Matt. 12:29). All these terms are in line with the language of Revelation 20:1–3 and are "associated with the first coming of our Lord Jesus Christ," involving the restraint of Satan for "the work of missions and . . . the extension of the witnessing Church among the nations."[10]

NO LONGER TO DECEIVE

In light of this overwhelming biblical evidence, a careful study of the binding of Satan reveals the thousand years as symbolically depicting the church age of gospel expansion. This argues for the amillennial view, as opposed to premillennialism, which ascribes this situation to an earthly reign after Christ's coming, and also the postmillennial view, which sees Satan as bound only at the end of the church age. Simon Kistemaker writes: "Since Jesus' ascension, Satan has been unable to stop the advance of the gospel of salvation. He has been bound and is without authority, while the nations of the world around the globe have received the glad gospel tidings."[11]

The vision of Revelation 20 begins with John seeing "an angel coming down from heaven, holding in his hand the key to the bottomless pit and a great chain. And he seized the dragon" (Rev. 20:1–2). In chapter 9, we saw the Abyss as the dwelling place of evil spirits, which, in that case, was opened by an angel to allow calamities on the earth (9:1–5). Now, Satan is symbolically locked in the Abyss. The angel brings a chain that Satan cannot break, with a key that locks the dungeon, so that the devil is thrown in, shut in, and sealed in (20:3). This vision shows "the complete and sovereign control that is being exercised over Satan."[12] God's plan for salvation must be fulfilled, and to this end, God's spiritual enemy is placed under wraps.

Four titles are given to this enemy, each of which shows why he must be restrained during the gospel age. He is the dragon, who according to chapter 12 had tried to destroy the Messiah before his birth (Rev. 12:4) and afterward had to be kept from destroying the witnessing church (12:15–17). He is the serpent who in Genesis 3 succeeded in deceiving our first parents

10. Hendriksen, *More than Conquerors*, 188.
11. Simon J. Kistemaker, *Revelation*, New Testament Commentary (Grand Rapids: Baker, 2001), 535–36.
12. Venema, *The Promise of the Future*, 317.

into sin and who would continue to "deceive the nations" if he was not restrained (20:3). He is "the devil," who is the great adversary of God's people, and "Satan," who "accuses" God's people "day and night before our God" (Rev. 12:9–10). Not only do these names sum up the charges against the devil, but they also prove why he must be bound for the gospel to advance.

This binding of Satan is not permanent, however, since after the thousand years "he must be released for a little while" (Rev. 20:3). This statement also conforms to the general New Testament teaching and confirms that the thousand years describes the church age. Paul wrote that before Christ's return, "the rebellion comes first, and the man of lawlessness is revealed" (2 Thess. 2:3). This describes the beast whom the dragon was seen calling out of the sea in Revelation 13:1, who wages a worldwide persecution of Christians and gathers the nations for the last battle. Paul is clear that this final time of great tribulation, characterized by Satan's "wicked deception" (2 Thess. 2:10), occurs at the end of the gospel age, just before Christ's return.[13] This corresponds to the "little while" after the thousand years when Satan is released so as to deceive the nations briefly before the final battle.

From this perspective, Christians look back on history, knowing that in Christ's first coming he defeated the devil and limited his authority. We look to the future and know that "for a little while" Satan will return to deceive the nations and persecute the church. What is most important now is our awareness of the current situation, when Satan is bound "so that he might not deceive the nations any longer, until the thousand years were ended" (Rev. 20:3). This defines our great opportunity in this life, our great calling as the church of Christ in the world, and our glorious privilege in service to the strong Savior who has defeated and bound our dreaded enemy. This was precisely Jesus' emphasis as he commissioned his disciples before ascending into heaven: "All authority in heaven and on earth has been given to me. Go therefore and make disciples of all nations, baptizing them in the name of the Father and of the Son and of the Holy Spirit, teaching them to observe all that I have commanded you. And behold, I am with you always, to the end of the age" (Matt. 28:18–20). As Jesus put it at the end of John's Gospel: "As the Father has sent me, even so I am sending you" (John 20:21).

13. The general pattern of Revelation 20:1–3 also fits the vision of Revelation 11, in which people of the witnessing church speak in the power of Moses and Elijah until the beast rises up to slay them, and are brought to life in the coming of Christ.

SERVANTS OF THE GOSPEL

Given the Bible's stated purpose for this present age, and Jesus' commission to the church, it is not surprising that the greatest heroes of the church have been those who most boldly spread the gospel. The early church saw the apostles taking the good news from Jerusalem to Rome. Over the centuries that followed, the Christian witness, empowered from heaven and made possible by the binding of Satan, astonished the nations by conquering the Roman Empire. Missionaries such as Boniface, Patrick, and Columba took the gospel to distant islands and the barbarian northern lands, until Europe became known as Christendom. When the light of the gospel blazed in the Protestant Reformation, the followers of Luther and Calvin spread salvation by grace alone in all directions, many sealing their testimony in fire or blood.

In the modern age, the zealous churches of Britain sent out the gospel to all lands in their empire: William Carey and Henry Martyn to India, Hudson Taylor and William Burns to China, David Livingstone to Africa, and John Paton to the New Hebrides. The gospel churches of America have spread the gospel to the farthest reaches of the world and in virtually every language. Our heroes include David Brainerd, missionary to the Native Indians; Adoniram Judson, gospel preacher to Burma; and Jim Elliot, who died preaching Christ's love to the native people of Ecuador. These and countless other servants of Christ have taken up his gospel banner, capitalizing on this present age when Satan is bound from holding the nations in darkness.

This age and the gospel opportunity will last until every single one of Christ's chosen people is called to salvation through faith. Jesus said, "This gospel of the kingdom will be proclaimed throughout the whole world as a testimony to all nations, and then the end will come" (Matt. 24:14). For a little while Satan will then be released to launch the rebellion of the final tribulation and last battle (Rev. 20:7–9), Christ will return, and the final judgment will bring a definitive end to this age (20:10–15).

What role are you playing in this grand advance of the gospel in history? Some will be called to preach the gospel full time, and those missionaries who carry the gospel to new lands are the very spearhead of the saving advance of Christ. All of us are called to the work of the gospel in the local church. Are you intentionally committed to the Great Commission through prayer, participation in evangelistic outreach, giving sacrificially to the support of the church and of missions, inviting non-Christian visitors to church, and bearing your individual witness to the saving grace of Jesus?

If you are not, what do you think this present world is for? Jesus taught that he has entrusted the gospel to each of us for our service to him in this life. When he returns, we will have the pleasure of presenting to him the fruits of our labor (Luke 19:11–19). As Jesus told it, it is inconceivable that a true disciple would have nothing to show for the work of the gospel in his or her life (19:20–27). Jesus tells us that in response to his own work in and through us by means of his saving Word, during the age in which he himself has bound Satan from opposing the gospel's spread, Jesus will say to every faithful laborer, "Well done, good servant!" (19:17). Given all that Jesus has done for us, dying for our sins and rising for our salvation, and all that he has done for the gospel in this present age, binding Satan while we bear testimony to the saving gift of Christ, surely the least that we can do is to give our all for this gospel, until the end comes and sinners will then be saved no more.

53

Reigning with Christ

Revelation 20:4—6

*Blessed and holy is the one who shares in the first resurrection!
Over such the second death has no power, but they will be
priests of God and of Christ, and they will reign with him
for a thousand years. (Rev. 20:6)*

n my senior year of high school, I was a sportswriter for the Madison Central High School newspaper, known as *The Trail.* I learned there the most basic rules of journalism. I was told that a news story must answer the questions *who, what, where, when, how,* and *why.* A preacher is a kind of reporter—a herald of God's holy Word—and these same rules often serve for expositing Scripture. As we seek to unravel John's visions in Revelation 20, these rules of journalism are a good way to structure our investigation. In an earlier vision, the angel asked John to be a good reporter: "Who are these, clothed in white robes, and from where have they come?" (Rev. 7:13). As we consider this vision of thrones and holy priests reigning with Christ, we can expand the question, asking: *Where* are these thrones, *who* are seated on them, and *what* is this first resurrection? We also need to consider: *When* is this thousand years, *how* do these saints reign with Christ, and *why* is this vision important to Christians today?

THRONES IN HEAVEN

John begins the vision, "Then I saw thrones" (Rev. 20:4). This raises the first question: *Where* are these thrones located? According to the premillennial view, these thrones are on earth, since the thousand years sees faithful Christians as reigning with Christ on earth. This claim is problematic, since of the forty-seven times that the word *throne* is used in Revelation, the thrones are almost always in heaven. The only exceptions are three occasions when the throne of Satan or the beast is mentioned on earth (2:13; 13:2; 16:10), and the references to God's throne after he has come down to reign in the new heaven and new earth (22:1, 3). On every other occasion, especially when the Lamb or the angelic representatives of the church are enthroned, the scene is in heaven. Moreover, Jesus earlier gave a promise that is fulfilled in this scene, locating it in heaven: "The one who conquers, I will grant him to sit with me on my throne, as I also conquered and sat down with my Father on his throne" (3:21).

The argument is made by premillennialists that the thrones have come to earth because of Christ's earthly millennial reign after his return. But the text states that John saw "the souls of those who had been beheaded" seated on the thrones (Rev. 20:4). It is true that the word for *soul* (Greek, *psuche*) does not always mean "disembodied spirits," but the fact that these are the souls of those who had been beheaded certainly suggests this meaning. Moreover, this verse clearly connects with an earlier vision of the souls of martyrs in heaven, who are described in nearly identical terms. Revelation 6:9 says that when the fifth seal was opened, John saw in heaven "the souls of those who had been slain for the word of God and for the witness they had borne." Revelation 20:4 explains that these souls had been "beheaded for the testimony of Jesus and for the word of God." These are evidently the same persons. Moreover, verse 5 contrasts these souls with "the rest of the dead," making it clear that "John is seeing a vision of the saints in glory, those believers who have died and are translated into the presence of Christ in heaven."[1]

We answered the question of the *when* of this thousand years in our study of Revelation 20:1–3, giving the amillennial answer that John describes the entirety of the church age. The millennium—the number one thousand symbolizing a lengthy and perfect duration of time—began with Christ's

---

1. Cornelis P. Venema, *The Promise of the Future* (Edinburgh: Banner of Truth, 2000), 329.

ascension to his throne and will conclude with his return to usher in the new heaven and new earth. During this present millennial age, Christ is reigning in heaven, and since these souls are reigning with him, the location can be only in heaven.

This means that Revelation 20:4–6 provides a heavenly counterpart to the events taking place on earth in verses 1–3. It describes what is known as the intermediate state: the state of believers' souls after death and before Christ's return and the resurrection of the body. John's vision shows these souls seated on thrones above during the gospel age. When Jesus returns, these spirits will be rejoined to their bodies to reign with Christ not merely for a thousand years—"they will reign forever and ever" (Rev. 22:5).

THE MARTYR CHURCH ENTHRONED

Having located these thrones in heaven, we must next identify *who* is seated on them. At the least, these are the souls of martyrs who suffered death for their faith in Christ: "I saw the souls of those who had been beheaded for the testimony of Jesus and for the word of God" (Rev. 20:4).

Some premillennial scholars argue that this vision shows martyrs of the faith receiving the special reward of reigning with Christ on earth during the thousand years.[2] Dispensational writers give a number of opinions, including the view that it is not martyrs but the saints who fought with Christ before his return (Rev. 19:14) who now exercise judgment with him on earth.[3] There can be no doubt, however, that John sees a vision of martyrs reigning with Christ on thrones above.

The heroism of martyrs provided a major inspiration to the Christians in the first-century churches to which John was writing. John the Baptist suffered the loss of his head because of his boldness in proclaiming God's Word (Matt. 14:3–12), as did John's brother, the apostle James, in Jerusalem (Acts 12:2). Tradition holds that the apostle Paul was beheaded outside Rome during Nero's persecution. Many of the first Christian leaders suffered death by a variety of means because of their "testimony of Jesus and for the word of God" (Rev. 20:4), including Peter and James, the brother of Christ.

2. See, for instance, George Eldon Ladd, *A Commentary on the Revelation of John* (Grand Rapids: Eerdmans, 1972), 263; Alan F. Johnson, *Revelation*, Expositor's Bible Commentary 12 (Grand Rapids: Zondervan, 1982), 582.

3. Robert L. Thomas, *Revelation 8–22: An Exegetical Commentary* (Chicago: Moody, 1996), 414.

By the time Revelation was written, only John remained unslain from the twelve apostles, and he was writing from exile. Many of those who first heard the reading of Revelation would seal their own testimony with death, refusing to burn incense at the imperial shrine or mutter the words, "Caesar is Lord," but giving worship only to Christ. The obvious question for such Christians was whether this suffering valor was worth it. In answer, William Hendriksen writes: "He describes these souls—together with those of all departed Christians who had confessed their Lord upon earth—as reigning with Jesus in heaven. He says, in effect, 'Here below: a few years of suffering: there, in that better land above, they live and reign with Christ a thousand years!' What a comfort!"[4]

The question is raised whether this vision offers this comfort only to those who died by beheading or by some other form of violent death. It is clear that John is not limiting this vision only to those who died violently, since he adds "and those who had not worshiped the beast or its image and had not received its mark on their foreheads or their hands" (Rev. 20:4). Some scholars see these as two distinct groups—those who died violently and those who were faithful without winning the martyr's crown. It seems best, however, to take these together as describing one faithful church in the midst of persecution. "Literal martyrs are spoken of . . . as representative figures for the whole of the church."[5] H. B. Swete writes: "The triumph of Christ is shared not by the martyrs only but by all who under the sway of the Beast and the False Prophet suffered reproach, boycotting, imprisonment, loss of goods, or other inconveniences . . . who were faithful in the age of persecution."[6] Dennis Johnson adds: "This fidelity, not the circumstances or the method of their death, distinguishes them as qualified to share in the Lamb's rule."[7]

So the question is asked of the entire church that boldly suffers for the gospel, a church typified by those who lost their lives for Christ: Have these believers lost everything by remaining loyal to Jesus? Leon Morris answers: "They have not lost everything. They have gained royalty and triumph."[8]

4. William Hendriksen, *More than Conquerors: An Interpretation of the Book of Revelation* (1940; repr., Grand Rapids: Baker, 1967), 191.

5. G. K. Beale, *The Book of Revelation: A Commentary on the Greek Text*, New International Greek Testament Commentary (Grand Rapids: Eerdmans, 1999), 999.

6. Henry Barclay Swete, *Commentary on Revelation*, 2 vols. (1911; repr., Grand Rapids: Kregel, 1977), 2:262.

7. Dennis E. Johnson, *Triumph of the Lamb: A Commentary on Revelation* (Phillipsburg, NJ: P&R Publishing, 2001), 290.

8. Leon Morris, *The Revelation of St. John: An Introduction and Commentary*, Tyndale New Testament Commentaries 20 (Grand Rapids: Eerdmans, 1969), 237.

John has emphasized throughout Revelation that Christians must persevere in faith during persecution in order to enter eternal life (Rev. 2:7, etc.). Now he reveals that all who remained faithful in their testimony "came to life and reigned with Christ for a thousand years" (20:4).

One Christian who was emboldened by this knowledge was the teenage English princess Lady Jane Grey. In 1553, her cousin, the young king Edward VI, died, leaving the throne of England contested. Politically minded Protestant lords put Lady Jane on the throne, but nine days later the Roman Catholic princess Mary, Henry VIII's first daughter, succeeded in pressing her more legitimate claim to the throne. The Duke of Northumberland, the political schemer who had put the crown on Lady Jane's head, immediately reverted to Catholicism. His famous explanation shows his ignorance of John's message in the vision of our text. Northumberland said: "Better to be a living dog than a dead lion."

There sat Lady Jane Grey in the Tower of London, awaiting execution for refusing to abandon her faith. In these circumstances, Queen Mary sent in her confessor, Cardinal Feckenham, to win the triumph of Jane's spiritual capitulation. Feckenham set one demand after another before her, but Jane refused each one with a clear defense from the Word of God. Finally, the cardinal gave in and expressed his disappointment. He said that he was sorry for her unwillingness to recant the gospel, since he was sure they would therefore never meet again. This was an unveiled warning of Jane's beheading. She answered, perhaps with Revelation 20:4 ringing in her heart: "True it is that we shall never meet again, except God turn your heart; for I am assured, unless you repent, and turn to God, you are in an evil case; and I pray God, in the bowels of his mercy, to send you his Holy Spirit . . . to open the eyes of your heart."[9] The next day, Jane was beheaded and her spirit soared to heaven to reign with Christ.

THE FIRST RESURRECTION

We have seen that the vision of Revelation 20:4–6 describes thrones in heaven on which the souls of faithful Christians are seated during the intermediate state between their death on earth and the return of Jesus from

---

9. Taken from Paul F. M. Zahl, *Five Women of the English Reformation* (Grand Rapids: Eerdmans, 2001), 110–13.

heaven. This has provided the *where, when,* and *who* of John's vision. The heart of this message is seen in the *what* of verses 4–6. John answers by saying that the saints "reigned with Christ," and called this reward "the first resurrection" (Rev. 20:4–6).

The premillennial view of history sees the statement that these souls "came to life" as requiring a physical resurrection. Premillennialists therefore teach that when Jesus returns, believers who died have their souls restored to their bodies in order to reign with Christ on earth. Only later, after the thousand years, are the bodies of unbelievers resurrected in order to stand in the final judgment (Rev. 20:10–15).

The strength of the premillennial argument notes a parallel between believers who "came to life" at the beginning of the thousand years and unbelievers who "come to life" when "the thousand years [are] ended" (Rev. 20:4–5), since the same Greek word is used in both cases (*ezesan*). George Eldon Ladd writes: "Natural inductive exegesis suggests that both words are to be taken in the same way, referring to literal resurrection."[10] In Revelation 2:8, this word is used to speak of Jesus' physical resurrection, saying that he "died and came to life." How, it is argued, can the word clearly mean a physical resurrection in 2:8 and 20:5 and yet mean a spiritual resurrection in 20:4? Since "came to life" must refer to a physical resurrection, the first resurrection must mean the believers' restoration to their bodies after Christ's return, followed by a second resurrection of unbelievers a thousand years later. Similarly, premillennial scholars insist that the use of the word *resurrection* (Rev. 20:5–6; Greek, *anastasis*) can refer only to a physical raising of the body.[11]

The amillennial view, which teaches that the thousand years symbolically refers to the present church age, has a number of compelling responses to this argument. The first response is to note not only that the Bible nowhere else speaks of a thousand-year interval between the physical resurrection of believers and of unbelievers, but also that the Bible positively rules out

10. George Eldon Ladd, "Historic Premillennialism," in *The Meaning of the Millennium: Four Views*, ed. Robert G. Clouse (Downers Grove, IL: IVP Academic, 1977), 37.

11. Premillennial scholars usually cite Henry Alford's classic argument based on this linguistic evidence: "If, in a passage where *two resurrections* are mentioned, . . . the first resurrection may be understood to mean *spiritual* rising with Christ, while the second means literal rising from the grave;—then there is an end of all significance in language, and Scripture is wiped out as a definite testimony to anything." Henry Alford, *The Greek Testament*, 4 vols. (Cambridge: Deighton, Bell, and Co., 1866), 4:733.

such a doctrine. An example is Jesus' teaching about his return to earth and the immediate judgment, for which all persons stand before him in their resurrected bodies: "When the Son of Man comes in his glory, and all the angels with him, then he will sit on his glorious throne. Before him will be gathered all the nations, and he will separate people one from another as a shepherd separates the sheep from the goats" (Matt. 25:31–32). Not only is there no thousand-year interval between Christ's return and the final judgment, but all persons—godly and ungodly—are resurrected at the same time for this event. In John 5:28–29, Jesus similarly placed the physical resurrection of all persons in a single event: "An hour is coming when all who are in the tombs will hear his voice and come out, those who have done good to the resurrection of life, and those who have done evil to the resurrection of judgment." By separating the return of Christ and the final judgment by a thousand years, and likewise separating the resurrection of believers and unbelievers by the millennium, the premillennial view contradicts these plain statements and must therefore be rejected.

Moreover, amillennial interpreters point out that both the words *ezesan* and *anastasis* may in fact be used to refer to a spiritual condition, rather than a physical raising. In Romans 6:4–5, Paul speaks of Christians' being raised into Christ's resurrection (*anastasis*) through our conversion, so that we may "walk in newness of life." He wrote similarly in Colossians 3:1: "If then you have been raised with Christ, seek the things that are above, where Christ is, seated at the right hand of God" (see also Eph. 2:4–6). In these passages, being raised and resurrected with Christ speaks of a spiritual change in believers. Jesus referred to the spiritual resurrection of our souls in the classic statement of John 11:25–26: "I am the resurrection [*anastasis*] and the life. Whoever believes in me, though he die, yet shall he live [future form of *ezesan*], and everyone who lives and believes in me shall never die."

Furthermore, in Revelation 20:5–6, John speaks not just of resurrection, but of "the first resurrection." Premillennialists assume that this implies a parallel *second* resurrection of unbelievers, but John does not say so. In the context of Revelation, it is more likely that "first" refers to the things of this present world rather than the "new" heavens and earth that are to come. Only the believer in Christ experiences two resurrections: the first a resurrection of the spirit to reign with Christ after death, and the second the bodily resurrection of all mankind for the final judgment in Christ's return.

Finally, when premillennial scholars insist that the expression "came to life" must be used in the same sense in both Revelation 20:4 and 5, amillennial writers point out that John is making not a positive comparison but a radical contrast. His point is that by suffering death for their faith in Jesus, believers enter into a resurrection that the ungodly never enjoy, whereas in the return of Jesus the ungodly suffer a resurrection to death that believers will never know. Believers suffer death in this life so as to enter the spiritual resurrection of their souls in heaven. Unbelievers are raised only at the end of the age to stand for judgment before the throne of Jesus Christ. Because of this contrast, the same word is used differently in verses 4 and 5, one a spiritual raising to heaven and the other a physical raising for the sake of hell.

The first resurrection, therefore, "is a reference to the life and blessing reserved for the saints . . . who have died," referring not to the future resurrection of their bodies, "but to a spiritual participation in Christ which brings the blessings of living and reigning as priests with him."[12] Hendriksen writes: "The first resurrection is the translation of the soul from this sinful earth to God's holy heaven."[13] Those who persevered in faith throughout this life, even under persecution, receive the crown of life and a throne from which to reign with Jesus. John writes: "They came to life and reigned with Christ for a thousand years" (Rev. 20:4).

I earlier mentioned the parallel between the vision of Revelation 6:9, where the souls of martyrs were shown in heaven, using virtually identical language to the description of martyrs in 20:4. The only difference is that in the first instance the souls were located under the altar of heaven, since their lives had been offered through faith in Christ's blood. Now these same souls appear as risen and enthroned, since they conquered "by the blood of the Lamb and by the word of their testimony" (Rev. 12:11). John's point to his first readers and to us is thus made clear: to suffer in this life for the blood of Christ is to reign with Christ in the resurrection life of heaven.

PRIESTS APPOINTED TO JUDGE

How, then, do Christians reign with Christ in heaven after their deaths? John answers: "Blessed and holy is the one who shares in the first resur-

---

12. Venema, *The Promise of the Future*, 332.
13. Hendriksen, *More than Conquerors*, 192.

rection! Over such the second death has no power, but they will be priests of God and of Christ, and they will reign with him for a thousand years" (Rev. 20:6).

The main point is that believers reign with Christ as priests who serve in God's presence. John has emphasized this calling from the very beginning of Revelation, saying in the benediction of 1:6 that Christ freed us from sin by his blood to be "a kingdom, priests to his God and Father." This indicates that believers in heaven have immediate access to the presence of God and enjoy the unimaginable blessing of perfect spiritual worship before the face of divine glory. Old Testament Israel was called to be a holy nation and a kingdom of priests before God, and Christ has brought this purpose to fulfillment in the triumphant session of the heavenly church. No wonder the apostle Paul said that while "to live is Christ," "to die is gain," and "to depart and be with Christ . . . is far better" (Phil. 1:21–23). Christians who die receive a glorious advance in their redemptive experience, reigning with Christ as priests above.

In Revelation 20:4, John also said that these enthroned souls "were those to whom the authority to judge was committed." The manner in which the saints exercise judgment is not specified, but at a minimum they have the pleasure of approving and taking part with Christ in his judgment of sin. This emphasis reflects Revelation's deep concern for God's justice on behalf of his persecuted church, including many of John's original readers, who would be martyred for their faith. Anthony Hoekema writes: "Needless to say, the vision here recorded would bring great comfort to the relatives and friends of these martyrs: John sees their souls as now sitting on thrones in heaven, taking part in the work of judging."[14] The vision that Daniel saw during an earlier age of persecution is thus fulfilled: "Judgment was given for the saints of the Most High, and the time came when the saints possessed the kingdom" (Dan. 7:22).

How do believers reign with Christ, as priests who sit on thrones to judge? John exclaims that they reign in blessing and holiness: "Blessed and holy is the one who shares in the first resurrection!" (Rev. 20:6). Having been exhorted throughout Revelation to overcome by faith, the saints above are now seen to have overcome, entering the blessing of spiritual communion

---

14. Anthony A. Hoekema, "Amillennialism," in *The Meaning of the Millennium: Four Views*, ed. Robert G. Clouse (Downers Grove, IL: IVP Academic, 1977), 166.

with God. Their bodies were destroyed on earth, but the souls reign with Christ in heaven. They are the holy ones whom God has set apart as his treasured possession forever and blessed to dwell before his glorious face.

John clinches the believers' hope of life after death in Revelation 20:6: "Over such the second death has no power." Christians suffer physical death, just as unbelievers do. The souls of believers are raised into heaven, awaiting the resurrection of their bodies, but with no fear of any further experience of death. How different is the fate of those who reject Christ! In death their souls do not go to heaven but to hell, and the resurrection of their bodies leads to the second death, which appears later in this chapter as eternal death in the lake of fire (Rev. 20:10, 15). To believe in Christ is to experience the first resurrection but never the second death. But to reject Jesus is to be denied the first resurrection and be condemned to the second and final death. Cornelis Venema explains: "Because of their participation in this first resurrection, [believers in Christ] are not liable to the power and dominion of death, including the second death of eternal separation from the presence and favor of God."[15] Or as C. Clemance writes: "They who are the Lord's rise twice, and die but once. They who are not the Lord's rise but once, and die twice."[16]

WHY NOT AFRAID?

We have nearly completed the journalist's assignment in reporting on the vision of John. He saw thrones in heaven, with the souls of faithful believers seated on them during the millennial reign that is the church age. In addition to this *where*, *who*, and *when*, John saw the *what* of the first resurrection. He further saw *how* they reign, as blessed and holy priests who share in Christ's judgment. This leaves only the final question: *why?*

There are a couple of ways to answer this question. We may ask why Christ provided this vision to John's readers. The answer lies in his desire to encourage them in the midst of struggles and the trial of persecution. As Jesus said in Luke 9:24, "whoever loses his life for my sake will save it." Sam Storms summarizes: "The apparent defeat of the Christian in physical

---

15. Venema, *The Promise of the Future*, 336.
16. Quoted in Geoffrey B. Wilson, *New Testament Commentaries*, 2 vols. (Edinburgh: Banner of Truth, 2005), 2:582.

death is, in point of fact, a spiritual victory that leads to life."[17] Jesus does not call his followers to sacrifice with him now without assuring us of what Paul anticipated as "an eternal weight of glory beyond all comparison" (2 Cor. 4:17).

An equally valuable way of considering the question *why?* is to consult those who joyfully endured suffering and death "for the testimony of Jesus and for the word of God" (Rev. 20:4). For instance, we might ask an Indonesian Christian named Stanley. In 1996, he graduated from Bible school and went to preach the gospel on an island where Islam was mixed with witchcraft and where official opposition to Christianity was intense. Stanley boldly testified to the saving love of Jesus, calling his converts to repent of idolatry and worship only the God of the Bible. One of these new believers burned an idol that had a copy of the Qur'an inside. When news of this reached the Muslim officials, Stanley was arrested. A pastor from home came to visit him, finding that Stanley had been so severely beaten with blows to the head that he lay in a coma. Shortly afterward, Stanley died and was raised in his spirit to reign with Christ in heaven.

If we ask why Stanley so recklessly proclaimed Jesus to such a hostile people, he would undoubtedly have answered in line with John's vision. He sacrificed his life because he knew the glory awaiting him in the first resurrection to life in heaven, and he knew the fate in the second death of sinners who have not embraced the gospel. He knew that he would reign with Christ in death, so he reigned with Christ in life through the gospel.

News of Stanley's death had a great impact on fellow believers in his home city. The immediate result was that seven more Bible students resolved to go to the same dangerous island to continue preaching the gospel. One of them was Stanley's mother, who gave her own answer to the question *why?* When asked, "Are you not afraid to die?" Stanley's mother showed that she, too, had learned the message of John's vision in Revelation. She gave her answer to the question *why?* with her own question: "Why should I be afraid to die?"[18]

---

17. Sam Storms, *Kingdom Come: The Amillennial Alternative* (Tain, Ross-shire, Scotland: Christian Focus, 2013), 465.

18. Taken from DC Talk, *Jesus Freaks: Stories of Those Who Stood with Jesus* (Minneapolis: Bethany House, 1999), 147–48.

54

GOG AND MAGOG

Revelation 20:7–10

And when the thousand years are ended, Satan will be released
from his prison and will come out to deceive the nations that are
at the four corners of the earth, Gog and Magog, to gather
them for battle. (Rev. 20:7–8)

O n the eve of Halloween in 1938, the CBS Mercury Theatre on
the Air broadcast a radio performance of H. G. Wells's science-
fiction thriller *The War of the Worlds*. The broadcast informed
listeners that it was a dramatization, yet as the actors simulated news reports
of Martians landing at Grover's Mill, New Jersey, panic spread around the
country. A fifth of the Americans listening believed that an army from
Mars had actually invaded the United States. As a result, traffic was clogged
nationwide, communications systems were overloaded, and hysteria reigned.
According to journalist Chris Jordan, the radio program touched a sensitive
nerve because the country "was on edge due to years of economic depression
and the winds of war swirling in Europe."[1]

Heightened anxiety in society produces a similar effect on the study of
biblical prophecy. In times of fear and stress, Bible readers tend to assume

---

1. Chris Jordan, "War of the Worlds Radio Broadcast Turns 75," *USA Today*, October 29, 2013.

that the foretold end is about to come. Perhaps no other passage in the Bible has been more subject to this tendency than the prophecy of Gog and Magog in Ezekiel 38 and Revelation 20. During the decline of the Roman Empire, the church father Ambrose insisted that Gog represented the Goths, who were then pressing on the territory of Rome. In the seventh century, Gog and Magog were the Muslim armies threatening the Holy Land. In the thirteenth century, Gog was identified as the Mongol Khan. Later times associated Gog with the Pope, the Turks, and the Russian tsar. The last of these is especially noteworthy because during the Crimean War of the nineteenth century, British Bible teachers developed the theory that Magog was Russia, with which the nation was then at war. This theory was reflected in the Scofield Study Bible that spread dispensational theology so widely. Still influenced by this theory a hundred years later, prophecy writer Grant R. Jeffrey wrote in 1991 that "Russia is the 'Gog and Magog' of Bible prophecy."[2] He then assured readers that Russian premier Mikhail Gorbachev would lead Magog-Russia to combine with Arab nations for an invasion of Israel. This war would trigger the rapture of the church, the discovery of the ark of the covenant, and the rebuilding of the temple in Jerusalem, all of which could be expected by the year 2000.[3]

Jeffrey's calculations proved false, but they represent a tendency that Iain Duguid explains: "With its vivid imagery and pictorial language, . . . literature such as [the prophecy of Gog and Magog] lends itself to a flexible application to whatever the contemporary dangers to world peace are perceived to be."[4] This approach unfortunately creates an attitude of hysteria among Christians not unlike the effect of the *War of the Worlds* radio broadcast—exactly the opposite of what the apostle John intended in Revelation 20.

SATAN'S GREAT REBELLION

The vision of Revelation 20:7–10 reflects the New Testament teaching of a great rebellion that will mark the end of the church age. Jesus spoke of this in Matthew 24:21: "For then there will be great tribulation, such as has not

---

2. Grant R. Jeffrey, *Messiah: War in the Middle East & the Road to Armageddon* (New York: Bantam, 1991), 47.

3. Ibid., 45–70.

4. Iain M. Duguid, *Ezekiel*, NIV Application Commentary (Grand Rapids: Zondervan, 1999), 451–52.

been from the beginning of the world until now, no, and never will be." Paul wrote that Christ "will not come, unless the rebellion comes first, and the man of lawlessness is revealed, the son of destruction" (2 Thess. 2:3). Revelation has variously depicted this intense attack against the church. In chapter 11, the church is represented by twin witnesses resembling Moses and Elijah. When their witness is concluded, "the beast that rises from the bottomless pit will make war on them and conquer them and kill them," until Christ raises them three and a half days later (Rev. 11:7–11). Revelation 20:1–3 shows Satan as bound during the church age, "until . . . he must be released for a little while" (20:3). John picks up this thought in verses 7–8: "And when the thousand years are ended, Satan will be released from his prison and will come out to deceive the nations that are at the four corners of the earth."

We should notice that Satan is "released" from his bonds, emphasizing the sovereign rule of God over him. This detail reminds us that however mighty the devil may be, he remains a finite creature of limited strength, unable to match the infinite might of God. Douglas Kelly writes: "He could never get loose from his bondage at his own will, until God in his sovereign timing takes off the chains from his hands and feet, opens the door and lets him out."[5]

We remember from our study of Revelation 20:1–3 that the binding of Satan has to do with God's forbidding him to "deceive the nations any longer" (Rev. 20:3), so that the gospel may spread throughout the world. The binding of Satan does not mean that his evil activities are totally curtailed but that he no longer has authority to bind the nations in the darkness of unbelief. It is noteworthy, then, that as soon as Satan is released, this is precisely what he does: he "will come out to deceive the nations" (20:8).

This combination shows us that Satan's chief instrument in this world is not violent persecution but deceptions that promote unbelief. This is why the Christian church is sent into the world with the truth. Whatever else the church does, it must boldly proclaim the truth of God's Word, refusing to compromise with the prevailing dogmas of secularist unbelief. We are constantly told today that Christians must be less doctrinally fixated and that we must be more tolerant of worldly ideas and practices. This approach should alarm us, given Satan's chief strategy of binding unbelievers with deception.

---

5. Douglas F. Kelly, *Revelation*, Mentor Expository Commentary (Tain, Ross-shire, Scotland: Mentor, 2012), 387.

Moreover, we see that the sinful tendencies of the human heart do not evolve upward over time. As soon as God lifts his restraint on Satan, "the nations" are deceived once more. Robert Mounce suggests that one reason why God releases Satan at the end of the age "is to make plain that neither the designs of Satan nor the waywardness of the human heart will be altered by the mere passing of time. Once loosed from prison, Satan picks up where he left off and men rally to his cause."[6] When the final judgment comes, immediately after these events, the justice of God's condemnation will be undoubted. George Eldon Ladd writes that Satan's success in leading the nations to rebellion "makes it plain that the ultimate root of sin is not poverty or inadequate social conditions or an unfortunate environment; it is the rebelliousness of the human heart."[7]

The purpose of Satan's deceptions has always been to lead darkened mankind into warfare against God, and so will be the great tribulation that ends the age. Satan will "deceive the nations that are at the four corners of the earth, Gog and Magog, to gather them for battle" (Rev. 20:8). The book of Revelation makes clear that this great battle is the same final conflict that earlier received the name "Armageddon" (16:16). Premillennial Christians deny this connection, asserting that Revelation shows a series of consecutive battles in the end times: the battle of Armageddon before the seventh bowl is poured; the great battle in which Jesus returns (19:19); and the final battle of Revelation 20:8–9, after the thousand years. These are best understood, however, as one and the same battle, with different details corresponding to different portions of Revelation. Notice that the battle of Armageddon takes place "on the great day of God the Almighty" (16:14) and is immediately followed by imagery associated with the final judgment. The great battle of chapter 19 draws the imagery of feeding carrion birds from Ezekiel 39, and the battle of Revelation 20 draws the names "Gog and Magog" from the same Old Testament chapter. Moreover, the language used in each of these battles is virtually identical. In each case, "the kings of the whole world" (Rev. 16:14) or "the kings of the earth with their armies" (19:19) are "gathered" to war against the Lord. Moreover, in the Greek text each of these is not merely a *battle* but *the battle*, all foretelling the final conflict that ends the

6. Robert H. Mounce, *Revelation*, rev. ed., New International Commentary on the New Testament (Grand Rapids: Eerdmans, 1997), 361.

7. George Eldon Ladd, *A Commentary on the Revelation of John* (Grand Rapids: Eerdmans, 1972), 269.

age. William Hendriksen writes: "We have here one and the same battle.... It is the final attack of antichristian forces upon the Church."[8] T. S. Elliot's famous poem "The Hollow Men" posits, "This is the way the world ends; not with a bang, but a whimper."[9] Revelation teaches exactly the opposite: history ends with the great battle of the world against the church. When the gospel has been preached to all the nations, the time of repentance will be gone and the end will come.

The news of Satan's release to deceive the nations reminds us of the urgency with which we should spread the gospel until that happens. The ease with which Satan wins over the nations shows that only the power of Christ through the gospel can bring salvation: as Paul wrote, the mind "set on the flesh is hostile to God" (Rom. 8:7). Christians must respond to this total depravity with the supernatural power of God's Word to grant new life. Moreover, we realize the significance of this present time when Satan is still restrained from deceiving everyone. Now is the time for you to be saved by trusting the gospel message of Jesus' salvation. For the day of grace will suddenly close, and Satan will once more bind all unbelievers in rebellion against God and for final destruction with himself.

SATAN'S GREAT ARMY

I mentioned that the three different accounts in Revelation of the final battle each have their own emphasis. Chapter 16 highlighted the destruction of sinful mankind, whereas chapter 19 showed the defeat of the beast. Chapter 20's version of the last battle emphasizes the capture and judgment of Satan himself. But it also vividly describes the great army that the devil gathers against God's people. Revelation 20:8 says that Satan "will come out to deceive the nations that are at the four corners of the earth, Gog and Magog, to gather them for battle; their number is like the sand of the sea."

Here, the assembled nations of the world are identified by the names "Gog and Magog." This reference originates in Ezekiel 38, where the prophet foretold a great assault on God's people after the age of their blessing. Ezekiel chapters 1–33 deal with God's judgment on wicked Jerusalem, involving the

8. William Hendriksen, *More than Conquerors: An Interpretation of the Book of Revelation* (1940; repr., Grand Rapids: Baker, 1967), 195.
9. Quoted in Kelly, *Revelation*, 387.

fall of the city to Nebuchadnezzar. In chapters 34–37, God promises the revival of his people through the gospel of Christ: "I will give you a new heart, and a new spirit I will put within you" (Ezek. 36:26). In chapters 38 and 39, however, Ezekiel foretells a final great assault on God's people, before showing the symbolic temple of chapters 40–48, which depicts the eternal age in Christ's return. Regarding the final battle, Ezekiel wrote: "Son of man, set your face toward Gog, of the land of Magog, the chief prince of Meshech and Tubal, and prophesy against him" (38:2). By using this same designation, Revelation is saying that its final battle is the same final battle anticipated by Ezekiel.

"Magog" first appears in the Bible as one of the sons of Japheth, the son of Noah (Gen. 10:2). Meshech and Tubal are usually associated with the area of the Scythian Empire, on the northern side of Assyria in the region of the Black Sea, where it seems that Gog was a leader. Despite the verbal similarities between *Meshech* and *Tubal* and the Russian cities of *Moscow* and *Tobolsk*, there is no actual connection. Ezekiel's point seems to be that Gog was a warrior from a very distant land, saying, "I will . . . bring you up from the uttermost parts of the north, and lead you against the mountains of Israel" (Ezek. 39:2). From the perspective of Westerners caught up in the Cold War of the late twentieth century, the uttermost north would be Russia or China, but from Ezekiel's it would be the kingdoms beyond Assyria, that is, the Scythian lands of Gog and Magog. G. B. Caird points out that this symbolism was picked up in rabbinic writings, which used the names *Gog* and *Magog* for the entire rebellious nations of Psalm 2.[10]

In other words, *Gog* and *Magog* played a role in Jewish end-times thought similar to the role of Martians in early science-fiction books: proverbial names for dreadful powers of chaos and worldwide war. John's terminology alerts us not to expect a literal correspondence with Ezekiel. Whereas in Ezekiel Gog is a person and Magog is his home, John uses both "Gog and Magog" to designate "the nations that are at the four corners of the earth" (Rev. 20:8). Ben Witherington writes: "Gog and Magog are symbols of evil in the nations of the earth, and this evil comes from all directions."[11]

John's language confirms the New Testament teaching of a final worldwide persecution of the Christian church (see Matt. 24:21; 2 Thess. 2:3–4). First,

10. G. B. Caird, *The Revelation of St. John the Divine* (San Francisco: Harper, 1966), 256.
11. Ben Witherington III, *Revelation*, New Cambridge Bible Commentary (Cambridge: Cambridge University Press, 2003), 250.

the nations are gathered from "the four corners of the earth . . . for battle" (Rev. 20:8). This shows that the final battle is launched not merely by a far-eastern nation such as Russia or China, as popular prophecy teaching often states. It is the entire world that gathers for a stand against the authority of God. Second, "their number is like the sand of the sea" (20:8), referring to the vastness of these enemies. The battle will not pit evenly matched forces, so that Christians may hope to succeed by their own strength. Rather, only the power of God is able to save them. This vast number of the wicked poses a problem for premillennialists. How can such a numberless host of enemies gather when Christ has been reigning on earth, with Satan bound from any activity? This language better fits the view that this great battle takes place at the end of our age, before Christ returns, when Satan has been restrained from stopping the gospel, yet is still working among those who rebel against God.

This vast worldwide army "marched up over the broad plain of the earth" (Rev. 20:9). The idea is of a great army marching over a vast tract of ground. Their objective is the church: "and surrounded the camp of the saints and the beloved city." This recaps the biblical model for the salvation of God's people. Throughout the Old Testament, Israel was placed at the mercy of wicked powers, yet was delivered by God's sudden intervention. It was the situation of John's readers, surrounded by pagan rulers who wielded the Roman sword. How often believers have experienced this plight, from David's exile in the caves of Judea, to the Chinese house churches that meet secretly to avoid arrest, to the Christian churches in Muslim lands that meet under the open threat of violence and attack. So in the end the entire church will be besieged, so that a refusal to worship idols and a bold witness to Christ will result in suffering.

Notice the language with which John describes the church: "the camp of the saints and the beloved city" (Rev. 20:9). The first description alludes to the camp of Israel in the exodus journey: the church is likewise the pilgrim body of believers passing through life toward a promised land beyond. We are reminded that we truly are exiles and aliens in this world. It is with this in mind that Peter urged Christians to avoid the pollutions of sin: "Beloved, I urge you as sojourners and exiles to abstain from the passions of the flesh, which wage war against your soul" (1 Peter 2:11). At the same time, though we are despised as aliens by the world, the church is God's "beloved city."

Paul Gardner writes: "How different this city is from the city of 'the inhab-itants of this earth,' the city of Babylon. In every way, Jerusalem stands as a contrast with Babylon."[12] Babylon stands for the prostitute world, just as Jerusalem represents the church as the bride of Christ. Whereas God will judge and condemn faithless Babylon, the faithful church bears his love and receives his promise of an eternal salvation. G. K. Beale writes: "The church is now and will be the true Israel in the midst of whose camp God's presence tabernacles."[13]

SATAN'S GREAT DEFEAT

We can tell that the people of God are God's beloved city because of his fiery defense of her from Satan's attack: "but fire came down from heaven and consumed them" (Rev. 20:9). In the Old Testament, God judged Sodom and Gomorrah with fire (Gen. 19:24–25), just as he sent down fire to protect his servant Elijah from the soldiers of wicked King Ahaziah (2 Kings 1:10–12). Here, as elsewhere in Revelation and the New Testament, Christ's second coming results in the immediate defeat of all the foes who afflicted his church. Paul wrote that God will "grant relief to you who are afflicted as well as to us, when the Lord Jesus is revealed from heaven with his mighty angels in flaming fire, inflicting vengeance on those who do not know God and on those who do not obey the gospel" (2 Thess. 1:7–8). Ezekiel specified that fire would fall on Magog both to defend God's people and to glorify his name (Ezek. 39:6). This point emphasizes that the church does not fight to defend herself. Revelation 12:11 described her warfare as trusting in Christ's blood, bearing testimony to God's Word, and offering our lives to seal our witness. This was the conquering power of the early church, which suffered greatly in its refusal to grant deity to Caesar, but displayed a power of grace that the world had never known. Likewise, the patient, suffering faith of the end-times church will glorify God when history concludes with "our blessed hope, the appearing of the glory of our great God and Savior Jesus Christ" (Titus 2:13).

The particular emphasis in this vision is the defeat and destruction of Satan himself. This will complete the judgment section that began in

12. Paul Gardner, *Revelation: The Compassion and Protection of Christ*, Focus on the Bible (Tain, Ross-shire, Scotland: Christian Focus, 2008), 278.
13. G. K. Beale, *The Book of Revelation: A Commentary on the Greek Text*, New International Greek Testament Commentary (Grand Rapids: Eerdmans, 1999), 1027.

Revelation 17 with the judgment of the harlot Babylon (chaps. 17–18), saw the judgment of the beast and the false prophet in chapter 19, and now witnesses the judgment of Satan himself. John writes that "the devil who had deceived them was thrown into the lake of fire and sulfur where the beast and the false prophet were, and they will be tormented day and night forever and ever" (Rev. 20:10).

Notice that the devil is primarily judged for deceiving the nations, reminding us again that the church's ministry of truth through God's Word is always the world's greatest need. The greatest victory of history is Jesus' conquest of sin by his blood, and that victory is joined with his defeat of Satan, the great tyrant and deceiver of the world. Knowing this, Christians face the future with a great hope, since God has ordained the judgment and condemnation of Satan. This judgment was anticipated in Matthew's Gospel, when demons whom Jesus had cast out admitted knowing of their coming judgment. "What have you to do with us, O Son of God?" they cried. "Have you come here to torment us before the time?" (Matt. 8:29). Jesus said that this time had not yet come, but Revelation shows that history ends with the greatest agents of evil receiving a terrible and just punishment from God.

John Bunyan's *Pilgrim's Progress* has a vivid scene when Christian is frightened from advancing on his path because of two deadly lions beside the road, until he learns that they are chained so as not to reach faithful disciples. This is a picture of Satan's restraint in this present age: he is a deadly lion, but bound from hindering the gospel work of Christ. Christians rejoice to know that Satan may not thwart Christ's gospel advance now, but how much more will we rejoice when even his intimidating roar is no more to be heard in the entire vast extent of God's whole creation!

Not only is Satan apprehended, but he is "thrown into the lake of fire and sulfur where the beast and the false prophet were" (Rev. 20:10). Satan is a spiritual being, so the language of his being thrown into a lake of fire is symbolic. This shows that whatever bodily suffering sinners may experience in hell, the greatest torment will be spiritual. Satan, together with his servants, "will be tormented day and night forever and ever" (20:10). This verse makes clear that hell involves never-ending conscious torment—a dreadful thought to human beings, yet still the clear teaching of Scripture. Grant Osborne writes: "Those who are offended by such teaching have too low a realization of the terrible nature of sin and the natural response that divine holiness must have toward it."[14] Revelation has reminded us of God's provision of his own Son, Jesus Christ, to die for the forgiveness of our sins. Those who suffer the torment of the lake of fire, together with Satan and his beasts (see 20:15), are all those who were hard-hearted toward their God in refusing to repent and scorned the Savior who shed his blood to offer them forgiveness.

FOREVER AND EVER

The final words of this vision are poignant and decisive: "forever and ever" (Rev. 20:10). This constitutes the gravest warning for those who enter into rebellion with Satan, reveling in sin and rebelling against God's rule. Their punishment is as eternal as God himself is. Sin, being an offense to God's justice and holy nature, is eternal, and so are its consequences. This same "forever and ever" provides the Christian with a ground for a most joyful hope. Just as Satan and sin played no role in the glorious creation of all things, so they will be completely removed from the completion of all things in the glory of Jesus Christ. Our own sin will be not only forgiven but actually removed. There will be no adversary to accuse us but only God's justice to demand our justification through faith in Christ. There will be no enemies to fear or hate, but as Isaiah foresaw, "They shall not hurt or destroy in all my holy mountain; for the earth shall be full of the knowledge of the LORD as the waters cover the sea" (Isa. 11:9).

What is the meaning of this "forever and ever" to believers now? It means that we have an antidote to the crippling fear of persecution that might otherwise undermine our faith. Why would we forsake Jesus Christ amid the afflictions of this world when we know how the story ends? Jesus wins! Why would we abandon his victorious cause, even though it may entail suffering for a little while in tribulation, and even if discipleship to him requires us to renounce the sinful pleasures of a condemned world?

The "forever and ever" of Revelation 20:10 warns the unbeliever not only of the futility of rebelling against God but even more about the folly of refusing the only Savior who can deliver us from a judgment that our sins deserve. Jesus promised, "Truly, truly, I say to you, whoever hears my word and

14. Grant R. Osborne, *Revelation*, Baker Exegetical Commentary on the New Testament (Grand Rapids: Baker Academic, 2002), 717.

believes him who sent me has eternal life. He does not come into judgment, but has passed from death to life" (John 5:24). But those who refuse to offer faith to Jesus are already under condemnation. He warned that "whoever does not believe is condemned already, because he has not believed in the name of the only Son of God" (3:18).

Finally, in a world where an entire society can be so gripped by anxiety that the radio-theater performance of *The War of the Worlds* drives millions of people to hysteria, the "forever and ever" of Revelation 20:10 sounds a clarion call of peace to believers in Jesus Christ. John's vision reminds us that when things look worst, victory is at hand. When the camp of the church is surrounded, Jesus' coming has drawn near. When sin has you cornered or the Gogs and Magogs of this world have brought you to despair, a Savior declares that he has loved you enough to die and is coming again to ensure that you live forever with him, calling you to live here and now for his glory. Douglas Kelly writes: "The worst that the devil, the demons, and mankind can do against the Lord and his church are going to bring stupendous hosannas and hallelujahs to God at the end."[15] Because we know this end, and the "forever and ever" beyond it without fear, sin, or death, let our worship, our service, and our lives now reflect the joy that belongs to the people of the beloved city that God has made his own.

15. Kelly, *Revelation*, 387.

55

THE FINAL JUDGMENT

Revelation 20:11–15

*And I saw the dead, great and small, standing before the throne,
and books were opened. Then another book was opened, which
is the book of life. And the dead were judged by what was written
in the books, according to what they had done. (Rev. 20:12)*

One evening in 1808, a young man named Adoniram Judson was lodging in an inn, while in the next room a man was struggling in the throes of death. Judson was a brilliant student at Providence College, where he had become enthralled with the Enlightenment ideas coming from Europe. On the urging of a witty upperclassman named Jacob Eames, he had adopted deism and its idea of an absent God. On his twentieth birthday, Judson told his distraught parents that he had abandoned the Christian faith and was moving to New York City to pursue a lifestyle of pleasure.

Shortly afterward, Judson listened to the terrible distress in the next room and wondered what the dying man was thinking. Moans passed through the walls, and he could hear the man's restless struggling. What would his "freethinking" friend Eames say to dismiss the man's anxiety and remove his concerns about eternity? Had this man, like Judson, rejected the gospel for a sophisticated worldly creed? Did his anguish suggest a fear of judgment beyond death? Judson wondered about his own fate in death, trying to remember the clever answers of the deist Eames to assuage his fears.

By dawn the sounds of struggle had subsided, and shortly afterward Judson gathered his things to leave the inn. On the way out, he passed the innkeeper and asked about the man next door. "He is gone, poor fellow!" was the reply. "The doctor said he would probably not survive the night." "Do you know who he was?" Judson asked. "Oh yes. Young man from the college in Providence," came the reply. "Name was Eames, Jacob Eames." Judson was stunned, and for hours a single thought occupied his mind: "Dead! Lost! Lost!"[1]

In that inn, hell had opened up and struck a blow close to Judson's heart. Although he was not immediately converted, this brush with death and judgment led him on a path to find forgiveness in Jesus Christ. He then became one of the greatest Baptist missionaries, suffering great pains to free others from the judgment of their sin.

THE REALITY OF FINAL JUDGMENT

As the apostle John presents the final vision of Revelation 20, he also wants his readers to face *the reality of the final judgment.* John wrote: "Then I saw a great white throne and him who was seated on it" (Rev. 20:11). The apostle Paul warned that God "has fixed a day on which he will judge the world" (Acts 17:31). Jesus defined this day as the day of his return: "When the Son of Man comes in his glory, and all the angels with him, then he will sit on his glorious throne" (Matt. 25:31). Bruce Milne comments: "Despite the humorous dismissal of the last judgment in our culture, its comparative neglect in much theological reflection, and the virtual silence on the subject in the modern pulpit, it is going to happen."[2] Whatever clever arguments may be made to urge us not to expect God's judgment, Revelation 20:11–15 starkly upholds the words of the Nicene Creed: Christ "will come again with glory to judge both the living and the dead."

1. Taken from Samuel Fisk, *More Fascinating Conversion Stories* (Grand Rapids: Kregel, 1994), 65–67.
2. Bruce Milne, *The Message of Heaven and Hell: Grace and Destiny,* The Bible Speaks Today (Downers Grove, IL: InterVarsity Press, 2002), 303.

John begins by describing the judgment seat: "Then I saw a great white throne" (Rev. 20:11). When John was invited into heaven, the first thing he saw was a throne (4:2), and now at the end it fills his vision. As a "great" throne, it exudes majesty and authority. As a "white" throne, it radiates perfect purity, holiness, and incorruptible righteousness. When Isaiah saw his vision of the heavenly courtroom, the seraphim were crying, "Holy, holy, holy" (Isa. 6:3). The great white throne conveys the same message of infinite perfect justice.

John does not specify who is seated on the throne, which suggests the presence of God the Father, as when this throne was first seen in chapter 4 (Rev. 4:2; see also 19:4; 21:5). In Daniel 7:9, from which John's vision likely draws, it was "the Ancient of Days" who sat on the throne, clothed as "white as snow." The Bible also states, however, that Jesus will judge the world, together with the Father. Paul said that "Christ Jesus . . . is to judge the living and the dead" (2 Tim. 4:1). John 5:22 tells us that the "Father . . . has given all judgment to the Son." Therefore, while Revelation 20:11 seems to focus on God the Father, it is clear that Jesus, God's Son, is the agent to whom judgment is committed, which is why he was seated at the right hand of the holy God (Eph. 1:20; Heb. 12:2).

Revelation 20:11 adds the striking statement: "From his presence earth and sky fled away, and no place was found for them." This imagery connects with earlier language in Revelation that was tied to Christ's return. After the sixth seal was opened, John saw a cataclysmic end to the physical order, with a great earthquake and the falling of stars. "The sky vanished like a scroll," he said (Rev. 6:12–14). This shows the upheaval that results from the absolute holiness and majesty of God when his throne is brought into the fallen world order. The prophet Micah spoke this way, saying that when God comes down to earth, "the mountains will melt under him, and the valleys will split open, like wax before the fire" (Mic. 1:3–4).

The reason for the fleeing of creation was "transgression" and "sins" (Mic. 1:5). Because it falls under the curse of the corruption of sin, J. Ramsey Michaels points out that "Mother Nature has taken a beating in the Revelation."[3] How ironic, in this light, that the anti-Christian "new age"

---

3. J. Ramsey Michaels, *Revelation*, IVP New Testament Commentary 20 (Downers Grove, IL: InterVarsity Press, 1997), 229.

movements are idolatrously fixed on the natural world that is destined to shatter in the coming of the glory of God.

In Revelation 6, the dissolution of nature left the human race unable to hide "from the face of him who is seated on the throne, and from the wrath of the Lamb" (Rev. 6:16). This same point is made by the fleeing of earth and sky in Revelation 20:11, leaving only God and his unavoidable judgment. Douglas Kelly writes:

> There is now nothing to hide any individual in an assembled universe from the Almighty, whose very existence some of these people spent their whole life trying to deny. All pretense is gone on that day. Each one of us will then be face to face with ultimate and final reality. No escape, no hiding place. The refuge of philosophy and false religion has vanished with the clouds. All is held captive by the face of God.[4]

THE SCOPE OF FINAL JUDGMENT

In addition to the reality of judgment, John's vision presents *the scope of the final judgment*: "And I saw the dead, great and small, standing before the throne" (Rev. 20:12). The meaning is that every human being who has ever lived will stand in this judgment. Milne notes: "The judgment, because it is the final act of history and the gathering up of the human story, is necessarily universal. The Lord of all life now passes all life under his all-determining review."[5]

John emphasizes the general resurrection of all the dead to stand before God's throne. Jesus said that "an hour is coming when all who are in the tombs will hear his voice and come out" (John 5:28). The universality of this resurrection is conveyed in Revelation 20:13: "And the sea gave up the dead who were in it, [and] Death and Hades gave up the dead who were in them." In the ancient world, burial was considered important to one's life after death. Dying at sea was therefore a troubling fate. Yet at Christ's return the sea will yield up all who died in her, though their bodies were thought to be lost. Moreover, the sea was a place of chaos that symbolized opposition to God, which perhaps explains its identification with "Death and Hades."

---

4. Douglas F. Kelly, *Revelation*, Mentor Expository Commentary (Tain, Ross-shire, Scotland: Mentor, 2012), 392.

5. Milne, *The Message of Heaven and Hell*, 297.

These places for the body and the soul in death will likewise yield up their victims to face the final judgment before God's throne.

The point is that all will stand before the judgment throne. John emphasizes that there will be no distinctions, since the "great and small" stand together before God. Kelly writes: "It will be the largest gathering of human beings in all of history. Not one descendant of Adam and Eve will be missing. . . . This will be God's final word on the personal, immortal destiny of every soul who has ever lived."[6]

THE BASIS FOR FINAL JUDGMENT

Since each of us will be present before God's throne, we should realize now what is *the basis for the final judgment.* John answers: "And I saw the dead, great and small, standing before the throne, and books were opened. . . . And the dead were judged by what was written in the books, according to what they had done" (Rev. 20:12).

Here we arrive at the vital matter. Since each of us must face God's judgment, what will be the basis of condemnation? The Bible is clear in stating that we are judged by our deeds. A book is opened, John reports, pointing out the divine record of our every thought, word, and deed, together with our sinful omissions. The early church theologian Augustine noted the symbolism of these books, ascribing them to the "Divine memory" that infallibly records all deeds, words, thoughts, and motives.[7] The infinite and omnipresent God has watched over every detail of history, with a perfect and infallible observation.

This thought is unsettling, to say the least. We often avoid people who knew us long ago, since they are likely to point out defects and embarrassing sins that we had thought to put behind us. Yet while we might forget our transgressions, the Righteous Judge of the universe remembers every single one. Not only are all our sins recorded in God's book, but that book will be opened before all creation and the great white throne of the holy God. Imagine if the sinful actions, words, and thoughts that you committed only today were written down. Imagine that list being given to the pastor to be

6. Kelly, *Revelation*, 391.

7. Quoted in Richard Bewes, *The Lamb Wins: A Guided Tour through the Book of Revelation* (Tain, Ross-shire, Scotland: Christian Focus, 2000), 142.

read from the pulpit of the church. You would want to crawl under the pew and get away. But unless your sins have been forgiven in advance through faith in Christ, there will be no getting away from God's judgment on your sins. Not only the guilt but also the shame of your sin will be brought to light for God's wrathful condemnation. Hebrews 4:13 states: "And no creature is hidden from his sight, but all are naked and exposed to the eyes of him to whom we must give account."

All the dead will be judged by God "according to what they had done" (Rev. 20:12). It is sometimes taught that the only sin for which we are judged is that of unbelief, since Jesus died for all other sins. This contradicts John's teaching. The Bible does not say that Jesus made atonement for the sins of unbelievers, and Revelation plainly states that *all* our actions will come under God's judgment. God's justice is not capricious or arbitrary, but perfectly fair. All the misdeeds that have ever violated God's law and brought harm to people—so many of them never brought to light in this world—will be laid bare in the punishment of a perfectly holy God.

In this world, people clamor for justice, seldom thinking of the full implications. Some go so far as to say that all they want from God is to get their due. But if all you want from God is justice, then you must be prepared for every sin to be exposed and the verdict of "guilty" to be pronounced against you. Imagine if you had sinned just three times a day—and that is a considerable underestimate—then you will have accrued a thousand offenses against God's law every year. Every time you offended proper authority, told a lie, lusted in your heart, or coveted another's goods, you sinned. Over a normal lifetime, you would thus accrue tens of thousands of offenses that will be read from God's book to your condemnation. And because of the sheer justice of that verdict, Paul says, "every mouth [will] be stopped, and the whole world [will] be held accountable to God" (Rom. 3:19).

Because of the precise fairness of God's judgment, different degrees of condemnation will be meted out. Jesus told the citizens of Capernaum that they could expect greater judgment than even famed cities of evil in the Old Testament: "For if the mighty works done in you had been done in Sodom, it would have remained until this day" (Matt. 11:23). How great, then, will be the guilt of those who reject Christ in spite of the warning of John's vision, which foretells the last judgment so that you might repent and believe! How great will be the judgment of those who hear the gospel of salvation through faith in Christ, yet reject it out of pride and a love for the world!

ESCAPE FROM FINAL JUDGMENT

When we understand the basis for God's judgment, we realize the great problem that all of us are guilty and stand worthy of condemnation. For this reason, the most important of all truths is how sinners can *escape from the final judgment.* John answers: "Then another book was opened, which is the book of life" (Rev. 20:12).

The Bible states that God has a record of every person chosen to be saved by his grace. This book contains not deeds but names: H. B. Swete calls it "the roll of living citizens of the New Jerusalem."[8] Daniel 12:1 spoke of God's saving "everyone whose name shall be found written in the book." This book was composed in eternity past, when, Paul teaches, God "chose us in [Christ] before the foundation of the world" (Eph. 1:4). John uses the same language in Revelation 17:8, stating that the names of the redeemed were "written in the book of life from the foundation of the world."

The full name of this book is given in Revelation 13:8: "the book of life of the Lamb who was slain." This makes clear that election and salvation are always in Christ. To say that it is the book "of the Lamb" is to affirm that the names recorded are those who belong to Jesus Christ. Moreover, in calling Jesus "the Lamb who was slain," this book records those who are saved by means of his atoning death for sin. Paul exclaims: "In him we have redemption through his blood, the forgiveness of our trespasses, according to the riches of his grace" (Eph. 1:7). This redemption is received through faith in Jesus. John 3:16 states, "For God so loved the world, that he gave his only Son, that whoever believes in him should not perish but have eternal life." First John 1:9 adds: "If we confess our sins, he is faithful and just to forgive us our sins and to cleanse us from all unrighteousness."

Jesus took up the cross as a sacrifice for his people. He was our Substitute, bearing the penalty of our sins as the wrath of God was poured out on them. Thus, as Paul wrote in Romans 8:1, "there is . . . now no condemnation for those who are in Christ Jesus." Moreover, instead of being judged by our own deeds, believers are justified by Christ's perfect deeds, the righteousness of which is imputed to us (Rom. 4:5–6; 2 Cor. 5:21). "Forgiven and reconciled," writes Philip Hughes, "they stand before the Judge justified,

---

8. Henry Barclay Swete, *Commentary on Revelation*, 2 vols. (1911; repr., Grand Rapids: Kregel, 1977), 2:272.

not in themselves but in Jesus Christ the righteous who is the propitiation for their sins and their advocate with the Father."[9]

Since the Book of Life was composed "before the foundation of the world" (Rev. 13:8), election precedes saving faith. We are not chosen because we believe in Christ, but we believe in Jesus by God's electing and regenerating grace. To believe, then, is to be assured that your name is written in the Lamb's Book of Life and that you will not be condemned in the final judgment. John Calvin writes: "How do we know that God has elected us before the creation of the world? By believing in Jesus Christ. . . . God has his eternal counsel, and he always reserves to himself the chief and original record of which he gives us a copy by faith."[10] Realizing this, believers give all the glory of salvation to the grace of God. We gain assurance, knowing that our faith is grounded not in our own choice, feeble as that would be, but in God's sovereign election before the creation of the world.

THE PENALTY OF FINAL JUDGMENT

The question is raised about believers' standing before God to be judged according to their deeds. It is clear in John's vision that while all mankind outside Christ must be judged by the book of their works, believers in Christ are vindicated by the record of their names in the Book of Life. Many, however, teach that Christians will nevertheless stand in the judgment to have their sins revealed and then pardoned. The basis for this teaching is 2 Corinthians 5:10, which says that "we must all appear before the judgment seat of Christ, so that each one may receive what is due for what he has done in the body, whether good or evil." Grant Osborne takes this view: "We will be faced with our evil deeds and then forgiven and will be rewarded for the good we have done."[11]

There are several reasons why I believe this teaching is in error. First, among the Bible's descriptions of forgiveness is the statement that God has forgotten all our sins. Indeed, this promise is at the heart of the new covenant fulfilled by Christ: "For I will be merciful toward their iniquities, and I will

9. Philip Edgcumbe Hughes, *The Book of Revelation* (Downers Grove, IL: InterVarsity Press, 1990), 219.
10. John Calvin, *Sermons on the Epistle to the Ephesians* (Carlisle, PA: Banner of Truth, 1973), 47.
11. Grant R. Osborne, *Revelation*, Baker Exegetical Commentary on the New Testament (Grand Rapids: Baker Academic, 2002), 722.

remember their sins no more" (Heb. 8:12, quoting Jer. 31:34). The point of this promise is that God will not keep a record of the sins of those who are forgiven through faith in Jesus. God will not even bring up our sins in the future, since he has erased them with the ink of Christ's blood. Isaiah uses similar language in saying that "you have cast all my sins behind your back" (Isa. 38:17). In Psalm 103:12, David rejoices: "As far as the east is from the west, so far does he remove our transgressions from us." These statements simply do not square with the doctrine that believers will be shamed by our sins, only to have them forgiven before God's holy throne.

Second, advocates of the judgment of believers for sin fail to consider how shattering it would be for our sins to be revealed before that holy throne. I once stood before a judge, accused of felony charges of which I was innocent. This took place when I was a young army officer and the Provost Marshal sought to make an example of a combat officer for a routine accident in the field. My defense attorney assured me that there was no basis for a charge. I, too, did not see how I could possibly be found guilty. Yet as I faced that judgment, I did not sleep a wink the night before. Why? Because even though the charges were ludicrous and my innocence was obvious, I yet had to stand for judgment. I showed up with a pale, drawn face, and sweat dripped from my palms even as the judge threw out the baseless charges against me. No Christian, justified through faith in Christ, should ever face the thought of the final judgment with that anxiety.

Third, as Jesus describes the final judgment in Matthew 25:32, the nations are gathered before his throne, but "he will separate . . . the sheep from the goats." This indicates that after the resurrection of all people, the righteous will be pulled out of the judgment in order to receive praise and rewards from Christ instead. Jesus will say to his people, "Come, you who are blessed by my Father, inherit the kingdom prepared for you from the foundation of the world" (Matt. 25:34). Moreover, with our sins forgiven through his blood, our good deeds will then be rewarded with the praise of our dear Savior and Lord (25:35–40). This is the meaning of Paul's statement that believers must appear before Christ and the reason that we should be zealous in our living. It is for this reason that Christians are taught to look forward to the return of Christ and the final judgment. Not only the guilt but also the shame of our sin was fully borne by Jesus on the cross. We will face not judgment but our coronation as joint heirs together with Christ in blessing.

Yet how dreadful is *the punishment of the final judgment* for those whose names are not written in the Lamb's Book of Life and who are judged for their sins. John writes: "And if anyone's name was not found written in the book of life, he was thrown into the lake of fire" (Rev. 20:15). This statement makes it clear that no one will ever be saved by his or her own works. The reason was stated by the apostle Paul: "None is righteous, no, not one; . . . for all have sinned and fall short of the glory of God" (Rom. 3:10, 23). Since all are sinners, none can be justified by their works before God. Salvation comes only through faith in Jesus, by grace, according to the Lamb's Book of Life. Bruce Milne writes: "We are shut up to one way of salvation and one alone. . . . It is Christ or eternal condemnation."[12]

THE WARNING OF FINAL JUDGMENT

John's vision of the final judgment concludes with God's ultimate victory—a triumph over even hell and death themselves: "Then Death and Hades were thrown into the lake of fire. This is the second death, the lake of fire" (Rev. 20:14). Death was the curse brought by sin into God's perfect creation. In order for Christ to bring the "new heaven and a new earth" of eternal glory (21:1), then he must put an end to the curse of death, along with Hades, the abode of the condemned. Paul wrote, "The last enemy to be destroyed is death" (1 Cor. 15:26). John depicts death and Hades as being thrown into the lake of fire, where Satan and his beasts were cast for eternal torment (Rev. 20:10). This "represents the final and unalterable victory of the triune God," in which his ultimate enemies "are overcome and subjected to his just wrath, and their threat to God's endless glory and reign is finally and eternally brought to an end."[13] Because of this victory, the final judgment is a day of rejoicing for the holy angels together with God's redeemed people. For then it will be truly declared by the exultant voices of heaven: "The kingdom of the world has become the kingdom of our Lord and of his Christ, and he shall reign forever and ever" (11:15).

But how bitter will be the judgment of sinners consigned to the lake of fire to "be tormented day and night forever and ever" (Rev. 20:10). "This is the second death," John says (20:14), not only the eternal death of the body

12. Milne, *The Message of Heaven and Hell*, 301.
13. Ibid., 298.

but the experience of death's darkness by the soul forever and ever. Henry Alford writes: "As there is a second and higher life, so there is also a second and deeper death."[14]

How tragic will be this end in the case of those who heard *the warning of the final judgment* but refused the gospel message of forgiveness in Christ! Was it because of pride that they would not confess their sin or bend the knee to Jesus? In repayment, they will feel the penalty of those sins forever while being forced to acknowledge in hell that "Jesus Christ is Lord, to the glory of God the Father" (Phil. 2:11). Was it through worldly wisdom that they rejected the pleas of the gospel of God's gracious love? Paul wrote: "For the word of the cross is folly to those who are perishing, but to us who are being saved it is the power of God" (1 Cor. 1:18).

If you visit medieval cathedrals, you will often see a semicircular carving over the front door that in Latin is called the *tympanum*. The carving portrays the last judgment, with Christ enthroned, the redeemed on his right, and the condemned on his left. When the people entered those doors every Sunday, they were being reminded of the same truth that Revelation sets before us in this vision of the last judgment: there are but two destinies in this world—heaven and hell—and those destinies are determined by our response to the gospel that is preached in the church, proclaiming God's judgment on sin and God's mercy to sinners who believe on Jesus Christ.[15]

Adoniram Judson faced those competing destinies as he listened to the death agonies of the man who had glibly encouraged him not to fear the judgment of God. Awakening to his peril, he turned back to the Bible and was saved through faith in Jesus. In John's vision of the final judgment, the Word of God warns you of judgment for sin and offers salvation through Jesus Christ. If you believe, you will be able to know that God placed your name in his Book of Life before all eternity and that the final judgment is for you a day of glory. Then, realizing how great is the need of sinners to be saved, you, like Adoniram Judson, must surely tell others the gospel message of the Lamb who was slain.

---

14. Henry Alford, *The Greek Testament*, 4 vols. (Cambridge: Deighton, Bell, and Co., 1866), 4:735.
15. Taken from Kelly, *Revelation*, 391.

56

A New Heaven and
a New Earth

Revelation 21:1–4

> *Then I saw a new heaven and a new earth, for the first heaven*
> *and the first earth had passed away, and the sea was no more.*
> (Rev. 21:1)

One of the top movies in 2012 was the film adaptation of J. R. R. Tolkien's *The Hobbit*. *The Hobbit* tells of a group of warrior dwarves whose home was lost to the assault of a terrible dragon. Once their mountain kingdom had been the wonder of the world and their wealth had seemed unending. They dwelt in the splendor of gold and jewels. But now their paradise had been lost, and they were forced to wander the world in poverty and shame. This presents an analogy to the state of our entire race since the fall of Adam and our expulsion from the garden of Eden.

Early in the movie there is a conversation between the dwarf leader, Thorin Oakenshield, and his uncle, a sage dwarf named Balin. The older dwarf argues the futility of Thorin's plan to return to the mountain kingdom and regain his throne. Balin says, "What are we? Merchants, miners, tinkers, toy-makers. Hardly the stuff of legend." So it is for mankind after the fall. We look back in Genesis to the glory of our creation in the image of God. Once we dwelt in the garden Paradise and walked with God "in the cool of the day" (Gen. 3:8). But like the dragon that swept upon the dwarven mountain, sin made a ruin of our once-glorious condition, leaving us adrift in the dust of the world. What are we? we ask. Businessmen, teachers, plumbers, and bakers. Hardly the stuff of glory. Christians look back on a Paradise lost, wondering if we can ever return.

Has the fall cut us off eternally from our original destiny, so that getting by in this life is the best we can do? The book of Revelation answers by directing our gaze both backward to the cross, where Jesus freed us by his blood from the penalty of our sin (Rev. 1:5), and forward to the return of Christ and the new heaven and new earth that he brings. In this way, the last book of the Bible answers the plight of the Bible's first book. The garden that was lost in the beginning is replaced at the end with "the holy city, new Jerusalem" (21:2). As John describes this coming new reality, he presents a future in which the chief banes of man's fallen condition have been removed: our evil spiritual enemies are no more, God's people are no more condemned by sin, and life is no longer made miserable by the specter of futility and death. With the effects of the fall reversed, God's original covenant aim is achieved: "Behold, the dwelling place of God is with man. He will dwell with them, and they will be his people, and God himself will be with them as their God" (21:3).

REPLACED OR RENEWED?

The opening statement of Revelation 21:1 provides some of the greatest encouragement that Christians could ever receive: "Then I saw a new heaven and a new earth, for the first heaven and the first earth had passed away." The Bible states that when Christ returns, the "heaven and [the] earth," which is a way of referring to both the physical universe and the spiritual world order, will be cleansed and renewed in glory. We are reminded by this that the Bible places the final destiny of God's people not in an ephemeral, wispy heaven but on a redeemed earth, where God's creation beginning comes to a glorious eternal end.

The New Testament contains abundant evidence concerning the cosmic transformation that takes place after Jesus' second coming. Revelation 20 showed the removal of Satan, his followers, and even death and Hades, which were all thrown into the lake of fire (Rev. 20:10, 14). With all his enemies thus finally defeated and forever put away, the victorious Christ advances to the crowning fulfillment of his work in the renovation of the entire cosmos. Paul anticipated this coming achievement in soaring terms of liberation: "The creation itself will be set free from its bondage to corruption and obtain the freedom of the glory of the children of God" (Rom. 8:21).

Some Christians teach a doctrine in which the present universe is consumed and replaced by a new one, largely on the basis of Peter's second epistle. Peter said that just as the world of Noah was destroyed by a flood, when Jesus returns "the heavens will pass away with a roar, and the heavenly bodies will be burned up and dissolved, and the earth and the works that are done on it will be exposed" (2 Peter 3:10). On the basis of this language, some Christians teach the eradication of this present world and its replacement with a new one.

A better understanding is that of the cleansing and renewal of the cosmos after Christ returns. Instead of making "all new things," Christ makes "all things new" (Rev. 21:5). In Matthew 19:28, Jesus spoke of "the new world" after he returns. In Greek, the word is *palingenesia*, that is, "regeneration," suggesting an analogy between the spiritual rebirth of believers in coming to Jesus and the transformation of heaven and earth after Jesus returns. The contrary idea, that Christ eliminates the original creation because of sin, holds alarming implications. Under this view, Satan would have succeeded in overthrowing the glorious work of God recorded in Genesis 1. Moreover, if God eradicates the present heavens and earth, then, as Cornel Venema writes, "we would have to conclude that the Triune God's redemptive work discards rather than renews all things."[1]

If Christ's return renews rather than replaces the universe, how do we understand Peter's statement that "the heavens will pass away" and "the heavenly bodies will be burned up and dissolved" (2 Peter 3:10)? The answer is seen in Peter's analogy with the destruction of the flood in Noah's time. The great flood did not destroy the world itself but rather removed sinners in judgment and cleansed the world of corruption. Just as Noah departed the ark into a renewed version of the old world, with sin swept away, Christ will usher his church into a creation that has been pristinely cleansed and

1. Cornelis P. Venema, *The Promise of the Future* (Edinburgh: Banner of Truth, 2000), 461.

made glorious. As Venema writes: "Once more, but now in a surpassing way, the creation will be a temple fit for the dwelling of God with his people."[2]

No More Sea

Revelation 21:1 adds a provocative statement that sums up the removal of all evil: "and the sea was no more." In the symbolism of Revelation, the sea has a theological rather than topographical meaning. The sea is the realm of evil and rebellion against God. Psalm 74 described salvation as God's breaking the head of "the sea monsters" and crushing "Leviathan," the great mythical sea beast that represents idolatrous opposition to God (Ps. 74:12–14). James Hamilton writes that for the Israelites, the sea was "the great dark unknown from which evil comes."[3] This provides the answer to the question: what is the shortest book in all history? The answer is *Naval Heroes of Ancient Israel*. There are no naval heroes in Israel! The reason is that God's covenant people avoided the sea as a source of chaos and destruction. In Revelation 12:17, Satan "stood on the sand of the sea," and then raised up his beast "out of the sea" (Rev. 13:1). In chapters 17–20, John was shown the removal of the dragon, his beasts, and the harlot, together with their entire wicked program. Finally, even the sea from which they came will be no more.

How wrong it therefore is for Christians to say, "We are destined to sin just like everyone else. We are hardly the stuff of legend." But we are future heirs of a sinless glory! Yes, we live now east of Eden in a wilderness of sin. But we are destined for a world in which the sea is no more. On this basis, Paul urged the Ephesians never to partner with the agents of evil. He explained: "For at one time you were darkness, but now you are light in the Lord." We are the stuff of biblical destiny! Therefore, Paul urged, "Walk as children of light" (Eph. 5:8). Do not give in to temptation or compromise with the evils of this wicked age. Christians are to anticipate now the renewed creation, where there will be no evil, no transgression, and not even the temptation to sin. Hebrews 6:5 says that believers in Christ "have tasted . . . the powers of the age to come."

2. Ibid. 460.
3. James M. Hamilton Jr., *Revelation: The Spirit Speaks to the Churches* (Wheaton, IL: Crossway, 2012), 383.

NO MORE CORRUPTION

The second feature of the new creation ushered in by Christ's return is a vision of the church as we will then be: "And I saw the holy city, new Jerusalem, coming down out of heaven from God" (Rev. 21:2). Isaiah had foreseen a redeemed Jerusalem that is made righteous by God's coming and that receives a new name reflecting a marriage relationship of love with God (Isa. 62:2–5). John sees this promise fulfilled not in Jesus' first appearing but in the second coming of Christ. Jerusalem was the earthly center of God's redeeming acts in history, especially in the atoning death of his Son. Therefore, just as creation is glorified in the new heaven and new earth, redemption comes to glorious consummation in the coming of the new Jerusalem.

The first characteristic of God's city is its *holiness*: "the holy city." Bruce Milne writes that this "reflects not simply—and negatively—the absence of sin and evil in all their forms, but the glorious positiveness of the outshining majesty of God in his resplendent otherness. . . . Because the city is the dwelling place of such a God, it cannot be other than a holy place."[4] When believers come to faith in Christ, they are spiritually renewed for the sake of this destination. By calling the new Jerusalem "the holy city," John identifies the chief characteristic and calling that is to define Christians and the church today. The Bible highlights the church not as "the affluent city," "the culturally progressive city," or "the entertaining city," but as "the holy city."

Second, God's people are a *community*. A city is defined not primarily by streets and buildings, but by its people. Eternity therefore consists not of a solitary pursuit of the beatific vision but of a corporate experience of God's glory. Hebrews 12:23 identified the heavenly Jerusalem as "the assembly of the firstborn[,] . . . the spirits of the righteous made perfect." This city now comes down to earth in renewed and glorified form. Just as God's own being involves the community of the Trinity, so the new Jerusalem involves a fellowship not merely of saints with God but of saints together with God.

Third, God's city is marked by his *sovereign grace*. When John says that the new Jerusalem is "coming down out of heaven from God" (Rev. 21:2), he means that God's activity results in his people's attaining to this place in

4. Bruce Milne, *The Message of Heaven and Hell*, The Bible Speaks Today (Downers Grove, IL: InterVarsity Press, 2002), 311.

eternal glory. The church was chosen, justified, adopted, and sanctified, and will finally be glorified by God's sovereign grace. For this reason, believers in Jesus can be certain of this glorious destiny: Peter promises "an inheritance that is imperishable, undefiled, and unfading, kept in heaven for you, . . . a salvation ready to be revealed in the last time" (1 Peter 1:4–5). For the same reason, the glory of the new Jerusalem belongs exclusively to God, reflecting on his people who are eternal mirrors of his grace.

Fourth, the new Jerusalem is marked by *loving intimacy*, since she is "prepared as a bride adorned for her husband" (Rev. 21:2). This love is enjoyed by Christians together with our Lord, the triumphant Jesus Christ. Many Christians struggle with the idea that earthly marriages, which are designed to foster our closest intimacy in this life, will end when we are separated by death and enter into glory (see Luke 20:34–36). But believers will suffer no loss in the eternal city. For just as earthly fathers are designed to hold in our hearts a place that God the Father will perfectly fill, so also God blesses us with marital intimacy now in order to ready our hearts for loving intimacy with Christ as his bride forever. Milne writes, "The experience of heaven is the bliss of being utterly and eternally loved."[5] As Paul wrote in his famous chapter on love, "then I shall know fully, even as I have been fully known" (1 Cor. 13:12).

Revelation 20:1 showed a new heaven and new earth, a regenerated creation in which all of Christ's enemies are removed. In the new Jerusalem, we see God's renewed people no longer condemned by sin. The flood cleansed the world until Noah and his family got out of the ark. Their entry brought a return of sin to the world (Gen. 9:18–25). It will not be so in the new heaven and new earth. Believers are qualified to enter eternal loving intimacy with God's Son because we are cleansed of our sin by his blood and justified in the garment of his imputed righteousness. This is why John says that the church is "prepared as a bride adorned for her husband" (Rev. 21:2). By the atoning sacrifice in his blood, Jesus has forever removed our sin, gaining forgiveness before God for all who believe. We have, Paul taught, "redemption through his blood, the forgiveness of our trespasses, according to the riches of his grace" (Eph. 1:7). So perfect is Christ's preparation of his bride that John sees the fulfillment of Isaiah's prophecy: "As the bridegroom rejoices over the bride, so shall your God rejoice over you" (Isa. 62:5).

5. Ibid., 312.

Here, too, Christians are reminded of their destiny as an incentive to loving zeal for Jesus now. The voice of Balin may tell us that we are "hardly the stuff of glory," but Revelation says that we are destined together to be the resplendent bride of God the Son, having been cleansed and glorified for the sake of his love. Realizing this, we are to live our present like a bride preparing for her wedding day, pursuing in faith the beauty of the holiness that our Savior loves. Indeed, Christ is now laboring "that he might sanctify her, having cleansed her by the washing of water with the word, so that he might present the church to himself in splendor, without spot or wrinkle or any such thing, that she might be holy and without blemish" (Eph. 5:26–27).

No More Death or Tears

Our present fallen world suffers the tyranny of Christ's enemies, so that we now live in a spiritual wasteland of corruption and temptation. To make matters worse, we have the calamity of our own sinful nature. A third evil of our present age is seen in the consequences of sin in terms of the ravages of grief and sorrow. Revelation 21:1–2 saw the sea and all evil removed from our future environment and God's people cleansed and adorned for glory. Now the life of the age to come is made new, with no more misery under the cursed reign of sin and death. John writes: "He will wipe away every tear from their eyes, and death shall be no more, neither shall there be mourning, nor crying, nor pain anymore, for the former things have passed away" (Rev. 21:4).

I am getting to be old enough that death is more a part of my life than it used to be. Both of my parents have died, and I deeply feel their loss. More than a few people around my age are suffering death, reminding me of my own mortality. Not long ago I was driving to a meeting in Philadelphia, and on the way I drove up the street where my wife and I had bought our first house when our children were little. There was the park with the big green turtle they played on. There was the driveway where they rode tricycles. It brought tears to my eyes, because those days are gone. I realize more than ever that the sweet things of today will soon have slipped away. This is true for the whole of our experience. Time and death stalk all who live in this present world. But the age to come will know no death, nor sorrow, nor tears, nor pain anymore.

A favorite verse for Christian funerals is Psalm 116:9: "I will walk before the LORD in the land of the living." It is pointed out that we currently inhabit the land of the dying—the land of the living is the heaven to which our beloved departed have gone. The sorrows of this life put tears on our cheeks and pain in our hearts. But when Christ returns, those who are joined to him by faith will experience the fullness of eternal life. George Eldon Ladd writes: "Tears here represent all human sorrow, tragedy, and evil. Accompanying the glorious vision of God will be a transformed mode of existence in which the sorrows and evils of existence in the old order are left far behind."[6] Isaiah foresaw that "the ransomed of the LORD shall return and come to Zion with singing; everlasting joy shall be upon their heads; they shall obtain gladness and joy, and sorrow and sighing shall flee away" (Isa. 35:10).

Most lovely of all, it will be God's own hand that wipes away our tears. The imagery of Revelation 21:4 poignantly has us entering into glory with the tears of our sorrowful lives still upon our cheeks. What image can more fully express the sheer pain of life in this fallen world! But our loving heavenly Father greets us, wiping the last tears we will ever shed from our faces, and bidding us to weep no more forever and ever. Indeed, in Revelation 21:4, God's hand reaches to us even now, gathering up our tears and showing us a time soon to come when Christ has returned and grief will be no more. Encouraged by his grace, we face the sorrows of this life with courage, heartened in our pilgrimage toward the promised land ahead.

DWELLING FOREVER WITH GOD

So far, Revelation's picture of the new creation has been primarily by way of negation: there will be no sea, no stain of sin, and no more weeping or sorrow. At the heart of the passage, however, is the great positive blessing awaiting Christ's people: "And I heard a loud voice from the throne saying, 'Behold, the dwelling place of God is with man. He will dwell with them, and they will be his people, and God himself will be with them as their God'" (Rev. 21:3). William Hendriksen describes this as "the climax of that entire process whereby God comes to His people. So close is this eternal

6. George Eldon Ladd, *A Commentary on the Revelation of John* (Grand Rapids: Eerdmans, 1972), 277.

communion between God and His elect that He, as it were, dwells with them in one tent—His tent, the glory of His attributes."[7]

The voice speaking from God's throne literally says, "The tabernacle of God is with men and he will tabernacle with them." This fulfills the promise given in Ezekiel 37:26–27, looking ahead to the time when God's Spirit came through the new and everlasting covenant in Christ: "I will . . . set my sanctuary in their midst forevermore. My dwelling place shall be with them, and I will be their God, and they shall be my people." Simon Kistemaker calls this promise "a golden thread woven into the fabric of Scripture from beginning to end."[8] God made this promise to Abraham: "an everlasting covenant, to be God to you and to your offspring after you" (Gen. 17:7). This was God's purpose in the founding of Israel: "I will take you to be my people, and I will be your God" (Ex. 6:7). When God had Moses construct the tabernacle in the desert, God said, "I will make my dwelling among you . . . . And I will walk among you and will be your God, and you shall be my people" (Lev. 26:11–12). Jesus fulfilled this promise in part by his incarnation: "And the Word became flesh and dwelt among us, and we have seen his glory" (John 1:14).

Christians enjoy greater privileges than God's people knew in the Old Testament. Then, only Moses and the high priests could enter God's tabernacle and see his glory, whereas now God's glory tabernacles in the heart of every believer through the Holy Spirit (2 Cor. 3:18). But in the age to come, the longing of every spirit to know God and see his face will be perfectly fulfilled. The communion that God has eternally purposed to enjoy with his people will be achieved.

Here is the longing of Abraham fulfilled, when he looked forward to "the city that has foundations, whose designer and builder is God" (Heb. 11:10). In this respect, it is noteworthy that where the English translations of Revelation 21:3 say that "they will be his people," the Greek text is plural: "they will be his peoples." God told Abraham that "in you all the families of the earth shall be blessed" (Gen. 12:3). As Abraham's faith directs us to Christ and the gospel is preached to all nations, every tribe and tongue is gathered for the possession of God.

7. William Hendriksen, *More than Conquerors: An Interpretation of the Book of Revelation* (1940; repr., Grand Rapids: Baker, 1967), 199.
8. Simon J. Kistemaker, *Revelation*, New Testament Commentary (Grand Rapids: Baker, 2001), 557.

Here, too, is the final realization of the Aaronic blessing: "The LORD bless you and keep you; the LORD make his face to shine upon you and be gracious to you; the LORD lift up his countenance upon you and give you peace" (Num. 6:24–26). Venema writes that when Christ's redeeming work is fully completed, the life to come "will consist in finding joy in God, living before his face. . . . Believers will stand unbowed before God, confident again in his presence that they are acceptable to him. The smile of God's countenance will shine upon the glorified members of Christ throughout all eternity."[9]

OUR BLESSED HOPE

It has been said that those who forget the lessons of history are doomed to repeat it. The converse is true when it comes to the Bible's revelation of the future. Without this vision of the new heaven and the new earth, we will live without the hope Christ offers, without the purpose he supplies, and without the glory he promises.

In *The Hobbit* movie, Balin tells Prince Thorin, "What are we? Hardly the stuff of legend." Don't let anyone say such things to you! The Bible teaches that you are children of God, coheirs with Christ for eternal glory, and the people in whom God himself will dwell and on whose faces the light of his glory will shine. How can this be? Because Christ has come to conquer sin and Christ is coming back to bring the fullness of salvation.

A holy city. A beautiful bride. A tearless everlasting life. A loving, Divine Savior who awaits the consummation of our love. Who will be there? All who confess their sins, trust in the blood of Christ, and believe in the gospel of his salvation. What now are we to do? Paul answered in terms of what God's grace has taught us:

> to renounce ungodliness and worldly passions, and to live self-controlled, upright, and godly lives in the present age, waiting for our blessed hope, the appearing of the glory of our great God and Savior Jesus Christ, who gave himself for us to redeem us from all lawlessness and to purify for himself a people for his own possession who are zealous for good works. (Titus 2:12–14)

9. Venema, *The Promise of the Future*, 482–83.

57

ALL THINGS NEW

Revelation 21:5–8

And he who was seated on the throne said, "Behold, I am making all things new." Also he said, "Write this down, for these words are trustworthy and true." (Rev. 21:5)

*I*n Revelation 21:5–8, the apostle John's long tour of church history brings him finally to the end of the world. Previous visions have brought us to the brink of the end. But the sixth cycle of visions, starting in chapter 17, has seen the judgment and removal of all of Christ's enemies. The great harlot Babylon has fallen. The beast and false prophet have gone into the lake of fire. Satan the dragon has also been cast into the fiery lake, together with even death and Hades. The sea itself—the symbolic source of chaos and evil—is no more. Now the end of history has been reached in the final verses of the sixth section of Revelation (six being the number of fallen mankind). And here, at the end, John and his readers face God himself: "And he who was seated on the throne said" (Rev. 21:5).

On only two occasions in the book of Revelation does God himself speak directly. The first occasion was at the beginning: "'I am the Alpha and the Omega,' says the Lord God, 'who is and who was and who is to come, the Almighty'" (Rev. 1:8). Now, at the end of history, we face God himself once more. In this way, Revelation makes a vital point: every living soul must deal with God. All through life we may follow the distractions that keep us from reckoning with God, but in the end we must all face him. Have you stood before God? Are you afraid to think of God, to realize that God sees you and knows you? Are you afraid to speak directly to him? Because we must all face God, we have no greater need than to know him. Revelation 21:5–8 shows God as he is and as he will be at the end of the world: a God of truth, a God of life, and a God of justice. We see him taking delight in his victory over all things, declaring his final purpose: "Behold, I am making all things new" (21:5).

THE GOD OF TRUTH

The truth of John's message was of vital importance to his first-century readers. Throughout Revelation they are exhorted to overcome in the face of deadly opposition. Some would have to sacrifice their lives rather than deny Jesus and submit to the imperial cult. Antipas had already died in Pergamum, and John's visions have shown a mounting number of martyrs (Rev. 2:13; 6:9–11; 20:4). What a tragedy if they were to suffer such loss for a misunderstanding! Today, there are terrorists who kill themselves and others because they believe that Allah will reward them in paradise. What they die for is false. But how do the Christians know that their own cause, for which they are peacefully dying, is true?

The answer is seen as God speaks to John: "Write this down, for these words are trustworthy and true" (Rev. 21:5). Here, God himself bears witness to the truth of his Word. He is able to establish truth because, as Hebrews 6:18 asserts, "it is impossible for God to lie." God's nature demands that he be faithful to his promises. Paul writes: "He who calls you is faithful; he will surely do it" (1 Thess. 5:24). In writing down the words that God has given him, John is fulfilling his apostolic office. When Paul said that the church is "built on the foundation of the apostles and prophets" (Eph. 2:20), he meant that by writing down the New Testament, they secured for us the truths committed to them by God for us to believe.

Not only was God speaking to John when he appeared in this vision on the Isle of Patmos, but God speaks to us now as this same Word is read and preached. Ultimately, it is by the Word itself that we know the truth of the Bible, as God speaks directly to us just as he did to John. Westminster Confession of Faith 1.5 notes that there are many reasons to receive the Bible as true. These include "the heavenliness of the matter, the efficacy of the doctrine, the majesty of the style, the consent of all the parts, . . . [and] the full discovery it makes of the only way of man's salvation," together with "many other incomparable excellencies" by which the Bible commends itself to us as the revealed truth of God. "Yet notwithstanding," the confession adds, "our full persuasion and assurance of the infallible truth and divine authority thereof, is from the inward work of the Holy Spirit bearing witness by and with the Word in our hearts." God reveals the truth of his Word by his Word as the Spirit applies it to our hearts. John writes in Revelation 21:5, "He who was seated on the throne said," and by his declaration that "these words are trustworthy and true," his people know and recognize the truth of God's Word. This is why John needed to write the book of Revelation, so that the persecuted believers of his day would receive God's truth by God's Word just as tempted believers today need the same. James Hamilton explains: "When we believe the Bible to be God's Word, we are believing what it tells us about itself," and then in our hearts "the Holy Spirit bears witness that these things are so and confirms the Bible's claims."[1]

Not only does God declare the truth of his Word by his own direct assertion, but he declares that the events foretold in Revelation are already fully established: "And he said to me, 'It is done!'" (Rev. 21:6). God is standing at the end of history, speaking to John in the midst of history to declare a future that is already certain. The Greek word is a perfect tense of the verb *to happen*, meaning "it has happened." Moreover, it is a plural verb (*gegonan*), so that it should be read "everything has happened," referring to all that is revealed in Revelation, including both judgment and salvation. George Eldon Ladd writes: "Contrary to the confusing and chaotic picture presented to man in his human experiences, the purposes of God in redemption are as certain as though they have already taken place. The future is not uncertain to those who trust God."[2] People say that the only certain things are death and taxes. But believers know that everything promised in God's Word is absolutely certain and worthy of our faith.

---

1. James M. Hamilton Jr., *Revelation: The Spirit Speaks to the Churches* (Wheaton, IL: Crossway, 2012), 386.

2. George Eldon Ladd, *A Commentary on the Revelation of John* (Grand Rapids: Eerdmans, 1972), 278.

We may note a relationship between God's assertion here, "It is done!" (Rev. 21:6), and earlier statements in John's writing. Most famous is Jesus' cry, "It is finished" (John 19:30), when he had made atonement for sin and was about to die on the cross. We note as well the cry of the angel, "It is done!" (Rev. 16:17), when he had poured out the seventh bowl of wrath. Jesus' cry on the cross marked the end of sin's guilt, and the angel with the seventh bowl marked the end of sin's reign. Grant Osborne writes: "Finally, God here says, 'They are over,' meaning that all the events of world history—including the world's destruction and inauguration of the final new age—are at an end."[3] Christ's death achieved the *ground* of salvation, the judgment of sin provided the *context* for salvation, and now God declares the *arrival* of salvation, having stated, "Behold, I am making all things new" (Rev. 21:5).

In addition to declaring the truth of his Word and the accomplished reality of his promises, God declares to John, "I am the Alpha and the Omega, the beginning and the end" (Rev. 21:6). *Alpha* is the first letter of the Greek alphabet, and *omega* is the last. By calling himself "the Alpha and the Omega," God speaks of his eternal being: he is the Creator who brought all things into existence, and he is the Judge who brings all things to their final end. The point is God's sovereignty over all things: he can ensure the end because he was Lord at the beginning and remains sovereign through every moment of history. As the Alpha and the Omega of history, God rules absolutely over all things in between.

God's sovereignty provides another reason to be certain of the truth of his Word. God told Jeremiah, "I am watching over my word to perform it" (Jer. 1:12). Robert Thomas writes: "His sovereign control over everything and His eternal nature guarantee His complete trustworthiness and the faithfulness and truthfulness of the words He has spoken. He is the unchangeable One by whom the old was and the new shall be."[4]

Like most other pastors, I am usually stationed in the church narthex after the service to greet those who have come. Kind people will often express their appreciation, saying that it was a good sermon. I like to respond not only by thanking them but by stating, "And it is true!" The preacher can declare the truth of his sermon only when he has faithfully preached God's

---

3. Grant R. Osborne, *Revelation*, Baker Exegetical Commentary on the New Testament (Grand Rapids: Baker Academic, 2002), 738.

4. Robert L. Thomas, *Revelation 8–22: An Exegetical Commentary* (Chicago: Moody, 1995), 448.

Word. Knowing the truth of God's Word is essential, since we are trusting it to reveal the way of salvation and eternal life. Knowing God's trustworthy and eternal nature and his sovereign control over all things, Christians who are called to suffer for their faith are comforted with the certain knowledge that they will not have believed in vain.

THE GOD OF LIFE

The God who stands at the end of the world is not only the speaker of truth but also the giver of life. He declares: "Behold, I am making all things new" (Rev. 21:5).

History records one failed human scheme after another to make a new world. Man has sought his own utopia through education, legislation, peace programs, and skillfully engineered environments. All of these fail because of the corruption of sin that has permeated all of life after the fall. God alone can truly renew because of the Spirit that he sends. He is doing this work now in the hearts of those who believe in Jesus. This is why Paul wrote: "If anyone is in Christ, he is a new creation. The old has passed away; behold, the new has come" (2 Cor. 5:17). The old life under the domination of sin comes to an end through the new birth into faith in Christ, and a new life begins with power from God for purity, truth, and love. What God is doing now on a limited scale in his people he will extend to all things at the end. John may have in mind Isaiah 43:19, where God said through the prophet, "Behold, I am doing a new thing." Only now God adds the word *all*: "I am making all things new" (Rev. 21:5). Those who are justified in Christ so as to stand before God in the end will have the glorious experience of witnessing the renewal of the entire creation.

The great tragedy of the world is that lost sinners resent God and avoid him as much as possible. Men and women recoil at the idea of facing God and try as hard as they can to avoid even thinking about him. Yet the God they are fleeing is a merciful giver of life. God thus says to John, "To the thirsty I will give from the spring of the water of life without payment" (Rev. 21:6). This is God's message to you, if you have never turned to him in faith. He offers you a life that has its origin in the spring of his own eternal vitality and being.

We can imagine a dry and weary land where travelers are parched. In that land there is a springing fountain, with green foliage all around. If only they will come, the thirsty may drink of this living water. This is an apt metaphor for the life in which we live. Souls are unsatisfied, hearts are grieved, and countless lives are embittered. Perhaps you are wrestling with a great disappointment. Perhaps you have felt a gnawing worry that this is all there is. Perhaps you have been broken by tragedy, like a cistern that has been emptied of water. God offers you water that restores life, satisfies the heart, and comforts those who are aggrieved. Jesus used this metaphor to speak of the Holy Spirit of God: "If anyone thirsts, let him come to me and drink. Whoever believes in me, . . . 'Out of his heart will flow rivers of living water'" (John 7:37–38). John explained, "Now this he said about the Spirit" (7:39). This image describes the experience of those who have turned to God through faith in Jesus Christ. J. C. Ryle writes:

> The saints of God in every age have been men and women who drank of this fountain by faith and were relieved. They felt their guilt and emptiness, and thirsted for deliverance. They heard of a full supply of pardon, mercy, and grace in Christ crucified for all penitent believers. They believed the good news and acted upon it.[5]

God offers through his Son everything that the soul needs in order to have eternal life: mercy, grace, pardon, peace, and strength from above. A man who owned the only refreshing spring in a dry wasteland would charge a fortune to allow others to drink. But God in his love "will give from the spring of the water of life without payment" (Rev. 21:6). God offers you eternal life as a free gift because of the grace of his generous heart.

This raises a vital question: what kind of person is welcomed by God to this spring of the water of life? Is there some quest to embark on? Must we accumulate a certain number of good deeds? Can a check written out to the church gain us entrance? Is there some ritual to perform? God tells John, "To the thirsty I will give" (Rev. 21:6). This is the sole requirement: to thirst for God and the spiritual life that he has to give. We come to God not with our feet but with our faith—with our hearts opened in need of his saving grace.

Having thirsted, we simply drink. Just as we dip into a fountain with a cup, our faith receives the gift of God's grace in Christ and we take it into our souls. Coming to God means receiving Jesus, the Son he sent to be the

---

5. J. C. Ryle, *Expository Thoughts on John*, 2 vols. (1869; repr., Edinburgh: Banner of Truth, 1999), 2:46.

only Savior of the world, and trusting ourselves to his care. It means bringing our sins to the cross, where Jesus' blood was shed for our forgiveness. It means walking with him in faith, our thirsty souls drinking daily from his Word, which is itself a spring of life (Ps. 1:3), receiving peace and purity and power from God.

The marvel is that the spring that God provides both satisfies our thirst and awakens in us deeper thirsts for more. The new world that God brings in the end will provide the fulfillment of our deepest longings, but at the same time our experience of God's glory will create still deeper longings so that our thirst is being eternally satisfied more and more. Bruce Milne thus writes, "To know God and to thirst to know him more and more is the paradox of heaven."[6] Bernard of Clairvaux captured the biblical idea of eternal blessing:

> We drink of thee, the Fountainhead,
> And thirst our souls from thee to fill.[7]

God's offer to provide salvation like a spring of water speaks to the experience of life that he offers the thirsty through Jesus. But he adds another aspect of life when he speaks of the relationship that the faithful will fully enter into at the end: "The one who conquers will have this heritage, and I will be his God and he will be my son" (Rev. 21:7).

The citizens of God's eternal city enjoy the privilege of knowing the true and living God as their own Father. Fathers are close to the hearts of their children and delight in their company. While earthly fathers often fail, Christians have a perfect heavenly Father who has gone to infinite lengths so as to spend eternity giving himself to his children. The longing of every child's heart is to know his or her Father and be sure of the Father's blessing and love. This experience of rich, deep, and growing love will be the inheritance of all who come to God now as children through faith in Jesus Christ.

Scholars note that John does not name God here as Father, though believers are named as sons. Some argue that this emphasizes Jesus' unique relationship to God as his natural Father. If this is true, however, this same relationship is enjoyed by Christians, since through the eternal Son we are

---

6. Bruce Milne, *The Message of Heaven and Hell: Grace and Destiny*, The Bible Speaks Today (Downers Grove, IL: InterVarsity Press, 2002), 315.

7. Bernard of Clairvaux, "Jesus, Thou Joy of Loving Hearts" (12th century).

received by God as adopted sons. Paul wrote, "For in Christ Jesus you are all sons of God, through faith" (Gal. 3:26). Included in this relationship is our status of heirs, since sons received the heritage of their fathers. Our heritage in eternity is to belong to God in the way that firstborn sons belong to the hearts of their loving earthly fathers (Heb. 12:23). God will be investing in us forever, even as he himself is the inheritance that we receive together with Jesus Christ (Rom. 8:17). Christians all have the foretaste of this heritage as we live now as God's children through faith. When God makes all things new, we will through the final resurrection "obtain the freedom of the glory of the children of God" (8:21).

If it is the thirsty who are invited to drink from God's living spring, it is "the one who conquers" who attains the heritage of eternal sonship with God (Rev. 21:7). Together, these two descriptions capture the beginning and the end of the Christian life. We first receive salvation by bringing our thirst to God in simple faith. But Christians then walk in that faith so as to persevere to the end. Some believers recoil from the idea that believers conquer. Some respond fearfully, knowing their weakness, forgetting that God is faithful to complete in us the good work he began in the day of our salvation (Phil. 1:6). Others respond with a false humility, considering it arrogant to speak of a conquering or triumphant life. They fail to realize, however, that believers overcome in the grace of Christ and not in their own strength, and for God's glory alone. Revelation 12:11 teaches that Christians conquer "by the blood of the Lamb and by the word of their testimony." This victory takes place in an active life of striving as we trust God and follow Christ. Derek Thomas concludes: "The guarantee of heaven for the redeemed does not lessen one whit the need for a diligent pursuit of holiness. Heaven is gained through perseverance and not apart from it."[8]

THE GOD OF JUSTICE

At the end of the world, God sits enthroned in truth and in the life that he gives. Those who have thirsted for salvation so as to drink from his grace and who have conquered in faith so as to be granted the status of sons will meet God there for an eternal experience of glory. Yet God was speaking to John while the apostle was still living on this earth. This means that a

8. Derek Thomas, *Let's Study Revelation* (Edinburgh: Banner of Truth, 2003), 175.

warning must accompany these soaring statements of grace. The God of truth and love must also be revealed as a God of justice who punishes all unforgiven sins. The Lord therefore concluded: "But as for the cowardly, the faithless, the detestable, as for murderers, the sexually immoral, sorcerers, idolaters, and all liars, their portion will be in the lake that burns with fire and sulfur, which is the second death" (Rev. 21:8). Those who thirst for sin and for the pleasures of the world, together with those who collaborate in the world's rebellion against God, will receive not the heritage of glory but the portion of condemnation reserved for all of God's spiritual enemies in hell.

The list given to John seems to have two groups, the first of which likely refers to those who had professed faith in Christ but abandoned their confession under worldly pressure or sinful enticement: "But as for the cowardly, the faithless, the detestable." The "cowardly" and "faithless" are not Christians who struggle with fear, but people who betray Christ under pressure. Such a person is the rootless one who Jesus said endures for a little while, but "when tribulation or persecution arises on account of the word, immediately he falls away" (Matt. 13:21). Such people do not lose their salvation but reveal by their faithlessness that they had never been saved (see 1 John 2:19). Christians should therefore approach trials with determination, realizing that they test us, both to prove the genuineness of our faith and to purify the faith by which we are saved (1 Peter 1:6–7).

Joined to the cowardly and faithless are "the detestable," which refers to those who imbibe the perverse practices of the harlot Babylon. This item may not seem to go with the previous two, until we realize that apostates very often become the most virulent haters of Christianity and promoters of the grossest sins. Those who betray Jesus do not abandon the gospel for nothing, but are generally like Paul's one-time colleague Demas, who was "in love with this present world" and so abandoned Christ (2 Tim. 4:10).

The remainder of the list involves sinners whose lives characterize the ungodliness of the world: "murderers, the sexually immoral, sorcerers, idolaters, and all liars" (Rev. 21:8). These are the kinds of sins that Jesus rebuked in the seven letters of Revelation, calling believers to purge them from their lives and fellowship. Jesus especially demanded a rejection of sexual immorality and idolatry (2:14, 20), although worldly violence, occult practices, and falsehood are also to have no place in the lives of those who are joined to Christ through faith.

This is not to say that Christians are people who have never committed such sins or that believers' lives are completely free from any such sins now. God is not telling John that anyone who has ever committed sexual immorality or who has lied is barred from eternal life. Christ came to redeem these very kinds of sinners (Mark 10:45; 1 Tim. 1:15), and the blood of Jesus, God's Son, cleanses believers from all their sins (1 John 1:7). The point is that those who are saved from such sins are called to renounce them in such a way that they cannot remain characteristic of a Christian's lifestyle. Yes, Christians have been guilty of all manner of sins, including some of the vile offenses mentioned here by God. But as Paul wrote in a similar passage, "you were washed, you were sanctified, you were justified in the name of the Lord Jesus Christ and by the Spirit of our God" (1 Cor. 6:11), so that if these sins belong to a Christian's past, they are not to belong to his or her future.

Since the God who is enthroned at the end of history is a God of justice, not all will enter into that glorious life. Not all will be saved in the end, but many will follow their rebellious life with an eternal portion "in the lake that burns with fire and sulfur, which is the second death" (Rev. 21:8). Just as believers will glorify God's truth and God's grace in eternal life, unbelieving sinners will glorify God's perfect justice in the eternal condemnation of hell.

YOUR MASTER PROCLAIM!

At the end of the world, God sits enthroned. Every human being will face him, and God's sovereign rule will be the arbiter of every person's eternal destiny. If God is the One who matters most in the end, then God also matters most now. For this reason, every person is called by God's Word to be reconciled to God through the forgiveness offered by Jesus (2 Cor. 5:20). It also means that the witness, worship, and prayers of believers have a decisive impact in history. Ben Witherington writes: "John is saying that faithful witness, faithful worship and faithful prayer can help change the world because they place matters in the hands of the only wise God who intends to work things out."[9]

Yet there is a single command that God gives to his servant in this passage: "Also he said, 'Write this down'" (Rev. 21:5). John was to write down God's

9. Ben Witherington III, *Revelation*, New Cambridge Bible Commentary (Cambridge: Cambridge University Press, 2003), 256.

message, recording the entire book of Revelation. This hails the Word of God as heaven's chief provision for mankind, by which sinners are warned of their future meeting with God and learn of his grace for salvation through faith in Jesus Christ.

As an author, I know that it is not enough for a book to be written. Every book also needs a publisher. Who will publish the book that God called John to write? Who will carry forth the message of God's truth, his gift of life, and his final judgment for sin? John's book was written to be published not by the booksellers in London or New York, but by the witness of the church and in the lives of Christians. This is the great need and calling of the believer today: to know God and publish abroad his message of truth, life, and justice. The enthroned God, speaking from history's end, called to John: "Write this down!" The apostle has done so, and now God's message is entrusted to his people. Charles Wesley thus urges us:

Ye servants of God, your Master proclaim,
And publish abroad his wonderful name;
The name, all victorious, of Jesus extol;
His kingdom is glorious and rules over all.

God ruleth on high, almighty to save;
And still he is nigh—his presence we have.
The great congregation his triumph shall sing,
Ascribing salvation to Jesus, our King.[10]

---

10. Charles Wesley, "Ye Servants of God, Your Master Proclaim" (1744).

PART 7

The Great Consummation and Eternal Glory

58

THE CITY WITH FOUNDATIONS

Revelation 21:9–14

And the wall of the city had twelve foundations, and on them
were the twelve names of the twelve apostles of the Lamb.
(Rev. 21:14)

One of the trite expressions we often read on bumper stickers or greeting cards says, "The Journey Is Better than the Destination." Many of us share this sentiment. Corporate heads look back fondly on the days of struggle when they were climbing the ladder. Parents of college students become misty-eyed over pictures of their children when they were little. How sad that this statement is often found to be true: the claim that the journey is better than the destination is a bitter indictment on life in this present world. When we achieve what we have long sought and arrived where we have long tried to go, we find in disappointment how little fulfillment and satisfaction there is in even the best things of this life.

One man who spent his whole life on the journey was Abraham, of the family of Terah, from Ur of the Chaldees, who lived about two thousand years before the birth of Christ. God came to Abraham with a call to follow him in faith to a land where he would be a stranger. There, God promised to make him a great nation and a blessing to all the families of the world (Gen.

12:1–3). These promises were never fulfilled during Abraham's life. Hebrews 11:9 summarizes: "By faith he went to live in the land of promise, as in a foreign land, living in tents with Isaac and Jacob, heirs with him of the same promise." Abraham persevered in faith, but not because he believed that the journey was better than the destination. Rather, he understood that his faith-sojourn was leading him to an eternal destination—not one of this world—that would satisfy his soul completely. Hebrews 11:10 explains: "For he was looking forward to the city that has foundations, whose designer and builder is God."

Abraham's journey was not completed in the book of Genesis, but at the end of the Bible in the book of Revelation. Here, all who follow in the footsteps of Abraham's faith, who are thus called the "sons of Abraham" (Gal. 3:7), see the destination of their journey as well. John writes that the Spirit carried him "to a great, high mountain, and showed [him] the holy city Jerusalem coming down out of heaven from God" (Rev. 21:10). With the faith of Abraham and the vision shown to John, we, too, may see "the city [with] foundations" and gain an eternal perspective on our lives as believers in Christ.

The Beautiful Bride

Revelation 21:9 begins the final of the seven visionary cycles in the book of Revelation and the last main section of the book. We see this in the angel's invitation, "Come" (Rev. 21:9). In Revelation 4:1, John was summoned into heaven to witness God's plan for the church age, beginning the cycles of visions from chapters 4 to 16. In Revelation 17:1, John was told, "Come," this time to witness the judgment and final destruction of Christ's enemies (Rev. 17:1–21:8). Now John is called to witness the bliss of Christ's people in the eternal glory.

John makes a point of stating that this summons came from "one of the seven angels who had the seven bowls full of the seven last plagues" (Rev. 21:9). G. B. Caird suggests that this assignment was a reward for the angels' prior faithfulness. "Perhaps," he writes, "John believed that the demolition squad had also an interest in the reconstruction for which they had cleared the ground."[1] From our perspective, this angel of wrath reminds us that the fulfillment of God's plan relies equally on God's work of judgment and of

1. G. B. Caird, *The Revelation of St. John the Divine* (San Francisco: Harper, 1966), 269.

salvation. Seeing this angel who earlier condemned the great prostitute (17:1) warns us that all history is summed up by the two women of Revelation: we must belong either to the harlot Babylon, doomed to perish for wantonness in this life, or to the bride of God's Son, blessed to enter into glory through a holiness that begins even now.

When the angel invites John to see the bride, he is looking ahead to the time when the sacred marriage between Christ and his church has taken place, leading to an eternity of loving intimacy and mutual sharing. The chief idea of marriage in this life is that of unity and oneness: as Genesis 2:24 stated, "they shall become one flesh." Correspondingly, the idea of Christ and his bride in the glory to come is that of spiritual oneness and mutual delight. The basis for this love is stated by the reference to Christ as the "Lamb." Jesus is referred to in this way seven times in this final section of Revelation, emphasizing that the union between Jesus and his people is based on his sacrificial death to remove the curse of our sins. The cross is sufficient not only to establish the beginning of the Christian life but to sustain our relationship with Jesus forever.

Believers learn from Revelation 21:9 not only what we will be but what we are now. Having come to Jesus in saving faith, we are cleansed by the blood of the Lamb so as to enter into his love. If you are a Christian, you are being prepared in the beauty of holiness so that the purifying of your character is a primary task of this life. But you are already betrothed to Christ, your eternal destiny in his love having been made certain by his sacrifice for you. You are fundamentally different from everyone who is not a Christian, and your lifestyle is to reflect this difference in holy obedience. Those cleansed by the Lamb are delivered from the judgment awaiting the harlot Babylon. Now, Simon Kistemaker writes, "as husband, the Lamb supplies his wife with everything she needs, honors her with great respect, and adorns her with attractive attire and exquisite accessories."[2]

The Radiant City

While John's vision begins with a reference to Christ's bride, the bulk of the passage describes the church as the holy city of God. These ideas may be joined to remind us that this vision of walls and gates describes the people

---

2. Simon J. Kistemaker, *Revelation*, New Testament Commentary (Grand Rapids: Baker, 2001), 563.

of Christ themselves. John was "carried . . . away in the Spirit to a great, high mountain" (Rev. 21:10), which he ascended spiritually, not physically, to see his own future together with the whole of the church.

The angel brings John to a high mountain where the eternal city is located. Isaiah foretold: "It shall come to pass in the latter days that the mountain of the house of the LORD shall be established as the highest of the mountains, and shall be lifted up above the hills; and all the nations shall flow to it" (Isa. 2:2). Looking ahead to this scene, Revelation 14:1 earlier revealed the Lamb standing on Mount Zion with the great host of his eternally blessed people (cf. Rev. 7:14–17). Three times in the Gospels we read that Jesus retreated to mountaintops to pray during times of difficulty (Matt. 14:23; Luke 6:12; 9:28). From Mount Sinai onward, mountains are associated with God's presence, so it was natural for Jesus to meet there with his Father, anticipating as well his future dwelling in eternal communion with his people on the high mount of God.

On this high mountain of eternity, John was shown "the holy city Jerusalem" (Rev. 21:10). Here we see the image, so often emphasized in Revelation, of God dwelling with his people to share his glory. God promised Abraham a vast multitude of spiritual offspring, as numerous as the stars in the desert sky, and a home in which they would dwell (Gen. 15:1–21). Now that promise is fulfilled in the holy city, true Jerusalem.

John sees the city "coming down out of heaven from God" (Rev. 21:10). He uses a present participle, "coming down," which suggests not merely that the city has come down from God but that "coming down from God" is "a permanent characteristic of the city," owing "its existence to the condescension of God and not to the building of men."[3] This city does not represent the achievement of man in finally erecting a self-glorying stairway to heaven. It is instead the culmination of God's working in redemptive history to bring about his loving eternal purpose. Its name, "Jerusalem," plainly identifies the city as the final result of his ancient working through the people of Israel and especially by the saving ministry of Christ for the sake of his covenant people.

John not only emphasizes that the city comes down as God's gracious gift but also highlights its special character: it is "the holy city" (Rev. 21:10). The purpose of this city is the fellowship of God with his people, and therefore it

3. Caird, *The Revelation of St. John the Divine*, 271.

is a holy place for holy ones. There are a couple of ways in which we should think of the people of this city as being holy. First, they have been separated by God out from the world to belong to and serve him. Second, they are people whose sins have been removed. The guilt of their sin was taken away by the Lamb when he died for them on the cross. The corruption of sin was removed from them when their souls entered heaven and when their bodies were resurrected in glory. Hebrews 12:22–23 speaks of the gathering of saints in heaven as "Mount Zion," "the city of the living God, the heavenly Jerusalem," which is inhabited by "the spirits of the righteous made perfect." This describes the souls of believers in heaven during this present age. In the coming age, that holy Jerusalem will have come down to earth forever, and its people not only will be free from sin but will partake of God's own holiness.

John describes this holiness by adding "having the glory of God" (Rev. 21:11). Moses possessed the glory of God shining from his face when he met the Lord in his tent (Ex. 34:30). Paul noted that Christians have this glory working inside them: "We all, . . . beholding the glory of the Lord, are being transformed into the same image from one degree of glory to another" (2 Cor. 3:18). John sees that in the end it is by perfecting the holy glory of his people that God completes his temple-building project for history. Bruce Milne writes: "To live in this city is to live continually in the presence of the unveiled glory of God."[4] This glory reflects not just from the body of God's people, as it did from Moses' face, but from their whole being as they fulfill mankind's original calling to bear the image of God for the display of his glory.

John compares the holiness and glory of God's city to a shining jewel: "its radiance like a most rare jewel, like a jasper, clear as crystal" (Rev. 21:11). We are not exactly sure about the identity of jewels called by ancient names, but the idea here is not so much of transparency as it is of a brilliant, sparkling gem. We should envision a diamond shining out in beautiful facets of light. Similarly, God's holy city, composed of his holy people, will reflect all his shining attributes in the perfection of their glory. Dennis Johnson summarizes: "The Lord of glory indwells his people and floods his new community with the beauty of his holiness."[5]

4. Bruce Milne, *The Message of Heaven and Hell: Grace and Destiny,* The Bible Speaks Today (Downers Grove, IL: InterVarsity Press, 2002), 317.

5. Dennis E. Johnson, *Triumph of the Lamb: A Commentary on Revelation* (Phillipsburg, NJ: P&R Publishing, 2001), 309.

We may wonder why John is shown this vision with its emphasis on the holiness and glory of God. The answer can only be that his readers were to coordinate their present lives in this world with their destination in the age to come. If our destiny is to dwell in a holy city in the light of God, to radiate the light of God's glory like a most radiant jewel, then this surely shapes our calling now. This is true of the church corporately. H. B. Swete wrote that the church is to shine as God's holy city in the whole of her witness to Christ: "her teaching, her sacraments, her whole corporate life—the light of tens of thousands of saintly lives."[6] Today, mass gatherings of Christians tend to emphasize the secular: worldly styles, worldly goals, and worldly methods; relying more on the splendor of the latest worldly technology than on the shining forth of God through his Word. In this world, holy churches may often seem small and insignificant, but they anticipate a great city in which all of God's people will be gathered in the end for the holy display of his glorious perfections.

What is true of the church corporately is true of Christians individually. If your destiny is to reflect the glory of God in holy beauty, then there should be a sacred quality about the entirety of your present life. Paul pointed out that Christians are not to blend into the dark world around us or to fall into the sin-corrupted lifestyles common to this age. Instead, he called Christians to be "blameless and innocent, children of God without blemish in the midst of a crooked and twisted generation, among whom you shine as lights in the world, holding fast to the word of life" (Phil. 2:15–16).

If God's Word is not changing you in the direction of spiritual holiness and moral purity, then on what basis do you expect to be part of "the holy city Jerusalem," which radiates the glory of God like a jasper? Christians will rightly answer that they expect to enter this glory through faith alone, trusting in the finished work of Christ as the Lamb of God who died for our sins. This is profoundly true. But many professing Christians fail to realize that Christ's finished work of justification invariably launches a present work of sanctification that will be finished only in the age to come. The mark of the Christian is therefore a growing holiness in faith-communion with God through Jesus Christ. Hebrews 12:14 warns that "without holiness no one will see the Lord" (NIV). Another way to say this is to note that

6. Henry Barclay Swete, *Commentary on Revelation*, 2 vols. (1911; repr., Grand Rapids: Kregel, 1977), 2:285.

all those who will shine with the radiance of a jewel in the holiness of the eternal city are starting to shine now through the transforming presence of the Holy Spirit working through God's Word.

Realizing that God's purpose in our lives now is not for happiness but for holiness will transform our attitude about trials and sorrows. The story is told of a Christian man who was staggered by great losses so that he wondered what God was doing in his life. As he walked dejectedly through the city, he encountered a construction site where a great cathedral was about to be finished. A stonemason caught his eye, working carefully on a decorative piece, and the man asked him what he was doing. The worker said, "I am shaping this down here so that it will fit up there." The Christian realized that this was the answer to God's working in his life. His destiny was not to be fulfilled in this age but in the next, and God was using trials to shape him in holiness for the holy city that is to come.

THE WELL-FOUNDED WALL

Not only is John shown the church as a beautiful bride and a holy city radiating the glory of God, but this opening section of the final visions in Revelation adds details about the wall that surrounds the Jerusalem to come: "It had a great, high wall, with twelve gates, and at the gates twelve angels, and on the gates the names of the twelve tribes of the sons of Israel were inscribed" (Rev. 21:12).

A wall surrounding a great city has the purpose of providing security. There are admittedly no enemies remaining after the final judgment. But the wall conveys the security of salvation inside the city as well as the protective character of God for his people. It is "a great, high wall," symbolizing the inviolable care of God in saving his own. John Newton expressed the safety that belongs to Christians not only in eternity but equally in this present world:

Glorious things of thee are spoken, Zion, city of our God;
He whose word cannot be broken formed thee for his own abode:
On the Rock of Ages founded, what can shake thy sure repose?
With salvation's walls surrounded, thou may'st smile at all thy foes.[7]

7. John Newton, "Glorious Things of Thee Are Spoken" (1779).

637

The walls of God's city are adorned "with twelve gates" (Rev. 21:12). Gates function to permit entry into a city, and these twelve gates show the abundant invitation for all people to enter God's city through faith in Christ. There are three gates on each side of the squared city: "on the east three gates, on the north three gates, on the south three gates, and on the west three gates" (21:13). In Revelation, the four corners speak of the entirety of the world from which God's people are gathered. These are not small gates, but large entry towers, fitting for a great multitude from every tribe, language, and nation that are assembled into God's city.

Each gate is assigned an angel: "and at the gates twelve angels" (Rev. 21:12). In Isaiah 62:6, God said, "On your walls, O Jerusalem, I have set watchmen," showing God's guardian care over his church and over the entry into the holy city. When Adam sinned, an angel was stationed with a flaming sword to bar the way into the garden and the Tree of Life (Gen. 3:24). With such guardians, none will enter the eternal Jerusalem except those who are sealed for entry through the blood of the Lamb. At the beginning of Revelation, John was shown the angels of the churches (Rev. 1:20). The Bible does indicate the idea of guardian angels, and as God's sentinels these angels know who belongs to the Lord and who does not. None will enter fraudulently or on any other basis than that established by God. Revelation 22:14 speaks in terms of faith in Christ's atoning blood: "Blessed are those who wash their robes, . . . that they may enter the city by the gates." Paul added in 2 Timothy 2:19, "God's firm foundation stands, bearing this seal: 'The Lord knows those who are his,' and, 'Let everyone who names the name of the Lord depart from iniquity.'"

Furthermore, "on the gates the names of the twelve tribes of the sons of Israel were inscribed" (Rev. 21:12). In Ezekiel's end-times temple-city, each gate bore the name of a tribe of Israel, the idea being that each tribe had its own territory. Here, the emphasis is not on the individual tribes but the twelve of them together. All through Revelation, twelve is the number of God's people (see 7:4), just as it was the number of the tribes of God's Old Testament nation. This city represents the fulfillment of Israel's hope and the result of God's redeeming work as revealed through his servants the prophets. God promised through Moses that "you shall be to me a kingdom of priests and a holy nation" (Ex. 19:6), and the names of the tribes on these gates signal the fulfillment of that ancient purpose.

Finally, "the wall of the city had twelve foundations, and on them were the twelve names of the twelve apostles of the Lamb" (Rev. 21:14). Ancient walls had large decorative foundation stones, and here the apostles are seen as the foundation of the eternal church. This imagery refers to the New Testament witness of Jesus Christ and the evangelistic labor of the apostles in founding the first churches. Paul had written similarly: "You are fellow citizens with the saints and members of the household of God, built on the foundation of the apostles and prophets, Christ Jesus himself being the cornerstone" (Eph. 2:19–20).

Here, as throughout Revelation, the essential unity between Old Testament Israel and the New Testament church is proved. God's old covenant people who looked forward to Christ have the same destiny through faith as the new covenant people who look backward on Christ. Both the twelve tribes and the twelve apostles adorn the wall that circumscribes God's people in eternity. George Eldon Ladd writes: "John indicates that the city encompasses both dispensations, and that both the Israel of the Old Testament and of the church of the New Testament have their place in God's final establishment."[8]

If you look to the foundation of your faith and your hope of salvation, you also find your answer in the mission of Christ's apostles. It is through the written testimony of God's Word, commissioned through the eyewitness disciples, that we are certain of our hope through Jesus Christ. The apostles themselves took their stand on God's Word. Peter wrote that while he had the privilege of seeing Jesus' ministry with his own eyes, "we have something more sure, the prophetic word, to which you will do well to pay attention as to a lamp shining in a dark place" (2 Peter 1:19). Our salvation hope rests securely on the apostolic testimony inspired by God's Holy Spirit, which declares salvation now even as that Word will form the foundation of God's eternal city. It is through this same foundation of God's Word that every true church is established and built up today. Jesus said this in response to Peter's faith in God's Word: "On this rock I will build my church, and the gates of hell shall not prevail against it" (Matt. 16:18). Jesus later declared: "Heaven and earth will pass away, but my words will not pass away" (24:35).

---

8. George Eldon Ladd, *A Commentary on the Revelation of John* (Grand Rapids: Eerdmans, 1972), 281.

FAITH BEHOLDING GOD'S CITY

As Christians look ahead to the holy city of the age to come, we thank God that the destination is better than the journey. We have what Paul called "our blessed hope" in the return of Christ and the glory he brings (Titus 2:13). For all the many blessings of this life, we like Abraham face present trials and disappointments by "looking forward to the city that has foundations, whose designer and builder is God" (Heb. 11:10). By faith, the things of the world to come become real to us now. We thus begin to reflect now some of the glory of God that in the end will radiate from us like a glittering jewel.

Since we follow in Abraham's steps, we might conclude by asking what the ancient patriarch's vision enabled him to do. First, Abraham's faith enabled him to be saved by answering God's call. Is God calling you through his Word? This vision of a glorious city gives you every reason to renounce this present world and its rebellion to God. God calls you to the cross of Jesus, to confess your sins and be forgiven where the Lamb of God paid the penalty of sin. The cross will be the beginning of a journey that leads to the most glorious destination, yet it is itself the most wonderful display of God's glorious love that history will ever know.

Second, Abraham's vision of the city to come enabled him to withstand temptations during his life. When his nephew Lot departed for the alluring setting of wicked Sodom, Abraham refused, knowing that his citizenship lay in a better city that called him to renounce the lifestyle of sin (Gen. 13). Likewise, your faith in Christ and in his promise of a glorious future will fortify you against temptation and embolden you to seek an increasingly holy life now.

Third, just as Abraham would father the vast nation of Israel through his faith in God's promise, you, too, may bear a gospel testimony that will lead others to faith and salvation. Fixing your eye on the city to come, you are freed from the fear of worldly scorn so as to boldly declare salvation through faith in Jesus Christ. In one of Daniel's visions, the angel said, "Those who are wise shall shine like the brightness of the sky above; and those who turn many to righteousness, like the stars forever and ever" (Dan. 12:3).

Fourth, after the course of your life has been run, and when history has burned out its candle so that Christ has come and the new age has begun, faith will enable you, together with Abraham and the entire great host of saints in Christ, to enter the holy city Jerusalem and live there forever. Jesus promised: "Whoever comes to me I will never cast out.... For this is the will of my Father, that everyone who looks on the Son and believes in him should have eternal life, and I will raise him up on the last day" (John 6:37, 40).

59

THE SHAPE OF GLORY

Revelation 21:15–21

The city lies foursquare, its length the same as its width. And he measured the city with his rod, 12,000 stadia. Its length and width and height are equal. (Rev. 21:16)

hen climbers ascend to the summit of Mount Everest, the highest spot on earth at 29,029 feet, they are greeted by the marks and artifacts left by those who arrived before them. Everest climbers join a fraternity that started when Edmund Hillary and Tenzing Norgay first summited in 1953. After descending, the ritual includes a stop at the Rum Doodle restaurant in nearby Katmandu to sign the famous wall reserved for those who have stood at the top of the world.

When the apostle John spiritually visited the eschatological mountain of Scripture, he also joined an elite fraternity. The first man to stand on the mountain of God was Moses, after redeeming God's people from Egypt. There, Moses dwelt in the presence of God's glory, received the Ten Commandments, and was also shown the pattern for God's tabernacle (Ex. 25:40). Centuries later, the prophet Ezekiel was taken to the high mountain of God, where an angel holding a measuring reed showed him the dimensions of a new temple for God (Ezek. 40:1–3). Now John ascends the theological apex of the earth to see the Bible's final vision of the city of God. Following Ezekiel's experience, he writes: "The one who spoke with me had a measuring rod of gold to measure the city and its gates and walls" (Rev. 21:15). The angel's golden rod, a fitting tool for the service of God, not only reveals the city's dimensions but marks out the realm where God has pledged his sovereign protection (see 11:1–2). John was shown "not physical geography but spiritual realities"[1] pertaining to the final home of God's people. John writes that this vision employs "human measurement, which is also an angel's measurement" (21:17). This means that the physical dimensions have a symbolic meaning regarding the heavenly glory of the city awaiting believers in Christ.

THE MEASUREMENTS OF THE HOLY CITY

The vision of the eternal city shown to John runs from Revelation 21:9 to 22:5. Revelation 21:15–17 provides the shape and measurements of the city, which convey truths regarding its character.

First, we consider the shape: "The city lies foursquare, its length the same as its width" (Rev. 21:16). This description reflects the model of the tabernacle given to Moses, which had God's abode constructed in rectangles and squares. Many important items in the tabernacle were "foursquare," including the altar of burnt offerings (Ex. 27:1), the altar of incense (30:2), and the high priest's breastpiece (28:16). Likewise, Ezekiel's temple vision featured square and rectangular structures. Richard Bauckham points out that the numbers used in Revelation for God's people are all square numbers, such as 144, whereas the number of the beast, 666, is a triangular number.[2] As a "foursquare" city, the eternal Jerusalem reflects perfect balance, harmony, and proportion. Many ancient writers used the expression *foursquare* to speak of integrity, completion, or perfection, and these qualities belong to the holy new Jerusalem.[3]

The new Jerusalem is constructed not only as a square but as a cube: "Its length and width and height are equal" (Rev. 21:16). Even more than the

---

1. Daniel I. Block, *The Book of Ezekiel: Chapters 25–48*, New International Commentary on the Old Testament (Grand Rapids: Eerdmans, 1998), 505.

2. Richard Bauckham, *Climax of Prophecy: Studies on the Book of Revelation* (London: T&T Clark, 2000), 390–407.

3. See G. K. Beale, *The Book of Revelation: A Commentary on the Greek Text*, New International Greek Testament Commentary (Grand Rapids: Eerdmans, 1999), 1075.

square, the cube speaks of perfect completion. In the tabernacle that Moses made, as with the temple of Solomon, there was only one cubical space: the holy of holies where God's presence dwelt (1 Kings 6:20). In the original tabernacle, the inner sanctum occupied only a small space at the center of Israel's camp and only one person could enter it, the high priest, only one day per year. But now all the people of God live in the inner sanctum to behold his glory all the time, since the entire city is the holy of holies. Vern Poythress writes: "Thus the whole city is not only architecturally perfect, but has become the most intimate dwelling place of God."[4]

In addition to the "foursquare" and cubical shape of the city, the angel gives its measurement: "And he measured the city with his rod, 12,000 stadia" (Rev. 21:16). The first thing we notice is the staggering immensity of this city. Taking a stadios as 200 yards, 12,000 stadia equals approximately 1,500 miles. A city this size would occupy the entire Mediterranean world from Jerusalem to Spain. It is obvious that this city is designed to house a vast number of people beyond human reckoning, especially when we remember that as a cube it is a high-rise tower that soars above any man-made construction to a celestial height. G. K. Beale writes that since the city is "the approximate size of the then-known Hellenistic world," this suggests that "the temple city represents not merely the glorified saints of Israel but the redeemed from all nations."[5] Christians are challenged by the resurrection to expand our expectations for the gospel: God is intending to save an incredibly vast number of people, not just a few here and there. For this reason, Christians should believe that there is a reasonable chance that people placed in our lives have been put there by God in order to hear the message of Jesus, believe, and receive salvation.

Not only can a great host of people live here, but there is plenty of space for them to grow and spread out. Non-Christians tend to think that life with God will hem them in, when exactly the opposite is the case. "This huge size symbolizes the immensity and profundity of God's purposes that will be realized."[6] The eternal city is therefore not only symmetrical and complete, but also vast beyond reckoning.

---

4. Vern S. Poythress, *The Returning King: A Guide to the Book of Revelation* (Phillipsburg, NJ: P&R Publishing, 2000), 191.

5. Beale, *Revelation*, 1074.

6. Poythress, *The Returning King*, 191.

Not only is the great size of the measurements significant, but the numbers themselves are highly symbolic. Each length of the city is 12,000 stadia, with twelve representing both the twelve tribes of Israel and the twelve apostles of the New Testament. This number is therefore intended to symbolize that this city not only *houses* the people of God but *is* the people of God. A cube has twelve edges; the sum of this city is 12,000 times 12, or 144,000. This is the very number used earlier for the assembled entirety of God's elect: twelve times twelve for the Old and New Testaments, multiplied by a thousand, which speaks of completion and fulfillment.

This emphasis on the number of God's people is extended to the measurement of the walls: "He also measured its wall, 144 cubits" (Rev. 21:17). Since a cubit is about 18 inches, this is a much smaller number, just over 200 feet. Physically, it is hard to imagine a wall this relatively short when the city itself extends 1,500 miles upward. The point is not the physical configuration, however, but the numerical symbolism. The meaning of 144 cubits is that the wall encompasses the entirety of God's elect from all times. In this holy and eternal city, all of God's covenant purposes and the promises of the Bible are fulfilled: the entire vast number of God's redeemed people will live in the glory of his immediate presence so as to experience the perfection of life as God designed it in eternity past.

The Preciousness of the Holy City

In addition to the city's dimensions, we are also told of the precious materials in its construction. John writes: "The wall was built of jasper, while the city was pure gold, clear as glass. The foundations of the wall of the city were adorned with every kind of jewel" (Rev. 21:18–19). Verse 21 adds, "And the twelve gates were twelve pearls, . . . and the street of the city was pure gold, transparent as glass." In popular parlance, this imagery is thought to promise material wealth to those who go to heaven. The actual point is that the glorified church reflects the glory and beauty of the holy God.

"Jasper" probably refers to a quartz that is flecked with various colors. The gold of the street is pure and transparent. In our world it is physically impossible for metal to be clear, but here the purity of the gold is such that God's light shines through it. The point is that the splendor of even the purest gold is inadequate to describe God's majesty, so here the gold is like a crystal that radiates with God's glory. William Hendriksen writes that the pure gold "symbolizes the pure, holy, gracious, and radiant character of the fellowship between God and his people."[7] This pure gold reflects God's goal in refining our character with trials, "so that the tested genuineness of your faith—more precious than gold that perishes though it is tested by fire—may be found to result in praise and glory and honor at the revelation of Jesus Christ" (1 Peter 1:7).

The impression of God's radiant glory is heightened by the foundation stones, which are "adorned with every kind of jewel." John lists them: "The first was jasper, the second sapphire, the third agate, the fourth emerald, the fifth onyx, the sixth carnelian, the seventh chrysolite, the eighth beryl, the ninth topaz, the tenth chrysoprase, the eleventh jacinth, the twelfth amethyst" (Rev. 21:19–20). The quartz of the first foundation is the same jasper from the walls. Among the other stones, sapphire and agate are blue; emerald and chrysoprase are green; onyx is streaked with reddish brown; carnelian and jacinth are red; chrysolite is golden; beryl is a blue-green crystal; topaz is typically yellow; and amethyst is purple. We remember that when John first saw God's throne in heaven, it, too, was resplendent in crystal colors: "He who sat there had the appearance of jasper and carnelian, and around the throne was a rainbow that had the appearance of an emerald" (4:3). The rainbow glory of God is now reflected in his glorified people, the new Jerusalem. The actual vision set before John was probably beyond description, so that the bright display of multiple hues is a pale reflection of the true glory that he saw.

These jewels are not the foundation stones themselves but are set into them. This connects with Peter's statement that Christians "like living stones are being built up as a spiritual house, to be a holy priesthood" (1 Peter 2:5). The eternal city is built of God's people themselves, and his grace within us is now working the glory that will then reflect the splendor of his beauty forever. Indeed, the multiplicity of hues that John describes points to the infinite combinations of grace that enable each individual Christian to make a unique and irreplaceable contribution to the glory of the new Jerusalem.

The idea of God's people as a holy priesthood is heightened by the realization that these jewels correspond to the gems that formed a rectangular

7. William Hendriksen, *More than Conquerors: An Interpretation of the Book of Revelation* (1940; repr., Grand Rapids: Baker, 1967), 202.

pattern on the breastplate of Israel's high priest. This makes sense when we realize that Aaron's garments were intended to replicate the tabernacle in miniature and that his breastpiece was designed to reflect the glory of the presence of God. Eight of the twelve gems that John mentions are identical to the Greek translation of the stones in Exodus 28:17–20, and the other four are probably John's own translation of the other gems. The twelve stones represented the twelve tribes of Israel, whose names were engraved on them (Ex. 28:21). The people formerly represented by those stones now are themselves the holy of holies in which God dwells with his glory within them.

By bearing the stones into God's presence, Aaron not only represented the people in making the atoning sacrifice for their sins, but also signified God's pledge that one day the whole people of God would live within the holy of holies. Revelation 21:16–20 sees the fulfillment of this promise in the eternal age to come. It is noteworthy that the foundation stones of Revelation 21 bear the names of the twelve apostles (Rev. 21:14), since the promise of Israel is fulfilled in the gospel-believing apostolic church. Jesus Christ is, of course, the Great High Priest who brings his people into God's presence through the true sacrifice of his blood, ensuring the saving blessing of God on every believer. Bruce Milne writes of this scene: "For the citizens of the New Jerusalem, the Great High Priest is now about and among them, and the jewel-strewn walls around the city vividly portray their life as enclosed within the heart of a God for whom each last individual is remembered and every person's concerns are his unceasing care."[8]

Yet another indication of the priestly nature of God's people is the statement that "the street of the city was pure gold, transparent as glass" (Rev. 21:21). I have already noted that this detail is not about the material riches accrued to believers in heaven but about the glory of God in the city. We remember as well that in Solomon's temple the floorboards were overlaid in gold (1 Kings 6:30). Those who walk on gold are those who are admitted into God's presence in order to serve and worship him as priests. Moreover, as Geoffrey Wilson notes: "The royal dignity of walking upon gold belongs to those who are joint-heirs with Christ."[9]

8. Bruce Milne, *The Message of Heaven and Hell: Grace and Destiny*, The Bible Speaks Today (Downers Grove, IL: InterVarsity Press, 2002), 319.
9. Geoffrey B. Wilson, *New Testament Commentaries*, 2 vols. (Edinburgh: Banner of Truth, 2005), 2:591.

The crowning detail of this spectacular vision is John's description of the city gates: "And the twelve gates were twelve pearls, each of the gates made of a single pearl" (Rev. 21:21). In the ancient world, pearls were valued far above gems; here the gate towers are each formed by a single gigantic pearl. William Barclay writes: "Gates of pearl are a symbol of unimaginable beauty and unassessable riches."[10] This is why Jesus used a "pearl of great value" to describe his kingdom of salvation. He told of a merchant who found such a pearl and because of its surpassing worth he "went and sold all that he had and bought it" (Matt. 13:45–46). Since these gates provide entry into Christ's eternal city, it is no wonder that they are formed of pearls. We are thus reminded that nothing is more valuable to us or more glorious in fulfillment than the salvation we receive through humble faith in the person and work of Christ. Matthew Henry writes: "Christ is the pearl of great price, and he is our way to God."[11]

Just as the measurements of the eternal city depict its staggering size, the multihued jewels and translucent gold express its precious value to God. Robert Mounce summarizes: "The city is magnificent beyond description. As the eternal dwelling place of God and his people, it is described in language which continually attempts to break free from its own limitations in order to do justice to the reality it so imperfectly describes."[12]

REDEMPTIVE FULFILLMENT IN THE HOLY CITY

In reflecting on this remarkable vision, we must consider a number of truths. The first is the unity of the Bible. I mentioned that Moses went up on a mountain and received instructions for building the tabernacle during the first exodus (Ex. 24:15–18). Ezekiel had a similar experience, receiving a much more elaborate temple vision as he anticipated the second exodus in the restoration of the Jews from their Babylonian exile (Ezek. 40–47). Now John is taken up in the Spirit to the same mountain in light of the final exodus redemption when Jesus returns, and he is shown a final vision of the holy city.

10. William Barclay, *The Revelation of John*, 3rd ed., 2 vols., New Daily Study Bible (Louisville: Westminster John Knox, 2004), 2:275.

11. Matthew Henry, *Commentary on the Whole Bible*, 6 vols. (Peabody, MA: Hendrickson, n.d.), 6:953.

12. Robert H. Mounce, *Revelation*, rev. ed., New International Commentary on the New Testament (Grand Rapids: Eerdmans, 1997), 383.

There are significant differences between these visions. Ezekiel's vision is dominated by a new temple building, whereas there is no temple *in* John's new Jerusalem (Rev. 21:22), for the simple reason that the entirety of the new creation is the temple of God's holy dwelling. Ezekiel's temple provides barriers between the clean and the unclean, while John's vision, looking into the time when all sin has been removed, sees a city without internal barriers. The differences occur because of their placement in the progress of God's redemptive work in history. But the theology is the same. Moses built his tabernacle in the mid–second millennium B.C., Ezekiel saw his temple around 600 B.C., and John wrote Revelation at the end of the first century A.D. All three temples form a progression moving forward to the final product of Revelation 21 and 22. All three visions direct the Bible's readers to worship a holy God by means of atoning sacrifices that pointed to the blood of the Lamb that Jesus shed (Ex. 25:22; Ezek. 43:18f.; Rev. 21:9, 14, 22). The promise embedded in Moses' more primitive tabernacle structure and in the high priest's breastpiece has in God's timing come to perfect fulfillment in the new Jerusalem to come. We are part of that history now, and the Bible that guides us presents a single redemptive purpose that can only be the work of the true and Sovereign God. The remarkable unity of this book that was written over fifteen hundred years, together with its transcendent message that was far beyond what Moses could have conceived, bears testimony to the divine nature of the Bible's origin.

In this way, John's vision shows how the Bible's themes "look when they are viewed through the lens of fulfillment in Christ."[13] If you look at Old Testament life and worship and ask, "What will this look like when God's purpose with these ancient tribes is fulfilled?" the answer is given in John's vision. Moses' tabernacle was divided by a thick curtain to keep sinners away from the burning terror of God's holy presence. Christ has come and removed the veil so that we are a kingdom of priests to serve God in his presence (Heb. 10:20). Ezekiel's temple had walls to separate Jews from unclean Gentiles (Ezek. 42:20), but when Christ came, his atoning blood broke down "the dividing wall of hostility" (Eph. 2:14). "For he himself is our peace," Paul writes, "that he might create in himself one new man" (2:14–15). Therefore, the Christian church unites all tribes and tongues together in Christ. Christ's coming has removed the guilt of sin and the division of sin,

---

13. Iain M. Duguid, *Ezekiel*, NIV Application Commentary (Grand Rapids: Zondervan, 1999), 482.

and finally in John's vision even the presence of sin is removed so that the entire city shines with the light of God's holy presence. John's vision shows what God wants to achieve in your life through Jesus Christ: not only to remove the guilt, shame, and alienation of sin but to advance you to a state of glory in which you, together with all other believers, fulfill the calling of mankind before sin first came into the world: to bear the image of the splendor of the glory of God.

THE PEARL OF GREAT PRICE

Another truth for us to emphasize is that God's eternal dwelling is not a place but is his people. This is not to say that after Christ's return there is no physical realm of God, for there will be "a new heaven and a new earth" (Rev. 21:1). Yet the symbolism of John's vision depicts not merely that there is a place for God's people to dwell, but also that God's people are the ultimate place where God intends to dwell in the radiance of his glory.

The key truth for Christians to understand today is not only that we are accepted as righteous through faith in Christ but that, having been justified, we have God living in us through the Holy Spirit. Paul summarized Christian spirituality when he wrote: "I have been crucified with Christ. It is no longer I who live, but Christ who lives in me" (Gal. 2:20). As Christ lives in us, he is preparing us as "living stones" who are together "being built up as a spiritual house" for God (1 Peter 2:5). The day is coming when we will finally put on the glory of God in order to be his fitting dwelling. Or, to put it differently, the jewels of the city in John's vision are the adornment of the divine Bridegroom for the bride he is taking into his love forever. In this life, Christ is working that beauty into us in order to "present the church to himself in splendor, without spot or wrinkle or any such thing, that she might be holy and without blemish" (Eph. 5:27).

Thoughts like these seldom penetrate the busyness of our daily lives. We are necessarily preoccupied with doing our jobs, raising our children, saving money, and trying to get by in this world. Yet John reminds us that the day is fast coming when everything we are working for in this life will pass away and our eternal reality will be the result of our relationship with God through Jesus Christ. If we take John's vision seriously, we will labor to seize time and passion away from our worldly pursuits in order to devote them to our walk with God. If we realize the inexorable pull of history toward the return of Christ, we will start praying, "Lord, be working in me to make me transparent, translucent, just a bit more today, to shine forth your glory!" How do Christians learn to become more and more open to God and more passionate about his work in us? How does a man fall in love with a woman? By exposure to her beauty and charms. John's vision is intended to expose us to the glory that God desires to work in us so that we will passionately seek an increasing work of his grace.

If this vision depicts our future, one mark of God's grace at work in Christians is an increasing commitment to things of true beauty. While secular society recedes into a mire of nihilistic cultural destruction, the Christian church should cultivate in its music, in its buildings, in its ministries, and especially in our character, relationships, and worship the beauty and goodness of God as revealed in his Word. In an age when secular opponents deride the God of the Bible as bigoted and ugly, exposure to actual Christians should reveal the beauty and goodness of his Word in a way that parallels the future shining forth of glittering jewels and translucent gold.

In recent years, thousands of climbers have flocked to Mount Everest, seeking to join the elite club of those who have reached its summit. As I write, over six thousand people have reached the top of the world and earned the right to inscribe their names on the famous wall in the Rum Doodle restaurant. A far greater host will ascend the mountain city of God and through faith in Christ enter its gates of pearl. Our names are already written in the Lamb's Book of Life, the most precious register in heaven or on earth. As Jesus taught, this salvation is like a pearl of great value that a merchant had sought. Finding it, he "went and sold all that he had and bought it" (Matt. 13:45–46). Nothing is more valuable to us than the salvation that God offers through Jesus Christ, and nothing of this world is worth holding if it will hinder us from entering the shining glory of God's eternal city.

60

The City without a Temple

Revelation 21:22–27

*And I saw no temple in the city, for its temple is the Lord God
the Almighty and the Lamb.* (Rev. 21:22)

he greatest Christians have thought often and much about
heaven and the eternal rest. St. Augustine said to God, "Thou
hast made us for thyself and our hearts are restless until they
find their rest in thee." John Calvin wrote that "the very summit of happiness [is] to enjoy the presence of God" in heaven. For this reason, he eagerly
embraced suffering in this present life and gladly anticipated death.[1] The
Puritan Richard Baxter looked forward to the eternal glory as "the most
happy state of a Christian," describing it as "the perfect endless enjoyment of
God by the perfected saints."[2] The Westminster divines wrote in answer 38
of the Westminster Shorter Catechism that when believers are resurrected at
the final judgment and enter into the city of God, they are "made perfectly
blessed in the full enjoying of God to all eternity."

We find the same emphasis on life after the final resurrection in the
prophets and apostles. King David rejoiced in the hope of glory, praying,

1. John Calvin, *Institutes of the Christian Religion*, trans. Henry Beveridge (Peabody, MA:
Hendrickson, 2008), 3.9.4.
2. Richard Baxter, *The Saints' Everlasting Rest*, ed. Benjamin Fawcett (New York: American Tract
Society, 2012), 13.

"In your presence there is fullness of joy; at your right hand are pleasures forevermore" (Ps. 16:11). The life of Abraham was summed up as "looking forward to the city that has foundations" (Heb. 11:10). Paul wrote, "For to me to live is Christ, and to die is gain" (Phil. 1:21). The apostle John anticipated: "We know that when he appears we shall be like him, because we shall see him as he is" (1 John 3:2).

We will find the same anticipation of heaven in the greatest Christians we know today. I was privileged to know Bobbie Houser, who spent her life as a missionary abroad and as a zealous Bible teacher. Bobbie's fervor for Christ and love for his people inspired multiple generations to live for the Lord. As she lingered near death at ages ninety-eight and ninety-nine, I would visit her and ask how I could pray for her. How often Bobbie replied, "Oh, I want my Lord to come. I want to see his glory."

A common theme in the writings of such great Christians is that believers cultivate a longing for heaven by meditating on it. This motive lay behind John's great description of the eternal city of God. In a book filled with important visions, the final vision depicts the new heaven and the new earth in the form of a temple-city. The book of Revelation was written to provide hope to suffering Christians in the church age and its persecutions. The final and greatest hope for every believer is the eternal glory awaiting us in Christ. A courageous faith will cultivate this hope by knowing the precious blessings awaiting us, anticipating glories that are beyond our present capacity by meditating on them as they are symbolized in Scripture.

A City with No Temple

The opening sections of this final vision identify the coming city as the glorified church of the Old and New Testaments (Rev. 21:12–14). The city's shape compares it to the holy of holies inside the tabernacle and temple, a perfect cube that marks the entire city as the inner sanctum of God's dwelling. The precious gems and pure gold that adorn the city show the preciousness of his people to God and their radiance in reflecting his surpassing glory (21:18–21).

Starting in Revelation 21:22, John looks inside to observe life in the eternal city. He makes three statements, each of which is in negative terms. Theologians take this same approach in defining the most essential attributes of

God, those that pertain solely to his deity. We describe the extent of God's being by saying that he is *infinite*—not finite. We describe the vigor of his life as *immortal*—he cannot die. God is *immutable*—he cannot change in his essence. In a similar way, John approaches a future glory that is incomprehensible to our finite minds by stating what we do not find in it.

The first of these negative statements notes the absence of a physical sanctuary: "I saw no temple in the city" (Rev. 21:22). All ancient cities had a temple or many temples. How remarkable it is, then, that when we gaze into the consummate fulfillment of the city of God, there is no temple within it. Temples existed as places where one went to meet with God. The new Jerusalem will need no such place, since "its temple is the Lord God the Almighty and the Lamb."

In the eternal city, God will fill the dwelling of his people so that he is met and known everywhere. William Hendriksen writes: "The radiance of God's majesty and glory, in all its fullness, fills the entire city. . . . No sanctuary is needed, for the fellowship of believers with their God is direct and immediate. God tabernacles with His people; they are constantly in His immediate and loving and abiding presence."[3] It was God's presence that made the old, physical temple sacred. In the end, God will have so reclaimed the entirety of creation that his glory will equally and fully pervade every square inch and light-year. Bruce Milne writes: "All is sacred, the *Shekinah* glory fills the entire city, and God is everywhere accessible to the priestly race."[4]

John's description of the city without a temple completes the Bible's development of the theme of God's dwelling with his people. When Moses met God on the mountain, the Lord told him to build the tabernacle, and from the inner sanctum of that tent God's shekinah glory shone forth in the midst of Israel. Later, Solomon built a permanent temple structure. Yet his prayer revealed that God was not contained in its cube-shaped holy of holies: "Behold, heaven and the highest heaven cannot contain you; how much less this house that I have built!" (1 Kings 8:27). When Jesus began his ministry, the presence of God extended outside the temple. John wrote that in his coming, "the Word became flesh and [tabernacled] among us, and we

---

3. William Hendriksen, *More than Conquerors: An Interpretation of the Book of Revelation* (1940; repr., Grand Rapids: Baker, 1967), 203.

4. Bruce Milne, *The Message of Heaven and Hell: Grace and Destiny*, The Bible Speaks Today (Downers Grove, IL: InterVarsity Press, 2002), 320.

have seen his glory" (John 1:14). No longer did people go to the temple to meet with God, but they went to Jesus and found God's saving grace in his person and works. Speaking of his body, Jesus said, "Destroy this temple, and in three days I will raise it up" (2:19). His death and resurrection are now the place of our meeting with God and the ground of our blessing.

The temple theme moved forward yet again when Jesus ascended to heaven and sent God's Spirit to live within his people. Paul wrote that the believer's own body is now sacred, "a temple of the Holy Spirit within you," and thus to be used only for God's glory (1 Cor. 6:19). Peter taught that the church is together the dwelling place of God on earth: "You yourselves like living stones are being built up as a spiritual house, to be a holy priesthood, to offer spiritual sacrifices acceptable to God through Jesus Christ" (1 Peter 2:5). In the final resurrection, after Christ returns, the church will be perfected in glory and will enjoy full communion with God in a regenerated cosmos designed for an infinite experience of God's holiness. Aaron prayed of old, "The LORD lift up his countenance upon you and give you peace" (Num. 6:26). An unmeasurable experience of this benediction is the destiny of believers in the presence of God's glory forever.

Notice that the temple in the eternal city is "the Lord God the Almighty and the Lamb" (Rev. 21:22). This statement makes clear the equality between Jesus and God; together with "God the Almighty," Jesus, "the Lamb," is the temple of his people. Not only do believers gain entry into the eternal glory through faith in Christ's death for our sins, but he reigns there as our Divine King and Mediator forever. From the moment a sinner puts his or her trust in Jesus and is forgiven of sins, there will never be a single second in all eternity when Christ's atoning mediation will not ensure our righteous standing before God and God's covenant favor toward us.

The fact that there will be no worship buildings in the new Jerusalem shows us how to think of such things now. Christian congregations rightly invest in physical surroundings designed to stimulate thoughts of majesty, looking forward to the time when we will worship God in the visual presence of his glory. Grand church buildings, rich worship services, and lovely sacred music play a valuable role in our worship now, but only as means to an end. The beauty of a church sanctuary, elegant choral music, and liturgical rituals are not themselves to capture our hearts but rather should direct us to God in anticipation of the reality that will soon replace them all. John

Calvin wrote that in the glory of the age to come, God "will give himself to be enjoyed by [his people]; and what is better still, will, in a manner, become one with them."[5] Week by week, as Christians gather in the church sanctuary to worship God, we are reminded to look ahead when all the symbols will give way to reality, and the glory that now sometimes pierces our hearts will one day be our all in all.

A CITY WITH NO LIGHTS

Not only is the new Jerusalem a city without a temple, but it also lacks physical lights: "And the city has no need of sun or moon to shine on it, for the glory of God gives it light, and its lamp is the Lamb" (Rev. 21:23). Grant Osborne writes: "As the Shekinah glory fills the temple, so the light of God's 'glory' fills the New Jerusalem."[6]

We are reminded here of the creation story in Genesis 1, when God spoke light into being on the first day. It was only on the fourth day that God made "lights in the expanse of the heavens . . .—the greater light to rule the day and the lesser light to rule the night" (Gen. 1:14–16). Secularists today insist that light cannot exist without the sun, moon, and stars, but the Bible declares that God is the source of light. Therefore, when his presence fills the eternal city, there is no further need for celestial lights. John's point is not about the astronomical situation in the renewed universe but "to affirm the unsurpassed splendor which radiates from the presence of God and the Lamb."[7] A candle burns brightly in the dark, but in the light of the sun its light can barely be seen. Likewise, the sun and its shining radiance would be lost in the shining glory of God that will fill the eternal city. G. K. Beale writes: "The light-giving sources of sun and moon were essential for the life and prosperity of the old Jerusalem when God's presence was limited to the temple. But now in the new cosmos God's complete presence among his people is what beautifies them and satisfies their every need."[8]

5. Calvin, *Institutes*, 3.25.10.

6. Grant R. Osborne, *Revelation*, Baker Exegetical Commentary on the New Testament (Grand Rapids: Baker Academic, 2002), 761.

7. George Eldon Ladd, *A Commentary on the Revelation of John* (Grand Rapids: Eerdmans, 1972), 284.

8. G. K. Beale, *The Book of Revelation: A Commentary on the Greek Text*, New International Greek Testament Commentary (Grand Rapids: Eerdmans, 1999), 1094.

Here again, the light belongs equally to the Father and the Son: "the glory of God gives it light, and its lamp is the Lamb" (Rev. 21:23). While they are coequal as God, the Son delights to display in his person and works the glory of the Father, as a lamp that reflects a light. When we consider the beauty of natural light, we can only imagine the surpassing glory of the light of God revealed by the lamp of Christ. Since John identifies Jesus as "the Lamb," we may be sure that God's end-times revelation of glory will highlight the love that gave his Son so that believers might be forgiven of our sins.

In the final book of J. R. R. Tolkien's *The Lord of the Rings*, the heroes Frodo Baggins and Sam Gamgee make slow progress through the foul and shadowed land of Mordor. Tolkien's Mordor provides a vivid depiction of life in a world ruled by sin and evil, so that Frodo and Sam are choked by its despair. Many of us feel this way about the present life: the future seems shadowed and threatening, and darkness presses on our hearts. In one scene, however, Sam peers up and sees the light of stars shining briefly through a hole in the shadow canopy. Seeking to encourage his downcast friend, Sam exclaims, "Look! There is light and beauty up there that no shadow can touch."[9] Christians can be similarly encouraged, despite our earthly woes and mortal failures, to see in John's vision the light of God shining beyond all darkness in the city to which we journey by faith in Christ.

Looking by the light of God into the city, John sees a teeming metropolis of activity. People from over the whole of the globe are gathered for worship and holy commerce: "By its light will the nations walk" (Rev. 21:24). Here is the fulfillment of God's ancient promise to Abraham: "In you all the families of the earth shall be blessed" (Gen. 12:3). Micah 4:1–2 foresaw this image: "The mountain of the house of the LORD shall be established as the highest of the mountains . . . ; and peoples shall flow to it . . . and say: 'Come, let us go up to the mountain of the LORD, to the house of the God of Jacob, that he may teach us his ways and that we may walk in his paths.'" It is to this end that the missionary labors of countless bold Christians have served the cause of Christ. The nations will walk by his light, having first seen that light in their witness of the gospel of Jesus.

John adds that "the kings of the earth will bring their glory into it" and "they will bring into it the glory and the honor of the nations" (Rev.

---

9. J. R. R. Tolkien, *The Return of the King* (New York: Houghton Mifflin, 1955), 898. I have quoted Peter Jackson's movie adaptation of *The Return of the King*, extended ed. (2004).

21:24, 26). This language seems confusing to some, since it implies Gentile peoples outside the city. But this scene takes place after the final judgment when all unbelievers and enemies of Christ have been cast into the lake of fire (20:15). Therefore, John sees not future people bringing the material wealth into the city, but rather believers from all the nations coming from this age into the eternal age, having believed in Christ and then offering themselves for worship to God. Isaiah foretold this scene in a passage to which John is referring throughout this vision, using language appropriate to his ancient setting: "Your gates shall be open continually . . . , that people may bring to you the wealth of the nations, with their kings led in procession" (Isa. 60:11). Ancient conquerors paraded their spoils of victory with captured kings led before them in chains. In Christ's eternal city, his "conquests" will have been won by grace, and they will fulfill their hearts' desire in yielding their fervent worship to God. As G. K. Beale puts it, the nations "are bringing . . . themselves as worshipers before God's end-time presence."[10] Our greatest treasure is our lives, offered up in service to Christ now and praising the glorious presence of God forever.

The statement that the nations "will bring their glory into it" (Rev. 21:24) suggests a continuity between our present lives and the eternal glory to come. Christians will bring all kinds of our godly culture into the new Jerusalem. This likely includes our hymnody, poetry, and tales of heroic faith. The perfect unity of the glorified church will retain a harmony of "all that is of abiding worth from within the national stories and the cultural inheritance of the world's peoples."[11] Douglas Kelly cites the legacy of the Ukrainian church under the godly ruler Jaroslav the Wise, who built St. Sophia Cathedral in Kiev for God's worship and tithed money from his royal lands for the Christian education of children. More recently, the persecuted Ukrainian church kept the light of Christ alive under Communist oppression. Kelly foresees the day when the saints of Ukraine go marching into the new Jerusalem under the banner of Christ. He wonders, "Will [their glory] include especially beautiful singing and poetry, because the Ukrainians are wonderful singers, musicians and poets to this day? Will the marks of seventy plus years of crucifixion as a church for the love

10. Beale, *Revelation*, 1095.
11. Milne, *The Message of Heaven and Hell*, 321.

of Christ under communism be turned into insignia of splendid beauty in their resurrected bodies and ransomed spirits?"[12]

Ancient cities closed their gates at night for security reasons, but in this city there is no need. John notes that "its gates will never be shut by day—and there will be no night there" (Rev. 21:25). The imagery speaks of peace and blessing in the city on which God's glory shines.

A City with No Sin

John's third statement regarding the new Jerusalem describes it as a city with no sin: "But nothing unclean will ever enter it, nor anyone who does what is detestable or false" (Rev. 21:27).

By "unclean" things, John means unregenerate people whose natures remain corrupted by sin and who "have defiled themselves through the abomination of idolatry and unfaithfulness to God."[13] By "what is detestable," John refers to the perverse evils condemned throughout the Bible as reprehensible to God. These sins are specified in the final chapter: "Outside are the dogs and sorcerers and the sexually immoral and murderers and idolaters" (Rev. 22:15). Paul gave an expanded list: "Do not be deceived: neither the sexually immoral, nor idolaters, nor adulterers, nor men who practice homosexuality, nor thieves, nor the greedy, nor drunkards, nor revilers, nor swindlers will inherit the kingdom of God" (1 Cor. 6:9–10). In a society as immoral as ours, it is essential that Christians speak the truth about God's hatred of sins such as adultery and homosexuality, together with the idolatry of greed and thievery. Recent examples show a gross intolerance toward biblical teaching about God's judgment on these sins, especially when it comes to deviant sexual lifestyles. Christians must nonetheless speak the truth boldly about God's condemnation of homosexuality, adultery, and other perversions, just as we must speak graciously about the forgiveness for all sins that is available in Jesus Christ. The fact that John concludes with those who are "false" may indicate God's special disgust for those who not only practice gross immorality but deny God's judgment in encouraging others to join in their sin.

12. Douglas F. Kelly, *Revelation*, Mentor Expository Commentary (Tain, Ross-shire, Scotland: Mentor, 2012), 420.
13. Beale, *Revelation*, 1101.

Bible believers know that what ultimately matters is not public opinion but God's teaching in his Word. J. C. Ryle writes: "You know well there are such people; they are not uncommon; they may be honourable in the eyes of men, they may be wise and knowing in this generation, admirable men of business, they may be first and foremost in their respective callings, but still there is but one account of them: . . . they are counted as defiled in [God's] sight, and nothing that is defiled shall enter heaven."[14]

Contrasted to the ungodly are those whose names are "written in the Lamb's book of life" (Rev. 21:27), who alone will enter God's glory. The Book of Life is God's eternal record of those elected by sovereign grace and called to salvation through faith in the blood of Christ. Whereas divine judgment is by just demerit, salvation is through the mercy of Christ for sinners, received by faith alone.

We are not permitted to look into God's Book of Life before the final judgment, but we can identify the distinguishing character of those whose names are there. J. C. Ryle points out that, first, "they are all true penitents."[15] Those destined for the new Jerusalem have felt the condemnation of their sins, have grieved before God for their guilt, and have hated the presence of sin in their lives. Second, "they are all believers in Christ Jesus."[16] Those who dwell in the eternal glory are those who trust the saving work of Christ, especially his atoning work as the Lamb of God who died for their sins. They found salvation nowhere else, but believed in Jesus, received his offered mercy, and continued in faith throughout their lives despite all manner of persecution.

Third, those whose names are written in God's Book of Life "are all born of the Spirit and sanctified."[17] This means that they began in this life, however imperfectly, the holy life they will enjoy perfectly in the age to come. They have been inwardly renewed by the Holy Spirit with a nature that inclines after God. Ryle writes: "The general bent of their lives has always been towards holiness—more holiness, more holiness, has always been their hearts' desire. They love God, and they must live to Him."[18]

This is how you know that you are destined to enjoy eternity in the glory of God's presence: not church membership alone, not fleeting spiritual

---

14. J. C. Ryle, *The Christian Race* (Moscow, ID: Charles Nolan, 2004), 261–62.
15. Ibid., 264.
16. Ibid.
17. Ibid.
18. Ibid., 264–65.

experiences, not money given to the church or good deeds that you think will overcome your sins, but a penitent heart that embraces the Lamb of God in faith and seeks thenceforth to live for the glory and honor of God.

WHAT GLORIFIES GOD?

The Westminster Shorter Catechism begins with the famous question and answer: "What is the chief end of man? Man's chief end is to glorify God, and to enjoy him for ever." Knowing that Christians will glorify God in the future in the marvelous ways that John describes calls us to glorify God now to the greatest extent that we are able. At the end of each year, many people take stock of their lives, and some make resolutions for the new year to come. In light of the blessings that we are destined to enjoy, John's vision supplies us with resolutions that will enable us to glorify and enjoy God more fully.

First, since God will fill the eternal city with the fullness of his presence, Christians should make it a priority to draw near to God and fellowship with him now so as to know him better. Jesus said, "And this is eternal life, that they know you the only true God, and Jesus Christ whom you have sent" (John 17:3). Why should Christians wait for the return of Jesus and the eternal glory to begin knowing God more intimately? John's vision should transform our ideas of Bible-reading and prayer from a dull ritual into a personal meeting with God that prepares us for the day when the whole of our life will be spent in the outshining radiance of his glory.

Second, if God intends to shine forth his light in the new heaven and new earth, then Christians should prioritize our witness to that light in this world. Jesus spoke of this in terms of our good works: "Let your light shine before others, so that they may see your good works and give glory to your Father who is in heaven" (Matt. 5:16). Paul added the testimony that shines from the holy lives of God's people: "Be blameless and innocent, children of God without blemish in the midst of a crooked and twisted generation, among whom you shine as lights in the world" (Phil. 2:15). To this we add our verbal witness to the gospel. Daniel 12:3 promises that "those who are wise shall shine like the brightness of the sky above; and those who turn many to righteousness, like the stars forever and ever." When we tell others about Jesus and God's grace in salvation, we reflect the very light that one day will bathe the new Jerusalem in glorious splendor.

661

Third, realizing that the ungodly will never enter God's holy, eternal city, we should not only warn sinners to repent and believe in Jesus, but first make sure that we ourselves come to him to be forgiven and cleansed from sin. Have you come to Jesus to deal with your sin and be justified before God? Until you admit your guilt, come to Jesus for forgiveness, and believe his gospel for salvation, there is no more important resolution for you to make. If you do not, you will be barred from God's eternal city as a rebel and cast into hell for your sin.

The day of judgment has not yet come, and the current age has yet to give way to the eternal glory. How urgent, then, is your need to embrace the opportunity to believe on Jesus Christ and be saved! John urges you to seek the only way of entry into the glorious city to come, through the Lamb of God who takes away our sins: "Blessed are those who wash their robes, . . . that they may enter the city by the gates" (Rev. 22:14).

61

THE RIVER OF THE WATER OF LIFE

Revelation 22:1–5

*Then the angel showed me the river of the water of life, bright
as crystal, flowing from the throne of God and of the Lamb.*
(Rev. 22:1)

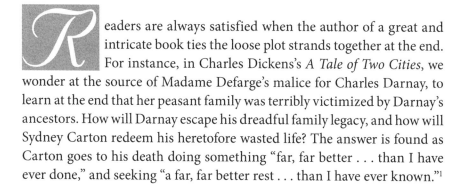eaders are always satisfied when the author of a great and intricate book ties the loose plot strands together at the end. For instance, in Charles Dickens's *A Tale of Two Cities*, we wonder at the source of Madame Defarge's malice for Charles Darnay, to learn at the end that her peasant family was terribly victimized by Darnay's ancestors. How will Darnay escape his dreadful family legacy, and how will Sydney Carton redeem his heretofore wasted life? The answer is found as Carton goes to his death doing something "far, far better . . . than I have ever done," and seeking "a far, far better rest . . . than I have ever known."[1]

FORWARD TO THE GARDEN

Even more satisfying than the conclusion of Dickens's great novel is the final chapter of the Bible, where the story begun in the dawn of creation

---

1. Charles Dickens, *A Tale of Two Cities* (1859; repr., New York: Random House, 1992), 482.

comes to perfect fulfillment in eternal glory. Revelation 22:1–5 provides the last images in the final vision of salvation in the entirety of Scripture. Here, we find images that we recognize from the garden of Eden, including "the river of the water of life" and "the tree of life" (Rev. 22:1–2). As the redeemed people of God are restored to these blessings, we find that God's original purpose in creation has not been thwarted a single iota by the rebellion of Satan and the scourges of sin. In the temple-city of Revelation's final vision, God's people do not go back to the garden but forward to what God intended when the first Paradise was born at the dawn of time. Simon Kistemaker writes that "John paints a picture of a renewed Paradise to complete the biblical account of human history."[2]

At the end, as in the beginning, the triune God reigns triumphantly in a paradise inhabited by his faithful, adoring, image-bearing people. G. K. Beale comments that this ending to the Bible's story confirms "that humanity's original purpose in the first garden sanctuary was to expand outward and spread the light of God's presence throughout the earth."[3] Every Christian who has taken up the missionary calling to spread the gospel message of Christ and by obedience to God's Word has sought to advance Christ's kingdom can rejoice to see that these labors were not in vain. By Christ's redeeming victory, the prophetic vision will be fulfilled: "The earth shall be full of the knowledge of the Lord as the waters cover the sea" (Isa. 11:9).

Life Flowing from God's Throne

Previously, John has looked on the eternal city and on the people living there. Now he concludes with the sources of life that bless the garden-city, the new Jerusalem: "Then the angel showed me the river of the water of life, bright as crystal, flowing from the throne of God and of the Lamb" (Rev. 22:1).

There are many biblical antecedents to this vision, but two stand out. The first was the river that "flowed out of Eden to water the garden" in Genesis 2:10. The second was the river that "was issuing from below the threshold of the temple" in Ezekiel's vision of God's end-times temple (Ezek. 47:1).

---

2. Simon J. Kistemaker, *Revelation*, New Testament Commentary (Grand Rapids: Baker, 2001), 581.

3. G. K. Beale, *The Temple and the Church's Mission: A Biblical Theology of the Dwelling Place of God* (Downers Grove, IL: InterVarsity Press, 2004), 326.

Whereas the first river flowed "out of Eden" and Ezekiel's river issued from the eastern temple door, the river of the new Jerusalem flows "from the throne of God and of the Lamb" (Rev. 22:1). The clear point is that the sovereign reign of God in history is the source of the life and refreshment that flows to his people in eternity. Since it is the throne not only "of God" but also "of the Lamb," we see that grace flows from the sovereign will of the Father by means of the saving death of his Son. Salvation's blessings are therefore "reserved . . . for those who have maintained their faith in the Lamb's atoning work and their testimony to his redemptive work."[4]

Moreover, the salvation depicted by this bright crystal stream consists of fellowship in the life that comes from God. This was Jesus' message to the woman by the well when he offered her "living water" (John 4:10). Jesus said, "The water that I will give him will become in him a spring of water welling up to eternal life" (4:14). Jesus was saying that by faith we may drink now of the spiritual life depicted in the river flowing through the new Jerusalem. Later in John's Gospel, he said, "I came that they may have life and have it abundantly" (10:10). When Jesus once offered "rivers of living water" to all who come to him (7:37–38), John explained that he was speaking "about the Spirit" whom Christ would send when he was glorified (7:39).

Here in Revelation, John provides details regarding this river of life. He says that its water is "bright as crystal," depicting the purity of life that God gives and the cleansing effect of the grace that we receive by faith. John adds that the river flows "through the middle of the street of the city" (Rev. 22:2). Earlier, we saw a street of "pure gold, transparent as glass" (21:21). Apparently the river flows either atop or beside the main thoroughfare, showing that divine life streams in the heart of the eternal dwelling place of God's people. Here is fulfilled the promise of Revelation 7:17: "The Lamb in the midst of the throne will be their shepherd, and he will guide them to springs of living water."

Ezekiel's temple vision showed the stream beginning at the temple doors as a trickle, then growing ankle-deep, then rising waist-deep, and finally getting so deep that it could not be crossed (Ezek. 47:1–12). This depicted the increasing power of God's grace as it advanced in redemptive history. As it flowed to the east, Ezekiel saw the brackish water becoming fresh,

---

4. G. K. Beale, *The Book of Revelation: A Commentary on the Greek Text*, New International Greek Testament Commentary (Grand Rapids: Eerdmans, 1999), 1104.

trees lining its banks, and fish swarming with life. Finally it reached the Dead Sea, purifying its salt water and cleansing it to produce life. Moreover, Ezekiel said that on its banks "there will grow all kinds of trees for food. Their leaves will not wither, nor their fruit fail, but they will bear fresh fruit every month . . . . Their fruit will be for food, and their leaves for healing" (47:12). John picks up this language to show that Ezekiel was foreseeing not a future physical blessing for the physical land of Israel but rather the vitality of life that God has in store for his people in the new Jerusalem: "on either side of the river, the tree of life with its twelve kinds of fruit" (Rev. 22:2).

The Genesis account of the garden highlighted not only the river flowing out of Eden, but also the "tree of life . . . in the midst of the garden" (Gen. 2:9), which conveyed eternal life to those who eat from it (3:22). Now John sees this Tree of Life growing on both sides of the river. Most scholars think that this image depicts not a single great tree but a grove of trees that give life, lining the banks of the river.

The nineteenth-century scholar James Hamilton sees an analogy between the Tree of Life and the incarnation of Jesus Christ, who brings God's presence to believers: it has pleased "the Father that in the Incarnate Son should dwell all the supplies of pardon, righteousness, strength, and wisdom which sinners need, all the life we lack, so Jesus is the Tree of Life."[5] It is noteworthy as well that the word *tree* was used in the apostles' preaching for the cross of Christ (Acts 5:30; 10:39; 13:29). Peter connected Christ's death to this scene, writing: "He himself bore our sins in his body on the tree, that we might die to sin and live to righteousness. By his wounds you have been healed" (1 Peter 2:24).

The redemptive source of eternal life is none other than the propitiatory sacrifice of the Lamb of God. Noting how the trees line both banks of the water of life with branches bending low to the hands of those who seek them, Hamilton writes that "all the blessings of salvation, all the sure mercies purchased by Christ's death, and all the sacred joys resident in Christ's person, are made as accessible as God's free gift."[6] As the gospel of Christ's death and salvation is preached today, this very life is freely available to all who believe and reach out for Jesus Christ.

---

5. James Hamilton, *Sermons and Lectures* (1873; repr., Stoke-on-Trent, UK: Tentmaker Publications, 2010), 521.

6. Ibid.

Ezekiel saw trees whose "fruit will be for food" (Ezek. 47:12), and John notes their fulfillment in the new Jerusalem: "the tree of life with its twelve kinds of fruit, yielding its fruit each month" (Rev. 22:2). The fact that "twelve kinds of fruit" are yielded "each month" indicates both the variety of blessings and their perpetual availability. There is an abundant provision of spiritual life and grace to meet every imaginable need. As Adam and Eve walked "in the garden in the cool of the day," enjoying "the presence of the LORD God among the trees of the garden" (Gen. 3:8), so will the vast multitude of God's redeemed people live in the blessing of the grove of the divine life forever.

According to Jeremiah, the principle depicted in this vision extends back into our present world. Jeremiah warned that those who trust in worldly strength, turning away from the Lord, become like "a shrub in the desert," shriveling up "in an uninhabited salt land" (Jer. 17:6). In contrast, the one who trusts in the Lord "is like a tree planted by water, that sends out its roots by the stream, and does not fear when heat comes, for its leaves remain green, and is not anxious in the year of drought, for it does not cease to bear fruit" (17:7–8).

This reality was experienced by Art and Wilda Matthews, the last missionaries to escape China after the Communist takeover. They lived with their family for months in a single room with only a stool for furniture. All contact with outside friends and financial support were cut off. With only a small stove, they often shivered, their food reduced to a daily meal of rice cooked over manure that Art gathered in the streets. By this means, the Chinese sought to wither up the Christians' faith, but the opposite happened. Throughout the trial they trusted God, spoke to him in prayer, and strengthened themselves by his Word. After they escaped they told their story, the title of which was drawn from Jeremiah 17:7–8, *Green Leaf in Drought-Time.*[7] "There is a river whose streams make glad the city of God," sang David of the gospel (Ps. 46:4). "Blessed is the man," he wrote, whose "delight is in the law of the LORD . . . . He is like a tree planted by streams of water that yields its fruit in its season, and its leaf does not wither. In all that he does, he prospers" (1:2–3).

Ezekiel's vision spoke of trees with "leaves for healing" (Ezek. 47:12), and John likewise notes that "the leaves of the tree were for the healing of the

---

7. Isobel Kuhn, *Green Leaf in Drought-Time: The Story of the Escape of the Last C.I.M. Missionaries from Communist China* (Chicago: Moody, 1957).

nations" (Rev. 22:2). Since there are no ills to heal in the city of the redeemed, the wounds that are healed probably come from life in this world. This is a wonderful idea. Think how even the strongest Christians depart from this life, whether tragically during their early years or feebly in old age, with the scars of battle and the grief of our own character failings. Though we depart from this life often battered and bowed down, we will receive in the life to come the complete restoration of both body and soul. In Psalm 23:5, David proclaims that "you anoint my head with oil." Ancient travelers arrived at an inn covered with dust and their skin cracked by the hot sun. A friendly host would greet them with soothing oil. Our Savior will do more for us in heaven, not only anointing our souls with the oil of his Spirit but healing us with leaves from his Tree of Life.

Moreover, every source of strife between tribes and nations will be alleviated in the new Jerusalem: "The nationalism, the racism, the acrimony, the bitterness, and the long history of warfare will be healed."[8] Here is regained the paradise that mankind lost through sin, not only at the personal but also at the corporate level. Only through the death of Christ for healing and forgiveness does mankind find its cherished utopia. Paul wrote, "He himself is our peace" (Eph. 2:14). In the eternal city, the work of Christ is ever present in its blessed effects. Having "been justified by faith," we "have peace with God" (Rom. 5:1) and peace in our relationships with others.

BLESSING IN THE LIGHT OF GOD'S THRONE

Theologians speak of Christ's redeeming work as both accomplished and applied. Revelation 22:1–2 shows the ultimate accomplishment of salvation by the sovereign will of the Father and the atoning death of the Son, culminating in the outflowing provision of eternal life. The final three verses depict the eternal application of redemption for those who come to Christ in faith. For them, the curse of sin will give way to the blessing of grace, eternity will be spent basking in the knowledge and service of God, and those joined to Christ will reign with him forever and ever.

When Adam and Eve first sinned against God, they fell under the curse of his just wrath. As a result, they were cast out of the garden and barred

8. James M. Hamilton Jr., *Revelation: The Spirit Speaks to the Churches* (Wheaton, IL: Crossway, 2012), 404.

from the Tree of Life (Gen. 3:22–24). No longer would they enjoy personal fellowship with God and serve as his people. The creation itself now struggled against them, making life frustrating and hard. The significance of sin can be seen in that the Bible has 1,189 chapters, all but four of which take place under the curse of sin. The first two chapters depict life before the entrance of sin, and the final two chapters show life after sin has been fully conquered by Christ. The intervening 1,185 chapters tell the story of how God redeemed his people from sin through the ministry of his Son, Jesus Christ.

When John says, "No longer will there be anything accursed" (Rev. 22:3), he declares that the entry of sin has been remedied and reversed. Now believers will enjoy the bounty of God's grace, which is richer in Christ than the joys of the original garden. We live now in the age when sin has not yet been removed. But by confessing our sins and bringing them to the cross for forgiveness, we escape the curse of sin and enter into the life of the children of God. The penalty paid by Jesus has restored us to God, and one day soon its effects will be cosmically removed for life in the new Jerusalem. Paul wrote: "Christ redeemed us from the curse of the law by becoming a curse for us—for it is written, 'Cursed is everyone who is hanged on a tree'" (Gal. 3:13).

The chief bane of Adam and Eve's fall into sin was their alienation from the presence of God. The chief blessing of the eternal glory is, correspondingly, the return of God's presence to his redeemed people. John thus writes that "the throne of God and of the Lamb will be in it" (Rev. 22:3). God's throne dominates the visions of Revelation. At first, John was permitted to peer into heaven to see the vision of God's throne (4:2). Now, at the end of the story, he sees "the throne of God and of the Lamb" in the very midst of his people.

This statement shows that redemption is a restoration to the presence and blessing of God, as well as to God's kingly rule. The calling for God's throne to reign in your life through obedience to his Word is a sign of your return to his favor. It is those under a curse who are left to wander in the blasted lands east of Eden, free to govern their own lives in folly and sin. Those who are placed under the authority of God's Word are those no longer cursed by sin but blessed by grace. Just as the curse of sin was removed by God's sovereign will and the Lamb's atoning work, his blessing is sustained by the enthroned presence of God in his truth and grace.

Note further that the people redeemed from the curse and blessed by God's presence are "his servants" who "will worship him" (Rev. 22:3). The Greek word *latreuo* can mean both "serve" and "worship." Of course, the two go together in the eternal city. Just as Adam was called to "work . . . and keep" the original garden (Gen. 2:15), making it be "fruitful and multiply" (1:28), so also will the redeemed pick up the work of spreading God's glory through the universe for all eternity. Here is the answer to those who worry that eternity will be a never-ending version of boring worship services that they may have endured on earth. Just as the presence of God in his Word makes worship enlivening now, so will his presence make our eternal service an exercise in glory.

In the new Jerusalem, we will be like the priests of Israel who marveled to enter the temple and serve in the midst of such precious things. We will share with Christ in the care and cultivation of the glorified cosmos, fulfilling our God-given desire to work for things of true value and glory. Undoubtedly, we will be filled with rapture in bowing before the living God and singing with angel choirs songs of grace and glory. Philip Hughes writes: "Clothed in robes of holiness that have been washed and made white in the blood of the Lamb, they are before the throne of God and serve him ceaselessly in his temple."[9] Our challenge today is to realize that through faith in Christ we are clothed in this very manner before God, and our sincere worship and witness constitutes a living sacrifice that is precious to him even now (Rom. 12:1).

Not only will we enter into the blessing of God, but we will spend eternity growing in our knowledge of him. John writes: "They will see his face" (Rev. 22:4). Richard Bauckham explains: "The face expresses who a person is. To see God's face will be to know who God is in his personal being. This will be the heart of humanity's eternal joy in their eternal worship of God."[10]

Here is a blessing denied to the greatest of God's servants during this present age. Moses pleaded to see God's face, but God answered, "You cannot see my face, for man shall not see me and live" (Ex. 33:20). Moses was instead placed in a cleft of the rock to see the back of God's glory. Jesus explained that man may not see God's face because of sin. But he said,

9. Philip Edgcumbe Hughes, *The Book of Revelation* (Downers Grove, IL: InterVarsity Press, 1990), 233.

10. Richard Bauckham, *The Theology of the Book of Revelation* (Cambridge: Cambridge University Press, 1993), 142.

"Blessed are the pure in heart, for they shall see God" (Matt. 5:8). In this life, none qualify for this vision, though we are justified by faith in Christ. Yet in the age to come, we will be holy like him and thus will see his face. John wrote: "Beloved, we are God's children now, and what we will be has not yet appeared; but we know that when he appears we shall be like him, because we shall see him as he is" (1 John 3:2). Knowing this, he added, is an incentive to our present pursuit of holiness: "And everyone who thus hopes in him purifies himself as he is pure" (3:3).

In this life, you will probably never meet a famous general, a head of state, or even a popular movie star. But if you belong to Christ through faith, you will see God's face. Indeed, the mark of a mature believer is an increasing desire to see God's glory in heaven and to be closer to him now. "I want to see his glory!" advanced believers will cry. They seek a privilege that only the high priest enjoyed in the Old Testament, when he entered the holy of holies once a year and beheld the ark of the covenant. The temple context of John's vision shows that the high priest's privilege would one day belong to all the people of God when they are restored in the resurrection. We anticipate and prepare now for this unimaginable delight by coming to know God better through his Word. It is not surprising that for people who are destined to see God's face, the most wholesome and enriching of all activities is the study of God in the teaching of his Word.

In addition to seeing God's face, believers will have "his name" written "on their foreheads" (Rev. 22:4). Whereas the mark of the beast signified loyalty to the tyrannical Antichrist, here the mark of God signifies the loyalty of those who belong to him. In an earlier vision, the sealing of God's name on his people indicated his care for their souls (7:3), in contrast to the unbelieving world marked with the sign of the beast. Moreover, the name of God stands for his character, which is reflected in the holiness of the glorified saints. God's mark indicates his ownership, his covenant union, and his acceptance of all who bear his name in eternity. None who bear his name will ever be forgotten or lost.

In one of his earlier letters, Jesus promised to the Philadelphians: "The one who conquers, . . . I will write on him the name of my God . . . and my own new name" (Rev. 3:12). Meredith Kline writes: "To say that the over-comers in the New Jerusalem bear the name of Christ in their forehead is to say that they reflect the glory of Christ, which is to say that they bear the image of the glorified Christ."[11] Christians read comments like this and marvel at what they think is really not possible for their lives. Is it feasible that you will "bear the image of the glorified Christ"? The New Testament says that through union with Christ in faith, as the Holy Spirit works in us by God's Word and by our prayers, we will increasingly display Christ's glory. Paul writes: "And we all, with unveiled face, beholding the glory of the Lord, are being transformed into the same image from one degree of glory to another" (2 Cor. 3:18). We increasingly bear the image of the glory of Christ in a sanctified character, through deeds of service, in biblically faithful worship, and in loving gospel witness as we grow spiritually in a life committed to knowing and glorifying God. As a Christian, you bear the name of Christ now! Why should you not consecrate yourself to him, asking Christ to display his glory in and through you by the power of his Holy Spirit?

John repeats in Revelation 22:5 his earlier statement that "night will be no more. They will need no light of lamp or sun, for the Lord God will be their light." Everything belonging to the old order will have gone, including both nighttime with its dangers and temptations and the celestial light needed for daytime. C. S. Lewis called this present life the "Shadow-Lands," meaning that here is the world of shadows and pale reflections of what will be possible in the light of God.[12] In the new Jerusalem, God's presence will always "be their light." Simon Kistemaker notes: "In the renewed world God's people will never need to rest and sleep; they will have boundless energy to serve God and praise his name forever and ever."[13]

REIGNING WITH CHRIST FOREVER

The very last statement of the final vision of salvation provided in Revelation must be significant. John concludes: "And they will reign forever and ever" (Rev. 22:5). Thus, at the end is fulfilled God's first calling for his people. God said, "Let us make man in our image, after our likeness. And let them have dominion" (Gen. 1:26). Sin made us slaves, but God intends by grace to make us kings. Bruce Milne writes: "Humanity will again raise their

---

11. Meredith G. Kline, *Images of the Spirit* (Grand Rapids: Baker, 1980), 54.
12. C. S. Lewis, *The Last Battle* (New York: Collier, 1970), 183.
13. Kistemaker, *Revelation*, 583.

heads and stand tall in God's presence, and in his world. The wretch will ascend the throne. The rebel will reign. The condemned will be crowned."[14]

Through union with Christ in faith, you are destined to reign with him in the land of glory. Of the one who conquers, he said, "I will grant him to sit with me on my throne, as I also conquered and sat down with my Father on his throne" (Rev. 3:21). This being true, why should sin reign over you now (Rom. 6:12)? Why should you succumb to anxiety, even in the midst of great trials, when God has sent his Son to die for your sins and has promised that you will reign with him forever? Remembering that John wrote the book of Revelation to churches facing terrible persecution for their faith and testimony to Christ, why should you fear to speak boldly the truths of God's Word, and especially the gospel offer of salvation? John said that Christ's faithful servants overcome evil now by the word of their testimony to the blood of Christ (Rev. 12:11). Of them, God's Word promises that "the saints of the Most High shall receive the kingdom and possess the kingdom forever, forever and ever" (Dan. 7:18).

The fantasy visions of C. S. Lewis excel in providing a foretaste of the glories depicted in Revelation. At the end of *The Lion, the Witch and the Wardrobe*, Lewis provides a vivid scene of the crowning of the servants of Aslan, the lion figure of Christ. Peter, the hero who wielded the sharp sword, was crowned with the name Magnificent. Lucy the healer was crowned as the Gentle. Susan with her deadly bow was named Queen Susan the Valiant. Even Edmund, who had betrayed his friends and disgraced himself in sin, was crowned. His title, heralding the righteousness that comes through faith in Christ, was King Edmund the Just.[15] There is a crown for you, too, together with a portion of the glory of Christ for you to display in this world. If you come to Jesus for salvation and yield yourself to his reign in this life, then the final words of John's vision will come true for you: the Lord God will be your light, and you will reign forever and ever.

14. Bruce Milne, *The Message of Heaven and Hell: Grace and Destiny,* The Bible Speaks Today (Downers Grove, IL: InterVarsity Press, 2003), 326.

15. C. S. Lewis, *The Lion, the Witch and the Wardrobe* (New York: Collier, 1970), 181.

62

Trustworthy and True

Revelation 22:6–9

And behold, I am coming soon. Blessed is the one who keeps the words of the prophecy of this book. (Rev. 22:7)

*W*hen a writer has finally completed the manuscript of a book, there is often a sense of relief joined with accomplishment. In some cases, the author is so convinced of the importance of his message that he begins promoting the book immediately. Having recorded messages of vital importance that he received from God, John in his concluding remarks in Revelation presses on the reader the truthfulness of his message along with the urgent need for this book to be received in faith.

John's appeal to the message of Revelation is reinforced when we compare the last chapter with the book's beginning in chapter 1, finding that they emphasize the same themes. The prologue in Revelation 1:1–3 stressed that John was writing a revelation from God, sent by an angel as a testimony from Jesus Christ concerning things that were soon to come. John wrote: "Blessed is the one who reads aloud the words of this prophecy, and blessed are those who hear, and who keep what is written in it, for the time is near" (Rev. 1:3). Now at the end of his remarkable book, John provides nearly the identical exhortation: "These words are trustworthy and true. . . . Blessed is

674

the one who keeps the words of the prophecy of this book" (22:6–7). John's concluding interest concerns the book's authenticity as a revelation from God and the urgent response merited by its message.

Included with these emphases is an implied challenge to us that comes not from John but from Jesus Christ: "How are you going to respond to reading this message?" All the information we need has now been provided; no further visions are needed for us to know what to do. The question now is whether we will do it! Will John's readers commit themselves to worship and serve only Jesus Christ, living faithfully as his people, relying on his sovereign rule over history to ensure our salvation, and rejoicing now to give our testimony to God's saving grace through the blood of Christ the Lamb?

THE TRUSTWORTHINESS OF SCRIPTURE

In order to respond properly to the staggering message of Revelation, we must first be persuaded of its truth. The angel thus said to John, "These words are trustworthy and true" (Rev. 22:6). By recording this testimony, John assures us that we may rely on Revelation's visions to accurately depict our present age as well as its ending. We may safely obey the exhortations that accompany the book's visions. If we commit ourselves to the faith and life urged by Revelation, we will experience the blessings promised with them.

John is commending not only the final vision of God's eternal city but the entire book of Revelation. The visions of the seven seals, seven trumpets, and seven bowls showed Christ's victory in judging evil, and John assures us that we can count on this happening. The visions of chapters 12–14 showed the church being opposed by Satan the dragon, with his tyrannical beast, deceiving false prophet, and seductive harlot Babylon. These truly are the spiritual powers that Christians face in this world, and Christ truly will cast each of them into the lake of fire when he returns in the last judgment. Concerning all these visions, including the final vision of a glorious city for the faithful people of God (chaps. 21–22), John writes: "These words are trustworthy and true" (Rev. 22:6).

We can see the significance of this matter by noting how Satan led our first parents into sin. Satan's first recorded words to Eve asked, "Did God actually say . . . ?" (Gen. 3:1). Satan challenged the truth of God's Word. By casting doubt on what God had said, Satan was able to cast our race into the fall. It is still by leading people to ignore or reject the Scriptures that Satan keeps unbelievers in bondage today.

When John claims that God's Word is "trustworthy and true," he is echoing the uniform teaching of the Bible about itself. According to the Bible, the Scriptures may be trusted completely because they are the Word of God. You see this view in Paul's writing. In 1 Corinthians 2, Paul criticizes his opponents for not understanding God's plan and purposes. Speaking of his own teaching, he adds, "These things God has revealed to us through the Spirit" (1 Cor. 2:10). Second Timothy 3:16 states: "All Scripture is breathed out by God." It is on this basis that what John says of Revelation is true of the entire Bible: "These words are trustworthy and true" (Rev. 22:6).

There are people who claim to believe what the Bible says about Jesus and salvation, but who dispute the Bible's teaching when it comes to matters that conflict with contemporary standards of thinking and morality. But how can we believe what the Bible says about Jesus and salvation when we do not even believe what the Bible says about itself? If the Bible is not true in declaring itself the Word of God, and therefore "perfect," "sure," and "true" (Ps. 19:7–9), then how can we accept what it says about anything? The only way for Christians to uphold God's Word in a hostile world and remain faithful to Jesus Christ is to stand on an authoritative, inerrant Bible, grounded on the infallibility of the God who has revealed his truth to us in it.

As the angel continues in Revelation 22:6, he describes God as "the Lord, the God of the spirits of the prophets." By referring to the "spirits" of the prophets in the plural, John speaks of the inward faculties of the various men who wrote the Bible books. The Bible was written by men in a wide variety of situations, and their spirits were fully engaged in writing their histories, poems, and prophecies. Yet God was ruling over this entire process: the Lord is "the God of the spirits of the prophets." Ben Witherington states that "God is the source of the prophet's inspiration because God is the ruler over human spirits."[1]

The angel's statement accords with the classic definition of *the inspiration of Scripture*, which states that the Bible's human authors wrote under God's control. Peter asserts that the Bible writers conveyed not their own thoughts, but God's message through the Holy Spirit: "For no prophecy was

---

1. Ben Witherington III, *Revelation*, New Cambridge Bible Commentary (Cambridge: Cambridge University Press, 2003), 279.

ever produced by the will of man, but men spoke from God as they were carried along by the Holy Spirit" (2 Peter 1:21). It is because God inspired the Bible writers that we can echo David's confidence, expressed in Psalm 119:105: "Your word is a lamp to my feet and a light to my path."

In the case of the book of Revelation, John's guide adds that God "has sent his angel to show his servants what must soon take place" (Rev. 22:6). In the Old Testament, angels often delivered God's Word, especially when it involved prophetic visions. John thus stands in the line of the prophets. Douglas Kelly writes: "What Revelation predicts is not brilliant human guesswork. It is not the product of human philosophy, or even religion. It is rather, a matter of God revealing to us what is true" through angelic messengers.[2]

John offers a final attestation to the truth of Revelation by noting that it was recorded by an eyewitness of the visions who was also an authorized apostle of Jesus Christ. Revelation 22:8 states: "I, John, am the one who heard and saw these things."[3] The apostles were Christ's authorized servants in recording the New Testament. What Paul said about his message is equally true of John's teaching: "I did not receive it from any man, nor was I taught it, but I received it through a revelation of Jesus Christ" (Gal. 1:12). For this reason, the teaching of the apostles is to be "accepted . . . not as the word of men but as what it really is, the word of God" (1 Thess. 2:13). Ephesians 2:20 notes that the church is built "on the foundation of the apostles and prophets, Christ Jesus himself being the cornerstone." Christ employed his apostles to reveal and record the truth on which his church would be built. In this capacity, John assures us that the visions he has seen and heard are "trustworthy and true" (Rev. 22:6).

COMING SOON?

The angels in Revelation were commissioned "to show [God's] servants what must soon take place" (Rev. 22:6). Assuming that the angel who spoke these words was referring to Jesus' return, some would argue that this statement cannot be taken as "trustworthy and true." Moreover, in verse 7, Jesus speaks, declaring, "And behold, I am coming soon." This statement, made roughly nineteen hundred years ago, would seem to undercut the truthfulness

2. Douglas F. Kelly, *Revelation*, Mentor Expository Commentary (Tain, Ross-shire, Scotland: Mentor, 2012), 429.

3. For the argument in favor of seeing Revelation's author as the apostle John, see chapter 1.

of John's message. How can this promise be taken seriously when Christ's return was not soon at all, but has been delayed for almost two millennia and may not occur for many more years to come? Does this not constitute an error that challenges the truthfulness not only of Revelation but of the whole Bible?

We might take Jesus' promise to come soon in a number of ways. First, the future events foretold in Revelation are "soon" in the important sense that they are the next events to occur on the prophetic calendar. The turmoil of the last days is near in that there are no great events in God's plan between our current situation and the events associated with Jesus' return.

A second approach takes Jesus as promising to come soon in the form of help for the churches under persecution. He would not abandon them to the sword of Caesar but would come to them with aid. This view accords with how Jesus spoke to the church in Pergamum, warning that if they did not repent, "I will come to you soon and war against them with the sword of my mouth" (Rev. 2:16). In his letter to the church of Philadelphia, Jesus promised, "I am coming soon," to deliver them "from the hour of trial" (3:10–11). These promises do not necessarily refer to the second coming, but promise Christ's sovereign lordship in ruling and protecting his people.

Still, the most natural way to take Jesus' promise to come soon pertains to his return from heaven to judge the world and inaugurate the eternal age. In this case, his coming does not seem to have come soon. Yet Peter urges us to consider God's perspective on time:

> But do not overlook this one fact, beloved, that with the Lord one day is as a thousand years, and a thousand years as one day. The Lord is not slow to fulfill his promise as some count slowness, but is patient toward you, not wishing that any should perish, but that all should reach repentance. (2 Peter 3:8–9)

Christians are therefore to anticipate Christ's coming at any time, looking often to the horizon for the appearing of our great hope. In the meantime, we are to live as those who are ready for our Lord's appearing, eager to be found faithful when he comes. Grant Osborne writes: "The church in every age is to await Christ's 'soon' return, but the actual timing is up to him."[4]

---

4. Grant R. Osborne, *Revelation*, Baker Exegetical Commentary on the New Testament (Grand Rapids: Baker Academic, 2002), 782.

How to Receive the Scriptures

Steve Wilmshurst compares the situation of believers awaiting Christ's return with that of the French Resistance fighters during World War II. During the four years of Nazi occupation, many of the people had started cooperating with the enemy. But small bands of brave fighters waged continuous guerrilla warfare. They sabotaged rail lines, raided military bases, and gave information to the Allied forces, whose coming they eagerly awaited. The Resistance did not know when British and American troops would finally land on their shores and parachute into their fields, but they had been given coded information to anticipate the event. On June 1, 1944, the BBC broadcast the first coded message, hidden in its normal programming. It read: "Stand by; we are coming soon." Jesus has likewise transmitted to his church the message that he will come soon, in order to encourage his church in its long fight against evil.[5]

While believers await the appearing of Christ, John gives clear instructions in Revelation's sixth beatitude: "Blessed is the one who keeps the words of the prophecy of this book" (Rev. 22:7). To "keep" God's Word is to receive it in faith, hold fast to it in hope, and obey it in action. The French Resistance fighters never thought that they alone could oust the German invaders, but were looking for deliverers to come. While they waited, however, they sought to do all that they could, upholding the cause in true faith and preserving their consciences from the stain of compromise. In a similar way, Christians awaiting Jesus' return keep his Word in true faith.

Revelation 22:7 informs us how to receive the entirety of God's Word. We are to keep its words and its prophecy. Receiving the words of the Bible means that we are to study it carefully, believing and putting into practice everything that it says. Christians believe not only the general message of the Bible but its actual words, since they are spoken to us by God. We therefore take seriously whatever the text of Scripture says. Jesus asserted, "Heaven and earth will pass away, but my words will not pass away" (Matt. 24:35). This is why evangelical Christians have emphasized *plenary, verbal inspiration*. *Verbal inspiration* means that the very words themselves are outbreathed by God and therefore to be placed into our hearts and minds,

5. Adapted from Steve Wilmshurst, *The Final Word: The Book of Revelation Simply Explained* (Darlington, UK: Evangelical Press, 2008), 271–72.

while *plenary inspiration* means that we receive all the Bible's words and sentences as divine truth, not just those that seem inspiring to us. We find an example of this attitude in the life of Jesus Christ, who declared the very words of God in his contest with the devil (4:1–11), and submitted his life and ministry in careful obedience to Holy Scripture. Jesus said in Hebrews 10:7, "Behold, I have come to do your will, O God, as it is written of me in the scroll of the book."

The angel especially emphasizes keeping "the prophecy of this book" (Rev. 22:7). This means that the history revealed in Revelation—some of it present and some future—becomes the truth by which we live. We are to resist evil, knowing that it is soon to be judged and that Christ will not allow his people to be defeated. Knowing the certainty of our victory in Christ, we are to do the will of God and bear testimony to Christ's blood. We keep the prophecy of Revelation by acting on the same conviction that kept the French Resistance fighting during World War II. Wilmshurst writes that they fought under the certain conviction "that this terrible occupation will not, *cannot*, last for ever. One day their enemies will be destroyed and liberation will come."[6] Verse 7 states that those who keep "the words of the prophecy of this book" will be blessed: "They will receive all God's covenant promises and inherit all that has been talked about through the book and especially in the last couple of chapters."[7] Geoffrey Wilson reminds us, "It is not in reading, or wondering, or talking, but in keeping, that the blessing comes."[8]

DO NOT DO IT!

This final section of Revelation not only teaches us the truthfulness of God's Word and shows us how to keep God's Word, but also indicates what will happen to faithful believers when we do. John has just witnessed the glorious vision of the new Jerusalem (Rev. 21:1–22:5). The angel had reminded him of the truth of these visions, and then, in Revelation 22:7, Jesus either interrupts to say that he is coming soon or says this to John through the

6. Ibid., 271.

7. Paul Gardner, *Revelation: The Compassion and Protection of Christ*, Focus on the Bible (Ross-shire, UK: Christian Focus, 2008), 301.

8. Geoffrey B. Wilson, *New Testament Commentaries*, 2 vols. (Edinburgh: Banner of Truth, 2005), 2:595.

angel. In response, John is so overwhelmed that he loses his bearings: "I fell down to worship at the feet of the angel who showed them to me" (22:8).

We see in John that when we receive God's Word as truth and keep its visions of glory, we will be cast down in an attitude of worship. Scholars take differing views of John's mistaken action in worshiping the angel, which previously occurred in Revelation 19:10. Some think that John is so dazzled that he wrongly thinks that angels are to be worshiped. Others hold that John confused the angel with Jesus Christ, perhaps because in 22:7 Jesus had spoken to John through the angel. Third, it is possible that John was simply so spiritually staggered that he lost himself in an attitude of wonder and praise. I think the last of these is at least one reason for John's behavior.

In responding to John's action, the angel instructs us in the vitally important matter of worship. Angels are worship specialists, so we should listen carefully when they teach us about this topic. Here, the angel responds in outraged horror: "You must not do that!" (Rev. 22:9). The English language does not fully reflect the strength of revulsion expressed in the original Greek, which says, "See that not!" "Don't do this, John!" the angel responds.

We should not think that this interplay between John and the angel is disconnected from the exhortation to keep the message of Revelation. John is being shown, and we with him, that the first and single most important element in keeping God's Word is to give to God alone the glory that he is due. The angel reacts out of a consuming passion for the exclusive glory of God, and this same passion must be seen in the hearts of all those who keep the words of God's Book.

The attitude of this angel is also seen in God's servants in the Bible. A notable example is that of the apostle Paul in Acts 17 when he worked his way through the streets of Athens. Acts 17:16 says that "his spirit was provoked within him as he saw that the city was full of idols." Paul was so grievously startled by idolatry that he suffered an inward convulsion. He suffered in his spirit something analogous to a heart attack. The reason for his paroxysm was the grievous thought that God's glory was being given to others who were not God. Paul was not overwhelmed because he did not know how to contextualize his ministry or because he lacked the sophistication of his pagan neighbors. Paul was stricken because through the Word of God he had obtained an overwhelming passion for the glory of God and a revulsion for the casting down of God's honor. This same spirit was seen in the great missionary Henry Martyn during his labors in Persia. On one occasion, Martyn heard from a Muslim that when Christians were persecuted, Christ himself would beg mercy from Muhammad. Martyn replied with utmost outrage at the blasphemy: "I could not endure existence if Jesus was not glorified—it would be hell to me, if he were always to be thus dishonored."[9]

When we read these glowing examples from the Bible and Christian biography, we should ask ourselves whether we know anything of this passionate concern for the glory of God. To keep the prophecy of Revelation calls us to walk through this world, not admiring its impressive idolatries and wishing that we could participate more fully in worldly things, but rather looking with broken hearts upon an age filled with men and women who were made for God's glory but who have foolishly offered themselves to serve idols and lies. We are to be as resolved to combat with spiritual weapons the idolatry of this age as the Resistance fighters were committed to opposing the Nazi rule in France. Instead of fearing what such a world might take from us, we should be stricken by realizing the glory it has withheld from God and determined to give a faithful living testimony to Jesus Christ so that many may be saved.

WORSHIP GOD!

We should consider the angel's reaction not only negatively but also in three essential and positive statements that he makes to John. First, he tells us that the worship of God is a command and duty for all his servants in Jesus Christ. "You must not do that!" the angel cries. Instead, he says, "Worship God" (Rev. 22:9). The call to "worship" is in the form of an imperative, which means that it is a command. We do not worship God merely when we think it would be pleasing to do so, or would otherwise serve our interests, but we are to devote ourselves fully and constantly to the praise of God. Answer 1 of the Westminster Shorter Catechism accurately sums up our duty: "Man's chief end is to glorify God, and to enjoy him for ever."

Here we see an instance of how good it is to obey God and how blessed it is to keep his commands. When we experience the blessing of worship, especially in corporate worship with God's people, we understand David's meaning in

9. John Sargent, *Life and Letters of the Rev. Henry Martyn, B.D.* (London: Seeley, Jackson, and Halliday, 1862), 343.

the Psalms, "Oh how I love your law!" (Ps. 119:97). Obedience to God always brings blessing, and how much more so when we are worshiping him.

Second, note that "worship" in Revelation 22:9 has a direct object. It is what we call a *transitive* verb, in contrast to an *intransitive* verb. The latter has no direct object. *Smile* is such a verb. But *worship* is a transitive verb that requires an object. Many people today say that they want merely "to worship." They may be listening to praise music in their car or singing repetitive verses in the church and declare that they are "just worshiping." But it is impossible "just to worship." Worship always has an object. The problem with many churches today is that the object or recipient of worship is man. The goal is to please the worshipers, or the visitors, or the observing unbelieving world. But the angel insists that only God is the true object and consumer of worship. "Worship God!" he says. This means that we come to church not primarily seeking what we will get out of worship but what God will get out of worship. The best way to achieve this is to worship according to God's Word. Through worship that follows the example of Scripture and fervently proclaims God's Word we fulfill the command of Hebrews 12:28, "Let us offer to God acceptable worship, with reverence and awe."

Third, the angel tells us that it is in true worship directed to God that we most thoroughly realize our high identity and privilege as God's people. The angel tells John, "I am a fellow servant with you and your brothers the prophets, and with those who keep the words of this book" (Rev. 22:9). What an incredible dignity the angel conveys upon John if he worships God as he should. As an apostle, John is a brother with the prophets of old. But in worshiping God, he becomes a fellow servant with glorious, unfallen angels in the splendor of their holiness. Moreover, the angel says that this is also true of "those who keep the words of this book." This is the true dignity of every Christian man and woman, when in the worship of God through Jesus Christ we are elevated into the fraternity and brotherhood of angels! In preaching on this verse, Eric Alexander exclaimed: "The thing that unites apostles and angels and the people of God with them in every generation is that their proper place is to be bowed together before the throne of the eternal God, exalting him to the unique place of honor and glory, and to give to him the worship which he is due."[10]

10. Eric J. Alexander, "Do Not Do It! Worship God," audio recording, Philadelphia Conference on Reformed Theology (Philadelphia: Alliance of Confessing Evangelicals, 1998). The concluding sections of this chapter are reflective of Alexander's sermon.

In light of this instruction, we must not think we have kept the words of the prophecy of the book of Revelation until we have imbibed the passion for the glory of God that we see in this angel. This is our true calling, and it is the purpose of Revelation that even in this present evil age we would enter into it: that we would possess an overwhelming concern for the glory of God in the person and work of Jesus Christ. Moreover, we must not think we have suitably given testimony before the world to the gospel message of this book until the world has seen in our lives the consuming passion for the glory of God that Revelation is intended to inspire.

63

THE LAST TESTIMONY
OF JESUS CHRIST

Revelation 22:10–16

Blessed are those who wash their robes, so that they may have
the right to the tree of life and that they may enter the
city by the gates. (Rev. 22:14)

evelation is the last book in the Bible, the final book of the apostolic era, and also the book that most clearly describes the end of history and return of Christ. As "the revelation of Jesus Christ" (Rev. 1:1), it has shown Christ reigning as Lord over his church, defending his people under persecution, slaying his enemies, and shining his glory on the eternal city. How fitting that Jesus should now speak at the book's end. Steve Wilmshurst writes: "On the last page of the Bible, before the canon of Scripture is closed for ever, Christ speaks one more time to his church, to *us*, reminding us of his identity, his return and his final summons to his people."[11]

Revelation 22:16 removes any doubt as to whose testimony is contained in the final message given to John: "I, Jesus, have sent my angel to testify to you

11. Steve Wilmshurst, *The Final Word: The Book of Revelation Simply Explained* (Darlington, UK: Evangelical Press, 2008), 273–74.

about these things for the churches." In the concluding verses of chapter 22, Jesus speaks as Sovereign, Judge, and Savior. In this last testimony, Jesus is himself the Last Word as the canon of Scripture closes and his people wait expectantly for his return.

JESUS THE SOVEREIGN

Throughout the book of Revelation, the sovereignty of God and of Christ has been emphasized as the basis of our hope for the judgment of evil and the salvation of believers. Chapter 1 declared God as "the Alpha and the Omega" (Rev. 1:8), who thus governs everything from beginning to end. Chapter 22 ascribes this same sovereign title to Jesus: "I am the Alpha and the Omega, the first and the last, the beginning and the end" (22:13). In this sovereign capacity, Jesus dictates to John how to handle the message of this book: "And he said to me, 'Do not seal up the words of the prophecy of this book, for the time is near'" (22:10).

We have observed the close relationship between Revelation and Daniel, whose prophecy was fulfilled in John's message. At the end of Daniel, the prophet was told to keep his message "sealed until the time of the end" (Dan. 12:9). Jesus gives the opposite command, telling John not to seal the message of his book (Rev. 22:10). Daniel was shown events that were far distant to his own generation, so his message had to be sealed to await the proper time. In John's case, Revelation must not be sealed because "the time is near."

Revelation described a situation that was urgent in John's time. These were churches facing the tribulations written of in Revelation, so they needed the courage that the book supplies by declaring Christ's sovereign victory. G. B. Caird writes that Revelation was needed so that "in the Roman court-room, at the Roman scaffold, in the Roman arena, the ears that are attuned to the songs of Zion may hear the lament, 'Fallen, fallen is Babylon the great', and the eyes of faith may see both the monster rising from the abyss and going to perdition and Jerusalem coming down out of heaven from God."[12] With the sword of the beast against their necks and the seductions of harlot Babylon alluring, it was necessary for John's readers to know the certain victory of the Lamb from his reigning throne on Mount Zion. It is in this same spirit that Jesus provides the message of Revelation to the church today, "for the time is near."

12. G. B. Caird, *The Revelation of St. John the Divine* (San Francisco: Harper, 1966), 284.

Jesus' instruction for the unsealing of Revelation proves that the book was not written merely for Christians who will live in the future period just before Christ's return. Jesus said that his message was urgent for the people of John's own time and thus for believers throughout the church age as well. According to the Bible, the last days began when Jesus ascended into heaven and established his church through the apostles, starting the final era of redemptive history (see 2 Tim. 3:1; Heb. 1:2). Jesus therefore gives his last testimony to John "about these things for the churches" (Rev. 22:16). Since Revelation is intended for the churches of this present age, the neglect of this book today will leave the church weakened under the assault of the world.

Jesus not only commands John's handling of Revelation, but speaks with sovereign authority to the world: "Let the evildoer still do evil, and the filthy still be filthy, and the righteous still do right, and the holy still be holy" (Rev. 22:11). This statement connects with the end of Daniel's prophecy, after the prophet was told to seal up his book. The angel added: "Many shall purify themselves and make themselves white and be refined, but the wicked shall act wickedly" (Dan. 12:10). There, the idea was that there would always be godly and ungodly people until Christ returns. In John's case, however, Jesus speaks with a command: "Let the evildoer still do evil" and "the righteous still do right" (Rev. 22:11). Jesus commands not only godly people to be godly but also evil people to do evil.

It is hard to understand Jesus' commanding people to be evil, which is why some commentators place this statement at the end of history when Jesus returns. The argument is made that Jesus is saying that there is no more chance of salvation, so that evil people will have to continue in evil. In this way, Jesus warns unbelievers to turn to him in faith while there remains time for salvation. This teaching urges that the worst thing that could happen to you is not that you could become sick or lose your job, or even lose your life. The worst fate possible is to be hardened in unbelief so as to be confirmed in evil and filth when Christ returns. This teaching is certainly true, but since Jesus wanted his message unsealed not merely at the end but also in John's time, it is not likely the whole point of this verse.

The language of Revelation 22:11 shows that Jesus is commanding, not merely commenting, and that he commands evil and filth just as he commands righteousness and holiness. In what sense can we understand Jesus to be commanding evil? The answer is that Jesus is commanding that

687

ungodliness be seen for what it is and that godliness be seen for what it is. One of the emphases of Revelation is that Christ will confront and judge evil throughout this age and especially at its end. Here, he commands that evildoing be seen as evil and moral corruption be displayed as the filth that it is. Is this not happening in Western society today, despite the propaganda that promotes sexual perversity, celebrates greed, and masks a culture of death? Despite the clever denials and deceptions, wickedness is nonetheless revealed by its effects. In this way, the Sovereign Christ exposes the evil of both sinful deeds and sinful character. The opposite will be true for godliness throughout this age and at the end: however misrepresented and despised biblical obedience may be in our time, Christ will ensure that its luster will nonetheless shine. Righteous deeds will be seen as being right, and Christ's holy people will be revealed as holy. This is the command of the Sovereign Christ, speaking at the end of his Word.

According to Jesus, there are only two kinds of people: evildoers with filthy natures and righteous people who are holy by God's grace. This is the important issue during this life—not the contest for the greatest amount of wealth, power, or prestige and not the quest for the most enjoyable experiences. What matters in this world is how we stand before God with respect to our sins and then how we will act in response to God's Word. Christ's sovereign command comforts his people with the certainty that however twisted events may seem in this world, darkness will be exposed in its evil and the light of true faith and holiness will be revealed in their beauty and glory.

JESUS THE JUDGE

In his last testimony, Jesus speaks not only as Sovereign but also as Judge: "Behold, I am coming soon, bringing my recompense with me, to repay everyone for what he has done" (Rev. 22:12).

This is the second of three times in this final chapter that Jesus declares his soon return (see also Rev. 22:7, 20). In this instance, he is emphasizing the need to be ready at all times. This statement echoes Isaiah 40:10, "Behold, the Lord GOD comes with might, and his arm rules for him; behold, his reward is with him, and his recompense before him." Jesus spoke similarly in his parable of the talents, in which he compared himself to a master who went away but then returned "and settled accounts" with his servants (Matt.

25:19). To those who had served him zealously, the master said, "Well done, good and faithful servant," and enriched them with rewards (25:21). But unfaithful servants who had done nothing for him were "cast . . . into the outer darkness" of "weeping and gnashing of teeth" (25:30).

The parable of the talents provides a background for Jesus' statement that he comes to recompense "everyone for what he has done" (Rev. 22:12). Simon Kistemaker writes: "The promise of Jesus' return means joy and happiness for the believer but fear and remorse for the unbeliever."[13] Those who have trusted Christ and served him will be rewarded: "You have been faithful over a little; I will set you over much" (Matt. 25:23). For those who rebelled against his claims and persisted in doing evil, Jesus returns to give retribution: "These will go away into eternal punishment, but the righteous into eternal life" (25:46).

Jesus' coming as Judge does not refer merely to his return at the end of the age, but also to his sovereign judgments within history. In his letter to Thyatira, Jesus warned about a woman he called "Jezebel," and those who followed her into "sexual immorality and to eat food sacrificed to idols" (Rev. 2:20). Jesus warned that he would visit the woman with sickness and bring great tribulation upon that church, unless they repented. He summed up his providential discipline, saying, "I will give to each of you according to your works" (2:23).

These statements raise the question whether Revelation is teaching salvation by works. The answer is made clear in 22:14, where it is seen that only those who wash their sins in Christ's blood can be saved. Salvation is not by works, since we are all sinners who would be condemned before God's law. The standard of works for salvation was given by Jesus in Matthew 5:48: "You therefore must be perfect, as your heavenly Father is perfect." Paul informs us that "all have sinned and fall short of the glory of God" (Rom. 3:23), so that we can be saved only by God's grace received through faith. Believers, Paul continues, "are justified by his grace as a gift, through the redemption that is in Christ Jesus" (3:24).

Salvation by grace alone does not mean, however, that the works of believers are of no importance. While good works are not necessary as a *condition* of a Christian's salvation, they are necessary as a *consequence* of salvation. Christians are God's "workmanship," Paul said, "created in Christ Jesus for

13. Simon J. Kistemaker, *Revelation*, New Testament Commentary (Grand Rapids: Baker, 2001), 589.

good works" (Eph. 2:10). Therefore, true believers must and will do good works, which alone can prove that our faith is real. James wrote that "faith apart from works is dead" (James 2:26). His point was not that we are saved by works instead of faith, but rather that a genuine saving faith is evidenced by the good works that it does. Without works, faith is empty and false, so that Jesus declared, "Not everyone who says to me, 'Lord, Lord,' will enter the kingdom of heaven, but the one who does the will of my Father who is in heaven" (Matt. 7:21).

A second reason why the works of believers are important concerns the rewards that Christ will give. Paul writes of a weak believer who enters heaven with little to show for his life. "Each one's work will become manifest," Paul explains, "for the Day will disclose it, because it will be revealed by fire, and the fire will test what sort of work each one has done" (1 Cor. 3:13). Some believers' works will not stand this test and will be burned up. Paul tells us that such a believer "will suffer loss, though he himself will be saved, but only as through fire" (3:15). This is not the way to enter heaven! Others, whose work that they "built on the foundation survives," that is, those whose lives and deeds responded obediently to God's Word, "will receive a reward" (3:14).

Jesus says, "Behold, I am coming soon, bringing my recompense with me, to repay everyone for what he has done" (Rev. 22:12). Christ clearly cares deeply about the kind of lives that we lead and the works that we do. Steve Wilmshurst writes: "If we are believers, our reward will depend on how we have served him and what we have done with the talents he entrusted to us."[14] Vern Poythress adds:

> Even during this life, the saints begin to live a holy life, and God is pleased to reward them for their works. The imperfections in these works, and the remaining contaminations from sinful inclinations, are covered by the blood of Christ. Good works are not the basis for eternal life, as if we earned life through our own efforts, but they are demonstrations of the genuineness of our faith and of the justice of God's judgment (1 Peter 1:7; 2 Thess. 1:5).[15]

It is likely that this context of judgment is the point of Jesus' statement in Revelation 22:13: "I am the Alpha and the Omega, the first and the

---

14. Wilmshurst, *The Final Word*, 277.
15. Vern S. Poythress, *The Returning King: A Guide to the Book of Revelation* (Phillipsburg, NJ: P&R Publishing, 2000), 196.

last, the beginning and the end." These words echo the claim made by God in 1:8, providing yet another proof of the full deity of Jesus Christ. It is as the eternal and Sovereign God who is there at both beginning and end that Jesus is able to give a recompense for everyone's life. The ungodly life begins in rebellion to Jesus' reign and ends in a righteous condemnation from Jesus' throne. The godly life begins with forgiveness through Christ's blood and culminates with Christ's blessing and reward in the last judgment. Christ is able to give the recompense of judgment for unbelief and sin, since he will sit enthroned at the end. Christ is able to receive his people into eternal life, since their salvation is established on his never-ending reign.

JESUS THE SAVIOR

It is appropriate that Christ appears at the end of Revelation as Sovereign and Judge, since these themes play such a large role in the book. His final testimony, however, is given as Savior, since Christ's true purpose in Revelation is to speak to his people for their deliverance from sin and salvation into eternal life. Indeed, when we speak of Christ's bringing a recompense for his people, his primary reward is stated in the final beatitude of Revelation: "Blessed are those who wash their robes, so that they may have the right to the tree of life and that they may enter the city by the gates" (Rev. 22:14). As judgment is by works, here we find that salvation is by grace through faith in the blood of the Lamb.

By saying that "those who wash their robes" are blessed, Jesus refers to the cleansing from sin that comes through faith in the blood of his cross. Paul said, "In him we have redemption through his blood, the forgiveness of our trespasses" (Eph. 1:7). As we earlier noted, this beatitude rules out the idea of salvation by works, since the believers' robes need to be washed. Through the blood of Christ our sins are cleansed, our penalty is paid, and we are made acceptable to enter into the presence of the glory of God and receive his blessing of eternal life. The cleansing of sin through Christ's blood is not only a past reality to believers but a present resource. The washing of robes in Revelation 22:14 is in the present tense: they are blessed who "wash" their sins, referring to the daily cleansing that comes through confession and faith in the blood of Christ (see 1 John 1:9).

The placement of this blessing at the end of Revelation indicates the central place of the atonement in the Christian faith. The church sometimes suffers attempts to marginalize the theme of cleansing blood, often out of a concern that the atonement seems barbaric to unbelievers. Yet the barbarism of sin and the violence of God's wrath are truths that non-Christians greatly need to hear. At the very heart of the gospel is the blood of Christ, received by faith, as the cleansing from sin needed for our entry into God's blessing. It is as "the Lamb" that Christ is constantly revealed in Revelation; it is "by the blood of the Lamb and by the word of their testimony" that believers conquer Satan (Rev. 12:11). And it is only those who confess their sin, come to the cross of Christ, and gain forgiveness through faith in the Lamb who will enter the eternal blessing of God.

We are cleansed from sin by Christ's blood, and thus through faith we receive eternal life. This blessing is symbolized by access to the Tree of Life and entry into the city gates. When Adam fell into sin, God barred him from the garden of Eden, "lest he reach out his hand and take also of the tree of life and eat, and live forever" (Gen. 3:22). Therefore, to "have the right to the tree of life" is to be restored by God to partake of eternal life. All that was lost by the breaking of God's covenant in the garden has been regained through the new covenant in Christ. Christians do not stand outside the gates of the glorious city described in Revelation 21 and 22. They do not vainly wonder how the wall may be scaled or the governing will of God might be breached. Instead, they have the right to enter the city by its gates.

John Bunyan envisioned the glorious conclusion of the Christian life when he depicted Christian and Hopeful as passing into the Celestial City at the conclusion of *Pilgrim's Progress*:

> I saw in my dream the two men enter the gate. As they did, they were transfigured. They had garments that shined like gold. Harps and crowns were given them. The harps for praise and the crowns for honor. Then I heard in my dream all the bells in the city rang again for joy. It was said to them, "Enter into the joy of your Lord."[16]

How great is the contrast for those who refused Christ and his gospel in this life, and who after his return are consigned to eternal darkness. John

16. John Bunyan, *Pilgrim's Progress* (Nashville: Thomas Nelson, 1999), 136–37.

writes: "Outside are the dogs and sorcerers and the sexually immoral and murderers and idolaters, and everyone who loves and practices falsehood" (Rev. 22:15). By describing the ungodly as "dogs and sorcerers," John indicates God's disgust with unforgiven and persistent, unflagging sinners, both the respectable unbeliever and the openly wicked. John earlier showed that in the final judgment, the ungodly are cast into the lake of fire for eternal torment (20:12–15). Here, he identifies those who violate God's law—"the sexually immoral and murderers and idolaters" (22:15)—with the wild creatures that belong in the howling wilderness outside, to whom the gates of God's city are permanently shut. Grant Osborne writes that "the idea is both exclusion and shame, perhaps with the added idea of the Valley of Hinnom, where the trash was burned outside the walls of Jerusalem."[17] In the ancient world, dogs were despicable creatures fit only to die. With this condemnation, the wicked likewise fall under God's contempt and condemnation.

The concluding emphasis on "everyone who loves and practices falsehood" (Rev. 22:15) shows God's special disdain for those who not only practice sin but call evil good and deceive others into joining their wickedness. There is probably as well a warning to professing believers and church members that our testimony must be true and consistent with our lives. Those who profess faith in Christ but show that their loyalty is with idolatry of this world have no reason to think they will enter the city of God or eat from the Tree of Life.

THE GREATEST SINNERS SAVED

We have been considering Jesus' last testimony in Scripture, but the time comes when each of us will give our final testimony as well. For Joachim von Ribbentrop, the end came on October 16, 1946, at the U.S. military prison in Nuremberg, Germany. Ribbentrop had been foreign minister to Adolf Hitler in the Nazi Third Reich and had plotted the deceptions that plunged the world into a bloody war. Now, condemned to die and standing on a scaffold with the noose around his neck, von Ribbentrop was asked for his final words. The last testimony that he gave would summarize his attitude as he departed from life and faced the judgment of God.

17. Grant R. Osborne, *Revelation*, Baker Exegetical Commentary on the New Testament (Grand Rapids: Baker Academic, 2002), 790.

Revelation 22:15 records Jesus' condemnation of evil men like Ribbentrop and his Nazi colleagues. They were like dogs who had defiled themselves in immorality, murder, and idolatry. Yet while they lived, they still had the opportunity to be saved by turning to Christ for cleansing through his blood. This was the belief of Henry Gerecke, the Lutheran minister assigned as chaplain to the Nazi war criminals. While others looked on the vile sinners with contempt, Gerecke met with them one on one to witness and pray, and he invited them to attend his regular worship services. After a few weeks under Gerecke's simple gospel preaching, eight of the Nazi hierarchy professed faith in Jesus Christ. Among them were Field Marshal Wilhelm Keitel, chief of the German Armed Forces; Fritz Sauckel, Nazi Head of Labor Supply; and Wilhelm Frick, the Minister of the Interior who oversaw a reign of terror that had targeted many Christians. At first, Ribbentrop had rejected Gerecke with scornful abuse, though he attended the worship services as a respite from the boredom of his cell. Under Gerecke's faithful preaching of the gospel, however, God's Word was pressed to his heart and Ribbentrop was converted.

The morning came when the Nazi war criminals left their cells to face execution. Ribbentrop was the first, and Gerecke walked with him to the scaffold. With the noose over his head, Ribbentrop plainly and clearly gave his testimony: "I place all my confidence in the Lamb who made atonement for my sins. May God have mercy on my soul."[18]

Can a Nazi war criminal be forgiven so as to stand spotless before the throne of God? He can through the blood of Christ, which fully pays the greatest debt of sin and washes clean all who come to God in Jesus' name. The same salvation is offered to everyone now through faith in Christ, before he returns to judge every soul. Jesus gives this as his last testimony in the Bible: "Blessed are those who wash their robes, so that they may have the right to the tree of life and that they may enter the city by the gates" (Rev. 22:14).

18. Taken from Don Stephens, *War and Grace: Short Biographies from the World Wars* (Darlington, UK: Evangelical Press, 2005), 253–71.

64

Come to the Waters

Revelation 22:16–17

The Spirit and the Bride say, "Come." And let the one who hears
say, "Come." And let the one who is thirsty come; let the one who
desires take the water of life without price. (Rev. 22:17)

*I*n the summer of 2000, I was present with a group of close friends and colleagues at the home of the well-known Bible teacher James Montgomery Boice. Dr. Boice had been suffering from an advanced cancer, and we had come to sing some of the hymns he had written, a couple of which had just been put to music by his collaborator, Dr. Paul Jones. Most beloved to me was a hymn titled "Come to the Waters," from the text of Revelation 22:17. The first verse reads:

> Come to the waters, whoever is thirsty;
> Drink from the Fountain that never runs dry.
> Jesus, the Living One, offers you mercy,
> Life more abundant in boundless supply.[1]

After we had sung this hymn, I was briefly sitting with Dr. Boice. He took my arm and, in a voice weakened by disease but alive with conviction, told

---

1. James Montgomery Boice, "Come to the Waters," *Hymns for a Modern Reformation* (Philadelphia: Tenth Presbyterian Church, 2000), no. 7.

me, "Never forget in your ministry that it all flows through Jesus Christ." That visit was the last time that I ever saw Dr. Boice, since he died and entered the presence of the Savior soon afterward. Needless to say, those last words made a deep impression on me and helped me always to remember that our ministry is one of inviting sinners to the life that God freely gives through his Son.

The Root and Morning Star

There is little doubt that the final verses of Revelation present the same emphasis as James Boice gave to me. Having given his testimony through the angel to the churches, Jesus identifies himself one last time: "I am the root and the descendant of David, the bright morning star" (Rev. 22:16). In response to this statement, the bride of Christ, his church, appeals for him to come. Jesus then promises to come soon, and John concludes the book by declaring the grace of Christ on his believing readers. Just as James Boice urged me to always keep Christ central, the conclusion of Revelation is centered on Jesus' salvation offer and his people's adoring praise.

When Jesus says that he is "the root and the descendant of David" and "the bright morning star," he declares himself the fulfillment of important Old Testament messianic prophecies. The first statement comes from Isaiah 11:1–10, where the prophet foretold, "There shall come forth a shoot from the stump of Jesse, and a branch from his roots shall bear fruit" (Isa. 11:1). Jesse was the father of David, to whom God promised an eternal kingdom (2 Sam. 7:12). Numerous commentators take Jesus' expression "the root and the descendant of David" to say that Jesus is both the origin of David in his divine nature ("root") and the offspring of David in his human nature ("descendant"). It is more likely, however, that Jesus is simply declaring himself as the fulfillment of Isaiah's prophecy concerning the Davidic Messiah. When Isaiah called the Messiah "the stump of Jesse" (Isa. 11:10), he was speaking not of Christ's divine nature but of the insignificant earthly remnant that David's line would have become when the Messiah came. All that would be left was not merely a stump of the line of Jesse but a root of that stump. Yet that root, being incarnated as the Son of God, would be blessed by God to bring salvation. "The Spirit of the LORD shall rest upon him," Isaiah wrote (11:2), and with divine power the "root" would fulfill God's promises and restore life.

By naming himself as "the root and the descendant of David," Jesus appears at the end of history as the One who fulfills the entire Old Testament hope of salvation. Isaiah said that the "stump of Jesse" would bring a cosmic peace, with the wolf and the lamb, the lion and the fattened calf, lying down together (Isa. 11:1, 6). Jesus says that his coming fully realizes Isaiah's vision: "The earth shall be full of the knowledge of the LORD as the waters cover the sea" (11:9). "I am," he proclaims, "the root and the descendant of David" (Rev. 22:16).

The second prophecy was made in Numbers 24:17 by the mysterious pagan shaman Balaam, whom God used to foretell Jesus Christ: "A star shall come out of Jacob, and a scepter shall rise out of Israel." Jesus now declares that his victory has achieved this prophecy: "I am . . . the bright morning star" (Rev. 22:16). Balaam spoke of Christ's rising not only to give light but sovereignly to crush his enemies, bringing redemption and salvation to the people of God. Donald Grey Barnhouse explains that in the ancient world, the stars "were the heavenly time pieces by which the shepherds told the different seasons of the year, and the various watches of the night. It was the 'morning star' which heralded the sunrise and the breaking of a new day." How fitting that Jesus should bear this designation, since "he will usher in God's eternal day."[2]

The impact of Jesus' self-description is felt not merely as we absorb the images but when we understand the doctrine that is realized in who he is and what he has done. In a world where salvation often seems unlikely, Jesus is the root from which an eternal peace has come to bless the renewed creation. Jesus is the rising morning star that signals the coming of an eternal age of glory and blessing. This is the Christian doctrine of salvation. Whereas humanism hopes for the cold advance of scientific progress, Christ speaks of eternal peace flowing from his saving work. Whereas Eastern mysticism hopes for the annihilation of the self in the cosmic sea, Jesus promises that his coming is the morning star that floods his people with life and light. "I am the root and the descendant of David, the bright morning star," Jesus proclaims. Christians best respond to this imagery in song:

How lovely shines the Morning Star!
The nations see and hail afar

2. Donald Grey Barnhouse, *Revelation: An Expositional Commentary* (Grand Rapids: Zondervan, 1971), 413.

The light in Judah shining.
Thou David's son of Jacob's race,
My bridegroom and my King of grace,
For thee my heart is pining.[3]

THE CRY OF THE SPIRIT-LED BRIDE

We know that we grasp Jesus' message if we respond to it in the way that the Spirit-filled church speaks in Revelation 22:17: "The Spirit and the Bride say, 'Come.'" The bride who calls to Jesus is his church. She is betrothed to him through faith and longs for the Bridegroom to return so that the marriage feast may begin. The "Spirit" is surely the Holy Spirit, speaking through and with the church that he indwells.

The main question in this verse concerns who is being addressed by the summons, "Come." The majority of commentators argue that in the first two instances, it is Christ who is called by his adoring people: "The Spirit and the Bride say, 'Come.' And let the one who hears say, 'Come'" (Rev. 22:17). Jesus has just declared himself as the Davidic Messiah whose coming brings God's new day. His people therefore plead with him to come now. In verse 20, Jesus responds to this plea: "Surely I am coming soon."

Christians who are familiar with John's Gospel are not surprised that the working of the Spirit in the church produces a fervent desire for Jesus Christ. You can know that the Spirit is working when you respond by calling out to Jesus. When Christ was departing from his disciples on the eve of his death, he promised to send the Holy Spirit. "He will glorify me," Jesus said, "for he will take what is mine and declare it to you" (John 16:14). The marks of a Spirit-led church, therefore, are the exaltation of Jesus Christ in faith and an obedient response to the teaching of his Word. J. I. Packer wrote that "the essence of the Holy Spirit's ministry, at this or any time in the Christian era, is to mediate the presence of our Lord Jesus Christ."[4]

Packer illustrates the Spirit's work by telling of a cathedral whose large stained-glass windows depict Jesus. At night, large floodlights are trained on the windows so that the image of Christ can be seen. This depicts the ministry of the Spirit. Some Christians focus on the Spirit himself and want an

---

3. Philipp Nicolai, "How Lovely Shines the Morning Star!" (1597).
4. J. I. Packer, *Keep in Step with the Spirit* (Old Tappan, NJ: Fleming H. Revell, 1984), 55.

immediate experience of the Spirit's power, apart from discipleship to Jesus. Packer compares this to turning to face the floodlights and being blinded by their rays. Instead, the Spirit desires to stand behind us, "throwing light over our shoulder, on Jesus, who stands facing us." The Spirit says to the bride, "Look at *him*, and see his glory; listen to *him*, and hear his word; go to *him*, and have life; get to know *him*, and taste his gift of joy and peace."[5]

This teaching indicates that the more we grow spiritually, the more we will find Christ exalted in our hearts. This happens in part because we become more aware of God's holiness and our sin, so that the cross of Christ looms higher as our only means of justification and his blood is deemed more precious for paying the penalty of our sin. Moreover, Christians who become more biblically minded begin to see this world for what it is: in the terms of Revelation, it is the realm of the beast, who opposes the Lamb, and of the harlot Babylon, in whose arms the souls of millions are destroyed. We begin to think like the apostle Paul, who described Christ's coming as "our blessed hope" (Titus 2:13). We begin to see the Lord's return as what Alexander Maclaren called "the Divine event to which the whole Creation moves; and in it all the world's dreams of a golden age are fulfilled, and all the world's wounds are healed."[6] To receive the gospel message of Revelation is to join the Spirit and the Bride as they call to us: "And let the one who hears say, 'Come'" (Rev. 22:17).

CHRIST'S MERCY TO SINNERS

While there is little doubt that at least the opening summons of Revelation 22:17 is directed to Christ, the second half of the verse calls to unbelievers who are present in the church or even in the world. John writes that "the one who hears" should say, "Come." Hearers of the gospel should call out to Jesus and then plead with his salvation offer to the world. The final sentence in the verse is clearly directed to sinners in need of grace: "And let the one who is thirsty come; let the one who desires take the water of life without price" (Rev. 22:17).

That this evangelistic appeal occurs at the end of Revelation, and of the Bible, tells us something important about Jesus. Revelation is a book that

---

5. Ibid., 66.
6. Alexander Maclaren, *Expositions of Holy Scripture*, 17 vols. (Grand Rapids: Baker, 1982), 17:392.

shows Christ as judging his enemies, imposing his kingdom on the world, and casting down Satan and his servants. Yet the compassion of Jesus' heart is not dimmed even in the midst of these scenes. While there remains time before the final judgment, Jesus still calls sinners to be saved. We discover the same mercy and zeal for salvation in the Gospels. Even after Jesus had been nailed to the cross, his first words were a prayer to the Father for the forgiveness of his tormentors: "Father, forgive them, for they know not what they do" (Luke 23:34). When one of the thieves crucified with him called out for salvation, Christ was ready to give it: "Truly, I say to you, today you will be with me in Paradise" (23:43). Despite suffering so dreadfully on the cross, Jesus was still evangelizing! After Christ was resurrected and ascended to heaven, his disciples' first witness was to the very Jewish leaders who had betrayed Jesus. His servants preached, "Repent therefore, and turn again, that your sins may be blotted out" (Acts 3:19). This is the Savior who sends his gospel out to you now, even as his Word is preached. The reason that he has not yet come in answer to the plea of his people is so that forgiveness of sins may still be offered until the last one has believed. What could keep you from calling on him for your own salvation, even as Jesus speaks from heaven offering salvation before he returns?

The same passion that Jesus shows for the lost will characterize a Spirit-led church. How astonishing that in a book that foretells so many trials and persecutions for God's people, and in which they must reject and oppose the sinful world in order to persevere and conquer, the Spirit still animates believers to cry out, "Come!" to those in need of salvation. The zeal of the first recipients of John's letter led to an explosive growth of the church even in the face of dire opposition. The same zeal is needed today and in every age, and if the Spirit moves in the heart of the bride, she will not only call out for Jesus to come but offer his salvation to all who can hear.

At age twenty-one, Joseph Hart became concerned about his soul. Feeling conviction under God's law, he resolved to lead a moral life. The bitterness of works-religion eventually turned his heart against God, and he became well known for writing a tract against the ministry of John Wesley, titled "The Unreasonableness of Religion." Hart became, in his words, "a loose backslider, an audacious apostle, and a bold-faced rebel."[7] Finally, at age

---

7. Quoted in William Petersen and Randy Petersen, eds., *The One Year Great Songs of Faith* (Wheaton, IL: Tyndale, 1995), 243.

forty-five, he attended a church where the good news of Jesus' saving grace was preached, and he heard that sinners may be justified simply by trusting in Jesus, apart from good works that they might do to appease God. He went home and cried out, "What me, Lord?" God's Word answered, "Yes, thee." He objected: "But I have been so unspeakably vile and wicked." The answer came to his heart, "I pardon thee fully and freely."[8] Joseph Hart became one of those who hear and say to Jesus, "Come!" He devoted himself afterward to extending that same invitation to other sinners. His famous hymn declares:

> Come, ye sinners, poor and wretched,
> Weak and wounded, sick and sore;
> Jesus ready stands to save you,
> Full of pity joined with pow'r;
> He is able, he is able, he is able,
> He is willing; doubt no more.[9]

THE WATER OF LIFE

Revelation 22:17 concludes with a great statement of the gospel as it invites us to "take the water of life." From the beginning of the Bible, where a "river flowed out of Eden to water the garden" (Gen. 2:10), to this statement at the Bible's very end, God's gracious stream has rippled with life-giving power for all who believe. David sang of "a river whose streams make glad the city of God" (Ps. 46:4), and Ezekiel foretold a stream issuing out from beneath the temple doors, bringing purity and life to a land poisoned by sin (Ezek. 47:1–12). Isaiah looked forward to the day of promise, declaring, "With joy you will draw water from the wells of salvation" (Isa. 12:3).

The writings of the apostle John especially teem with life-giving streams. At the wedding of Cana, Jesus performed his first miracle by turning water into wine. The water came from jars used for the Jewish rites of cleansing (John 2:6), so John was contrasting empty, formal religion with the life-giving relationship that Jesus offers to believers. When the Spirit and the bride call you to "take the water of life," they are offering you the joy of the wedding feast that Jesus gives by his power. In John 4, Jesus came to Jacob's well, offering the Samaritan woman "living water" (John 4:10). Contrasting

---

8. Ibid.
9. Joseph Hart, "Come, Ye Sinners, Poor and Wretched" (1759).

it with the stagnant well water that symbolized worldly pleasures, Jesus said, "The water that I will give him will become . . . a spring of water welling up to eternal life" (4:14). During the Feast of Tabernacles, Jesus cried out: "If anyone thirsts, let him come to me and drink. Whoever believes in me, as the Scripture has said, 'Out of his heart will flow rivers of living water'" (7:37–38). Finally, when Jesus' body was pierced on the cross, out from his side flowed a stream of blood and water (19:34). It is by the striking of Christ for the forgiveness of sins that salvation flows to his people, even as Moses once struck the rock in the desert and caused life-giving streams to issue forth (Num. 20:11). In light of these images, the water of life stands "for the whole aggregate of the blessings which come to men through Jesus Christ, and which, received by men, make them blessed indeed."[10]

Alexander Maclaren notes three vital points made by Jesus' offer of the water of life. First, "where it does not run or is not received, there is death."[11] Sin involves a living death and finds its end in the eternal death of God's final condemnation. The curse of death is escaped only at the cross, where Jesus offered his own death to pay the penalty of sin. He therefore said, "Whoever feeds on my flesh and drinks my blood has eternal life" (John 6:54).

Second, the water of life offers spiritual satisfaction now. Think of a hot, thirsty day when a cool glass of lemonade is placed into your hand and passes down your throat. This is the spiritual experience that Jesus offers you. Jesus said, "I came that they may have life and have it abundantly" (John 10:10). Jesus gives the blessings of "righteousness and peace and joy in the Holy Spirit" (Rom. 14:17), the very blessings that mankind desires but cannot gain apart from Christ. Through faith in him, we are reconciled to walk with God as beloved children and know the power of his grace in our lives.

Third, the water of life offers even greater satisfaction after death when Christ returns. Revelation 22:1 showed the eternal city, where "the river of the water of life, bright as crystal," flows from the throne of God and of the Lamb. On its banks grows the Tree of Life with its never-failing fruit and with leaves "for the healing of the nations" (Rev. 22:1–2). "Blessed are those who wash their robes," Jesus said, referring to faith in his blood, "so that they may have the right to the tree of life and that they may enter the city by the gates" (22:14), there to drink from the river of the water of life forever.

10. Maclaren, *Expositions of Holy Scripture*, 17:398.
11. Ibid.

Summarizing Christ's invitation, Maclaren writes:

> Brother, here is the offer—life eternal, deliverance from the death of sin both as guilt and power; the pouring out upon us of all the blessing that our thirsty spirits can desire, and the perpetuity of that blessed existence and endless satisfaction through the infinite ages of timeless being.[12]

TAKE THE FREE GIFT

Christ stands at both the end of the Bible and the end of history and together with his church offers you the water of salvation life. What remains is only for you to come and take it: "And let the one who is thirsty come; let the one who desires take the water of life without price" (Rev. 22:17).

Notice the kind of person to whom Christ offers salvation. He speaks to "the one who is thirsty." Here is a universal appeal, for the entire human race thirsts from souls that are unfulfilled and dissatisfied with life. Man is created with a universal need to know his Maker and a craving in the soul for the life that only God can give. The heart longs for acceptance by One who is wholly worthy to be loved. The mind cries out for truth. The will desires a truly noble cause, to which we may offer our lives and find transcendent meaning. None of these desires can be satisfied by worldly things so as to fulfill our nature, which is stamped by the image of God. Thus, David wrote, "My soul thirsts for God, for the living God" (Ps. 42:2).

The tragedy of life arises when men and women know their thirst but have forgotten the only object of satisfaction. They move from one pursuit in life to another, seeking fulfillment in romance, in career success, in family and child-raising, in politics, in sports, or in the arts. However worthy these pursuits are in themselves, they are not designed by God to quench the thirst of the soul made by him and for him. It is therefore with mercy and love that Jesus Christ presents himself before everyone—even the greatest sinners—as "the root and the descendant of David, the bright morning star" (Rev. 22:16). He calls, "Let the one who is thirsty come" (22:17). Here is the general call of the gospel, offered universally to every soul, promising life if only you will come. It is the call given by the church today, proclaiming the gospel in every ear with the genuine offer of forgiveness and life.

12. Ibid., 17:400.

Jesus further speaks to "the one who desires" (Rev. 22:17). Here is the special call of the gospel, which only Jesus can give to the souls of those made willing by his power. If we only choose to be saved, we may come to Christ and drink. But the great problem of life is that men and women in sin are not willing and do not choose salvation. In their pride they will not bow before the Son of God. With hardened hearts they cast down the cup of faith by which alone they may drink from the waters of life. Without having heard the gospel, we may not realize the true thirst that we feel. But having heard the gospel, many still perish in moral rebellion against their Sovereign and Redeemer. This is why Jesus said, "No one can come to me unless the Father who sent me draws him" (John 6:44). It is the special, personal grace of God through the Holy Spirit that makes sinners willing and brings them to the Savior for eternal life.

Finally, there is a condition—you must receive Christ's salvation as a free gift: "Let the one who desires take the water of life without price" (Rev. 22:17). God has grace for sinners who need to be saved and can do nothing for themselves. I mentioned earlier the hymn written by James Montgomery Boice, which in a sense was his final testimony to the gospel. In it, he directs you to a Fountain of free grace:

> Come to the Fountain without any money;
> Buy what is given without any cost.
> Jesus, the gracious One, welcomes the weary;
> Jesus, the selfless One, died for the lost.[13]

You must receive salvation as a free gift, because you have nothing of your own with which to buy it. All your supposedly good works are corrupted by sin and are unacceptable to God (see Isa. 64:6). Every quest you might perform, every dollar you might give, and every prayer you might offer is invalidated by the guilt of sin that lies heavy upon you. You must be saved by grace alone. Isaiah wrote: "Come, everyone who thirsts, come to the waters; and he who has no money, come, buy and eat! Come, buy wine and milk without money and without price" (55:1). Jesus offers you the salvation that he has achieved, which you receive as a gift through simple faith. Salvation is "the water of life without price" (Rev. 22:17), to the glory of God's grace, which he generously extends freely to everyone who comes.

13. Boice, "Come to the Waters."

This appeal forms the final verse of Boice's hymn "Come to the Waters." Its offer comes to you from Jesus himself, who died and rose to free us from our sin. Its appeal is urgent, since he is coming soon:

Come to the Savior, the God of salvation.
God has provided an end to sin's strife.
Why will you suffer the Law's condemnation?
Take the free gift of the water of life.[14]

14. Ibid.

65

COMING SOON!

Revelation 22:18–21

He who testifies to these things says, "Surely I am coming soon."
Amen. Come, Lord Jesus! (Rev. 22:20)

*A*t the end of Israel's exodus from Egypt and journey through the Sinai desert, Moses assembled the twelve tribes on the plains of Moab. There, Moses gave the book of Deuteronomy as a constitution for the nation of Israel in the promised land. Deuteronomy was different from Genesis, Exodus, and Numbers, which recounted past history and its lessons, and from Leviticus, with its procedures for the priesthood. Deuteronomy explicitly looked forward to the life that the Israelites were entering as a people, with promises and commands pertaining to their covenant life as the people of God.

In this respect, Revelation is like the book of Deuteronomy. The four Gospels record the life, death, and resurrection of Jesus. The book of Acts tells of the apostolic founding of the church, and the Epistles record the doctrinal and practical instructions of the apostles to those churches. Revelation looks explicitly to the church age that was then beginning and would continue until Jesus returns, looking ahead even to an eternity of glory. As Deuteronomy was written directly to Israel as it departed the exodus generation, Revelation was given to the churches emerging out of the apostolic age into the gospel millennium. It details the promises and obligations of the church's life as God's covenant people in Jesus Christ.

A WARNING FOR HEARERS

One sign that the apostle John saw Revelation as a new book of Deuteronomy is the warning he attaches in Revelation 22:18–19. Directed to "everyone who hears the words of the prophecy of this book," the warning threatens anyone who "adds to them [and] . . . anyone [who] takes away from the words of the book of this prophecy." This warning mirrors similar words that occur in Deuteronomy. Moses commanded, "You shall not add to the word that I command you, nor take from it, that you may keep the commandments of the LORD your God that I command you" (Deut. 4:2).

In John's plain language, the apostle is warning readers neither to add to nor to take away from Revelation, saying that for the one who adds to it, "God will add to him the plagues described in this book." To him who takes away, "God will take away his share in the tree of life and in the holy city, which are described in this book" (Rev. 22:18–19).

While the language of this warning is clear, John's precise meaning requires some thought. First, John is not insisting that Revelation is the final book of the biblical canon, so that no other books can be added after it. It is true that no Holy Scripture was written after Revelation, as the early church affirmed and as Christians should insist today.[1] It is also true that John wrote by the inspiration of the Holy Spirit, and the divine Author surely knew that Revelation would conclude the biblical canon. Still, John's warning specifically concerns "the words of the prophecy of this book" (Rev. 22:18), that is, Revelation itself.

Second, some scholars have suggested that John's remarks were directed to scribes who would later copy Revelation and who must be exact and correct in their work. One reason for this view is that the early church *Letter to Aristeas* contains just such a warning, in similar language to John's. This

---

1. The earliest extant canonical list is the Muratorian Canon, dated approximately 170 A.D., which includes Revelation on the list of biblical books. For more information on this subject, see Michael J. Kruger, *Canon Revisited: Establishing the Origins and Authority of the New Testament Books* (Wheaton, IL: Crossway, 2012).

is not likely John's meaning, however, since he speaks to "everyone who hears" the prophecy of Revelation (Rev. 22:18), not just to those who copy it.

Third, John does not teach here that true believers who have been saved through faith in Christ can subsequently lose their salvation because of a sin against this text. This idea may be suggested by the language that "God will take away his share in the tree of life and in the holy city" (Rev. 22:19). Yet John's writings elsewhere make it clear that a true believer can never lose salvation. In John 6:37, Jesus promised, "Whoever comes to me I will never cast out." In 1 John 2:19, John explains that those who seem to have fallen away were never true believers, "for if they had been of us, they would have continued with us." John's warning does not therefore mean that true believers can lose a salvation that they once possessed, but rather that those who are unfaithful to God's Word will be barred from salvation's blessings.

Fourth, John is not condemning well-meaning believers who make mistakes in teaching Revelation. We have sometimes noticed differing interpretations between those who hold dispensational, historic premillennial, amillennial, and postmillennial views of eschatology. These differing views and any errors made by them are not "wilful perversions of its teaching,"[2] which John means by the idea of adding to or subtracting from his book. Still, John's warning should cause Bible teachers to take their work seriously and remind them not to take lightly the solemn duty involved in teaching God's holy Word.

What, then, does John precisely mean by the concept of adding to or taking away from the words of Revelation? George Eldon Ladd writes: "He is not concerned about possible mechanical errors in transmission or mistakes of judgment in interpreting his message, but in deliberate distortions and perversions of it."[3] This answer is suggested by Moses' similar warning in Deuteronomy, since the opposite of adding or taking away was to "keep the commandments of the LORD" (Deut. 4:2) and to hold "fast to the LORD" (4:4). Those who were judged under this warning were the faithless and disobedient (4:3).

2. Henry Barclay Swete, *Commentary on Revelation*, 2 vols. (1911; repr., Grand Rapids: Kregel, 1977), 2:311.

3. George Eldon Ladd, *A Commentary on the Revelation of John* (Grand Rapids: Eerdmans, 1972), 295.

In the time of Jesus, the Pharisees and Sadducees best fit the description of this warning. Raymond Brown writes: "The Pharisees added to the word of God hundreds of detailed prohibitions which were not contained in canonical Scripture. In the same period, the Sadducees subtracted from the word the things they found unacceptable—anything about the supernatural, the doctrine of the resurrection, angels and spirits."[4] These two groups find their analogies today in legalists who add man-made works to salvation and liberals who deny plainly taught biblical doctrines. Moreover, adding to or subtracting from Revelation's message is a hallmark of the cults and their false prophetic leaders. Examples are Ellen G. White of Seventh-day Adventism, whose claim to prophecy alters the message of Revelation, and Joseph Smith, the Mormon leader who also claimed to add to Revelation. Those who take away from its message include Charles Taze Russell, whose Jehovah's Witness movement denies Christ's deity and his personal return. Such heretics fall under judgment because in rejecting Christ and his gospel, they presumptuously tamper with God's Holy Scriptures.

In recording this threat, John is emphasizing the divine character of the book he has written. Revelation is true "prophecy," the revealed Word of the God who now defends its sanctity. Dennis Johnson writes: "This divine Witness is not to be toyed with! He jealously guards the integrity of his word, for it is through this word that he jealously guards his beloved bride from the devil's lies."[5] G. K. Beale adds: "The punishment for disobedience is severe, since . . . John is not merely writing his own words, but the very words of God."[6]

The solemn warning to keep the message of Revelation underscores the particular significance of this book for the church in our time. We should avoid giving any book of Scripture a superior place over the others, since each book has its particular role to play in God's revealed Word. Yet just as Deuteronomy gave covenant rules that applied directly to Israel in the promised land, the enthroned Jesus Christ speaks in Revelation directly to his covenant people in the church age. At the very least, Revelation ought therefore to be given careful and reverent attention by Christians today. In

4. Raymond Brown, *The Message of Deuteronomy: Not by Bread Alone*, The Bible Speaks Today (Downers Grove, IL: InterVarsity Press, 1993), 63.

5. Dennis E. Johnson, *Triumph of the Lamb: A Commentary on Revelation* (Phillipsburg, NJ: P&R Publishing, 2001), 330.

6. G. K. Beale, *The Book of Revelation: A Commentary on the Greek Text*, New International Greek Testament Commentary (Grand Rapids: Eerdmans, 1999), 1153.

the seven letters of chapters 2 and 3, Jesus commands his churches to reject false doctrine, to guard themselves against idolatry and sexual impurity, and to keep alive their zeal for his gospel mission. Christians today should treat these obligations seriously. Later in Revelation, Jesus makes clear that his people must never worship tyrants who usurp the place of God. If John's first readers chose to die rather than worship the image of Caesar, in this way taking the mark of the beast, Christians today must likewise refuse to grant ultimate authority to any state or political leader. Jesus commands that his church not participate in the filthy practices taught by the harlot Babylon in the form of seductive secular culture. The Sovereign Lord commands his people to persevere in true faith and godliness until he returns to complete our salvation. "Be faithful unto death," he commands, "and I will give you the crown of life" (Rev. 2:10).

There are voices today that urge Christians to downplay Jesus' sovereign demands. We are told to mention only the promises and comforting phrases of the New Testament, without the requirements and warnings. Some even hold that to teach commands and laws for the Christian life amounts to an antigospel legalism. The book of Revelation shows, however, that Jesus did not hold this view. The Sovereign Lord puts commands before his people even as he provides the grace needed to keep them. Having insisted that his people must overcome the power of evil by faith, Jesus commands his church to reverently keep his Word. "Only hold fast what you have until I come," Jesus says. "The one who conquers and who keeps my works until the end, to him I will give authority over the nations" (Rev. 2:25–26).

A Promise to Come Soon

In addition to the warning that concludes Revelation, Jesus adds a promise to return soon: "He who testifies to these things says, 'Surely I am coming soon'" (Rev. 22:20). Jesus is not far off and inattentive but will soon return to bring both judgment and salvation. His primary emphasis here is to encourage his faithful disciples who are suffering in the world. In verse 17, the Spirit and the bride called out to the beloved Lord, saying, "Come." He answers now, "Surely I am coming soon."

Skeptics point out that nineteen centuries have passed since Jesus promised to return soon, yet still he has not come. The idea, however, is that

Jesus will return without delay. At the very moment when God's redemptive timeline has run its course, the Savior will immediately come to gather his followers. While there remain people of his to be saved, Jesus' coming is delayed, and for this reason the witness of his gospel occupies Christians' attention. Meanwhile, with every day Jesus' coming has been brought nearer. We know that in terms of God's prophetic calendar we are on the brink of his glorious coming. Philip Hughes writes: "It is an event that is always imminent, hence the need always to live in the expectation of his appearing."[7]

Most significant is the response of the true church, which replies in excitement: "Amen. Come, Lord Jesus!" (Rev. 22:20). By saying, "Amen," the church expresses satisfaction and agreement in Jesus' promise. The prayer—the final prayer of the Bible—"Come, Lord Jesus" indicates the joyful hope of believers in the return of Christ. The Greek translates the Aramaic expression *maranatha*, so that John's Gentile believers are carrying over the language and the piety of the first believers in Jerusalem; "Come, Lord Jesus" is therefore "one of the oldest creedal prayers in existence."[8] The *Didache*, a church manual dated to the late first century, connects this prayer to the early church liturgy of the Lord's Supper. We can see the fervor of the original disciples in that the same prayer for Christ's spiritual presence in the sacrament also expressed their longing for his physical return in the second coming.

This prayer shows the fervent longing of the early Christians for Jesus' glorious return. Tragically, many believers today have been taught to dread the return of Christ as an event that may prove disastrous to them. Revelation, however, presents the church as a bride longing for the Lord and Bridegroom to come. Animated by the Spirit, she cries, "Come," in 22:17. Jesus answers, "Surely I am coming soon" (Rev. 22:20). The bride replies with surging hope, "Amen. Come, Lord Jesus!" His coming is, Paul said, "our blessed hope" (Titus 2:13). We are awaiting from heaven, he writes, "a Savior, the Lord Jesus Christ, who will transform our lowly body to be like his glorious body, by the power that enables him even to subject all things to himself" (Phil. 3:20–21).

7. Philip Edgcumbe Hughes, *The Book of Revelation* (Downers Grove, IL: InterVarsity Press, 1990), 241.

8. Grant R. Osborne, *Revelation*, Baker Exegetical Commentary on the New Testament (Grand Rapids: Baker Academic, 2002), 797.

One reason that Christians dread rather than rejoice in Christ's return is the way that warning passages have been preached to suggest that we may lose everything by slipping up at the fatal hour. In the parable of the ten virgins, Jesus tells of five brides who kept their lamps lit and were there to welcome the Lord, and five who did not and were kept out of the wedding feast (Matt. 25:1–13). The parable does not, however, discriminate between two kinds of faithful Christians: those who were watching when Jesus returned and were saved and those who were careless and lost their blessing. Rather, it distinguishes between true Christians in whom the Holy Spirit is alive and false professors of Christianity who do not possess the Holy Spirit. The parable's final appeal to "watch therefore, for you know neither the day nor the hour" (25:13), is not meant to lurk in the nightmares of Christians but to give a standard exhortation regarding our need to persevere in faith.

In Jesus' parable of the talents, the Lord's promise to reward his faithful servants should inspire us with a joyful hope (Matt. 25:14–30). It is true that all his loyal disciples must trust and serve Jesus in this life. When he comes, Jesus will greet them all—not just the famous and hyperproductive—with words of blessing: "Well done, good and faithful servant. . . . Enter into the joy of your master" (25:21). Jesus' words of welcome in Matthew 25:34 should cause us both to serve him faithfully and to pray for his soon return: "Come, you who are blessed by my Father, inherit the kingdom prepared for you from the foundation of the world."

Craig Keener tells a story from early in his Christian life that should challenge us all. As a young adult, he greatly longed for a marriage partner, and this desire dominated his daily prayer life. One day, however, he walked in on a worship service where Christians were fervently singing about Jesus' return. He was struck that while he longed for a wife and prayed constantly for this earthly companionship, which God had not necessarily promised him, he was thinking nothing about and praying little for the greatest companionship that God has promised. Keener exhorts us: "Any other longing we have will be but a shadow of our desire for the greatest and truest love available, the love to which the Lamb's shed blood stands as an eternal testimony."[9] Jesus says, "Surely I am coming soon." May our hearts respond in the spirit of John and the first Christians, saying, "Amen. Come, Lord Jesus!" (Rev. 22:20).

9. Craig S. Keener, *Revelation*, NIV Application Commentary (Grand Rapids: Zondervan, 1999), 522.

IMPLICATIONS OF CHRIST'S SOON RETURN

So central is the theme of Christ's soon return to the Christian faith that we should point out some of its important implications.

First, the return of Christ should produce a serious concern to lead faithful, Bible-obeying lives. Christians have no need to fear condemnation in the coming of Christ, yet the Bible does teach that he will look to each of us to see the return on his grace in our lives. Faithful Christians will desire to do as much for Jesus as we can in these days and will desire that Christ receive a great profit from his investment in our salvation. Moreover, the church should always conduct herself as accountable to her Lord, who though absent in the body is present by the Spirit. Not only will Christ physically return to take accounts, but Revelation shows that he rules us now through the Holy Spirit, disciplining wayward believers and supporting his obedient disciples in their need.

Second, knowing that Jesus will soon return should animate all believers with a fervor for evangelism and world missions. We should be concerned about the spiritual condition of all people, realizing that without faith in Jesus they are under God's wrath and in danger of terrible judgment when Christ returns. Moreover, we are told that Jesus will return only when the last of his people has been gathered to faith. In this sense Peter writes that Christians are now "waiting for and hastening the coming of the day of God" (2 Peter 3:12). Therefore, having offered our prayer of *maranatha!* with the early church believers, we should follow their example of departing from the worship service as devoted witnesses to Christ and his gospel.

An excellent example of this attitude was given by ten-year-old Archibald Alexander Hodge and his sister Mary Elizabeth on June 23, 1833. On that day, the Rev. James R. Eckard was departing from Princeton Seminary, where the children's father was a professor, for missionary service on the island of Ceylon. During the farewell, the children came forward with a letter they had addressed to the people of that island. It read:

Dear Heathen: The Lord Jesus Christ hath promised that the time shall come when all the ends of the earth shall be His kingdom. And God is not a man that He should lie nor the son of man that He should repent. And if this was promised by a Being who cannot lie, why do you not help it to come sooner by reading the Bible, and attending to the words of your teachers, and loving

713

God, and, renouncing your idols, take Christianity into your temples? . . . My sister and myself have, by small self-denials, procured two dollars which are enclosed in this letter to buy tracts and Bibles to teach you.

The letter was signed, "Archibald Alexander Hodge and Mary Eliz. Hodge, Friends of the Heathen."[10] Like these wise children, we should become friends of the unbelievers through the gospel and be eager to make sacrifices in support of their salvation.

Third, the soon return of Christ calls on nonbelievers to repent, acknowledge the lordship of Jesus, and come to him now in faith. Christ is coming soon to save his faithful people and also to judge rebels who have refused him homage. I mentioned Jesus' parable of the talents, which shows him as coming back to reward his faithful servants. That parable concludes with a warning of judgment on those who did not trust or serve him, who are cast "into the outer darkness. In that place there will be weeping and gnashing of teeth" (Matt. 25:30).

The urgency of the sinner's need to turn to Christ for salvation is illustrated by the events of December 26, 1811, when all the fashionable society of Richmond, Virginia, crowded the city's theater for the opening performance of a popular play. Just before the last act, a lamp caused the stage scenery to catch fire, and within minutes the building was wrapped in flames. Seventy-five people perished, including the governor of the state and many other prominent citizens, including some of the most fashionable ladies of the city.[11]

Sermons were preached throughout America in response to this tragedy. In one of them, Archibald Alexander pointed out the response of Jesus to a similar calamity in Jerusalem, when the Roman governor slew a crowd of Galileans at the temple. Jesus asked, "Do you think that these Galileans were worse sinners than all the other Galileans, because they suffered in this way?" He answered that their death was not warranted by any special sins they had committed, but provided a general warning of God's wrath on all who refuse to submit in faith. "I tell you," Jesus concluded, "unless you repent, you will all likewise perish" (Luke 13:2–3). Preaching on this theme, Alexander urged his hearers in words that might be equally suited

---

10. Quoted in David B. Calhoun, *Faith and Learning 1812–1868*, vol. 2 of *Princeton Seminary* (Edinburgh: Banner of Truth, 1994), 193.

11. Taken from Wayne Sparkman, *This Day in Presbyterian History*, http://www.thisday.pcahistory.org.

to the message of Christ's soon return in Revelation. He pleaded: "Receive the warning then, and suffer the word of exhortation. . . . You may never in the whole period of your lives, find a season so favourable to shake off the undue influence of the world, and . . . become real Christians."[12]

A BENEDICTION OF GRACE

John concludes Revelation with a benediction that reminds us that Revelation was a letter sent by the apostle for the benefit of his churches. He concludes: "The grace of the Lord Jesus be with all. Amen" (Rev. 22:21).

A benediction is both a prayer appeal and a declaration of God's blessing on his people. As was Paul's practice, John in his benediction proclaims the grace of Christ for believers. When we speak of salvation "by grace," we mean that salvation is a free *gift* from God. Here, "grace" refers to the *attitude* of the Lord toward his people: Christ is filled with merciful love for all those who call on his name. Revelation has shown Jesus as the Lion and Lamb who is worthy to unseal the scroll of God and establish the divine purpose for heaven and earth. This victorious Lord looks upon his struggling people—then and now—with grace in his heart, acting in compassion for their sufferings and determining by his redeeming work to bring them with him into the new Jerusalem that is to come.

"Grace" further refers to the *power* that God provides to his people in need. In Revelation, Christ has commanded believers to overcome through faith. Will we? The answer is yes! By his grace the people of Christ will persevere in faith so as to stand triumphant on Mount Zion together with the Lamb (Rev. 14:1). Christians are commanded to hold fast to God's Word and uphold our testimony to Jesus to the end. By the grace of Jesus, we will: the stars of the churches will shine brightly in the darkness of this world until the morning star rises to bring a new day. Christians are required to withstand the allures of the harlot and must refuse to worship the beast. We must reject false teaching from the false prophets of this world. Will the church and will Christians maintain their faith against such potent opposition? The answer, for which John prays and that he declares on Christ's behalf, is found in

12. Archibald Alexander, *A Discourse Occasioned by the Burning of the Theatre in the City of Richmond, Virginia, on the Twenty-sixth of December, 1811* (1815; repr., London: Forgotten Books, 2013), 28.

his closing benediction: "The grace of the Lord Jesus be with all. Amen" (22:21). Not merely some of Christ's people are strengthened, empowered, and secured by this grace, but, John insists, the grace of the Lord Jesus will save all who hear, believe, and call on his name in true faith.

This grace is sufficient to our need because it is the grace of Jesus, who bears to us the love of God the Father. Charles Hodge writes: "The grace of our Lord Jesus Christ is the undeserved love of a divine person clothed with our nature, whose love has all the attributes of sinless human love; the love of one who owns us, who is invested with absolute dominion over us and who is our protector and preserver."[13] The grace of this Lord and Savior, Lion and Lamb, who reigns forever from the throne of God, is now and will always be "able to save to the uttermost those who draw near to God through him" (Heb. 7:25).

With this benediction, John concludes the book of Revelation right where he began. Chapter 1 presented the "revelation of Jesus Christ, ... who loves us and has freed us from our sins by his blood" (Rev. 1:1, 5). Looking now in faith to the same Lord and Savior at the end, experiencing the power of his grace, and hearing his promise soon to come for our salvation, we know that we can continue in faith and conquer in his name until he returns. With his promise of grace ringing in our ears, we hear our Sovereign Lord claim, "Surely I am coming soon." We answer, "Amen. Come, Lord Jesus!"

---

13. Charles Hodge, *Princeton Sermons* (1879; repr., Edinburgh: Banner of Truth, 1958), 63.

Bibliography

Aikman, David. *Jesus in Beijing*. Washington, DC: Regnery, 2003.

Alexander, Archibald. *A Discourse Occasioned by the Burning of the Theatre in the City of Richmond, Virginia, on the Twenty-sixth of December, 1811.* 1815. Reprint, London: Forgotten Books, 2013.

Alexander, Eric J. "Do Not Do It! Worship God." Audio recording, Philadelphia Conference on Reformed Theology. Philadelphia: Alliance of Confessing Evangelicals, 1998.

———. *Our Great God and Saviour*. Edinburgh: Banner of Truth, 2011.

Alexander, J. W. *God Is Love: Communion Addresses*. Edinburgh: Banner of Truth, 1985.

Alford, Henry. *The Greek Testament*. 4 vols. Cambridge: Deighton, Bell, and Co., 1866.

Anderson, Ken. *Bold as a Lamb: Pastor Samuel Lamb and the Underground Church of China*. Grand Rapids: Zondervan, 1991.

Aune, David E. *Revelation 1-5*. Word Biblical Commentary 52a. Dallas: Word, 1997.

Bainton, Roland H. *Here I Stand*. New York: Penguin, 1955.

Barclay, William. *The Revelation of John*. 3rd ed. 2 vols. New Daily Study Bible. Louisville: Westminster John Knox, 2004.

Barnhouse, Donald Grey. *Expositions of Bible Doctrines, Taking the Epistle to the Romans as a Point of Departure*. 10 vols. Grand Rapids: Eerdmans, 1959.

———. *Revelation: An Expositional Commentary*. Grand Rapids: Zondervan, 1971.

Baron, David. *The Visions and Prophecies of Zechariah*. Grand Rapids: Kregel, 1972.

Bauckham, Richard. *Climax of Prophecy: Studies on the Book of Revelation*. London: T&T Clark, 2000.

———. *The Theology of the Book of Revelation*. Cambridge: Cambridge University Press, 1993.

Baxter, Richard. *The Saints' Everlasting Rest*. Edited by Benjamin Fawcett. New York: American Tract Society, 2012.

Beale, G. K. *The Book of Revelation: A Commentary on the Greek Text*. New International Greek Testament Commentary. Grand Rapids: Eerdmans, 1999.

———. *The Temple and the Church's Mission: A Biblical Theology of the Dwelling Place of God*. Downers Grove, IL: InterVarsity Press, 2004.

Beasley-Murray, Paul. *The Message of the Resurrection: Christ Is Risen!* The Bible Speaks Today. Downers Grove, IL: InterVarsity Press, 2000.

Bewes, Richard. *The Lamb Wins: A Guided Tour through the Book of Revelation*. Tain, Ross-shire, Scotland: Christian Focus, 2000.

Block, Daniel I. *The Book of Ezekiel: Chapters 25–48*. New International Commentary on the Old Testament. Grand Rapids: Eerdmans, 1998.

Boice, James Montgomery. *Acts: An Expositional Commentary*. Grand Rapids: Baker, 1997.

———. *Foundations of the Christian Faith*. Downers Grove, IL: InterVarsity Press, 1986.

———. *The Gospel of John*. 5 vols. Grand Rapids: Baker, 1999.

———. *Revelation*. Unpublished manuscript, n.d. On file with author.

———. *Romans*. 4 vols. Grand Rapids: Baker, 1991–95.

———. "Testimony." http://www.tenth.org/articles/000507jmb.pdf.

Bonhoeffer, Dietrich. *The Cost of Discipleship*. 1937. Reprint, New York: Macmillan, 1959.

Brown, Dan. *The Da Vinci Code*. New York: Doubleday, 2003.

Brown, Raymond. *The Message of Deuteronomy: Not by Bread Alone*. The Bible Speaks Today. Downers Grove, IL: InterVarsity Press, 1993.

Bunyan, John. *Pilgrim's Progress*. Nashville: Thomas Nelson, 1999.

Butterfield, Rosaria Champagne. "My Train Wreck Conversion." *Christianity Today* 57, 1 (January–February 2013): 212–14.

———. *The Secret Thoughts of an Unlikely Convert*. Pittsburgh: Crown & Covenant, 2012.

Caird, G. B. *The Revelation of St. John the Divine*. San Francisco: Harper, 1966.

Calhoun, David B. *Faith and Learning 1812–1868*. Vol. 2 of *Princeton Seminary*. Edinburgh: Banner of Truth, 1994.

———. *Our Southern Zion: Old Columbia Seminary (1828–1927)*. Edinburgh: Banner of Truth, 2012.

Calvin, John. *Institutes of the Christian Religion*. Translated by Henry Beveridge. Peabody, MA: Hendrickson, 2008.

———. *Sermons on the Epistle to the Ephesians*. Carlisle, PA: Banner of Truth, 1973.

Carson, D. A. "This Present Evil Age." In *These Last Days: A Christian View of History*, edited by Richard D. Phillips and Gabriel N. E. Fluhrer, 17–37. Phillipsburg, NJ: P&R Publishing, 2011.

Carson, D. A., et al. *An Introduction to the New Testament*. Grand Rapids: Zondervan, 1992.

Chalke, Steve, and Alan Mann. *The Lost Message of Jesus*. Grand Rapids: Zondervan, 2003.

Charles, Tyler. "(Almost) Everyone's Doing It." *Relevant* 53 (September–October 2011).

Charnock, Stephen. *The Existence and Attributes of God*. 2 vols. Grand Rapids: Baker, 1996.

Chilton, David. *Days of Vengeance: An Exposition of the Book of Revelation*. Ft. Worth, TX: Dominion Press, 1987.

Cromarty, Jim. *King of the Cannibals: The Story of John G. Paton*. Darlington, UK: Evangelical Press, 1997.

Dawkins, Richard. *The God Delusion*. New York: Houghton Mifflin Harcourt, 2006.

DC Talk. *Jesus Freaks: Stories of Those Who Stood with Jesus*. Minneapolis: Bethany House, 1999.

DeYoung, Kevin. "A Great Multitude and a Great Hope." *The Gospel Coalition* (blog). https://blogs.thegospelcoalition.org /kevindeyoung/2013/01/21/a-great-multitude-and-a-great-hope/.

Dickens, Charles. *A Tale of Two Cities*. 1859. Reprint, New York: Random House, 1992.

Duguid, Iain M. *Daniel*. Reformed Expository Commentary. Phillipsburg, NJ: P&R Publishing, 2008.

———. *Ezekiel*. NIV Application Commentary. Grand Rapids: Zondervan, 1999.

Edwards, Jonathan. *Altogether Lovely: Jonathan Edwards on the Glory and Excellency of Jesus Christ*. Morgan, PA: Soli Deo Gloria, 1997.

———. *The Distinguishing Marks of a Work of the Spirit of God*. In *Jonathan Edwards on Revival*. Edinburgh: Banner of Truth, 1965.

Eusebius. *The History of the Church*. New York: Penguin, 1989.

Fisk, Samuel. *More Fascinating Conversion Stories*. Grand Rapids: Kregel, 1994.

Foxe, John. *The New Foxe's Book of Martyrs*. Edited by Harold J. Chadwick. Gainesville, FL: Bridge-Logos, 2001.

Gardner, Paul. *Revelation: The Compassion and Protection of Christ*. Focus on the Bible. Tain, Ross-shire, Scotland: Christian Focus, 2008.

Green, Joel B., and Mark D. Baker. *Recovering the Scandal of the Cross: Atonement in New Testament & Contemporary Contexts*. Downers Grove, IL: InterVarsity Press, 2000.

Hamilton, James. *Sermons and Lectures*. 1873. Reprint, Stoke-on-Trent, UK: Tentmaker Publications, 2010.

Hamilton, James M., Jr. *Revelation: The Spirit Speaks to the Churches*. Wheaton, IL: Crossway, 2012.

Hendriksen, William. *More than Conquerors: An Interpretation of the Book of Revelation*. 1940. Reprint, Grand Rapids: Baker, 1967.

Henry, Matthew. *Commentary on the Whole Bible*. 6 vols. Peabody, MA: Hendrickson, n.d.

Henry, O. "The Assessor of Success." In *One Hundred Selected Stories*. London: Wordsworth, 1997.

Hitchens, Christopher. *God Is Not Great: How Religion Poisons Everything*. New York: Twelve Books, 2007.

Hodge, Charles. *Princeton Sermons*. 1879. Reprint, Edinburgh: Banner of Truth, 1958.

Hoekema, Anthony A. "Amillennialism." In *The Meaning of the Millennium: Four Views*, edited by Robert G. Clouse, 155–87. Downers Grove, IL: IVP Academic, 1977.

———. *The Bible and the Future*. Grand Rapids: Eerdmans, 1979.

Hughes, Philip Edgcumbe. *The Book of Revelation*. Downers Grove, IL: InterVarsity Press, 1990.

Hughes, R. Kent. *John: That You May Believe*. Wheaton, IL: Crossway, 1999.

Ironside, Henry A. *Addresses on the Gospel of Luke*. Neptune, NJ: Loizeaux Brothers, 1947.

Jacobi, Peter. *The Messiah Book: The Life & Times of G. F. Handel's Greatest Hit*. New York: St. Martin's Press, 1982.

Jeffrey, Grant R. *Messiah: War in the Middle East & the Road to Armageddon*. New York: Bantam, 1991.

Johnson, Alan F. *Revelation*. Expositor's Bible Commentary 12. Grand Rapids: Zondervan, 1982.

Johnson, Dennis E. *Triumph of the Lamb: A Commentary on Revelation*. Phillipsburg, NJ: P&R Publishing, 2001.

Jordan, Chris. "War of the Worlds Radio Broadcast Turns 75." *USA Today*, October 29, 2013.

Keener, Craig S. *Revelation*. NIV Application Commentary. Grand Rapids: Zondervan, 1999.

Kelly, Douglas F. *Revelation*. Mentor Expository Commentary. Tain, Ross-shire, Scotland: Mentor, 2012.

King, Martin Luther, Jr. *Strength to Love*. New York: Harper & Row, 1963.

Kistemaker, Simon J. *Revelation*. New Testament Commentary. Grand Rapids: Baker, 2001.

Kline, Meredith G. "The Covenant of the Seventieth Week." In *The Law and the Prophets: Old Testament Studies in Honor of Oswald T. Allis*, edited by J. H. Skilton, 452–69. Nutley, NJ: Presbyterian and Reformed, 1974.

———. "Har Magedon: The End of the Millennium." *JETS* 39, 2 (1996): 207–22.

———. *Images of the Spirit*. Grand Rapids: Baker, 1980.

Kruger, Michael J. *Canon Revisited: Establishing the Origins and Authority of the New Testament Books*. Wheaton, IL: Crossway, 2012.

Kuhn, Isobel. *Green Leaf in Drought-Time: The Story of the Escape of the Last C.I.M. Missionaries from Communist China*. Chicago: Moody, 1957.

Ladd, George Eldon. *A Commentary on the Revelation of John*. Grand Rapids: Eerdmans, 1972.

———. "Historic Premillennialism." In *The Meaning of the Millennium: Four Views*, edited by Robert G. Clouse, 17–40. Downers Grove, IL: IVP Academic, 1977.

Legg, John D. "John G. Paton: Missionary of the Cross." In *Five Pioneer Missionaries*, 303–45. Edinburgh: Banner of Truth, 1965.

Lenski, Richard C. H. *The Interpretation of St. John's Revelation*. 1943. Reprint, St. Louis: Augsburg Fortress, 2008.

Lewis, C. S. *The Last Battle*. New York: Collier, 1970.

———. *The Lion, the Witch and the Wardrobe*. New York: Collier, 1970.

———. *The Weight of Glory and Other Addresses.* New York: Macmillan, 1962.

Liddell Hart, Sir Basil, ed. *History of the Second World War.* New York: Exeter Books, 1980.

Lloyd-Jones, D. Martyn. *Knowing the Times: Addresses Delivered on Various Occasions, 1942–1977.* Edinburgh: Banner of Truth, 1989.

Loane, Sir Marcus. *Masters of the English Reformation.* Edinburgh: Banner of Truth, 2005.

Luther, Martin. "Preface to the Revelation of St. John." In *Word and Sacrament,* ed. E. Theodore Bachmann. Vol. 35 of *Luther's Works.* Philadelphia: Fortress, 1960.

MacArthur, John. *Twelve Ordinary Men.* Nashville: Thomas Nelson, 2002.

Machen, J. Gresham. *Christianity and Liberalism.* 1923. Reprint, Grand Rapids: Eerdmans, 1996.

Maclaren, Alexander. *Expositions of Holy Scripture.* 17 vols. Grand Rapids: Baker, 1982.

McCullough, David. *John Adams.* New York: Simon and Schuster, 2001.

McIlvaine, Charles P. *Truth & Life: 22 Classic Christ-Centered Sermons.* 1854. Reprint, Birmingham, AL: Solid Ground, 2005.

Michaels, J. Ramsey. *Revelation.* IVP New Testament Commentary 20. Downers Grove, IL: InterVarsity Press, 1997.

Milne, Bruce. *The Message of Heaven and Hell: Grace and Destiny.* The Bible Speaks Today. Downers Grove, IL: InterVarsity Press, 2002.

Mohler, R. Albert. "Christian Values Cannot Save Anyone." September 11, 2012. http://www.albertmohler.com/2012/09/11/christian-values-cannot-save-anyone/.

Morgan, G. Campbell. *The Westminster Pulpit: The Preaching of G. Campbell Morgan.* Grand Rapids: Baker, 1995.

Morris, Leon. *The Revelation of St. John: An Introduction and Commentary.* Tyndale New Testament Commentaries 20. Grand Rapids: Eerdmans, 1969.

Mounce, Robert H. *Revelation.* Rev. ed. New International Commentary on the New Testament. Grand Rapids: Eerdmans, 1997.

Niebuhr, H. Richard. *Christ and Culture.* 1951. Reprint, San Francisco: HarperSanFrancisco, 2001.

———. *The Kingdom of God in America.* 1937. Reprint, New York: Harper & Row, 1959.

Osborne, Grant R. *Revelation*. Baker Exegetical Commentary on the New Testament. Grand Rapids: Baker Academic, 2002.

Packer, J. I. *Keep in Step with the Spirit*. Old Tappan, NJ: Fleming H. Revell, 1984.

———. *Knowing God*. Downers Grove, IL: InterVarsity Press, 1973.

Palmer, Chris. "Reinventing the Wheel." *ESPN the Magazine* 11, 15 (July 28, 2008): 52–58.

Petersen, William J., and Randy Petersen, eds. *The One Year Great Songs of Faith*. Wheaton, IL: Tyndale, 1995.

Pink, Arthur W. *The Attributes of God*. Grand Rapids: Baker, 1993.

Piper, John. *God Is the Gospel: Meditations on God's Love as the Gift of Himself*. Wheaton, IL: Crossway, 2011.

Pitzer, A. W. "Why Believers Should Not Fear." In *Southern Presbyterian Pulpit: A Collection of Sermons from the Nineteenth Century*. 1896. Reprint, Birmingham, AL: Solid Ground, 2001.

Pliny the Younger. "On the Christians." http://www.earlychristianwritings .com/text/pliny2.html.

Poythress, Vern S. *The Returning King: A Guide to the Book of Revelation*. Phillipsburg, NJ: P&R Publishing, 2000.

Prothero, Rowland E. *The Psalms in Human Life*. New York: E. P. Dutton, 1904.

Ramsey, James B. *Revelation: An Exposition of the First III Chapters*. Geneva Commentaries. Edinburgh: Banner of Truth, 1977.

Roberts, Alexander, and James Donaldson, eds. *Ante-Nicene Fathers*. 10 vols. Peabody, MA: Hendrickson, 1999.

Russell, Bertrand. *Why I Am Not a Christian*. New York: Simon & Schuster, 1957.

Rutherford, Samuel. *The Letters of Samuel Rutherford*. 1664. Reprint, Edinburgh: Banner of Truth, 2006.

Ryken, Philip Graham. *Discovering God in Stories from the Bible*. Wheaton, IL: Crossway, 1999.

———. *Jeremiah and Lamentations: From Sorrow to Hope*. Preaching the Word. Wheaton, IL: Crossway, 2001.

———. *My Father's World: Meditations on Christianity and Culture*. Phillipsburg, NJ: P&R Publishing, 2002.

Ryle, J. C. *The Christian Race*. Moscow, ID: Charles Nolan, 2004.

———. *Expository Thoughts on John.* 2 vols. 1869. Reprint, Edinburgh: Banner of Truth, 1999.

Sargent, John. *Life and Letters of the Rev. Henry Martyn, B.D.* London: Seeley, Jackson, and Halliday, 1862.

Scofield Reference Bible. New York: Oxford University Press, 1909.

Smalley, Stephen S. *The Revelation to John: A Commentary on the Greek Text of the Apocalypse.* Downers Grove, IL: InterVarsity Press, 2012.

Solzhenitsyn, Alexander. *The Gulag Archipelago.* New York: Harper, 1974.

Sparkman, Wayne. *This Day in Presbyterian History.* http://www.thisday.pcahistory.org.

Sproul, R. C. *The Holiness of God.* Wheaton, IL: Tyndale, 1985.

Spurgeon, Charles H. *Metropolitan Tabernacle Pulpit.* 63 vols. Pasadena, TX: Pilgrim Publications, 1969–1980.

———. *Spurgeon's Sermons on the Second Coming.* Edited by David Otis Fuller. Grand Rapids: Zondervan, 1943.

Stephens, Don. *War and Grace: Short Biographies from the World Wars.* Darlington, UK: Evangelical Press, 2005.

Storms, Sam. *Kingdom Come: The Amillennial Alternative.* Tain, Ross-shire, Scotland: Christian Focus, 2013.

Stott, John R. W. *The Cross of Christ.* Downers Grove, IL: InterVarsity Press, 1986.

———. *What Christ Thinks of the Church: An Exposition of Revelation 1–3.* Grand Rapids: Baker, 2003.

Suetonius. "Domitian." In *Lives of the Caesars*, trans. J. C. Rolfe. Rev. ed. Loeb Classical Library 38. Cambridge, MA: Harvard University Press, 1997.

Swete, Henry Barclay. *Commentary on Revelation.* 2 vols. 1911. Reprint, Grand Rapids: Kregel, 1977.

ten Boom, Corrie. *The Hiding Place.* New York: Bantam, 1971.

Thomas, Derek. *Let's Study Revelation.* Edinburgh: Banner of Truth, 2003.

Thomas, Robert L. *Revelation 1–7: An Exegetical Commentary.* Chicago: Moody, 1992.

———. *Revelation 8–22: An Exegetical Commentary.* Chicago: Moody, 1995.

Tidball, Derek. *The Message of the Cross: Wisdom Unsearchable, Love Indestructible.* The Bible Speaks Today. Downers Grove, IL: InterVarsity Press, 2001.

Tolkien, J. R. R. *The Return of the King.* New York: Houghton Mifflin, 1955.

Tozer, A. W. *The Knowledge of the Holy*. San Francisco: HarperSanFrancisco, 1992.

Travis, Stephen H. *Christ and the Judgment of God: Divine Retribution in the New Testament*. Basingstoke, UK: Marshall Pickering, 1986.

Venema, Cornelis P. *The Promise of the Future*. Edinburgh: Banner of Truth, 2000.

Vos, Geerhardus. *Grace and Glory: Sermons Preached in the Chapel of Princeton Theological Seminary*. 1922. Reprint, Edinburgh: Banner of Truth, 1994.

Warfield, Benjamin Breckinridge. *Faith and Life*. 1916. Reprint, Edinburgh: Banner of Truth, 1974.

———. "'Redeemer' and 'Redemption.'" In *The Person and Work of Christ*. Philadelphia: Presbyterian and Reformed, 1950.

Wells, David F. *Above All Earthly Pow'rs: Christ in a Postmodern World*. Grand Rapids: Eerdmans, 2005.

———. *God in the Wasteland: The Reality of Truth in a World of Fading Dreams*. Grand Rapids: Eerdmans, 1994.

Wilcock, Michael. *I Saw Heaven Opened: The Message of Revelation*. The Bible Speaks Today. Downers Grove, IL: InterVarsity Press, 1975.

Williams, Garry J. "Penal Substitution: A Response to Recent Criticisms." In *The Atonement Debate: Papers from the London Symposium on the Theology of Atonement*, edited by Derek Tidball, David Hilborn, and Justin Thacker, 172–91. Grand Rapids: Zondervan, 2008.

Wilmshurst, Steve. *The Final Word: The Book of Revelation Simply Explained*. Darlington, UK: Evangelical Press, 2008.

Wilson, Geoffrey B. *New Testament Commentaries*. 2 vols. Edinburgh: Banner of Truth, 2005.

Witherington, Ben, III. *Revelation*. New Cambridge Bible Commentary. Cambridge: Cambridge University Press, 2003.

Wright, N. T. *Revelation for Everyone*. Louisville: Westminster John Knox, 2011.

Yeats, William Butler. "The Second Coming." In *Modern American and Modern British Poetry*, edited by Louis Untermeyer. Rev. ed. New York: Harcourt, Brace and Company, 1955.

Zahl, Paul F. M. *Five Women of the English Reformation*. Grand Rapids: Eerdmans, 2001.

Index of Scripture

733

EXTRA-BIBLICAL CITATIONS

1 Enoch

3 Maccabees

Index of Subjects and Names